Management Decision Making

The Irwin Series in Management

Consulting Editor   John F. Mee *Indiana University*

MANAGEMENT

DECISION MAKING

by

Max D. Richards

Head, Department of Management

and

Paul S. Greenlaw

Professor of Management

both of

The Pennsylvania State University

1966

RICHARD D. IRWIN, INC.

Homewood, Illinois

PRINTED IN THE UNITED STATES OF AMERICA

Library of Congress Catalog Card No. 66–11815

To
Wimp and Shirley

PREFACE

The original impetus to writing this book was our perceived need for teaching materials in the basic management theory course which would integrate with "traditional" management concepts both (1) scientific knowledge from the behavioral sciences about organizational behavior, and (2) the newer quantitative approaches to decision making. Our perceptions as to this need were reinforced with the appearance of the Carnegie and Ford Foundation reports on business education.

The integrative conceptual framework utilized in this book is one which views the business organization as an information-decision system, in which decision making represents the focus of activity performed by managers. This view emphasizes that in dealing with problems in all areas of organizational endeavor—from those involving interpersonal relationships to those requiring an economic analysis of revenue, costs, and profits—the manager is faced with choice situations, in which numerous alternative courses of action are possible, and for which certain information is prerequisite for effective decision making.

To provide the reader with a theoretical basis for understanding managerial decision making in the context of an information-decision system, considerable attention is given to the growing body of concepts and research findings from the social sciences which has been developed to explain and predict organizational behavior. Although at our present state of understanding, many organizational problems are not amenable to quantitative treatment, some of the variables and relationships developed theoretically can be explicitly described by mathematical models. To the extent that such models can assist in understanding the decision-making process (without involving sophisticated mathematics), they are utilized in this text. Attention is also given to the "practical" application of these theoretical concepts and to an examination of specific approaches which have been developed to handle business problems. In the presentation of these approaches, an overly descriptive orientation is avoided. For example, no attention is given to the different kinds of computer hardware in common use nor to the design of inventory record-keeping forms. Rather, emphasis is placed upon the analysis of problem-solving approaches as they relate to key decision variables. What affect may different styles of leadership have upon employee motivation under various conditions? How may linear programming be utilized in making allocation decisions? These are some of the kinds of problem areas calling for managerial decisions upon which this text centers.

This book is intended to be an introductory general management text. That is, its use requires no previous study of management on the part of the reader; while its focus is upon the kinds of decision problems faced by managers at all levels and functional areas in the business organization. As such, one function of the text is to provide a basic foundation for the subsequent study of more specialized fields such as sales, production and personnel management, organization theory, etc.

Some prior study of college algebra, economics, and accounting will be of considerable value to the reader of this text; while having taken basic courses in psychology, sociology, and statistics will also be helpful. However, the materials in the text have been utilized successfully with students who have not completed prior work in each of these areas. We have utilized most of the textual materials in an undergraduate management theory course required of all College of Business Administration students at The Pennsylvania State University. Ordinarily, this course is taken during the last half of the Sophomore or the first half of the Junior year. Additionally, many of our graduate students have found numerous chapters of the text useful as reference sources in their graduate management theory courses.

It is possible to utilize this book at several different levels of sophistication, depending on the materials employed with it. If case studies and problems are used along with the textual materials, for example, students can both intensify their *understanding* of the subject matter, while at the same time develop a degree of *skill* in applying concepts and analytical tools to specific problems. To help provide for various degrees of sophistication in usage, we have included numerous questions, problems, and/or short cases at the end of each chapter. Some of the questions so included are simply designed to test the student's knowledge of specific points covered in the chapters. Others, which are case and problem oriented, are intended to provide a vehicle for skill development in the application of concepts and tools to specific problem situations. Still others are geared toward having the student explore unresolved theoretical questions, examine overgeneralizations derived from management "folklore" in light of current theory, etc. For some questions of these latter types, there may be few final answers—the chapter materials may merely provide a general basis for discussion.

This book has been organized in the following manner. Chapters 1–3 are designed to summarize the major historical and current trends in management thinking; to introduce the reader to the key phases of the decision-making process; and to provide an introduction to various basic approaches to decision making.

Chapters 4–10 focus attention on individual and group behavior, leadership, and organizational design. In these chapters, considerable attention is given to concepts and research findings from the social sciences which help to explain human behavior in organizations.

Chapters 11–19 focus attention on organizational planning and control. In these chapters, considerable emphasis is placed on the use of economic models to describe and explain decision processes. Since these models are quantitatively the most highly developed of those utilized to deal with organizational problems, these chapters generally have a greater quantitative orientation than do the previous ones. It is not our purpose in these chapters, however, to help enable the reader to become a mathematician or "operations researcher"; rather emphasis is placed upon helping the student without a sophisticated mathematical background to better understand how quantitative approaches can be useful to managers in their decision making.

Finally, Chapter 19 provides an overview of decision making in a systems context, and attempts to tie together some of the more basic conceptual themes presented in the preceding chapters.

Our basic rationale for placing most of the quantitatively oriented materials in latter chapters of the text was that their values and limitations become more meaningful to the student if he first understands the "behavioral environment" of the firm in which such quantitative techniques will be utilized. On the other hand, some instructors who have utilized the textual materials have found the following chapter sequencing also to be an effective one: Chapters 1–3; Chapters 11–18; Chapters 4–10; and Chapter 19.

We have been aided greatly in our writing efforts by the willingness of our colleagues at Penn State to utilize the materials in this book in their classes; to critically review the manuscript; and to provide materials from which we have drawn in developing numerous of the cases and problems at the end of the chapters. We would like to thank especially Professors M. William Frey, John Yanouzas, Ned Shilling, and Rocco Carzo, Jr., for such assistance.

We are also appreciative of the efforts of Mr. Robert D. Smith, who aided us considerably in developing both our discussion questions and problems and our Teacher's Manual. Appreciation is also expressed to Professor R. H. "Sam" Wherry, who gave us continuing encouragement to develop these materials as a means of upgrading our basic management theory course. As further encouragement, both he and Dean Ossian R. MacKenzie have been most helpful in providing secretarial assistance and other resources which have made it possible to utilize these materials on an experimental basis in our classes. Finally, without the determined conscientiousness of Miss Jean Rusnak, who has typed the manuscript several times, it is doubtful that this work could have been completed. We appreciate the inestimable aid of all who have helped bring this project to fruition while recognizing our own complete responsibility for it.

MAX D. RICHARDS
PAUL S. GREENLAW

University Park, Pennsylvania
December, 1965

TABLE OF CONTENTS

CHAPTER 1

MANAGEMENT:
PAST AND PRESENT

THE purpose of this chapter is to introduce the study of management by describing the panorama of management thinking and practice as viewed in different time periods by diverse schools of academic thought. In succeeding chapters of this book, we will attempt to interweave many of these different concepts about management into an integrated framework which may be utilized by the reader to guide his thinking as a manager in the business world.

This chapter consists of two parts. In the first section, we will present a brief history of management thought and summarize the major current trends in management thinking. The second part of the chapter considers several differing ideas about the nature of the managerial process. We will conclude the chapter with a summary of the basic approach to be undertaken in this book: an eclectic view which integrates many of the diverse approaches to management thought into a framework which focuses attention upon decision and information systems.

HISTORICAL FOUNDATIONS OF MANAGEMENT

As an art, management has been practiced since the early beginning of time. As John F. Mee has pointed out in his award winning book, however: "Management thought is a product of the Twentieth Century." [1] Although we can find traces of managerial concepts in the Bible, in the writings of the Greek and Roman philosophers, [2] and

---

[1] John F. Mee, *Management Thought in a Dynamic Economy* (New York: New York University Press, 1963), p. xviii. This book was a winner of the Academy of Management's McKinsey Book Award in 1963.

[2] For example, Cicero's, *De Officiis*, Book II, Chaps. 3–5.

1

in the works of early political economists,[3] no systematic or comprehensive approach for the study of management was developed until relatively recently. The foundations of probability theory, now frequently applied in analysis for decision making, were developed by Cardan (1501–1576) and Pascal (1623–1662), but were not systematically incorporated into business decisions at a practical managerial operating level until the middle of the Twentieth Century, even though Laplace (1749–1827) had developed applications of probability theory to other types of decision making. Or, to cite another illustration, Charles Babbage (1792–1871), a professor at Cambridge University, developed the concept of the automatic computer in the Nineteenth Century. At the time, however, only mechanical devices were available for constructing his computer and friction prevented the practical application of his ideas. Babbage also wrote an essay in 1832—*On the Economy of Machinery and Manufactures*—which contained numerous forward-looking recommendations to management. Although his essay received some attention, it did not foster fundamental or widespread changes in management practice.

Probably the most important stimulus to management thought was the so-called "industrial revolution" which started in England around the middle of the Eighteenth Century. Prior to this time, most business enterprises were small, characterized by hand craftsmanship rather than mechanization, and faced problems much simpler than those faced today by many firms in our complex industrial society. In consequence, relatively little need was perceived for giving systematic attention to the problems of management.

During the industrial revolution, many new inventions and technological developments occurred which made it possible to transform manufacturing from in-the-home production into large-scale factory operations, as, for example, was the case with textiles. Furthermore, developments within one industry spurred invention within others. For instance, the development of the metal-working screw lathe in 1797 made practical the extensive use of metals and interchangeable parts. The resulting demand for metals encouraged the development of Bessemer and open-hearth steel-making methods which rendered large-scale steel production possible.

Of considerable impetus to the industrial revolution was a legal, social, and technological environment which tended to generate in-

---

[3] For example, Adam Smith, *Wealth of Nations*, Book I, Chap. 1, p. 5 in Cannan's edition.

dustrial growth and encourage entrepreneurs to invest in new industries. This environment was characterized by the protestant ethic, which held that what was best for the individual coincided with God's will as well as with the general social welfare. Such an ethical philosophy of individualism gave encouragement to business promoters and owners while, at the same time, tended to silence business critics. In the United States those who may have been injured through business excesses during this period could exercise the alternatives of settling new lands in the West or of forming their own businesses. The relatively large number of choices in employment which were available freed the individual from dependency upon business firms or the government for a livelihood.

This ethical philosophy of individualism was mirrored in the political-economic philosophy of laissez faire, which postulated that the greatest social good is realized when the individual business firm attempts to maximize its profits. Restraints upon business activities by governmental or social institutions should, therefore, according to this doctrine, be minimized so that the individual entrepreneur can be quite free to do whatever he wants in order to maximize his profits. Given these social and economic philosophies, it was often highly profitable to expand industry and to form new businesses.[4]

By 1850, England had been transformed from an agricultural and trading society to one characteristic of an industrial country. The industrial revolution occurred later in the United States and continued into the Twentieth Century. In the later stages of the industrial revolution, the closing western frontier in the United States reduced the opportunities for individuals to seek alternate employment opportunities. As the American society became an industrial one, individuals tended to become more and more dependent upon each other. Individual initiative became less relevant as a practical philosophy. No longer did the protestant ethic and its emphasis on freedom and individualism provide such a realistic guide to a person's behavior. If one had a factory job the alternatives in employment open to him often were few. Social progress tended to become dependent upon

---

[4] It is interesting to speculate whether the industrial revolution would have taken place as quickly if the legal, social, and technological environment of the times had been different. If communism or the divine right of Kings had been the prevailing political-economic philosophy during the Eighteenth Century, the benefits of industrialization and technological development would have accrued to the state rather than to individuals. Under either system, would individual entrepreneurs or inventors have been motivated to create as they did? Or, would the state have been willing to risk the capital resources necessary to build factories and to design and utilize new previously untried machinery?

cooperative effort and organization as well as upon individual effort. Fewer and fewer individuals were able to rely solely upon their own abilities and resources to earn their livelihoods. Reflections of this greater dependency came in many forms. The clergy paid less praise to the great captains of industry and pointed with alarm at the industrial "robber barons." Trade unions emerged to help protect the often relatively powerless individual worker against many business excesses. Legislation, such as the anti-trust laws, were enacted to curb still other forms of business individualism.

At the same time that these changes in the socio-economic environment were taking place, a basic change in the form of management in many business firms was occurring. When the corporate holdings of an individual became very large, he needed assistance to manage and operate his enterprises. This need generated a *separation of ownership of business from its management*. The hired manager could not depend upon his ownership rights to insure his livelihood. He usually had little, if any, stock ownership. Rather, he needed to rely upon his own competence as a manager in order to maintain his job. The owners were interested in employing those managers who could maximize the stockholders' returns. Managerial tenure became dependent upon performance rather than ownership.

The Scientific Management School

The development of a complex, interdependent society, in which large-scale business firms operated by professional managers became predominant created a need for much greater attention to the problems of managing. One of the first and most significant persons to attempt to develop ways to meet this need was Frederick Winslow Taylor, often referred to as the Father of the "scientific management" school of thought.

Taylor was able to show, through both the logic of his writings and the application of his ideas as a manager, that the work of management could be *analyzed scientifically* so as to arrive at better decisions.[5] In 1878, Taylor started working at the Midvale Steel Works. As he progressed upwards through the ranks of management, he was impressed by the lack of accurate knowledge at the disposal of managers. In attempting to set incentive pay rates for jobs, for example, no reliable estimates of the time required for performing the work were available. Taylor found that it would not be desirable to take

---

[5] Probably Taylor's most definitive and comprehensive work is his *Principles of Scientific Management* (New York: Harper & Brothers, 1911).

the actual time of the best worker as a standard since the methods of some of the slower workers on certain parts of a particular job might be superior to those of the fastest worker. What was required was to determine the best possible method for each job segment by observing the performance of numerous workers, and from these data develop a best method for the job as a whole. Once the best method had been determined and taught to all workers, a time standard derived for it could be used for incentive purposes. This led to his development of a relatively accurate method of timing jobs called time study.

Taylor's success in setting time standards and incentives led him to apply the same methods of analysis to a wide variety of management problems including those involved in inventory control, production planning, metal cutting, cost accounting, and quality control. These analytical methods included: (1) *research* into the nature of the variables bearing upon problems; (2) *standardization* (applying the methods developed to *all* applicable jobs); (3) *selection* of workers best suited to performing the jobs analyzed and; (4) *training* them in the best method developed for performing the work. These research techniques implied that management could best determine the way that the work was to be performed, whereas previously trade skills had been passed down from master craftsman to apprentice. Thus, there was a separation of *planning* how the work was to be done from the actual performance of jobs by employees.

Managers and workers alike found it difficult to believe that an individual unskilled in a task could tell a master craftsman how to perform his job better. Consequently, Taylor's ideas were resisted by many whose positions were challenged by his work. When Taylor left the Bethlehem Steel Corporation after three years of work there, for example, many of his applications were discarded. His successes could not be ignored, however, and other analysts extended similar concepts into many industries. Frank and Lillian Gilbreth,[6] Harrington Emerson,[7] H. L. Gantt, and Henry Towne, among others, continued working along the lines followed by Taylor and were extremely active in formulating and applying scientific management approaches in business firms.

The advancement of these scientific management ideas—which

---

[6] Frank B. Gilbreth, *Motion Study* (New York: D. Van Nostrand Co., 1911).
[7] Harrington Emerson, *The Twelve Principles of Efficiency,* 1913. H. L. Gantt, *Industrial Leadership,* 1916.

have focused attention upon managerial problems faced at relatively low levels of administration in the firm, and upon the actual work performed by non-managerial employees—continues today in industrial engineering and production management departments at many universities. Depending upon the university involved, these departments are located organizationally either in colleges of engineering or of business administration.

The Functional or Process School

As indicated above, during the early part of the Twentieth Century, the management movement in the United States centered its attention upon managerial problems at the worker or shop level. Contemporary developments in European management thought, on the other hand, proceeded by concentrating attention at upper management levels. Henri Fayol, a French industrialist, conceived of the job of managing as consisting of several distinct *functions* or *processes:* planning, organizing, commanding, coordinating, and controlling.[8] Fayol's work was based less upon detailed research (illustrative of Taylor's work) than upon generalizing from his observations and his experience as a manager. Fayol's writings, however, were not translated into English until 1925 nor did they become widely available in the United States until 1949.

Fayol's work initiated what is referred to as the functional management school, or now frequently as the "classical" approach to management. Later contributions and elaborations of the functional approach came from Ralph C. Davis,[9] William Newman,[10] George Terry,[11] and Koontz and O'Donnell.[12]

The central focus of the classical school has been upon what the manager should do. The thinkers of this school have attempted to develop a set of principles to prescribe how the managerial functions should be performed. For example, one of the basic principles developed by the classical school is that the manager is limited in the number of subordinates which he can effectively manage. These principles have been derived largely from the experience and per-

---

[8] Henri Fayol, *Administration Industrielle et Générale,* 1916.

[9] R. C. Davis, *The Fundamentals of Top Management* (New York: Harper & Brothers, 1951).

[10] William Newman, *Administrative Action* (Englewood Cliffs, N.J.: Prentice-Hall, Inc., 1950).

[11] George Terry, *Principles of Management* (Homewood, Ill.: Richard D. Irwin, Inc., 1953).

[12] Harold Koontz and Cyril O'Donnell, *Principles of Management* (New York: McGraw-Hill Book Co., Inc., 1955).

sonal observation of managers and from studies by academic scholars.

The proponents of functional principles consider them applicable to management in all types of institutions (e.g., business, government, educational) and to all levels of management from the first line supervisor to the highest executive.

Human Relations and Behavioral Science

A third school of management thought of significance today is the so-called "human relations movement." This movement may be traced back to a number of experiments which were carried out at the Hawthorne Plant of the Western Electric Company in the 1920's. These experiments were initially directed toward determining, under controlled conditions, the effect of certain physical conditions upon worker output. For example, in one experiment, illumination levels were systematically varied at the work place. In this experiment, it was found that worker output increased with increased illumination but when the illumination was then *decreased*, output *continued* to increase.

At first perplexed by their discovery, the researchers finally came to the conclusion that the productivity increases with lessened illumination were due to psychological factors—the performance of employees being studied was influenced to a considerable extent by the special attention that they were receiving as subjects of the experiment. This finding led the researchers to conclude that social and human factors in the place of work were often much more important than physical factors in influencing productivity.[13]

Whereas the scientific management school had focused attention upon the technology of work place arrangement, the human relations movement gave major consideration to individual and group relationships in organizations. Numerous disagreements between proponents of these two schools of management thought have been generated. The human relationists often have argued that irrespective of the technical efficiency of the physical layout, say for the mass-production of an item on an assembly line, productivity would be impaired unless the psychological and sociological factors affecting worker output were considered. Certain persons in the scientific management school, on the other hand, have tended to

---

[13] Reported in Elton Mayo, *The Human Problems of an Industrial Civilization* (New York: The Macmillan Co., 1933), and F. J. Roethlisberger and W. J. Dickson, *Management and the Worker* (Cambridge, Mass.: Harvard University Press, 1939).

accuse the human relationists of placing too much emphasis on the feelings and needs of workers while ignoring costs and profitability.

The work of human relations continues as an intellectual pursuit in the management departments of colleges of business administration as well as in departments of psychology, sociology, and in institutes dealing with human relations problems. Also giving consideration to the human problems of business organization has been another group of thinkers—a group often referred to as the behavioral scientists. Although the work of both of these two groups focuses attention on human variables, they may be distinguished on the basis of the differing emphases which they place on theory. Much of the early work of the human relations school was undertaken with relatively little theoretical background to explain or to predict why a particular management technique worked or did not. In contrast, the behaviorists have put more emphasis on analyzing the functioning of a management system with reference to basic theory in the social sciences—psychology, social psychology, sociology, etc. Rather than applying a technique on the basis that it has worked elsewhere in the past, the behavioral scientists have attempted, with sufficient prior knowledge of the particular system under consideration, to predict the theoretical impact of the application of various types of solutions to problems.

The Quantitative School of Management Thought

Another focus of managerial thought which has originated in the Twentieth Century is that of quantitative, mathematical analysis. During World War II, major applications of mathematical approaches to the solution of managerial decision problems were developed. Such problems as convoy make-up and submarine deployment were studied, analyzed, and solved mathematically. Then, after the war, many similar forms of quantitative analysis were developed by business firms. Many problems and sub-problems that theretofore had been subjected only to intuitive experience-based analysis came under mathematical probing and scrutiny. The postwar development of automatic electronic computers greatly increased the ability of management analysts to perform complex quantitative studies of business problems since the large number of computations necessary in many types of these analyses cannot be handled easily without computers.

The rise of mathematical techniques has spawned new areas of business interest. One of these is often referred to as *operations research*. Operations research techniques are quantitatively-based analytical methods useful in shedding insight into and in generating recommendations for action on a wide range of managerial problems. Also, a group of scholars, known as *management scientists* have developed additional and complementary quantitative techniques. Although it is often difficult to distinguish the operations researcher from the management scientist, the management science movement is generally considered (by management scientists) to encompass a broader range of problems than does operations research, in that it also includes quantitative behavioral science approaches within its confines.[14]

Trends in Management Thought

In the previous sections we have examined the major schools of management thought as they have developed since just prior to the turn of the Twentieth Century. The chronology of these developments is portrayed graphically in Figure 1–1. We will now consider these ideas in light of the most significant current trends in the field of management.

FIGURE 1–1. Chronology of Management Thought

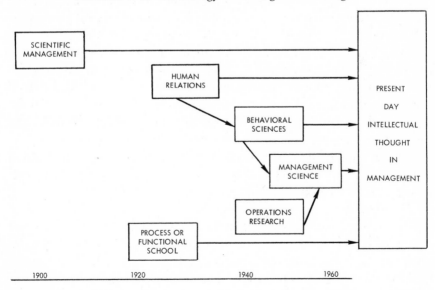

---

[14] It is interesting to note that many scholars are members of both the Operations Research Society of America (ORSA) and The Institute of Management Sciences (TIMS).

Three basic trends seem to be significant today in management thinking: (1) a broadening of the knowledge deemed to be relevant to management; (2) an increasing use of and dependence upon quantitative methods; and (3) greater application of the underlying behavioral sciences to managerial understanding and decision making.

Broadening of Management Knowledge.   Prior to the Twentieth Century, management was often practiced in a way similar to the apprenticeship system with sons typically relieving fathers in administrative positions. Little conscious intellectual thought was given to improving or professionalizing practice, until the emergence of the scientific management movement. This movement introduced the idea that scientific methods of analysis could be applied to managerial activity. Its applications were concerned primarily with factory-oriented relatively low-level managerial jobs, and with technological and cost considerations.

The classical school emphasized the notion that *all* levels of management in a wide variety of institutions warranted intellectual thought. The classicists pointed up the importance of analyzing what managers should do as well as planning what workers should do.

Those scholars focusing attention on the human problems of organizations have brought us to the realization that knowledge of the social sciences (in addition to economics) could both aid the understanding of management and help improve managerial decision making. Neither the scientific management nor the classical schools of thought ignored human and social problems relevant to management, but the human relationists and behavioral scientists placed much greater emphasis upon these factors. Without doubt, these thinkers have broadened our ideas about the variables that management needs to consider in its day-to-day functioning.

Finally, the quantitative school of management thought has added mathematics and statistics as areas of knowledge important for effective decision making by managers.

Each of these schools of thought has broadened the scope of knowledge considered important to management. At the same time, their work has resulted in the management field becoming more complex and more difficult to conceptualize in any overall integrated sense. Further, sometimes these diverse approaches have arrived at quite opposing views as to how management problems ought to be analyzed and dealt with.

To cope with the dilemmas presented by this diverse and complex set of management ideologies, many scholars have restricted their attention to only those few management concepts most congruent with their own ideas. Such an approach runs the risk of ignoring important developments in other management areas. What management thought needs at this time is an integrating concept or focus through which knowledge from all sub-sets of management knowledge may be viewed. At the conclusion of this chapter, we will view the decision-information system concept as an integrating mechanism through which, in the remainder of this book, knowledge from these many diverse schools of management thought will be brought together.

The Increasing Use of Quantitative Methods. The second basic current trend of management thought is the increasing use of quantitative methods. Although, for example, statistical quality control dates from Shewhart's work in the mid-1920's, the application of mathematical approaches to management problems received its greatest impetus during World War II. Since that time, utilization of mathematical techniques by managers has extended considerably. The range of quantitative decision-making tools useful to management is becoming broader with the appearance of each issue of the scholarly journals. Present day management makes use of linear, nonlinear and dynamic programming, statistical decision theory, inventory decision models, simulation and Monte Carlo methods, and many other quantitative decision tools. These have been applied to problems existing within the several functional areas of business such as production, marketing, and finance. In addition, these techniques have found application by managers of many other kinds of organizations such as hospitals, universities, both military and civilian governmental agencies, farms, and unions.

This increasing emphasis on quantitative approaches to management parallels earlier developments in the physical sciences. As problems, and the variables bearing on these problems, can be measured and stated in quantitative terms, a more precise prediction of behavior is possible. Progress in the physical sciences paralleled quantification and measurement in these fields. It is not coincidental, then, that many scholars and students of management thought consider progress in management theory closely related to the degree of quantification and measurement that can be associated with it. This also explains, to some extent, the emphasis which some managers and students place upon quantification and on the development of mathematical models for management.

Increasing Emphasis on the Behavioral Sciences. The third current trend in management thought is the growing emphasis on the behavioral sciences. Economics has long been recognized as the mother science of management. Much of the study of management has been focused upon the application of economic principles to administrative problems of organizations. For example, numerous inventory models have been utilized for a number of years as a means of minimizing the costs associated with the production or procurement of raw materials and parts. These models represent applications of cost-minimization principles from micro-economic theory. Since administrators are charged with the responsibility of achieving goals with limited resources, economics will continue to be one of the fundamental sciences underlying management.

As management thought has become more sophisticated both in theory and in practice, it has become evident that economics cannot explain or predict many types of organizational behavior of interest to managers. As an example, one of management's continuing problems is the training of its employees. Here, several concepts developed by learning theorists in the field of psychology have been helpful in designing more effective training programs. Similarly, personality theory has helped provide a basis for the design of the so-called sensitivity training approach, which is utilized to train executives in developing more effective interpersonal relationships with others.

In addition to economics and psychology, knowledge from other social sciences, such as sociology, cultural anthropology, and political science can be useful to the manager. Managers must deal with the behavior of work groups as well as that of individual employees in the organization; in the management of the firm's operations abroad, the cultural values of other nations and societies become important considerations, and many managerial problems must be dealt with in the light of existing governmental regulations and/or possible future legislation.

The relationship of management to the behavioral sciences is similar to that between engineering and the physical sciences or to that between the practice of medicine and the biological sciences. Medicine, management, and engineering are professional occupations whose activities are concentrated upon the solution of problems within their respective areas of endeavor. Doctors utilize the biological and physical sciences as a basis for analyzing health problems; engineers use the physical sciences in solving design problems in connection with chemical, electrical and mechanical systems. Managers utilize the social sciences in an analogous manner since they are engaged in the solution of individual and group problems related to the achievement of organizational goals. The behavioral sciences furnish the underlying understanding of the behavior of individuals and groups necessary to arrive at knowledgeable solutions.

DIFFERING CONCEPTS OF MANAGEMENT

As we have indicated previously, during the relatively short history of the management movement, a great number of different ideas have been presented to explain the nature of management. Management thought may, in a sense, be likened to a many-faceted gem, any one side of which is interesting and contributes to an understanding of the whole. Yet no one facet can, in itself, provide a complete picture of the managerial process. To help develop a better understanding of these many facets and gain a broader perspective of the managerial process, we will now examine several differing views about management.

External and Internal Studies of Management

Since managers may exert considerable influence outside of their firms by the decisions they make, social scientists have often examined the direction that these influences take in the community and society. These studies of management have usually not been directly concerned with improving the internal operations of organizations; rather, their purpose has been to learn more about the external impact of management upon other social institutions and/or upon individuals in our society. For example, studies of interlocking directorates have focused attention upon the degree of centrality of power in economic life. From the vantage of society as a whole, studies of this type are important since they may be able to reveal or to clarify general social issues or problems to which the citizenry or its institutions may wish to address themselves. Externally oriented studies of management are also of significance to managers since they may be able to reveal potential business excesses which, in the opinion of the public, require remedy. Being forewarned, management may be able to forestall drastic public reactions (e.g., legal restrictions) to these problems.

In contrast to such external studies of management, the goals of most studies which focus attention on the internal problems of the firm are directed toward the improvement of managerial perform-ance. Theories to explain managerial behavior are developed so that they may be applied by management practitioners in their jobs. The vast majority of these endeavors are not intended to be critical of the manager's role; rather, they are intended as means for better-ment of the managerial job. Most of the data with which we will deal in this book have been derived from internal analyses of or-ganization and are geared toward the improvement of managerial decision making.

Cultural Influences Upon Management

Numerous observations about management made in this volume are valid and relevant in their entirety only in the United States since the problems faced by management are often conditioned con-siderably by cultural factors. For example, the Japanese manager does not have to be concerned about a high degree of labor turn-over common to industry in the United States because most workers remain with a single employer for life.[15]

The scope of this book does not allow an extensive discussion of the impact that cultural influences have upon management. In sub-sequent chapters, however, we will cite a few examples of how cul-tural influences may affect the practice of management. These kinds of influences may not be so great as to require a manager to make *drastic* changes in his patterns of behavior if he were to, say, move from a position in New York to one in Los Angeles, although certain cultural differences do exist in various sections of this country. For companies which engage in international operations, however, pay-ing specific attention to and making careful analyses of cultural in-fluences are of considerable importance.

Management as a Profession

In the writings about management, one often finds reference to professional managers and the need to make management a profes-sion.[16] Consequently, we will now (1) examine the meaning of the word "profession" and then, (2) evaluate the relevance of the term "profession" to present-day management.

---

[15] James Abegglen, *The Japanese Factory* (Cambridge, Mass.: Massachusetts In-stitute of Technology, 1959).

[16] See, for example, Mary Parker Follet, "When Business Management Becomes a Profession," *Advanced Management,* 20 (July, 1955), 22–26.

A profession is an occupation or calling possessing certain unique characteristics for admission to and for remaining in practice. The requirements for admission are often set by the states in conjunction with professional associations in the field. Minimum educational and/or experience requirements may be established as prerequisites for a license to practice a profession (e.g., medicine and law). In addition, an examination may be required (e.g., licensed professional engineers). Further, standards for being permitted to continue in practice may be established by law and by the professional associations (e.g., the prohibition against euthanasia by members of the medical profession). Members of a profession are also usually considered as having responsibilities to their profession above and beyond their responsibilities to their employer. An accountant who is a C.P.A. is expected to adhere to professional accounting standards in his work while at the same time helping meet the objectives of his employer.

In viewing management as a profession, we find that managers perform similar activities, the sum total of which provides an occupational focus for a profession. In contrast to the more established professions, however, there are no common or widely accepted standards for admission to the practice of management. Although particular companies may establish and maintain a set of qualifications for managership in their firms, other enterprises may utilize quite different standards. Similarly, the standards for continuing in the practice of management show wide variability among different firms and even within the same firms. Furthermore, no government agency or professional association controls admission to or the practice of management. We may conclude, therefore, that although management is comprised of a set of occupational activities which form the basis for professional practice, the other accouterments normally associated with a "profession" are absent. As science evolves in management, it may be possible in the future to develop professional standards for management practice, but no agreement about what these standards are or might be exists at the present.[17]

---

[17] One argument opposing the establishment of a professional society to develop admission and practice standards for managers is as follows: There is a need for some people in our society to undertake risks and to perform the entrepreneurial functions of business. If a professional society were to restrict individuals from initiating business enterprises on the basis that they had not met certain standards, this might have the effect of reducing competition. See for example Peter F. Drucker, *The Practice of Management* (New York: Harper & Brothers, 1954), pp. 8–11, 47–48.

The Art and Science of Management

In the previous sections we have made several references to "management science." Discussed considerably by management thinkers has been the question "Is management really a science, or is it rather an art?" In this section, we will both (1) make some observations about the characteristics of an "art" as opposed to a "science," and then (2) present several views on the question of whether management is an art or a science.

Art and Science. An art is a "skill in performance acquired by experience, study, or observation; knack." [18] In contrast, a science is "A branch of study concerned with observation and classification of facts, especially with the establishment of verifiable general laws, chiefly by induction and hypotheses." [19] Management or administration has long been considered as a practicing art. Since the days of Taylor, however, management scholars have been attempting to reduce the art to a science of management.

It is important to understand the difference between these two concepts. The term "art" emphasizes the *skills* employed in solving problems. Management as an art is concerned with performance, with getting things accomplished. The art in management is decision and action oriented. The knack of achievement implied by the "art of management" is often considered to have been acquired through experience. Good managers are often said to have a definite "feel" for the situations facing them and to be able to intuitively size them up and make decisions.

Let us now contrast the concept of management as an art with that of management as a science. In any branch of endeavor, science is usually conceived of as consisting of a *theory* or a set of theories designed and interrelated in such a way as to *explain* phenomena and behavior. Thus, the orientation of a science is toward *knowledge* about behavior. In any science, many theorems of behavior remain unproven until sufficient research has been undertaken to validate them. When, however, substantial evidence of an impartial nature accumulates, the theorem becomes an accepted one and may be stated as a principle or a law. If the scientist is able to *describe* managerial behavior and *why* it occurs, he may be able to predict the outcomes of specified courses of management action. By comparing different courses of action on some preference scale

---

[18] *Webster's Collegiate Dictionary* (5th ed.; Springfield, Mass.: G. & C. Merriam Co., 1946), p. 60.
[19] *Ibid.,* p. 890.

(such as profitability), the most desirable ones may then be determined. In the development of a science, then, progression takes place from description to explanation to prediction to prescription.

Since knowledge is the basis upon which science is founded, we should be aware of the acceptable scientific methods for the development of knowledge. The ideal research method is the reproducible experiment. If an experiment conducted by one researcher is reproducible, the reliability and validity of the knowledge obtained from it can be confirmed by other observers. Management is one area of knowledge, however, that does not readily lend itself to reproducible experimentation because operating organizations are run for profit. Managers are often hesitant to permit experiments to be conducted within their organizations which may be costly in terms of both time and expense. The Western Electric Hawthorne experiments are one notable exception to this hesitancy.

Many additional valid research techniques, however, do exist for developing managerial knowledge. For example, considerable data about the functioning of organizations have been obtained by survey research approaches, analytical case studies, and interview methods. In addition, one recently developed approach—simulation—has permitted controlled experimentation without disrupting the operation of organizations through the study of certain business conditions in artificial laboratory situations.

As indicated previously, theory is considered basic to all sciences. Thus, some observations are also in order about the role of theory in applying the scientific method to management. A primary function of theory is to suggest to the researcher the phenomena most worthy of studying in order to further knowledge. Without theory, the collection of data for its own sake is questionable. Unless we had some theory to indicate that executives with red hair are more successful than other managers, for example, it would be highly speculative to look for any relationship between hair color and managerial success on the bare chance that some such relationship does exist. We can increase the probability of experimental success if data are collected to prove or disprove one of the yet unproved hypotheses derived from theory.

To illustrate, there is a growing body of knowledge about the behavior and characteristics of executives. Some of this knowledge supports the theory that executives are, on the whole, in better physical and mental health than are workers and that the higher his position the healthier the executive tends to be.[20] Using this theory, we might further hypothesize that executives enjoy better adjusted marriages than do workers. Then, to test this hypothesis, a measure of marriage adjustment or maladjustment might be developed (e.g., divorce and separation rates). If a representative sample of both executives and workers were taken and marital maladjustment measured and compared for the two groups, differences, if any, could be noted and the hypothesis accepted or rejected. In this way theory about executive behavior could be extended or modified based upon research results.

The purpose of the above example is to illustrate that hypothetical relationships developed on the basis of theory (mental health and executive level) are much more probable of being relevant and useful extensions of knowledge than are relationships based upon pure speculation (e.g., red hair and executive success). Funds and time available for research are often extremely meager. We can ill afford research projects to test speculative whims of researchers or research supporters.

Finally, in discussing the application of scientific methods to management, we should emphasize that the development of a body of knowledge does not assure its proper application. In spite of considerable knowledge about the adverse physiological effects of certain drugs upon the body, for example, drug addiction continues. In a similar way, managers may or may not utilize existing knowledge as they operate their businesses from day to day.

We would consider a doctor to be derelict or criminal if he ignores new scientific developments in treating patients. In management, however, some businessmen tend to discount the value of new scientific theories for they consider themselves extremely practical men. However, if it can predict the outcomes of various courses of action open to the manager, theory can be an extremely valuable tool. Managers can learn to *use* and *apply* management theory to their problems. The doctor and engineer have learned to apply the sciences underlying their practices. There is little reason to believe that managers cannot do the same.

Scientific data can be detrimental, of course, if it is misapplied to business problems. One firm, for example, undertook a study to determine the product characteristics desired by the largest propor-

---

[20] This evidence contradicts the old wives' tale of the executive ulcer. See John R. P. French, Jr., "Status, Self-Esteem and Health," *Proceedings*, CIOS XIII (New York: Council for International Progress in Management, 1963), pp. 735–38.

tion of its customers, and then redesigned its product along these lines. However, the company ignored the additional fact that all of its competitors had similar designs. If the firm had selected a different, but exclusive design, preferred by fewer consumers, the company might have had a market segment all to itself and been much more successful. This points up the fact that *applying* knowledge obtained through scientific investigation to the solution of management problems remains, to a considerable extent, an art, dependent upon the skill and expertise of the executive.

Management: An Art or Science? Now that we have discussed several facets of the meaning of the terms "art" and "science" and their implications for management, we will examine several views as to whether management is an art or a science.

There is one school of thought which contends that management can never become a science. This belief is partly based upon the complexity of the problems with which managers deal—there are so many variables which must be considered in making certain decisions and some of these are so ill-defined that the degree of precision and predictability usually attributed to a science do not appear capable of attainment. While conceding that a portion of managerial activity may be amenable to scientific analysis, some persons who conceive of management as an art contend that these portions comprise a relatively unimportant segment of the total managerial job. This is considered to be especially true at the highest and most important positions in an organization, where the problems which must be dealt with are most complex.

Taking a somewhat different view are those who believe that although knowledge about management can be classified and organizational behavior predicted and even prescribed, the science characterization is irrelevant. When managers decide or act, they do so not as scientists but as practitioners—as employers of science in the solution of their problems. They view the scientist's goal as truth and its discovery. Where knowledge exists, managers may use it. But even if knowledge does not exist, *the manager must still decide.* He must, in spite of knowledge or the lack of it, achieve results.

Those who view management as a science often admit that it is an emerging one. Generally acceptable techniques exist for the solution of some managerial problems, but there are still substantial gaps in the theory of management. In these areas, managerial decision making is based largely upon experience, judgment, and intuition. Yet scientific analysis of management problems progresses at a substantial pace. Projecting these developments over time, one might visualize a future in which comprehensive prescriptive laws for management behavior may be based upon sound verifiable theory.

The growing utilization of science in management may be exemplified by a study of short-term demand forecasting for power by a public utility. Over a long period of experience, repeated daily, one manager had developed a high degree of skill in anticipating what customer demand for power would be. By means of a scientific study of the variables influencing demand, two researchers with no experience in the utility industry were able to incorporate this and other knowledge into an efficient computer program which was substantially more accurate in its predictions than the experienced executive.

In some cases, however, the utilization of scientific methodology may not yield results better than those achieved by experienced-based decision approaches. In a study of the scheduling methods used by foremen in one plant, for instance, an attempt was made to classify and simplify the decision rules currently being used. The researcher discovered that more than 30 different scheduling rules were being used by the foremen. These rules were being applied under different conditions of product demand, shop conditions, and worker availability. The study found that the varying conditions in the shop warranted the apparently large number of scheduling rules, and that the set of rules which had been established through experience were comprehensive enough to meet almost all contingencies which arose in the plant. Further, the results of the scientific analysis coincided with the same conclusions derived from long experience on the job. In this particular case, science was not able to improve upon the art of management in the scheduling function.

In conclusion, we suggest that scientific analysis of managerial problems often provides opportunities to improve managerial decision making. Conversely, management as a practicing art has provided many examples of success, some of which science has been unable to improve upon. Although management has not yet been reduced to a set of verifiable laws of behavior, continuous inroads have been made toward the development of a science of management.

OVERVIEW: DECISION–INFORMATION SYSTEMS

In the introduction to this chapter, we indicated that the basic approach to be taken in this book would be one in which the information-decision system would provide a central integrative focus. We will now elaborate upon this conception as a means of providing an overview to some of the basic ways in which we view the managerial process.

Our decision-information focus may be better understood if attention is first given to certain developments in scientific thought which have occurred in the Twentieth Century outside the field of management. As the reader is undoubtedly aware, many "revolutionary" scientific developments have taken place in this century—Einstein's theory of relativity, the emergence of quantum theory in physics, Freud's psychoanalytic approach to the human personality, etc.

A number of prominent thinkers of our day have held that in spite of the wide diversity of scientific development which has occurred in different fields of endeavor, many basic similarities in trends of ways of thinking may be noted among this diversity of thought. Among those scholars who hold that there is a basic unity in the way that thinkers in various disciplines are coming to view the world is the biologist Ludwig von Bertalanffy, sometimes referred to as the father of General System Theory. In his book, *Problems of Life*, Bertalanffy has the following observation to make about the unity of scientific thought:

> If we survey the various fields of modern science, we notice a dramatic and amazing evolution. Similar conceptions and principles have arisen on quite different realms, although this parallelism of ideas is the result of independent developments. . . .
>
> . . . a stupendous perspective emerges, a vista towards a hitherto unsuspected unity of the conception of the world. Similar general principles have evolved everywhere, whether we are dealing with inanimate things, organisms, mental or social processes.[21]

In answering the question: "What is the origin of these correspondences?" Bertalanffy goes on to say:

> We answer this question by the *claim for a new realm of science*, which we call General System Theory. It is a logico-mathematical field, the subject matter of which is the formulation and derivation of those principles which hold for systems in general. A "system" can be defined as a complex of elements standing in interaction. There are general principles holding for systems, *irrespective of the nature of the component elements and of the relations or forces between them*. . . . In modern science, dynamic interaction is the basic problem in all fields, and its general principles will have to be formulated in General System Theory.[22]

---

[21] Ludwig von Bertalanffy, *Problems of Life* (New York: Harper & Brothers, Harper Torchbook Edition, 1960), pp. 176, 199.
[22] *Ibid.*, pp. 199, 201. The second emphasis in this quotation is ours.

In addition to Bertalanffy's General System Theory, a second "interdisciplinary" view intended as a unifying approach for science, has been developed in this century by the late Norbert Wiener, that of *cybernetics*. Cybernetics—taken from the Greek word, *kubernētēs*, meaning "steersman"—is defined as the science of communication and control. Wiener's thesis is that:

> . . . society can only be understood through a study of the messages and the communication facilities which belong to it; and that in the future the development of these messages and communication facilities, messages between man and machines, between machines and man, and between machine and machine, are destined to play an everincreasing part.[23]

In paralleling the function of some of the newer automatic machines (e.g., computers) with that of man, Wiener has emphasized that both receive information to provide the basis for action; both possess memory mechanisms; both utilize the feedback of information from "outside" their own system as a means of comparing actual performance with intended performance; and both possess central decision organs which determine what is to be done on the basis of the informational feedback received. As Bertalanffy has viewed General System Theory as a unifying one in science, so also have Wiener and others held that "information theory, cybernetics, and other associated areas possess sufficient generality to warrant their extension into most every facet of the animate universe." [24]

As of the writing of this book, relatively few of Bertalanffy's specific notions concerning systems have been explicitly incorporated into management thought or applied in the analysis of managerial problems. However, in recent years, an increasing number of management scholars and practitioners have come to view the business organization as an information-decision system and, in doing so, have emphasized, as did Wiener, analyzing problems in terms of informational inputs, feedback, etc.[25] Although many managerial and organizational processes have not yet been adequately conceptualized in terms of their dynamic interaction with other facets of the organizational system, we nonetheless believe that the most broadly based integrative conception of managerial and organizational be-

---

[23] Norbert Wiener, *The Human Use of Human Beings* (Garden City, N.Y.: Doubleday & Company, Inc., Anchor Books Edition, 1954), p. 16. Quoted with permission of the Houghton Mifflin Company, original publishers of the book.

[24] William G. Scott, *Human Relations in Management* (Homewood, Ill.: Richard D. Irwin, Inc., 1962), p. 211.

[25] See, for example, Elias H. Porter, "The Parable of the Spindle," *Harvard Business Review*, 40 (May–June, 1962), pp. 58–66; Paul S. Greenlaw, "Management Development: A Systems View," *Personnel Journal*, 43 (April, 1964), pp. 205–11.

havior existing at this time is one in which organzations are viewed in cybernetic and systems terms to the extent possible. In this conception the business organization is viewed as: (1) an open system in interaction with its environment, (2) comprised of many interdependent and interacting parts, and, (3) central to which are managerial decisions which provide the basis for actions designed to meet business objectives and which are "linked together" by feedback and other informational flows. Although admittedly many important facets of organizational behavior have not yet been adequately integrated conceptually into this framework, we further believe that the *basic* foci of the various schools of management thought discussed earlier can be viewed in information-decision systems terms. For example, time-study based performance standards (scientific management school) provide information for making decisions about employee incentives, and when feedback data about actual performance indicates that certain of such standards are not being met, a basis for taking corrective action may be provided. The effect of certain types of informational flows in the organizational system in creating psychological stresses for the recipients of the messages has been analyzed both in psychological-behavioral and cybernetic terms. The so-called principles of management of the classical school of thought can be analyzed in terms of their validity as guides to decision making. Or, most of the mathematical models of the operations researcher are oriented toward providing better tools for decision making; while certain of these models, especially some of those of the simulation variety, focus direct and explicit attention upon problems in a systems context.

One final comment concerning the approach to be taken in this book is in order. Although certain sections in succeeding chapters have a heavy "systems flavor," many others do not—numerous topics covered are treated largely "in isolation" from other facets of the organizational system. In some cases, such a non-systems treatment is utilized because we believe it to provide an adequate conceptualization; in other cases, it is taken because the problems under consideration have not yet, to our knowledge, been adequately framed in systems terms. For similar reasons, but to a much lesser extent, not all of the materials in this book are directly and explicitly treated in terms of the decision-making process. Our basic focus, however, is upon managerial decision making, and our basic premise is that the most unitary conception of the managerial process may be provided by a systems framework.

DISCUSSION AND STUDY QUESTIONS

1. What are the primary differences between the following schools of management thought: (a) scientific management and the functional school? (b) human relations and the behavioral sciences? (c) scientific management and "management science"?

2. In what ways can we differentiate management from professions such as medicine, engineering, and law?

3. Scientifically conducted experiments within business firms have represented the primary source of knowledge comprising intellectual management thought. Comment on this statement.

4. Is the *application* of scientific knowledge to the solution of business problems considered primarily an art or a science? Explain. Would the same answer be true for medicine or engineering?

5. What historical developments have tended to bring about a greater need for improving the practice of management while also stimulating the intellectual study of management?

6. In what ways did existing social, ethical, and political philosophies tend to encourage the industrial revolution?

7. Why did the protestant ethic become less useful as a philosophy for individual behavior during the later stages of the Industrial Revolution?

8. Would you say that practicing managers are more concerned with the solution of problems or with furthering the development of scientific knowledge about business behavior? Explain.

9. For an electronics manufacturer in New York City, what differences might there be in the usefulness of (a) a scientific analysis of a quality control problem in its production department and (b) a scientific study of the decision-making behavior of managers in a representative sample of Pennsylvania manufacturing firms?

10. "In many companies, too much reliance these days is being placed upon management theory. In our firm, we don't care whether a proposed course of action is 'theoretically' sound or not. All we are concerned about is whether or not it works." Comment.

SELECTED REFERENCES

BARNARD, CHESTER I. *The Functions of the Executive.* Cambridge, Mass.: Harvard University Press, 1938.

CHURCHMAN, C. W.; ACKOFF, R. L.; and ARNOFF, E. L. *Introduction to Operations Research.* New York: John Wiley & Sons, Inc., 1957.

COCHRAN, THOMAS C. *Basic History of American Business.* Princeton, N. J.: D. Van Nostrand Co., Inc., 1959.

COPLEY, FRANK B. *Frederick W. Taylor: The Father of Scientific Management,* Vols. I and II. New York: Harper & Bros., 1923.

DAIUTE, JAMES R. *Scientific Management and Human Relations.* New York: Holt, Rinehart & Winston, 1964.

DAVIS, RALPH C. *The Fundamentals of Top Management.* New York: Harper & Bros., 1951.

DRUCKER, PETER F. *The Practice of Management.* New York: Harper & Bros., 1954.

FAYOL, HENRI. *General and Industrial Management.* London: Sir Isaac Pitman & Sons, Ltd., 1949.

FILIPETTI, GEORGE. *Industrial Management in Transition.* Rev. ed. Homewood, Ill.: Richard D. Irwin, Inc., 1953.

FORRESTER, J. W. *Industrial Dynamics.* New York: John Wiley & Sons, Inc., 1961.

GRAS, N., and LARSON, H. *Casebook in American Business History.* New York: F. S. Crofts & Co., 1939.

HERRMANN, C. C., and MAGEE, JOHN F. "Operations Research for Management," *Harvard Business Review,* 31 (July–August, 1953), 100–112.

KOONTZ, HAROLD. "The Management Theory Jungle," *Journal of the Academy of Management,* 4 (December, 1961), 174–88.

KOONTZ, HAROLD (ed.). *Toward a Unified Theory of Management.* New York: McGraw-Hill Book Co., Inc., 1964.

KOONTZ, H., and O'DONNELL, C. *Principles of Management.* 2d ed. New York: McGraw-Hill Book Co., Inc., 1959.

MAYO, ELTON. *The Human Problems of an Industrial Civilization.* Boston: Harvard Graduate School of Business Administration, 1946.

MAYO, ELTON. *The Social Problems of an Industrial Civilization.* Boston: Harvard Graduate School of Business Administration, 1945.

MEE, JOHN F. *Management Thought in a Dynamic Economy.* New York: New York University Press, 1963.

MERRILL, HOWARD F. (ed.). *Classics in Management.* New York: American Management Association, 1960.

MILLER, D. W., and STARR, M. K. *Executive Decisions and Operations Research.* Englewood Cliffs, N. J.: Prentice-Hall, Inc., 1960.

MOONEY, JAMES. *The Principles of Organization.* Rev. ed. New York: Harper & Bros., 1954.

RICHARDS, M. D., and NIELANDER, W. A. (eds.). *Readings in Management.* 2d ed. Cincinnati: South-Western Publishing Co., 1963.

ROETHLISBERGER, F. J. *Management and Morale.* Cambridge: Harvard University Press, 1941.

SIMON, HERBERT. *Administrative Behavior.* 2d ed. New York: The Macmillan Co., 1957.

SMIDDY, HAROLD F., and NAUM, L. "Evolution of a 'Science of Managing' in America," *Management Science,* 1 (October, 1954), 1–31.

SUMMER, CHARLES E., JR. *Factors in Effective Administration.* New York: Columbia University Graduate School of Business, 1956.

SPRIEGEL, W. R., and MYERS, C. E. (eds.). *The Writings of the Gilbreths.* Homewood, Ill.: Richard D. Irwin, Inc., 1953.

TAYLOR, FREDERICK W. *Scientific Management*. New York: Harper & Bros., 1947.

URWICK, LYNDALL. "Have We Lost Our Way in the Jungle of Management Theory?" *Personnel*, 42 (May–June, 1965), 8–18.

URWICK, LYNDALL. *The Elements of Administration*. New York: Harper & Bros., 1944.

VILLERS, RAYMOND. *Dynamic Management in Industry*, Chap. II. Englewood Cliffs, N. J.: Prentice-Hall, Inc., 1960.

CHAPTER 2

VALUES, OBJECTIVES, AND DECISION MAKING

INTRODUCTION

DECISION making has received increasing attention as a focal point for the study of business management during recent years. In fact, some leading authorities, such as Herbert Simon, have considered decision making and management as synonymous terms.[1] With few exceptions, the work performed by managers involves or is related to the making of organizational decisions. When, for example, a manager studies a report dealing with his competitors' pricing policies, the information which he obtains from it may provide a basis for pricing decisions which he will subsequently make. When a manager communicates with his subordinates, this behavior results from some decision or choice. Additionally, the information communicated by him provides a basis for the further making of decisions by his subordinates. When a manager decides to restructure his organization, he may have as an objective the improvement of interpersonal relationships and information flows so as to provide for more effective decision making in the future.

Although we do not claim all management to be decision making, decision making does prove to be a highly useful focus for the analysis and study of management. Further, if one considers the entire decision-making process of gathering and processing information, making choices from among alternatives, and effectively communicating decisions made to other members of the organization, there is little managerial activity which could not be considered within a decision-making framework.

---

[1] Herbert Simon, *The New Science of Management Decision* (New York: Harper & Brothers, 1960), p. 1.

Rationality in Decision Making

Sound and logical reasons seem to be lacking to explain why certain decisions in organizations were made the way that they were. Some decisions appear to have been based upon personal reasons or emotional factors. Still other decisions appear to have been ill-considered. When attempts are made to prescribe *how* decisions should be made, however, exhortations are given that managers ought to be "rational"—that they should put aside their personal feelings and emotions and base decisions on the facts of the situation. It is appropriate, then, to examine the concept of rationality in decision making and the extent to which managers are able to approach rationally the problems that arise within organizations.

The concept of "rational man" is not a perfectly clear one. Some hold that the rational man acts in the same way as does the economic man of classical economic theory. This means that the manager would weigh the economic factors bearing upon organizational problems and decide solely with the objective of maximizing profits for the firm. Noneconomic factors, however, have an important bearing on the outcome of many decisions in organizations. During the early days of the union movement, for example, many managers were baffled at the actions of their union members. These managers often made decisions based on the assumption that if the organization provided sufficient economic benefits to its workmen, this ought to suffice in satisfying their wants. Many workers, however, were interested in such "non-rational" factors as their individual dignity and treatment as human beings. Since that time, psychological and sociological factors have gained increasing recognition as key ones in influencing the outcome of decisions, and the view that decision making involves only purely economic considerations has tended to disappear.

Not only may noneconomic factors have a bearing on whether a firm will meet its economic objectives; rather, some enterprise objectives themselves may be noneconomic in nature. One firm, for example, has an objective of providing steady employment to its employees as a means of maintaining a satisfied work force. Decisions which may appear incongruent with achieving a company's economic (profit) goals may, in fact, he considered "rational" ones, if these choices are directed toward such noneconomic objectives.

Another clarification of the concept of rationality comes from the fact that managers usually do not have complete information at their disposal for making decisions. Ignorance of this fact is still with us in some books and courses given in decision making; there is often the exhortation to the decision maker to get "all the facts" before he considers alternatives in making a decision. Compare this concept of rationality with an example of a decision to select a person for the position of controller in a large organization.

The person in charge of selecting a man to fill the controller's position indicated that his objective was to obtain the most highly qualified person in the country since some of the decisions contemplated for the new man would be of critical importance to the future of the company. An intensive search for candidates within the company's several divisions was undertaken. In addition, an executive search consultant was engaged to obtain candidates from outside the company. All possible candidates from these sources were evaluated and the total number of persons seriously considered was limited to twelve. Eventually a person from within the company was selected for the position.

How close to an optimum solution to this problem was the organization able to come? Did the company have perfect knowledge or foresight? Did the person making the decision have all the facts? Obviously, there were a great many more people in the nation who could have been considered for the position than the group from which the firm's selection was made. Although the individual selected may have been a good choice for the position, the "best" person in the country probably wasn't even contacted. The search for candidates probably uncovered a group of *satisfactory* individuals. There is a difference, however, between a *satisfactory* solution to a problem and an *optimum* solution. Rationality to achieve the optimum solution was restricted by the time and costs associated with the search activity necessary for its attainment.

This example is not an unusual one. Humans cannot always make optimum decisions because their choices are bounded by the time and the costs involved in making such decisions. Rather than assay all possible candidates, the company in the above example satisfied itself with the selection of the best person from among a limited supply. This decision may have been optimum in the sense that the marginal cost of further search activity may have exceeded the marginal value of considering additional candidates. That is, a better man may have been uncovered through more search activity, but the extra cost of this search may have exceeded the added value of finding him. This limitation in decision making is sometimes referred to as the principle of *bounded rationality* [2]—the manager can rarely make

---

[2] Herbert Simon, *Administrative Behavior* (2d ed.; New York: Macmillan Co., 1957), pp. 52 ff.

decisions in the sense of having complete information and perfect foresight.

In summary, the managerial decision process culminates in choices which tend to elicit further organizational actions or decisions. A rational decision for an enterprise is one in which the manager consistently attempts to achieve maximum goal attainment giving consideration to the time and costs involved in obtaining information. Goals, as well as the factors bearing upon their achievement, may be economic or noneconomic in nature.

Phases of Decision Making

It is convenient to think of decision making as involving several phases or steps.[3] First, the manager has to determine whether or not a decision needs to be made. This step is concerned with finding the problems that require solution in an organization. To discover whether or not problems exist, it may be necessary to refer back to the organization's objectives. The second phase of decision making is that of developing or generating alternative strategies or courses of action to solve existing problems. Finally, the decision maker must select the most appropriate alternatives from those available. Although some writers treat the implementation of decisions as an additional phase of decision making, we will consider implementation as still another problem requiring another decision.

DETERMINING THE NEED FOR DECISIONS

Since the initial phase of decision making involves the determination that a decision is required on the part of the manager, we will first consider the rise of problems and their identification. If an organization were confronted with no problems, there would be no need to inject an explicit decision into the operation. This ideal situation rarely, if ever, exists in organizations, however, and the *need for decisions arises because of the existence of problems.* Organizational problems may be created by either of the two following conditions: (1) When the performance of the firm does not meet the goals which it has set and/or (2) When its objectives are inappropriate. A discussion of each of these conditions giving rise to problems —and thus the need for managerial decisions—follows.

---

[3] Peter Drucker utilizes five phases of decision making in *The Practice of Management* (New York: Harper & Brothers, 1954). Other writers consider anywhere from 1 to 20 steps or phases as comprising the decision process. Simon, in *The New Science of Management Decision,* Chap. 1, uses the three phases discussed below.

Performance Inadequacies

Inadequate performance in meeting the objectives of an organization may be the result of either or both of two factors. First, the work of the organization may be directed toward activities which do not assist or aid in meeting the stated objectives. This is a case of misdirected effort on the part of the organization. Perhaps the organization could easily meet its objectives if its efforts were directed toward activities which would further these ends rather than being frittered away in meaningless (in terms of objectives) activities. If a businessman has the singular objective of obtaining a maximum profit but engages in many tangential activities which do not contribute toward meeting this objective, a problem may well exist.

Even though the activities of an organization are directed toward meeting its objectives, the performance may not be adequate and problems will result. That is, the level of effort is insufficient to meet the objective. Some businessmen, for example, may direct all of their efforts toward the profit objective and still be unable to meet it. Inefficiency in this effort or insufficient input of effort itself may cause the level of performance to fall short of meeting the objective.

Need to Change Objectives

Under relatively static conditions, there may be little need to make decisions about the nature of the objectives of an organization. Under changing conditions, however, objectives tend to become obsolete. When such is the case, many major decisions requiring attention in the firm will center around revision of its objectives to meet the changed conditions. Decisions effecting the implementation of existing objectives assume less importance because any such decisions are likely to be worthless if the objectives themselves are changed.

As an example of the revision of objectives let us consider the commercial banks of the United States which have historically provided checking and savings account services to their depositors. For many years the investment activities of these banks had been directed mainly toward commercial firms and investments in mortgages and bonds. With the development and growth of small loan companies to extend credit for consumer durables purchases, the profitability of and relatively low risk for large numbers of consumer loans became known. These changing conditions led many commercial banks to increase their consumer loan business and a number of banks changed their marketing objectives to encourage consumer loans.

A second reason why decisions may be required is that an organization's objectives may be unrealistic. If a firm finds that it is extremely easy or difficult to obtain its objectives there is usually sufficient cause for their reconsideration. If General Motors, for example, set an objective of obtaining a profit of $100 per year, the company would, in most years, have a problem. Considering its investment in facilities and personnel, this level of profit is ridiculously small. Similarly an objective by NASA of "colonizing the moon" within the next 12 months would be out of the question under the present state of the art of space flight. Although these two examples are extreme ones, many problems in organizations come about because the performance that can reasonably be expected is widely at variance with the objectives which have been set.

The sources of organizational problems which we have discussed are summarized in Figure 2–1. It should be recognized that most managers spend a great deal more of their total time on decisions arising from performance inadequacies than from the need to reset objectives. This does not mean that setting objectives is unimportant. Obviously if the company has established inappropriate objectives and if activity is directed toward meeting them, serious problems will occur in the long run. When basic objectives are established, however, they tend to remain in effect over a relatively long period of time. There is a periodic, but not a continuous need for their review.

Since the problems and the decisions with which managers deal are related either directly or indirectly to the objectives of the organization, the remainder of our discussion of the "need for a decision" will center on this subject.

FIGURE 2–1. Sources of Problems

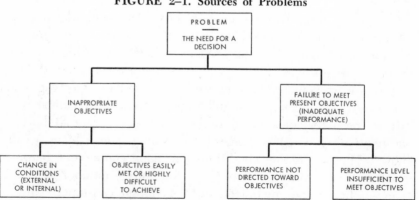

Values and Business Objectives

Organizations, like individuals, are goal-seeking organisms. Their activities are performed so as to achieve some goal, some end, some objective. It is appropriate, therefore, to consider the sources or origins of objectives which organizations develop.

From the viewpoint of society as a whole rather than that of the individual firm, businesses exist to provide economic goods and services. The concept of profit is a measure of how well the firm is able to provide these goods and services to society. Economic analysis shows that the maximization of profit by individual business firms is consistent in the long run with the maximization of goods and services in a strictly competitive society.

Business institutions in the United States represent not only suppliers of goods and services but also sources of jobs, places to work and social institutions in which friendships develop and interpersonal relations with others assume importance. As business has become more successful in supplying goods and services (economic values), there has been a tendency for society to expect business to provide other values as well, such as fair and equal treatment to their employees. Today, businessmen are continually being called on to meet these and other social responsibilities. Some writers have summoned businessmen to forego profit as their sole objective and to give attention to sociologically derived values.[4] Others have placed emphasis on psychological values,[5] spiritual values, and human dignity.[6]

The extent to which the objectives of a particular firm are oriented toward such values will vary considerably depending upon the personal philosophies and attitudes of its managers. In general, however—as Howard Bowen has concluded from his study of businessmen and their responsibilities to society—most managers have not and probably will not rise much above what the public expects of them.[7] That is, although managers must be attuned to what society expects of them, they tend to follow, rather than lead, public opin-

---

[4] See, for example, Douglas McGregor, *The Human Side of Enterprise* (New York: McGraw-Hill Book Co., Inc., 1960), Chap. 8.

[5] For example: Chris Argyris, *Personality and Organization* (New York: Harper & Brothers, 1957).

[6] O. A. Ohmann, "Skyhooks with Special Implications for Monday through Friday," *Harvard Business Review*, May–June, 1955, as reprinted in Max D. Richards and William A. Nielander (eds.), *Readings in Management* (Cincinnati: South-Western Publishing Co., 1958), pp. 49 ff.

[7] Howard Bowen, *Social Responsibilities of the Businessman* (New York: Harper & Brothers, 1953), pp. 103–107.

ion in terms of accepting social responsibilities. Social expectations will set the lower limits of the values which organizations supply, although these may sometimes be exceeded by the manager.

The reader may wonder at this point how business organizations are able to produce a profit if the manager spends his time and resources providing a wide number of social values. Are efforts directed toward furnishing psychological values to employees, for example, consistent with the profit objective, or do they conflict with it? Unfortunately, there is no universally applicable answer to this question. Chris Argyris, for example, holds that some of the very activities which are most effective in maximizing profits produce a psychological climate that is unhealthy in terms of the development of individuals toward maturity.[8] On the other hand, Douglas McGregor argues that the more a manager is able to provide conditions under which the psychological needs of his employees are satisfied, the greater will be the economic output of his company.[9] We will undertake further discussion of human motivation and the needs of individuals in our society in Chapter 4.

Multiplicity of Objectives

A multiplicity of objectives exists for all business firms. Common among the key areas in which overall firm objectives are set are those recommended by Peter Drucker: Market standing; innovation; productivity; physical and financial resources; profitability; manager performance and development; worker performance and attitude; and public responsibility.[10] One reason for the existence of multiple objectives is that business firms attempt to provide multiple values. Another reason for this phenomenon is that to be of value for day-to-day decision making, the overall objectives of the firm must be supplemented with more narrowly circumscribed sub-objectives. Consider the difficulty in decision making at the lower echelons of an organization if long-run profitability were the only objective toward which each manager were to direct his decisions. How could the production manager of a plant, for instance, realistically gear his efforts toward profit maximization unless he developed such more specific sub-goals as number of units to be produced, acceptable quality standards, number of man-hours to be scheduled during each week, and so on? Nor is it probable that even such relatively specific

---

[8] Argyris, *op. cit.*
[9] McGregor, *op. cit.*, Chap. 8.
[10] Drucker, *op. cit.*, Chap. 7.

sub-objectives as these could be optimally implemented unless they, in turn, were further refined into even more narrowly defined sub-goals. To attain an acceptable level of quality for its product, for example, the firm may find it necessary to increase the skills of its workers, improve its materials, or develop a greater degree of precision in its machining processes. Thus, most objectives of the firm may be viewed simultaneously as both *ends* toward which numerous sub-goals are directed and as *means* geared toward the achievement of higher level objectives. A somewhat similar pattern may be observed when we view the relationships between the long- and short-run objectives of the firm. A manufacturer of space systems, for example, may establish the development of a military missile as a short-run objective which in the longer run may provide the expertise for designing rockets for communications satellites. This latter objective, in turn, may provide a stepping stone for someday sending a manned space craft to Mars.

Conflict Between Objectives: Suboptimization

Conditions frequently exist in which the achievement of one organizational objective results in a less than optimum attainment of the others. This problem is often referred to as *suboptimization*.[11] From the point of view of the economist, an optimum overall condition for the firm exists when its marginal revenues are equal to marginal costs; and suboptimization occurs whenever the latter either exceed or fall below the former. In either case, greater profitability could be achieved by changing the firm's level of expenditures. In actuality, however, many types of expenditures cannot be directly related to revenue since they produce both economic and noneconomic values. Although theoretically it is possible to measure and weight all of the noneconomic objectives of a company—such as employee satisfaction—and thus relate them to its economic outputs so as to achieve overall optimization, in practice this would probably involve such a level of complexity as to be economically unfeasible.

From a less theoretical point of view, there are many cases in which (1) the attainment of two or more objectives is dependent upon a particular decision or set of decisions, and (2) no matter which course of action is chosen, some objectives will be realized only at the expense of the others. Two or more of the firm's overall objectives may conflict with one another; sub-objectives may not be

---

[11] See Edward H. Bowman and Robert B. Fetter, *Analysis for Production Management* (rev. ed.; Homewood, Ill.: Richard D. Irwin, Inc., 1961), pp. 24 ff.

congruent with the overall objectives; or one sub-objective may be in opposition to another. As an example of how these suboptimization conditions may arise, let us consider the production scheduling problems of a toy manufacturer whose demand reaches a high peak during the Christmas season. Should his production of toys be leveled over the year in which case inventories would build up during the slack season? Or, should production be geared directly to consumption with output greatly expanded and additional workers hired on a temporary basis each year to meet the period of peak demand? The production leveling alternative would be more congruent with the objectives of the personnel department, for the costs associated with the hiring, training, and laying off of the temporary employees would be eliminated. These savings, however, would be realized only at the expense of one of the prime objectives of the inventory manager—i.e., the reduction of inventory levels and their carrying costs. Further, from the point of view of the overall firm, neither of these two alternatives may represent an optimum course of action as far as profitability is concerned. Analysis of the problem may indicate, for example, that a partial leveling of production coupled with the hiring of just a few temporary workers during the peak season will result in the lowest total cost to the firm. Still this alternative might not be the optimum one if the company had established as one of its basic objectives the provision of steady year-round work for all of its employees.

There is still another important aspect of suboptimization. The attainment of short-run objectives may result in a lesser achievement of the long-run objectives of the organization. Our toy manufacturer may be able to improve his long-run profit considerably by increasing his expenditures for the development of new and different kinds of toys. Since such developments often do not pay off for some time, however, the achievement of this long-run objective may well be at the expense of profitability in the immediate future.

Measurement and the Weighting of Objectives

If the manager is to be able to evaluate effectively the success of his decision efforts, he must be able to measure the extent to which they contribute to the attainment of his objectives. In addition, when he seeks the achievement of a number of objectives which cannot all be directly translated into dollars of profit, it is important to develop means of weighting their relative importance. These two problems will be discussed briefly in the following sections.

Measurement. There are usually a number of different ways in which any given facet of organizational performance may be measured. For example, if the plant manager of a manufacturing firm has set as one of his objectives the prompt delivery of his product to his customers, several measures could be employed such as:

1. Number of orders shipped late.
2. Percentage of orders shipped late.
3. Total dollar value of the late orders.
4. Percentage of the company's total dollar volume shipped late.
5. Percentage distribution of orders shipped late by the number of days late.

Choice of any particular measures such as these should be conditioned not only by the value of the information so provided, but rather by the marginal value of the information as compared to its marginal cost. That is, the increased value of the decision payoff accruing from the marginal information should exceed the costs of obtaining the data.

In addition to measuring organizational performance, it is necessary for the decision maker to develop performance *standards* as a means of relating these measures to his objectives. For example, let us assume that the plant manager in our above illustration has decided that the best measure of the delivery objective is the "percentage of dollar volume shipped late." Suppose further that after having made this decision he observes that these percentages over the past four week period have been 3.5, 4.2, 2.9, and 3.4. Is his objective being met? Does a problem exist? These questions cannot be answered until a specific percentage figure has been set to represent the successful attainment of the objective. If this standard has been set at 10%, for example, the delivery objective so defined would have been achieved in each of the four weeks indicated above. On the other hand, if the manager had decided that any number of delivery failures over 1% would represent failure on the part of the organization to meet its objective, a problem would have existed in each of these weeks.

Weighting of Objectives. If performance relative to the attainment of each of the sub-objectives of a firm could be measured in dollars of profit, and the latter was the sole overall objective being sought, the manager would not be faced with the problem of determining the relative importance of each objective. In such a case, he would have a single criterion which could be applied to all organizational performance. As indicated previously, however, such a condition probably never exists, and, thus, the weighting of objectives is an important requisite for effective decision making. To illustrate, let us assume that a manager has decided that he wants to achieve three objectives, A, B, and C, and that he has developed an appropriate measure for each of these objectives. The basic question which he must then determine is: "How important is the attainment of objective A in relation to that of B and C?" If the manager believes that all three are equally important, for example, he might develop the following "model" to express the desired relationship between each and (O) his overall objective: $O = \frac{1}{3}A + \frac{1}{3}B + \frac{1}{3}C$. Although some authorities, such as Peter Drucker, believe that such attempts at weighting may prove fruitless at the overall level of company operations,[12] this process is essential for the development of certain types of operations research models.[13] An example of the establishment and weighting of objectives in such a specified decision-making situation is provided by the experience of the following company:

Company X manufactured a number of products, each of which required several different machining operations. Each time a different product was scheduled on any particular machine, change-over and set-up costs were incurred. The company attempted to develop an optimum set of decision rules to guide its dispatchers in scheduling the various products on the machines. Before this could be done, it was necessary to determine what objectives the firm was seeking to attain in its scheduling. Management decided that meeting its delivery promises to its customers and the minimization of operating costs were its two prime objectives, and an appropriate measure was developed for each. In deciding upon the relative importance of these two objectives, each was given equal weight. A mathematical model was then developed to represent the production operation and a series of past orders were "fed" into the model. Several different scheduling rules were tried out during these simulated production runs to determine which rule would provide for the greatest attainment of the two equally weighted objectives, cost and delivery. In addition, the process was subsequently simulated with a different relationship between the two objectives incorporated into the model. This subsequent simulation indicated that different decision rules for the scheduling would be required whenever the weighting of the two objectives was modified.

This latter finding is what one would expect. If a firm's prime objective is to manufacture the highest quality product in the industry, its decisions would probably be quite different than if it were at-

---

[12] Drucker, *op. cit.*, p. 62.

[13] C. West Churchman, Russell L. Ackoff, E. Leonard Arnoff, *Introduction to Operations Research* (New York: John Wiley & Sons, Inc., 1957), p. 112 presents a discussion of the weighting of objectives.

tempting to undersell all competition. Thus, the relative importance given to various objectives conditions the problems faced by, and consequently, the decisions required by an organization.

Values, Objectives and Problem Identification: Summary

In the previous sections we have been concerned with organizational values, objectives, and problem identification. A summarizing flow chart of these aspects of the managerial process is presented in Figure 2–2. We have noted that problems exist when: (1) there is a difference between the current performance of an organization and its objectives, and/or (2) the objectives of the organization are

FIGURE 2–2. Problem Identification in Organizations

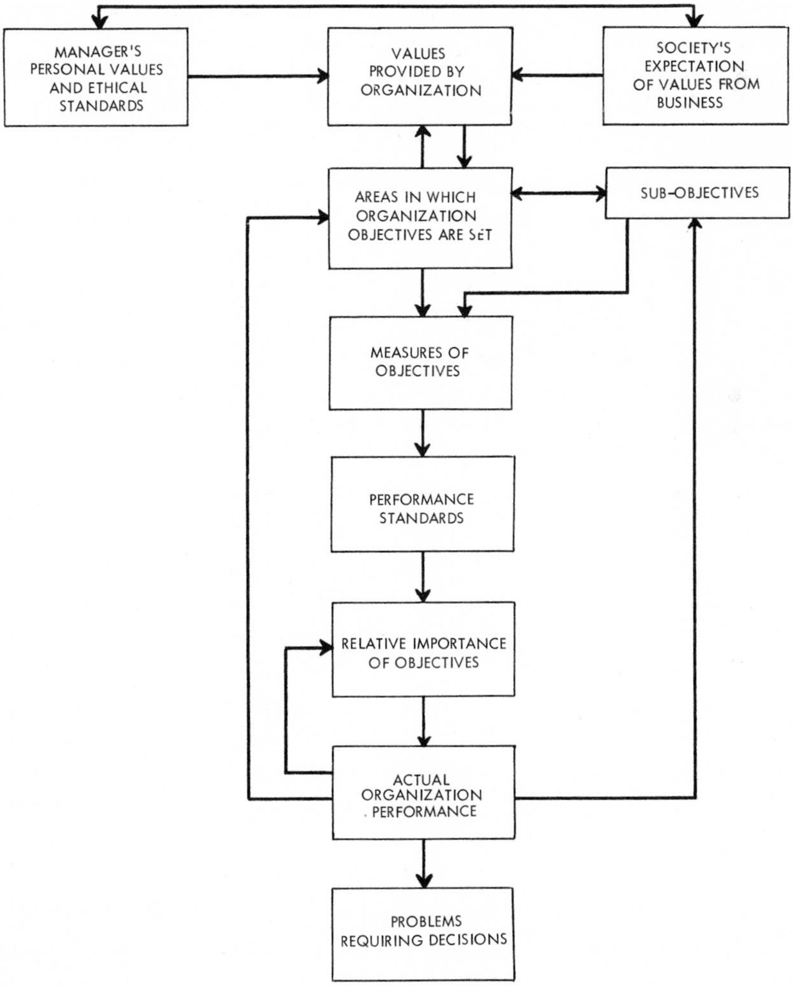

inappropriate. Thus, the first requirement for decision making is the determination of objectives. The objectives are derived from the values which the company is attempting to provide to society—both economic and noneconomic. The manager's choice of values is conditioned both by what society expects of him and by his own philosophy and beliefs. A multiplicity of values and objectives exists for all business firms. In many cases, the full attainment of one objective results in a less than optimum achievement of others, and thus, suboptimization occurs. In relating the overall objectives of the firm to day-to-day decision making, it is necessary to develop additional detailed operational sub-objectives, measures and standards of performance, and often, means for determining the importance to be attached to each objective. In addition, the decision maker will need to develop alternative courses of action to achieve his objectives. It is to this aspect of decision making that our discussion now turns.

DEVELOPING ALTERNATIVE STRATEGIES

The second phase of decision making involves the generation of alternative strategies or courses of action which the manager may take to solve his problems. While analysis is of central importance in discovering the problems of an organization, creativity tends to predominate in the generation of alternatives. In this section, consideration will be given to identifying the relevant factors involved in decision problems together with the creative means that the manager may use to generate alternative strategies.

Models of the Factors Influencing Achievement of Objectives

To improve the performance of an organization, any decision must modify the factors which have a bearing on the attainment of its objectives. If we know, for example, that the number of rejects of a particular product depends upon worker skill, degree of supervision, type of machine used and machine maintenance, any decision aimed at reducing the reject rate must effect a modification of one or more of these variables. To develop meaningful strategies for the solution of problems, then, it is important to understand both the objectives desired and the variables which influence the attainment of the objectives.

If the variables—including the objectives—can be identified and measured and the relationships between them explicitly stated, it is possible to construct a mathematical model of the behavior of the organization to the extent that it is influenced by these variables. Many readers of this book may be familiar with the representation of the value, A, of an investment, P, drawing interest, i, at the end of each year for n years as $A = P(1+i)^n$. In this equation, the initial investment, the interest rate, and the number of years are *independent variables,* and the resultant value is the *dependent variable* in that it depends upon the values of the other variables. This model is a simple one in that the number of variables are few and the relationships between them not too complex. Many behavior patterns in organizations, however, cannot be represented by such elementary models, since a great number of variables are involved and the relationships between them are extremely complicated.

A model of the variables influencing the attainment of objectives is a highly useful device for generating alternative strategies. By substituting different values for the independent variables, it is possible to see what effect various changes in the firm's operations would have upon achieving the objective. For example, the manager may not need to actually increase his machine maintenance effort to observe how it would affect the reject rate. If he has developed a model of reject rate behavior, he can simulate modifications in this behavior by changing the values of the maintenance variable in the model and experimentally arrive at a satisfactory solution to the problem.

Although models may be highly useful tools for generating alternative strategies, their employment is often limited because the manager is unable to identify all factors which may have a bearing on the decision problem. Nor is it always possible to explicitly define the relationships between the decision variables, even when the manager is aware of their existence. In such cases, it may be necessary to develop novel strategies and approaches for the handling of problems. This development—as is also true with the formulation of new models—calls for creative thinking on the part of the manager.

Creativity in Decision Making

A new idea or a creative thought is the result of combining certain elements into new and different patterns. Consider as an example the ball point pen. Although none of its separate parts were new, in and of themselves, their combination represented a new and radical departure in writing instruments. This was a case in which old elements were brought together in a new combination. On the other hand, creativity sometimes results from a novel combination comprising previously unknown elements. The physicists have been discovering new and different parts of the atom for years, and the search for new sub-atomic particles continues. These discoveries, combined with knowledge already in existence, have provided a basis for creating new conceptions of the atom and of the universe itself.

As indicated above, creativity in the generation of alternatives is often required of managers in making decisions for their organizations. Unique strategies to overcome organizational problems may defy developments by any other means. Although an advertising manager may have a general idea of the effect of advertising on the sales of products for which he has responsibility, for example, each new advertisement requires creativity in the development of layout, copy, format, and, perhaps, media. The precise combination of factors for insuring the success of the advertisement is not known for certain. It may not be possible to develop a formal model to ensure that a particular combination of elements will have the desired effect in attaining the objective. Furthermore, even if a model were developed to solve this problem, there is no assurance that the same combination of elements would bring about an equal degree of success over an extended period of time. That is, the model, if developed, may portray a dynamic and, perhaps, unstable condition. The existence of dynamic variables and relationships is not necessarily confined to advertising. Other decision problems exhibit similar characteristics. The manager who makes most of his decisions on the basis of intuition or hunch may maintain that such an approach is necessitated because his job involves dynamic variables and relationships. To some extent this may be true. It is equally true, however, that the variables and relationships in many types of managerial decisions can be identified. The manager relying on science in management recognizes this possibility. This is not to imply that in the future creativity will decline in importance for decision makers. On the contrary, as managers are better able to identify the key factors contributing to the success of their organizations, they will be free to make greater use of creativity in dealing with the remaining unsolved problems.[14]

---

[14] It has been estimated that most people usually use only a small part of their creative ability, and considerable attention has been devoted in industry to devising means to develop this unrealized potential. Among the methods contrived to encourage greater creative output are brainstorming, buzz sessions, forced association and planned adaption. For a survey of creative techniques, see C. S. Whiting, "Operational Techniques of Creative Thinking," *Advanced Management,* 20 (Oct., 1955), 24–30.

SELECTION OF ALTERNATIVE STRATEGIES

Once the decision maker has developed a number of possible decision strategies, he will attempt to select one which contributes most to the attainment of his objectives. This choice is influenced by the resources which he has available. These are the *means* at his disposal.

The attainment of objectives is dependent not only upon the means applied by the manager, but also upon two other types of variables over which he has no direct influence or control. These are (1) *states of nature* and (2) *competitive strategies.* Either may have an effect upon the ability of the manager to meet his objective *regardless* of the strategies he chooses. For example, when a manager decides to spend $500,000 during a year to advertise his company's products, he expects the advertising to have a direct and positive effect on sales. The advertising may not be as effective as planned in meeting this objective, however, if a depression occurs or if competition spends larger sums on advertising than had been anticipated. In this instance, the depression is a state of nature, and the action of competitors in increasing the amount of advertising for their products is a competitive strategy. Although these variables are beyond the direct control of the decision maker, he may nonetheless be able to force a competitor into particular competitive strategy by the actions which he takes.

Decision Making Under Certainty

If a manager can determine what his competitors' strategies will be and what external conditions he will face, his decision simply involves (1) calculating the return or payoff that he can expect from each alternative strategy developed and (2) then selecting that strategy which provides the highest return in terms of his objective. In such a case, his primary task is that of determining what these returns will be. Assuming that the objective is to maximize profit, the decision under certainty consists merely of selecting the strategy offering the greatest profitability.

In most cases, however, the manager will not be able to determine with certainty what his competitors will do or what states of nature will occur. In some cases, he will have no estimate at all of these two variables. This condition is known as "decision making under ignorance or uncertainty." In other cases, he will be able to estimate the probability that competition will choose certain strategies or that certain states of nature will occur. If so, we have a condition referred to as "decision making under risk." Since the manager is required to make decisions irrespective of his knowledge, it is appropriate that we turn to an examination of decision making under these less certain conditions.

Expected Value, Conditional Value, and Decision Making Under Risk

The concept of expected value is employed in decision making when the states of nature or competitive actions which will have a bearing on the effectiveness of the alternative decision strategies are not certain. The *expected* value of any event (EV) is defined as: the value if it occurs (conditional value, [CV]) multiplied by its probability of occurrence, (p); or $EV = (CV) \cdot (p)$.[15] Suppose, for example, that a company has the alternatives of bidding on only one of two potential contracts and that: (1) the probability of receiving from customer A a $100,000 contract is .10; and (2) the probability of receiving a contract from customer B of $50,000 is .25. On which contract should the company bid? The expected value of the contract from customer A is $10,000 ($100,000 × .10); while the expected value of the contract from customer B is $12,500 ($50,000 × .25). Assuming maximization of sales dollars is the objective, the company should bid for the contract of customer B, for the expected value of this contract is $2,500 more than that for customer A. It should be noted, however, that there is no assurance that the company's sales will be $2,500 greater *this particular time* if the company bids for the contract of customer B rather than that of customer A. The company may obtain sales of either $50,000 or $0 if the contract from customer B is bid upon. The reason for selecting customer B over customer A is based on the fact that if the company is faced with a great number of such decisions in which both the conditional values and probabilities remain the same, it will maximize its sales objective *over the long run* if it selects the strategy with the greatest expected value. That is, the *average* payoff for many such contracts would be $12,500 from customer B, as compared with $10,000 from customer A. This reasoning assumes, of course, an ability to estimate the conditional values of the events and the probabilities of their occurrence.

---

[15] For a simplified explanation of the mathematical theory of probability see Harold Bierman, Jr., Lawrence E. Fouraker, and Robert K. Jaedicke, *Quantitative Analysis for Business Decisions* (Homewood, Ill.: Richard D. Irwin, Inc., 1961), Chaps. 2, 3, and 4.

A convenient way of summarizing the expected values of the alternative decision strategies is by the use of a *payoff matrix,* an example of which is illustrated in Figure 2–3. The rows on the table

FIGURE 2–3

Conditional Payoffs for Warehousing Strategies (in $)

	D1	*D2*	*D3*
	States of Nature: Demand		
Strategies	*D1*	*D2*	*D3*
WS1............	100,000	50,000	50,000
WS2...........	1,000	80,000	125,000

represent the strategies open to the decision maker; the columns represent the different states of nature or competitive actions which may occur. In the example presented in Figure 2–3, the decision involves a choice between two warehousing strategies that a company is considering. These strategies are represented by the two rows designated WS1 and WS2. The three possible conditions of product demand which may occur during the time period under consideration are represented by columns D1, D2, and D3. The body of the table indicates the payoffs to the company under all possible combinations of demand and available strategies. These values represent the conditional values of the strategies. For example, if the decision maker selected strategy WS1, and a demand of D2 occurs, the payoff, or conditional value, would be $50,000. Once these conditional values have been determined, it is next necessary to calculate the expected values for all possible combinations of strategies and states of nature. These values are illustrated in Figure 2–4. The total expected value for each strategy is equal to the sum of its expected values under each possible state of nature; and represents the aver-

FIGURE 2–4

Expected Values for Warehousing Strategies (in $)
(Conditional Values Times Probability of Occurrence)

Strategies	*D1*	*D2*	*D3*	*Total Expected Value*
	States of Nature: Demand			
	D1	*D2*	*D3*	
	Probability of Occurrence			
	.10	*.50*	*.40*	
WS1........	10,000	25,000	20,000	55,000
WS2........	100	40,000	50,000	90,100

age payoff that would be obtained if the decision were made a great number of times. The total expected value for strategy WS1 is $55,000, and for WS2, $90,100. Thus, the latter represents the decision maker's best choice in order to achieve maximization of profits.

Determining Probabilities: Objective and Subjective Probability

An *objective* probability is one that can be determined on the basis of some past experience. We know, for example, that the probability of obtaining a head in the toss of a fair coin is .5 from experience in flipping a large number of such coins in the past. Similarly, previous company experience in the use of a particular psychological test to select managers may provide a basis for establishing the probability that a person obtaining a certain score on the test in the future will be successful. The process under analysis must be a stable one, however, if the experience of the past is to provide a valid basis for establishing the probabilities of events occurring in the future. If, for example, the managerial position referred to above now entails greater responsibilities than ever before, the probabilities associated with past use of the psychological test may not be valid for predicting the expected success rate for people now being hired.

In many cases the manager will not be able to determine from specific experience a suitable estimate of objective probability. Under such circumstances, however, he may be able to make a subjective estimate of the risks entailed in the decision making on the basis of his general knowledge of the problem under consideration. This involves what is referred to as *subjective* probability.[16] Although less precise, the use of subjective probabilities is better than completely ignoring the probabilities of occurrence of the different states of nature or competitor actions pertinent to the decision problem. Subjective probabilities are used in decision making the same way objective probabilities are used to arrive at the expected values for the various alternative strategies under consideration.

Decision Making Under Uncertainty

In some decision problems, it is not possible to develop estimates of the probabilities that certain competitive strategies or states of

---

[16] For a discussion of the concept and rationale of subjective probability, see Robert Schlaifer, *Probability and Statistics for Business Decisions* (New York: McGraw-Hill Book Co., Inc., 1959), Chap. 1.

nature will occur. Thus, the manager cannot calculate the expected values of the alternative strategies which are available. In such cases, there is no single optimum criterion for selecting any one strategy over the other. There are, however, a number of criteria which have been suggested as rational ones to follow in evaluating the strategies under consideration. Regardless of the criterion employed, the initial step in decision making under uncertainty is to calculate the conditional values for each alternative strategy under each possible competitive strategy or state of nature. This step is identical to that employed in making decisions under conditions of risk. The next step involves the selection and application of a criterion for handling the conditional values that have been derived. To illustrate this process, we will first pose a hypothetical decision problem under conditions of uncertainty, and then indicate its solution by each of several different criteria.

As an example, let us assume that an aircraft manufacturer is considering the possibilities of designing a new high-performance jet fighter for the air force, and that three strategies are available: (1) the company can design a completely new plane from the ground up; (2) it can redesign an existing craft to meet the new military requirements; or (3) it can elect to not design a plane at all. Let us further assume that there are four possible states of nature which might occur that could affect the payoff of any one of the strategies: global war, limited war, cold war, and peace. After examining all evidence that might give some indication of the likelihood of which state of nature will occur, the company concludes that there is no basis for believing that any one is any more or less probable than the other. Given the conditional profit matrix indicated in Figure 2–5, let us examine some of the possible criteria that the company might employ in making this decision.

FIGURE 2–5

Conditional Values for Aircraft Producer
(in $ Millions)

	States of Nature			
Strategies	N1 Global War	N2 Limited War	N3 Cold War	N4 Peace
S1–New Craft......	−5	6	4	4
S2–Redesign........	2	2	2	1
S3–No Design......	0	0	0	1

The Laplace Criterion. If there is no good reason to believe that any one event is more likely to occur than any other, there is similarly no good reason for assuming that it will *not* occur with the same probability as the others. This concept, which is referred to as the *principle of insufficient reason,* provides the basis for one well-known criterion for decision making under conditions of uncertainty —the Laplace criterion.[17] This criterion simply applies equal probabilities to the occurrence of each state of nature or competitive strategy. In the aircraft problem, application of equal probabilities to the conditional values of each of the states of nature indicated in Figure 2–5 provides the expected values for each of the three strategies shown in Figure 2–6. Figure 2–6 was arrived at by assigning an equal probability to each of the four possible states of nature (i.e., $100/4 = .25$), and multiplying this figure by each conditional value in Figure 2–5. These values indicate that strategy S1, the design of a completely new jet fighter, should be chosen.

FIGURE 2–6

Expected Values for Aircraft Producer Applying Laplace Criterion
(in $ Millions)

Strategies	N1 Global War	N2 Limited War	N3 Cold War	N4 Peace	Total Expected Value
S1–New Craft..	−$1.25	1.5	1.0	1.0	$2.25
S2–Redesign....	0.5	0.5	0.5	0.25	1.75
S3–No Design..	0	0	0	0.25	0.25

The Pessimism Criterion: The Maximin.[18] The pessimism criterion assumes that the manager should always be pessimistic in assessing which competitive strategies or states of nature will occur. He should always act on the premise that the worst is going to happen, and then select the strategy which will maximize the payoff which he will receive under such adverse conditions. This guiding principle is often referred to as the *maximin,* because the manager attempts to maximize his gain under minimally favorable conditions—i.e., he tries to *maximize* the *minimum* possible gain. Inspec-

[17] This criterion is also referred to as the criterion of rationality, although it is no more rational than any other of the criteria discussed below.
[18] This criterion was first suggested by Abraham Wald. For a discussion of it see David W. Miller and Martin K. Starr, *Executive Decisions and Operations Research* (Englewood Cliffs, N. J.; Prentice-Hall, 1960), Chap. 3.

tion of Figure 2–5 indicates that if the aircraft producer were to apply the criterion of pessimism he would choose strategy S2—the redesign of his present jet fighter—for the following minimal conditions apply:

Strategy	Worst Condition	Payoff
S1............	N1	−$5,000,000
S2............	N4	1,000,000
S3............	N1, N2, N3	0

This strategy (S2) results in a maximin payoff of $1,000,000.

The Criterion of Optimism: Maximax.[19]   The maximin has been criticized on the grounds that to expect the most pessimistic conditions to occur all the time is not a rational approach to the selection of decision alternatives. One could just as well be completely *optimistic* about the occurrence of all future events. If the decision maker were to do the latter, he would select that strategy under which it is possible for the most favorable payoff of all to occur, on the optimistic assumption that *it will* occur. Our aircraft producer, for example, would select strategy S1 in Figure 2–5 since the most favorable payoff condition ($6,000,000) prevails when this strategy and state of nature N2 occur.

Neither complete optimism nor pessimism is probably very realistic. At any given time, the decision maker may be more or less optimistic, but not completely so. In such a case, it is possible for him to develop a scale—from 0 to 1.0—to indicate the extent to which he is optimistic or pessimistic. For example, assume that the aircraft manufacturer decides that he holds a .7 degree of optimism and a .3 degree of pessimism about the occurrence of the states of nature which bear on his design decision. If so, he would multiply the conditional value of the most optimistic state of nature for each strategy by his coefficient of optimism (.7). Then the conditional value of the most pessimistic state of nature for each strategy would be multiplied by his coefficient of pessimism (.3). Finally, these two values for each strategy would be added together, and the strategy with the highest value as weighted by the optimism-pessimism scale selected. Figure 2–7 illustrates these calculations for the aircraft producer and indicates that S1 (new craft) would be the most preferable strategy.

---

[19] First suggested in the form discussed below by Leonid Hurwicz.

FIGURE 2–7

Application of Optimism Scale to Conditional Values for Aircraft Producer
(.7 Optimism and .3 Pessimism)
(in $ Millions)

| | Conditional Value * | | | | Weighted Value | | |
| | Best Condition | | Worst Condition | | Best Condition | Worst Condition | Sum of Weighted Values |
Strategy							
S1–New Craft	N2	$6	N1	−$5	$4.2	−$1.5	$2.7
S2–Redesign..	N1, 2, 3	2	N4	1	1.4	.3	1.7
S3–No Design	N4	1	N1, 2, 3	0	.7	0	.7

* From Figure 2–5.

The Criterion of Regret.[20]   A fourth criterion for decision making under conditions of uncertainty is the *criterion of regret.* It provides a method of selecting a strategy that *minimizes the maximum regret* that could be realized. The regret of a strategy is defined as *its payoff* under any given state of nature and/or competitive strategy *subtracted from* the *maximum payoff that is possible* with the occurrence of this event. For example, if state of nature N1 in our previous example occurs, the payoff for S1 is—$5 million; that for S2, $2 million; and that for S3, zero (see Figure 2–5). The regret for each strategy under the N1 state of nature is the difference between the maximum payoff ($2 million for S2) and its own payoff. Thus, the regret in this case for S1 is $7 million; for S2, zero; and for S3, $2 million. The amount of regret for all strategies and states of nature for the aircraft manufacturer is shown in Figure 2–8. This figure indicates that the maximum regret which the manufacturer may realize will be minimized if he selects strategy S2—$4 million.

FIGURE 2–8

Regret for Aircraft Producer in Selection of Alternative Strategies
(in $ Millions)

| | State of Nature | | | | |
Strategy	N1 Global War	N2 Limited War	N3 Cold War	N4 Peace	Maximum Regret
S1–New Craft.....	7	0	0	0	7
S2–Modify........	0	4	2	3	4 *
S3–Nothing.......	2	6	4	3	6

* This is a minimax solution—i.e., we try to *min*imize our *ma*ximum regret.
Source: Calculated from Figure 2–5.

[20] L. J. Savage, "The Theory of Statistical Decision," *Journal of the American Statistical Association*, 46 (Mar., 1951), 55–67.

If he chooses S1, he might incur a regret of $7 million (if N1 occurs); and with strategy S3, a regret of $6 million is possible (with N2). If N1 does not occur, of course, the selection of S2 may not minimize the manufacturer's regret; however, he is assured that, no matter what state of nature prevails, his regret will never be more than $4 million.

Selection of an Uncertainty Criterion. As we have indicated previously, there is no single best criterion for selecting decision strategies under conditions of uncertainty. In fact, to assess the effectiveness of any of these measures, it would probably be necessary to develop a set of criterion-evaluating criteria. One such set has been devised by Milnor; [21] and the criterion of regret appears to satisfy a greater number of the Milnor criteria than any other presented in this chapter. In spite of the development of such criteria, however, the selection of an uncertainty criterion remains a matter of managerial judgment.

Utility

Thus far in our discussion of decision making under conditions of risk and uncertainty we have assumed that the manager attempts to maximize the attainment of his objectives in terms of dollars. In many decision situations that the manager faces, this assumption is a valid one, providing that the decisions involve economic values. In other instances, however, the assumption of monetary maximization is inappropriate. Such a case—involving a small bakery—is examined in Figure 2–9. Two strategies are available to the baker and either one of two competitive actions may occur. The probability of occurrence of each competitive strategy has been determined. S1 results in an expected value of $44,000 and S2, only $10,800.

FIGURE 2–9

Payoff Matrix for a Small Baker

	Conditional Value		Expected Value		
	CS1	CS2	CS1 *	CS2 **	Total
Strategy S1......	−$60,000	$200,000	−$36,000	$80,000	$44,000
Strategy S2......	10,000	12,000	6,000	4,800	$10,800

* Probability of Occurrence .60.
** Probability of Occurrence .40.

[21] John Milnor, "Games Against Nature," in R. M. Thrall, C. H. Coombs, and R. L. Davis, *Decision Processes* (New York: John Wiley & Sons, Inc., 1954), pp. 49–59. See especially the table on p. 52.

According to the expected value criterion, the baker should obviously select strategy S1. This choice will maximize this payoff in the long run. It should be noted, however, that if the baker selects this "optimum" strategy, and competitive strategy CS1 should occur, the bakery will suffer a loss of $60,000. Although the average value of strategy S1 *if made a large number of times* would be $33,200 greater than that for S2, the baker may never have an opportunity to make the decision more than once if the selection of S1 is coupled with competitive strategy CS1 because the $60,000 loss might well spell bankruptcy! Thus, the manager of the bakery might be unwilling to select any strategy, regardless of its average value, if it could result in the incurrence of such a large loss. Or, to put it another way, the value of the possible gain to the baker by choosing S1 ($200,000) is less than the disvalue of the possible loss of $60,000, even though in dollars the gain greatly exceeds the loss. The reader should not infer that this example indicates that probability theory is useless in decision making, however. Rather, it points up the fact that payoff measures in dollars are often not satisfactory guides when the amounts of money involved in the decision making are very large in relation to a firm's total assets. In terms of the economist, the *utility* of money to the manager is different when relatively large sums are an important consideration in decision problems. That dollars have a different utility to individuals under different conditions may be seen in the manner in which items are purchased just before and just after payday. Immediately prior to payday, many persons are quite cautious about how and upon what they spend their money. Immediately after receiving their paycheck, however, they usually exhibit much less inhibition. In general, as the amount of money possessed by an individual (or firm) increases, its utility decreases, and vice versa.[22] When money and expected values are employed as criteria for decision making, there is an assumption that the relationship between utility and money is approximately linear. For most business decisions, this assumption of linearity is probably valid, for the sums of money involved are not large in proportion to the total assets of the firm. The value of utility to decision making, then, is its appropriateness as a measure in those cases in which large variations in the utility of money exist for the different payoffs which may occur as a result of decisions.[23]

---

[22] For alternative methods of measuring utility in its relation to money see Miller and Starr, *op. cit.*, p. 57 and Bierman, *et al.*, *op. cit.*, pp. 82 ff.

[23] Schlaifer, *op. cit.*, Chap. 2.

FIGURE 2–10. The Decision-Making Process in Organizations

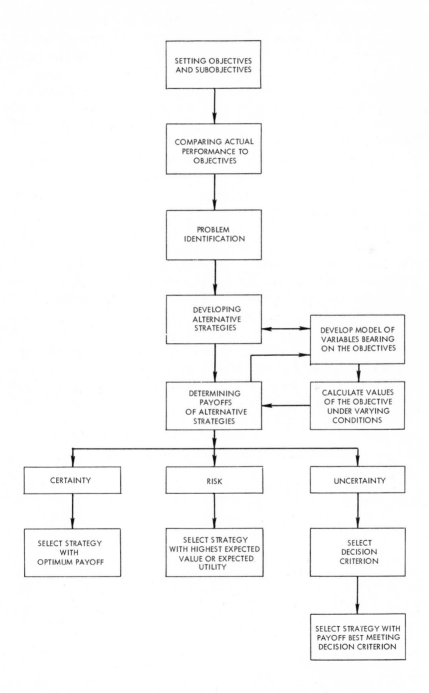

SUMMARY

In this chapter we have discussed the major phases involved in managerial decision making. These phases are summarized by the flow diagram in Figure 2–10 (page 53). After the firm has established its objectives and identified its problems, it is necessary to develop alternative decision strategies. One or more of these strategies is then chosen as representing the most appropriate course(s) of action. In the development and selection of strategies, it is sometimes possible to design mathematical models as decision tools. In other cases, the key decision variables and their interrelationships defy explicit quantification. Often, a considerable degree of creativity is required in the development of alternative strategies. In those rare instances in which the future events which will condition the effectiveness of various strategies are certain, the task of the manager simply involves the selection of that course of action which provides the greatest payoff to his firm. When some degree of risk is involved in the decision making, it is necessary to determine both the conditional and expected values of the alternative courses of action. If future events are completely uncertain, any one of a number of criteria may serve as guides to decision making. Although decision payoffs are frequently stated in terms of dollars of profit, many objectives of the firm involve noneconomic values. In addition, when the dollar value of different payoffs varies greatly, utility may be the most appropriate objective criterion.

DISCUSSION AND STUDY QUESTIONS

1. If a firm has multiple goals, each can be viewed in "means-end-means" terms as a subgoal directed toward attaining long-run profitability. Discuss.

2. Under what conditions might a firm's clearly-stated objectives be inappropriate?

3. Evaluate the following statement about business behavior made by an executive from a multi-national firm: "What may be illegal may be ethical. In the United States, the Justice Department would be quick to prosecute us if we joined competitors to set common prices or to divide up the market. In Europe, in contrast, we are expected to join a monopolistic consortium, take our assigned share of the market, and not reduce prices agreed upon. The very actions expected of us in Europe are illegal in the United States, but that does not make them unethical."

4. What might motivate a business firm to supply social values to its em-

ployees and the community in which it operates? (Examples of social values would be provision for family picnics for its employees, support of a community theater, active participation in a hospital expansion program, etc.)

5. What is the difference between an objective probability and a subjective one? Give a clear-cut example of each.

6. The sales manager of one firm complained that his company's sales were being hurt because the credit manager was refusing to grant credit to numerous poor-risk customers. The credit manager replied that the sales manager wanted to "give away" the company's products to some customers who would not or could not pay for them.
    a) When operating in a credit-competitive environment, can a firm ordinarily maximize its sales while simultaneously minimizing its losses from bad debts?
    b) How might an expected value approach be used to resolve differences in viewpoints such as those of the sales and credit manager expressed above?
    c) Was the sales manager "rational" in attempting to maximize sales volume?
    d) If an optimum solution in terms of profitability were developed, would the goals of each department be optimized or suboptimized? Explain.

7. Discuss the following judgment: "Ethical business practice dictates that declining production costs should eventually be reflected in lower selling prices, or improved quality or service to the consumer."

8. Historical data for an automobile dealer indicates that 3 out of every 15 persons who have taken a demonstration ride in its new model, the NONSEL, actually purchased a car from him. If the gross profit made on the sale of each NONSEL is $400 and demonstration costs average $5.50 per demonstration, what is the expected value of each demonstration ride?

9. An individual with $400,000 in capital is considering two investment alternatives. The first is the purchase of $100,000 in bonds, which pay a return of 4%. The second alternative is to buy several hundred acres of land, which cost $400,000. The land purchase would lead to either of two possibilities. First, the government is considering the purchase of this land for a recreation area; and if this purchase were effected, the investor would receive 3% more than his purchase price for the land.

    The investor, however, would prefer to develop the land for a housing project which would return a profit of about 12%. Government condemnation would preclude this alternative. The investor would like to know what probability of government acquisition would allow him to equate his return from purchasing the land to that from buying the bonds. (Assume that all yields would be received in one lump sum at the end of the current year.)

    Of what value would this information be to the investor?

10. A merchant buys and sells a perishable commodity on a daily basis. The commodity costs $5.00 per unit and sells for $10.00 per unit. Fresh stock must be obtained each day and any unsold stock at the end of the day has

a salvage value of $1.00 per unit. The merchant, having recently completed a course in decision making, has developed the table of demand probabilities given below based on his past daily sales.

Probabilities of Sales

Units Demanded per Day	Mon.	Tues.	Wed.	Thurs.	Fri.	Sat.
0	.10	.05	.05	.05	.02	.40
1	.20	.15	.20	.10	.08	.40
2	.30	.20	.35	.15	.10	.10
3	.25	.40	.20	.20	.20	.05
4	.10	.10	.12	.22	.30	.03
5	.02	.05	.04	.20	.20	.02
6	.02	.03	.03	.06	.06	.00
7	.01	.02	.01	.02	.04	.00
	1.00	1.00	1.00	1.00	1.00	1.00

a) Based on the above information, determine how many units of the commodity should be stocked each day by the merchant for the following week.

HINT: First construct a table of conditional values.

b) Assume that the merchant knows only that demand in any given day may range from 0–7, but that he has no basis for assigning probabilities to any particular demand level within this range. How many units should be stocked on any given day if he follows the Laplace criterion to decision making under uncertainty? If he follows the criterion of optimism? The pessimism criterion? The criterion of regret? A weighted optimism-pessimism approach, assuming that he entertains a .6 degree of optimism and a .4 degee of pessimism?

11. Jonathan's is a high quality clothing store in a midwestern city of a population of approximately 175,000. The store has built its reputation as a quality-minded store carrying national brand merchandise in men's wear and to a lesser extent women's and children's wear. Jonathan's is the largest clothing store in the city and it is thought to do more clothing business, at least in dollar terms, than any of the large department stores in the city.

Jonathan's main store is located in a new, modern downtown store. The store is expensively furnished and the store provides many services to its customers. Jonathan's policy is to carry a wide range in lines of merchandise. These lines range from medium-priced to high-priced goods. Jonathan's prices are competitive with department store prices for the same quality or brands of merchandise. The expensive building and furnishings are justified by high volume selling in these lines. This policy is implemented through an aggressive advertising program.

A second smaller Jonathan's is located adjacent to several exclusive suburbs. Its lines of merchandise, buying, and other service activities are handled by the main store staff.

On December 15, one of the buyers came across an opportunity to purchase a sizeable amount of clothing from a store in another city. This store had gone out of business and was trying to dispose of its remaining inventory. Approximately 15% of the merchandise was the same merchandise that Jonathan's was purchasing or had purchased in the recent past. The rest of the goods was of varying degrees of lower, although good quality. The offer to Jonathan's to purchase the goods stipulated that the price to be paid by Jonathan's would be 66% of the cost of the goods to the original store providing the total amount of goods would be bought. The Jonathan buyer was unable to purchase a portion of the merchandise.

The Christmas selling season had been extremely good for the Jonathan stores. Most of the department heads in charge of selling operations were predicting low inventories to start the new year. Although the buyer could not get delivery on the proposed merchandise in time to be of much value for the Christmas rush, it could be made available for the traditional Jonathan's "After-Christmas Sale." During the week following Christmas it was customary to offer a store-wide sale during which each department head attempted to sell most of his normal stock. Some had thought that it would be necessary to eliminate the sale during this year due to the rush of pre-Christmas business.

The buyer thought that the offer of the distressed merchandise presented an excellent buying opportunity that would provide merchandise for the After-Christmas sale. Since the amount of the purchase exceeded the buyer's authority, he made the following recommendation to Mr. Jonathan:

1. Advertise the After-Christmas sale as usual except for some adjustments to reflect differences in prices.
2. Buy the merchandise from the closed-out store.
3. Use the newly purchased merchandise in the sale.

a) With what problems is Mr. Jonathan faced?
b) What caused these problems?
c) What alternatives are available to Mr. Jonathan?
d) What additional information would you like to have prior to resolving these problems?
e) What decision(s) would you make if you were in Mr. Jonathan's position?

SELECTED REFERENCES

ANSOFF, H. I.   "A Quasi-Analytic Approach to the Business Policy Problem," *Management Technology*, 4 (June, 1964), 67–77.

BIERMAN, HAROLD, JR., *et al.* *Quantitative Analysis for Business Decisions.* Rev. ed. Homewood, Ill.: Richard D. Irwin, Inc., 1965.

BORKO, HAROLD. *Computer Applications in the Behavioral Sciences,* chap. ii. Englewood Cliffs, N. J.: Prentice-Hall, Inc., 1962.

BOWEN, HOWARD. *Social Responsibilities of the Business Man.* New York: Harper & Bros., 1953.

BOWMAN, EDWARD H., and FETTER, ROBERT B. *Analysis for Production Management.* Rev. ed. Homewood, Ill.: Richard D. Irwin, Inc., 1961.

BRONOWSKI, JACOB. "Science as Foresight," *What Is Science* (ed. Newman, James R.). New York: Washington Square Press, Inc., 1961.

CHERNOFF, H., and MOSES, L. E. *Elementary Decision Theory.* New York: John Wiley & Sons, Inc., 1959.

CHURCHMAN, C. W. *Prediction and Optimal Decision.* Englewood Cliffs, N. J.: Prentice-Hall, 1961.

CHURCHMAN, C. W.; ACKOFF, R. L.; and ARNOFF, E. L. *Introduction to Operations Research.* New York: John Wiley & Sons, Inc., 1957.

DENT, JAMES K. "Organizational Correlates of the Goals of Business Managements," *Personnel Psychology,* 12 (Autumn, 1959).

DRUCKER, PETER F. "Business Objectives and Survival Needs: Notes on a Discipline of Business Enterprise," *The Journal of Business,* 31 (April, 1958), 81–90.

DRUCKER, PETER F. *The Practice of Management.* New York: Harper & Bros., 1954.

EELLS, RICHARD, and WALTON, CLARENCE. *Conceptual Foundations of Business.* Homewood, Ill.: Richard D. Irwin, Inc., 1961.

GREENWOOD, WILLIAM T. *Issues in Business and Society.* New York: Houghton Mifflin Co., 1964.

MANNE, ALAN S. *Economic Analysis for Business Decisions,* chap. x. New York: McGraw-Hill Book Co., Inc., 1961.

McGUIRE, JOSEPH W. *Business and Society.* New York: McGraw-Hill Book Co., Inc., 1963.

MILLER, D. W., and STARR, M. K. *Executive Decisions and Operations Research.* Englewood Cliffs, N. J.: Prentice-Hall, Inc., 1960.

SCHLAIFER, ROBERT. *Probability and Statistics for Business Decisions.* New York: McGraw-Hill Book Co., Inc., 1959.

SIMON, HERBERT. *Administrative Behavior.* 2d ed. New York: Macmillan Co., 1959.

SIMON, HERBERT. *The New Science of Management Decision.* New York: Harper & Bros., 1960.

SIRI, GIUSEPPE CARDINAL. "Management and the Spiritual Needs of Man," *Proceedings CIOS XIII International Management Congress,* 1 (1963), 37–42.

SMITH, GEORGE ALBERT, JR. *Business, Society, and the Individual.* Homewood, Ill.: Richard D. Irwin, Inc., 1962.

THRALL, R. W.; COOMBS, C. H.; and DAVIS, R. L. (eds.). *Decision Processes.* New York: John Wiley & Sons, Inc., 1952.

TOWLE, JOSEPH W. (ed.). *Ethics and Standards in American Business.* Boston: Houghton Mifflin Co., 1964.

WILLIAMSON, OLIVER E. *The Economics of Discretionary Behavior: Managerial Objectives in a Theory of the Firm,* chap. ii. Englewood Cliffs, N. J.: Prentice-Hall, Inc., 1964.

CHAPTER 3

APPROACHES TO
DECISION MAKING

I N the preceding chapter, we presented a basic framework for understanding the decision-making process. We will now turn our
attention to a number of approaches which managers employ in
making decisions—experience and judgment, management principles, decision models, systems analysis and heuristic programming.
There is a wide range in the degree of optimization possible with
these different approaches. Some are relatively unsophisticated,
while others are based on rather complex analytical processes. We
will discuss the less sophisticated approaches first, and then examine
the more complex and "scientific" ones.

EXPERIENCE AND JUDGMENT IN DECISION MAKING

One widely used approach to decision making is that of depending on one's own personal experience and judgment.[1] Such experience-based decision methods are subject to certain limitations. Each
manager's background is limited and his previous experience may
not provide an adequate sample upon which to base current decisions. For this reason, decisions in new situations may fail because
of false premises derived from past experience. Further, human
memory, observation, and interpretation of data are fallible. Therefore, even if a manager's assumptions are correct, incomplete knowledge and faulty interpretation of data can undermine the effectiveness of experience-based decisions.

On the other hand, if the manager can avoid overgeneralizing

---

[1] For an attempt to systematically study the judgmental, "intuitive," and "insight-
ful" aspects of managerial decision making, see: Adrian J. Grossman, "An Approach
for Formalizing Entrepreneural Processes in Business," *Proceedings, CIOS XIII
Management Congress* (New York: Council for International Progress in Management
[USA], Inc., 1963), pp. 239–248.

from past experience and accurately perceive how the key variables existing in new decision problems are similar to or different from those in previously encountered situations, experience-based decision making may prove quite effective. Further, experienced-based methods may be necessary for dealing with the many problems which confront managers daily and for which there are no analytical or "scientifically-based" solution methods available. Also, decision problems often have to be made quickly, and there may not be sufficient time to apply complex, time-consuming scientific analysis to their solution. Finally, the manager may sometimes deem it more profitable to purposely ignore scientific approaches even though he realizes that by doing so he may achieve less than optimum results. Achieving an optimum solution may not be sufficiently important to justify the considerable time and expense required to apply scientific approaches. The expense of developing an analytical solution may equal or exceed its contribution to improved decision making.

Notwithstanding their continued wide usage, managers rarely place sole reliance upon experience-based judgmental decision approaches. Most blend scientific and experience-based methods. Further, the adoption of more scientific analytical tools is beginning to take place at a more rapid rate than ever before. Wide availability of electronic computers has made possible the application of highly sophisticated tools for decision making, the use of which was not possible in the past because of prohibitive computational work. With rapid advances in decision theory, operations research, model building, and systems analysis, there is little doubt that the manager of tomorrow will rely on scientific methodology to a much greater extent than his counterpart of today.

PRINCIPLES OF MANAGEMENT IN DECISION MAKING

A principle is defined as a "settled rule of action; a governing law of conduct . . ." [2] To the extent that principles exist and are valid in their application to managerial problems, they may be valuable decision-making guides for managers. If a retailing chain has the problem of determining who is to have the responsibility for deciding which items of merchandise should be carried in each store, for example, the organizing principle of "delegation" of responsibility is one guide which may be followed. This principle states that the

---

[2] *Webster's Collegiate Dictionary* (5th ed.; Springfield, Mass.: G. C. Merriam Co., 1941).

responsibility for decision making should be passed down in an organization to the lowest level at which competence to make a decision exists. We will examine the conditions under which principles such as this are valid in our later chapters on organization.

Development of Principles

Managerial principles may be derived in a number of ways. One source of principles is the experience of managers. If a manager finds one course of action successful in his practice, he tends to allow this to become a principle of action for him. If large numbers of managers in diverse situations find that the same course of action is successful in handling their problems, the principle may become generally accepted.

Experimentation and research may also be used in developing principles. The effectiveness of a course of action may be determined by observing its impact under controlled conditions, either in an actual organization or in a laboratory situation. If the observation reveals that a particular strategy is successful only under certain conditions, the principle prescribing its effectiveness must be modified to take into account these conditions. Control of as many variables as possible is attempted while the principle is being tested so that differences in results can be attributed to the effect of the principle rather than some other factor. Research by observational and experimental means is preferable to personal experience as a means of developing principles since extraneous or unobserved variables in experience may influence the effectiveness of the principle. Competent observation and experimentation isolate the effect of the principle from such variables.

In addition to the above methods, deduction may be used to develop principles. If a general theory of behavior exists, principles consistent with the theory may be logically deduced. For example, let us assume that one manager's theory about the behavior of individuals in organizations is as follows: "All people are inherently lazy and they abhor work." One principle which may be derived from this theory is that since people dislike work, "employee productivity can be increased only if forceful and threatening supervisory methods are employed." If the theory is valid, the principle should prove effective. We will examine the validity of this particular theory and its derived principles in a later chapter.

When first developed, no real life evidence of successful use of such logically deduced principles necessarily exists. The principles merely represent a logical extension of the general theory. When the principles are applied in practice they may or may not be verified. If not, either the original theory or the logic of the deduction is in error.

Values and Limitations of Management Principles

There is considerable disagreement as to whether many of the so-called principles of management have the strength of truth implied by the definition of a principle. While some authorities title their books *Principles of Management,*[3] others writing about the same subject matter discuss instead the ". . . bases of effective thinking that condition the formulation of executive decisions"[4] or state that ". . . there are gaps in the information we possess, inconsistencies in other places, and frequently hypotheses not substantiated by demonstrated fact."[5] These authors do not make excessive claims about the validity and reliability of their generalizations concerning managerial behavior. Still other scholars sharply criticize the validity of behavior prescribed by most principles of management[6] pointing out that one principle is often contradicted by another. When such contradictions exist, the decision maker has little basis for selecting the most appropriate principle.

Theoretically, it should be possible to learn from experience. Each time that a manager encounters a problem he should not have to consider it as entirely new and unique since countless managers before him have undoubtedly faced similar situations. If the causes of successful and unsuccessful results can be determined and understood, it should be possible to form generalizations about the appropriateness of prospective courses of action. This attractiveness of principles to guide decision making, however, has led some to leap to their formulation without sufficient factual data to support their applicability under varying conditions.

At the same time, the so-called "principles" of management do have some value. In almost every case, there is some evidence to support their applicability, at least *under certain conditions*. If a

[3] See George Terry, *Principles of Management* (rev. ed.; Homewood, Ill.: Richard D. Irwin, Inc., 1956) and Koontz and O'Donnell, *Principles of Management* (rev. ed.; New York: McGraw-Hill Book Co., Inc., 1960).

[4] Ralph C. Davis, *The Fundamentals of Top Management* (New York: Harper & Brothers, 1951), p. 29.

[5] William Newman, *Administrative Action* (Englewood Cliffs, N. J.: Prentice-Hall, Inc., 1951), p. 8.

[6] For example, Herbert A. Simon, *Administrative Behavior* (2d ed.; New York: The Macmillan Company, 1960), Chap. 2.

manager's problem corresponds to the kind of situation under which the principle is applicable, it may provide him with a valuable guide for expediting and simplifying his decision making. In other situations, the principle may just be one factor or variable to be taken into consideration along with several others in making a decision.

MODELS FOR DECISION MAKING

In current management practice, models are receiving increased attention as aids to decision making. The purpose of this section is to explain what models are, how they are constructed and how they may be used in handling decision problems. Models of business behavior represent one of the more sophisticated and scientific tools at the disposal of managers. They represent an approach offering considerable promise for the manager of tomorrow. Although knowledge and skill in the use of mathematics and statistics are desirable for expertise with models, the following discussion and the application of the models presented throughout this book can be mastered with a minimum background in these subjects.

A model is a representation of some real situation or object. Lead soldiers and toy guns can be set up to represent a battle of war. Similarly, a model can represent the elements of a decision problem for a manager. It is not necessary for the model to duplicate in all the richness of life every detail of the real object or situation. It may serve its purposes by representing only the essential features. Few, if any, toy soldier battles represent the noise, emotion, and courage of combat. Yet the mock battle may serve a purpose by illustrating the effects of a military strategy. In a similar way, most decision models are abstractions from reality. In a model designed to aid in the selection of an individual for a job, for example, it may be unnecessary to show the color or existence of his hair or many other of his personal characteristics. Such abstraction from detail allows concentration on the essential or vital factors in decision problems.

Different models vary in their degree of abstraction (and conversely of reality). There are a number of factors which will condition the degree of abstraction desirable in a model. If a model is too abstract, the manager may lose confidence in it because it seems unrealistic to him. On the other hand, if the model is too concrete, he may feel that there are so many variables and relationships in it that he cannot move directly to the heart of the decision problem. For these reasons, a balance between abstraction and reality is desirable. In addition, there are cost factors related to the degree of abstraction appropriate for a model. Defining and quantifying each variable takes time on the part of the model builder, and thus, more highly abstract models may be cheaper to construct.

Model Types

Models may be classified in many different ways.[7] Our classification is based upon the type of model construction. Three general types of construction can be distinguished: descriptive, analogue, and symbolic.

A *descriptive* model [8] attempts to represent a situation by picturing the way that it looks. A picture or a drawing of an automobile plant allows the viewer to imagine what the real plant looks like. A scale model, a blueprint, a pilot plant, a scale layout, a painting, all represent reality through imagery. These models possess a high degree of concreteness and relatively little abstraction. Descriptive models are relatively easy to construct but difficult to manipulate— e.g., it is cumbersome to change the variables in a picture. For this reason, the descriptive model is limited in application to the particular situation which it portrays and does not have general applicability to other situations. For the same reason, descriptive models usually do not lend themselves to portraying dynamic situations or causal relationships between variables although they may sometimes do so. Descriptive models, however, are valuable for obtaining a "feel" for a situation and for providing a stepping stone for the development of other models with more abstract representations.

The second type of model is the *analogue* model. It represents the elements of a real situation by substituting for them other elements with different properties or forms. An airplane is represented by a blip on a radar screen. Lakes are represented by blue colors on maps. Different materials for parts are represented by different types of cross-hatching on drawings. The flow of money and credit in the economy has been represented in a hydraulic analogue model by colored water, pipes, and valves. Analogue models are often more difficult and expensive to construct than descriptive models,

---

[7] D. W. Miller and M. K. Starr, *Executive Decisions and Operations Research* (Englewood Cliffs, N.J.: Prentice-Hall, Inc., 1960). In their Chapter 7, models are classified by a) degree of abstraction, b) dimensionality, c) degree of model development, d) subject, and e) quantification.

[8] C. West Churchman, Russell L. Ackoff, and E. Leonard Arnoff, *Introduction to Operations Research* (New York: John Wiley & Sons, Inc., 1957), refer to descriptive models as "iconic" p. 159.

but their value for decision making is also greater. Analogues may be constructed to portray more general conditions than is often possible with descriptive models and thus may be applicable to a greater variety of situations. They also may be more easily manipulated than most descriptive models, and causal and dynamic relationships may be more easily shown. In the money-flow analogue, for example, the effects of a policy reducing the rates of interest paid by savings institutions could be traced throughout the system. Theoretically this policy would encourage additional consumption and discourage individuals from saving their incomes. These effects could be traced to other variables such as production, investment, etc., by increasing or decreasing the water flows in the analogue model. The changes in water flow are analogous to the changes in the money and credit variables they represent.

The third type of model is the *symbolic* model in which symbols are employed to represent the variables existing in real life situations. Mathematical models or those based on symbolic logic are examples of this type of model. A major advantage of symbolic models is that the manipulation of variables as symbols is usually easier than the manipulation of analogues. Further, symbolic representation often permits the use of powerful mathematical problem-solving techniques which are not applicable when situations are represented in descriptive or analogue terms. Symbolic models usually abstract from reality to a greater extent than do other models; however, the danger of misrepresentation is greater. Solutions to highly abstract models may have little applicability to real situations.

Model Choice

The manager's choice of the type of model he wants to use will depend on the kind of problem with which he is dealing and the relative importance of the problem. As we indicated above, descriptive, analogue and symbolic models differ in the degree to which they possess several characteristics. These differences are summarized in Figure 3–1.

If the manager is faced with a dynamic decision problem in which analysis of causal relationships is critical, a symbolic model would usually be most appropriate, provided it could be developed at a reasonable cost. On the other hand, if the manager wanted an easily constructed highly concrete representation of a relatively static operation, he might prefer a descriptive model. Whatever his choice may be, cost is an important consideration, as implied above. Model

FIGURE 3–1

Model Characteristics by Type of Construction

Model Characteristic	Descriptive	Type of Model Construction Analogue	Symbolic
Degree of Abstraction	3	2	1
Concreteness	1	2	3
Generality	3	2	1
Ease of Construction	1	2	3
Ease of Manipulation	3	2	1
Ability to Handle			
Dynamic changes	3	2	1
Causal relationships	3	2	1

Note: The type of model possessing the greatest degree of a characteristic is denoted by a 1, the least by a 3.

building may consume considerable time on the part of highly-skilled personnel, and if a problem is relatively insignificant, the costs of developing a model may equal or exceed the benefits which may be derived from its usage. Consideration should also be given to the inclinations of the managers who will use the results generated from a model. If top management has a negative and suspicious attitude toward sophisticated mathematical analysis, the results obtained from a highly technical mathematical model may stand little chance of ever being used.

Objectives Served by Model Utilization

In the previous sections we have indicated that models may be highly useful aids to decision making. We will now examine in detail the specific functions which models may serve. A fundamental advantage of model utilization is that it permits the manager to "try out various decision alternatives without interfering with the real system. The major advantage of this approach is that new policies and procedures can be tested without disrupting the operations of an organization, which would often be extremely costly and difficult, if not impossible to do." [9] For example, miniature machines in a scale-model plant can be moved around in order to determine their optimum layout much more easily than could real machines installed in the plant. Or, it might be more desirable for a firm to experiment with inventory reorder rules via a mathematical model than to try out the rules in "real life" where failure could be very costly. In short, the manager may experiment and make mistakes with models and then apply this knowledge to his actual operations.

---

[9] Paul S. Greenlaw, Lowell W. Herron, and Richard H. Rawdon, *Business Simulation* (Englewood Cliffs, N. J.: Prentice-Hall, Inc., 1962), p. 9.

Development of and experimentation with models may be carried out with either one or more of three specific objectives in mind: (1) to simply provide insight into an operation; (2) to predict organizational behavior; or (3) to prescribe managerial behavior. We will now examine each of these types of model utilization in detail.

Understanding and Insight.   One purpose which models may serve is to provide the manager with a better understanding of certain phases of his operations. For example, the development of organization charts—in which each position in the company is represented by a box, and lines are drawn connecting these boxes to show the relationships between positions—may aid the manager in obtaining a better picture of his company's organizational relationships. Models such as this do not prescribe any specific courses of action for the manager to take, although they may enable him to predict, at least in a general way, how certain phases of his operations will function. Rather, their primary purpose is to help him gain insight which ultimately may provide the basis for improved decision making.

Prediction of Behavior.   In certain other cases, models are designed primarily to aid in predicting the behavior of an organization or the conditions which it will experience, rather than simply providing understanding. For example, one company was interested in the impact that the successful introduction of a new product would have upon its operations. In analyzing the introduction of the product, the treasurer prepared pro-forma balance sheets and profit and loss statements of company operations during the proposed engineering, preproduction, testing, and production phases. These predictions in the form of financial models of the business operations showed that prior to any return of income through the sale of the product, a substantial outlay of cash would be required. If other cash needs of the company were to be met, additional outside capital would be needed. Having been shown by the model the extent and timing of the cash shortage, management was able to negotiate a flexible loan agreement with a banking group to alleviate the predicted cash need. It should be noted that although highly useful in guiding the decisions of the company's officers, this model did not show management what to do. It merely predicted a cash shortage. Given this prediction, management might have chosen other alternatives such as: (1) acquiring more funds through equity financing, and/or (2) slowing down the introduction of the product.

Prescribing Behavior.   A third purpose of models is to prescribe managerial decisions. If the manager is able to develop a model closely representing the operations of his organization, analysis or experimentation with the model may allow development of a preferred course of action. In this way, decisions can be said to be prescribed through the use of models.

Assume for purposes of illustration that a simple symbolic model of profit for a company is as follows:

$$P = 78Q - \left(\frac{Q^2}{1520} + 53Q + 70{,}000\right)$$

where P equals profit and Q equals the number of units produced and sold. The company may want to determine the level of output at which it will maximize its profit. In this case, by applying analytical techniques to the model, the manager can arrive directly at the optimum level of production, which is 19,000 units. For other models, however, no analytical methods may be available. In still other cases, the computation by analytical methods may be so cumbersome and time consuming that it would be cheaper to experiment with the model—i.e., try out different values for the independent variables and evaluate their effect on the dependent variable. This process of experimentation is sometimes referred to as *simulation*, which we will discuss more fully in Chapter 18. Figure 3–2 illustrates experimentation with four values of Q in the company profit model indicated above. The profit level is calculated for four different levels of output: 10,000; 20,000; 30,000; and 40,000 units. It should be noted that the simulation alternative of 20,000 units ap-

FIGURE 3–2

Simulation and Analysis of a Profit-Quantity Model

Units Produced	Sales Revenue ($000) (78Q)	Total Costs ($000) $\left(\frac{Q^2}{1520} + 53Q + 70{,}000\right)$	Profit ($000) (Revenue − Total Costs)
10,000	780	666.8	113.2
20,000	1560	1393.2	166.8
30,000	2340	2252.1	87.8
40,000	3120	3242.6	−122.6
* 19,000	1482	1314.5	167.5

Model: $P = 78Q - \left[\frac{Q^2}{1520} + 53Q + 70{,}000\right]$, where P represents profit, and Q, the number

of units produced and sold. 78Q represents sales revenue; and, $\frac{Q^2}{1520} + 53Q + 70{,}000$, represents

total costs.

* Analytical solution obtained as follows: $\frac{dP}{dQ} = 25 - \frac{Q}{760}$; and Q = 19,000 when $\frac{dP}{dQ}$ is set

equal to zero.

proaches the optimum solution of 19,000 units. However, in this case the optimum may be directly arrived at by the use of the calculus, while reaching it by simulation may require substituting so many values for the independent variable, Q, as to be quite time consuming and expensive. For this reason, analytical means are preferred when they are available and when they do not require excessive computation.

Whether analytical or simulation techniques are used in manipulating models, they are intended to provide either optimum or highly satisfying solutions. Thus, the results obtained by their application prescribe courses of action for the manager to follow.

Model Construction

We will now describe the steps involved and some of the methods employed in constructing decision-making models. The reader will note that these steps are similar to the phases of the decision-making process described in the previous chapter. It should also be noted that the construction approaches which we will describe are applicable primarily to symbolic models, and to a lesser extent, analogue models.

Objective Definition and Measurement. The initial step in model construction is to determine the objective to be optimized. In scientific terminology, an objective is referred to as a *dependent* variable. The same considerations in setting objectives that were discussed in Chapter 2 apply in determining dependent variables in model construction.

After the dependent variable has been defined, a measure of effectiveness or ineffectiveness of it is necessary. The measure of effectiveness of a sales organization might be total sales in dollars. Cost of production is a measure of ineffectiveness for a manufacturing plant. Effectiveness measures are intended to be maximized and ineffectiveness measures minimized.

In some models, it is desirable to optimize more than a single dependent variable, such as cost and quality—i.e., multiple objectives exist. When this is the case, it is most desirable to combine the measurement of all dependent variables in a single overall measure of effectiveness or ineffectiveness. If this is not done, manipulation of the model will result in no overall optimum solution, but merely a set of values for each dependent variable. For example, application of a simulation model in which product cost and quality are the dependent variables might indicate that a particular set of production decisions would (1) result in a reject rate of 3% and (2) a cost per piece of $.50. For a different set of decisions however, the reject rate might be 2.7% and the cost per piece, $.54. Which of these two conditions is preferable depends upon the relative value of the 3% reduction in rejects compared to the four cent increase in cost. Weighting the relative importance of objectives such as these may be accomplished after results are attained from the model, or the weighting decision may be built into the model itself. This latter alternative is usually preferable since it obviates the need for management to consider the question of weighting each time data are to be run through the model.

Determining Model Variables and Their Relationships. After the decision maker has determined the measures of effectiveness he wants to optimize in the model, the next step is to determine those factors which have some bearing upon the attainment of his objectives. Then factors are referred to as *independent* variables. In developing a model, it is necessary to determine the type of relationship existing between each independent variable and the dependent variables. The following example will illustrate this process.

The management of a manufacturing operation wished to discover the relationship between the number of inspectors it employed and the number of poor pieces turned out by its employees. In a discussion of this problem, one manager held that when only a few inspectors were employed, some employees became careless, and more poor pieces were turned out than when the inspection force was adequate. Another manager agreed that, while such an inverse relationship between the number of inspectors and the number of poor pieces turned out did exist, the employment of additional inspectors led to fewer rejects only up to a point. He believed that when too many inspectors were utilized, some machine operators became antagonistic to their "snooping," and that this probably caused more rejects. From this discussion, management concluded that within a certain range, the number of rejects turned out was inversely and linearly related to the number of inspectors utilized, but that outside this range, the relationship had "tails" as illustrated in Figure 3–3.

In this example, we included only one independent variable. However, others can be treated in a similar manner. For example, management might also explore the relationship between employee scores on psychological tests and the number of rejects turned out. Such an analysis might indicate that there is an inverse relationship between an employee's performance on a manual dexterity test and the number of rejects he produces, up to a point, but that there is no significant relationship between intelligence test scores and the quality of production.

FIGURE 3–3. Relationship Between Poor Pieces Produced and Number of Inspectors

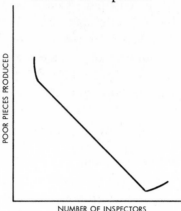

NUMBER OF INSPECTORS

The method of determining relationships between variables described in the above example is essentially subjective in that it relies on the opinions of managers. Such opinions, however, may be checked against company records of past performance to discover if the managerial estimates are consistent with historical data. Another approach to model building is to start by analyzing company data rather than by obtaining executive opinions. Even when this is done, however, it may still be necessary for management to judge whether the periods covered by the data are representative of the company's operations. Thus, this approach also utilizes both data and opinion to serve as checks on each other.

If reliable data covering past operations exist, statistical techniques may be used to determine the importance and the effect of different variables upon the attainment of objectives. If, however, no reliable data are available and if opinion is considered unreliable, models may still be developed by experimentation. Experimentation may also be desirable when an operation has not been performed in the same way that it is planned for the future. For example, if we wanted to determine the factors which influence typist productivity with electric typewriters when none had been used previously, an experiment using the new machines might generate sufficient data to develop a model. The model builder has, then, several options open to him in identifying and measuring the independent variables of the proposed model: opinion and discussion, statistical and mathematical analysis of company data, and experimentation.

Historically, managers in organizations have not always considered decision variables and their relationships in explicit, precise ways. Instead, a great deal of vagueness and many implicit assumptions about the behavior of organizations have existed in the minds of managers. When attempting to define and describe these variables from managerial descriptions then, the model builder may have considerable difficulty in arriving at satisfactory representations.

In addition, some important variables may be essentially qualitative in nature. A plant location decision model, for example, may require a consideration of community relations, but it may be quite difficult to derive a precise definition or measurement of this variable. The model may be constructed and tested, however, without this "soft variable." Then when the analysis is complete, explicit consideration of the community relations factor can be made. Thus this factor is not ignored, yet the difficulty of incorporating it into the model is avoided. Excessive use of this technique with several variables in one decision model, however, may lessen the value of the model as the decisions become primarily dependent upon non-quantifiable variables.

Refining the Model. Examination often will show that some independent variables are relatively unimportant and that others have the same or a similar effect upon the dependent variable. Unimportant variables *may* be discarded from further consideration in order to ease the job of manipulating the model. If, for example, through analysis, worker age is found to be unrelated to productivity, it can be ignored in the construction of models in which productivity is *the* dependent variable. This approach creates a degree of abstraction, to be sure, but at the same time, it allows concentration on the most important elements comprising the decision problem. Further, independent variables affecting the dependent variables in the same way may sometimes be grouped together and considered as a single variable in constructing models. For example, "material costs" and "direct labor costs" often vary in exactly the same way and can be combined as "variable costs." Conversely, the manager may find that an independent variable affects an objective differently when tested with different sets of data or at different time periods. If so, the model builder should suspect that the definition and/or measurement of such a variable masks two or more separate sub-variables operating in different ways. In this case, instead of combining variables, the independently acting sub-variables should be separated for individual treatment in the model.

Symbolizing. The final step in model building is to assign symbols to the dependent and independent variables. Basically, this amounts to developing abbreviations for the variables; such as P for profit, C for costs, etc. This process is applicable primarily in the development of symbolic models. However, in the hydraulic analogue models we could assign green tubes to the pipe representing consumption and red tubes to that pipe representing savings. The basic purpose in developing symbols is to facilitate manipulation of the model.

Following the above procedures results in an abstract representation of a real situation. The model-building process is useful in and of itself because it forces us to focus attention upon the key elements in decision problems and to disregard unimportant variables. Moreover, the existence of the model allows the use of powerful analytical and simulation techniques which would not be feasible unless this abstract mathematical representation existed. The cost of model building for business systems may be high, however, and these costs usually cannot be justified unless the model is subsequently manipulated to shed considerable light upon how a decision or a set of decisions should be made.

Use and Modification of Models. Upon completion, a model can be tested to determine its applicability to the decision problem for which it was designed. This testing can utilize data from past periods to show what decisions would have been best had the model been used during those times. A more rigorous test of the model with present and future data will disclose whether it can perform satisfactorily under less certain conditions.

If the tests of the model are successful, its use is justified under the conditions and within the limitations indicated in its design. It should be recognized, however, that the model was constructed under conditions of the past. If the variables are dynamic, modification of the model during its use may be necessary. At times it is possible to predict during the construction of the model that the variables and/or their interrelationships are subject to change. In such cases, it is sometimes possible to build self-modifying features into the model. In other instances, the variables may change without forewarning. If so, redesign of the model may be required. At a minimum, management should be aware of the assumptions underlying the models it uses for decision making. Additionally, a periodic, if not continuous, monitoring of the reality of the assumptions will allow management to modify decisions based on use of models as conditions change.

THE SYSTEMS CONCEPT

In our previous discussion we considered decision making from the manager's point of view and of the tools which he has available to help him make his decisions. We are now going to broaden our consideration of decision making by examining this process in terms of a "systems" framework.

The term "system" is used to describe many different kinds of phenomena such as the solar system and the social security system. Utilities send electricity over a distribution system. Even within businesses, there are many different types of systems. The engineering department of a tractor company designs a hydraulic system for power steering on its products. Personnel departments develop wage and salary systems to achieve equitable wage payments. There are accounting systems, management control systems, electronic systems and many others. Further, as we indicated in Chapter 1, a body of knowledge contributing to a general system theory is beginning to evolve. In this section we will consider one type of systems view of the organization—that which focuses attention on information and decision making.[10]

The systems concept may be applied in examining informational and decision processes of an organization in two different ways. First, we may view the decisions made by management and the information flows associated with these decisions as constituting an *information-decision* system. This view focuses attention on decisions as representing the transformation of information into courses of action. For example, when a gasoline station manager learns that a competitor has reduced prices by two cents a gallon, he may decide to follow suit. In systems terms, the manager's *decision* repre-

---

[10] In a more general representation of a system, physical as well as informational inputs may be considered. For example, if the human body is considered as a system, its inputs would include food, water, air, and environmental conditions (light, sound, heat, etc.). If a manufacturing plant is considered as a system, the raw materials, personnel, equipment, and supplies as well as information would be considered inputs. Similarly, physical transformations and outputs occur within all business organizations. For example, a man and a milling machine, as operating elements, take bar stock as input and transform it into a part for a product as output. In this system, physical transformations are made. We will discuss in greater detail managerial decision making relative to such physical inputs, transformations and outputs in later chapters.

sents the *transformation* of the *information* that was obtained about his competitor into a specified course of action, or *output*.

Second, data processing operations in business firms may be viewed as *pure information* systems.[11] In pure information systems, as distinguished from information-decision systems, information is simply changed into different forms. No decisions are made, except those specifying what information is to be processed and how it is to be processed. In a job cost system, for example, data from manufacturing operations may be obtained, coded, sorted, and summarized. Although these data may ultimately be transformed into decisions by management, the data processing *per se* simply effects a change in form of the information.

Whether we examine information-decision or pure information systems, their basic design is similar. Both types are comprised of the same kinds of *elements* (the basic building blocks of a business system). These elements can be grouped into three general classes: (1) information elements, (2) transformation elements, and (3) control elements.

There are several different types of information elements. First is the *input* element, which represents data *received* from outside the system. These data may come from other systems within the firm or from outside the organization. A special type of input is the *feedback* element, which refers to information reflecting results of the previous operations of the system which is fed back into the system to help guide future performance. Another type of information element is *output*, which centers around transmission of the results of a system to other systems. Finally, the *memory* element of a system stores and updates information in the system.

There are two basic types of *transformation* elements. As we indicated above, when we are considering an information-decision system, data from input, feedback and memory are weighed and translated into a *decision;* whereas in a pure information system, data are simply changed into a different form.

The third basic type of element in business systems is the *control* element. This element, which is comprised of plans, policies, rules, etc., guides the way the total system of information and transformation elements are to function.

The different types of systems elements and their interrelation-

---

[11] See, for example, Ned Chapin, *An Introduction to Automatic Computers* (Princeton, N. J.: D. Van Nostrand Company, Inc., 1957), Chap. 4 and especially Figure 8, p. 51.

ships are illustrated in Figures 3–4 and 3–5. Before examining each of these elements in detail, we will illustrate their role in the business system with an example.

Consider the manager responsible for buying raw materials for a business firm. A certain portion of his time is devoted to the receipt

FIGURE 3–4. Schematic Representation of a System and Its Elements

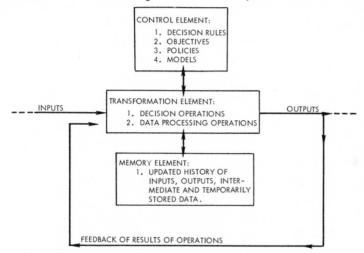

Note: Arrows indicate flow of information and its directions in the system. Examples of element contents are not necessarily all-inclusive.

FIGURE 3–5. Types of System Elements

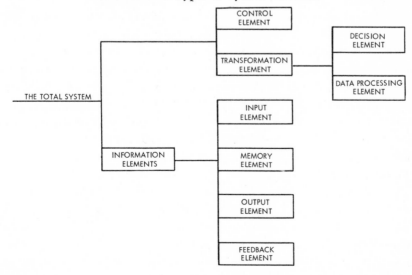

of information. He needs to know the materials requirements of his organization. He also receives market information about materials from suppliers and salesmen. This portion of his activity spent in obtaining and receiving data represents an input element in the buying system.

After these data have been obtained they may be processed into a standard form useful for reference. For example, a file of potential suppliers classified by type of material available from them is common. Similarly, a specification file is often maintained. These and similar parts of the information system constitute the memory element.

The decision to purchase a specified amount of material from a particular supplier represents the transformation element in the system. Thus, information pertaining to the supplier and to needs of the firm is transformed into a specific purchasing decision.

The output element of the buying system consists of purchase orders and follow-up communications sent to suppliers. Further, information showing the status of outstanding purchase orders may be sent to the departments within the firm using the various materials for future planning. Most buying decisions of this type are not unique. Similar decisions have been made in the past. Company policies, objectives, and past decisions of buyers influence the transformation of data into decisions. The portion of the system which guides this transformation of data is the control element. In purchasing, one rule might be to restrict the total amount of any one order from a given supplier to a specified amount (e.g. $10,000). Other guides to making the decision might include the following: "Change suppliers for each material once each year." "Purchase from suppliers located within 100 miles." "Give preference to suppliers who buy from us." "Fifty percent of purchases shall be from small businesses." "Long-run lowest price is the primary criterion for selection of supplier." "For standard items, carload quantities are preferred if volume of usage allows." "Acceptance of gratuities from suppliers is cause for dismissal." These portions of the control element effect the supplier chosen as well as the data that is maintained.

Dividing a decision-information system into its elements may appear artificial since a particular buyer may perform duties simultaneously which include all of the elements. He may not make these distinctions between parts of his job. It is extremely useful to examine each system element separately, however, in order to focus attention on those parts creating difficulties and requiring revision.

In large volume complex buying organizations, different parts of the system will be performed by separate individuals or machines. Under these conditions, consideration of each systems element becomes highly useful for analysis of decisions and information flows.

Inputs

The information inputs to a system are those data which are externally derived or developed and are helpful in making decisions. When we say that the information is externally derived, we mean that it is not developed within the decision system under consideration. These data may come from other systems within the organization or from outside the company.

A common decision in plants operating assembly lines for the manufacture of their products is that of determining the number of hours per week that the plant should work. This decision may be made each week. One of the pieces of information valuable in arriving at this decision is the inventory of items in the possession of distributors and dealers. Trade association data or the company's own marketing operations may be the source of such data. Whatever its source, dealer inventories are useful in making the "hours per week" decision and would be considered as inputs.

The design of information inputs for a system is dependent upon the nature of the decisions and outputs desired from the system. If certain data are necessary to perform any of the functions required by a system, an input element must provide them. Thus, input element design is related to the design of other elements of the system. Further, input design is influenced by the following factors:

1. The availability of data useful to the system. (Is it possible to obtain dealer inventory data?)

2. The cost of obtaining the desired inputs. (What is the relative cost of obtaining inventory data from the trade association as compared to a questionnaire financed by a company?)

3. The usefulness of available data to the system as a whole. (Can data more useful than dealer inventories be used?)

4. The timing need in the data receipt and use. (What if dealer inventory information were available monthly and the scheduling decision were made once per week?)

Memory

When a system relies on past actions, or when the arrival of the data inputs does not coincide with the time when they will be used, the memory element furnishes a means of storing these data for future use. In any office one observes file cabinets, safes, and desk drawers full of papers. These constitute the memory of past operations, decisions, and data stored for future use. For example:

> In calculating social security deductions from employee earnings, a record of the total deductions for the year to date for each individual is necessary. The memory element of this system contains deductions identified by employee's name and social security number. The memory element is updated as further deductions are credited to each employee's account. If total deductions reach the maximum for an employee, no further deductions are made for him.

The form of the information in the memory element will vary considerably depending on the needs of the operation. However, certain generalizations may be made concerning memory design.

1. Its size is determined by the number of items to be sorted, their identification requirements, and the size of the items to be stored. For example, storing data for social security purposes requires a larger memory if (a) there is a larger number of employees; (b) an additional identification of each employee (such as age or sex) is desired; or (c) cumulative earnings as well as deductions are stored.

2. Its content is determined by the operation's or system's needs. Income tax rates would be superfluous in the social security deduction system.

3. It is updated by input (or feedback) and the transformation element. As the employee works more hours (from input) the cumulative deductions in memory are updated. The addition of these to prior deductions is performed by the transformation element and the result is stored in memory.

4. The memory must be able to forget information on some planned basis. For the social security system, the memory is made to forget cumulative deductions at the end of each year or when an employee terminates employment.

Feedback

When the decision of a system is implemented, data about the *results* of the operation may be returned to the system so that the effect of past decisions can be evaluated and taken into consideration in making future decisions. This information flow in systems terms is referred to as "feedback."

> The personnel department of one company selects and hires key punch operators. During the selection process, considerable information concerning each applicant is obtained. These data are filed in the personnel jacket (a

memory document) of each employee. Semi-annually, supervisors rate the performance of the key punch operators. These ratings are used for several purposes, and one copy of them becomes available to the person making the selection decisions. High and low production operators are grouped and compared with the criteria by which they were originally hired. One such analysis showed that there was no significant correlation between favorable personal recommendations given by former employers and the supervisors' ratings of the operators. By indicating that these recommendations were of little value in selection, the feedback of past results permitted decision refinement.

In the above example, the results of the decision were fed back into the system twice a year. Other systems may feed back data continuously and with little delay. One airplane landing system constantly monitors the position of each approaching aircraft in relation to a pre-selected guide path. As the position of the plane deviates from this path, the ground control operator feeds this information back to the pilot who makes flight corrections. One proposed model of a landing system has a computer monitoring the radar data showing the position of each plane. As deviations from planned positions occur, the computer is to send radio messages to a control mechanism in the plane for realignment of its position relative to the guide path. Thus, the information flow and the reactions or decisions in this projected system will become completely mechanized.

The feedback element of a system has several characteristics and requirements:

1. Some recording of the results of past decisions is required, as were supervisor evaluations in our example of the key punch operators.

2. Processing of the recorded data into a useful form for subsequent decisions is usually necessary (as was interpretation of radar scope data by the ground control operator in our example).

3. Feedback information has time as well as content requirements (as may be noted by comparing the need for continuous and instantaneous data in the aircraft landing system with the delayed feedback in the selection of the key punch operators).

4. Some systems require that certain information be designated more *urgent* or *important* than other data. The lack of precautionary movements by Army and Navy commanders at Pearl Harbor on December 7, 1941, has been attributed in part to the great mass of intelligence data flowing into the system with insufficient emphasis placed upon those pieces which would have triggered precautionary decisions. Similarly, when the ground control operators sees a plane

leaving the guide path, he may raise the pitch and intensity of his voice to notify the pilot that this information is not ordinary.

5. Feedback of data is intended to stabilize the outputs of a system by focusing attention on deviations from planned output. If, however, the output of a system is oscillating between two points, it is possible for feedback to amplify deviations from planned performance rather than to dampen them. This will happen when the output operations are *out of phase* with the feedback—i.e.; when information concerning the low phase of a cyclic operation is fed back at the time at which the system is performing at the high phase of the cycle. This feedback implies that the operations should be pushed higher in the cycle at a time that they are already too high, and vice versa.[12] The danger in delayed feedback can be seen by imagining that an incoming airplane is oscillating 20 feet above and below the guide path, If feedback is delayed to such an extent that the ground control operator indicates that the plane is 20 feet too high when it is 20 feet below the path, the consequences could be serious. Thus, the timing of feedback should be designed so that deviations from planned performance may be reduced. Operating oscillations are not uncommon. Feedback which amplifies variations can destroy the tendency toward equilibrium desirable in a system.

Output

The output of a system is information transformed into a useful form. An executive's decision is merely a mental concept until it has been translated into oral or written form. These forms of information represent the output of a system.

The design of system outputs depends, first of all, upon the use to which they are to be put. If an output is to be used as an instruction to an employee, it may be merely a verbal statement. If it is a decision to introduce a new product to the company's line, on the other hand, the output may consist of a detailed plan of action which will in turn initiate additional studies, decisions, and actions throughout the company.

The prime criterion for designing systems outputs is the subsequent use to be made of them. However, the manager must also consider the cost of obtaining the output. Such costs are influenced by the availability of system inputs and the transformation of these

---

[12] If a system employs *negative* feedback, oscillations of output are reduced. Instability results when feedback is *positive*. Oscillations are then amplified and overcorrections occur. See, for example, Churchman, Ackoff, and Arnoff, *op. cit.*, p. 78.

into the desired output. For example, obtaining some kinds of market research data may be so expensive that any gains made possible through their use are not sufficient to justify their cost. Thus, the optimum specification for outputs is determined by their value to the system and by the costs of their production.

Transformation Elements

Although our primary concern in this book is with managerial decision making, we have focused attention in the preceding sections on non-decision elements. This was done because of the critical importance of information transmission and processing in decision making. Most managers spend considerable portions of their time developing and managing information systems to obtain adequate data for their decisions. In fact, some managers are concerned solely with the selection of the most appropriate data collection, transmission and processing methods.

We will now turn our attention to the transformation element which is at the heart of the decision-making process. As we indicated earlier, there are two basic types of transformation elements. Sometimes decisions are made to transform data into plans of action and orders. We will refer to these as *substantive* transformations. For example, a substantive transformation is involved when a manager determines that he is going to reduce the number of hours his department will work the following week on the basis of feedback of his costs from last week's operation. Similarly, on the basis of inputs of market research data and cost projections, a company president may decide not to develop a new product. These decisions represent the transformation of information into a course of action to be taken.

Other transformations, as we have indicated, consist simply of data processing operations. We will refer to these as *procedural* transformations. When a clerk extends quantity and price per unit information on an invoice, he transforms these two bits of data into a total price. When an employee files outstanding invoices by customer, he transforms data organized in a random manner to customer accounts receivable. The latter type of organized data can be used for decisions (e.g., credit for future orders from the customer), but the clerk does not perform decision transformations, merely data processing ones.

The design of a transformation element depends to a considerable extent upon the kind of outputs required from and the kind of inputs available to the system. Unless the form and content of the outputs are known, logical systems design is not possible. Consider a typical payroll operation in a plant manufacturing products to customer order. First, a timekeeper fills out a form indicating each job performed, the operator who performed it, the time taken, and the number of pieces produced. The payroll system then takes these pieces of data as inputs and transforms them into a paycheck for each employee. This involves adding each employee's time on all job slips during a given period, multiplying these times by the appropriate rate or rates, calculating deductions and net pay, and transforming these results into appropriate records and paychecks.

These same timekeeping data inputs could be used for determining departmental labor costs each week. This would require the transformation of the timekeeping slips into total labor costs for the plant and segregating these for each department. If the original timekeeping form identified the department in which the individual worked, this transformation could be performed by sorting the forms weekly by department, multiplying the hourly rate for each employee by the hours on each job, and adding the results. Although the inputs to the payroll and the labor cost system are the same, the *transformations* are different because the outputs required from the two systems are different.

It should be noted that if both of these outputs are required by the same organization, savings could be accomplished by integrating the two transformation operations. In both cases, hours worked are multiplied by the rate per hour, and duplication could be avoided by carrying out this operation only once. Once the multiplication has been accomplished, the data then could then be separated by employee's name for the payroll system and by department for the labor cost system. Further, the transformation of other data useful to the system such as the following could also be integrated with the multiplication operation:

1. Product costs. (The costs would need to be separated by job and the costs for all jobs on each product totaled.)
2. Time standards and estimates. (A time standard for an operation could be calculated by determining the total costs for each job and dividing by the number of pieces produced. This per unit cost could then be averaged with previous per unit costs for the same operation to arrive at a historical time standard for the job. These standards might provide a basis for estimating future costs.)

The above example points up that there may be considerable common usage of certain system inputs. Thus, systems design, as a whole, should recognize the possibility of combining elements of the different systems into one system with multiple transformations and multiple outputs. This concept of integration has wide applicability, and represents an important reason for considering decision making and information processing from a systems viewpoint.

Not only does the design of transformation elements depend upon the nature of the inputs available and outputs desired, as we have indicated above, but it also must take into consideration two other factors. The first of these is the nature of the physical operations upon which the inputs may be based. For example, if an employee is paid the same rate per hour for each job he performs, the payroll system can total the hours he works in a period and make one multiplication to arrive at his gross pay. If, however, the employee receives a different rate of pay for each job, a separate multiplication must be made for each job and the results of these intermediate multiplications must be totaled to arrive at the employee's gross pay. Transformation element design also depends upon the availability of data in memory that may be transformed into an acceptable output. For instance, it may be difficult to generate departmental labor costs if the department in which the job was performed is not identified on the timekeeping form at the time the original record was made. The labor cost output could still be calculated, however, if the memory element contained a record of each employee's department. Since the timekeeping form contains the name of the employee, labor costs could be allocated to the various departments by reference to the intermediate memory record identifying the employee as a member of a particular department.

The Control Element

The "control" element in a system is that unit with the function of determining how the other elements of the system are to operate. It is the brains of the system. It tells the transformation element what shall be done with the input and memory in order to produce the output required.

The control unit comprises objectives, policies, models, procedures, and programs as well as plans and controls. Any specific system might not include all of these types of controls, but it would include enough of them so that the people in charge of the system may meet their responsibilities to the organization (in terms of system outputs required) at a cost deemed reasonable. The choice of control methods will be conditioned by the effect that these different measures will have upon the efficiency of the system.

The control element can offer *general* guides to how the system is to operate or it may provide highly *specific* operating rules. If only the objectives of the firm are given as a guide, the persons performing the transformation operation have considerable leeway as to how operations will be performed. In some cases the output of an organizational system is not even specified. For example, one man was hired by a machine tool manufacturing firm as "Chief Industrial Engineer." His duties were not specified. In general, he had a feeling that he was supposed to act "as industrial engineers act." Supposedly he could do this with respect to the office organization, the production group, or the sales staff. Here the industrial engineering system was able to determine its own outputs as well as the methods it would use to accomplish them.

Contrast this rather general specification control to the following situation: Through analysis of the flow of rejects of parts from a machining operation, one quality control organization determined that if the operating rejection rate exceeded a fixed percentage, the machines should be shut down for adjustment. This rule, made available to the foreman, provided a specific rule for operating decisions.

Overall Systems Design

As we have seen in the previous sections, each element of a system is dependent on each of the other elements. The output is determined by the transformation, memory, and the input, and each of these is, in turn, related to each of the other elements. At what point, then, should the design of a system begin? It is usually desirable to start at either the input or the output stage. Further, it is recommended that design begin with an analysis of the objectives that the manager wants accomplished by the system. Thus output design is primary. Then it is possible to determine whether the desired outputs can be produced economically or whether they must be modified in light of the costs of attaining them through the design of each of the other system elements.

In considering the design of a system as a whole, it is not possible to stop after a consideration of a single output and the accompanying elements necessary to provide that output. As was shown in the discussion of the payroll system, several different outputs useful in decision making in the organization can be developed from the same input data. Rather than design three or four different information systems to provide such needed data as these, it is more typical for organizations to combine input, memory, and transformation elements so as to minimize systems costs. However, it should be recognized that excessive combination can result in compromises in the form and availability of the outputs. These compromises tend to reduce the effectiveness of the data as it is used in decision making. Consider a multiple payroll and departmental labor cost system. If labor costs are needed for decision making on a daily basis and payrolls are calculated semi-monthly, the integration of these two systems tends to compromise the costs savings theoretically possible.

Self-Regulating and Automatic Systems

A self-regulating system is one which automatically takes action to keep its outputs in line with the objectives desired. In order to accomplish self-regulation, a system must be able to monitor its outputs and compare them with the *desired* outputs. Detection of significant variances allows the system to adjust its operations in such a way as to bring about the reduction or elimination of these deviations. It should be noted, however, that self-regulation depends upon the ability of the system not only to monitor its outputs but also to change its methods of operations so as to correct output errors. Not all systems are able to change operating methods in this way. Some payroll systems, for example, cannot *correct* an overpayment although the system may be able to *detect* an overpayment. Output correction would, in such cases, be performed outside the payroll system. In contrast, a self-regulating payroll system would not only detect the error but also recalculate the paycheck to correct the potential overpayment. With no self-regulation, however, other means (such as the addition of an individual or group to monitor the outputs) will be required to achieve the same results.

Self-regulating systems in business firms have become more widely used with the advent of automation. Self-regulation is a necessary component for the operation of automatic factories. In the operation of an automatic oil refinery, for example, the outputs desired from each intermediate stage of refining are specified within certain ranges of composition (temperature, pressures, etc.). Flow meters, pressure and temperature gauges, and product analyzers continuously or intermittently monitor the values of these variables in the operating stages. The results of these measurements are fed into a control center (usually some type of computer). At the control center, the actual measurements are compared with the ranges that these values must take if the system or one of its stages is to operate successfully to produce the desired outputs. When deviations outside the allowable limits for these variables appear, the control center dispatches messages automatically to servomechanisms. These actuate valves and initiate other appropriate action to bring the operations into line with what is desired. Thus, the functioning of the automatic factory and its sub-parts are closely related to systems theory as we have described it. The alternative to the automatic refinery, of course, is to have men compare the actual performance of the system with the desired outputs, and to take corrective action when required—such as reading a thermometer and turning down the heat when the temperature in a particular process gets too high.

Information and Decision Systems: Summary

Our previous discussion has focused attention on the various interrelated elements in business systems. Underlying this discussion has been the view that the business organization may be thought of as either a single information-decision system, or as comprising a set of interrelated sub-systems, both of the information-decision and pure information variety. Or, to put it another way, the organization may be viewed as a network of interconnected decision and information transformations. This conception is illustrated in Figure 3–6. The nodes of the network represent the transformations, while the links of the network represent the flows of input and output. The reader will note that—although we have previously treated

FIGURE 3–6. Linking of Decisions and Data-Processing Operations

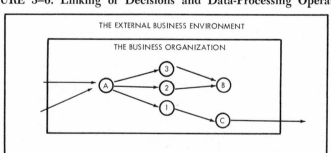

Legend: Letters indicate decision transformations.
Numerals indicate data transformations.
Arrows indicate directions of information flows.

input and output separately for the purposes of exposition—the outputs from one transformation serve as inputs to another. For example, the president of a company decides (a transformation) that he wants to obtain certain data from the industrial engineering department, and sends the chief industrial engineer a memo to this effect. From the president's point of view, the memo represents an information output, but at the same time the communication serves as an input to industrial engineering. Figure 3–6 also illustrates that the firm must be viewed as interacting with its external environment. Inputs are received from outside the organization (such as supplier information in our purchasing department example given earlier); while at the same time some of the firm's information outputs are externally oriented. For example, information may be developed to maintain legally required records, for tax returns, or for reporting to company stockholders.

Finally, we should reemphasize that our concept of an organization as an information-decision system focuses attention upon the data requirements of decision making. That is, the end goal of the development of a business system is to enable management to make better decisions in terms of meeting its objectives. We will give further attention to the role of systems in organization design when we consider organization structure in later chapters.

A THEORY OF COMPLEX DECISION MAKING

Traditionally we have looked at complex top-management decisions with awe and admiration. An aura of mysticism has surrounded the executive with his battery of assistants as he rolls out decisions with ease. This view attributes a great deal of acumen, "sixth sense," and similar qualities to managers.

In contrast to this mystical concept of the executive, a new view of decision making is emerging. The essential elements of this theory can be stated as follows:

1. Complex problems can be broken down into similar sub-problems and in turn into sub-sub-problems.
2. Sub-problems possessing similar characteristics may be classed into a number of basic problem types. Few sub-problems are so unique that they have no similarity to other (sub) problems.
3. For some types of sub-problems, analytical or simulation solutions exist. For these, optimum solutions may be approached.

4. For other types of sub-problems, it is possible to identify a series of methods which may be tried out to seek a solution. That is, a repertoire of possible solution techniques which satisfices may be developed.

5. Given various classes of sub-problems and a series of solution techniques for each, successive application of these techniques provides a high probability that the sub-problems can be solved.

6. As each sub-problem is solved, that portion of the overall problem no longer remains.

7. By successive reiteration of available solution techniques to each sub-problem, the solution to the overall problem can be obtained or its magnitude can be reduced.

To what extent does evidence exist that such an atomistic theory of complex decision making is valid? The air-defense command SAGE system exhibits some of the characteristics postulated by this theory. Each of the many decisions that are necessary to repel an attack upon the United States has been identified and broken down into atomistic sub-problems, and these sub-problems have been classified into a few simple decision types. Thus, the whole system may be viewed as a network of simple decisions. H. Goode classifies these decisions and their sequence in Figure 3–7. His "multiple

FIGURE 3–7

Air Defense System: Functions and Decisions

Class of Function	Function	Class of Decision
Front end analysis	Detection	Go, no-go
	Track determination	Estimation
	Height determination	Estimation
	Split targets	Go, no-go
	Merge targets	Go, no-go
	Identification	Go, no-go
Raid decision	Speed	Estimation
	Direction	Estimation
	Strength	Estimation
	Attack	Go, no-go
Attack	With what	Multiple choice
	How many	Multiple choice
	From which base	Multiple choice
	When	Estimation
	Kill or no-kill	Go, no-go
Weapon direction	Acquisition	Go, no-go
	Track	Estimation
In missile	Seeker acquisition	Go, no-go
	Warhead detonation	Estimation

Source: H. Goode, "A Decision Model for a Fourth-Level Model in the Boulding Sense," in Donald P. Eckman (ed.), *Systems: Research and Design* (New York: John Wiley & Sons, Inc., 1961), p. 108. Reproduced by permission.

choice" class of decisions merely represents a series of go-no-go decisions. Since the latter are simple "yes or no" decisions, the number of decision types are not only few, but also relatively simple.

When the air-defense system was first proposed, there was considerable opposition to it by the executives in the then existing system. Disbelief that a great many complex decisions could be simplified and programmed was widely expressed. Few persons working in the old system believed that the work of the mystical executive could be analyzed and explained as consisting of relatively simple sub-parts. The system's success is legend, however. Persons who opposed the automated system initially now support it and hold that people alone could not do the job as well as does the successor combination of people and computers operating the programs.

The air-defense system reduced a complex decision process into a logical step-by-step program, parts of which could be operated by computers. Thus this system exhibits some of the characteristics of our theory of complex decision making. Another approach to decision making—heuristic programming—appears to apply this theory to a broader scope of problems. We will now examine this approach in some detail.

HEURISTIC PROGRAMMING

Heuristic programming is a systematic approach to solving relatively unstructured problems. Ill-structured problems have three general characteristics:

1.　The objective or the goal of the problem is not well defined or is non-quantifiable.

2.　Many of the independent variables are qualitative, symbolic or verbal rather than quantitative.

3.　Computational means or algorithms are not available.[13]

Heuristic programming consists of three basic types of procedures which, when applied to a problem, may be able to produce a solution. The first classifies the type of problem to be solved. The second breaks down large problems into smaller problems if the larger ones cannot be solved. The third calls for the application of problem-solving techniques. These techniques are known to be able to solve certain types of problems that probably comprise the overall prob-

---

[13] From Fred M. Tonge, *A Heuristic Program for Assembly Line Balancing* (Englewood Cliffs, N. J.: Prentice-Hall, Inc., 1961), p. 49.

lem. In any heuristic program there may be a library or bank of these techniques, classified by the kinds of sub-problems to which they apply. The following description of the heuristic programming process will serve to illustrate the application of each of these three basic types of procedures:

1. Identification of the overall problem.
2. Determining the type of the overall problem.
3. Application of problem-solving techniques which may be able to solve problems of this type. If these techniques are successful, the overall problem is solved.
4. If not, sub-problems are then derived, classified into types, and appropriate problem-solving methods are applied to each. If each sub-problem can be solved, an aggregate solution exists.
5. If not, those sub-problems which are not soluble are broken down into sub-sub-problems. These may be classified by type, and problem-solving techniques known to be applicable to the various types derived may be applied.
6. The above procedure may be continued until either (1) the solution of all levels of sub-problems permits the solution of the overall problem, or (2) it is determined that all or certain parts of the overall problem are not soluble.[14]

A schematic portrayal of this process is illustrated in Figure 3–8.

It is important to note that heuristic programming does not guarantee a solution to problems—the problem-solving techniques built into the program in some cases may be unable to generate solutions. Further, the solutions which are provided are not necessarily optimum ones. Usually satisfactory, rather than optimum solutions are generated, although procedures for achieving solutions closer to the optimum may be applied to first approximations of solutions which have already been obtained. Heuristic programs do not provide a completely exhaustive examination of problems. Rather, heuristic programs often limit the examination of alternative solutions to each problem or sub-problem. This is because consideration of *all* alternatives to problems and their consequences involves prohibitive time and expense whether the solution is by human or computer methods.

The concepts in heuristic programming are important because

---

[14] After Herbert Simon, *The New Science of Management Decision* (New York: Harper & Brothers, 1960), pp. 21–34; and Tonge, *op. cit.*, p. 17.

FIGURE 3–8

Heuristic Programming Procedures

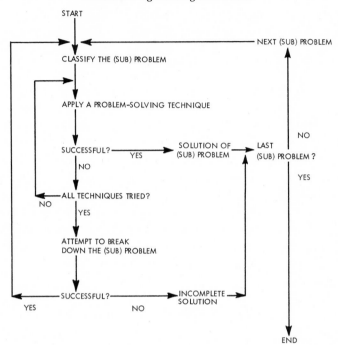

most model construction and application has been restricted to decisions made at relatively low or middle levels of the organization structure. Theoretically, heuristic programs offer a technically feasible method for the solution of any problem at *any* level. In actuality, however, the use of heuristic programs has been limited to date. Heuristic programs have been used to play games such as chess and checkers and to prove theorems in logic. Further, a number have been applied to business problems.[15]

As the reader may gather, heuristic programs may simulate the activities of human problem solving. The techniques and procedures for carrying out these activities can be programmed for computer use. The complex human thought processes used in solving ill-structured problems become (in heuristic programs) procedures for applying relatively simple techniques recursively to problems and

[15] See, for example, William S. Gere, *Heuristics in Job Shop Scheduling,* O. N. R. Memorandum No. 70, Graduate School of Industrial Administration, Carnegie Institute of Technology, June, 1960; also, G. P. Clarkson and A. H. Meltzer, "Portfolio Selection: A Heuristic Approach," *Journal of Finance,* 15 (December, 1960), pp. 465–80.

sub-problems.[16] Theoretically, complex problems are merely complex chains or sets of simple problems. These sub-problems are amenable to solution by relatively few types of problem techniques.

SUMMARY

The purpose of this chapter has been to introduce several decision approaches useful to the manager. We have considered their relative effectiveness and examined some of the kinds of problems to which they may be applied. Figure 3–9 presents a comparison and evaluation of the usefulness of each approach for managerial decision making. These approaches together with the concepts developed in Chapter 2 are basic to management. In the following chapters, we will undertake an examination of types of decisions managers face. Using the framework developed in this and the preceding chapter, the reader can bring perspective and deeper understanding to his study of these managerial decisions.

DISCUSSION AND STUDY QUESTIONS

1. Evaluate the validity of the following reasoning: 75% of the time, a firm's performance is appreciably improved by undertaking action Y instead of action Z. Therefore, the principle: "follow action Y" is established for the firm.

2. What values may a firm be able to gain through the careful design and use of models?

3. Consider the following items and classify them as elements of an information-decision system. In each case give the reason for your decision.
    a) Estimates of industry sales volume as provided to a company's vice-president for marketing which he will utilize as a partial basis for establishing the firm's advertising budget.
    b) A daily report of the number of defective items produced in a plant as: (1) provided to the superintendent of the production department; and (2) distributed by the quality control manager.
    c) A company policy which states that each employee with over fifteen year's service is entitled to a three-week vacation with pay each year.
    d) A report of monthly shipments developed by a company's transportation manager.
    e) A supervisor's selecting an employee for a position.

---

[16] This is not to imply that the procedure operates the same as the human brain does. We do not know exactly how the brain handles a problem. We do, however, know that the *results* from the heuristic procedures are roughly equivalent to those attained by human problem solving.

FIGURE 3–9

Tentative Rating of Decision Methods and Techniques by Characteristics

Type of Decision Approach	Ability to Handle Complexity	Probable Frequency of Managerial Use	Need for Computational Aid	Degree of Optimization	Decision Validity	Degree of Quantification	Organization Level of Primary Applicability	Stage of Development
Judgment and Experience	2	1	3	3	3	3	All	High
Principles	3	2	5	4	3	4	All	Moderate
Analysis with Models	2	3	2	1	1	1	Middle and Lower	Moderate High
Simulation with Models	1	4	1	2	2	1	Middle	Moderate
Heuristic Programming	2	5	2	3	2	2	Top-Middle	Low
Systems Concept	2	4	3	3	2	3	All	Low

NOTE.: These ratings are based upon an overall estimate of the use of the various approaches in businesses, and there may be certain exceptions. A rating of (1) indicates the greatest degree of the characteristic indicated, a rating of (5), the least.

    f) Employee personnel records on file in the firm's employee relations department.

    g) The calculation of trends in the sales of a firm's product by a clerk in its marketing research department.

4. Indicate whether each of the following models is a symbolic, descriptive, or analogue model: (Give your reasons in each case.)

    a) A flow diagram of the paths that a purchase order and its copies take in being processed in a firm.

    b) A formula describing the impact of pressures, temperatures, and rates of flow upon the output in a chemical process.

    c) An organization chart.

    d) A set of wooden blocks used to represent the layout of equipment in a machine shop.

    e) A scale model of a manufacturing plant on display in the plant manager's office.

5. What problems may arise in utilizing symbolic models to deal with managerial decision problems?

6. Some experts contend that experienced-based decision methods are completely unreliable approaches to decision making. Comment.

7. To what extent do you agree or disagree with the tentative evaluation of decision methods given in Figure 3–9?

8. Discuss the hypothesis: "There is no such thing as a true principle of management."

9. What characteristics of most descriptive models deter their manipulation by computerized methods?

10. The personnel manager of one firm suggested a wage increase to help improve the satisfaction of its workers. The company's production manager replied: "We *know* that a wage increase will hurt our cost picture. While I agree that a wage increase will tend to improve worker satisfaction in the plant, we can't measure such satisfaction or go to the stockholders with such a fuzzy explanation of why we increased costs and reduced profits." Can an optimum choice ignore a variable because its impact can't be measured? Explain. If profitability is the firm's sole objective, would the wage increase necessarily be beneficial, assuming that it did lead to an improvement in worker satisfaction? Explain.

11. For what types of managerial decision problems is heuristic programming most useful?

12. Think of a decision problem with which a college student is typically faced (e.g., getting a certain grade in a course, purchasing a textbook for a course). Break this decision problem down into as many sub- and sub-sub-problems as you can think of. Indicate (1) the informational inputs which would be necessary for the student to make a decision with respect to each sub-problem, and (2) the informational outputs which he would generate in dealing with each sub-problem. Develop a schematic diagram indicating sequentially each step undertaken by the student in resolving his decision problem.

SELECTED REFERENCES

ANSHEN, MELVIN, and BACH, GEORGE L. (eds.). *Management and Corporations 1985, A Symposium.* New York: McGraw-Hill Book Co., Inc., 1960.

BELL, D. A. *Intelligent Machines, An Introduction to Cybernetics.* New York: Blaisdell Publishing Co., 1962.

BORKO, HAROLD (ed.). *Computer Applications in the Behavioral Sciences.* Englewood Cliffs, N. J.: Prentice-Hall, Inc., 1962.

BOULDING, KENNETH E. "General Systems Theory—The Skeleton of Science," *Management Science*, 2 (April, 1956), 197–208.

CHAMBERS, R. J. "The Role of Information Systems in Decision Making," *Management Technology*, 4 (June, 1964), 15–25.

CHAPIN, NED. *An Introduction to Automatic Computers.* Princeton, N. J.: D. Van Nostrand Co., Inc., 1957.

CHURCHMAN, C.; ACKOFF, R. L.; and ARNOFF, E. L. *Introduction to Operations Research.* New York: John Wiley & Sons, Inc., 1957.

GAGNE, ROBERT M., *et al. Psychological Principles in System Development.* New York: Holt, Rinehart & Winston, 1962.

GELERNTER, H. L., and ROCHESTER, N. "Intelligent Behavior in Problem-Solving Machines," *IBM Journal of Research and Development*, 2 (October, 1958), 336–345.

GRAHAM, RICHARD W., JR. "Total Systems Concept," *Management Technology*, 4 (June, 1964), 1–6.

GREENLAW, P.; HERRON, L.; and RAWDON, R. *Business Simulation.* Englewood Cliffs, N. J.: Prentice-Hall, Inc., 1962.

GREGORY, R. H., and VAN HORN, R. L. *Automatic Data-Processing Systems.* San Francisco: Wadsworth Publishing Co., Inc., 1960.

JOHNSON, D. M. *The Psychology of Thought and Judgment.* New York: Harper & Bros., 1955.

JOHNSON, RICHARD A., *et al. The Theory and Management of Systems.* New York: McGraw-Hill Book Co., Inc., 1963.

KLEINMUNTZ, B. "A Portrait of the Computer as a Young Clinician," *Behavioral Science*, 8 (1963), 416–418.

KUEHN, A., and HAMBURGER, M. "A Heuristic Program for Locating Warehouses," *Management Science*, 9 (July, 1963), 643–666.

McDONOUGH, ADRIAN M. *Information Economics and Management Systems.* New York: McGraw-Hill Book Co., Inc., 1963.

McDONOUGH, ADRIAN M., and GARRETT, LEONARD J. *Management Systems.* Homewood, Ill.: Richard D. Irwin, Inc., 1965.

MILLER, D., and STARR, M. *Executive Decisions and Operations Research.* Englewood Cliffs, N. J.: Prentice-Hall, Inc., 1960.

OPTNER, STANFORD. *Systems Analysis for Business and Industrial Problem Solving.* Englewood Cliffs, N. J.: Prentice-Hall, Inc., 1965.

PORTER, ELIAS H.   "The Parable of the Spindle," *Harvard Business Review,* 40 (May–June, 1962), 58–66.

SAMUEL, A. L.   "Some Studies in Machine Learning Using the Game of Checkers," *IBM Journal of Research and Development,* 3 (July, 1959), 210–29.

SCHANCK, RICHARD L.   *The Permanent Revolution in Science.* New York: Philosophical Library, 1954.

SIMON, HERBERT.   *Administrative Behavior.* 2d ed. New York: The Macmillan Co., 1957.

SIMON, HERBERT.   *The New Science of Management Decision.* New York: Harper & Bros., 1960.

SIMON, H. A., and NEWELL, A.   "Information Processing in Computer and Man," *American Scientist,* 52 (September, 1964), 281–300.

TONGE, FRED M.   *A Heuristic Program for Assembly Line Balancing.* Englewood Cliffs, N. J.: Prentice-Hall, Inc., 1961.

CHAPTER 4

MOTIVATION
AND BEHAVIOR

Introduction

IT has been stated often that "management involves getting work done through people." Although this statement does not tell very much about the managerial process, it cannot be denied that human behavior is a key variable with which the manager must deal. In fact, all managerial decisions—from formalized policies and rules which guide the organization as a whole to a manager's interpersonal relationships with his subordinates—have an ultimate impact on the behavior of members of the organization. The installation of new machinery and equipment requires new work procedures to be followed by production employees. The decision to increase levels of production may necessitate overtime work or the hiring of additional employees; production cutbacks may effect layoffs or shorter working hours. The manner in which a supervisor decides to handle disciplinary problems in his department may have a marked effect on both the attitudes and behavior of his employees.

To perceive the ways in which decisions influence the behavior of the members of an organization, managers need to *understand* why people behave the way they do. As Douglas McGregor has pointed out: "Behind every managerial decision or action are assumptions about human nature and human behavior." [1] If the manager's decisions are to be appropriate ones, therefore, it is important that his assumptions about human behavior be valid. From a somewhat different point of view, an understanding of human behavior is essential in that it provides a basis for prediction and control.

---

[1] Douglas McGregor, *The Human Side of Enterprise* (New York: McGraw-Hill Book Co., Inc., 1960), p. 33. Copyright © 1960 by and used by permission of the McGraw-Hill Book Company.

Chris Argyris in emphasizing this need for understanding has likened the manager to the scientist:

> The administrator and the scientist are basically interested in the same question, namely, *why* people behave the way they do in organizations.
> Once they *understand*, it is an easy matter to *predict* and *control* behavior. Predictions and control of behavior are the fruits of understanding. Too often administrators *and* scientists try to take short cuts and go directly to predicting and controlling. For example, the latter create such techniques as intelligence tests to try to predict how to control human beings without knowing what intelligence is. . . . The former develop complex production records and budgets which, within reasonable limits, predict how much the company will produce and at what costs but lack understanding of *why it is so.*[2]

In addition to understanding human behavior, effective managerial decision making also requires *skills* in dealing with people in specific problem situations. A manager needs not only to understand why people are motivated to behave the way they do—he must also be able to make the kinds of decisions which will encourage his employees to direct their efforts toward the goals of the organization. Similarly, a thorough understanding of how people learn and modify their behavior is insufficient if the manager is unable to apply this knowledge when the need arises for him to make decisions relative to the training of one of his workers.

Unfortunately, the development of skills in dealing with other people is usually a slow and difficult process, requiring both breaking well-established habits and considerable practice in trying out new ways of behavior. This is because our attitudes, perceptions, and ways of relating to other people are the product of life-long learning processes—many of our behavioral patterns are deeply ingrained in our personalities. Consequently, the development of skills in "human relations" is not something which can be accomplished simply by reading a textbook such as this or by taking an introductory course in management. For this reason, our primary objective in this chapter is to help the reader develop a better understanding of human behavior, rather than to foster skill development. In doing so, we intend to provide (1) a basis for future skill development, and (2) a framework for our analysis in succeeding chapters of the influence of group membership, leadership, and organizational arrangements on the behavior of members of the business firm.

Attention in this chapter will be focused on several different aspects of human behavior. First, we will treat behavior as being

---

[2] Chris Argyris, *Personality and Organization* (New York: Harper and Brothers, 1957), pp. 5–6.

basically oriented toward the satisfaction of needs, and will examine the more important types of human needs and the implications of the individual's success or failure in their satisfaction. Second, we will consider the influences of personality on motivation and behavior. Third, we will examine the conditions under which learning of new patterns of behavior seems to be most effective. Finally, we will turn our attention to a basic behavioral question of concern to the manager: To what extent can and should the business organization provide the individual with opportunities for satisfying his basic needs?

Before proceeding further, a few brief comments are in order regarding the difficulties involved in the study of human behavior. Although philosophers have speculated on the nature of man at least as far back as Plato, over 2300 years ago,[3] very little systematic scientific investigation of human behavior was undertaken until the present century. Sigmund Freud, for example, the father of psychoanalysis, and to whose work so much of contemporary psychological, sociological, and anthropological thought may be traced, did not publish his first book, *The Interpretation of Dreams*, until 1900.[4] Because the study of human behavior is still in its infancy, many psychological hypotheses have not been fully tested as yet, and one has to be cautious in ascribing too great a degree of validity to them. The problem of developing valid descriptions and predictions of behavior is further complicated by the extraordinary complexity of the human organism. The determinants of behavior are many; their interrelationships are extremely complex; and they are difficult to define and measure. For these reasons, few if any behavioral models yet exist which are quantifiable to the extent that are those models dealing with the economic variables with which we will deal later in this text.

Notwithstanding these problems in definition and measurement, research in the field of human behavior has grown enormously in the past few decades. A number of concepts and propositions have been developed upon which there is fairly wide agreement, and many of these can be useful in providing the manager with a basic frame-

---

[3] See, for example, Plato's *Republic*.

[4] This book "which is now considered to be one of the great works of modern times, is more than a book about dreams. It is a book about the dynamics of the human mind." Calvin S. Hall, *A Primer of Freudian Psychology* (New York: The New American Library of American Literature, Inc., 1955), p. 15. Copyright 1954 by The World Publishing Company. Reprinted by arrangement with The World Publishing Company, Cleveland and New York.

work for the analysis of the human problems of his organization. The next section will be devoted to a discussion of one class of these concepts—those which seek to explain why people are motivated to behave the way they do.

Need Satisfaction, Motivation, and Behavior

Why do people behave the way they do? Why does one manager closely watch the office clock prior to the close of each working day and leave the job promptly at quitting time, while his colleague at the next desk puts in two or three additional hours of work every evening after everyone else has gone home? Why does one person strongly prefer working alone with figures and cost data while another cannot tolerate "being chained to a desk all day" and enjoys only work which calls for him to make a large number of daily contacts with other people? Why are some individuals "yes men" and afraid to express any disagreement with their bosses, while others are not at all reluctant to criticize their superiors?

There is general agreement among psychologists that—with a few exceptions which will be noted below—all behavior is *motivated;* people have reasons for doing the things that they do, and that behavior is oriented toward meeting certain goals and objectives. Such goal-directed behavior centers around the desire for *need satisfaction.* All individuals have certain needs for which they are continuously seeking satisfaction. Among the human needs which have been distinguished by psychologists are: hunger, thirst, sex, companionship and belonging, love, recognition, security and safety, knowledge, and self-realization. One way of viewing the relationship between needs and behavior is that the existence of unsatisfied needs produces tension in the individual and that the motivation underlying behavior is to reduce these tensions. Although need satisfaction is generally accepted as constituting the prime determinant of behavior, disagreement exists among psychologists as to the number of human needs which exist and the relative importance of each. Before presenting a framework for viewing human needs which we believe is most useful to the manager, a few comments are in order about these differences of opinion.

Human Needs: Some Differing Views

Most classical economists and early contributors to the scientific management movement placed primary emphasis on the individual's *rational* pursuit of *economic* objectives. These views hold that since man consciously and rationally strives to maximize his economic gain or utility, a prime means of motivating individuals is by providing them with monetary incentives. Although money is undoubtedly an important motivator for most people, practically all psychologists emphasize that individuals seek to satisfy needs other than purely economic ones. Further, as Freud was the first to publicize widely as a central tenet of psychological thought, our behavior is often not rational and, in fact, is sometimes even self-destructive—many times our actions are conditioned by unconscious motives of which we are not aware.[5]

Although psychologists generally agree that man is motivated by the desire to satisfy a number of needs, some of which he is not consciously aware of, differences of opinion exist as to the nature and relative importance of these needs. Some psychologists have attempted to reduce all human needs to a few underlying types. Freud, for example, emphasized two basic classes of needs—the life instinct and the death instinct;[6] Adler focused primary attention on the drive for power or mastery; and Horney considered as a primary motive "the need for security and safety in a potentially dangerous world."[7] Other thinkers, however, have taken a more pluralistic position, emphasizing that there are many different types of needs, the satisfaction of which is a prime determinant of behavior. This latter approach appears to us to be a more useful one for the manager in understanding and analyzing human behavior in organizations. We will now turn our attention to one such pluralistic framework—that presented by the psychologist, A. H. Maslow, in his work, *Motivation and Personality*.[8]

The Hierarchy of Needs

Maslow's theory of motivation stresses that individuals are motivated to satisfy several different kinds of needs, some of which are more *prepotent* than others. Prepotency as it is used here means taking precedence over, and Maslow's theory states that if a number of a person's needs are unsatisfied at any given time, satisfaction of the most prepotent ones will be more pressing than that of the

---

[5] Not widely known is the fact that the concept of the unconscious mind was developed and explored long before Freud. See Lancelot Law White, *The Unconscious Before Freud* (New York: Basic Books, 1960).

[6] See Hall, *op. cit.*, pp. 57 ff.

[7] See David C. McClelland, *Personality* (New York: The Dryden Press, 1951), pp. 402–403.

[8] A. H. Maslow, *Motivation and Personality* (New York: Harper and Brothers, 1954), Chap. 5.

others. Maslow postulates the following five classes of needs in order of their prepotence: (1) physiological; (2) safety; (3) belongingness and love; (4) esteem; and (5) self-actualization.[9]

This conceptual framework, referred to as the *hierarchy of needs* because of the different levels of prepotency indicated, is diagrammatically illustrated in Figure 4–1.

FIGURE 4–1. Hierarchy of Needs

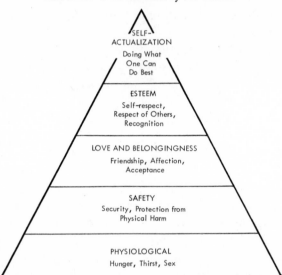

The prime prepotence of man's physiological needs is explained by Maslow as follows:

> Undoubtedly these physiological needs are the most prepotent of all needs. What this means specifically is that in the human being who is missing everything in life in an extreme fashion, it is most likely that the major motivation would be the physiological needs rather than any others. A person who is lacking food, safety, love, and esteem would probably hunger for food more strongly than for anything else.[10]

Once the individual's physiological needs are largely satisfied, the next level of needs in the hierarchy begins to emerge. These are the safety needs, among which are the avoidance of physical harm, illness, economic disaster, etc. In a similar manner, satisfaction of the safety needs gives rise to the emergence of belongingness and love needs, and so on, until the satisfaction of all other needs leads

---

[9] Maslow also considers cognitive and aesthetic needs as important, although he does not formally fit them into the hierarchy framework. *Ibid.*, pp. 93–98.

[10] *Ibid.*, p. 82.

the individual to be primarily concerned with the highest level needs, those for self-actualization. Self-actualization is described by Maslow in the following terms:

> Even if all these needs . . . [the lower level needs] . . . are satisfied, we may still often (if not always) expect that a new discontent and restlessness will soon develop, unless the individual is doing what he is fitted for. A musician must make music, an artist must paint, a poet must write, if he is to be ultimately at peace with himself. What a man *can* be, he *must* be. This need we may call self-actualization.[11]

Several observations are necessary to clarify the needs hierarchy concept. First, the framework which Maslow presents is *not* intended to be a static, rigid portrayal of the individual, in which each class of needs is unchanging and unrelated to the others. Rather, Maslow views human behavior in *dynamic* and *holistic* terms—i.e., the individual's personality may be conceived of as a dynamic system in which any given aspect of behavior can be understood only in light of his *whole* personality structure.

Second, the reader should not infer that only one class of needs exists for a person at any given time, and that once satisfied, it completely disappears giving way to the next higher level of needs. Rather, all levels of needs probably exist to some degree for the individual most of the time. Rarely, if ever, is any one need completely satisfied, at least for very long. Our hunger, for example, may be fairly well satisfied after eating breakfast, only to emerge again before lunch time (or perhaps to a lesser extent even sooner at the mid-morning coffee break). It is important to recognize, however, that certain types of needs are generally of much greater importance to certain individuals than others. In our "affluent society," for example, the hunger and safety needs are generally fairly well satisfied and are not of overriding concern as in some of the impoverished nations in which getting enough to eat represents the primary focus of behavior for many. Or, in our own business world, some individuals are strongly motivated by a need for recognition, while others are more interested in job security. We will discuss some of the reasons for such differences more fully later in this chapter when we treat the subject of personality.

Third, it should be noted that there are certain exceptions to the relative degree of prepotency indicated by Maslow for each of the various levels of needs. That is, the physiological needs, although

---

[11] *Ibid.*, p. 91.

generally more prepotent than the safety needs, and so on up the hierarchy, are not always so. Among such exceptions is the behavior of those individuals who are martyrs, and are willing to sacrifice all other needs for the sake of an ideal or a religious, political or social value.[12] The fasting of India's political and religious leader, Mahatma Gandhi, provides a good example of this type of behavior.

It is also important to recognize that much behavior simultaneously satisfies several different needs, rather than just one. Participation in the mid-morning coffee break, for example, may simultaneously satisfy a person's hunger needs, his need to belong and be accepted by the group in which he works, or even as a possible means of letting the boss know about some important work in which he is engaged.

Finally, we should reemphasize a central tenet of Maslow's theory of motivation—if a need is largely satisfied at any given point in time, it ceases to serve as an important motivator until reemerging again. This characteristic of needs is of considerable importance to managerial decision making. As we will indicate in greater detail later, organizations may be in a position to provide opportunities for the satisfaction of all five basic classes of employee needs, although the satisfaction of some is often difficult in work situations. If management places emphasis on meeting needs which are not largely satisfied, rather than those already highly satisfied, its employees are likely to be more highly motivated to direct their efforts toward the goals of the organization. Let us consider an engineer, for example, who is earning $12,000 a year, who is fairly secure in his position, owns his own home, and lacks few of the physical comforts of life, but who has a strong need for self-actualization which is not being met because much of his current work is semi-routine in nature. An opportunity to engage in more creative and challenging engineering projects would probably serve more to increase this individual's level of motivation than would a salary increase of $500 a year. On the other hand, a $5000-a-year purchasing clerk whose wife is expecting their fifth child might welcome such a raise much more than the opportunity for more creative work. In short, when management is interested in providing optimum motivational conditions for its employees, it is important that its decisions be based on the recognition that human behavior is primarily directed toward the fulfillment of *unsatisfied* needs.

---

[12] For other exceptions see, *Ibid.*, pp. 98–99.

Lack of Need Satisfaction: Frustration

As we indicated previously, unsatisfied needs produce tensions in the individual, and behavior is motivated to relieve these tensions. When an individual is unable to satisfy his needs, and thus reduce tension, we say that he experiences *frustration*. The student who studies conscientiously every week only to flunk out of college at the end of his freshman year provides an example of a person who would be quite frustrated. His goal, that of receiving a college degree, the attainment of which would have represented the satisfaction of many needs—status, prestige, greater earning power, pleasing his parents, etc.—has been blocked. Although most of us hopefully do not experience such serious frustrations most of the time, all of us are continuously frustrated to one degree or another, for our needs are never completely satisfied.

People react to frustration in different ways, just as the importance of different needs varies from person to person. Sometimes individuals react to frustration in a positive manner—that is, they search for realistic and constructive approaches to meet their unsatisfied needs. In other cases, however, when frustrated, people attempt to protect themselves from a threatening situation by evoking *defense mechanisms*. We will now examine each of these two kinds of reactions to frustration.

Constructive Behavior

Relatively little needs to be said about constructive problem-solving approaches since we are all familiar with this form of behavior. An employee frustrated because promotional opportunities in his company are not open to him because his education is limited may work for a college degree by taking evening courses at a local college. An individual who fails to achieve the recognition for his work which he desires may increase his effort on the job. In order to satisfy unmet belonging needs and gain acceptance from his fellow workers, an employee may conform to the values and standards of the work group of which he is a member. These are but a few of the wide variety of constructive strategies which individuals may employ to satisfy needs and lessen frustration.

Defensive Behavior

When need satisfaction is blocked and frustration is experienced, a person may react by evoking one or more defense mechanisms instead of adopting constructive, realistic approaches to solving his problems. We will discuss this phenomena in somewhat greater detail than we did constructive behavior, not because it is more important or more common, but rather because it is not as generally well understood.

The concept of the defense mechanism appeared early in the writings of Freud.[13] The following summary of Freud's conception of the defense mechanism will serve to clarify its nature:

> One of the major tasks imposed upon the ego is that of dealing with the threats and dangers that beset the person and arouse anxiety. The ego may try to master danger by adopting realistic problem-solving methods, or it may attempt to alleviate anxiety by using methods that deny, falsify, or distort reality and that impede the development of personality. The latter methods are called *defense mechanisms* of the ego.[14]

All of us employ defense mechanisms to one degree or another. As Freud has hypothesized, they serve an important protective function in the development of the individual, since in infancy we are not strong enough to face up to all of the demands that reality imposes upon us by rational means.[15] As the psychologically healthy individual matures, however, he becomes more and more able to cope realistically with the demands imposed on him, and his need for irrational defenses decreases. Those adults whose behavior continues to be dominated by defense mechanisms find it difficult to adapt to their work, responsibilities, and other people.

There are several different types of defense mechanisms which have been identified by psychologists. Among the more common of these are the following:

Rationalization. Rationalization refers to excusing one's behavior by presenting a reason for it which the individual sees as less ego destructive or more socially acceptable than the real reason. An employee's lack of proficiency on the job may be perceived as "poor working conditions," "low quality materials," or "worn tools" rather than his own ineptitude which would be ego-deflating for him to ad-

---

[13] For a discussion of the development of the defense mechanism concept, see Ruth L. Munroe, *Schools of Psychoanalytic Thought* (New York: The Dryden Press, 1955), pp. 90–93.

[14] Hall, *op. cit.*, p. 85. We should also note that the defense mechanisms must be evoked unconsciously if they are to be effective in reducing an individual's anxiety.

[15] Or, as Hall summarized Freud's thinking: "Why then do defenses exist if they are so harmful in so many ways? The reason for their existence is a developmental one. The infantile ego is too weak to integrate and synthesize all of the demands that are made upon it. Ego defenses are adopted as protective measures. If the ego cannot reduce anxiety by rational means, it has to utilize . . . [the defense mechanisms]." *Ibid.*, p. 96. At the expense of considerable over-simplification the term "ego" here may be considered synonymous with the "self."

mit to others. Lucy's elaborate explanation of her failure as a batter in the Peanuts cartoon shown in Figure 4–2 provides a humorous illustration of rationalization.

FIGURE 4–2. Rationalization

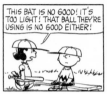

Projection. Projection involves attributing one's own feelings or the reasons for one's own behavior to someone else. An employee may intensely dislike a colleague and attempt to make him look bad in the eyes of others whenever possible. At the same time, however, he may feel very guilty about this hostility, and attempt to justify it in terms of "my colleague is always out to get me." Projection of this type serves the purpose of changing an internal danger (one's own hostile impulse) which is difficult to cope with to an external danger (his dislike for me) which is much easier to handle.[16] Or, to put it another way, it is less ego deflating to view someone else as trying to make life difficult for us than to think of ourselves as hostile individuals.

Reaction Formation. Reaction formation is a defense mechanism aimed at avoiding an unpleasant situation. "Here the person is so anxious to prevent the occurrence of the painful situation that he does the direct opposite of the thing he wishes to avoid."[17] In our previous illustration, for example, the employee may have felt so guilty about his hostility toward his colleague that instead of trying to make the colleague look bad, he expressed nothing but praise and admiration for him.[18] The purpose of such reactive behavior would have been to *conceal* the real feelings of hostility about which so much guilt existed.

---

[16] Hall, *op. cit.*, pp. 89–90.
[17] McClelland, *op. cit.*, p. 508.
[18] Expressed admiration such as this which is a product of reaction formation may be distinguished from real admiration in that it is exaggerated behavior. "Reactive love protests too much; it is overdone, extravagant, showy, and affected. It is counterfeit, and its falseness, like the overacting of the player-queen in Hamlet, is usually easily detected." Hall, *op. cit.*, p. 92.

Repression. Individuals sometimes *repress* unpleasant experiences or feelings from the conscious to the unconscious mind as a means of denying their existence. An occasion on which we were severely criticized by our parents (or boss), feelings of jealousy of which we are guilty, or fears experienced at one time or another may be "forgotten" because they are too painful to remember. Or, we sometimes find ourselves forgetting to take care of unpleasant tasks —they simply "slip our mind."

Regression. When frustrated, people sometimes revert back to earlier, more childish forms of behavior as a means of escaping from the unpleasantness of reality. This phenomenon is referred to as regression. One of the more common forms of regression of concern to the manager is horseplay on the job. Although a certain amount of regressive behavior may help to relieve tensions in stressful work situations, immoderate horseplay may not only interfere with productivity but also lead to accidents and injuries.

Aggression. A common reaction to frustration is aggression. In fact, some authorities believe that "the existence of frustration always leads to some form of aggression." [19] Essentially, aggression involves an attack (physical or non-physical) with the intent of injuring the object of the attack. Sometimes aggression may be directed toward the person whom we perceive as the source of our frustration, e.g., a boss who is a perfectionist may engage in a bitter diatribe against a subordinate who has made a minor clerical error. In other cases, an individual's aggression may be *displaced* (or projected), i.e., directed toward a person or object other than the source of the frustration. The manager who comes to work after a heated argument with his wife at the breakfast table and finds fault with everything his subordinates do provides an example of displaced aggression. In addition, aggression is sometimes directed against oneself. In its milder form, the self-aggression may be simply denying ourself some pleasure because we have done something "wrong"; at its extreme, the self-punishment may manifest itself in suicide.

Avoidance (Withdrawal). Sometimes people defend themselves against a painful reality by avoiding or withdrawing from those situations which are laden with frustration for them. Avoidance manifested in excessive absenteeism or tardiness, or a high turnover rate is not uncommon among workers holding jobs which provide little need satisfaction.

As may be noted from our above discussion, many forms of de-

---

[19] John Dollard, *et al., Frustration and Aggression* (paperbound ed.; New Haven: Yale University Press, 1961), p. 1.

fensive behavior such as aggressive acts or horseplay (regression) are basically nonproductive in orientation, and their occurrence on the job may interfere with the attainment of organizational objectives. Since all people rely on defense mechanisms to at least some extent, such behavior can never be completely eliminated in business organizations. However, its occurrence may sometimes be prevented by managerial decisions which provide conditions under which employees will be able to satisfy many of their needs (and, thus, not experience considerable frustration) in the performance of their work. We will explore a number of decision approaches with this objective in mind in later sections of this book. Further, the manager may be able to deal with employees who do exhibit defensive behavior in such a way as to help overcome the frustrations of which the behavior is symptomatic. In many cases, counseling with an employee may enable the manager to pinpoint the source of the frustration, and provide insight as to possible actions which may be taken to help overcome the problem. For example, the manager's counseling with a subordinate who has become apathetic toward his job since being passed over for a promotion recently may lead to a training and development program for the man which will place him in a much stronger position to be considered for the next promotional opening.

Unmotivated Behavior

Although most behavior can be thought of as being motivated by the existence of unsatisfied needs, there are certain exceptions. Maslow, for example, has distinguished goal-oriented behavior from expressive or stylistic (style of life) behavior which is "simply a reflection of the personality." [20] In the latter category is included such behavior as the random movements of a child, the way in which a person walks, the pitch of an individual's voice, or one's preference for one type of music over another. Some expressive behavior, however, may be partially conditioned by a person's need structure. An executive may choose to play golf rather than tennis, for instance, to gain the acceptance of his boss who regularly shoots in the low 80s.

Behavior is also sometimes motivated by needs which *no longer exist*. This phenomenon has been referred to as *functional autonomy*.[21] To satisfy our needs at one time in our lives, we engage in

---

[20] Maslow, *op. cit.*, p. 103.
[21] This term was coined by Gordon W. Allport. See his *Personality* (New York: Henry Holt and Co., 1937), pp. 191 ff. for a fuller discussion of the concept.

certain types of behavior; we then continue these patterns of behavior even though they no longer serve to satisfy a currently existing need. The behavior which was once a *means* to an end now becomes an end in itself, largely through habit. Many examples of functional autonomy exist which may be of concern to the manager. An individual who was given high praise as a child by his parents for performing to perfection may, as an adult worker, be compelled to perfectionism even though his output and earnings suffer accordingly. A person who was mistreated by his father as a youngster may show hostility toward his present boss even though the latter does not mistreat him and such behavior is decidedly detrimental to his best interests. In fact, as we shall indicate later, our adult personalities are conditioned considerably by our experiences early in life.

Needs, Motivation, and Behavior: Summary

We have indicated that most human behavior is motivated by the desire to satisfy needs. Among the exceptions are certain forms of expressive and functionally autonomous behavior. We have suggested Maslow's framework of the hierarchy of needs as a useful approach for understanding behavior. When needs are not satisfied, the individual experiences frustration. Frustration may be dealt with either by constructive behavior aimed at satisfying one's unmet needs, or by the evocation of defense mechanisms. A schematic portrayal of our motivational model is presented in Figure 4–3. We

FIGURE 4–3. Motivational Model

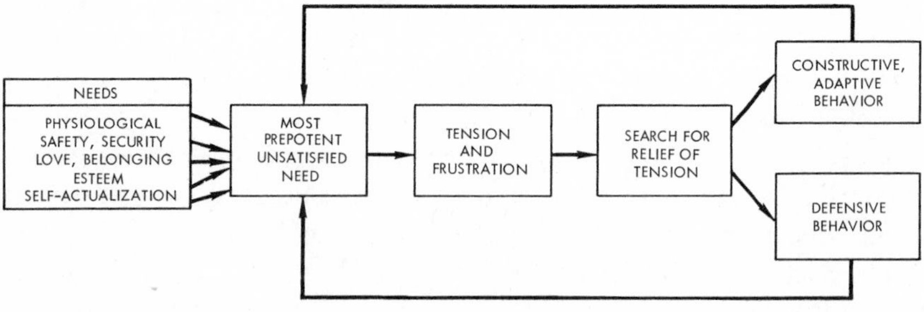

reemphasize that this model is not intended to be a static, rigid one, in which the individual's various needs and behavior are neatly segregated or pigeon-holed. Rather, it is meant to represent a dynamic process of interrelationships among all aspects of the individual's behavioral system.

Personality and Behavior

We have presented a conceptual framework for understanding the needs and motivation of people in general, and have only made passing references to individual differences in motivation and behavior. Although all of us may be motivated to satisfy the same general kinds of needs, our particular motivational and behavioral patterns are different from those of anyone else, for we each possess a unique personality. In this section, we will put forth some observations about personality differences, with the view in mind of relating them to the motivational model presented earlier.

Personality and Personality Characteristics

The term "personality" is one which has been defined in many different ways. Most definitions, however, signify personality as representing the totality of a person's characteristics, and emphasize that each of an individual's characteristics are interrelated with all of the others. That is, personality represents an *organization* of forces within the individual—it may be viewed as a dynamic system.

Many different generalized personality characteristics have been defined and described by psychologists, such as mental ability, physical ability, feelings, attitudes, beliefs, interests, and emotional makeup. In turn, each of these has been broken down into a number of more specific characteristics. In the area of mental ability or intelligence, for example, measurements have been made of such abilities as verbal reasoning, mathematical reasoning, symbolic reasoning, and creative problem solving. As one might expect—considering the complexity of the human being and the difficulties involved in measuring such characteristics—considerable disagreement exists among psychologists in the analysis of personality. To delve into any of the many difficult problems of personality definition or measurement is beyond the scope of this text. Rather, we will focus our attention on three aspects of personality which have special relevance to the manager's understanding of behavior and motivation: (1) personality differences and motivation, (2) the determinants of personality, and (3) the development of personality.

Personality Differences and Motivation

Our motivational model indicated that most behavior is directed toward need satisfaction, that when need gratification is blocked the individual experiences frustration, and that he may react to frustration either by adopting constructive problem-solving approaches or by the evocation of defense mechanisms. From the frame of reference of this model, personality differences may manifest themselves in several different ways:

1. The relative strength and importance of different needs varies considerably from individual to individual depending upon one's personality structure. Some people have a very strong need for security, which may reflect itself in an intense desire for a job which offers steady employment above all else. On the other hand, those individuals whose need for security is fairly well satisfied, but for whom esteem is highly important, may be primarily interested in work for which they can gain considerable recognition.

2. Different individuals have different levels of aspiration depending upon the strength of their needs. One manager may never be very satisfied until he achieves the presidency of his firm, while another may aspire only to a middle management position. As the following Peanuts cartoon indicates, not everybody wants to be "somebody important."

FIGURE 4–4. On Being Important

3. The strategies which an individual develops and employs for attempting to gain the satisfaction of a particular need is also a function of his personality. One person may strive to meet his esteem needs by gaining recognition on the job, while another may seek to meet the same needs by taking an active role in some community activity, such as the Boy Scouts. Or, in the choice of one's occupation, the boy who finds that he has an exceptional ability as an athlete may decide that he can gain the most recognition and earn the most money by becoming a professional baseball player, while the student highly proficient in mathematics may decide that he can meet these same needs best by entering the field of operations research.

4. Similarly, the manner in which a person reacts to and handles frustration is also a function of his personality. Individuals differ as

to: (1) the kinds of situations in which they experience frustration, (2) the degree to which they evoke defense mechanisms when confronted with frustration, and (3) the kinds of defense mechanisms resorted to under different conditions. Some persons seems to have a relatively high *frustration tolerance,* while others do not. Some managers, for example, are able to function effectively without becoming emotionally upset in jobs in which considerable pressure exists, while others become easily upset and find emotional control difficult in such situations.

In summary, within the context of the needs hierarchy-motivation framework, motivational and behavioral patterns vary considerably from individual to individual in several ways, depending upon differences in personality structure. These relationships are illustrated diagrammatically in Figure 4–5. We will now turn our attention to a brief examination of the basic reasons for such personality differences among individuals.

Determinants of Personality

The development of the human personality is influenced by the mutual interaction of two basic kinds of factors—*constitutional and environmental.* By constitutional factors we mean those inborn characteristics with which the individual is endowed through the processes of heredity. There are many different ways in which con-

FIGURE 4–5. Personality and Motivation

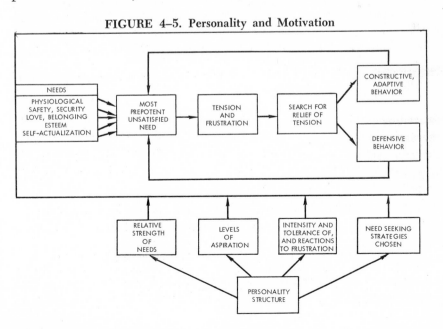

stitutional factors may condition a person's behavior, attitudes and ways of viewing life. As Kluckhohn and Murray have pointed out:

There are substantial reasons for believing that different genetic structures carry with them varying potentialities for learning, for reaction time, for energy level, for frustration tolerance. Different people appear to have different biological rhythms: of growth, of activity, of depression and exaltation. The various biologically inherited malfunctions certainly have implications for personality development, though there are wide variations among those who share the same physical handicap (deafness, for example).

Sex and age must be regarded as among the more striking constitutional determinants of personality. Personality is also shaped through such traits of physique as stature, pigmentation, strength, conformity of features to the culturally fashionable type, etc. Such characteristics influence a man's needs and expectations. The kind of world he finds about him is to a considerable extent determined by the way other people react to his appearance and physical capacities.[22]

The personality of the individual is also shaped by a number of environmental factors. One of the most important of these is the culture in which we live. The customs, traditions, standards, and values of our society, which are transmitted (and modified) from generation to generation, condition our behavior to a considerable extent.

The life history of the individual is first and foremost an accommodation to the patterns and standards traditionally handed down in his community. From the moment of his birth the customs into which he is born shape his experience and behavior. By the time he can talk, he is the little creature of his culture, and by the time he is grown and able to take part in its activities, its habits are his habits, its beliefs his beliefs, its impossibilities his impossibilities. Every child that is born into his group will share them with him, and no child born into one on the opposite side of the globe can ever achieve the thousandth part.[23]

As anthropologists have discovered, behavior considered appropriate in one society may be highly frowned on in another. To note the extreme differences which may exist between different patterns of culture, compare, for example, the culture of the Dobuans of New Guinea with that of our own.

The motivations that run through all Dobuan existence are singularly limited. . . . All existence is cut-throat competition, and every advantage is

---

[22] Clyde Kluckhohn and Henry A. Murray, "Personality Formation: The Determinants," in Clyde Kluckhohn and Henry A. Murray, *Personality in Nature, Society, and Culture* (2nd ed., rev.; New York: Alfred A. Knopf, 1956), p. 57.

[23] Ruth Benedict, *Patterns of Culture*, (New York: New American Library of World Literature, 1934), p. 2.

gained at the expense of a defeated rival. . . . The good man, the successful man, is he who has cheated another out of his place. . . .

Life in Dobu fosters extreme forms of animosity and malignancy which most societies have minimized by their institutions. Dobuan institutions, on the other hand, exalt them to the highest degree. . . . according to his [the Dobuan's] view of life virtue consists in selecting a victim upon whom he can vent the malignancy he attributes alike to human society and to the powers of nature.[24]

Although one will not find such extreme differences as those between the Dobuan culture and our own among today's highly industrialized societies, even here significant variations exist in cultural attitudes, beliefs and standards. As one would expect, many of these differences reflect themselves in the behavior of individuals in their roles as members of business organizations. In the Japanese business firm, for example, attitudes and policies toward such factors as pay, promotions, and responsibility for decision making are quite different from our own.

Japanese workers are hired for life. They are practically never fired. Promotions go largely by seniority even at managerial levels. The incompetent executive moves up with advancing years to positions with titles appropriate to his age—even when this means devising types of duties that will keep him from interfering with the progress of the firm. The pay of workers bears no relation to their productivity. The pay envelope is the sum of a complex set of factors, in which length of service and number of dependents figure prominently. All management decisions are made on a group basis—at least normally. If an individual were credited with a certain decision that turned out to be unwise, then the individual would lose face. To spare management people from such humiliation, to all appearances the group as a whole shares responsibility in all decisions.[25]

Within a particular culture many different kinds of personality patterns may be found. One reason for such variations is that the constitutional characteristics of individuals vary, as indicated above. In addition, different persons within any given culture are exposed to the values, beliefs and standards of their culture in different ways. Culture is transmitted to the individual by educational and religious institutions, by various groups with which he comes into contact during his life, and most important of all by the family. There is almost universal agreement among psychologists that a most critical factor in the development of personality is the child's relationships with his parents. The child's earliest and closest associations are with his family; he is rewarded or punished depending upon whether his

---

[24] *Ibid.*, pp. 130–31, 151.
[25] William F. Whyte, *Men at Work* (Homewood, Ill.: Dorsey Press, Inc., and Richard D. Irwin, Inc., 1961), p. 66.

behavior is approved or disapproved by his parents; and he learns their values, beliefs, and ways of behaving. The reader who is a parent has undoubtedly observed on many occasions how quick junior is to copy the behavior of father and mother (unfortunately, sometimes in public to the latter's considerable embarrassment). Whether the parents show love or hostility toward the child, whether they are overprotective and rarely let the child make any decisions of his own, or whether they are supportive of him and encourage his development—such relationships are likely to have a lasting influence on his behavior and ways of viewing life.

Finally, personality is molded by the experiences which befall the individual during his life, many of which may be quite accidental. Traumatic war experiences may lead to serious emotional disturbances; or a chance meeting of a high school student with his Congressman may serve to inspire this student to pursue a career in politics. Similar experiences, of course, may be reacted to quite differently by different individuals, for their impact is a function of the personality structure as it has been molded previously by constitutional, family, and cultural influences.

This brings us to an important point. In viewing *any* of the determinants of personality, it is extremely important to recognize their interdependence and not consider them as isolated influencing factors. For example, if a child with a high degree of mental capacity is encouraged by his parents and teachers to develop this ability, and is given the opportunity for a college education, he may become a highly successful professional man. If, on the other hand, his brightness is ridiculed by his parents, and his cleverness supported by his peers only when it is directed toward antisocial ends, he may engage in juvenile delinquency and ultimately become one of a prison's most "intelligent" inmates. Thus, no single determinant may be viewed as being *the cause* of one's personality; rather the development of the individual's personality system must be considered as having been conditioned by a number of interdependent factors in mutual interaction with one other.

To summarize the ideas presented in this section and to relate them to our previous observations about motivation and behavior:

1. Most human behavior is motivated by the desire to satisfy needs, some of which are more prepotent than others. When needs are not satisfied, the individual experiences frustration, which may be dealt with either by constructive adaptive behavior, or by the evocation of defensive behavior.

2.   The relative strength of a person's different needs, his levels of aspiration, the strategies which he employs to meet his needs, and his reactions to frustration are a function of his personality system.

3.   The individual's personality system is molded by a number of factors in mutual *interaction*—both constitutional and environmental. Culture is an extremely important environmental influence, which is transmitted primarily by the family, and to a lesser extent by other social institutions and groups. Personality is also molded by the experiences which befall a person during his life, many of which may be chance happenings. The relationship of these personality determinants to the motivational model we presented earlier is illustrated diagrammatically in Figure 4–6.

FIGURE 4–6. Personality and Motivation

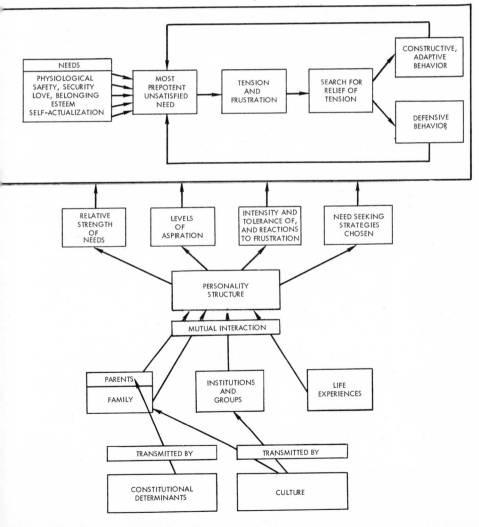

Personality Development

In the previous section we indicated that personality development and structure may take quite different forms in various cultures. We will now present some observations about certain aspects of personality development in our own culture which have special implications for management.

Although each individual is unique, the personality development of most psychologically healthy people in our culture seems to proceed in certain similar directions. As Argyris has pointed out, individuals:

1.   Tend to develop from a state of passivity as infants to a state of increasing activity as adults. . . .

2.   Tend to develop from a state of dependence upon others as infants to a state of relative independence as adults. . . .

3.   Tend to develop from being capable of behaving only in a few ways as an infant to being capable of behaving in many different ways as an adult. . . .

4.   Tend to develop from having erratic, casual, shallow, quickly-dropped interests as an infant to having deeper interests as an adult. . . .

5.   Tend to develop from having a short time perspective (i.e., the present largely determines behavior) as an infant to a much longer time perspective as an adult. . . .

6.   Tend to develop from being in a subordinate position in the family and society as an infant to aspiring to occupy an equal and/or superordinate position relative to their peers.

7.   Tend to develop from a lack of awareness of self as an infant to an awareness of and control over self as an adult.[26]

As we shall note in a later section, many observers such as Argyris believe that the demands of formal business organizations placed upon the individual are often incongruent with the adult modes of behavior described here.

Two other observations should be noted concerning the development of personality. First, there are considerable differences in the extent to which various individuals develop along the lines suggested above. The reader has undoubtedly met adults who are highly dependent upon others, whose interests are shallow and quickly dropped, or who show little awareness of their own behavior. With their development having somehow been stunted, such individuals may find it difficult to assume job responsibilities and may present problems to the manager. Second, regardless of the degree to which an individual has developed, his basic personality pattern tends to remain relatively constant once he reaches

---

[26] Argyris, *op. cit.*, p. 50.

adulthood, and is extremely difficult although not impossible to change. For example, the degree to which an individual feels secure in life usually does not vary greatly even in the face of considerable environmental change.

> No matter what the level of security may be, it is difficult either to raise or to lower it. . . . we find some tendency to hang on to the life style in the healthy as well as in the unhealthy person. The person who tends to believe that all people are essentially good will show the same resistance to change of this belief as will the person who believes all people are essentially bad. . . .
>
> Personality syndromes can sometimes maintain a relative constancy under the most surprising conditions of external change. There are many examples of the maintenance of security feelings in emigres who have undergone the most grueling and harrowing experiences. Studies of morale in bombed areas also give us proof of the surprising resistance that most healthy people have to external horrors.[27]

The reason for such constancy is that our ways of perceiving, thinking, and behaving have been repeated so many times by the time we are adults they become deeply ingrained habits.

The difficulty of changing many of the adult's basic ways of behaving has important implications for management. In personnel selection, managers should be wary of hiring an individual lacking the personality characteristics desired for a job in the pious hope that "he's basically a nice guy and perhaps somehow he'll change once he's employed with us"—for such changes are usually not forthcoming. Those responsible for management training and development programs have also found that behavioral and attitudinal change is often very difficult to induce. Although much money is being spent for such efforts every year by industry, research has shown that managers exposed to many such programs often show little positive change in their behavior after the training; and in some cases, negative change occurs.[28] These observations do not mean that people never change, for all of us are learning new ways of doing things all the time. Rather, we are indicating that our *basic* patterns of behavior and *fundamental* attitudes remain relatively constant and are difficult to alter.

---

[27] Maslow, *op. cit.*, p. 39.

[28] There are probably a number of reasons for such negative training results. In some cases, the training itself may be ill conceived. Or, when managers return to their jobs and attempt to try out new ideas and ways of behavior learned in a development program, these efforts are rejected by other members of the organizational system who have not been exposed to the training. For a discussion of this problem in systems terms, see: Paul S. Greenlaw, "Management Development: A Systems View," *Personnel Journal*, 43 (April, 1964) 209.

Learning and Behavior

In the preceding sections, we have made numerous references to learning. We have indicated that although certain capabilities and predispositions are inborn, much of our behavior is learned. We have also pointed out that although many of our basic personality patterns have been learned so thoroughly by the time we reach adulthood that their modification is difficult, we all continue to learn new ways of behaving throughout life.

An important task of management is to provide the conditions under which members of the organization will be able to learn the most effective and appropriate ways of behaving in order to meet the firm's objectives. The new employee in the organization must become familiar with company rules, regulations, and policies and must master the skills called for on his job. In our current era of rapid change, members of the organization are continually being compelled to respond to new technological developments, work processes, and competitive conditions. Crucial to the manager as he prepares himself for and assumes positions calling for greater responsibility in the organization are the development of greater knowledge and the learning of new skills and ways of behaving. In this section, we will examine some of the important conditions for effective learning.

There is considerable disagreement among learning theorists as to the conditions under which individuals learn most effectively. However, there are a number of generally accepted statements about learning [29] that can be of value to the manager not only in the design of formalized training programs but also in his day-to-day assignment and development of subordinates.

Capacity of the Learner. "In deciding who should learn what, the capacities of the learner are very important. Brighter people can learn things less bright ones cannot learn. . . ." [30] Recognition

---

[29] To cite the opinion of one leading authority as to the degree of agreement existing on principles of effective learning (Ernest R. Hilgard, *Theories of Learning* [2nd ed.; New York: Appleton-Century-Crofts, Inc., 1956]): "While the state of knowledge is not therefore as bad as the parade of points of view make it out to be, it is still rather unsatisfactory. There are no laws of learning which can be taught with confidence." (p. 457). "It turns out, however, that many of the quarrels of the theorists are internal ones, not very important in relation to immediate practical problems; there are, in fact, a great many practically important experimental relationships upon which the theorists are in substantial agreement. That is, they accept the facts as demonstrated, even though they disagree about the interpretations of these facts." (p. 485). Copyright, © 1948, 1956 by Appleton-Century-Crofts, Inc. Reprinted by permission of Appleton-Century-Crofts, Inc.

[30] *Ibid.*, p. 486. Copyright, © 1948, 1956 by Appleton-Century-Crofts, Inc. Reprinted by permission of Appleton-Century-Crofts, Inc.

of this fact has obvious implications for personnel selection, promotion, and the assignment of work. Considerable attention has been given by many business firms to the measurement of the individual's learning capacity by means of psychological testing.

Repetition. Repeated practice is important for the effective learning of skills and certain types of factual information. The value of repetition has been recognized and its use incorporated into many training efforts in business organizations. For example, the Job Instruction Training (J.I.T.) method—which has been widely used in training employees in new job skills—prescribes that the trainer should demonstrate the job at least twice, and that the trainee should perform the job at least twice under the guidance of the trainer.

Knowledge of Results. In learning, it is important for us to know how well or how poorly we are doing. Feedback of information as to the effectiveness of our learning enables us to correct our errors and modify our behavior in the desired directions. The feedback will be most effective if it is immediate, for unless we correct our errors at once, we may continue learning the wrong things, and thus develop bad habits which may be difficult to unlearn. Knowledge of results and corrective feedback as a basis for modifying behavior are important not only in the learning of specific tasks, but are also central to organizational controls. In fact, the entire control process, which we will consider later in this book, may be thought of as a learning mechanism. Performance standards are established, information is fed back to the decision maker which enables him to compare actual with planned performance, and efforts then may be undertaken to correct for any variance which exists among the two.

Motivation. As the needs theory which we discussed earlier would indicate, learning for which there is a strong motivation is generally more effective than relatively unmotivated learning. However, motivation that "is too intense (especially pain, fear, anxiety) may be accompanied by distracting emotional states, so that excessive motivation may be less effective than moderate motivation for learning some kinds of tasks. . . ."[31] Somewhat relatedly, learning which is motivated by the desire to obtain a reward seems more effective than that which is undertaken in order to avoid punishment. These observations raise serious questions as to the effec-

---

[31] *Ibid.* Copyright, © 1948, 1956 by Appleton-Century-Crofts, Inc. Reprinted by permission of Appleton-Century-Crofts, Inc.

tiveness of excessive supervisory pressures, under which emphasis is placed on the fear of losing one's job as a means of motivation.

Participation and Involvement. It is generally more effective for an individual to participate in and become actively involved in the learning rather than simply assuming a passive role in the training. In learning a new job skill, for example, simply observing someone else's performance is of limited value by itself. If the trainee has an opportunity to perform the skill himself, more rapid learning will take place. Similarly, the neophyte manager will probably never learn to be an effective decision maker simply by watching his boss. He will learn faster if given the opportunity to participate actively in the decision making.

Realistic Goal Setting. In Chapter 2, we indicated the inappropriateness of organization objectives which are either too easy to accomplish or at the other extreme impossible to attain. Similarly, it is important in learning for realistic goals to be set by both the trainer and trainee. If goals are set too high, the learner will experience frustration and failure. On the other hand, goals which are too easily met will provide little learning challenge to the individual.

In the above paragraphs we have indicated some of the conditions under which individuals tend to learn new ways of behaving most effectively. As may be inferred from these comments, effective learning conditions in organizations may be influenced by a number of variables, such as supervisory behavior, organizational arrangements, and the types of rewards and/or punishments provided by the organization. We will explore these variables further with respect not only to learning but also to many other facets of human behavior in succeeding chapters.

ORGANIZATIONS AND NEED SATISFACTION

In the preceding sections we have presented a number of basic concepts and ideas useful to the understanding of human behavior in general, with only passing references to the implications of these concepts to organizational decision making. Building on our premise that most behavior is motivated by the desire to achieve need satisfaction, we will now explore some of the ways in which organizations both provide and fail to provide opportunities for need satisfaction to their members. We will also consider the relationship between meeting the needs of the individual and achieving the objectives of the organization.

Needs Met by Organizations

The business organization may provide its members with opportunities to help satisfy a number of their needs. Our paycheck enables us to meet a number of our basic physiological and safety needs through the purchase of food, clothing and shelter. Money also performs a symbolic function. That we are able to earn more than our neighbors, own the largest home in the community, afford a membership in the country club, or be a three-car family gives us status and prestige in the eyes of others. Or, in terms of the hierarchy of needs discussed earlier, money makes it possible for us to meet certain of our esteem needs.

Organizations also provide many noneconomic rewards to the individual. Being accepted by one's boss and fellow employees is an important way in which the individual's needs for belonging are satisfied. Having our work recognized and performance praised by other members of the organization serves to satisfy our esteem needs. Further, certain types of work provide the individual with an opportunity for self-actualization. The manager who is given responsibility for making complex and difficult decisions or the engineer who develops new and creative production methods may be deriving considerable satisfaction from doing what they can do best. Unfortunately, however, as we will note in the next section, many jobs in business organizations provide very little opportunity for such self-actualization.

Success and Failure of Organizations in Meeting Needs

Without question, American business organizations have been exceptionally successful in providing their employees with an opportunity to meet many of their physiological and safety needs. Nothwithstanding poverty in some quarters, most American workers are well fed, well clothed, and enjoy a relatively high standard of living. Although the nation is plagued with some unemployment problems, a fairly high level of economic security is enjoyed by most Americans. Among the forms of protection against economic insecurity which exist today are: unemployment compensation, workman's compensation, seniority provisions in union-management contracts, health and medical insurance, retirement programs, and social security.

Earlier we observed that needs once largely satisfied cease to serve as important motivators. In light of this, one may question the effectiveness of management's continuing to focus its attention on economic rewards as a primary basis for the further motivation of its employees. As Zaleznik, Christensen and Roethlisberger have pointed out:

> Because management has been so successful in satisfying its workers' subsistence needs, and because workers whose subsistence needs are satisfied are no longer motivated to satisfy these needs, management can no longer use its traditional rewards to motivate them. No amount of good wages, fringe benefits, and good working conditions in and by themselves will motivate workers to give more than minimum effort. Thus management seems to be left with obsolescent motivational tools on its hands that have not been "written off" for new ones.[32]

With employees' physiological and safety needs largely satisfied, it is important to appraise management's effectiveness in providing motivation through the opportunity for satisfaction of the higher level needs. Considerable evidence has been marshalled by contemporary observers to indicate that in many cases business firms have not been too successful in providing organizational conditions under which their employees are able to meet their belonging, esteem, and self-actualization needs. A salient characteristic of many firms, especially those geared toward mass production and assembly line operations, is a high degree of specialization of work. The work to be performed by production employees is broken down into simple repetitive tasks which often require little skill.[33] In many cases, assembly line work is machine paced, and even when it is not, the worker has relatively little control over the way in which he has to perform his job—he is expected to follow closely detailed step-by-step instructions for doing the work which have been developed by management. In addition, some assembly line jobs provide the worker with little chance for social interaction, either because of the need to give close continuous attention to his job, noise which renders conversation difficult, or because of physical isolation from other employees. Work of this type is often not conducive to the individual's satisfaction of his higher level needs. In those jobs where there is limited social interaction, the belongingness needs may easily be thwarted. When a person feels that his work is so simple that

---

[32] A. Zaleznik, C. R. Christensen, and F. J. Roethlisberger, *The Motivation, Productivity, and Satisfaction of Workers, A Prediction Study* (Boston: Harvard University, Division of Research, Graduate School of Business Administration, 1958), p. 402.

[33] For an interesting study of the automotive assembly line, which exhibits these characteristics, see, Charles R. Walker and Robert H. Guest, *The Man on the Assembly Line* (Cambridge, Mass.: Harvard University Press, 1952).

"a five-year old can come in and do it now," [34] it may be difficult for him to develop a high level of self-respect or consider himself esteemed by others for the work that he does. Further, there is quite obviously little opportunity for self-actualization, unless, of course, one's abilities are extremely limited.[35] Nor are highly specialized, routine production jobs the only ones in organizations which may fail to substantially provide opportunities for the individual to satisfy his higher level needs. In many organizational positions, both managerial and nonmanagerial, the individual's behavior is closely directed and controlled; he has little opportunity to assume major responsibilities or make many important decisions himself, and is not able to fully utilize his abilities.

A number of contemporary management observers such as Chris Argyris and Douglas McGregor have expressed concern over the lack of higher level need satisfaction provided in many jobs in industry today. Argyris has taken the position that the requirements of formal organizations are basically incongruent with the needs of the mature individual in our culture. He contends that:

If the principles of formal organization are used as ideally defined, employees will tend to work in an environment where (1) they are provided minimal control over their workaday world, (2) they are expected to be passive, dependent, and subordinate, (3) they are expected to have a short time perspective, (4) they are induced to perfect and value the frequent use of a few skin-surface shallow abilities and, (5) they are expected to produce under conditions leading to psychological failure.[36]

To highlight this incongruency, the reader may wish to refer back to Argyris' description of the mature adult which we cited earlier.

McGregor also concludes that many of the individual's higher level needs are thwarted in organizations, although his position is stated somewhat differently. He contends that traditionally management has tended to direct and control closely the behavior of its employees because it has adhered to a fallacious set of assumptions about human behavior. At the heart of this thinking (which is referred to as Theory X) are the following beliefs:

---

[34] This is a statement by a worker on an automotive assembly line. Cited in *ibid.*, p. 57.
[35] It is interesting to note that there have been cases in which mentally retarded individuals have proven to be highly satisfactory employees in routine production jobs. See, for example, Argyris, *op. cit.*, pp. 67–68.
[36] *Ibid.*, p. 66.

1. *The average human being has an inherent dislike of work and will avoid it if he can. . . .*

2. *Because of this human characteristic of dislike of work, most people must be coerced, controlled, directed, threatened with punishment to get them to put forth adequate effort toward the achievement of organizational objectives. . . .*

3. *The average human being prefers to be directed, wishes to avoid responsibility, has relatively little ambition, wants security above all.*[37]

In refutation of Theory X, McGregor stresses that people do not inherently dislike work, and that they will assume responsibility and willingly direct their efforts toward the objectives of the organization *provided that* in doing so they are able to satisfy their higher level needs.

To what extent are criticisms such as those raised by Argyris and McGregor valid? To what extent are the demands of the organization incongruent with the needs of its members? To what extent do managements assume that people are inherently lazy and dislike work, and as a consequence closely control and direct the activities of their employees? As we indicated previously, when an individual's needs are not satisfied, he experiences frustration, and may react with negative and nonproductive behavior. Considerable evidence exists to indicate that when employee needs are thwarted on the job, workers may display hostility and aggression toward management, become apathetic and indifferent toward their work, or engage in some of the other forms of defensive behavior discussed previously. Tardiness, absences, strikes, slowdowns, and excessive numbers of grievances are among the more common forms of behavior which are often symptomatic of job frustrations. When confronted with such behavior, management may be tempted to conclude that employees are inherently lazy, dislike assuming responsibility, and must be coerced into directing their efforts toward the goals of the organization. Such a conclusion may lead management to exert more pressure on its employees and attempt to control their behavior more closely, which in turn often creates greater frustration and more nonproductive behavior. Thus, we may have what amounts to a vicious cycle. In jobs in which individuals are unable to fulfill many of their needs, frustration and behavior, not in accordance with management's objectives, occurs. This in turn convinces management to take actions which tend to magnify the kinds of problems underlying the behavior which it wishes to avoid.

Just how widespread management's "failure" to provide oppor-

---

[37] McGregor, *op. cit.*, pp. 33–34.

tunities for members of the organization to meet their higher level needs is, however, open to considerable question. The reader should not infer that the individual's higher level needs are rarely if ever met in business organizations. Many managerial and some nonmanagerial positions afford the individual with considerable opportunity for creative endeavor, recognition, and self-actualization. Nor should we assume that all people want to engage in work in which they will be called on to assume considerable responsibility and make important decisions. Some persons are satisfied with routine work, like to be told exactly what to do and how to do it, and do not wish to assume any major responsibilities.[38] Thus, in appraising an organization's effectiveness in providing opportunities for on-the-job need fulfillment, one must guard against overgeneralization. It is necessary to look at each position within the organization separately and examine the demands of the job *in relationship to* the needs of the particular person who is filling it.

Organization Objectives and Member Needs: Integration

One further question needs to be explored before we conclude our discussion of the effectiveness of organizations in meeting member needs. To what extent *should* management attempt to provide conditions under which members of the organization can more fully meet their needs (especially the higher level needs)? We have indicated that the thwarting of employee need satisfaction often leads to behavior of a nonproductive type. As we pointed out in Chapter 2, however, it is possible that by devoting too much attention to member need satisfaction, organizations may be diverted from the attainment of their primary objectives, such as profitability. On the other hand, as McGregor has contended, it may be possible in many cases to create conditions under which individuals may satisfy their own needs *best* by directing their efforts toward the goals of the organization. This tenet, which is referred to as the principle of *integration* by McGregor, is based on the assumption that the individual does not need to be coerced to work toward the goals of the organization, but will willingly assume responsibility for meeting these goals under conditions which provide him with need satisfaction.

---

[38] In some cases this may be because the individual has continually been told exactly what to do and given few responsibilities since early childhood; in other cases a very limited mental capacity may be an important reason for one's desire for routine and uncomplicated work. See, for example, footnote 35, above.

To what extent can such integration be achieved? Although there is no clear cut answer to this question, it appears that a greater degree of integration of organization goals and member needs is possible than has existed in many traditionally managed firms in the past. A number of managerial approaches have been designed and utilized which have been aimed at more fully meeting individual need satisfaction while *at the same time* improving organizational effectiveness. We will discuss a number of these in succeeding chapters. Unfortunately, however, most jobs will always contain aspects which are unpleasant, provide little need satisfaction, and are frustrating. Integration, thus, may be best thought of as an ideal objective, never to be fully realized, for some conflict will probably always exist between the objectives of the organization and the needs of its members.

SUMMARY

Most behavior is motivated by the desire to satisfy needs. Useful for analyzing human motivation is the hierarchy of needs framework which emphasizes that some needs are more prepotent than others. Although none of our needs are ever fully satisfied, at least for very long, those which are largely satisfied at any given time cease to serve as important motivators. When needs are not satisfied, the individual experiences frustration, which may be dealt with either by constructive behavior or by the evocation of defense mechanisms. Although the behavior of all individuals is geared toward need satisfaction, the importance of different needs and the approaches taken to satisfy them vary considerably from individual to individual. The personality of each person is unique. An individual's personality is influenced in its development by certain inborn characteristics and environmental factors in mutual interaction. Although each personality is unique, the personality development of most normal individuals in our culture seems to proceed in similar directions. Important in this development and in all of our behavior is learning; and we have examined some of the conditions under which learning seems to take place most effectively.

Business organizations are in a position to provide their members with opportunities for satisfying many different types of needs. Although American business firms generally have been successful in enabling their members to meet most of their physiological and safety needs, many observers consider business organizations have failed to provide opportunities for the fulfillment of the higher level needs.

The organization, however, has to be concerned not only with endeavoring to provide for the need satisfaction of its employees, but also with attaining its primary objectives, such as profitability. An ideal objective in managerial decision making would be the creation of conditions under which organization members could satisfy their own needs best by directing their efforts toward the objectives of the firm. However, it is likely that there will always be some degree of incongruency between organizational objectives and member needs.

DISCUSSION AND STUDY QUESTIONS

1. What is meant by the statement "most behavior is motivated"?
2. What does it mean to say that one need is more prepotent than others? Illustrate.
3. The manager of a textile mill was overheard saying "I don't want happy, satisfied employees working for me. Unless they are dissatisfied, they tend to coast along, and don't put forth their best efforts. I want them dissatisfied so as to avoid complacency." Evaluate this statement.
4. What is meant by functional autonomy? Give an example of someone whom you know personally or whom you have read about whose behavior might be described as "functionally autonomous."
5. "Experience is the best teacher." Evaluate this statement in light of the discussion of learning theory in the text.
6. In general, what employee needs has management in the United States today been most successful in satisfying? To what degree? What are some of management's major problems today in providing conditions under which its employees will be highly motivated to gear their efforts toward organizational objectives?
7. What objective does McGregor seek with his "principle of integration"? Discuss the extent to which you believe that this objective can be attained within a business organization.
8. Based upon what you have read in Chapter 4, evaluate the following statements about human behavior and motivation.
   a) "The military type of discipline would be very useful in our large business organization if we could get away with it."
   b) "Obtaining maximum production from each employee is what is important to the organization. Managers should strive toward meeting this objective and avoid complicating matters by giving attention to the feeling, attitudes, and emotions of their employees."
   c) "The large organization can provide little opportunity for individuality, and this fact of life must be accepted realistically."
   d) "Supervisors should be made to realize that both a reasonable amount of discussion among employees while on the job and providing limited coffee breaks are compatible with getting the job done."

9. In discussing the advisability of promoting qualified employees who are also union stewards to supervisory positions, one manager stated, "Once a union man, always a union man. We don't want people with union attitudes infiltrating our management hierarchy." What assumptions underly this manager's prediction as to the future behavior of supervisors who previously held union positions? To what extent may the manager's apprehensions be well-founded?

10. Assume that in each of the following situations you are sufficiently familiar with the individual involved to conclude that he is employing a defense mechanism in reaction to frustration. What type of defense mechanism is being employed in each case? What is the reason for your selection?

a) You have been the manager of a small shoe store for the past fifteen years. Two able employees have worked with you for ten of those years and you have just decided to make one of them assistant manager. On the following day, although obviously upset by your choice, the one who was *not* selected tells you at least a half-dozen times what an excellent decision you made, and expresses nothing but praise toward you as a decision maker.

b) Your roommate has been having trouble with a particular course. The night before the mid-term examination in the course (for which he has done very little studying) he decides to go into town to a movie.

c) As foreman of a manufacturing plant, you have noticed that one of your men's quality of work started deteriorating a few weeks ago, shortly after his request for a transfer to a higher paying job was denied because he lacked certain qualifications for the job. You decide to ask him if anything is wrong and he replies that his raw materials have been of poor quality lately.

d) As president of the Canadian Swim Suit Company, you are confronted one day by your marketing manager who remarks: "Gee boss, Fred, our controller, says we are in terrible financial shape because you insist on devoting so much of our advertising budget to selling swim suits to the Eskimos."

e) After an especially difficult day at work, your next door neighbor comes home and explodes at his children for having left their bicycles in the driveway.

f) In the firm for which you work, numerous managers have recently been laid off each payday due to poor business conditions. You notice that several of your younger managerial colleagues have spent considerable time lately placing bets with each other as to who is going to "get the ax" the next payday.

11. You have been asked to teach a friend how to drive a car so that he can obtain a driver's license. Indicate step-by-step how you would go about conducting this training. Indicate how you might incorporate each of the "principles of learning" covered in the text into your training efforts.

SELECTED REFERENCES

ALLPORT, GORDON W.   *Personality.* New York: Henry Holt & Co., 1937.

ARGYRIS, CHRIS.   *Personality and Organization.* New York: Harper & Bros., 1957.

DOLLARD, J., and MILLER, N. E.   *Personality and Psychotherapy.* New York: McGraw-Hill Book Co., Inc., 1950.

DOLLARD, JOHN, *et al.   Frustration and Aggression.* New Haven: Yale University Press, 1939.

HALL, CALVIN S.   *A Primer of Freudian Psychology.* New York: The New American Library of World Literature, Inc., 1955.

HALL, CALVIN S., and LINDZEY, GARDNER.   *Theories of Personality.* New York: John Wiley & Sons, Inc., 1957.

HILGARD, ERNEST R.   *Theories of Learning.* 2d ed. New York: Appleton-Century-Crofts, Inc., 1956.

KLUCKHOHN, CLYDE, and MURRAY, HENRY A.   *Personality in Nature, Society, and Culture.* 2d ed. New York: Alfred A. Knopf, 1953.

MASLOW, A. H.   *Motivation and Personality.* New York: Harper & Bros., 1954.

McCLELLAND, DAVID C.   *Personality.* New York: Sloane, 1951.

McGREGOR, DOUGLAS.   *The Human Side of Enterprise.* New York: McGraw-Hill Book Co., Inc., 1960.

MUNROE, RUTH L.   *Schools of Psychoanalytic Thought.* New York: Holt, Rinehart & Winston, Inc., 1955.

WALKER, CHARLES R., and GUEST, ROBERT H.   *The Man on the Assembly Line.* Cambridge, Mass.: Harvard University Press, 1952.

WHYTE, WILLIAM F.   *Men at Work.* Homewood, Ill.: Dorsey Press, Inc., & Richard D. Irwin, Inc., 1961.

WITKIN, H. A., *et al.   Personality Through Perception.* New York: Harper & Bros., 1954.

CHAPTER 5

THE LEADERSHIP PROCESS

OUR discussion in the previous chapter focused attention on several aspects of *individual* behavior of importance to the manager—motivation, learning, and personality. An understanding of the managerial process also requires that we examine *relationships among individuals,* for the functioning of the business firm centers around a complex network of interrelationships among many persons working together to meet organizational objectives.

There are two facets of human interaction which are of special concern to the manager. One of these is the impact of group membership upon individual behavior, which we will examine in the following chapter. The other is the phenomenon of leadership, to which we will now turn our attention. In the ensuing discussion, we will suggest that leadership may be best thought of as an influence process. We will examine this process in terms of both need satisfaction and social power. We will also consider the question of what constitutes successful leadership; and an examination will be made of various leadership styles (or strategies) available to the manager and some of the conditions under which each seems to be most effective.

In discussing leadership we face some of the same kinds of problems that were encountered in our examination of motivation, learning, and personality. The variables involved in the leadership process are complex and not well defined; and considerable disagreement still exists among authorities as to their role and significance. However, a number of concepts have been developed which may provide the manager with a useful framework for understanding the phenomena of leadership and influence in business organizations. These concepts may be of value to him in analyzing his own role both as a leader and as a follower, and in selecting leadership strategies which will be effective for him in his interpersonal relationships with other members of his organization.

LEADERSHIP: A DEFINITION

Many different conceptual frameworks have been developed for examining the phenomenon of leadership. Our preference is to view leadership as an *influence process,* the dynamics of which are a function of: (1) the personal characteristics of the leader,[1] (2) those of his followers, and (3) the nature of the specific situation in which the influence efforts take place. This view is often referred to the *situationist* approach to leadership. It suggests that leadership may be defined as *efforts* on the part of one person (the leader) *directed at influencing* the behavior, attitudes, beliefs, or values of another person or persons (followers) toward specified goals in a given situation.[2]

Several observations are in order to further clarify this conception of leadership. First, the reader will note that we define leadership not as influence *per se,* but rather as influence *efforts*—i.e., we consider any attempt on the part of one person to influence others as leader behavior whether or not the effort is successful. We find this distinction useful since it permits us to examine the leadership process itself separately from the difficult question of what constitutes effective leadership, thus simplifying our analysis.

Second, it should be noted that the leader's influence efforts may

---

[1] It should be noted that a considerable amount of research has been carried out in an attempt to isolate personal characteristics differentiating leaders from other individuals. Although many authorities question whether there are any personality traits universally characteristic of leaders, certain traits do seem to be important factors in leadership. For example, it has been found that "leaders are more intelligent than followers, but one of the most interesting results emerging from studies in this area is the discovery that they must not exceed the followers by too large a margin, for great discrepancies between the intelligence of leaders and followers militates against the emergence of the leadership relation, presumably because such wide discrepancies render improbable the unified purpose of the individuals concerned." Cecil A. Gibb, "Leadership," in *Handbook of Social Psychology,* ed., Gardner Lindzey, Vol. II (Cambridge, Mass.: Addison-Wesley Publishing Company, 1954), p. 886. For a discussion of the traitist approach to leadership, see also: Alex Bavelas, "Leadership: Man and Function," *Administrative Science Quarterly,* 4 (March, 1960), 491–98.

[2] This definition is quite similar to that presented in Robert Tannenbaum, Irving R. Weschler, and Fred Massarik, *Leadership and Organization* (New York: McGraw-Hill Book Company, Inc., 1961) p. 24. It should also be noted that one person may influence the behavior of others merely by his presence, rather than by any overt efforts. A policeman, for example, may influence the driving behavior of passing motorists simply by standing at an intersection.

be directed either toward or against changing the behavior, attitudes, etc., of others. For example, a manager may attempt to influence one of his employees to do something—such as to agree to overtime work. Or, the efforts may be aimed at dissuading the employee from doing something—such as refraining from taking his vacation at a time when the firm's workload is at its peak for the year.

Finally, our definition of leadership encompasses leader efforts directed toward influencing both the behavior of another individual and that of a group of followers. In the following discussion, primary attention will be given to concepts which are applicable to both types of influence efforts. Then in Chapter 6, we will consider certain special facets of the leader-group relationship.

LEADERSHIP, FOLLOWERSHIP AND NEED SATISFACTION

Although some individuals are obviously more influential than others, all people assume both leadership and followership roles to varying degrees. Our purpose in this section is to explore the nature of these roles and of the influence process by raising the following questions: (1) Why do individuals desire to seek influence over others and conversely, (2) why are people attracted by situations in which they are in a position to be influenced by others? Since— as we have indicated in Chapter 4—most human behavior is motivated by the desire to satisfy needs, we will seek answers to these questions by analyzing the need satisfactions gained by both the influencer and the influencee.

Need Satisfactions of the Leader

An individual may help satisfy many different needs by assuming the role of leader—in fact, possibly all of the five basic classes of needs discussed in the previous chapter. The financial rewards given to those holding positions of considerable influence in our society are generally greater than those realized by persons exerting relatively little influence in their work. Such rewards, as we indicated earlier, may enable the individual to help meet a number of his physiological, safety, and esteem needs. Further, some individuals may also derive feelings of security simply by being in positions in which they have the power to control the behavior of others. This may be especially true for those insecure persons who have relatively little confidence in their own abilities and view others as a threat to themselves—e.g., the boss who fears that his subordinates may take his job away from him may feel less insecure if he controls their behavior closely in such a manner as to stifle their creativity and prevent them from fully utilizing their abilities. As this example points out, leader behavior is not always constructively goal-oriented —it may also be defensive in nature.

Assumption of a position of leadership may also put the individual in a better position to satisfy both his belongingness and esteem needs. The reason for this is that individuals holding positions of influence in organizations and groups usually attain higher *status* than those who do not. By "status" we mean roughly the degree of prestige which an individual enjoys as a member of a group. As one observer has pointed out:

> The higher levels of status are believed to be, and usually are, the more pleasant to occupy. They involve more power and influence and they may bring higher financial returns. But the important factor in considering status as a motive in itself is that higher status gives entrée into attractive associations; it makes possible friendships and group memberships which, in turn, tend to maintain status and thus to satisfy important ego needs. This may indeed be one of the most important, and most general, satisfactions, to be had from occupancy of a leader role in any group.[3]

Finally, assuming the role of leader may provide the individual with an opportunity to help meet his self-actualization needs. Many leadership positions in our society call on the individual to direct and coordinate the efforts of others toward the solution of complex and difficult decision problems—e.g., the presidency of a corporation or the job of directing a large scale research and development program. Some persons find that this type of endeavor is what they are best fitted for, and that they will experience "a new discontent and restlessness," to use Maslow's words, unless they are continually called on to deal with such challenging problems.

Need Satisfactions of the Follower

Many different types of needs may also be satisfied by assuming the role of follower. Acceding to the influence efforts of others may help provide satisfaction of some of the individual's physiological, safety, and belongingness needs. For instance, modifying one's behavior in the business organization in the directions indicated by the boss's influence efforts may lead to economic rewards in the form of a pay raise or promotion, greater assurances of job security,

---

[3] Gibb, *op. cit.*, p. 904.

or a feeling that one is accepted by his superior. Moreover, an individual may help meet his esteem and self-actualization needs by taking the role of influencee in at least two different ways. First, there is strong evidence to suggest that some of a person's esteem needs may be satisfied as a follower, at least *vicariously* through the psychological process of *identification*. Identification, a concept attributed to Freud,

> provides a means of incorporating the strength of another in ourselves. We can identify with strong individuals and with groups. The classic example of the vicarious strength obtained through identification is found in the small boy's assertion "My dad can whip your father." The individual feels strong if he has a close tie with another strong person. . . . Paradoxical as it may seem, followership may represent to the follower satisfactions of status needs very similar to those represented to the leader by his leadership.[4]

Second, satisfaction of the follower's esteem and self-actualization needs may be contributed to when the leader directs his efforts towards inducing the employee to behave in such manner that he will gain esteem and recognition and more fully utilize his abilities. For example, a manager may exert strong influence on an employee to take some night courses at the university which will enable him to develop certain skills and thus be in a position to perform better on the job and gain more recognition in the organization.

The Problems of Leadership and Followership

Although need satisfactions may be gained from assuming both leader and follower roles, either may present problems for the individual. The leader-follower relationship may be difficult for all concerned when the leader, in order to meet his needs and objectives, must exert influence aimed at inducing followers to behave in a manner incongruent with the satisfaction of certain of their needs. For example, in order to meet his responsibilities the manager may have to call on one of his employees to put aside some creative and highly interesting work and devote several weeks to a routine, monotonous project which the employee dislikes intensely. In this case, the employee may gain the satisfaction of some needs by acceding to the influence of the manager (e.g., obtaining the approval of his boss, or conversely, avoiding being fired); but only at the expense of having certain other needs thwarted (e.g., esteem or self-actualization). Further, the manager, too, may find such a situation difficult and may experience some feelings of guilt because he is exerting influence toward inducing the employee to behave in a man-

---

[4] *Ibid.*, p. 906.

ner which is unpleasant for him. Such conflict between leader and follower needs is not uncommon, and probably exists to some degree in most influence relationships. For this reason, a better understanding of leadership may be gained by an analysis of both the power of the influencer and of the follower's resistance to influence. Before undertaking such an analysis, however, it will be useful to examine the problems involved in the leader-follower relationship from another point of view—in terms of the independence and dependence needs of the individual, and of his ambivalence toward the leader.

We indicated in Chapter 4 that as the psychologically healthy individual matures, he moves from a state of dependence on others to a state of relative independence. Whereas the child has to turn frequently to his parents (and other elders) for help with his problems, the adult generally neither needs nor has the desire to rely as heavily on others. As adults most of us want to assume responsibilities, make our own decisions, and have some control over our own destinies. Such wants and desires are often referred to as *independence* needs.

There are limits, however, to the individual's desire for independence and freedom from direction and control by others. To rely primarily on ourselves rather than others, to stand alone in a complex, difficult, and uncertain world, to assume the responsibility not only for our own well-being but possibly also that of many others—can be very frightening for the individual. Consider as an extreme example of the heavy burdens of responsibility that the individual may be called on to bear, President Truman's problem of whether or not to employ the atomic bomb against Japan in World War II. Although the President was able to seek counsel from many of his advisers, it was he, and he alone, who had to bear the ultimate responsibility for his decision—a decision which meant the unleashing of a highly destructive force, but also one which might in the long run save many thousands of American lives.

Fortunately, most of us do not have to face up to such difficult decisions. However, all of us are at times confronted with complex and uncertain situations in which it is frightening to stand alone and depend on ourselves rather than to seek direction from and rely on others. For this reason, persons sometimes attempt to "escape from freedom," as Erich Fromm has put it, by seeking out a strong leader upon whom they can depend.[5] As a child it was comforting

---

[5] Erich Fromm, *Escape from Freedom* (New York: Farrar and Rinehart, 1941). One of Fromm's interesting theses is that the rise of Hitler can be explained to a considerable extent by a strong need on the part of many Germans for a strong leader figure.

to have a "strong powerful father" to whom we could go for help with our problems; similarly, as adults, it is often comforting to have a strong leader or "father figure" to whom we can turn. Such yearnings for someone else to depend upon (especially at difficult times) are often referred to as *dependence* needs.[6]

However, as much as we *sometimes* like to rely on others and seek strong leadership, most of us do not want to be completely dominated and controlled by someone else. As we indicated earlier, acceding to the influence of others may often mean that we must sacrifice certain of our own needs, goals, and objectives. As a consequence, most of us have mixed feelings toward leadership—we want to be able to depend on a leader to an extent, but not completely so. Or, in terms of the psychologist, we all have *ambivalent* feelings toward leaders, "ambivalence" meaning an emotional attitude toward an individual involving the opposite feelings of love and hate. As one observer has pointed out:

> Whatever the culture, followers have an ambivalent attitude toward the leader. Satisfactions of dependency needs are rarely without conflict for the individual. Particularly is this true for the male adult, since in most cultures he is less free to express dependence and seems to sacrifice virility by doing so. . . . Almost any leader-follower relation one can think of involves this ambivalence because the follower needs the leader and his control but does not want to be exploited. . . . the father "may be an object of fear in one mood; in another an object of affection. The same is true of all the father surrogates, all the grandfathers and uncles, all the policemen and martial heroes, all the kings, presidents, and popes, who derive their first place in the child's experience as configural duplicates of his first experiences." [7]

We may feel great affection for the leader when his support helps us to satisfy our needs for dependence. On the other hand, we may become quite hostile toward him when his influence efforts thwart our needs for independence and self-assertiveness. Further, such hostility may also be felt when an individual perceives that the leader has failed to give him the support that his dependence needs require. An employee who needs to rely heavily on his boss for directions, for example, may feel "let down" and angry when the boss

---

[6] The dependence and independence needs discussed in this section should not be considered as being distinct from and unrelated to those needs included in Maslow's hierarchy. Rather, they simply represent a different way of viewing some of the same kinds of motivational phenomena upon which Maslow's framework focuses attention. For example, the desire to have someone else to depend on reflects a basic need for security; while the need to assume responsibilities and make one's own decisions may represent the need for self-esteem and/or self-actualization.

[7] Gibb, *op. cit.*, p. 906. The quotation cited by Gibb is from G. Murphy, *Personality* (New York: Harper, 1947), pp. 845–46.

requires him to make more decisions on his own. The relative strength of these dependence and independence needs, of course, varies considerably from individual to individual, as do most all facets of personality.

THE FORCES OF INFLUENCE AND OF RESISTANCE

Our preceding discussion has indicated that satisfaction of certain of the follower's needs may sometimes be thwarted if he permits himself to be influenced by the leader. Nevertheless, the individual often does allow himself to be influenced by others to behave in a manner distasteful to him—we are all persuaded at times to do things which we do not want to do. Such behavior may be best understood if it is examined from two different points of view—in terms of (1) the influencee's need system and of (2) the nature of the forces which the influencer may bring to bear on the influencee.

The Need System of the Influencee

From the point of view of the influencee's need system, we suggest that a person will decide to permit himself to be influenced by another if he perceives that he will probably gain greater net need satisfaction by doing so than by refusing to do so.[8] Such a decision is often a highly complex one, for the satisfaction of many different needs, each to varying degrees, may be at stake. Further, the decision is not always "reasoned out" consciously, but rather is often influenced, at least in part, by unconscious forces in the individual of which he is not fully aware. To the extent that a person does "rationally" reason out the consequences of his willingness or refusal to accede to the influence efforts of others, however, he will probably consider both (1) the relative importance of those of his needs which may be affected by the influence acceptance decision, and (2) the probability of gains or losses in need satisfaction which will accrue from various alternative strategies open to him. We use the phrase "various alternative strategies" here because in addition to the complete acceptance or outright rejection of an influence attempt, a person may go along partially with the wishes of another, or do so in a half-hearted way.

To illustrate the ideas which we are conveying, let us consider

---

[8] To the extent that the difference between the attractiveness of acceding to the influence efforts and that of not doing so is sufficiently great to be perceptible by the influencee. If not, there would be no basis for predicting the behavior of the influencee.

some of the questions which might be raised in the mind of the employee in our previous example who was asked by his boss to devote several weeks to distasteful work:

1.   If I refuse outright to do the work, what are my chances of being fired? Of losing a chance for a promotion? Of losing the approval of the boss? How important are each of these needs to me as compared with the frustration that I will experience if I consent to do the task?

2.   If I cheerfully undertake the distasteful work, will my chances of getting ahead in the firm or of gaining the boss's approval be materially enhanced?

3.   If I choose another strategy—such as not openly refusing to do the work but avoiding as much of it as possible perhaps by taking longer lunch hours or coffee breaks each day and by calling in "sick" on several occasions—what will be the consequences?

Sources of Leader Power

The above example illustrates the role of influencee needs in the leadership process; it also points up that the leader has certain *powers* to provide, withhold, or take away need satisfactions which he may utilize to induce influence acceptance—e.g., the boss's power to fire the employee or to grant a promotion. To provide further insight into the influence process we will now examine the bases of social power of the leader.

A useful framework for understanding the bases, or sources of social power that an individual may possess has been developed by French and Raven.[9] The term "social power," as utilized in this framework may be roughly defined as the *potential* ability of one person to influence another. Or, to put it another way, social power represents the maximum *possible* influence that one person may have on another as distinguished from the influence which he actually exerts—i.e., people often choose to exercise less than the full power at their command. A manager, for example, may have the power to influence an employee to work overtime, but not insist on the employee's doing so.

French and Raven have distinguished five different bases of social power: (1) reward power, (2) coercive power, (3) referent power,

---

[9] John R. P. French, Jr., and Bertram Raven, "The Bases of Social Power," in *Studies in Social Power*, Dorwin Cartwright, ed. (Ann Arbor, Mich.: Institute for Social Research, 1959), pp. 150–67. Our discussion in this section draws heavily on French and Raven's conceptual framework.

(4) expert power, and (5) legitimate power. We will now examine each of these.

Reward Power. "Reward power is defined as power whose basis is the ability to reward." [10] That is, an individual may be able to influence others because he is in a position to reward them if they accede to his influence efforts. Notice here that reward power is *not* the same as the power to reward. Rather it is one's power to *influence based on* his power to reward. In fact, a person may be in a position to dispense rewards, and yet possess little or no reward power. For example, the parent may have the power to reward junior with a candy bar if he stops hitting sister; but be unable to induce the desired behavior by promising such a reward.

The reward which the influencer has at his disposal may represent either (1) an increase in positive need satisfaction or (2) a reduction in need dissatisfaction. For example, the manager may influence one of his employees to do an exceptionally good job on a work project by promising him, if he does so, either an increase in pay or relief from certain unpleasant aspects of his job in the future. These two different types of reward are illustrated in Figure 5–1.

The reader will note that we have used the word "promised" to describe the rewards or lack of rewards in Figure 5–1. This is because the influencer may or may not actually provide the reward to the influencee once the prescribed influence efforts have been conformed to. Whether or not the influencer *does* live up to his promises

FIGURE 5–1. Types of Reward

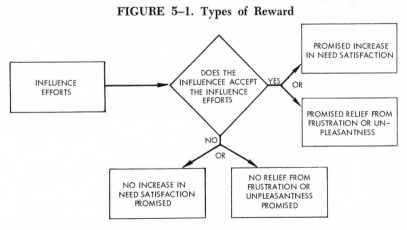

Note: For the purposes of simplification the possibility of partial acceptance of influence efforts has been ignored here.

---

[10] *Ibid.*, p. 156.

of reward, however, is of considerable importance. If he does so:
(1) his reward power will tend to be augmented because the influencee is likely to attach a greater probability to the fulfillment of
future reward promises, and (2) his attractiveness as a person to
the influencee will tend to increase, thus enhancing his referent
power, the nature of which will be discussed below. Conversely, the
failure to fulfill reward promises will tend to reduce both the influencer's reward power and his attractiveness to the influencee. From
these observations, two prescriptive statements may be made about
leader behavior: the leader should refrain from promising rewards
(1) that he cannot fulfill, and (2) for behavior which it is not possible for the influencee to attain (e.g., a pay raise for a level of production so high as to be impossible for the influencee to meet).

Coercive Power.   Coercive power refers to the potential ability
of the individual to influence others because he is in a position to
punish them if they do not follow his wishes. The parent may influence junior to stop jumping up and down on the living room sofa
by threat of a spanking; the professor may influence his students to
attend class by virtue of his power to fail them if they do not do so;
the manager may influence his employees to produce at high levels
by threat of dismissal. Again—as with reward power—it is important
to distinguish between the power to punish and the power to *influence* others by threat of punishment. The professor, for example,
may be unable to induce certain students to come to class even
though he has the power to give them a failing grade.[11]

Referent Power.   A third basis of social power, which we have already mentioned in passing, is referent power—we accede to the influence efforts of another person because we are attracted to him, wish
to identify with him, and want to be like him. The young son may
be more than willing to help daddy build a cupboard for mother
because he wants to be like his father and do the things his father
does. Or the employee may be very enthused about carrying out a
request of his boss because he admires his superior and wants to
identify with him. As we indicated in an earlier section, such identification enables the individual to incorporate, psychologically, the
strength of another in himself.

---

[11] As the reader may observe, coercive power is in some respects quite similar
to reward power, and at times it may be difficult to distinguish between the two.
Withholding a reward may be much the same as doling out a punishment; or conversely, withholding punishment may be equivalent to giving a reward, depending
on the way that the influencee *perceives* the influence effort. French and Raven, however, contend that the dynamics of these two types of power are different. See *ibid.*,
p. 158.

It should also be pointed out that a person may identify with *groups* of people as well as with individuals, and that such identification may provide a basis for his being influenced by the values, standards, and modes of conduct considered desirable by the group. In fact, groups also derive social power from their ability to provide punishments and rewards in much the same way as do individuals, as we will indicate in the following chapter.

Expert Power. The fourth basis of social power distinguished by French and Raven is *expert* power. Expert power refers to the potential ability of one person to influence others because of his superior knowledge or understanding of a particular situation. Many examples of the exercise of expert power could be cited—the patient's acceptance of his doctor's prescribed treatment, the student's acceptance of his professor's recommendation to read a particular book as preparation for a term paper, or the plant superintendent's acceptance of his personnel manager's interpretation of a psychological test.

Generally, the *range* of expert power is fairly narrow—i.e., we tend to be influenced by another person because he is an expert only within his area of expertise. For example, we would probably not pay much attention to our doctor's advice regarding our legal matters. In fact, a person's expert power may be reduced if he attempts its exercise in an area in which he is not truly knowledgeable. We recall one labor relations assistant, for example, who proclaimed to be an expert on everything from high fidelity systems to the preparation of exotic oriental foods, and who was continually trying to get his colleagues to accept his "expert" advice on all sorts of different matters. Although this individual was highly competent in his own field of labor relations, even here his colleagues began to become suspicious of his expertise because "he was such a phony" in his claims to knowledge in other areas.

Legitimate Power. The fifth, and perhaps most complex, basis of social power is *legitimate* power. Legitimate power refers to the individual's permitting himself to be influenced by others because he believes that it is the right thing to do. That is, our conscience, or our own internalized value system, tells us that another person has the right to influence our behavior and that we have an obligation to accept his influence.

There are at least two different types of legitimate power. First, we may feel an obligation to do as another person requests us because we have previously made a promise to do so and feel that it would be morally wrong to break that promise. Second, and of greater relevance to organizational behavior, is legitimate power based on our belief that other individuals *holding certain positions* have the right to influence our behavior. If a person

> . . . accepts as right the social structure of his group, organization, or society, especially the social structure involving a hierarchy of authority, . . . [he] . . . will accept the legitimate authority of . . . [a person] . . . who occupies a superior office in the hierarchy. Thus legitimate power in a formal organization is largely a relationship between offices rather than between persons. And the acceptance of an office as *right* is a basis for legitimate power—a judge has a right to levy fines, a foreman should assign work, a priest is justified in prescribing religious beliefs, and it is the management's prerogative to make certain decisions.[12]

Legitimate power of this second type is quite similar to the idea of formal "authority," which has long been a central concept in management thinking.

Sources of Social Power: The Formal and Informal Leader. Up to this point, we have not mentioned a distinction frequently made in analyzing the influence process—that between *formal* and *informal* leaders. A *formal* leader is defined as one, like the business manager, who derives considerable power by virtue of having been appointed to a position in an organization. An informal leader, on the other hand, is one whose position of influence is conferred on him solely by the membership of his group itself—e.g., a work group in a manufacturing plant may choose one of its members to be its spokesman, to present its grievances to management, etc.[13] Although many of the concepts which we are examining in this chapter are applicable in the analysis of both formal and informal leadership, there are certain differences between these two types of influence relationships which we will point up later.

Reliance on the Bases of Social Power. In the preceding sections, we have treated separately each of the five different bases of social power. In analyzing the influence process, however, it is usually necessary to consider simultaneously more than one power base. This is because we rarely find only one base underlying any given influencer-influencee relationship in the business organization (or elsewhere, for that matter). When a subordinate agrees to carry out

---

[12] *Ibid.*, p. 160.

[13] It should be mentioned that a person may assume the role of both formal and informal leader depending upon the specific influence situation in which he is involved. For instance, in his relationships with his subordinates, a first line supervisor would be viewed as a formal leader; while the same individual may have emerged as an informal leader within a group of first line supervisors of which he is a member.

a work assignment in the manner specified by his boss, for example, it may be because he not only feels a moral obligation to do so, but also has confidence in his superior's expertise and identifies with him.

It should also be noted that most managers probably derive their power from all five of the sources which we have mentioned to varying degrees. All managers, by the very fact that they occupy positions in the organization hierarchy (as formal leaders) possess certain legitimate rights to influence others, and, unless they are extremely ineffective, are able to derive *some* power from this source. Most managers also possess some power to reward and punish on the basis of which they are able to influence, and hopefully have attained some degree of expertise and have some qualities which will lead others to want to identify with them. Of course, there are wide differences among managers as to the degree to which they not only are able to draw on but actually do utilize the various forms of power. For example, the manager of a research department doing work in cryogenics in an aerospace firm may be a recognized authority in his field and rely heavily on his expertise in influencing his colleagues. On the other hand, a newly appointed production supervisor with little technical knowledge of the operations of which he is in charge, but who is supportive of and has the ability to inspire others, may draw largely upon his referent power. Further, the same manager may rely more heavily on one source of power in some situations and another source in others. A supervisor may find, for instance, that some of his subordinates both recognize his expertise and identify with him, while others are somewhat hostile toward him and at times can only be induced to accept his influence efforts if he threatens punishment for their failure to do so.

Social Power and Organization Analysis. The social power framework may be quite useful in analyzing organizational problems and developing courses of action aimed at their resolution. To illustrate how this framework may be applied to organization analysis, we will examine a problem which has been of concern to many companies in recent years—the declining importance of the first-line supervisor—and some of the steps managements have taken to help resolve this problem.[14]

---

[14] For a fuller discussion of this problem, see George Strauss and Leonard R. Sayles, *Personnel: The Human Problems of Management* (Englewood Cliffs, N. J.: Prentice-Hall, Inc., 1960), pp. 346–52.

Fifty or sixty years ago, many first-line supervisors (or foremen) in production operations had considerable power—power to hire, fire, and promote their employees, and to make decisions regarding many phases of their operations. With the growth of unionism, however, both disciplinary and promotional procedures have come to be spelled out in many union-management contracts. For example, whereas the foreman once could fire a man for being absent a day without a justifiable reason, today under some union-management contracts he can only give the employee an oral warning for the first such offense.[15] In addition, some companies have taken the hiring decision from the foreman and transferred it to the personnel department. Thus, the coercive, reward, and legitimate bases of the foreman's social power have all been reduced in scope. Further, as business organizations have become technologically more complex, the foreman has come to be surrounded by a myriad of staff specialists in production control, quality control, industrial engineering, personnel, maintenance, etc., all of whom have some say as to the way in which his department should be run. This has often led to an erosion of the supervisor's expert power.

In recent years some companies have taken certain steps to help overcome the problem of the first-line supervisor's diminished importance. A few have taken the position that the foreman has become obsolete, and have restructured their organizations so as to abolish the position.[16] A number of others, on the other hand, have attempted to deal with the problem by attempting to strengthen the foreman's bases of social power. Some companies have given back to the foreman the right to hire new employees—a least partially on the assumption that a new man may be more attracted to and identify more with a supervisor who has personally chosen him, than with one who has been forced to hire him by the personnel department.[17] Firms have also attempted to augment the foreman's referent power by training him in human relations skills. The reasoning here is that if a person is able to develop more effective interpersonal relationships with others, they will tend to be more attracted to him and identify with him to a greater extent. Business

---

[15] For further offenses, more serious measures are usually in order—e.g., a one-day layoff for the second such offense, a one week layoff for the third, and discharge for the fourth. This type of disciplinary approach is often referred to as *progressive discipline*.

[16] See, for example, " 'Upgrading' Foreman with an Ax," *Business Week* (February 11, 1961), pp. 110, 112.

[17] Giving the foreman responsibility for hiring his own men also makes it more difficult for him to "pass the buck"—i.e., when things go wrong to blame the personnel department for the "poor" men which it compelled him to hire.

firms have not overlooked the possibility of enhancing the foreman's expert power. Efforts have been made to increase the foreman's knowledge and understanding of many different phases of his company's operations—e.g., by providing him with training programs on the meaning of the provisions in the firm's union-management contract, on time study procedures employed in the plant, etc. In addition, some companies have attempted to augment the supervisor's expert power by (1) communicating to him more information about decisions being made by top management and/or (2) permitting him to sit in on higher-level management committee meetings and participate actively in these discussions.

THE LEADERSHIP PROCESS: SUMMARY

We have indicated that the leadership process centers around the efforts of one person (the leader) to influence others (the followers) either to change their behavior, attitudes, etc., or to refrain from doing so. The leader possesses social power—reward, coercive, referent, legitimate, and expert—essentially by virtue of his ability to provide, withhold, or take away certain need satisfactions of the follower. We have suggested that a person will choose to accept the influence of another when he perceives that he will gain greater net need satisfaction by doing so than by refraining from doing so. These concepts are summarized graphically in Figure 5–2.

LEADERSHIP EFFECTIVENESS

We will now turn our attention to the question of how one may determine whether the leadership efforts of an individual are successful or not. The evaluation of leader effectiveness is an extremely difficult problem, and there are no simple, clear-cut approaches for its resolution. However, insight into the problem may be gained by analyzing it from two different points of view. First, we will explore the question of leader effectiveness in terms of leader objectives and strategies. We will then examine a continuum of leader approaches or strategies available to the manager—from highly directive to highly permissive leadership—and indicate the conditions under which each seems to be most appropriate.

Leader Objectives and Strategies

We indicated in Chapter 2 that organizational performance must be measured against objectives which have been established by the

FIGURE 5–2. A Model of the Leadership Process

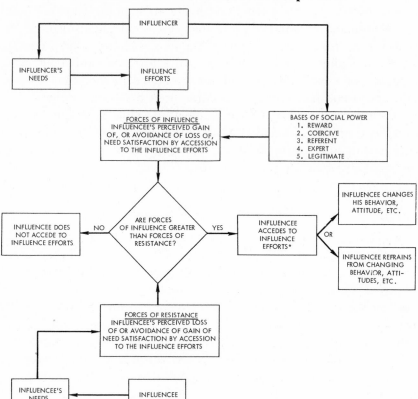

*Accession may be either complete or partial.

firm. We pointed out that problems exist for management when its objectives are either (1) inappropriate or (2) not attained. A similar frame of analysis may be applied in the evaluation of leader behavior. That is, in examining leadership we may ask (1) are the objectives which the leader seeks to achieve by means of influencing others appropriate, and (2) assuming that they are, to what degree are his influence efforts successful?

Leader Objectives. As shown in Chapter 2 objectives are derived from values. Thus, in considering leader objectives we must first appraise the values upon which they are based. Whether or not we judge a particular leader's objectives to be appropriate depends on our own value system and to the extent that we use our values in appraising the behavior of others. Many leaders have enjoyed considerable success in light of their own standards, yet have been vigorously condemned by others with different values. Hitler, for example, was very "successful" in influencing the heads of his concentration camps to develop and apply new and "improved" methods of mass extermination. Yet if we apply our own standards to such behavior we must consider it highly abominable.

Of course, the position could be taken that a leader is effective as long as his efforts are successful in inducing influence behavior which leads to the attainment of his objectives, *regardless* of the values from which they are derived. That is, we could discard our own value system, and consider only that of the leader in evaluating his behavior. Or, we could take a somewhat less extreme and amoral position and accept the leader's own values as appropriate even though we may not agree with them, as long as the values do not grossly conflict with our own. For example, we might believe that a particular manager is directing the efforts of his employees too much toward "good public relations" at the expense of profitability, but still evaluate his behavior in terms of his own values since we find nothing very morally "wrong" with placing a high value on good public relations. In short, we can judge a leader's behavior on the basis of our own values, his values, or take a position somewhere in between.

Several other observations must be made in order to clarify the problem of the appropriateness of leader objectives. Turning to leader behavior in the business organization, we must first raise the question as to how congruent a manager's objectives are with those of his organization. A manager may successfully influence his subordinates to direct their efforts toward his own personal objectives; yet such influence behavior may be incongruent with the goals of the organization. For instance, in order to "strengthen" his own position in the firm, a supervisor may induce his employees to develop an inaccurate report which will make one of his managerial rivals look bad in the eyes of top management. Such a report may have negative repercussions in terms of the firm's attainment of its objectives, yet possibly enhance the supervisor's own personal ambitions.

The question may also be asked as to what extent the leader's influence efforts are congruent with the needs and objectives of those he is attempting to influence. In Chapter 4, we indicated that the needs of employees will probably never be completely congruent with the objectives of the organization toward which management may direct their behavior. However, does the manager not have a moral obligation to refrain from exerting influence on his subordinates which, if accepted, would be seriously detrimental to their interest? For example, is it legitimate for a manager to coerce, by threat of dismissal, an employee—for whom it would be extremely difficult to find a job elsewhere if he were fired—into performing some work which would be injurious to his health? Again, answers to questions such as these depend upon one's own value system and the extent to which one uses his own values in appraising the behavior of others. If one accepts the manager's viewpoint that organizational objectives should be attained at all costs, the threat of dismissal in our previous example might be justified.[18] On the other hand, if we hold that the manager does have certain moral obligations to his employees, such coercion would probably be considered inappropriate.

Finally, we should note that the manager (as a formal leader) usually does not have to give as much consideration to the objectives of his group as does the informal leader. This is because his leadership is imposed upon his employees by virtue of his having been appointed to the position in the organization which he holds; whereas the informal leader is chosen by and derives his powers from the group itself.

The Means Chosen to Achieve the Leader's Organizational Objectives. The above discussion has raised questions concerning leader objectives and the means chosen to attain these objectives. In examining leader influence means, a further question must be asked: Is the behavior of the follower which the leader is attempting to influence going to contribute to the leader's attainment of his objectives, assuming they are appropriate? If not, the leadership must be considered ineffective, even though the leader is successful in inducing the influence to behave as he desires. This type of ineffective leadership may be illustrated by the following example.

The manager of a manufacturing plant wanted to increase production on a particular operation because of a large backlog of customer orders. As a means of achieving this quite legitimate objective, he instructed the head of the maintenance department to not shut down a particular machine for 3 hours for its monthly preventative maintenance check. The maintenance manager argued strongly against this action, pointing out that the machine was one of the oldest in the plant, that the "normal" preventative maintenance check had also been skipped the previous month because of a similar production problem, and that he believed that the machine was on the verge of breaking down. After a heated discussion, the plant manager ordered the maintenance man-

---

[18] This is not necessarily so. Such coercion, for example, might over a period of time alienate the manager's entire department, and contribute to lower productivity.

ager to "do as I say or else." The latter acceded to these influence efforts, and the machine was not checked. Shortly thereafter, the machine broke down and three days of production, rather than three hours was lost.

In this example the plant manager's objective was legitimate and his influence efforts were successful, yet his leadership was ineffective since the means of accomplishing his objective toward which he directed the influencee's behavior were inappropriate.

Acceptance of the Leader's Influence Efforts. Finally, in evaluating leadership effectiveness, we must obviously consider the extent to which the leader is actually able to gain acceptance of his influence efforts, assuming that they are appropriately directed toward the attainment of valid objectives. Little needs to be said further about this aspect of the influence process except to reemphasize the need to examine the influencee's *degree* of acceptance. As we indicated previously, an influencee may neither completely accept nor outright reject the leader's influence efforts, but rather may often choose any one of many strategies of partial acceptance.

Effective Leadership: Summary. We have indicated in the previous sections that several different questions must be raised when we attempt to evaluate leadership effectiveness. We must take into consideration values, objectives, the means toward which the leader directs influence behavior, and the degree to which the leader is able to gain acceptance of his influence efforts. A leadership model indicating these factors is illustrated in Figure 5–3.

Leadership Approaches

The influence process is a complex one as our previous discussion has indicated, and there are many different ways of viewing the types of influence strategies which may be chosen by the leader. Research which has been carried out on leadership, however, suggests one conceptual framework for examining leader strategies which seems especially useful. This framework, which we will now explore in some detail, focuses attention on the *degree of direction* exercised by the leader in his relations with his followers.

The Authoritarian—Democratic—Laissez-Faire Continuum. Individuals holding positions of leadership in organizations and groups differ widely as to the degree to which they attempt to direct and control the behavior of those in subordinate positions. At one extreme of the directiveness continuum is a pattern of leader behavior which is often referred to as *authoritarian* leadership. The highly authoritarian leader:

FIGURE 5–3. Leader Effectiveness

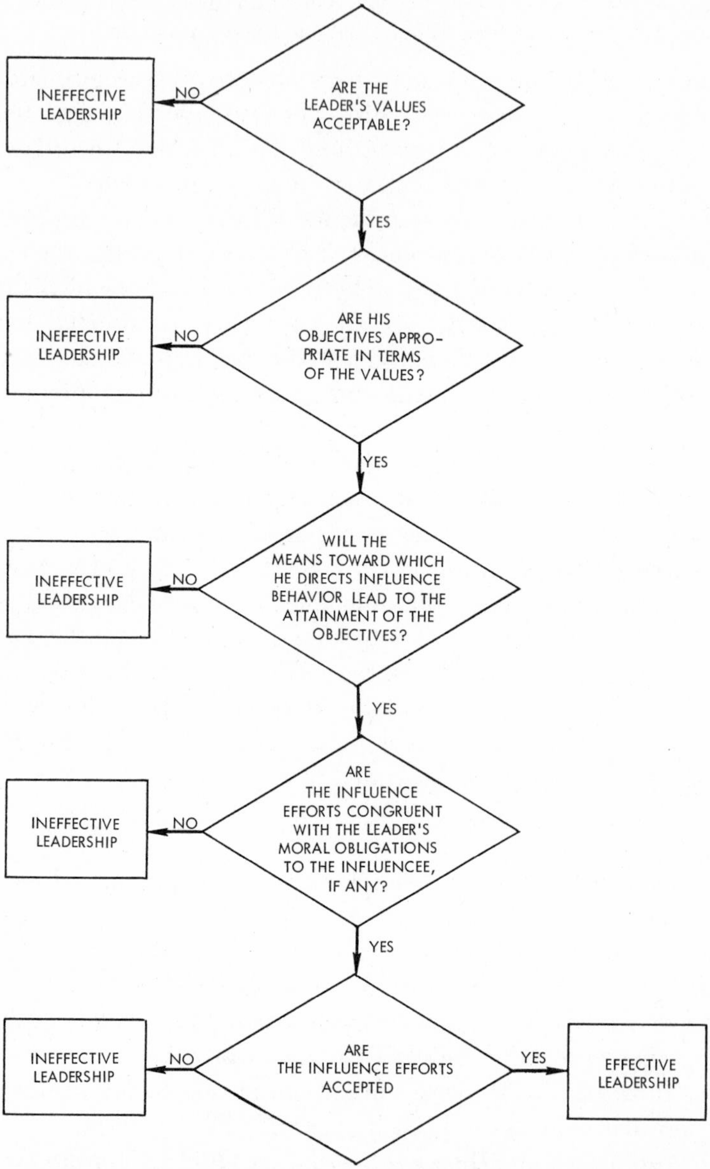

1.   Makes decisions and gives directions often without consulting with his subordinates. He supervises his people closely, checks on their behavior frequently, spells out in detail how they should perform their work, and gives them little latitude in making decisions on their own.

2.   Places emphasis on obedience and upon the status differences

between himself and his subordinates. As the leader, he is the most important, the central person, the individual with the greatest status and prestige, and it is the duty of those working under him to defer to him.

As the reader may note, such behavior represents a highly boss-centered type of leadership, in which the leader is the focal point of attention and wields considerable power:

> . . . he alone determines policies of the group; he alone makes major plans; he alone is fully cognizant of the succession of future steps in the group's activities; he alone dictates the activities of the members and the pattern of interrelations among the members; he alone serves as the ultimate agent and judge of rewards and punishments for the individual members and hence of the fate of each individual within the group structure.[19]

At the other extreme of the directiveness continuum is a type of behavior which is sometimes called *laissez-faire* leadership. The laissez-faire leader rarely sets or helps set objectives for his work group, and gives his followers little or no direction. Rather, he allows them almost complete freedom to do what they wish to do. Or, as the term "laissez-faire" implies, he "lets his people alone" and attempts to exercise very little influence over them. As an example of laissez-faire leadership, we cite the following experience:

> The manager of a research-oriented staff function in a large corporation found it extremely difficult at times to decide just what his department's objectives should be or what kind of work his employees should be engaged in. His employees would frequently complete a particular study or work project and submit it to the manager. (These were often filed away by the manager because he couldn't decide just what should be done with them). The manager would then be asked: "Boss, what project do you think we should work on next?" The reply: "Well, I don't know. Do whatever you want to do." The employees would then raise some suggestions as to possible courses of action which might be appropriate. Again, however, the manager would find it difficult to commit himself, and the conversation would often end with no conclusions being reached as to what work should be undertaken.

The behavior of many managers falls somewhere in the middle range, rather than at either extreme of the directiveness continuum. This middle range is often referred to as *democratic* leadership or general supervision.[20] The democratic leader:

---

[19] David Krech and Richard S. Crutchfield, *Theory and Problems of Social Psychology* (New York: McGraw-Hill Book Company, Inc., 1948), p. 423. Copyright © 1948 by and used by permission of the McGraw-Hill Book Company.

[20] Some researchers in examining the directiveness variable have utilized only two categories to describe leader behavior—"close supervision" as contrasted with "general

1.   Unlike his laissez-faire counterpart, sets objectives, makes decisions, gives direction and does not give his subordinates extreme latitude in their behavior;

2.   Unlike the authoritarian, however, does not attempt to control his subordinates closely or insist on spelling out in detail the ways that they should behave. Rather, he encourages his followers to help set objectives and make decisions, gives them considerable freedom to act on their own within certain prescribed limits, and encourages their creativity and development. Although he recognizes status differences, he does not emphasize them—rather he treats his followers more as equals than does the authoritarian leader. Nor does he stress obedience as does the authoritarian—he invites criticism of his own ideas and welcomes the suggestions of others when they are appropriate.

An Evaluation of Leadership Approaches.   We will now turn our attention to an analysis of the conditions under which the different types of leadership previously described seem to be most effective. Before doing so, however, two preliminary observations are in order. First, we should reemphasize that we are examining a *continuum* of behavior ranging from highly directive to highly permissive, and that we are using the terms "authoritarian," "democratic," and "laissez-faire" simply to describe general ranges on the continuum, rather than clear-cut, neatly distinguishable categories of behavior.

Second, the reader should recognize that any given leader—although he *generally* exhibits behavior which may be described as authoritarian, democratic, or laissez-faire—will usually vary in the degree of directiveness which he exerts from time to time. In fact, we contend that the most effective leader is one who *is* flexible in his behavior and who *does* appropriately adjust his influence strategies to meet the requirements of different situations. This observation leads us to the key question which we intend to explore in this section: Just what are the conditions under which various types of leadership patterns seem most effective?

A number of research studies which have examined the influence process in groups and organizations *in our culture* have suggested that the democratic leadership pattern (or general supervision) is

---

supervision." See, for example, D. Katz, N. Maccoby and N. Morse, *Productivity, Supervision and Morale in an Office Situation* (Ann Arbor, Mich.: Institute for Social Research, 1950). Their conception of general supervision, however, does not imply the complete or near complete lack of direction characterized by laissez-faire leadership but rather is similar to the democratic leadership pattern as we describe it.

generally the most appropriate.[21] Supporters of democratic leadership have pointed out that when followers are permitted to participate in making decisions for their group or organization they will tend to: (1) gain a greater understanding of the work in which they are involved, and (2) give greater support for the programs developed and decisions made. Further, the democratic pattern seems to provide a better answer to the problem of leader succession than does the authoritarian pattern. If, in the business organization, a manager allows none of his subordinates to make any important.decisions or to assume any major responsibilities, it is not likely that any of them will be prepared to take over his duties when he leaves the company or is promoted to a higher position. On the other hand, if he has given his subordinates considerable responsibility, one or more of them may be ready to step into his job immediately should the need arise.

Other observers, however, have seriously questioned the efficacy of the democratic pattern, at least in the modern business organization.[22] Robert N. McMurry, for example, in suggesting as an ideal managerial leadership philosophy one which he refers to as "benevolent autocracy," takes the following position:

I do not doubt . . . [that the humanistic or democratic-participative philosophy of management] . . . is superior to blind autocracy, especially when the latter leads to the development of a great inchoate and bumbling bureaucracy. Democratic leadership is obviously more productive. It stimulates and builds men; it invariably enhances morale. It has everything to recom-

---

[21] Much of this research has been conducted by the Institute for Social Research at the University of Michigan. See, for example, *ibid.*, and D. Katz, N. Maccoby, G. Gurin, and L. G. Floor, *Productivity, Supervision, and Morale Among Railroad Workers* (Ann Arbor, Mich.: Institute for Social Research, 1951). Many of the ideas drawn from the research of the Institute may also be found in Rensis Likert, *New Patterns of Management* (New York: McGraw-Hill, 1961). It should also be noted that other research has indicated that a greater degree of leader direction may be more effective in certain other nations, where cultural values are different. As Cecil Gibb has noted: "Many studies, particularly of the German culture, have given support to the hypothesis that authoritarian leadership is more highly valued, and more efficient, in authoritarian cultures." *Op. cit.*, p. 910.

[22] Some small group research has also indicated that under certain conditions the democratic pattern may be less effective than the authoritarian. For example, in one such study, it was found that in making repetitive routine decisions with a computerized business simulation, groups comprised of both authoritarian leaders and followers (as measured by a psychological test) performed more effectively than groups comprised of either: (1) equalitarian (democratic) leaders and equalitarian followers or (2) equalitarian leaders and authoritarian followers. See M. William Frey, "An Experimental Study of the Influence of Disruptive Interactions Induced by Authoritarian-Equalitarian Leader-Follower Combinations upon the Decision-Making Effectiveness of Small Groups." Doctoral Dissertation, The Pennsylvania State University, 1963.

mend it except for the one fact that only in a relatively few small, socially well-integrated, and homogeneous groups—for example the New England town meeting, the British Foreign Office, or some types of family-run firms—can it really be made to work.[23]

To support these observations, McMurry argues that many individuals prefer regimentation, that most top level managers in business organizations tend to be autocratic, and that most decision making in the firm must be centralized and structured.

Unlike the democratic and authoritarian approaches, the laissez-faire pattern of leadership has few supporters today, and generally does not seem to be too effective. As indicated earlier, most people have some needs for dependence and at times want to rely on and receive direction from a leader figure. A complete, or almost complete lack of direction, usually leads to a highly ambiguous and unstructured situation for the followers, tends to frustrate their dependence needs, and is likely to result in chaos, confusion, and hostility toward the leader. In the department headed by the highly laissez-faire oriented manager in our previous illustration, for example, the employees spent considerable time discussing "what was wrong with the boss" and reading or working on mathematical problems unrelated to their work just to keep themselves occupied.

The key question for managerial analysis, however, is *not which* leadership approach is *generally* most effective, but rather is, *under what specific conditions* do the varying degrees of directiveness seem most appropriate? Unfortunately, research dealing with leadership has not provided us with precise or complete answers to this question. However, certain observations may be made regarding the kinds of situations in which more or less directive leader influence efforts seem to be most effective.

One useful framework for analyzing this problem has been developed by Tannenbaum and Schmidt.[24] These observers suggest that in analyzing the manager's choice of a leadership pattern, one must examine certain forces: (1) in the subordinate, (2) in the situation, and (3) in the manager. We will now examine each of these three classes of variables.

The Follower Variable. In selecting influence strategies, it is important for the manager to consider the personality system of the follower first of all. As we have indicated previously, some in-

---

[23] Robert N. McMurry, "The Case for Benevolent Autocracy," *Harvard Business Review,* 36 (Jan.–Feb., 1958), p. 85.

[24] Robert Tannenbaum and Warren H. Schmidt, "How to Choose a Leadership Pattern," *Harvard Business Review,* 36 (March–April, 1958), 95–101.

dividuals have fairly strong dependence needs and function best when they are closely directed and controlled; while others prefer to assume more responsibility, to be given greater freedom, and to rely less heavily on the leader for direction. In addition, the knowledge and experience of the follower are important considerations in the leader's choice of an influence pattern. A new and inexperienced employee, for example, or one who possesses only a modicum of intellectual ability, may be unable to deal with the problems he faces on the job unless the method of handling them is spelled out in detail for him by his supervisor. On the other hand, a highly capable, seasoned employee may have the knowledge and ability to perform most of his duties with very little supervision. Finally, as Tannenbaum and Schmidt point out, less direction tends to be required on the part of the manager for those situations in which subordinates "are interested in . . . [a] . . . problem and feel that it is important" and "understand and identify with the goals of the organization." [25]

The Situation Variable. Optimally, the leader's degree of directiveness should be conditioned by the follower variable and by certain other forces existing in the particular situation where his influence is exerted. The *time available* for making a decision is one variable which must be considered when a leader is deciding to what extent he should permit his subordinates to participate in making a particular decision. When decisions have to be made quickly, there may not be time for consultation, and he may be forced to act on his own. Leader decisions involving the amount of subordinate participation should take into consideration the nature and complexity of the problem involved. In some situations,

> the more complex a problem, the more anxious a manager will be to get some assistance in solving it. However, this is not always the case. There will be times when the very complexity of the problem calls for one person to work it out. For example, if the manager has most of the background and factual data relevant to a given issue, it may be easier for him to think it through himself than to take the time to fill in his staff on all the pertinent background information.[26]

It is also important to know how serious the consequences may be if a problem is handled improperly. Failure on the part of a subordinate to deal correctly with a relatively minor problem may cost the company only a few dollars; and the loss may be offset by the learning

---

[25] *Ibid.*, p. 99.
[26] *Ibid.*, p. 100.

gained from the experience. If, however, a poor decision may cost his company many thousands of dollars, the manager may be much more likely to make the decision himself, rather than delegating its handling to any of those who work for him.

The type of organization or group in which the leader functions will have a bearing on the varying degrees of directiveness which seem to be appropriate. As we indicated earlier, the informal leader generally needs to consider the needs and objectives of his group to a greater extent than the formal leader. For this reason, he "is more restricted in his behavior . . . [than the formal leader] . . . both as regards the degree of authoritarian control he can exert and the degree of *laissez-faire* he can get away with." [27] Furthermore, in the formal organization the behavior, attitudes, and philosophy of top-level members often condition the directiveness pattern of its lower level managers to a great extent. For example, if the president of a corporation believes in and practices either close or general supervision, his pattern will often be transmitted to his subordinates, in turn to their subordinates, and so on, down through the organization.[28] The basic reason for this is that the manager may find it necessary to practice the type of leadership that his own supervisor believes in if he wants to gain his boss's approval and move ahead in the organization.

There are also many other organization variables which may have an influence on the leadership pattern of the manager. For example, if a manager is called on to supervise a large number of subordinates, he may not have time to direct each of them closely, and may be forced into a pattern of general supervision. Or, if a manager's subordinates work in locations quite distant from him geographically (e.g., a field sales force), he may be compelled to give them considerable freedom in making day-to-day decisions. We will discuss in greater detail organizational variables such as these in our later chapters on organization.

The Leader Variable. Finally, it should be recognized that both the needs and values of the leader may have a considerable influence on the type of leadership pattern which he will choose. In this respect, the leader's choice of an influence strategy may often be *constrained* by the nature of his own personality system. That is, even though a specified degree of directiveness may be optimal with

---

[27] Gibb, *op. cit.*, p. 908.

[28] Katz, Maccoby, and Morse, for example, in their study of productivity and morale among office workers, found that close supervisors more frequently worked under managers practicing close supervision and that general supervisors more often worked for supervisors who practiced general supervision.

regard to the follower's needs and abilities in any given situation, the leader may find it uncomfortable and difficult or in some cases impossible to make such a choice. For example, the individual who has learned to function, say in an authoritarian manner, may be unable to tolerate psychologically the thought of giving his subordinates considerable latitude in making decisions on their own. Or, the manager's general level of confidence in himself and others may have a bearing on his choice of a leadership pattern. "Managers differ greatly in the amount of trust they have in other people generally, and this carries over to the particular employees they supervise at a given time." [29] If a manager has relatively little confidence in his subordinates, he may believe it necessary to supervise their work closely; whereas if he has considerable faith in their abilities, he is less likely to do so. Furthermore, confidence in his own ability to function in uncertain situations is likely to condition his choice of leadership strategies. This is because the manager becomes less certain as to how it will be handled when he turns the responsibility for dealing with a problem over to a subordinate. For this reason those individuals who have a strong need for predictable and unambiguous situations often find it very difficult to delegate major responsibilities to others.

The Directiveness Variable: Some Further Observations. At this point some further observations are in order concerning leader directiveness. First, although we have treated separately three classes of variables in our discussion above—the leader, the follower, and the situation—it should be recognized that all three must be considered simultaneously, and in mutual interaction with one another in the analysis of any particular situation. For instance, in deciding on how closely he wants to supervise an employee whom he plans to have handle a certain problem, the manager might simultaneously consider his general level of confidence in the man, the employee's previous experience in handling similar problems, and the complexity of the problem.

Second we should point out briefly some of the ways in which the leader's social power, discussed earlier, is interrelated with his choice of directiveness strategies. With respect to this interrelationship, it may be postulated that:

1. The leader's social power may be enhanced by his choice of directiveness strategies which are *perceived* as appropriate by the

---

[29] Tannenbaum and Schmidt, *op. cit.*, p. 99.

follower. For example, a subordinate who has a strong preference for general supervision would more likely be attracted to and identify with a superior who does not direct him closely than to one who does, all other factors being the same.

2. The stronger the leader's bases of social power, the more likely it is that the influencee will *attempt* to accede to his influence efforts, no matter how directive or permissive they may be, all other factors being the same. We emphasize the word "attempt" here to take into account the fact that the influencee may *lack the ability* to follow instructions successfully which have been spelled out for him only in a very general manner, even though he tries to do so.

SUMMARY

Leadership may be most appropriately thought of as an influence process. A number of needs may be satisfied by the assumption of either the leader or follower role, although neither is without its problems. Analysis of the individual's inclination to accept the influence efforts of others may be undertaken in terms of both his own need system and of the social power of the influencer. Evaluating the effectiveness of any given leader behavior is a complex problem for we must consider not only whether the influence effort is accepted, but also the leader's values and objectives and the means toward which the influence behavior is directed. Many different degrees of directiveness may be chosen by the leader in his attempts to influence others, ranging from highly directive to highly permissive. The appropriateness of these strategies will vary considerably depending upon the leader, the follower, and the specific situation in which they are utilized. In essence then, our approach to leadership is a situationist one, in which we ask not what kind of leadership is universally best, but rather, *under what conditions* do each of various types of leader patterns seem most effective.

DISCUSSION AND STUDY QUESTIONS

1. How might occupying the role of a follower satisfy an individual's needs?
2. Discuss Fromm's concept of "escape from freedom" in terms of dependence and independence needs.
3. Select from among your friends and acquaintances a person whom you consider possesses considerable "leadership" ability. Can you think of any instances in which this individual was not effective in influencing others? In each case, indicate why.

4. Do you subscribe to the philosophy "once a leader, always a leader"? Why?

5. What problems might arise if an employee with very strong dependence needs were supervised by a manager whose leadership style was generally quite permissive? Why?

6. "Successful top level managers do not reach their positions by letting others make their decisions. Management is decision making; managers cannot avoid choices. Rather, the very aggressiveness and drive necessary to reach the top in a competitive firm requires heavy reliance on decisive authoritarian leadership methods. Thus, we cannot expect top managers to utilize democratic leadership techniques even if such methods might be effective in motivating subordinates." Evaluate the above statements.

7. "Empathy" has been defined as the ability to imagine oneself in the situation of another. How would this ability be useful in the leadership process?

8. Discuss the hypothesis "If a manager in an organization consistently employs authoritarian leadership methods, many attempts by his subordinate managers to employ democratic leadership techniques may be ineffective."

9. "Strong leaders" who employ authoritarian methods in directing their followers tend to have strong independence needs. Do you agree? Why?

10. Evaluate the leadership effectiveness of a manager who successfully influences one of his employees to take a job with a competitor firm so he can steal a number of their latest engineering designs.

11. Identify the bases of power implied in these statements by leaders to subordinates:
    a) I know that you disagree with me on this project, but I've made up my mind, and since I'm the boss, it's your obligation to accept my thinking.
    b) If you continue being obstinate, I'll have to lay you off for three days.
    c) If you take on this work, I'll recommend you for a raise.
    d) If you don't take on this work, I'll have to cut your salary.
    e) On the basis of my computer analysis, we should try to diversify our product line.
    f) You'd make me very pleased if you did an especially good job on this project.
    g) These activities were recommended by our management consultants.

12. Joe Blasco, co-captain of a large university's nationally-ranked football team, is well thought of by both players and coaches. Other members of the team seek his advice regarding running, tackling, blocking, and throwing. Joe exerts considerable influence upon his teammates both on the field as well as in the general "skull sessions" held by the team. When the team is traveling, Joe is always around to give advice and answer questions about future opponents.

      One evening, as Joe and his girl friend are returning from a dance, they come upon the scene of a serious automobile accident immediately after two cars have crashed. Joe slams on his brakes, and leaps from the car, only to become stunned at the sight of the near fatal conditions of the passengers of the wrecked automobiles. While Joe is deliberating on a course of action, another motorist, Bill Runt, drives up in an old pick-up truck, steps down and hands Joe a flashlight telling him to direct traffic around the scene of the accident. Next, Bill commands Joe's date to hurry to a neighboring farmhouse and call first an ambulance and second the state police. Then he quickly begins to apply pressure to a badly bleeding wound of one of the victims.

Bill is a "pint-sized" office clerk, and is a high school graduate with average intelligence. For some time, he has attended weekly meetings of a first aid class given by his local Red Cross Chapter.

Discuss the above situation in light of what you have read in Chapter 5 regarding leadership and influence.

SELECTED REFERENCES

BASS, BERNARD M.   *Leadership, Psychology and Organizational Behavior.* New York: Harper & Brothers, 1960.

FRENCH, JOHN R. P., JR., and RAVEN, BERTRAM.   "The Bases of Social Power," in Dorwin Cartwright (ed.). *Studies in Social Power.* Ann Arbor, Mich.: Institute for Social Research, 1959.

FROMM, ERICH.   *Escape from Freedom.* New York: Farrar and Rinehart, 1941.

GIBB, CECIL A.   "Leadership," in Gardner Lindzey (ed.). *Handbook of Social Psychology,* Vol. II. Cambridge, Mass.: Addison-Wesley Publishing Company, 1954, 877–920.

GOULDNER, ALVIN W. (ed.).   *Studies in Leadership.* New York: Harper & Brothers, 1950.

JENNINGS, EUGENE E.   *An Anatomy of Leadership: Princes, Heroes, and Supermen.* New York: Harper & Brothers, 1960.

KATZ, D.; MACCOBY, N.; and MORSE, N.   *Productivity, Supervision and Morale in an Office Situation.* Ann Arbor, Mich.: Institute for Social Research, 1950.

KRECH, DAVID, and CRUTCHFIELD, RICHARD S.   *Theory and Problems of Social Psychology.* New York: McGraw-Hill Book Company, Inc., 1948, Chapter 11.

LIKERT, RENSIS.   *New Patterns of Management.* New York: McGraw-Hill Book Company, Inc., 1961.

McMURRY, ROBERT N.   "The Case for Benevolent Autocracy," *Harvard Business Review,* 36 (Jan.–Feb., 1958), 82–90.

STRAUSS, GEORGE, and SAYLES, LEONARD R.   *Personnel: The Human Problems of Management.* Englewood Cliffs, N. J.: Prentice-Hall, Inc., 1960, Chapter 6.

TANNENBAUM, ROBERT; WESCHLER, IRVING R.; and MASSARIK, FRED.   *Leadership and Organization: A Behavioral Science Approach.* New York: McGraw-Hill Book Co., Inc., 1961.

CHAPTER 6

GROUP BEHAVIOR

T HE behavior of the member of the business firm is influenced by a number of variables in mutual interaction with one other. One of the most important of these is his membership in one or more social groups within the organization. Beginning with the now famous "Hawthorne" studies conducted at the Western Electric Company in the late 1920's,[1] research into organizational behavior has indicated that employees usually do not react to their work environment as isolated individuals. Rather, their behavior and attitudes toward their jobs and toward management are conditioned to a considerable extent by the values, standards, and expectations of the work groups to which they belong. For this reason, it is important for the manager to have some understanding of the dynamics of those groups in the organization with which he must deal so as to have a basis for predicting the impact of his decision strategies on their attitudes and behavior.

Our purpose in this chapter is to provide a conceptual framework for understanding the behavior of organizational work groups. In doing so, we will focus attention on both (1) some of the kinds of work group behavior of greatest concern to managerial decision making, and (2) certain major classes of variables which influence these patterns of behavior.

GROUP BEHAVIOR: SOME FUNDAMENTAL CONSIDERATIONS

People belong to many different groups. Some are comprised of many members; others are small in size. Some function for only short periods of time; others may endure for many years. Membership in some groups is extremely important for the individual, while his

---

[1] For a report of this research, see F. J. Roethlisberger and W. J. Dickson, *Management and the Worker* (Cambridge, Mass.: Harvard University Press, 1939).

association with other groups may contribute only slightly to his need satisfaction.

The primary and most basic group to which the individual belongs is his family. Here, he is cared for as an infant and child; frequent interaction with others takes place, and close and enduring relationships are developed. In addition, most people belong to a number of other groups—school groups, church groups, social clubs, civic groups, and, of most concern to us here, business organizations and small face-to-face work groups within business organizations.

Definition of a "Group"

Although we are all familiar with many of these different kinds of groups, the meaning of the term "group" is subject to many different interpretations. Our preference is to view a group as *two or more persons, working together in pursuit of some common objective or objectives, the attainment of which through concerted effort will provide some need satisfaction for each.*[2] Thus, we would consider a number of teen-age boys who associate with each other as a "neighborhood gang" as a social group. Or, in the business organization, a team of engineers working together toward the development of an intercontinental ballistic missile would constitute a group, as would a number of employees who band together to protest to their supervisor about a new work rule which they consider to be unfair.

One further observation needs to be made concerning our meaning of the term "group." Above, we have referred to work groups as existing *within* organizations. However, we may also consider the organization *itself* as a group in light of our definition. Business firms (except for small one-man operations) are comprised of two or more persons working together to meet certain organizational objectives; and the attainment of such objectives enables their individual members to gain some needed satisfaction. As Krech and Crutchfield have pointed out:

Although we can distinguish between psychological groups and social organizations, these two have much in common. In the first place, the very same social group can, at certain times and under certain conditions, simultaneously qualify as either. . . . In the second place, and this is of the greatest significance . . . many of the most basic generalizations about psychological

[2] Our definition is somewhat similar to that suggested by: Cecil A. Gibb, "Leadership," in *Handbook of Social Psychology*, ed. Gardner Lindzey, Vol. II (Cambridge, Mass.: Addison-Wesley Publishing Company, Inc., 1954), p. 879.

groups apply to social organizations. This is merely a reflection of the fact that both kinds of groups are special instances of social groups.[3]

In effect then, the business firm may be viewed as one larger group comprised of many smaller sub-groups. It will be upon these sub-groups that we will focus primary attention in this chapter. Then, in Chapters 7–10, we will examine the organizational structure of the firm as a whole, and its relationship to the behavior of these smaller groups.

Group Membership and Need Satisfaction

People join groups and organizations for many different reasons. In some instances, an individual's membership in a particular group may be completely involuntary—e.g., the baby has no choice whatsoever as to the family group into which he is born. In other cases, a person has some choice as to his group memberships, although there may be strong pressures imposed upon him to join (or not to join) a particular group. For example, an employee in the business firm who has been transferred to a department in which he does not care to work, may be able to avoid membership in the new work group only by giving up his job and leaving the organization. In still other cases, one's group memberships may be on a highly voluntary basis. For instance, the individual may be under little or no pressure from others to join, or not to join, a bridge club, bowling team, or civic group.

As is true with most behavior, people are motivated to join groups and participate in their activities in order to help satisfy certain needs. More specifically, the following observations may be made concerning group membership and need satisfaction.

1.   The satisfaction of any or all of the five basic classes of needs discussed in Chapter 4 may be contributed to by virtue of an individual's membership in a group. For example, satisfaction of many of the child's physiological, safety, and other needs obtain from his membership in the family group; the individual may gain considerable acceptance and recognition from his association with the other employees in his work group; or a person's endeavor in a civic group may contribute to the satisfaction of his self-actualization needs.

---

[3] David Krech and Richard S. Crutchfield, *Theory and Problems of Social Psychology* (New York: McGraw-Hill Book Company, Inc., 1948), p. 370. Copyright © 1948 by and used by permission of the McGraw-Hill Book Company.

2.   Groups are not equally responsive to the needs of their various members. As we will indicate more fully later, some group members usually enjoy greater prestige and status, and have more influence than others. In fact, groups are often dominated by a few individuals, while the remaining members assume a relatively passive role in making group decisions. In consequence, most groups serve to meet the current needs of their more influential members and "the function of any group can be better understood in terms of the major needs of its more dominant members than in undifferentiated terms for all of its members." [4]

3.   A certain amount of conflict will probably always exist between group objectives and the needs of its members. The reader will recall from our discussion in Chapter 4 that some observers have held that the requirements of formal organizations are incongruent with the needs of the mature individual. Although the small face-to-face group may often be more responsive to its member needs than the large organization, even in such groups we may expect to find some degree of incongruency. One reason for this is that, as indicated above, these groups are often dominated by a few members, with the remaining membership having relatively little say in making group decisions. In addition, the individual may find himself in a conflict situation by virtue of his membership in a number of groups of which two or more have opposing objectives. For example, an employee (1) whose family group places a high premium on hard work, and (2) who has considerable loyalty to the business organization for which he works, may find himself a member of a work group within the firm which imposes strong pressures on him to restrict production.

The above discussion raises the questions: (1) Under what conditions will an individual decide to join or leave any given group (assuming he has any choice in the matter); and (2) To what extent will he be inclined to accept the values and objectives of any group of which he is a member? In answering these questions, we suggest —as we did previously in Chapter 5 with respect to the individual's acceptance of leader influence efforts—that a person will join, withdraw from, or accept the values of a group when he perceives that he will probably gain greater net need satisfaction by doing so, than by not doing so. For example, as we will point out more fully below, an organizational employee may restrict his production and hence his

---

[4] *Ibid.*, p. 382.

earnings in order to avoid being rejected by his work group because the belongingness needs at stake loom more important than the economic rewards involved.

WORK GROUP BEHAVIOR: A SYSTEMS ANALYSIS

Now that some general observations have been made about groups, we will turn our attention to a description and analysis of some of the kinds of organizational work group behavior of greatest interest to management and to an exploration of certain important variables which influence such behavior.

Analysis of work group behavior is complex because of the multiple interrelationships existing among the many variables which are involved. In developing a conceptual framework geared toward considering these complexities, we find it useful to draw on some of the concepts from our discussion of the systems approach in Chapter 3. In doing so, we will: (1) view the work group as a sub-system within the total organizational system of the firm, and (2) focus attention on certain classes of sub-system inputs and outputs, and their interrelationships. A schematic model of this systems view is illustrated in Figure 6-1.

In our model, the behavior and attitudes of the work group represent the *outputs* of the sub-system, and are generated by member decision *transformations*. For the purposes of conceptualization, we have grouped these outputs into three general classes:

1.   Group objectives, norms and standards,
2.   Concerted action taken by group members, and
3.   Patterns of differentiated member behavior—i.e., differences among individuals in the kinds of attitudes and behavior which they exhibit as members of any particular group.

The decision transformations made by any group, are in turn, influenced by many different kinds of *inputs* into the sub-system. In our model, these are grouped into two major classes:

1.   Group membership—i.e., the output of any group is influenced considerably by the needs, values, etc., of the *particular* personalities of which it is made up.
2.   The organizational environment in which the group functions —types of work performed, supervisory actions taken affecting the group, etc., also influences the output.

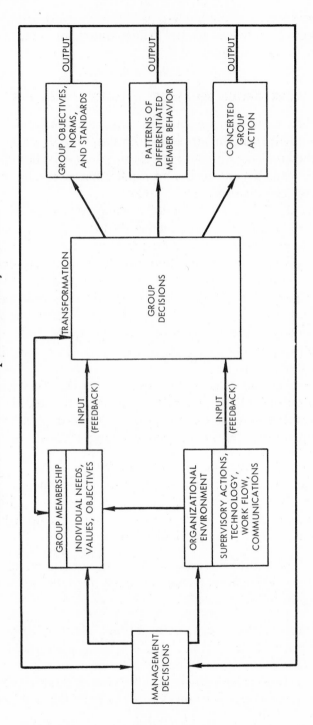

FIGURE 6–1. Work Group Behavior: A Systems View

The nature of each of these two input classes is conditioned considerably by various types of managerial decisions, as we will indicate later.

The basic reason why our work group model is framed in terms of inputs and outputs rather than independent and dependent variables is that the variables with which we are dealing are *interdependent*. For instance, not only may concerted action by a work group be influenced by management decisions, but it in turn may also influence actions taken by management. Such interdependence among the variables with which we are dealing may be illustrated by the following example:

A number of employees in a manufacturing plant where the work performed was frequently quite dirty made it a habit of leaving their work places fifteen or twenty minutes before quitting time to wash up. This was done even though no provision existed for clean-up time in the union contract. Their departmental supervisor decided to curb this practice and posted a notice to the effect that those who left early in the future would be disciplined. The members of his work group resented this action, and decided that they would ignore the supervisor's warning. The following day all but three members of the group left their work places seventeen minutes early and were subsequently given an oral warning (the first step in the company's disciplinary procedure) by the supervisor. Angered by the action, the group decided that it would engage in a production slowdown and restrict its output to the minimum acceptable level. After the slowdown had been in effect for three days, the matter was brought to the attention of top management. Shortly thereafter, a compromise agreement was negotiated with the union whereby employees in the department were given ten minutes of clean-up time at the end of each day.

As the reader will observe, we have illustrated in the above example what might be termed a "behavioral chain reaction" in which a series of mutually interdependent actions were taken by management and a work group. From the point of view of the group as a sub-system, the supervisor's actions constituted information inputs on the basis of which group decisions (substantive transformations) were made to engage in protest behavior (output). On the other hand, if we were to view this situation from the viewpoint of management and the total organizational system, the group's behavior would represent information inputs from a sub-system, with the supervisor's decisions constituting transformations, and his actions, outputs. The behavior illustrated in our example is viewed from the vantage point of both the total organizational system and the group sub-system in Figure 6–2.

FIGURE 6–2. The Work Group Sub-System and the
Organizational System
As Viewed by the Total Organizational System

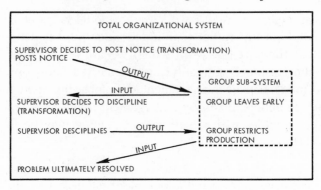

As Viewed by the Work Group Sub-System

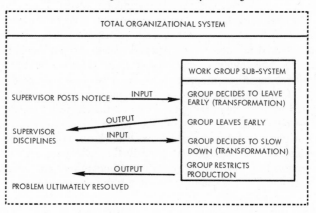

We will now turn our attention to a more detailed analysis of work group behavior. In doing so we will first make some observations about managerial decisions and the work group membership input. Then, we will examine the three major classes of outputs in our model, and some of their relationships to the sub-system inputs.

Managerial Decisions and the Group Membership Inputs

In examining work group behavior, it is important to recognize that the employee in the business organization frequently is *not* a member of a *single* group. Rather, he often enjoys membership in more than one such group. Our purpose in this section is to describe briefly four different *types* of work groups which have been observed to exist frequently within the business organization, and to indicate

how managerial decisions may influence the formation and composition of each.[5] These types of groups are:

1. The *command* group, which is comprised of all employees reporting to the same supervisor.

2. The *task* group, which is made up of those employees who
collaborate in some way on a given job or task. Within a research
and development department, for example, four or five engineers
may work closely together over a period of time on a particular sub-
phase of a project.

3. The *interest* group, which includes those employees who have
banded together in order to promote some common objective relating
to the organization. Employees forming such groups may or may
not work together on a common task, or be under the command of
the same supervisor. A number of milling machine operators in a
plant, for example, regardless of department, may unite to press
management for looser production standards, or improved seniority
rights.

4. The *friendship* clique, comprised of those members of the
organization who associate together on the basis of ties of friendship. Such groups may converse with each other during working
hours, take their coffee breaks together, or sometimes extend their
on-the-job associations to such outside activities as a bowling team
or monthly poker club.

The composition of any given command or task group within the
organization is basically determined by managerial *selection* and
assignment decisions. Although once employed by the organization,
an individual may succeed in being transferred away from the command of a particular supervisor, or may have some say as to the tasks
to which he will be assigned, it is management which ultimately
decides which employees it will hire, to which department they will
be assigned, and upon which tasks they will work.

Management, on the other hand, does not assign particular organizational members to any given interest group—groups of this type
are voluntarily formed. However, the composition (membership
inputs) of interest groups may be influenced considerably by any

---

[5] Our classification of work groups by type in this section is drawn from Leon-
ard R. Sayles, *Research in Industrial Human Relations*, Industrial Relations Research
Association (New York: Harper, 1957), pp. 131–45, as reprinted in "Work Group
Behavior and the Larger Organization," in I. L. Heckmann, Jr. and S. G. Huneryager,
Human Relations in Management (Cincinnati, Ohio: South-Western Publishing Co.,
1960), pp. 231–43.

one of a number of different kinds of managerial decisions. For example, the manner in which pay and seniority provisions, production standards, and other working conditions have been effected for those selected for and assigned to various jobs in the firm will determine to a considerable extent just which members of the organization do have interests in common which may lead them to band together to enhance their position.

Membership in the friendship clique is also basically voluntary. These groups represent

. . . the diverse interests of the workers placed there by the organization. The boundaries of these clusterings appear to reflect the employees' off-the-job interests and associations or previous work experience. Age, ethnic background, outside activities, sex, marital status, and so on, comprise the mortar that binds the clique together.[6]

Even though membership in the friendship clique is largely voluntary, its composition is influenced by the formal command and task structure of the organization to the extent that physical proximity tends to facilitate friendship associations. That is, there is a greater opportunity for those employees who see each other every day on the job to get to know one another; and, hence, by assigning particular employees to physically proximate work stations, management is, in effect, influencing considerably the membership inputs of those cliques which form in the organization.

From the above discussion we can see that both of the two major input classes in our group sub-system model are influenced by managerial decisions. Through employee selection and assignment, management determines where specific personalities are to be placed within the organization. Such placement decisions, coupled with those establishing the types of work environment in which each member of the firm is to function, influence considerably the formation and composition of particular work groups. *Once formed,* the behavioral and attitudinal outputs of any such group will also be a function of the specific personalities which comprise it and the organizational environment in which it exists. We will now turn our attention to the first of our three major classes of work group outputs —objectives, norms and standards.

Group Objectives, Norms and Standards

Work Group Objectives. Work groups, as indicated previously, establish objectives; these objectives are conditioned considerably

---

[6] *Ibid.,* p. 233.

by member needs, and are also influenced by the organizational environment.

Although the objectives of different work groups will vary considerably, certain general observations may be made about the goals of the four different types of work groups described above. Both the command and task groups are formed to meet organizational objectives—employees are assigned to specific departments and tasks in order to carry out the work to be undertaken by the firm. Task and command groups, however, may or may not fully accept the objectives laid down for them by management, and may develop goals of their own.

For example, task groups often develop work methods that may depart from the organization's original conception of the job, or at least . . . ["fill in"] . . . the specific details of the operation not specified in the formal work plan . . . employees may exchange repetitive jobs, although such trading is illegal; one worker may do two jobs while a colleague rests; or, . . . they may change the sequence of the operations to reduce tensions and provide short cuts.[7]

Both interest groups and friendship cliques, on the other hand, are voluntarily formed to meet member objectives rather than those of the organization. The objectives of the interest group, as indicated above, are geared toward enhancing or protecting some common interest of its membership—improved work methods, pay, etc. A primary goal of the friendship clique, on the other hand, is to meet the belongingness needs of its members on the job. Somewhat relatedly, membership in the friendship clique also "provides a source of personal security in an impersonal environment." This is because:

Loyalty, even attachment, to the total organization with its impersonality, extended hierarchy, and social distance becomes ambiguous. However, attachment to the immediate and easily perceived face-to-face group is the predominant reality of organization experience.[8]

Work Group Norms and Standards. As a means of gearing member actions toward their various objectives, work groups invariably develop certain attitudinal and behavioral standards to which it is expected that their members will conform. The attitudes and viewpoints which group members are expected to share are often referred to as *norms;* those patterns of behavior toward which conformity is expected, *standards.* We have already observed the manifestation of a group standard in the illustration presented in a pre-

---

[7] *Ibid.*, p. 235.
[8] *Ibid.*, p. 233.

vious section—i.e., concerted action to restrict output in protest of
the supervisor's efforts to curb the practice of leaving the job early
to wash up. The following are some examples of work group norms
which might be found in the business firm: "Our jobs are the most
important in the plant"; "Our supervisor tries to help us whenever
he can"; or, "We are not being paid enough considering the high
level of skill required for our jobs."

Enforcement of Norms and Standards. Various degrees of conformity to different norms and standards may be found among members of any particular work group. While some group attitudes and
standards of behavior may be accepted by all members, others may
conflict strongly with the needs and values of certain individuals
within the group, and for this reason be rejected. For example, an
employee in a work group in which the restriction of production
is viewed as an important standard may refuse to limit his output
because he feels a strong need to earn as much money as he can so
as to be able to send his children to college.

Notwithstanding such differences, however, strong pressures are
often exerted by the work group on its individual members which
renders nonconformity to norms and standards difficult if they are
to remain within the group. The nature and effectiveness of these
pressures can perhaps be best understood by drawing on some of
the concepts which we have examined previously—by viewing the
group's ability to influence its member's behavior in terms of member needs and the bases of social power which the group possesses.

A basic reason why individuals are often inclined to be influenced
by group norms and standards even though such conformity may
conflict with certain other needs experienced and values held is that
they want to identify with, be a part of, and be accepted by the
group. In much the same way as with identification with authority
figures which we discussed in Chapter 5, identification with the
group may enable the individual to incorporate psychologically the
strength of others in himself. Further, groups often have considerable power to reward those members who conform to its values and
standards, and to punish those who do not. In addition to bestowing
acceptance—a most powerful reward—upon the "regular" member,
the group may be in a position to provide assistance to its members
and help "protect" them from management. For example, the older,
and more experienced members of a group may inform those newer
members who have become accepted of short cuts in work methods
unknown to the supervisor which will result in greater earnings with

less effort, ways of avoiding being caught by supervision for breaking unpopular work rules, etc. On the other hand, the group can be
extremely punitive to those of its members who do not abide by the
norms and standards which exist. The nonconformist member may
face ostracism—his fellow workers may refuse to talk with him, or
permit him to engage in any of their social activities. Or, some cases
have even been noted in which the machines of nonconformists
have been sabotaged as a punitive measure by other members of
a group. As suggested earlier, whether any *particular* individual will
accede to the influence efforts exerted upon him by the group, will
depend upon whether he perceives that he will probably gain greater
net need satisfaction by conforming than by not doing so.

Directionality of Norms and Standards. Some observations are
now in order regarding the *direction* toward which work group
norms and standards are geared in terms of management's objectives—i.e., to what extent are such attitudinal and behavioral standards directed toward meeting organizational objectives, or, conversely, toward thwarting the aims and goals of management?

Many research studies to date have focused attention on norms
and standards *negatively* directed in terms of organizational objectives. One of the most significant areas of negatively directed work
group behavior which has been observed in a number of firms, and
especially among production employees in manufacturing enterprises, is that of output restriction. Even in cases where incentive
systems are in effect, under which employees are rewarded by additional pay for each piece of work turned out above a standard established by the firm, many work groups have been known to develop
and enforce output restriction standards. For example, where company work standards are set at 100 pieces per hour for all members
of a particular task group, and where a majority of the employees
could turn out 140 pieces with relatively little extra effort, the group
may, nevertheless, attempt to enforce the restriction of output by
its members to not more than 110 pieces.

There seem to be at least three basic reasons for such behavior.
First, work groups may attempt to restrict output because they fear
that if they do not some of their members will be out of jobs. Such
fears may be well justified, especially when the demand for a firm's
products is relatively inelastic. When this is the case, the company
may not be able to sell the increased production that would be
turned out if all workers put forth their maximum efforts, and consequently, some employees might have to be laid off. Further, in

some firms subject to highly fluctuating seasonal demand patterns, policies are followed by which numbers of employees are temporarily laid off each year during slack periods. Here also, work groups may feel that the magnitude of such layoffs will be reduced if output is restricted.

A second motive for output restrictions is to protect group members against the "tightening" of work standards by management. Sometimes incentive standards on a particular job may be set so that they can be exceeded by, say sixty or seventy percent, by most employees with maximum effort. Production at such high levels, however, might well convince management that the standards have been too loosely set, and that they need to be restudied and made more realistic.[9] On the other hand, if the group makes sure that member output never exceeds the company established standards by perhaps twenty to twenty-five percent, such actions on the part of management are less likely to be forthcoming.

A third reason for the development and enforcement of output restriction standards is to protect the older members of the work group. In our culture a commonly held value is that older and more experienced employees should enjoy greater earnings than their younger and less experienced colleagues. In the professions and in many skilled non-professional jobs, the individual's earnings normally do increase as he gains experience and becomes more competent in his work. However, in many production jobs in which (1) earnings are directly related to output and (2) considerable physical effort and vigor are called for, this cultural value may be violated in the absence of output restrictions. This is because individuals in such jobs often slow down physically as they grow older to the extent that they could be outproduced by their younger, more vigorous colleagues if the latter were to put forth maximum effort. If this were permitted to occur, many of the more experienced workers would be dealt a serious status blow, for their weekly earnings might be considerably less than those of even some of the newest men in their work group.

Although work group norms and standards are sometimes geared in directions which conflict with organizational objectives, often they are not. In fact, some work groups develop and attempt to en-

---

[9] Although some authorities insist that management should never "cut rates," others have pointed out that in practice this policy is difficult to follow. For a discussion of this problem, see George Strauss and Leonard R. Sayles, *Personnel: The Human Problems of Management* (Englewood Cliffs, N.J.: Prentice-Hall, Inc., 1960), pp. 648–49.

force upon their membership performance standards calling for both a high quality and quantity of work. Members of a firm's research and development department, for example, may adhere to high professional standards, and look down upon and reject any of their colleagues whose sloppy performance does not meet these standards. Or, in some university departments, one's prestige, status, and acceptance by his fellow professors are enhanced by a high level of output in research and writing.

Patterns of Differentiated Member Behavior

We will now turn our attention to the second major class of outputs in our sub-system model—the many differences found among members of the work group in their attitudes, behavior, and participation in group activities. In doing so, we will examine member differentiation from the point of view of: (1) role; (2) status; and (3) informal leadership.

Role Differentiation. One way of viewing differences among individuals as members of groups is to focus attention on the *roles* which they assume.[10] A role has been defined as:

. . . a patterned sequence of learned *actions* or deeds performed by a person in an interaction situation. The organizing of individual actions is a product of the perceptual and cognitive behavior of person A upon observing person B. B performs one or a number of discrete acts which A observes and organizes into a concept, a role. On the basis of this conceptualization of the actions of B, A expects certain further actions from B. . . . Once having located or named the position of . . . [B] . . . A performs certain acts which have been learned as belonging to the reciprocal position; these actions are conceptualized as A's role.[11]

There are a number of variables which determine the roles which individuals are expected to assume in their relationships with others —age, sex, and other personality characteristics, job or position held, values of the particular culture in which they live, etc. In the family, a different role is expected for the father than for the mother. At the university, the professor and the student assume different roles. Similarly, different roles are assumed by different members of organizational work groups. New members may be expected to show deference to those with greater seniority in the group; a

---

[10] For a more detailed but not overly technical discussion of the concept of a "role," see William G. Scott, *Human Relations in Management* (Homewood, Ill.: Richard D. Irwin, Inc., 1962), pp. 103 ff.

[11] Theodore R. Sarbin, "Role Theory," in *Handbook of Social Psychology*, Vol. I, p. 225.

member who is highly intelligent and adept at communicating ideas
to others may be looked to as a spokesman for the group in presenting complaints to the foreman; an individual whose religious or
ethnic background is different from that of the majority of group
members may be looked down upon and expected to play a passive
role as far as influencing group decisions is concerned.

Status Differences. Implied in the above discussion is the fact
that in the work group (as in other groups) some members enjoy
a greater degree of status than others—i.e., they are viewed as being
more important or prestigeful.[12] Within the business firm, an individual's status is a function of two major classes of variables: (1) certain of his personal characteristics and (2) his position in the "formal" organization. *In general,* men enjoy a higher status than
women; individuals of the same ethnic and religious background
as the majority of the members in their group enjoy a greater status
than those with different backgrounds; and a person's status is enhanced by personality characteristics which appeal to others—e.g.,
intelligence, a "warm and friendly" disposition, etc. As far as one's
position in the formal organization is concerned, those persons holding more important, more highly paid, and more skilled jobs will
often enjoy a higher status than those who do not, all other factors
being equal. In addition, a person's status may be enhanced if his
job calls for him to be physically located in such a manner that he
can interact frequently with other members of his group—as opposed
to being physically isolated from his colleagues.

From the above discussion, the reader may observe that an individual may possess some attributes which would tend to give him
a high status position within his group, and others which would
tend to lower his status. For example, a member of a race or religion
different from that of most of his colleagues might be the most intelligent and most highly paid employee in a particular work group.
When such is the case—i.e., when a person's status indicators are
considerably "out of line" with each other—the individual is referred to as being characterized by a low degree of *status congruence.*

Both the individual's total status and his status congruence seem
to have considerable influence on his relationships with the work
group. In a study conducted by Zaleznik, Christensen and Roethlisberger, for example, it was found that both the individual's need

---

[12] For a more thorough discussion of the concept of status, see William G. Scott,
op. cit., pp. 95–103.

satisfaction and his inclination to conform to group standards were conditioned by these two variables.[13] It was found that those individuals possessing both high total status and status congruence were more likely to be accepted by the group as "regular" members. Further, these regular members tended to be satisfied and to conform to the output standards of the group, while the nonregulars (those not accepted by the group) tended to be less satisfied and not to conform to the standards. Or, in terms of needs and motivation, those individuals who were in a position to gain some satisfaction of their belongingness needs by virtue of their acceptance by the group were willing to abide by its standards, while those for whom such acceptance was not forthcoming were not inclined to do so.

Informal Leadership. In Chapter 5 we indicated that employee behavior in the business organization is influenced not only by formally appointed supervision, but also by members of work groups who evolve as "informal leaders." We will now examine the phenomenon of informal leadership within the work group in greater detail.

Many different patterns of member influence may be observed among organizational work groups. In some groups, little or no informal leadership may evolve. In others, efforts directed toward influencing the behavior and attitudes of the group membership may be centered largely in one individual. In still others, we may find more than one person assuming the role of informal leader.

Many of the observations which we made about leadership in Chapter 5 apply to the informal as well as the formal leader—e.g., those concerning the needs satisfied by assuming the leader role, the ambivalence of the followers toward the leader, etc. There is, however, one important difference between the formal and the informal leader—the latter lacks many of the powers which the former enjoys. Unlike the formally appointed manager, the informal leader within the work group lacks both the power to discipline (or fire) his colleagues if they do not accede to his influence efforts, and the power to reward them with promotions or pay increases based on meritorious performance. Neither may he have the power to make many other types of decisions which may have an important bearing on member need satisfaction, such as scheduling overtime work, as-

---

[13] A. Zaleznik, C. R. Christensen, and F. J. Roethlisberger, *The Motivation, Productivity, and Satisfaction of Workers: A Prediction Study* (Boston: Harvard University, Division of Research, Graduate School of Business Administration, 1958).

signing employees to jobs or work projects which they may especially like or dislike, etc.

Why then, is the informal leader, although he lacks many of the powers of the formal leader, often in a position to induce other members of his group to accede to his influence efforts? Probably the most fundamental reason for the work group's acceptance of one or more of its member's assumption of the leader role is that it is necessary for this role to be fulfilled if many of the group's objectives are to be achieved. Plans of action must be initiated by one or more members of the group and then communicated to the rest of the membership. Someone must attempt to compromise differences of opinion which may exist among the group and to influence members to take a common stand on basic issues if concerted action is to be undertaken. Dealings with management can often be facilitated if one or more members are chosen as spokesmen to communicate the group's position to supervision. In short, the informal leadership serves to plan, organize, coordinate, and provide direction for the work group in its efforts to achieve its objectives.

One final question should be raised concerning informal leadership within the organizational work group: What are the characteristics of those individuals who emerge as informal leaders? As the situationist analysis presented in the previous chapter would indicate, there are few, if any specific personality characteristics universally possessed by those assuming such leader roles.[14] Rather, the characteristics of informal leaders will vary considerably from group to group. However, the informal leader will usually be a member who lives up to "the group's idealized conception of what a group member should be." [15] In a work group dominated by French-Canadian membership and values, he is likely to be of French-Canadian origin. In a work group, the majority of whose members prefer strong authoritarian "leader figures," he is likely to be an individual whose techniques of influencing others are authoritarian. In a work group in which output restrictions have been developed, he is likely to be a member whose productivity comes close to the standard set by the group. In short, the informal leader's values, objectives, behavior, etc., will tend to be congruent with that considered desirable by the group.

---

[14] Nor are supervisory styles universally effective; except, as we mentioned in Chapter 5, it is usually more difficult for the informal leader than the formal leader to practice highly authoritarian or highly laissez-faire leadership.

[15] Strauss and Sayles, *op. cit.*, p. 64.

Concerted Group Action

Now that we have discussed some of the basic differences among member behavior within the work group, we will turn our attention to those conditions under which group members behave similarly— i.e., unite to take concerted action to meet their objectives. In our discussion we will examine the concept of "cohesion" and some of the more important relationships between the inputs into the group sub-system and the concerted action output.

Work Group Cohesion. One concept which has frequently been utilized by researchers in their study of organizational work groups is that of *cohesion* or *cohesiveness.* To date, two different major approaches have been followed in attempting to measure group cohesion. Some researchers have given attitude questionnaires to various groups, and have judged as highly cohesive those groups "in which the members express positive sentiments toward the group and negative reactions toward the possibility of being transferred out of it"; [16] while others have considered cohesive groups as "ones in which the members act together toward some common goal." [17] As the reader may note, the latter approach focuses attention on one of the three general classes of output in our group sub-system model—concerted action. Considering this view more useful than the "positive sentiments" concept of cohesiveness, we will use the terms "cohesion" and "concerted action" synonymously in the following discussion.

Sub-System Inputs and the Concerted Action Output. Research has shown that different work groups in the business organization vary considerably in their cohesiveness. In this section, we will indicate some of the relationships between our two major classes of sub-system inputs—group membership and the organizational environment—and work group cohesion. In doing so, we will make some observations about the impact on cohesiveness of certain sub-variables within each of these two classes, *assuming in each case that all other factors are held the same.* The reader should recognize that for any given work group, some of these inputs may tend to predispose the group to a high degree of cohesion, while others may have an influence in the opposite direction. Thus, in attempting

---

[16] William F. Whyte, *Men At Work* (Homewood, Ill.: The Dorsey Press, Inc., and Richard D. Irwin, Inc., 1961), p. 540. A major study utilizing this approach in examining groups is: Stanley Seashore, *Group Cohesiveness in the Industrial Work Group* (Ann Arbor, Mich.: Survey Research Center, 1954).

[17] *Ibid.* A major study utilizing this approach to cohesion: Leonard R. Sayles, *The Behavior of Industrial Work Groups* (New York: John Wiley & Sons, Inc., 1958).

to predict the degree of concerted action to be exhibited by any particular work group, one would have to consider and weigh each of the inputs in relationship to each other.

Before discussing the impact of the sub-system inputs on cohesion, it should be reiterated that concerted work group actions may be directed toward the objectives of the organization or in opposition to them. For this reason, it may be either desirable or undesirable in the eyes of management for a particular work group to be highly cohesive, depending upon the nature of the objectives toward which its concerted actions are taken. Thus cohesiveness, *per se,* can be considered as neither "good" nor "bad" by the organization.

The Group Membership Input.[18] In general, homogeneous work groups—i.e., those whose members possess similar personal and social characteristics—tend to be more cohesive than heterogeneous groups. Among such characteristics which seem to have an influence on homogeneity are ethnic affiliation, and, perhaps to a lesser extent, social class background. In addition, at least one leading researcher believes that "a one-sex work group is likely to be more cohesive than one in which both sexes are represented."[19] There is also some evidence to suggest that the degree to which a group's members' psychological orientation is toward their peers rather than their superiors has some influence on its cohesiveness. For example, William F. Whyte has observed on the basis of his research that:

> Some people seem to look primarily to their organizational superiors for approval, whereas other people seem to look primarily to their peers. . . . These orientations represent two extremes; of course, many people seem to fall somewhere in between, being pulled in both directions. A work group consisting of members who are oriented toward their peers will naturally be more cohesive than those in which a substantial proportion of the members are oriented toward their organizational superiors.[20]

As Whyte suggests, such personality differences are probably conditioned to a considerable extent by the degree to which the individual grew up under firm parental control and has had previous peer group experiences.[21]

---

[18] Our discussion in this and the following section is influenced considerably by William F. Whyte, *op. cit.,* pp. 539 ff.

[19] *Ibid.,* p. 541.

[20] *Ibid.,* p. 542.

[21] To quote Whyte: "The individual who grows up under the firm (and accepted) control of his parents and who has little peer group experience will tend to be vertically oriented; the individual who does not experience such parental control and who has led an active peer group life will tend to be horizontally oriented." *Ibid.,* p. 543.

The Organizational Environment Input. There are a number of
organizational factors which also seem to have an important influence on the degree to which work groups will engage in concerted
behavior. In general, homogeneous groups with respect to *jobs performed* are more likely to be cohesive than those groups in which
members hold dissimilar jobs. A basic reason for this relationship
is that individuals performing the same kind of work, earning the
same pay, and subjected to the same working conditions are more
likely to be affected *uniformly* by management decisions, and hence
have a more common basis for uniting to take concerted action.

A second organizational input which seems to have an important
bearing on cohesion is the degree to which interactional opportunities are available to members of the work group. In general, those
groups whose members find it difficult to converse with each other,
either because of a high noise level or physical separation will find
it more difficult to effect concerted action than those groups in which
greater communication among members is possible.[22]

The importance to management of the jobs performed by work
groups is another organizational input affecting cohesion—especially
when concerted action is taken to pressure management to improve
the position of the work group. As William F. Whyte has pointed
out:

> If the group's work is exceedingly important to management, the group is
> likely to perceive this importance and assume that management is more likely
> to respond to this group's collective pressures than it would to the pressures
> of some work group whose operations seemed more peripheral to the enter-
> prise.[23]

In a study conducted by Leonard Sayles,[24] for example, those work
groups which engaged in concerted action to the greatest extent
were frequently found where: (1) there was a flow of work among
departments, and (2) a production slowdown or wildcat strike on
their part would have halted total plant operations more readily
than would have similar behavior on the part of many other work
groups in the organization.

A final organizational input influencing cohesion which should be

---

[22] However, if members of work groups who perform identical jobs work very
closely together, and an extremely great degree of interaction is possible, emotional
support for concerted action may develop rapidly and lead to uncontrolled outbursts.
This seemed to be the case with a number of so-called "erratic groups" described by
Leonard Sayles in *The Behavior of Industrial Work Groups.*

[23] Whyte, *op. cit.,* p. 545.

[24] Sayles, *op. cit.*

mentioned is the degree to which the work group has been previously successful in achieving its objectives through concerted action. There is evidence to suggest that if a particular work group finds that it can effectively pressure management into giving in to its demands by concerted behavior (such as a wildcat strike) it will be more predisposed to engage in such tactics on future occasions. Strong management resistance to the group's demands, on the other hand, tends to reduce the probability of the recurrence of such behavior. This relationship again points up the interdependence between the group sub-system inputs and outputs. Concerted action (output) will touch off a response on the part of management (input), the nature of which will influence the group's concerted action output in the future.

MANAGERIAL DECISIONS AND WORK GROUP OUTPUTS

As has been pointed out in previous sections, work group behavior is quite complex, and may be influenced by many different kinds of managerial decisions. For this reason, prescriptive statements as to *specifically* how management should deal with *any particular* work group cannot be made validly without first analyzing its membership, objectives, norms and standards, the organizational environment in which it functions, etc.

It is possible, however, to make some observations about certain *general* approaches which may be useful to the manager in influencing work group behavior and attitudes. We will now examine three of these.

Deference to Group Norms and Standards

Work group norms and standards, as emphasized earlier, may sometimes conflict with organizational objectives. For example, a norm which holds that dirty or unpleasant tasks should not be performed by the high status members of a group may conflict with the optimal assignment of work in a department.

In cases such as this, the supervisor is often faced with a dilemma or, in decision-making terms, a suboptimization problem—if he takes actions which violate a norm or standard, his objective of good relationships with his group may suffer, while, on the other hand, if he defers to the group, certain other organizational objectives may not be as fully achieved. To resolve such problems, the supervisor must assign some weight to each of the conflicting objectives and assess the strategies open to him accordingly. If the organizational objectives at stake are major ones, he may decide to disregard group norms or standards, even though he recognizes that his actions may lead to strong protests and negative group behavior. On the other hand, if the objectives are minor in comparison with the negative group actions which he believes will follow if the norms or standards are violated (e.g., a production slowdown), it may be more advisable for him to defer to them. For example, in a department examined in the Hawthorne studies, one supervisor permitted his men to falsify their output records (to effect a belief held by the group that output should be kept relatively constant) because, to have enforced the company's rules:

. . . would have required his standing over the men all day, and by so doing he would have sacrificed all hope of establishing good relations with them. . . . He would have lost even that minimum of influence that he needed if he was to do any kind of a job at all. Under these circumstances he chose to side with the group and wink at much that was going on. . . .[25]

In short, what we have been emphasizing in this section is that the supervisor must be sensitive to the attitudinal and behavioral standards of the group, and that in some cases deference to them, even at the expense of certain organizational objectives, may enhance his overall influence with the group in the long run.

Working Through the Informal Leader

Another influence strategy which the supervisor should be aware of is the possibility of working through his work group's informal leadership. As we indicated earlier, one or more individuals often emerge as informal leaders within the work group, and are in a position to exert considerable influence on the remaining membership. If the supervisor can (1) identify such individuals, and (2) build and maintain good relationships with them, he may be able to persuade them to influence the group to take action in accordance with his objectives. For example, obtaining a group's acceptance of a new work rule may be facilitated considerably if the informal leadership has been first convinced of its merits by the supervisor.

There is, however, one danger in working through informal group leadership which the supervisor should recognize. If the informal

---

[25] George Homans, *The Human Group* (New York: Harcourt, Brace, 1950), p. 63. This supervisory strategy apparently created no serious problems for the company. In fact, in spite of the falsification of records, output was generally considered good by management.

leader identifies too greatly with the supervisor or comes to be regarded as his "pawn," his influence within the group may diminish greatly. Moreover, the strategy of working with the informal leader is sometimes not possible because (1) little, if any informal leadership exists within a group, and/or (2) group attitudes are strongly antimanagement rendering any form of cooperation with the supervisor difficult.

Group Participation in the Decision Making

In some cases, the supervisor may gain a group's support for certain of his objectives by permitting its membership to participate in determining how the objectives are to be realized. For example:

> One unpleasant task which had to be performed by members of a group of car hops in a drive-in restaurant after closing hours each night was that of picking pieces of broken soda pop bottles from a wire mesh bin—a job that often resulted in cut fingers. When particular car hops were assigned to the task by the supervisor, they frequently balked and offered excuses as to why they couldn't stay on to do it. Finally, the supervisor called the group together, pointed out that the job had to be done and asked the group to assign the responsibility for deciding which of its members were to perform the task each night. The group agreed, worked out a system of taking turns, and exerted strong pressures on any of its members who attempted to avoid their turn. From that point on, the supervisor was relieved from all haggling as to who was to perform the unpleasant job each night.

Several comments are in order concerning the group participation approach. First, the theory underlying the approach is that (1) individuals will tend to identify with, and hence give greater support to decisions which they have participated in making, and (2) groups tend to exert influence on their membership to conform to courses of action agreed upon—influence which may be more effective than that of the supervisor. In the illustration given above, for example, the car hop group would "needle" any member who offered what the group considered a "lame" excuse for avoiding his turn to pick up the broken bottles.

Second, the group participation approach has certain limitations. In some cases, groups may resist any such participative efforts on the part of the supervisor because they are apathetic or hostile toward management. Moreover, work groups usually do not possess the knowledge and skills which would permit them to contribute effectively to the making of some kinds of decisions affecting their work—e.g., whether or not the introduction of a new machine is economically justifiable. Finally, we should mention that group participation has sometimes been used as a means of helping to overcome resistance to changes within organizations. We will illustrate this application of the participative approach in Chapter 10.

SUMMARY

The behavior of the organizational employee is influenced considerably by his membership in one or more work groups. For this reason, it is important for the manager to have an understanding of the nature of work groups, and of the impact of his decisions on such behavior.

For conceptual purposes, the work group may be viewed as an organizational sub-system. Its behavior is influenced by two major classes of sub-system inputs—group membership and the organizational environment—both of which are influenced considerably by decisions made by management. To achieve their objectives, groups develop both attitudinal and behavioral standards, and are often in a position to exert strong pressures on their membership to abide by such standards. Accession to these standards permits concerted group action, which may be directed either toward or in opposition to the objectives of the organization. Although groups often take concerted action to meet their objectives, many differences exist among their membership in roles played, status enjoyed, and influences exerted. These three classes of group attitudes and behavior—objectives, norms and standards, concerted action, and member differentiation—may be viewed as the outputs of the group sub-system. Important to recognize in analyzing organizational work groups is the interdependence which exists among the system's elements. Group inputs, such as managerial decisions, not only influence such outputs as concerted action, but the latter may in turn condition the nature of future organizational decision inputs.

DISCUSSION AND STUDY QUESTIONS

1. How might you as a manager go about determining the composition of any informal groups which might exist within the command group which you supervise?
2. What functions does the informal leader perform? Explain.
3. What limitations are there in the use of group participation in decision making?
4. Give an illustration of a situation which you have personally observed in which the existence of a friendship clique has been either helpful or det-

rimental to achieving the goals of a group or organization. Why did the clique exert influence?

5. Which of the following are "groups" as defined in Chapter 6? Give reasons in each case.
   a) A group of people waiting on a street corner for a bus.
   b) A pilot and co-pilot of an airplane in flight.
   c) Seventeen freshmen drinking cokes in the cafeteria.
   d) Two honeymooners.
   e) The president of a firm and a management consultant team he has just called in to help him deal with a personnel problem.
   f) A hunter and his guide.

6. Jack, Bill and Fred are accountants, all reporting to the comptroller. Jack works closely with the production manager in determining standard costs. Bill and the comptroller have recently spent considerable time together trying to get top management to allow them to make a revision in the company's accounting system so that their work would be easier. Fred, the comptroller, and the production manager often have lunch together and talk about golf or fishing which are activities that all three are interested in.
   a) Jack, Bill, and Fred constitute a _____ group.
   b) Jack and the production manager constitute a _____ group.
   c) Bill and the comptroller constitute a _____ group.
   d) Fred, the comptroller, and the production manager constitute a _____ group.

7. Why might an individual allow himself to be influenced by group norms and standards even when conformity to them conflicts with his own values and needs?

8. Cohesiveness within informal work groups cannot be considered as inherently good or bad for the business organization. Discuss.

9. May an informal leader utilize authoritarian leadership techniques? Explain.

10. In terms of Maslow's hierarchy of needs, explain how membership in an informal group may provide need satisfaction to an individual.

11. Evaluate the following statement: "Business firms are not institutions designed to allow individuals to socialize. If our employees want to join a lodge or social club, that is all right, but we expect them to spend all of their time on the job performing their work. Our supervisors have been instructed to discourage social conversations on the job and the formation of disruptive cliques."

12. Discuss the following evaluation of the role of informal groups: "In my department, the jobs are so interesting and challenging that informal group activity is not needed as a means for breaking up monotony. My workers can satisfy all their needs without informal group participation."

13. "I'm not a participant of the 'in-group,' so I can't tell you what is going on in this department."
   a) Why might an individual resist becoming a member of an informal group?

b) Why might he not be accepted as a group member even though he
would like to become one?

14. The Edgewater Company is a small producer of equipment used in steel
mills. It is located in a small town of about 15,000 in the Spring Creek
Valley of Western Pennsylvania. Like many small steel-town communi-
ties in this area, the population is composed of a number of different na-
tionality groups.

The Edgewater Company and Hyde Park Steel Company, which is
located in the same town, employ most of the working people of this small
town. Hyde Park Steel employs about 2,500 men and Edgewater, 700
men.

Ted Nichols is the foreman of a group of about 30 men doing semi-
skilled work in the Molding Department of Edgewater. This group is
composed of three distinct ethnic groups and a few others belonging to
none of these ethnic groups. Even though most workers understand English, when conversing within the group, they usually prefer using their
native language. An informal leader has developed in each of the groups.
Each group leader assumes spokesmanship for his particular group.

Each of these groups is usually assigned a particular kind of job by the
foreman. In the past, each ethnic group was given certain jobs that were
traditionally reserved for it. Each informal leader, then, would assign and
explain work to each member of his group. Production has been satisfactory under this arrangement. Nichols, who has been a foreman for the
past two years, inherited this arrangement from his predecessor. He has
not made any changes because production has been adequate. Furthermore, the work operations of the department lend themselves to the
utilization of crews and team work.

Recently Nichols noticed that some discord has been developing between groups. Occasionally, quarrels between groups have resulted because certain members of a group were temporarily assigned to work with
one of the other groups involved. Although this did not happen frequently, it did occur often enough to create some antagonism between
groups.

a) Should Nichols do anything about this situation?
b) Should Nichols continue to recognize the informal leaders, or should
he work directly with the men?
c) Why did the quarrels arise? How might they be reduced?
d) If you were an employee of one group and were asked by Nichols to
work with another group for a few days, would you be willing to do
so? Explain.
e) Are there any ethical questions involved in operating under the present system? Explain.

SELECTED REFERENCES

Asch, S. E. *Social Psychology*. Englewood Cliffs, N. J.: Prentice-Hall, Inc.,
1952.

BERELSON, BERNARD, and STEINER, GARY A. *Human Behavior an Inventory of Scientific Findings*, Chaps. viii–xvi. New York: Harcourt, Brace & World, Inc., 1964.

CARTWRIGHT, DORWIN, and ZANDER, ALVIN. *Group Dynamics Research and Theory*. 2d ed. Evanston, Ill.: Row, Peterson & Co., 1960.

DAVIS, KEITH, and SCOTT, WILLIAM G. *Readings in Human Relations*, Chap. ii. 2d ed. New York: McGraw-Hill Book Co., 1964.

DUBIN, ROBERT. *Human Relations in Administration*, Part II. 2d ed. Englewood Cliffs, N. J.: Prentice-Hall, Inc., 1961.

HECKMANN, I. L., JR., and HUNERYAGER, S. G. *Human Relations in Management*. Cincinnati: South-Western Publishing Co., 1960.

INDUSTRIAL RELATIONS RESEARCH ASSOCIATION. *Research in Industrial Human Relations*. New York: Harper & Bros., 1957.

KRECH, DAVID, and CRUTCHFIELD, RICHARD S. *Theory and Problems of Social Psychology*. New York: McGraw-Hill Book Co., Inc., 1948.

LINDZEY, GARDNER (ed.). *Handbook of Social Psychology*, Vol. I and Vol. II. Cambridge, Mass.: Addison-Wesley Publishing Co., Inc., 1954.

LITTERER, JOSEPH A. *Organizations: Structure and Behavior*, Part II and Part IV. New York: John Wiley & Sons, Inc., 1963.

PORTER, DONALD E., and APPLEWHITE, PHILIP B. *Studies in Organizational Behavior and Management*, Section 4. Scranton, Pa.: International Textbook Co., 1964.

SCOTT, WILLIAM G. *Human Relations in Management*. Homewood, Ill.: Richard D. Irwin, Inc., 1962.

TUCKER, W. T. *The Social Context of Economic Behavior*. New York: Holt, Rinehart & Winston, Inc., 1964.

WHYTE, WILLIAM F. *Men at Work*. Homewood, Ill.: Richard D. Irwin, Inc. & Dorsey Press, Inc., 1961.

ZALEZNIK, ABRAHAM, and MOMENT, DAVID. *The Dynamics of Interpersonal Behavior*. New York: John Wiley & Sons, Inc., 1964.

CHAPTER 7

DESIGN OF THE
ORGANIZATIONAL
STRUCTURE

I N the previous three chapters we have discussed several facets of the behavior of both individuals and groups within the business organization. We will now shift our attention to the design of the firm's organization structure.

To organize, according to *Webster's Dictionary*, means: "To arrange or constitute in interdependent parts, each having a special function or relation with respect to the whole. . . . To become systematized or constituted into a whole of interdependent parts." [1] In the business firm, the total work to be performed must be broken down into various sub-tasks and jobs, and the sub-tasks assigned to various individuals then interrelated and coordinated in such a way as to meet organizational objectives.

In this and the following chapter, we will consider several basic decision problems which must be faced by the management in structuring the work to be performed by the organization. Then, in Chapters 9 and 10 we will focus attention upon organizational change —giving recognition to the fact that most organization structures, once designed, do not remain static, but rather become dynamic and characterized by frequent change.

ORGANIZATIONAL DESIGN: SOME BASIC CONSIDERATIONS

Before examining any of the specific types of organizing decisions which the manager is called on to make, three general obser-

---

[1] *Webster's Collegiate Dictionary* (5th ed.; Springfield, Mass.: G. & C. Merriam Co., 1946), p. 699.

vations about the design of the firm's organization structure are in order.

First, organizational design can be approached both analytically and synthetically. That is, we might first consider the overall task or tasks which the firm must accomplish if it is to meet its objectives, and then break these down, progressively, into smaller sub-tasks and sub-sub-tasks, until the division of work has reached a point at which the content of each sub-part approximates the job which one individual in the organization can be expected to perform. Conversely, organizational design can be approached synthetically—we could first attempt to enumerate various jobs which need to be performed in the firm, and then consider how these might be grouped together into various departments, how the departments might be combined into different divisions, and so on, until the complete organizational hierarchy has been established. These two ways of viewing organizational design are illustrated in Figure 7–1.

FIGURE 7–1. Two Approaches to Organizational Design

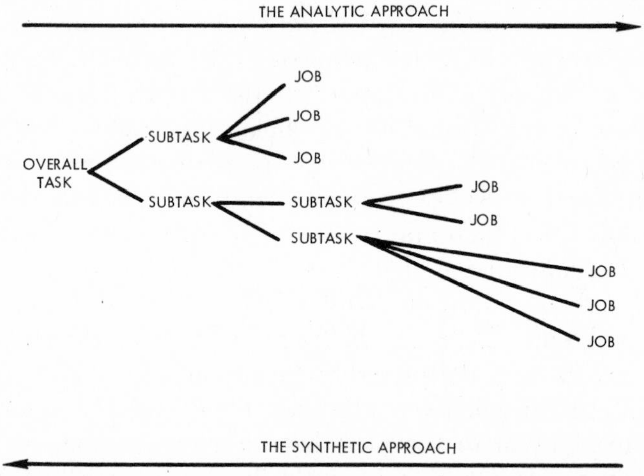

The analytical approach of viewing the organization "from the top down" has been supported on the grounds that it permits focusing greater attention on the relationships between sub-tasks to overall company objectives than does the synthetic approach of designing an organizational structure from "the bottom up." On the other hand, the synthetic approach has been deemed superior by such writers as Chapple and Sayles, who hold that it facilitates organizational design which provides a smoother flow of work from one department to another.[2] Our position on the issue is that it is probably most useful for the manager to view the design of his organization *both* analytically and synthetically, so as to gain the merits of both approaches. Thus, in our subsequent discussion, we will conceive of the process of organizing as being both combinational and divisional in nature.

Second, our approach to organizational design in this and succeeding chapters will be similar in fundamental orientation to that which we utilized in considering leadership in Chapter 5—i.e., a situationist one. We will focus attention on several of the key variables involved in a number of different types of organizing decision problems and on some of the conditions under which various alternative forms of organizational structure seem to be most appropriate. Some of the variables which will be considered are human ones, of the types previously discussed in Chapters 4–6; while others may be classed as economic and/or technological. In the analysis of any given organizing decision problem it is, of course, important for the manager to simultaneously consider all pertinent variables of these types and their interrelationships with one another.

Finally, in our subsequent discussion, we will sometimes utilize *organization charts* to depict structural relationships among positions in the firm. On an organization chart, which is essentially a simple analogue model, positions are represented by boxes, with superior-subordinate relationships being indicated by lines connecting the boxes. For example, in the simple organization chart illustrated in Figure 7–2, the managers of both the firm's east and west

FIGURE 7–2. Illustrative Organization Chart

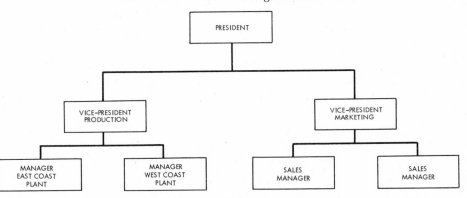

² See, for example, Eliot D. Chapple and Leonard R. Sayles, *The Measure of Management* (New York: The Macmillan Company, 1961), especially Chap. 2.

coast plants report to the vice-president of production, who in turn reports to the company's president.

Organization charts are useful for facilitating visualization of some of the basic relationships between positions, and individuals holding these positions, within the firm. The reader should recognize, however, that the organization chart does not depict many of the "informal" individual and group relationships which may evolve in the organization—e.g., influence and friendship clique patterns, etc. Further, such charts are basically static in nature. As is sometimes true with analogue models, they present a "still picture" of structural relationships existing at a given point in time, and are not geared to the portrayal of the dynamics of organizational change.

SPECIALIZATION OF WORK IN NONMANAGERIAL POSITIONS

Most organizations are structured so as to provide some degree of specialization of activity for each of their members. Rather than calling on each employee to perform all of the different kinds of work necessary to meet a firm's objectives, certain individuals may be assigned to the task of selling, others may be assigned to devote their full time to operating a particular machine, and so on.

A key decision problem involved in designing an organizational structure is that of determining just how much specialization should exist—i.e., of deciding how large or small the scope of work performed by each employee should be. For example, in a manufacturing operation comprised of three steps—setting up a machine, operating the machine, and inspecting the pieces turned out on the machine—should management:

1. Structure the work so that each employee performs all three of these tasks? or
2. Provide for even greater specialization by having some workers just do the set-up work; others, just the machining; and still others do nothing but inspection?

In general, specialization of activity, *up to a point* enables the individual to be more productive than would be the case were he to try to perform a job calling for the application of a wide variety of different types of skills. Certain tasks in organizations, however—especially at the nonmanagerial level—have become so highly specialized as to lead to problems which may tend to reduce the productivity of the majority of employees performing them. In this section we will first focus our attention upon some of the advantages of specialization and some of the problems of overspecialization at nonmanagerial levels in the business organization.[3] We will then examine some of the approaches utilized by business firms to help overcome such problems.

Advantages of Specialization

Most highly specialized nonmanagerial positions have short *cycle times*—i.e., a task requiring only a short duration of time to complete is repeated over and over again. As we indicated in Chapter 4 in our discussion of learning theory, learning generally is more effective when there is repetition of the activity being taught. Further, activities requiring only very short cycle times often require only relatively low skill levels in their performance. Thus, highly specialized nonmanagerial jobs, such as those found on many production lines, often can be learned more quickly than those calling for a broader scope of activities to be performed. In one study of assembly-line positions, for example, it was found that jobs with three-minute cycles required approximately three times as many repetitions as jobs with one-half minute cycles before standard levels of production were reached.[4]

Shorter learning times required for jobs are advantageous to the firm for several reasons. For one, the cost of training employees to perform on new jobs is reduced. Further, interruptions in production due to absences, vacations or resignations can be minimized because new workers can be quickly trained as replacements. When such is the case, the organization becomes less dependent upon any one employee—his skill becomes relatively unimportant since it can be so easily replaced.

Not only may training time be less on short-cycle jobs; additionally, workers may often become more proficient on such jobs as compared with less highly specialized ones. As the short-cycle job is repeated over and over, the individual learns to eliminate wasted and ineffective motions. False starts and mistakes tend to be reduced. In one study, for example, it was found that the ultimate

---

[3] The reader should recognize that specialization of work, with both its advantages and disadvantages, also occurs at *managerial* levels in most business organizations. In consequence, certain of the observations which we will make in this section have some degree of applicability to at least certain managerial positions. Specialization of work at the managerial level, however, is rarely, if ever, carried to the extreme that it often is at the worker level in many firms.

[4] Maurice Kilbridge, "A Model for Industrial Learning Costs," *Management Science*, 8 (July, 1962), 522.

attainable level of proficiency for certain TV chassis assembly jobs with one-minute cycles was 16% above that of those with three-minute cycles.[5]

Disadvantages of Overspecialization

There are at least two basic kinds of disadvantages which may accrue to the organization when jobs become overspecialized. First, as we indicated previously in Chapter 4, when employees are called on to perform simple repetitive tasks which require little skill, satisfaction of their esteem and self-actualization needs may be thwarted; and the resultant frustrations may lead to defensive behavior such as excessive absenteeism, hostility toward supervision, etc. Moreover, by greatly reducing the firm's dependence upon the skills of any single employee, specialization has sometimes tended to threaten the security needs of workers. When an employee performs a low-skill-level job which almost anyone can do, his boss may be more inclined to fire him for arbitrary or capricious reasons, than if he possessed skills not easily replaceable. One way of the employee's overcoming such problems has been through unionization and the design of union-management contracts protecting workers from arbitrary discipline or dismissal by their supervisors. In fact, some observers of the labor scene attribute much of the organizing success which unions have enjoyed to the failure of management to provide job security to operating employees as their jobs have become highly specialized.

In addition to these psychological problems, the specialization of work beyond a certain point may effect inefficiencies due to technological considerations. For instance, shortening cycle times to an extreme degree may result in an increasing amount of handling time required in the performance of a task, as may be illustrated by the following hypothetical example.

A firm has an assembly-line job in which the operator: (1) picks up a subassembly, (2) drills and reams four holes in it, (3) assembles inserts into the holes, and (4) replaces the subassembly on the line. We will assume that the standard times for each of these four elements of this task are those shown in Figure 7–3.

The firm's industrial engineers estimate that if this job were further broken down with the machining tasks assigned to some workers, and the assembly of inserts to others, an overall increase in efficiency of 20% could be expected for these two work elements. If

[5] *Ibid.*, 520.

this further specialization of the job were effected, however, both the machining operator and the assembler would have to pick up the subassembly and replace it on the line, whereas these steps have to be performed only once for each subassembly under the present set-up. Given the standard times shown in Figure 7–3, the total

FIGURE 7–3

A Technological Limit to Specialization
(Illustrative Example)

Present Job		Proposed Additional Specialization			
Job: Drill, Ream and Assemble		Job 1: Drill and Ream		Job 2: Assemble	
Operation	Time in minutes	Operation	Time in minutes	Operation	Time in minutes
Pick up	.04	Pick up	.04	Pick up	.04
Drill and Ream	.26	Drill and Ream	.22	Assemble	.16
Assemble insert	.19	Replace	.04	Replace	.04
Replace	.04	Subtotal	.30	Subtotal	.24
Total work and handling time	.53		.54 min.		
Total work time	.45		.38 min.		
Total handling time	.08		.16 min.		
Handling as % of work	18%		42%		
Increased efficiency in work elements	—		20%		

time required for the job would be lengthened by .01 minute by the further specialization, rather than decreased, because the additional handling time required more than offsets the increased efficiency which could be realized in the performance of the work elements.

Techniques for Dealing with Specialization Problems

To help overcome the adverse psychological effects of overspecialization, several techniques have been developed and utilized by business firms. We will now examine several of these.

Employee Selection. One way of offsetting some of the adverse psychological effects of specialization is to *select* workers who do not perceive the firm's highly specialized jobs to be monotonous. Although it may be difficult to predict how a potential employee will view a particular job, this approach theoretically offers a solution to the monotonous tendencies induced by specialization and sometimes has been effective, as we noted in Chapter 4. However, most people may consider a large majority of a company's highly specialized jobs as monotonous. If, for example, a firm were to build a new plant calling for 3,000 highly specialized jobs to be filled in an area with a labor supply of 5,000 individuals available for work, perhaps as many as 4,500 or ninety percent of them might view practically all of these jobs as monotonous. That such a 90 percent figure may not be unreasonable for mechanically paced, repetitive jobs is indicated by the following finding from a study of workers on an automobile assembly line:

> Roughly 10 percent of our sample of workers preferred or were indifferent to jobs with basic mass production characteristics such as mechanical pacing, repetitiveness, and so forth. The great majority expressed in varying degrees a dislike of these features of their job situations at Plant X.[6]

Thus, although sometimes practicable, worker selection oftentimes may not provide a widely applicable means of overcoming the psychological problems associated with high degrees of specialization.

Participative Methods.   Frustration in achieving higher level needs arising from specialized job design may be partially overcome by utilizing the participative management approach discussed in Chapter 6. If this approach is employed, it may be possible to provide decision opportunities which allow employees to achieve some degree of fulfillment of their self-actualization needs. However, in many cases participation may not be consistent with job specialization. If a job is highly routinized and its steps prescribed in engineering detail, to what degree can an employee's decisions affect his own work? Yet some latitude for employee participation in decision making may exist even in highly repetitive routine jobs. For example, in one toy manufacturing firm, a paint spraying operation, staffed by girls, was plagued by absenteeism and employee turnover. The girls doing this work were called in to talk with their supervisor to discuss the problems which they faced on their jobs. Among other complaints, the girls pointed out that they were frustrated by the constant speed of the conveyor belt which brought them the toys to paint. They suggested that they be permitted to "adjust the speed of the belt faster or slower depending on how we feel." [7] Then,

---

[6] Charles R. Walker and Robert H. Guest, *The Man on the Assembly Line* (Cambridge, Mass.: Harvard University Press, 1952), p. 141. It should be noted that some observers believe that a higher percentage of individuals than the figure cited here can find satisfaction in repetitive work; and that greater advantage may be gained from utilizing the selection approach for jobs of this type. See for example, Theodore O. Prenting, "Better Selection for Repetitive Work," *Personnel*, 41 (Sept.–Oct., 1964), 26–31.

[7] William F. Whyte, *Money and Motivation* (New York: Harper & Brothers, 1955), as reprinted in Charles R. Walker, *Modern Technology and Civilization* (New York: McGraw-Hill Book Company, Inc., 1962), p. 117.

With great misgivings, the foreman had a control with a dial marked "low, medium, fast" installed at the booth of the group leader; she could now adjust the speed of the belt anywhere between the upper and lower limits that the engineers had set. The girls were delighted. . . . Production increased, and within three weeks . . . the girls were operating at 30 to 50 percent above the level that had been expected. . . .[8]

As the reader may note, not only was the approach utilized here participative in nature; it also resulted in the employees being freed to a considerable extent from machine-pacing, a mass production characteristic objectionable to many workers.

Job Enlargement. Another approach sometimes utilized to help offset the adverse effects of extreme specialization is *job enlargement*. As its name implies, job enlargement is the opposite of dividing up work into minute sub-tasks—it is a form of *de*specialization in which work is restructured so that each job contains *more*, rather than fewer, elements. Although enlarged jobs require longer training time, monotony tends to be reduced and job interest increased in comparison with that in extremely specialized jobs. In this way, job productivity (after training) may be increased.

An example of job enlargement is provided by the I.B.M. Corporation.[9] The work of certain of its machine operators at one time consisted solely of placing a part into their machine, and removing it when the machine processing was completed. These jobs allowed little ingenuity or challenge. Job enlargement was effected by additionally assigning both the set-up of the machines and the inspection of completed parts to the machine operators. This broadening of responsibility necessitated a higher level of operator skill because set-up (formerly performed by a specialized set-up man) is a more highly-skilled function than is machine operation.

Increasing the operator's skill, of course, required commensurate upgrading of their rate of pay. Additionally, as a result of the job enlargement, certain increased costs had to be incurred due to the need for extra inspection equipment. The company believed, however, that these costs were worth their investment because three valuable benefits accrued from the enlargement:

1. A better product quality resulting from an increased sense of worker responsibility.

---

[8] *Ibid.*
[9] Information about the I.B.M. experience described in this and the following paragraphs was drawn from C. R. Walker, "The Problem of the Repetitive Job," *Harvard Business Review,* 28 (May, 1950), 54–58.

2. Less idle worker time, with a 95% reduction in set-up and inspection costs because the workers no longer needed to wait for a setup man to come along before starting on a new batch of parts, or for an inspector to check their parts.

3. "Job enrichment" due to greater job interest, variety and responsibility than was present before.

In spite of numerous successful applications, however, there are limitations to the applicability of job enlargement. If jobs are too greatly expanded in scope, many of the advantages of specialization discussed earlier will be lost. Further, due to technological constraints, no job enlargement may be possible for certain classes of jobs. For example, at certain stages of some manufacturing operations, set-ups may be very infrequent, with no inspection being carried out until later stages in the production process. In such cases, there may be no additional tasks available for enlarging the scope of the work of those individuals tending the machines, unless the technological process were to be considerably revamped.

Job Rotation. A final approach designed to help overcome some of the problems arising from specialization which deserves mention is that of *job rotation*. With job rotation, neither the worker's task nor its cycle time is extended as with job enlargement. Rather, workers are trained in performing several jobs, rather than one. Then, periodically during the day (or at less frequent intervals), they are rotated from one job to another by switching jobs with one another. For example, an employee may be assigned to rotate among three jobs along with two other workers.

Job rotation is usually a simpler approach to inaugurate than job enlargement, since it does not call for the redesign of jobs. Further, it tends to provide more flexibility in relating the assignment of workers to their own skills and capabilities. Since skill levels, capabilities, and perceptions of monotony vary from worker to worker, the enlargement of all jobs in a particular operation may be highly beneficial for some workers while less so for others. Under job rotation, on the other hand, it may be relatively easy to schedule the work so that: (1) those individuals with limited capabilities, and who experience little or no boredom when assigned to routine tasks, be given just one job and not rotated, while at the same time (2) those individuals who want to switch jobs periodically be provided with an opportunity to do so.

Specialization: Summary

The factors which must be considered in determining how specialized jobs at the worker level should be, consist of two opposing types: (1) those which tend to increase productivity with greater degrees of specialization (e.g., faster learning), and (2) those which may result in decreased productivity as specialization increases (e.g., boredom, monotony, and lack of job interest). The magnitude of these tendencies will vary considerably from one situation to another. A particular repetitive, machine-paced job may be quite satisfying to one individual, for example, while being equally unsatisfactory for another. Thus, both in the initial design of jobs of the types we have been discussing, and in considering organizational modifications by such approaches as job enlargement and job rotation, a situational approach is called for.

MANAGERIAL COORDINATION: INFORMATION AND INFLUENCE

In the previous section, our attention was focused upon the nature and scope of the task content of particular nonmanagerial jobs. We will now give consideration to certain key aspects of the *interrelating* of different jobs in the organizational hierarchy.

Work performed by different individuals in the firm must obviously be *coordinated* if company objectives are to be met. If each organizational member were to define his own performance output without giving consideration to its relationship to work performed by other individuals in the firm, a high degree of organizational chaos could result.

A basic function of and need for managers in the business organization is to provide such coordination. The plant manager in a manufacturing firm, for example, must coordinate the work of engineering, production, and quality control so that the items produced meet specifications; the production and sales efforts of the firm must be coordinated so that there is sufficient number of salesmen to sell the units of product produced, or so that production can turn out a sufficient number of units to meet customer orders.

Essentially managerial coordination is effected by (1) *providing information* to subordinates and other organizational members, and (2) *influencing* these individuals *to accept* the content of their communicational messages. The foreman, for example, needs to inform his workers as to what work he wants them to accomplish; then he must influence them to direct their efforts toward meeting these work objectives.

These information-providing and influence needs of the coordinative process have two basic implications for organizational design. First, in structuring jobs, not only must the work content of the job be considered, but attention must also be given to its *informational* requirements. If the production worker is to be able to operate a particular machine, he must be given information as to how to do it; if the manager is to make effective decisions, his informational inputs must be adequate, etc. Further, not only must information *content* be defined, informational *flows* and communications *channels* must be given explicit attention in organizational design. *From whom* is the production control manager to obtain information needed to establish the plant's production schedules for the following week? Once a scheduling decision has been made, then *to whom* must such information be communicated if the decision is to be effectively implemented?

Second, organizational design implies the structuring of *power* and influence relationships among individuals holding various positions in the firm. By virtue of the fact that he has been appointed to a position of "boss," the first line foreman is usually perceived by his subordinates as possessing a certain amount of legitimate power. By designing a managerial position so that its holder has the power to hire, fire, promote, demote, and give or withhold salary increases to subordinates, coercive and reward bases of power are established.

In summary, the design of an organizational hierarchy, in which managers at one or more levels are called on to coordinate and direct the efforts of their subordinates toward organizational goals, implies the structuring not only of work content, but also of informational flows and power and influence relationships among various members of the organization.

SPAN OF CONTROL

In our previous discussion, we indicated that the job of organizing involves subdividing a total task into smaller and smaller sub-tasks until jobs are defined for individual workers. Then, we pointed out that in order to coordinate specialized tasks, formal leadership in the firm is necessary. Reliance on both specialization and coordination implies that organizations be comprised of a set of groups, each consisting of a number of specialized workers and a formal leader or manager. In determining how these groups should be designed, two corollary questions emerge:

1. What size group is optimum?
2. What kinds of tasks should be grouped together?

We will focus attention on the first of these questions in this section and upon the second when we discuss the bases of departmentation and line and staff in the following chapter.

Quite obviously, any individual is limited in what he is able to accomplish. We are limited by time, and by our knowledge, skills, interests, and motivation. These limitations upon the scope of a manager's activities within any given period of time are considered explicitly in organization design by the notion of span of control.[10] The concept of span of control may be stated as follows: "There is a limited number of subordinates who may be *supervised effectively* by any single manager." We will now examine the subject of span of control. In doing so we will point up both some of the organizational implications of different size spans of control, and some of the key variables which must be considered by management in determining what the span of control ought to be at various levels in the organization.

Implications of Differing Spans of Control

Management's choice as to the width of the span of control at each level in the organizational hierarchy can have numerous implications of significance for the firm. Several of these implications may be visualized by examining three possible alternative spans of control for a small (hypothetical) organization consisting of 16 operating employees: (1) a narrow span of 2, (2) an intermediate span of 4, and (3) a wide span of 16. These three possibilities are illustrated graphically in Figure 7–4, and some of the organizational implications of each summarized in Figure 7–5. For purposes of simplicity, we are assuming in this example that the span of control is the same at each level in the organization, although, as we will indicate later, spans usually do (and should) vary at different organizational levels.

Generalizing from Figures 7–4 and 7–5, we may note that, all other factors being the same, the smaller the span of control in an organization, the larger will be the number of: managers, total em-

---

[10] "Span of control" is also sometimes referred to as "span of management" or "span of supervision."

FIGURE 7–4. Alternative Spans of Control

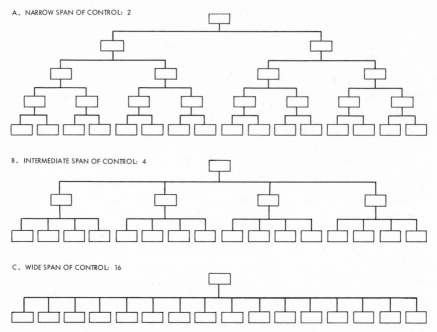

A. NARROW SPAN OF CONTROL: 2

B. INTERMEDIATE SPAN OF CONTROL: 4

C. WIDE SPAN OF CONTROL: 16

ployees, and both managerial and total organizational levels. In consequence, increasing the span of control in an organization tends to decrease administrative costs, since salaries do not have to be paid to as large a number of managers.[11] Further, *vertical* communications—i.e., the transmission of verbal messages, written reports, etc., from top management down to lower levels in the organization, and, conversely, from lower level managers up to the top—tend to pose fewer problems when wider spans of control are utilized. This is because with a smaller number of levels in the organization, there are fewer managers through whom messages must pass in going from their source to their ultimate destination. For example, suppose that in the hypothetical organization of 16 operating employees discussed previously, a problem involving certain work procedures on a particular job arises that should be decided upon by top management, rather than at any lower level, because it has several important implications for the overall operations of the firm. With a span of control of four, as illustrated in Figure 7–4, pertinent information on

---

[11] Decreasing the number of managers in an organization by increasing span of control may not always result in lower administrative costs. For example, each manager whose span is increased may be paid more than he previously was due to the added responsibilities which he has been given; and such salary increases may more than offset any cut in costs resulting from the employment of fewer managers.

FIGURE 7–5

Effects of Alternative Spans of Control

	Narrow	Intermediate	Wide	Organization Level
Span of Control	2	4	16	
Number of Non-supervisory				
Employees	16	16	16	1st
1st Level Supervisors	8	4	1	2nd
2nd Level Supervisors	4	1	0	3rd
3rd Level Supervisors	2	0	0	4th
4th Level Supervisors	1	0	0	5th
Total Management Levels	4	3	1	
Total Organization Levels	5	4	2	
Number of Managers	15	5	1	
Total Employees	31	21	17	
Managers as a Percent of				
Total Employees	49%	23%	6%	

the problem would have only to be transmitted from the manager of the department in which the problem arose to the president of the firm. With a span of control of two, on the other hand, the information would have to be additionally brought to the attention of two other managers (the first line supervisor's boss, and, in turn, his boss) before it was received by the president. One disadvantage of such "longer" communications channels as opposed to shorter ones is that messages tend to become *distorted* as they pass from one individual to another, since different individuals' knowledge, levels of understanding, perceptions, needs, etc. are different. Further, more time is usually required for a message to reach its destination when it must be transmitted to and then be retransmitted from numerous individuals in the organization. In consequence, delays in obtaining information needed quickly to provide the basis for decision making may pose a greater problem in multi-level firms where the vertical communications channels are quite "long" than in those organizations characterized by a relatively small number of hierarchical levels.

Now that we have considered some of the positive implications of a wide span of control, let us consider the disadvantages of this form of organizational structuring. As indicated earlier, the primary disadvantage accruing from a span of control which is "too wide" is that the job of supervising may become so great that the manager cannot perform his work effectively. In explaining the increased supervisory burden facing managers as their span of control is increased, attention has often been given to the fact that:

As the number of individuals reporting to a manager increases, the number of supervisor-subordinate *relationships* which may exist in this department increases at a *much faster rate*.

To illustrate, if a supervisor, A, has only a single subordinate, B, only one relationship may exist within the department—that between A and B, which may be denoted A:B. With two, three, or four subordinates, however, the number of possible supervisor-subordinate relationships increases to three, seven, and fifteen respectively as is illustrated in Figure 7–6.

FIGURE 7–6

Possible Supervisory-Subordinate Relationships
with Two, Three, and Four Subordinates

Two Subordinates	Three Subordinates	Four Subordinates	
A:B	A:B	A:B	A:CD
A:C	A:C	A:C	A:CE
A:BC	A:D	A:D	A:DE
	A:BC	A:E	A:BCD
	A:BD	A:BC	A:BCE
	A:CD	A:BD	A:BDE
	A:BCD	A:BE	A:CDE
			A:BCDE
3	7	15	
	TOTAL		

Important to recognize is the fact that the supervisory-subordinate relationships which we have been discussing are simply *possible* ones. In some instances some of them may rarely, if ever, exist or, even if they occur relatively frequently may involve only a very small amount of supervisory time. Referring back to Figure 7–6, for example, supervisor A may have to spend only ten minutes a month instructing, helping to resolve problems among, or in other ways communicating with subordinates B, C, and E, as a group—the relationship A:BCE. On the other hand, he may find it necessary to spend several hours each week in his supervisory relationship with B and D (A:BD). Thus, although wider spans of control do mean the existence of increasingly larger numbers of possible supervisor-subordinate relationships, the *importance* of such relationships in terms of supervisory burden is often influenced considerably by other variables. We will now turn our attention to some of the key variables which do influence span of control.

Variables Affecting Size of Span

Considerable variations may be found in the number of subordinates considered most desirable for managers to supervise in different organizational situations. In some cases, firms have found a span of control of as small as two or three to be the largest which certain of their managers could handle effectively; while in others, effective supervision with spans of thirty or more have been reported. Our purpose in this section is to examine some of the variables of importance in determining what the manager's span of control should be under various conditions.

Interrelated Work Among Subordinates. In the previous section, we indicated that certain of the supervisor-subordinate relationships which may exist in a department may place fairly heavy demands upon the manager while others may not. One important variable which will influence the amount of attention which a manager will have to give in helping to resolve problems *among* his subordinates (relationships of the type A:BC, A:BCD, etc.) is the degree to which the work performed by the subordinates is *interdependent*. In general, other factors being the same, a manager may effectively supervise a larger number of subordinates when the work performed by each is relatively *independent*, since fewer problems of *coordination* arise. This point may be illustrated by reference to two research studies which have been made on span of control.

In a study of Sears, Roebuck retail stores, James Worthy found that a large span of control (sometimes over 30) for store managers seemed to be more effective than a small span.[12] In contrast, a study made by James Healey of manufacturing firms in Ohio indicated that a relatively narrow span of control for plant managers was more often used and considered desirable.[13] These opposing research results may be reconciled if the differences in the relationships requiring management attention in each are examined. In Sears, Roebuck stores, the work of various departments is relatively *independent*. Work in the hardware department, for example, is only loosely related to work in the women's clothing, sports, or appliance departments. Thus, few interrelationships among the work of the department managers require attention by the store manager and a relatively large span of control is feasible.

---

[12] James Worthy, "Organizational Structure and Employee Morale," *American Sociological Review*, 15 (April, 1950), 169–79.

[13] James H. Healey, *Executive Coordination and Control* (Columbus, Ohio: Bureau of Business Research, The Ohio State University, 1956).

In contrast, the plant managers studied by Healey supervised a number of departments performing interrelated work—such as engineering, tooling, production planning and control, manufacturing and inspection. In such manufacturing operations when the engineering department has completed a design and the drawings for a part or a product, the tooling department must then design and manufacture tools for its production. After obtaining estimates as to what volume of sales can be expected, production planning must determine when and on what machines parts are to be produced; manufacturing produces the product and quality control inspects it. Since actions in one department may seriously affect the operations in others, a much greater degree of coordinative supervision is required by plant managers in manufacturing than by store managers in retailing operations such as Sears.

Complexity of Work Performed. Another variable influencing span of control is the complexity of the work performed by the manager's subordinates. If the work carried out by employees in a department is highly programmed, routine, and not subject to frequent change, less supervisory attention will usually be required than if the work is of a more dynamic and complex nature. It is for this reason that organizations typically exhibit wider spans of control at lower levels than at upper levels. First line supervisors, who are able to rely upon precise job descriptions, operating instructions and work rules to aid them in defining and coordinating subordinate actions, often are able to effectively supervise 20, 30 or more employees. At upper levels in most organizations, on the other hand, managerial problems tend to be much broader in scope and more dynamic, with fewer precise *precedents* for decision making and action available. Under such non-routine conditions in which many problems are ill-defined, executives must spend considerable time working out plans for action with their subordinates; and hence, the effective span of control tends to be fairly narrow.

Leader and Follower Characteristics. The personality characteristics of both the manager and his subordinates may also have an important bearing on span of control. If a manager's subordinates are well trained, competent, and able (and willing) to plan their own work and make decisions for themselves, there will be less need for supervisory attention; and a larger span of control will be possible. Moreover, if the manager himself is highly skilled in planning, instructing subordinates, handling employee problems, etc., it may be possible to give him a larger span than would be the case with a less adept supervisor.

Physical Contiguity.   When a manager's subordinates are separated physically from one another, it may be necessary for his span of control to be narrower. This is because supervision is rendered more difficult by his inability to "oversee" all of his subordinates at any given time. Physical separation inhibits instruction, and other forms of communications. Organization analysts sometimes try to offset the span-narrowing impact of physical separation by utilizing approaches to make the manager's supervisory task less burdensome. For example, short written forms to ease superior-subordinate communications are often introduced (e.g., salesman report forms). Or, individuals selected for remotely located positions may be given special instruction and training, necessitating less supervisor attention and communication. All other factors remaining the same, however, physical separation does tend to reduce the manager's effective span of control.

Administrative Assistance.   Another factor influencing span of control is the amount of assistance or aid available to the manager in coordinating the efforts of his subordinates. As Ernest Dale has suggested, it was possible for General Eisenhower to allow 50 corps commanders direct "access" to him because he had an intervening level of staff officers who relieved him from handling numerous day-to-day problems.[14] Or, in the Sears stores mentioned previously, an assistant manager, who was responsible for dealing with several managerial functions, can be considered as contributing to the effectiveness found with a wide span of control. Somewhat similarly, by assigning a training assistant and a paper-work clerk to certain of its first line foremen, I.B.M. was able to widen their span of control and as a result eliminate one level of management.

Just how much coordinative assistance should be provided the manager will, of course, depend on a number of variables. For example, consider providing a manager with one administrative assistant, which would have the effects shown in Figure 7–7. Whether the additional $7,500 in salary paid to the assistant would be justified would depend on such factors as the following: How much more effectively can the manager run his department with the assistant? By increasing his span of control (and possibly that of other managers by providing them with assistants) would it be possible to reduce the number of managers and organizational levels in the firm? In short, providing administrative assistance will tend to in-

---

[14] Ernest Dale, *Planning and Developing the Company Organization Structure,* Research Report No. 20 (New York: American Management Association, 1952), pp. 56–57.

FIGURE 7–7

Addition of an Administrative Assistant
(Hypothetical Example)

	Without Assistant	With Assistant
Manager's Salary	$10,000	$10,000
Assistant's Salary	—	7,500
Span of Control Possible	10	15
Administrative Cost/Subordinate	$1,000	$1,167

crease the manager's effective span of control; but whether such assistance is desirable depends upon a number of factors.

A Model of Span of Control

In the previous sections we have illustrated how several different variables may influence the appropriateness of different sized spans of control. We have not, however, examined the *relative importance* which should be given to each of these variables in determining what span of control is most effective in any given organizational situation.

Unfortunately, no research evidence yet exists which will permit the development of any definitive quantitative model explicitly specifying the relationship between the variables involved in making span of control decisions. However, one firm—the Lockheed Missile and Space Company—has experimented with the design and utilization of a simple span of control "model," in which several variables believed to be of considerable influence on span of control have been weighted.[15]

What Lockheed did was to first weight six separate factors believed to affect span of control. These factors, and their maximum ratings (and hence, relative weights) were as follows:

1. (Dis)similarity of functions performed by subordinates—5
2. Geographic separation of employees—5
3. Complexity of jobs performed by subordinates—10
4. Degree of subordinate direction and control required—15
5. Degree of coordination of subordinates required—10
6. The scope and complexity of and precedents available for the planning required in the supervisory position—10

Then, each managerial position was rated by these factors and the

[15] The material in this and the following paragraphs was drawn from: Harold Stieglitz, "Optimizing Span of Control," *Management Record*, 24 (September, 1962), 25–29.

ratings were summed to give a supervisory "index." Next, by analyzing numerous supervisory positions, several different suggested
spans of control were established based on the point value of the
supervisory indices. For example, for middle management positions,
an index of 40–42 indicated a suggested span of four or five subordinates, an index of 31–33, of from five to eight subordinates, etc.[16]

Once designed, the Lockheed "model" was applied to a few units
of the company, and the following results reported:

> One . . . [application] . . . extended the average span from 3.8 people
> to 4.2 and reduced supervisory levels from five to four; another broadened
> the average span of middle managers from 3.0 to 4.2 and cut levels from six
> to five; and in a third case, the average span went from 4.2 to 4.8 persons and
> levels dropped from seven to five. The reductions in managerial personnel and
> supervisory payroll were "substantial." [17]

Admitting to its successful application in a few cases, let us now
consider the question: "How may the Lockheed approach in general
be evaluated?" In our opinion, a primary advantage of this approach
is that it focuses *explicit* and *systematic* attention on the problem of
span of control in organization design. In doing so, it may warn
against developing a small-span, many-level organization which is
expensive in supervisory salaries, and which tends to magnify problems in vertical communications; while at the same time, it may help
assure narrow enough spans of control for effective supervision.

As the analysts who designed this approach have been quick to
point out, however, the index cannot be applied "blindly" and without thought to supervisory positions; rather its successful application requires considerable reliance on managerial judgment.

> Judgment, for example, is called for in evaluating the extent to which the
> six factors are present in a particular job situation. And even greater judgment
> is needed in deciding whether the "suggested span" is truly appropriate in a
> given situation.[18]

Thus, the model should not be viewed as one in which the manager
can routinely "plug in" values and obtain optimum results. Rather,
it is intended as a general guide, which, when supplemented with
managerial judgment, may aid in making more effective span of
control decisions.

---

[16] It should be noted that in utilizing the supervisory indices, consideration was
also given to the amount of administrative assistance which various supervisors had.
[17] Stieglitz, *op. cit.*, 29.
[18] *Ibid.*

SUMMARY

Organizational design involves both the breaking down of the overall work of the firm into numerous sub-tasks; and providing for coordination of the work performed by each organizational member. An important characteristic of many business firms today is that the tasks assigned to individuals have often become highly specialized, especially at the nonmanagerial level. Although specialization is advantageous up to a point, overspecialization may create numerous problems. To help overcome some of these problems, business firms have utilized such approaches as job enlargement, job rotation, and employee participation in decision making.

In order to coordinate the many specialized jobs performed in the organization, numerous managers are appointed, each given the responsibility for supervising a certain number of subordinates. Just how many subordinates a manager may effectively supervise is the central focus of attention in the span of control concept. In considering what a manager's span of control ought to be, numerous variables must be taken into consideration—both the interdependence and complexity of the work performed by subordinates, personality characteristics of both the manager and his subordinates, the physical contiguity of subordinates, and the amount of coordinative assistance given the manager. Offering promise of helping management to make better span of control decisions has been the Lockheed approach in which weighting was given to numerous variables believed to have an important influence on how many subordinates can effectively be supervised by the manager.

DISCUSSION AND STUDY QUESTIONS

1. Why has it sometimes been said that specialization of work at the employee level has contributed to the growth of unions? Explain in motivational terms.
2. What effect does interdependence among jobs have upon the span of control? Why?
3. What effect would the existence of numerous established precedents for decision making in an organization have on span of control? Explain why.
4. Discuss the usefulness and limitations of models such as that designed by Lockheed which attempt to quantify the variables involved in span of control problems.
5. Discuss: The extent of monotony perceived as existing in a job is dependent upon the job and the individual. Consequently, job design factors

tending to induce job monotony may be offset by the proper selection of employees.

6. Indicate for each of the following pairs of management positions the one for which you believe the span of control would normally be smaller. In each case, give your reasons in terms of the variables conditioning span of control discussed in the chapter.

    a) The foreman of a machine shop vs. the foreman of a group of brick-layers.

    b) The head of a research and development department vs. the head of a bookkeeping department.

    c) A district supervisor of supermarket store managers vs. a supervisor of waitresses in a restaurant.

7. "Establishing an organizational hierarchy and bestowing formalized power on individuals occupying positions in this structure may account for 10 per cent or more of our total costs. If we were to eliminate the man-agement structure and delegate all managerial duties to our workers, not only would they be more highly motivated as a result of being given greater responsibilities, but also an immediate 10 per cent cost reduc-tion could be gained." Evaluate such an approach.

8. In a firm employing 100 non-supervisory employees, what would be the ratio of total supervisory to total non-supervisory employees if the span of control utilized at each level in the organization is (a) 5, (b) 10? How many managerial levels would there be in each case? Draw an organization chart depicting each of these two organizations.

9. Are the advantages of job rotation inconsistent with those obtained from job specialization? Explain.

10. Increased job specialization is consistent with both motivational and learning theory as discussed in Chapter 4 of this text. Discuss.

11. Think of some job which you have performed, perhaps during summer vacation. Indicate for this type of work how its specialization beyond a certain point might effect inefficiencies due to technological considera-tions.

SELECTED REFERENCES

(See end of Chapter 8.)

CHAPTER 8

FORMAL ORGANIZATION: DEPARTMENTALIZATION

BECAUSE the manager's span of control is limited, it is necessary for business firms (except very small ones) to develop numerous sub-groups, which, in turn, are combined into larger and larger groups until the organization is encompassed as a pyramidal whole. A key managerial problem is that of determining what areas of work responsibility will be assigned to each such departmental grouping at each level in the organization.

The purpose of this chapter is to focus attention upon the problems involved in departmentalization in the business firm. In doing so, we will first describe four basic forms of departmentalization. Then we will consider some of the more important variables which must be considered in deciding upon the types of departments which should be established in an organization. In succeeding sections of this chapter, we will examine: (1) a modified type of departmentalization which has received attention in recent years— project organization, (2) the creation and functioning of staff departments, and (3) the utilization of managerial committees to deal with interdepartmental problems.

ALTERNATIVE BASES OF DEPARTMENTALIZATION

There are four basic ways in which departmental areas of responsibility may be defined in the business firm—by function, process, territory, or by product.[1] We will now examine each of these.

---

[1] In addition to these four bases, work activities are sometimes grouped on the basis of customers served. For example, one sales department might sell certain products to one group of customers, while another sales department sells the same products to a different group of customers. This form of work grouping which is sometimes referred to as departmentalization by *clientele* is not nearly as widely utilized as the four bases which we will discuss in this section.

Functions Performed

A common form of organizational structuring is that of departmentalization on the basis of functions performed. In a manufacturing firm, for example, all activities involved in purchasing might be assigned to one department, and all engineering work to another department, with production, sales and finance activities assigned to still other major departments. In retailing, a department store organized on the basis of functions performed might include the following major departments: (1) merchandising, to decide upon, purchase, and promote the lines of goods to be sold; (2) receiving, to inspect, store, and distribute goods to the selling floor; (3) sales, to which all the store's sales clerks are assigned; (4) credit, to grant credit, and handle collections; and (5) delivery, responsible for distributing goods to the store's customers. These two examples of functional departmentalization are illustrated in Figure 8–1.

Processes Employed

A second common form of departmentalization found in business firms is that based on technological processes employed. In process departmentalization, workers operating the same (or similar) types of machinery or equipment are grouped together and report to the same supervisor. In a machine shop, for example, one might find drill press, milling machine, lathe, screw machine, punch press, and stamping departments, as illustrated in Figure 8–2. Although process departmentalization is probably most common in manufacturing

FIGURE 8–1. Examples of Functional Departmentalization

A. MANUFACTURING

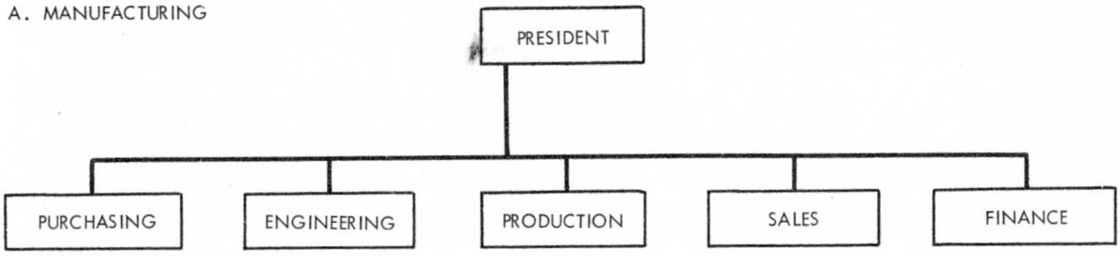

PRESIDENT

PURCHASING — ENGINEERING — PRODUCTION — SALES — FINANCE

B. RETAILING

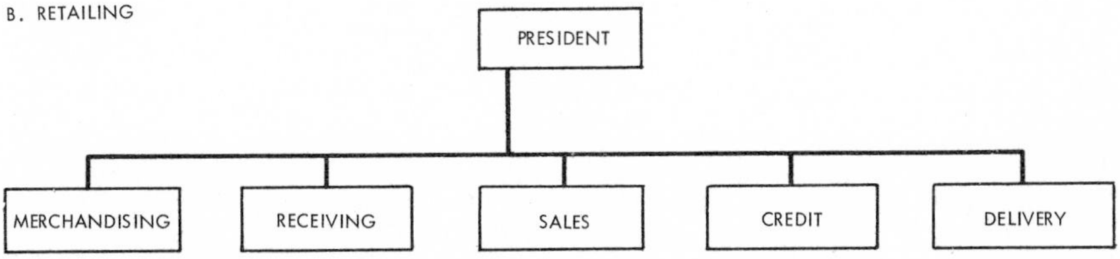

PRESIDENT

MERCHANDISING — RECEIVING — SALES — CREDIT — DELIVERY

FIGURE 8–2. Example of Process Departmentalization

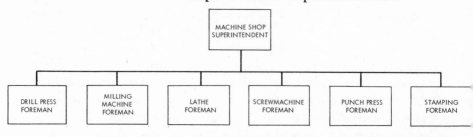

operations, this form of organizational structuring may be found elsewhere as well. For example, in an office situation, numerous typists may be grouped together into a typing pool; or, in a large computer center, all key punch operators may report to the same supervisor in a key punch department.

Product or Service Departmentalization

In many cases, all duties related to one or more products or services may be assigned to a particular department. In a large chemical firm, for example, the major operational departments might be plastics, oils, and chemicals, as is illustrated in Figure 8–3. Within each of these three major divisions, all activities involved in producing and selling the product classes assigned to the division would be carried out. As is also illustrated in Figure 8–3, the basis of departmentalization *within* a major product division may vary—the work performed within the chemical division in our example is broken down on the basis of product; while functional departmentalization exists within the oil division.

Conceptually similar to departmentalization based on products is that based on the grouping of similar services. Illustrative of a service departmentalized organization would be that of a large bank, in which departments were established to handle: (1) customer

FIGURE 8–3. Example of Product Departmentalization

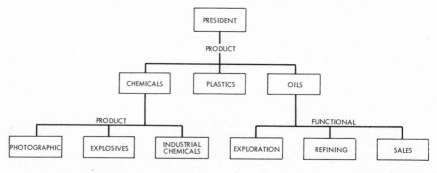

deposits and withdrawals, (2) mortgage and other loans, and (3) trusts.

Geographical Departmentalization

In many instances, firms will assign the activities involved in servicing a given geographical area to a particular department. In one large supermarket chain with which the authors are familiar,[2] for example, over twenty geographical divisions exist—a division encompassing all stores in the greater Cincinnati area, a Pittsburgh division, a Detroit division, etc. In addition, in this organization the activities carried out by these major geographical divisions are further broken down on the basis of territory serviced—the divisions are divided into a number of zones or districts, each comprised of several stores.

In addition to retailing operations such as the above in which a number of physically dispersed stores exist, many firms' sales and international operations are departmentalized geographically. It is fairly common for firms selling goods throughout this country to have a number of major territorial sales divisions (and offices)— e.g., Eastern, Midwestern, Southern, and Far Western—with, in many cases, further geographic sub-departmentalization within each region. For instance, a company's Eastern sales region might be divided into the following districts: (1) New England, (2) New York, (3) Pennsylvania, and (4) New Jersey, Maryland and Delaware. Because of the many special problems involved in doing business abroad, many companies have established separate divisions to encompass all of their international operations, and in many cases the activities of international operations departments are subdivided on a geographical basis. For example, in 1960 the Quaker Oats Company "owned twenty-one plants located in ten countries in Latin America, Canada, and Europe,"[3] and its international operations division was divided into three departments, one responsible for operations in each of these three geographical areas.

In some cases, the scope of responsibilities assigned to a geographic unit may be quite broad. Such is sometimes the case with department store chains which give each branch store considerable latitude to operate as a quasi-autonomous unit. In other instances, however, the scope of functions performed by territorial divisions or

---

[2] The Kroger Company.
[3] Thomas J. McNichols, *Policy Making and Executive Action*, (2nd ed.; New York: McGraw-Hill Book Company, Inc., 1963), p. 533.

FIGURE 8–4. Several Possible Basic Departmentalization
Alternatives for a Hypothetical Firm

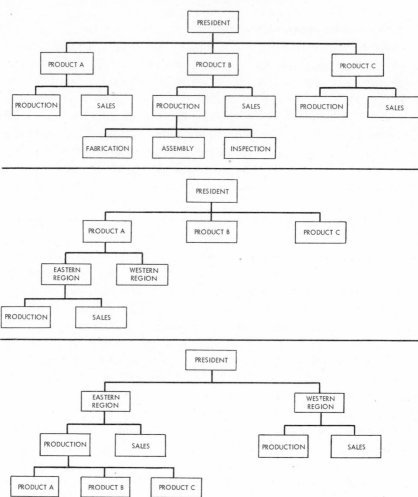

departments may be much narrower. Many regional sales divisions,
for instance, are permitted only to contact customers and obtain
orders, with advertising, pricing, marketing research, promotion and
other activities encompassed by the marketing function assigned to
a centralized marketing department.

VARIABLES INFLUENCING DEPARTMENTALIZATION DECISIONS

The departmentalization problem is an extremely complex one in
large business organizations, and especially those in which many

FIGURE 8–4. *Continued*

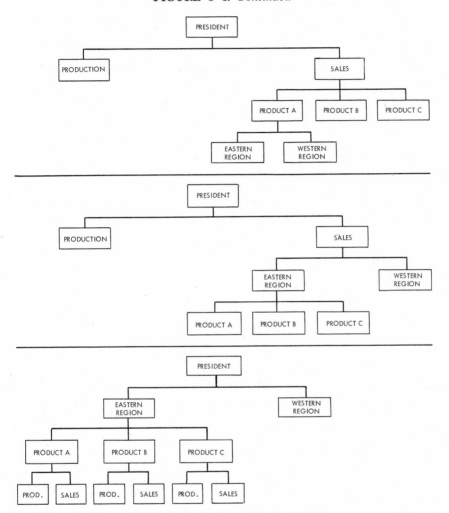

products are manufactured and sold to many different customer groups in diverse geographical areas. As we pointed out previously, departmentalization involves determining which activities should be grouped together at *each level* in the firm, and in large multi-level firms, the range of possible departmentalization alternatives which could be chosen may be quite large. To illustrate, Figure 8–4 depicts only a few of the many different forms of basic departmentalization which might be conceived of for a company manufacturing three products for sale throughout the United States. Further, the variables which will influence the effectiveness of any particular work grouping choice are often both considerable in number and interdependent. In the following sections we will consider several of these variables which we consider to be of importance.

The Nature and Physical Location of Operations

The nature and physical location of the firm's operations are important variables which often must be considered in making departmentalization decisions. For example, in one plant which manufactures automobile tires:

> The raw rubber is received at one end of the plant, and compounded at a nearby location. Then the various components of the tires (treads, beads, etc.) are turned out and transported to the tire building machines where tires are "built" from these components. The tires are next placed on conveyors and moved to another building, where they are later cured and finally to another building where they are finished and inspected. The plant manufactures several hundred different sizes of tires; although a majority of its production is comprised of a relatively small number of popular sizes. Different-sized tires are manufactured in "batches" or "lots" and the particular "mix" of sizes produced on any given day varies.

The nature and physical layout of these processing operations makes it almost mandatory to set up departmentalization by *process* within the tire plant—a receiving department, a tire building department, a curing department, etc. Departmentalization by product—with each supervisor responsible for all production stages for certain sizes and/or lines of tires—would not be feasible. Not only would each supervisor have to direct and instruct workers scattered all over the plant; but on any given day, each group of workers might be producing several different kinds of tires, falling under the jurisdiction of different supervisors—i.e., they would have several different bosses.

The physical dispersion of a firm's operations may also dictate to a considerable extent the types of departmentalization which are most effective. As we mentioned previously, firms with widely dispersed operations frequently utilize some form of geographic departmentalization. Some of the reasons why physical dispersion of operations may render geographic departmentalization an effective choice may be noted by considering the operations of a supermarket chain with stores in numerous locations. In most firms of this type, each separate store will have its own manager, with a head meat cutter, and head clerks for produce, grocery, and sometimes dairy departments reporting to him. Rather than such geographical departmentalization at the overall store level, however, product departmentalization would theoretically be possible. For example, in a

12-store chain encompassing a geographical area with a 200-mile radius: *one* meat manager might supervise the head meat cutters in *all* 12 stores, one produce manager might supervise all 12 head produce clerks, etc., with no one serving as manager of the overall operations of any one store. Among the reasons why most grocery chains do prefer to have one manager responsible for all operational areas of each store, rather than the alternative form of product departmentalization are as follows:

1.   Some one person with full responsibility for the operations is physically proximate and available for handling emergencies or other problems affecting the store as a whole—e.g., fire, theft, power failure, customer injuries in the store, etc.

2.   Better coordination of efforts among the product departments may be obtained. For example, the store manager could instruct his head grocery clerk to temporarily assign one of his people to help handle a work overload in the produce department; whereas, if the head produce and grocery clerks reported to different product managers, neither of whom was physically proximate, such reassignments would often be much more difficult to effect.

Additionally, giving one person the responsibility for coordinating all efforts in one geographical location may help develop his co-ordinative skills, which may better qualify him for higher-level managerial work. We will discuss this variable with respect to departmentalization more fully in the next section.

Decentralization, Coordination and Managerial Skills

A second important variable affecting departmentalization is the degree to which various alternative structural forms will permit the *decentralization* of decision making in the organization—i.e., the delegation of decision-making responsibilities by upper-level managers to their counterparts at lower levels in the organization. The decentralization of decision making may be desirable not only because it may help relieve the work burden of upper level managers, but also because it may provide lower level managers with more challenging work, and hence, greater opportunities for meeting their higher level needs.

Decentralization tends to be feasible when the delegated decision responsibilities do not have an impact on departmental sub-systems in the organization other than those under the jurisdiction of the manager making the decisions. Decisions made in the firm will differ widely in the extent to which they have an interdepartmental impact. To illustrate, one manager, upon assuming a position in a firm, found that he was expected to approve all salaries in his division above $5000 per year. He decentralized this decision-making responsibility by setting up constraints in terms of a salary budget and salary policies, and allowing his subordinate managers to make salary decisions within these defined limits. The establishment of the constraints minimized any possible negative interdepartmental impact of the decisions delegated—e.g., inconsistencies in salaries from one department to another resulting from different policies followed by each of his subordinate managers.

Decentralization of salary decisions as discussed above could be effected with any form of departmentalization—product, functional, process, or geographical. Some types of managerial decisions, however, can be delegated to a much greater extent with certain types of departmentalization than with others. For example, suppose a manufacturing plant produces three products, each requiring three processing operations, fabrication, assembly, and inspection, in that order; and that the technology is such (e.g., ways in which the machinery and equipment could be located) that either a product or process type of departmentalization were possible—as is illustrated in Figure 8–5. In these operations, the decentralization of certain types of decisions would be possible under the product departmentalization alternative, whereas it would not be with the process structure. For example, important to such operations is the coordinated scheduling of each operation so that there is a smooth flow of work from one process to the next. If, for instance, only enough workers were scheduled to permit the fabrication of 500 units a day, while the assemblers assigned to work could turn out 2000 units per day, the latter would not have a sufficient number of pieces to keep them busy (unless large inventories of fabricated, but yet unassembled units were available). With the product form of departmentalization illustrated in Figure 8–5, worker scheduling decisions could be delegated to the *general foreman* since each would have responsibility for all of the three *interdependent* phases of work flow required in turning out his product. With the process structure, however, these interdependent scheduling decisions would have to be made *centrally* by the *plant manager* (or one of his assistants), since coordination of work schedules among all three major process departments is necessary.

FIGURE 8–5. Example of Product vs. Process Departmentalization

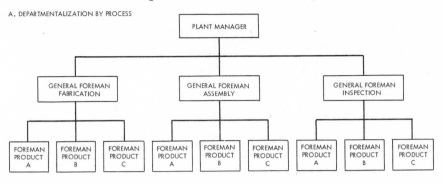

A. DEPARTMENTALIZATION BY PROCESS

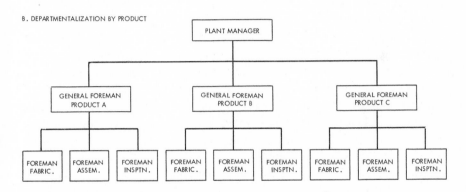

B. DEPARTMENTALIZATION BY PRODUCT

Several other observations are in order concerning the impact of departmentalization on decentralization, coordination, and managerial decision making. First, departmentalization by either process or function tends to result in *interdependent stages* of work flow being assigned to *different supervisors* (as illustrated in our above example) to a greater extent than does either product or geographical departmentalization. For this reason, the decentralization of many decision-making responsibilities tends to be more difficult with either a process or functional grouping of activities than with either a product or geographical one. This does not mean, of course, that all, or even most, decision responsibilities can easily be decentralized to lower level managers in a product or geographical-based organization structure. For example, if a supermarket chain with 20 stores in a large city were to permit each store manager to determine what meat specials (and prices) would be offered in his store each week:

1. The firm often would not be able to obtain as good prices on its meat purchases as it would if larger quantities of the same meat item were bought for sale in all stores; and,

2. Its problems of local newspaper and television advertising would be complicated, since no single ad could apply to all stores.

In consequnce, most chains operating under such conditions generally do not delegate the responsibility for determining and pricing weekly specials to their store managers.

Second, observations are sometimes made that a firm employing product or geographical departmentalization is, *because of* its departmentalization choice, *necessarily* a "decentralized" organization. While we have shown that it is generally easier to decentralize certain decision-making responsibilities in product or territorial based departments, it may also be quite easy to *centralize* decision making in such departments. Consider, for example, a "Five-and-Ten" retail chain with several hundred stores. Since the operations of each store are basically similar, many of the decisions made for one store would be applicable to others in the chain. To the extent that such is the case, firms of this type often have found it more economical to have experts in store layout, merchandising, counter display, employee training, etc. make these decisions for all of their stores. It is inappropriate, therefore, to refer to a firm as "centralized" or "decentralized" in its decision making simply on the basis of the type(s) of departmentalization it employs. Whether a company decentralizes many of its decision responsibilities depends more upon other factors. Again, however, the decentralization of many decisions can be more readily effected in product or territorial-based departments than in functional or process based ones.

A third aspect of departmentalization of importance to managerial decision making is that the coordination of activities tends to be a more complex problem for managers of product and geographical based departments than for those managing process or functional departments. This is especially true when several *interdependent* work processes are placed under the jurisdiction of a product or territorial manager. In our previous example of the plant manufacturing three products, each calling for fabrication, assembly, and inspection, relatively little coordinative work scheduling could be carried on by the general foremen under the process form of departmentalization discussed; whereas, under the product structure, each general foreman could be permitted to schedule his fabrication, assembly, and inspection operations so as to provide for a smooth flow of work through these interdependent processes.

The additional coordination which may be required with a product or territorial grouping leads to two important implications for management. First, and somewhat related to our previous discussion of decentralization, is that one of the basic reasons why many large, multi-product firms establish separate product divisions is to allow the delegation of many coordinative responsibilities from the presidential level to lower levels in the organization. For example, consider a large electrical firm manufacturing household appliances, light bulbs, and power generation equipment. In such a firm, coordinating the various functions and stages involved in producing and selling any particular product would involve many more complex problems than would inter-product coordination. For instance, for each product: production schedules have to be coordinated with sales forecasts (or orders sold); pricing policies may have to be made in light of production costs; customer complaints as to defective products received by the firm's salesmen may have to be worked out with quality control; etc. If such a firm's primary departmentalization were functional, the burden of resolving all coordinative problems among production and sales for all products would be placed upon the shoulders of its president, whereas with primary product divisions, such problems could be handled at one level lower in the organization, by the product vice-presidents. These effects of departmentalization are illustrated in Figure 8–6.

A second important implication is that the more frequently product and geographical managers are faced with coordinative problems, the more *experience* they will gain in dealing with these problems. At the top levels in a firm, the manager must perceive and deal with the operations of his organization as an integrated whole, and in doing so, manage the interrelationships among numerous organizational sub-systems. Managerial experience at lower levels in the organization constitutes probably the most important experience that aspirants to top level executive positions can have. As a training experience for top level positions, the management of process and functionally-based departments has limitations, since the problems which managers deal with in such departments tend to be relatively narrow in scope, focusing upon a work stage or a processing technology rather than upon the coordination of many interdependent activities. A manager's advancement within a functional department such as engineering may depend to a considerable extent upon

FIGURE 8–6. Coordinative Problems—Functional vs.
Product Departmentalization

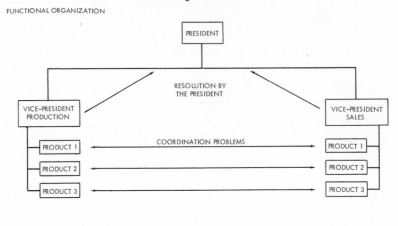

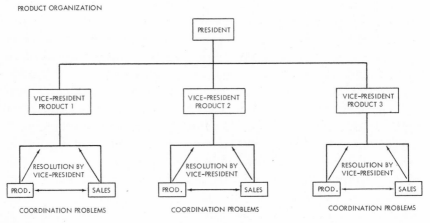

his becoming a more and more skilled and knowledgeable specialist in engineering. If encouragement is given to learning more about such specialized areas as this, expertise in the function may be developed at the expense of perceiving and dealing with interrelationships among different functions—i.e., those executive qualities considered of prime importance at upper levels in the organization. The manager may gain experience in perceiving and dealing with interrelated work stages before he reaches top executive levels if he is given an opportunity to manage departments organized in such a way as to require inter-functional or inter-process coordination—i.e., departments established on a territorial or product basis comprising multiple interdependent functional and process responsibilities.

Duplication of Work

In most large organizations many of the same types of work are carried on at more than one location. For example, checking out customers at the cash register will take place in every one of a firm's 150 physically dispersed supermarkets; interviewing prospective applicants for employment may be done at each of a company's eight manufacturing plants, etc. In many cases, such simultaneous performance of identical (or very similar) activities at numerous locations in a firm is necessitated, not because of the way its organization is structured, but because a need exists to provide services on a dispersed basis. For example, customers would have to be checked out in each of the 150 supermarkets mentioned above regardless of whether the chain was organized on a product or geographical basis.

In some cases, however, business firms will be afforded a choice as to whether certain types of similar activities should: (1) be all grouped together in one process or functional department, or (2) be dispersed, with some of them being performed in each of a number of product or territorial based departments. One problem which sometimes may occur when the performance of similar tasks is so dispersed is that an uneconomical *duplication of effort* takes place. For example, in one firm in which several product divisions existed, each of two of its divisions was simultaneously developing a complex computer program for handling payrolls. Neither division was aware of the fact that the other was engaged in what was essentially the same project. If the firm had been organized such that the development of all such computer programs were carried on in one functionally based department, the duplication of effort probably would not have occurred. We should point out that problems such as this may be minimized when those managers responsible for the performance of similar functions in different product or geographical divisions are in communication with each other regarding the projects which they are working on and/or contemplating for the future.[4] Nonetheless, the problem of unnecessary duplication of work tends to be a greater one with both product and territorial departmentalization than with either functional or process forms.

---

[4] Further, some firms will have additional centralized departments dealing with the same functional areas as those assigned to the product divisions. In such cases, the centralized functional managers may help insure that unnecessary duplication does not occur in the product divisions. We will discuss the employment of both centralized and divisional departments dealing with the same functional area more fully in a later section.

The Balancing of Work Loads

Another reason for establishing process and functional based departments which we have not yet discussed is to permit a balancing of work loads. To illustrate, in one manufacturing plant with which the authors are familiar, three different product lines are produced; and the basic departmentalization is a product one, with a general foreman responsible for each product reporting to the plant manager. However, all time study work in the plant is assigned to one centralized industrial engineering department; rather than having three or four industrial engineers reporting to each general foreman. One reason for the functional grouping of all industrial engineering activities is to provide greater balance in the work loads of the engineers.[5] Frequently, during certain time periods considerable time study work is required in one of the product departments, with relatively little work called for in the others. With the functional departmentalization, any or all of the engineers can be assigned to any of the product departments as the need may arise, whereas if a few engineers were assigned to work only in one department, they would on occasion be overloaded with work, while those engineers assigned to the other product departments might have little to do. It is for a similar reason that in many office operations—in which clerical work relative to several different functions (or products) is carried on—typist pools are established. In such cases, numerous typists are grouped together under one supervisor (process departmentalization), and handle work sent to the typing pool from executives, who may be responsible for such diverse areas as marketing, engineering, personnel, and finance.

PROJECT DEPARTMENTALIZATION

In recent years, a special type of product departmentalization which deserves special attention has been developed in certain types of organizations. This structural form is referred to as *project* departmentalization. Under project departmentalization, personnel from existing functional departments are typically assigned on a semi-permanent basis to work for a project manager, who is respon-

---

[5] Such a functional grouping of all industrial engineers under the same department head may also help ensure that the engineers are consistent in establishing work standards—i.e., that some engineers do not set rates which are much "tighter" or "looser" than others. For a discussion of the problem of consistency in developing time standards, see George Strauss and Leonard R. Sayles, *Personnel: The Human Problems of Management* (Englewood Cliffs, N. J.: Prentice-Hall, Inc., 1960), pp. 626 ff.

sible for all activities required to turn out a relatively short-lived project. As soon as the project is completed, the personnel who had been assigned to it are reassigned either to their functional departments or to other projects.

In "pure" project departments, the project manager has direct supervisory power over all personnel assigned to him from the various functional departments. Under such an arrangement, individual engineers, research personnel, etc., typically report to project supervisors, who in turn report to the project manager (since the number of personnel working on large projects would normally be greater than the project manager could supervise directly by himself).

In American firms, a major impetus to project departmentalization has been the missile and space race touched off by the Soviet launching of Sputnik. After that time, numerous crash programs aimed at insuring the delivery of space systems were undertaken. Under such conditions of urgency, separate project departments were established so that special managerial attention could be given to high-priority programs. When a project is in progress, a project department is in many ways quite similar to a product-based department. In each case, the departmental manager has control over the functions, activities, and resources necessary to achieve a specified output. The generation of output in a product department is expected to continue more or less indefinitely, but the work of a project department has a limited life span. The work required for the completion of some projects may take only a few months or less. For others, however, several years of effort may be needed—e.g., work on a complex manned space-vehicle system.

During the life cycle of many large projects, numerous changes will occur in the types of work activities which need to be performed. In a 5-year missile project, for example, the bulk of the engineering efforts required might be expended during the first two years, with the peak utilization of tooling facilities subsequently following. Then, at a later time, the number of production man hours required for the project would be at its maximum. Thus, a problem faced by many project managers is that of frequently having to build up certain functions while, at the same time, having to decelerate or disband others.

In general, project departments have been utilized, and tend to be justified to the greatest extent, when one or more of the following conditions exist:

1.   The size of the project is *large* relative to the capacity of the organization, and the per unit dollar value is high.

2.   Some aspect of the project (e.g., delivery or cost) is considered *critical* to the success of the organization, either in the short or long run.

3.   When required by the customer. (To obtain a large space system contract, one contractor firm felt compelled to guarantee the contracting government agency that it would initiate a complete product organization to manage the design and production of the system).

Even when the above conditions do exist, project departments have been criticized as resulting in over-organization and over-manning in a company. With this type of organizational arrangement, a firm not only has to employ functional maagers but also a number of project managers and supervisors. Also, the question has been raised: "What is so different about the work of one-time contracts that the work required on them could not be assigned sequentially to each of a firm's functional departments, as would be work on a *special order*, say, of furniture for a new hotel? A furniture company can merely sequence work on such an order in its regular stream of work along with its other orders, even though it might require some special and unique operations. Many firms do produce specially-ordered, unique items for which there is no recurring demand. Why couldn't contract work on a large defense project be handled in a similar manner?

On the other hand, project departmentalization—which is fairly common in some industries which do considerable contract work, such as in the aerospace industry—has been defended on the grounds that it does help assure the meeting of project goals. As the general manager of an aerospace division employing almost 10,000 people, doing contract work for several military organizations and foreign countries, and handling several hundred contracts at a time, has pointed out:

> I have a project manager for every contract, no matter how small. Perhaps we don't need them for spare parts contracts since these are almost production runs, but project managers are vital for research and development contracts where numerous uncertainties exist with respect to performance, delivery, and cost. With project managers, I am assured that someone is seeing to it that we meet our commitments and that we make a profit on each contract if at all possible. If we just ran these projects through our functional departments without individual attention, many of them would get lost in the shuffle.

Some people refer to project managers as glorified expediters, but they are responsible for more than just getting the work out on time. They are responsible for working with the customer to insure that our designs meet their needs. They are responsible for costs and profits. The expense of project management is justified in my mind since it relieves me from having to worry and getting involved in running down these problems. I couldn't keep on top of them all by myself. The manager of our largest contract has a staff of eleven people, but his contract comprises about 45 percent of our total business at present. He has about 4,500 people working for him. The expense incurred in operating his office is relatively small. In contrast, for some of our smaller contracts, one manager may supervise up to a dozen separate contracts.

Furthermore, functional departmentalization, as an alternative approach, also has its limitations. For example, under a functional type organization in the Department of Defense, each functional service in the Army often felt the need for a detailed review of proposals for new weapons systems, and a lengthy evaluation of the performance of contractors on such systems contracts. With many different groups responsible for different phases of development and procurement, it was believed that the lead time on Army weapons "was excessive, that in some cases costs were higher than necessary and that performance once in the field, was not always equal to the needs of combat." [6] As a result, separate project organizations were established for different major systems.

One further observation is in order concerning project departmentalization. If a firm has a large number of smaller contracts, each of a relatively short duration but still utilizes project managers, personnel tend to be shifted frequently from one project (and project manager) to another. In some such cases, individuals may be assigned to one project for one week or more, and then be shifted to another. In other cases, personnel from the functional departments may be called on to work part-time on several projects during any given time period. Under either of these conditions, some firms will employ a modified type of project departmentalization, sometimes referred to as a *matrix* type of organization. With the matrix form, personnel remain permanently assigned to their functional departments, although working at various times for the different project managers.

When an individual works for a project manager on a part-time or temporary basis, he will normally take orders from and report to

---

[6] Lt. General F. S. Besson, Jr., "Project Management Within the Army Matériel Command," in Fremont E. Kast and James E. Rosenzweig, eds., *Science, Technology and Management* (New York: McGraw-Hill Book Company, Inc., 1963), p. 92.

the project manager. Yet, the basic responsibility for deciding upon any pay raises and promotions which he may obtain is in the hands of the manager of the functional department to which he is permanently assigned. In effect, then, he is working for two supervisors, which violates one of the so-called principles of management—unity of command—which prescribes that an individual should have only one "boss." While the functional manager and the project manager may work closely together in guiding and evaluating an individual's work performance, if conflicts arise among the two managers, the subordinate would tend to follow the lead of his functional supervisor, upon whom his future in the organization depends to a greater extent. The existence of this problem again points up the fact that project departmentalization tends to be more suited to firms working on large projects of relatively long duration.

STAFF DEPARTMENTS

There is a considerable breadth of knowledge necessary for a manager to perform his work effectively. In fact, Frederick W. Taylor, the "father of scientific management" held that the knowledge required of supervisors is generally so broad and extensive that they cannot be expected to be an expert in each area for which they are responsible. As a result of this belief, Taylor devised a form of organization structure referred to as *functional foremanship*. In it, each worker was supervised by eight different foremen, each of whom was an expert in a specialized area of operations. This form of organizational structuring is illustrated in Figure 8–7.

FIGURE 8–7. Functional Foremanship

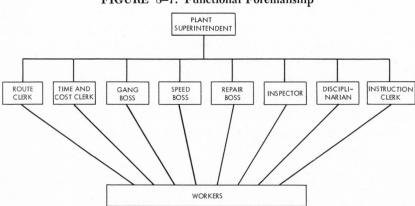

Taylor's functional foremanship never became widely used, primarily because of the confusion engendered with the workers being given directions—sometimes in conflict with one another—by eight different supervisors.[7] The need for managerial expertise, however, is just as important today, if not more so, than it was in Taylor's day.

Practically all business firms of any size today attempt to meet this need by employing individuals, or groups of individuals, who are experts on certain particular aspects of management. Such experts, who deal with some limited part of the total managerial job, and who provide specialized knowledge or services to the rest of the organization, are commonly designated by the term *"staff."* Among the more common staff departments found in business organizations today are personnel, accounting, marketing research, engineering, legal, public relations, and production control. To differentiate such specialists from those managers who supervise workers *directly engaged* in the firm's primary activities of producing or selling its goods or services, the latter are commonly referred to as *line* managers. For example, on the organization chart illustrated in Figure 8–8:

1. The firm's president is its top line manager with the production and sales vice-presidents, the foremen in charge of fabrication

FIGURE 8–8. Hypothetical Organization Chart Illustrating Line and Staff Managers (and Departments)

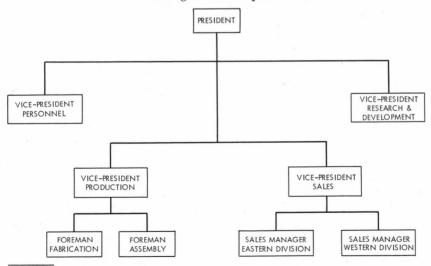

---

[7] As the reader may note, this arrangement violates the "unity of command" concept mentioned previously.

and assembly, and the sales managers for each division all being line officials;

2. The vice-presidents for personnel and research and development are designated as staff managers.

Two other observations concerning the concepts of line and staff are in order at this point. First, not all managers designated as "staff" are experts in some particular specialized area as described above—there are certain exceptions. For example, in some firms staff assistants who are "generalists" are employed to relieve top managers of many of the burdensome details of their work. These staff assistants are frequently designated "assistant to"—e.g., "Assistant to the President."

Second, we should point out that the distinction between "staff" and "line" is in many ways a blurred one; and considerable differences of opinion exist as to what precisely are the differences between the two.[8] Furthermore, some departments (and functions) are designated as "staff" in some firms, but as "line" in others. This is perhaps especially true for the finance function in business organizations.

Types of Staff Work

To clarify the functions which staff personnel perform in organizations, we will now examine three types of specialized assistance which staff departments may provide to the business organization.

One of the most common functions performed by staff managers is that of studying and analyzing problems and developing problem-solutions. The personnel department, for example, may design psychological tests for use in selecting job applicants, and through the utilization of such tests and other selection techniques, make recommendations as to whether specific job applicants should be hired. Or, the firm's operations research department may develop a mathematical model for inventory control; its marketing research department may analyze the market potential for a proposed new product, etc.

In addition to analyzing managerial problems, staff specialists may undertake the function of preparing and processing data which

[8] Compare, for example, the discussion of line and staff in John M. Pfiffner and Frank P. Sherwood, *Administrative Organization* (Englewood Cliffs, N. J.: Prentice-Hall, Inc., 1960), Chap. 10, with that in Harold Koontz and Cyril O'Donnell, *Principles of Management* (2nd ed.; New York: McGraw-Hill Book Company, Inc., 1959), Chap. 9.

line managers need for making decisions. Top- and middle-level line managers, who usually do not have close daily contact with work being performed at lower levels in the organization, must rely heavily upon indirect methods, rather than direct observation, to determine what is going on at these levels. Information about operating performance may be provided by various staff departments— cost data by accounting, labor turnover and accident rate data by personnel, etc. Since many managers in a firm may require similar types of information about operating performance, integrated systems for data collection and processing are often economical. For example, accounting departments frequently collect all types of cost and financial data from all parts of the organization for use by all managers in the firm. Since they often are experts in data *analysis* as well, such departments are frequently charged with preparing financial analyses, cost estimates on new projects, etc. Thus, many staff groups, such as accounting, perform the function of problem analysis as well as that of data collection and processing.

Finally, we should point out that not all organizational personnel engaged in staff work are managers. Rather, non-managerial staff *service* groups exist in many business firms. For example, maintenance crews may be assigned the responsibility for all maintenance activities in a plant from repairing machines which have broken down to replacing burned out light bulbs in the plant manager's office; or, draftsmen may be employed to provide drafting assistance to the firm's engineers. One basic advantage of such non-managerial staff specialization is that it may enable a firm to reduce its wage costs by permitting its more highly skilled employees to concentrate their efforts upon the most highly skilled aspects of their jobs; while relegating those parts of their work calling for less skill to lower-paid workers. For example, draftsmen develop drawings for engineers so that the latter may concentrate their efforts on design work and avoid "wasting" their talents on doing their own drawings.

Staff Powers

When staff positions and departments are created separate from the line organization, the question is posed: "What powers shall the staff personnel be given" to *study* problems only, to *provide the results* of those studies undertaken to line managers for their use, to *recommend* actions that line managers should undertake or, to *"tell"* or *dictate to* line management those courses of action which should be taken based upon staff study and analyses? The range of powers given to staff may fall anywhere on this continuum—from simply studying problems to actually "calling the shots" as to what line management should do—and may be illustrated by the following story about the president of a small brewery:

The president of the brewery found himself so burdened with work that he hired an economist to help him keep his knowledge of the raw materials market up to date. Since the cost of grains constituted such a large percentage of the firm's total expenses, the president had personally purchased all these raw materials.

The president first explained to the economist the data he needed, their sources, and the kinds of analyses he had been utilizing. He trained the economist in the *collection* and *preparation* of these data.

After a few months had gone by, the president requested *recommendations* from the economist as to which grains should be purchased. In many cases, the recommendations were discussed at length by the two. The president, however, continued to make all final decisions on grain purchases. Before long, the president gained considerable confidence in the economist's work. He became dependent on the economist to prepare the *purchase orders,* and to submit these to him along with the economist's recommendations.

One day when he was exceptionally busy, the president signed the purchase orders without bothering to read the recommendations. Soon thereafter, he regularly omitted reading the orders and eventually prepared a rubber stamp with his signature for use by the economist. Some time later, the rubber stamp was lost, and from that time on, the economist signed all purchase orders himself.

The gradual expansion of staff power as illustrated in this example is not uncommon. In many cases, staff personnel may initially simply provide information sought by the line, then, be called on to make recommendations, and ultimately, as line management gains more and more confidence in their abilities, be given the power to make decisions formerly made by line.

We should also note that staff personnel actually possess what might be termed *"implicit decision powers"* even when they are only called on to study problems and make recommendations. If staff has the power to recommend, it has, at the same time, the power *not to recommend.* The number of possible alternatives which staff personnel *might* recommend in many cases may be very large. When a staff manager recommends considering only one or two such alternatives, he may, in effect, be conditioning to a considerable extent the ultimate decision which will be made. This is because line managers—lacking time to research problems further and having confidence in their staff advisors—often have a tendency to consider only those alternatives explicitly recommended by the staff.

The powers which staff possess may also be examined in terms of their *control over information*. As we emphasized in Chapter 3, decisions made by managers are strongly influenced by the informational inputs at their disposal. For this reason, staff managers, who generate the basic data on which line decisions will be largely based, may influence these decisions considerably by the way in which the information is developed and presented to line management. The methodology which a staff manager employs in developing information may be biased by his educational and/or professional background. Further, his own personal prejudices may lead to his "slanting" the information in one direction or another. For example, if a personnel researcher has a strong anti-union bias, this bias may well influence the data he prepares with respect to the firm's contract negotiations. Although such biases may not be conscious or intentional, they nonetheless, may have a considerable impact on decisions made by line management.

Line-Staff Frictions

A problem which appears common to most large organizations is that of numerous conflicts and frictions existing between line and staff departments. There are many different reasons why line-staff conflicts may arise. We will examine some of the more important of these in this section.

In many firms, staff departments have expanded their scope of activities considerably over the past several decades. In many cases, this expansion has led to an erosion of the power of certain line managers. As we pointed out in Chapter 5, many of the decision areas for which first-line foremen were once responsible in many companies have been assigned to various staff departments—e.g., personnel, quality control, industrial engineering, etc. Although first-line foremen have undoubtedly welcomed the opportunity to have staff departments relieve them of certain responsibilities, in numerous instances they have grown resentful of staff personnel "usurping" more and more of their powers.

A second reason for the emergence of problems in line-staff relationships is that in some cases both line and staff may have certain responsibilities for dealing with a particular problem, but there may exist no clear definition as to what powers each possesses with respect to resolving the problem. To illustrate, in one manufacturing plant, the manager of training, who reported to the personnel manager (as is illustrated in Figure 8–9), was given the responsibility

FIGURE 8–9. Partial Organizational Chart for Plant Situation
Illustrating Line-Staff Conflict

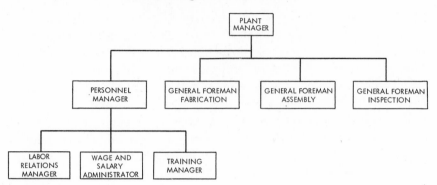

of developing a training program for a number of new production
workers who had recently been assigned to the plant's fabrication
department. The general foreman, who *also* had the responsibility
of making sure that his new employees were trained adequately,
resisted many of the training manager's ideas for the program as
being "new-fangled" and "too theoretical"; and he took the position
that his people should be trained by certain methods which had
been followed in the past, but which the training manager considered unsound in terms of learning theory. In this case, the training manager had no power to command the general foreman to
follow his program, even though if his program was rejected and
the training of the new employees, as a consequence, was to be ineffective, he would be held (at least partially) responsible for the
failure. On the other hand, the general foreman realized that if he rejected the training manager's program, and the training then failed,
he might be severely criticized by the plant manager for not bowing
to the wishes of the staff specialist. Further complicating the relationship between the training manager and general foreman were
numerous *status incongruences*. The training manager held a graduate degree while the general foreman had never finished high school;
he was considered an expert in training methodology while the foreman was not. Yet, the general foreman held a higher level position
in the firm's organizational hierarchy, earned several thousand dollars more per year than the training manager, and had been with
the company about twenty years longer. Such incongruences, we
should point out, are not uncommon in line-staff relationships. In
general, staff groups tend to be better educated, more articulate
and younger than many of their line counterparts, whereas many

of the line managers with whom they must deal enjoy higher level and better salaried positions in the organizational hierarchy.

One additional observation is in order concerning our above illustration. Ultimately, the disagreements between the training manager and general foreman were brought to the attention of the plant manager. Among the decision alternatives available to him for resolving this problem were: (1) to support the staff specialist's position, (2) to support the general foreman, or (3) attempt to get the two to work out some sort of compromise solution themselves. In this case, the plant manager chose the latter alternative.

The bringing of this dispute to the plant manager's attention illustrates another common problem emanating from the existence of line and staff departments—the problem faced by top line managers as to what to do when line-staff frictions do exist. If top management consistently supports the staff in such situations, the lower level line manager may come to perceive that he might as well take orders directly from the staff, since he will ultimately be directed by his superior to bow to the wishes of staff. On the other hand, consistent support of lower line by top management may lead staff to feel frustrated because of an inability to gain acceptance for their programs.

Two further sources of conflict between line and staff deserve mention. First, in some cases staff managers are called on to develop and to present to top line management data for control purposes on the operations of lower-line managers, which makes the latter appear in an unfavorable light. For example, a personnel manager's monthly safety report may indicate that the accident rate among workers under the supervision of the plant's fabrication foreman is exceptionally high. Or, cost data developed by the accounting staff for the plant manager may indicate that costs are way out-of-line in the foreman's department. Since this type of work performed by staff may pinpoint weaknesses in the line departments, the line managers may come to perceive the staff as posing a threat to them. This threatening aspect of staff work may be minimized if the staff reports any performance inadequacies detected in the line manager's department directly to the line manager himself, rather than to his superior. For instance, the head accountant might inform the fabrication foreman that his costs are out-of-line, discuss with him ways for dealing with the problem, and the problem might readily be overcome by the foreman himself.

Second, conflicts may sometimes arise in organizations when several line departments are competing for services performed by staff groups. For instance, if all maintenance crews in a plant are already overloaded with work, and each of two production supervisors has a machine which "has just broken down and must be repaired at once if production schedules are to be met," the maintenance manager would be faced with the problem as to which of the two line supervisor's requests should be given priority. Such problems—which, of course, tend to occur more frequently when staff services are being fully utilized—may in some cases be resolved not so much on the basis of which priority choice is optimal for the firm as a whole as upon friendships among the staff and certain line supervisors and/or staff's perception of the status and power of the different line supervisors making the requests for services.

One final observation is in order concerning line-staff frictions. The reader should *not* infer that all conflict between line and staff managers is *inherently bad*. In some cases, a line and staff manager may have differing perceptions as to how a certain problem should be handled, each of which has some merit. In the situation involving the training manager and general foreman discussed previously, for instance, the training manager's program as originally conceived was probably too theory-oriented, while the general foreman's thinking did not give sufficient emphasis to some valid theoretical concepts. In this situation, a compromise solution was ultimately worked out which incorporated the thinking of both the line and staff manager. In many respects, the compromise program was probably more effective than the training would have been had just the ideas of either of the two managers been followed. Because different managers will have different backgrounds, perceptions, and objectives, some degree of conflict will always exist in organizations, not only among line and staff, but among different line managers, and different staff managers as well. What is important to the firm is that the disruptive effects of conflict be minimized, and that a constructive resolution of conflicting viewpoints be effected.

Location of Staff Activities

Another decision problem often faced by management is that of determining where staff departments are to be located in the organization. If the services of a staff department are utilized extensively throughout an organization, there may be a need to locate it relatively high up in the hierarchical structure. Many firms, for example, have centralized staff departments handling legal, public relations, and personnel problems relative to all divisions in the company and headed by a vice-president, who reports directly to the president. If all staff groups of this type should report to the president, however, his span of control may become so large that he cannot give adequate attention to them. Some large organizations, with many staff groups, have attempted to overcome this problem by combining numerous staff functions into a smaller number of departments, each with a fairly broad scope of responsibility. General Electric, for example, has utilized a Vice-President of Relations, given responsibilities encompassing personnel and industrial, as well as public relations.

If a staff group is designed to provide services to a single function in contrast to many throughout the firm, on the other hand, it is only logical to subordinate the staff to that function. For example, draftsmen, who assist engineers, would normally be grouped within a firm's engineering department. Or, even though they may provide some services to many departments in an organization, purchasing and quality control groups may report to a firm's top manufacturing manager because the major portion of their assistance is provided to manufacturing.

One further observation needs to be made concerning the location of staff departments. In many large organizations with multiple product or territorial divisions, staff departments dealing with the same functional area will be created both: (1) centrally, and reporting to the president, and (2) within each product or geographical division, and reporting to the divisional manager. This phenomenon is often referred to as *staff parallelism*. In a large geographically dispersed supermarket chain, for example, parallel staff departments as illustrated in Figure 8–10 might well be found. In such a case, the centralized staff departments would normally be responsible for such activities as research, developing overall company policies, and providing technical assistance to the geographical divisions; while the divisional staff groups would focus attention on implementing company policies and on the day-to-day operational problems of their divisions. For example, consider the area of personnel selection:

1. The centralized personnel staff might develop and validate psychological tests for use in all divisions, determine what scores on the tests should be attained by job applicants if they are to be considered for employment by the firm; develop brochures for use by

FIGURE 8–10. Staff Parallelism

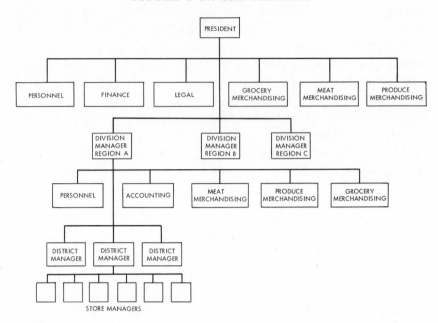

the divisional personnel managers outlining the company's selection procedures, and possibly train the divisional staff in such facets of selection as interpretation of the psychological tests; while

2. Each divisional personnel department might be responsible for: placing ads announcing job openings in the supermarkets in local newspapers; interviewing, giving the psychological tests to job applicants, and interpreting the test results; arranging for physical examinations and credit checks on applicants; making recommendations to its divisional line management as to whether particular job applicants should be hired, etc.

When parallel staff departments exist, not only must the organization be concerned with line-staff relationships (and frictions), but staff-staff relations must also be given consideration. To illustrate, a divisional personnel manager in our above example reports to his divisional manager, yet at the same time he may be expected to follow the policies and procedures developed by the central personnel staff. Although the central staff has no direct command power over him, he may feel strong pressures to abide by their wishes. One reason for this is that he may be aiming for a future promotion to the central staff (or to a personnel position entailing greater responsibilities in another of the firm's divisions) rather than to a higher level position outside his speciality in his own division; and, thus, want to be looked upon favorably by the central staff group, who probably would have considerable influence on any such promotional decisions. Thus, divisional staff personnel may often have divided loyalties—loyalties to both their own division and to the central staff group in their function. This condition may lead to no special problems in many instances, for the divisional manager may be in full accord with the policies, procedures, etc., which the central staff wants his own staff to follow. However, when the central staff's influence efforts are incongruent with the philosophy and wishes of the divisional manager, his staff may find themselves in a conflict situation.[9]

ORGANIZATIONAL COMMITTEES

Up to this point, we have focused attention upon work assigned to individual members of the organization who are grouped together into a department headed by a supervisor or manager. Many firms, governmental agencies, and educational institutions, however, also employ committees—often comprised of individuals from different departments—to deal with certain kinds of problems. Committees may be classed into two general types. First, there are *ad hoc*, or special committees, which are charged with dealing with temporary or nonrecurring problems such as exploring the question as to whether the firm should purchase or rent an electronic computer. Second, are *standing* committees, which are concerned with problems or problem areas of a continuing nature. For example, in many manufacturing plants, production committees comprised of the plant manager and his department heads will meet once or twice a week to deal with common problems. We will now discuss some of the values and limitations of the utilization of committees.

As a means of promulgating and obtaining information more quickly, a department head may meet in committee with his subordinate managers rather than communicating separately with each. Further, if the work flow between the departments headed by the subordinate managers requires coordination, information from one

---

[9] There are, of course, many different strategies that the staff might employ in dealing with such problems, depending on their objectives and perception of the situation—e.g., following central staff's policies completely and ignoring their own boss's reactions; attempting to influence their superior that the central staff position should be adhered to; following their superior's position while trying to placate the central staff, etc.

department that affects the others can be brought forth and areas of conflict among departments can be discussed in committee. Such discussions may make possible greater mutual understanding of common problems among the manager and his department heads.

In addition to providing a vehicle for the exchange of information and discussion of common problems, committees may also be utilized to make decisions or recommendations with respect to problems which affect numerous different departments. For instance, the evaluation of new products is often undertaken by committees, since new product proposals must be satisfactory from the viewpoint of a number of different functional managers in the firm: engineering, production, marketing, finance, etc. The utilization of committees permits representatives from each of the affected departments to evaluate the impact of the proposals upon his own operations.

Additionally, for dealing with special and nonrecurring problems, *ad hoc* committees make it possible to avoid the disruption which would occur if managers were taken completely off their normal duties to work on these problems. Although serving on such committees does require the manager to divert some of his attention from his regular operations, this disruption is relatively slight compared to that which would occur if a single individual were called on to accomplish the entire committee task.

The utilization of committees, however, has certain limitations. In some cases, committees will be dominated by an individual, or by a small clique, so that decisions arrived at do not really represent the thinking or wishes of many committee members. Furthermore, the *implementation* of many decisions cannot be effected by committees, and responsibility for obtaining the desired results of such joint decisions may be difficult to pinpoint. Also, there is sometimes a tendency for committees (whether they be set up simply for exchanging information or for assuming decision responsibilities) to waste members' time by discussing irrelevant subjects. This latter problem, however, may be largely overcome if the manager chairing the committee sessions is effective in guiding the group discussions.

SUMMARY

A basic problem facing business firms is that of determining which work activities will be grouped together under each manager at each level in the organization. Four commonly utilized means of departmentalization are by product, process, function, and territory. Additionally, numerous firms carrying out work on large contracts have employed a modification of product departmentalization—departmentalization by project. The departmentalization problem is a complex one involving consideration of a number of interdependent variables. Some of the factors which may have a bearing on departmentalization decisions are the nature and physical location of the firm's operations, the degree to which decision responsibilities may be decentralized, the coordinative problems at different organizational levels arising under alternative departmentalization forms, tendencies toward the uneconomical duplication of work, and the balancing of work loads.

Most larger business firms employ staff groups to provide specialized assistance to line management in various functional areas. The powers granted to or assumed by staff groups may vary widely —from simply providing information to line management to actually making decisions. One problem which is common to most organizations is that of line-staff conflicts, which may arise for numerous reasons. In many large firms, staff departments are created both at the corporate and divisional levels, giving rise to staff parallelism, and the emergence of staff-staff as well as line-staff relationships. To deal with problems of an interdepartmental nature, business organizations frequently employ committees, both *ad hoc* and standing. These committees may provide a vehicle for communication among managers and be utilized for making recommendations and decisions with respect to the resolution of organizational problems.

DISCUSSION AND STUDY QUESTIONS

1. Under what forms of departmentalization does the decentralization of many decision-making responsibilities tend to be more difficult? Why is this so?

2. Which type(s) of departmentalization tend to render the coordination of activities a more complex problem for the manager? Why? Illustrate by giving an example of some of the coordinative problems faced in a firm with which you are familiar.

3. What are some of the reasons for conflict between line and staff personnel?

4. Indicate some of the types of conflicting objectives that might be faced by the head of a divisional accounting department in a large corporation in which a centralized accounting department exists at the firm's corporate headquarters.

5. What are some advantages and disadvantages of corporate committees?

6. Explain how staff members designated purely as advisors to line officers may obtain considerable power to influence decisions made by line personnel.

7. Staff parallelism represents a form of work duplication. Comment on this statement.

8. On a visit to a company division responsible for the design, production, and sales of industrial material-handling equipment, the firm's president discovered that the division engineering department was running a series of tests on hydraulic fluids for use in the division's products. The president was disturbed because he recalled that a similar study had been carried out by another division of the firm producing earth-moving equipment. (a) Does this firm have a problem? (b) If so, what is it and how might the problem be minimized? (c) Might the present practice be beneficial?

9. For which firm in each of the following pairs might a project organization be preferred? Explain.
   a) A national supermarket chain or a large-scale road builder.
   b) A producer of large sailing yachts or a producer of 16-foot rowboats.
   c) A firm producing an established television situation-comedy series or a firm engaged in the production of television specials covering a wide variety of newsworthy current events.
   d) A building contractor engaged in constructing large office buildings or a building contractor specializing in the construction of low-cost prefabricated housing with a volume of 1500 houses per year.

10. The Claxton Manufacturing Company is one of the nation's largest producers and distributors of ceramic sewer pipe, drain tile, and brick products. Its manufacturing operations are located in Central Pennsylvania and in Southern Illinois. The Pennsylvania plant produces sewer pipe and the drain tile, while the Illinois plant produces brick products. Company headquarters are located in Pittsburgh, where one finds the accounting, finance, and marketing offices as well as the production headquarters.

   The manufacturing process is quite similar for the Pennsylvania pipe and tile plant and for the Illinois brick plant. The clay, shale, and coal are extracted from a mine near each plant. The clay and shale are next pulverized and blended with water. The molding or firming of the product then takes place. The same machinery is used for the drain tile as for the sewer pipe. Following this stage, drying and firing or burning of the product occurs. The finished product is then shipped to one of the three warehouses of the company by motor freight.

   The three warehouses are located in Pittsburgh, Pa., St. Louis, Mo., and Oakland, Calif., and are located so as to serve three different regional markets. The markets are identified as East Coast, Midwest, and West Coast. Regional sales offices are also located in the three cities mentioned. Each market region is further broken down into five districts. Within each district in each region, the company has a sales force to serve two basic customer groups, which are building supply distributors and building contractors. The East Coast and Midwest regions, however, serve two additional customer groups: governmental agencies, and retail outlets.

Develop an organization chart representing the firm's organizational structure as it now exists.

What alternative forms of departmentalization might be utilized by Claxton? Discuss the advantages and disadvantages of each.

11. The Q.R.M. Pharmaceutical Corporation is one of the leading producers of drugs in the United States. Its main manufacturing division is located in Brooklyn, New York, and two other small plants are situated in the Midwest.

The products of this corporation have a wide distribution thoughout the United States and in 56 foreign countries. Domestic sales are assigned to a sales division and the foreign sales are consummated by manufacturer's agents in the foreign countries.

Like most pharmaceutical producers, the company's product line is undergoing continual change. It has been estimated that approximately 50 percent of the firm's product line has changed during the past 10 years. The company has a Research Division comprised of both product and economic research departments.

The Production Manager, J. S. Rexworth, is responsible for producing a product line which is determined by a committee composed of representatives from each of the firm's Manufacturing, Sales, Research, and Finance Divisions. Mr. Rexworth is also responsible for maintaining the proper level of inventories, and supervising the activities of the firm's Warehouse and Shipping Department.

Over the past few years, Mr. Rexworth has fallen into the habit of adjusting the volume of production to the predictions of Mr. Erhardt, the company economist. Mr. Erhardt heads the Economic Research Department, which is a part of the Research Division. Previous to his present assignment, Mr. Erhardt was affiliated with a management consulting firm in New York. His work assignment with his former firm involved monthly economic forecasts which were used by businessmen in planning their sales.

Recently, the Sales Manager, Mr. Vais, found that one of his best selling products was in short supply. He immediately carried his complaint to Mr. Ross, the President of the Corporation. When questioned by Mr. Ross about the problem, Mr. Rexworth explained that the economist, Mr. Erhardt, gave him "incorrect information" on which he had based his production schedules.

With what organizational problems is Q.R.M. faced? How might these problems be overcome?

SELECTED REFERENCES

ALLEN, L. A. *Management and Organization.* New York: McGraw-Hill Book Co., Inc., 1958.

BARNARD, CHESTER I. *The Functions of the Executive.* Chaps. v–xii. Cambridge, Mass.: Harvard University Press, 1938.

BARNES, L. B. *Organizational Systems and Engineering Groups.* Boston: Division of Research, Graduate School of Business Administration, Harvard University, 1960.

BAUM, BERNARD H. *Decentralization of Authority in a Bureaucracy.* Englewood Cliffs, N. J.: Prentice-Hall, Inc., 1961.

DALE, ERNEST. *Planning and Developing the Company Organization Structure.* Research Report No. 20. New York: American Management Association, 1952.

DALTON, MELVILLE. *Men Who Manage.* New York: John Wiley & Sons, Inc., 1959.

DAVIS, R. C. *The Fundamentals of Top Management.* Chaps. viii–xiv. New York: Harper & Bros., 1951.

DUBIN, ROBERT. *Human Relations in Administration.* Part 2, "Organizations." 2d ed. Englewood Cliffs, N. J.: Prentice-Hall, Inc., 1961.

FISCH, GERALD G. "Line-Staff Is Obsolete," *Harvard Business Review,* 39 (September–October, 1961), 66–79.

HAIRE, MASON (ed.). *Modern Organization Theory.* New York: John Wiley & Sons, Inc., 1959.

HENSKEY, ROBERT L. "Organizational Planning," *Business Topics,* 10 (Winter, 1962), 29–40.

HILL, LAWRENCE S. "The Application of Queuing Theory to the Span of Control," *Academy of Management Journal,* 6 (March, 1963), 58–69.

HOLDEN, PAUL E.; FISH, L. S.; and SMITH, H. L. *Top Management Organization and Control,* Part B. New York: McGraw-Hill Book Co., Inc., 1951.

KAST, FREMONT E., and ROSENZWEIG, JAMES E. (eds.). *Science, Technology, and Management.* New York: McGraw-Hill Book Co., Inc., 1963.

LEIBENSTEIN, HARVEY. *Economic Theory and Organizational Analysis.* New York: Harper & Bros., 1960.

LITTERER, J. A. *Organizations: Structure and Behavior.* New York: John Wiley & Sons, Inc., 1963.

MARCH, JAMES G., and SIMON, H. A. *Organizations.* New York: John Wiley & Sons, Inc., 1958.

MILLMAN, R. WILLIAM. "Some Unsettled Questions in Organizational Theory," *Academy of Management Journal,* 7 (September, 1964), 189–195.

MOONEY, J. D. *The Principles of Organization.* Rev. ed. New York: Harper & Bros., 1939.

MYERS, C. A., and TURNBULL, JOHN G. "Line and Staff in Industrial Relations," *Harvard Business Review,* 34 (1956), 113–124.

PFIFFNER, JOHN M., and SHERWOOD, F. P. *Administrative Organization,* Chaps. i and iv. Englewood Cliffs, N. J.: Prentice-Hall, Inc., 1960.

RUBENSTEIN, ALBERT H. "Organizational Factors Affecting Research and Development Decision-Making in Large Decentralized Companies," *Management Science,* 10 (July, 1964), 618–633.

RUBENSTEIN, ALBERT H., and HABERSTROH, C. J. (eds.). Rev. ed. *Some Theories of Organization.* Homewood, Ill.: Richard D. Irwin, Inc. & Dorsey Press, 1966.

SAMPSON, ROBERT C.   *The Staff Role in Management.* New York: Harper & Bros., 1955.

SCOTT, WILLIAM G.   "Organization Theory: An Overview and an Appraisal," *Journal of the Academy of Management,* 4 (April, 1961), 7–26.

SMITH, G. A., JR.   *Managing Geographically Decentralized Companies.* Boston: Division of Research, Graduate School of Business Administration, Harvard University, 1958.

STIEGLITZ, HAROLD.   "Staff-Staff Relationships," *Management Record* (February, 1962), 2–13.

SUTERMEISTER, ROBERT A.   *People and Productivity,* Chap. vi. New York: McGraw-Hill Book Co., Inc., 1963.

URWICK, L.   *Profitably Using the General Staff Position in Business.* General Management Series, No. 165. New York: American Management Association, Inc., 1953.

WALKER, CHARLES R. (ed.).   *Modern Technology and Civilization.* New York: McGraw-Hill Book Co., Inc., 1962.

WARNER, W. LLOYD, and LUNT, P.   *The Social Life of a Modern Community.* New Haven: Yale University Press, 1941.

WICKESBERG, A. K., and CRONIN, T. C.   "Management by Task Force," *Harvard Business Review,* 40 (November–December, 1962), 111–118.

CHAPTER 9

FORMAL ORGANIZATIONAL CHANGE

A SALIENT characteristic of most business firms is that their organizational structures undergo frequent changes. Modifications take place in tasks performed by individual workers, in the way jobs are grouped together, in the areas of responsibility for decision making held by various managers, in the patterning of communications, etc.

Some organizational modifications effected by business firms are of considerable magnitude—e.g., a major redepartmentalization may be made in which the areas of responsibility of the department heads reporting directly to the president of a company are changed from functional-based ones to product-based ones. Changes such as these, which are usually geared toward overcoming major organizational problems, and which often lead to considerable upheaval in the firm, are generally effected at infrequent intervals. On the other hand, many more minor organizational changes take place almost continuously in most firms—e.g., a manager may modify the work assignments of one or more of his subordinates; his own span of control may be temporarily enlarged by the hiring of part-time help during a rush period of work, etc. Unlike major restructurings of the organization, which represent "formal" planned changes by management, many of the minor day-to-day organizational modifications are effected "informally," and, in fact, sometimes even without the knowledge of management. For example, production employees in a manufacturing operation may modify their work procedures, or perhaps engage in job trading with one another without their foreman's being aware of such task modifications. In short, the changes which one may find taking place in the way organization structures are designed may vary considerably in magnitude and scope, frequency of occurrence, and degree of formality.

In the previous two chapters our view of the organization has been primarily a static one, although we have given some attention to such organizational redesign techniques as job enlargement and job rotation. Our purpose in this and the succeeding chapter is to focus more explicit attention on several basic facets of organizational change. In this chapter, our discussion will cover: some of the reasons for restructuring organizations, the identification of problems necessitating such changes; and certain approaches to organizational redesign utilized by business firms. Then, in Chapter 10 we will examine the behavior and reactions of individuals and groups within the firm with respect to organizational change.

PROBLEMS NECESSITATING ORGANIZATIONAL CHANGE

In some cases, firms find organizational change necessary because their task assignments, spans of control, etc., were inadequately structured in the first place. In defining the scope of work for numerous production workers, for example, a company may have given insufficient attention to the psychological problems of over-specialization, only to find that absenteeism and turnover have become an acute problem with these individuals.

In many other cases, however, organizational restructuring may be necessitated by changed environmental conditions facing the firm rather than by ineffective initial organizational design. We will now examine three basic types of environmental change which may give rise to the need for organizational redesign.

Changes in Types of Output Desired

When the firm desires to modify its output specifications—e.g., changing its product line or providing for new services to meet changed competitive conditions—its work loads, assignment of tasks, skills required by its workers, etc., may also need to undergo modification, thus necessitating some degree of organizational redesign.

An illustration of organization changes accompanying shifts in product objectives is afforded by the airframe industry. Prior to the time that missiles began replacing airplanes as prime Air Force defensive and offensive weapons, the organizations of major airframe contractors were frequently characterized by a ratio of from .2/1 to .5/1 between (1) research and development, and engineering personnel and (2) production workers. As missile systems advanced to the state in which they were able to replace airplanes, it became evident for airframe concerns going into missiles that:

1.   These systems would utilize rocket engines instead of jet, jet-prop, or reciprocating engines. In fact, the latter two had already become obsolete through the use of the pure jet engine for many other purposes.

2.   Rather than using airframes—the manufacture of which was a complex and expensive operation requiring large amounts of labor— these systems would utilize relatively simple "stovepipes" in which the fuel for the engines would be stored.

3.   Automatic electronic systems for the control of missiles would become more important, complex, and expensive as compared to the human-electronic systems in airplanes.

4.   The reliability needs would be greater in missile systems, with less dependence upon human correction or compensation.

For those firms entering the missile business, these changes in product, and therefore in output objectives, were reflected in major differences in the costs of components. Notable was the large reduction in the labor to produce the carrier (missile fuselages as opposed to airframes). Concurrently an increased number of engineers was needed to design, test, and mate the complex electronic equipment. For example, after it had gone into missiles, at one time Martin's Denver facility is said to have required a ratio of seven engineering personnel to one laborer.

If the objectives of an airframe company were to encompass missile production, rather major organization changes were required. For example, North American Aviation Company set up separate divisions designed to produce: (1) sub-systems for missiles, (2) electronic control and communication devices, (3) rocket engines, etc., as well as (4) one to continue airplane manufacture. Some other companies decided not to enter the missile business, but rather to attempt to gain a larger share of the dwindling airplane business. Still others decided to enter the missile business but to subcontract from established electronic and engine firms those subsystems for which they did not have superior capabilities. In one such firm, even though sales were not reduced substantially, a major cut in employment took place as considerably fewer manufacturing employees were required. At the same time, however, there was a large increase in the employment of scientific, research, engineering, and test personnel. These major organizational changes were necessary because of modified product objectives and because of the particular methods that the company chose to meet these objectives.

In addition to changes in product objectives, changes in other objectives such as public or personnel relations may also require organizational restructuring. For example, recognition of a union by the management of a firm will require an output of relations not theretofore needed—i.e., preparing for and conducting contract negotiations, designing and following an agreed upon grievance procedure, etc. In some companies, such tasks may simply be handled by enlarging the scope of responsibility of existing managers; while in others new staff specialists may be hired and staff departments either expanded or created to deal with labor relations.

Transformation Changes

A second reason for the need for organizational change is that the firm's technological processes (or methods of *transforming* its raw materials, etc., into output) have undergone modification; even though its basic output specifications have not changed. The invention of the linotype has eliminated hand typesetters. In many business firms computers have eliminated many clerical jobs in recent years. In one large firm, for example, approximately 35 people had been engaged in preparing the payroll each two-week period. Then, payroll computation and check-writing were computerized, and the payroll department was reduced to five people, including the department head. After computerization, the work of these personnel consisted primarily of checking exceptions and making corrections. In addition to these major changes in the clerking function, modifications were required in the firm's computer operation which had existed previously to handle other company problems. The payroll work had to be programmed, checked, debugged, tested, and run. Computer personnel and facilities had to be reorganized to accomplish these changes.

That transformation changes may have considerable impact on the firm's organization may be further illustrated by the experience of another company, which produced industrial equipment, motors, and pumps. Although the company's management believed that it had a reasonable market share for the products which it manufactured, its volume on any one product was not sufficiently large to justify mass-production methods. Many of the parts for its various products were machined on the same general-purpose equipment in relatively small lots. Some of its products were designed in such a way that they had several different end uses. For example, certain motors were designed so that they could be used by several different customers. This alleviated but did not overcome completely the problem of short machine runs on parts. In analyzing their competition on each product, company executives noted that they and their five competitors had approximately equal market shares for one particular pump. Each firm's sales volume was relatively low; and none could produce the pump as cheaply as could be done with mass-production methods. The executives predicted that if they had fifty percent of the market, they could afford to invest in special-purpose equipment and tooling so as to mass-produce the pump. Since mass-production would reduce costs considerably below that of its competitors, the company would be able to price the pump sufficiently low to obtain a greater market share. The decision was made to go ahead with the plan, and within several years, the company had captured a major share of the market.

In the above example, the firm's basic product was not changed. Both its market share objective and transformation methods, however, were modified. A new building was constructed, new special purpose equipment was installed, and a new organizational division was created. With mass production of the pump, a greater degree of worker specialization was effected on many jobs, and lesser skill levels were required for these jobs. Thus, both departmental and task restructuring resulted from the change in transformational methods of producing the firm's product.

Organizational Growth

In the example given in the previous section, we saw how transformation changes coupled with organizational growth (i.e., the production and sale of more pumps) necessitated organizational redesign by a firm. Of importance also in understanding the business firm is the fact that organizational growth *per se*, even in the absence of changes in basic technological processes utilized, may render organizational change necessary or desirable. A number of researchers have found that as firms become larger, not only do their departments become larger, with simply more people doing the same kinds of jobs—but certain changes usually occur in their organizational "*shape.*"

Several investigators have attempted to show that the shape an organization takes as it grows is a *natural* phenomenon. Mason Haire has suggested that the square-cube law might be utilized in explaining organization shape.[1] In living organisms, the square-cube law has been used to explain changes in the relationship between an organism's area and volume as it grows. In applying this "law" to companies, Haire has classified employees as being either "outside" or "inside." Outside employees include salesmen, purchasing agents, labor negotiators, and other individuals performing work dealing with entities outside the firm. The square-cube law, as applied by Haire to organizational growth, predicts that for any size of firm the square root of the number of external employees (area) varies as the cube root of the number of internal employees (volume); or, $\sqrt{\text{external employees}} = \sqrt[3]{\text{internal employees}}$. Haire's evidence shows that, when plotted, data from a number of actual companies over a period of time seem to indicate that the rate of growth in the number of internal employees is less than that predicted by the formula.

A somewhat different type of relationship has been postulated by Ralph C. Davis in examining organizational growth. In predicting the relative size of staff groups as opposed to line, Davis has stated:

> The complexity of functional relationships tends to increase in geometric progression as the volume of work that the organization must handle increases in arithmetic progression. Staff organizations tend to grow faster than the line organizations they serve. There is some evidence that the growth relation between them also involves geometric progression until we approach the optimum organization size.[2]

Haire's data indicates that this tendency for rapid staff expansion in relation to that of the line is descriptive of early stages of company growth; but that line and staff groups tend to grow at similar rates after reaching some "established" (and indefinite) size.[3] This conclusion has been supported by data by Despelder.[4]

Still another study, conducted by Alan Filley, however, disputes all of the above-mentioned conclusions:

> The fact that either line or staff executives may perform necessary supportive functions seems to have been generally overlooked in management litera-

---

[1] Mason Haire, "Biological Models and Empirical Histories of the Growth of Organizations," in his *Modern Organization Theory* (New York: John Wiley & Sons, 1959), pp. 272–306.

[2] Ralph C. Davis, *The Fundamentals of Top Management* (New York: Harper & Bros., 1951), p. 232.

[3] Haire, *op. cit.*, Figures 13, 14, 15, and 16.

[4] Bruce Despelder, *Ratios of Staff to Line Personnel* (Columbus, Ohio: Bureau of Business Research, The Ohio State University, Research Monograph No. 106, 1962).

ture and research. Research designs which purport to measure a natural-order result of growth are, in fact, measuring only the extent to which circumstances or policy has dictated the creation or restriction of staff units. Nor do such designs consider the conditions militating toward the retention of such functions by top management and against delegation to subordinates.[5]

Filley found the data from the various studies so different and conflicting he concluded that there is no *natural* order to organizational growth or to the shape of this growth. His contention is that the staff units formed in organizations are dependent upon management *decisions*. In one growing firm that he studied staff personnel remained at an approximately constant ratio of one to nine to line personnel. But Filley indicated that this firm could probably have economized by adding more staff units to benefit from greater managerial staff specialization.[6]

It is obvious that a staff group cannot be initiated without managerial decision and action. The fact that some managements do not choose to differentiate their management functions by forming staff *departments* as the firms become larger does not deny that there is some relationship between the staff *work* to be performed and the size of the firm. On the other hand, there are probably more basic reasons for staff growth than any "natural order." A basic reason why it is "natural" for a personnel staff to form when a firm reaches a size of approximately 175 people,[7] for example, is that by that time the number of personnel activities and problems being handled by the line has usually become large enough to justify the addition of a specially trained and competent professional personnel manager.

PINPOINTING ORGANIZATIONAL PROBLEMS

In the previous sections, we have shown several different types of conditions under which organizational restructuring may be needed by a firm. In order for management to undertake organizational redesign (or any other approach) for dealing with its problems, it is first necessary to identify and analyze the nature of those problems

---

[5] Alan C. Filley, "Decisions and Research in Staff Utilization," paper delivered at the Midwest Management Conference, April 26, 1963, p. 13.

[6] Filley, comments made following the presentation of his paper cited above.

[7] Haire, *op. cit.*, p. 293. It should be noted that in companies whose employment is dependent to a considerable extent upon obtaining one or more large contracts, the growth in some staff or auxiliary functions (e.g., purchasing, engineering) tends to *lead* increases in worker employment whereas the workload of other functions (e.g., handling accounts receivable) may lag peak worker employment.

facing it. The purpose of this section is to explain some of the approaches used by management in pinpointing organizational problems.

Before discussing any of these, it is important to emphasize that an inappropriate organizational structure is only *one* possible cause of a firm's problems. Difficulties can and do arise from many other sources. A combination of many factors, including organizational design, often contribute to the problems of a firm. Since organization structure, job design, leadership, the personal capabilities of the firm's members, etc., are often all interdependent in influencing the output of an organization system, one manifestation of a firm's problem may simply be the result of another variable in the system. For example, the supposed weakness of a manager may be due more to faulty organization design which fails to provide the timely data necessary to make the decisions assigned to him, than to his own inadequacies.

Analysis of Day-to-Day Operations

Many times organizational redesign arises from problems identified by managers in their day-to-day operations of the firm. Management may find that its costs are increasing, that an increasing number of late deliveries on its products are taking place, etc., and, after subsequent analysis of such problems, decide that one or more kinds of inadequacies exist in its organization structure. An example of this type of problem identification and analysis is provided by a manufacturing firm which experienced a late delivery problem.

For over a year, the firm in question had been plagued by frequent late deliveries. To help overcome this problem, several expedients were attempted by the production department: overtime; splitting processing runs on parts into two or more lots; using expediters to push particular jobs through the shop; utilizing rush and special rush orders which took precedence over ordinary jobs, etc.

These actions resulted in high costs from duplicate machine set-ups and overtime work. The late deliveries, however, continued. Analysis showed that twenty per cent of the lots *entered* the machine shops up to one month after machining on them had been originally scheduled to start. Eighty per cent of the parts *left* the machining shops behind schedule partially because rush orders took priority in processing and delayed other orders which previously had been on schedule. The work flow of an order through the organization was as is shown in Figure 9–1.

FIGURE 9–1. Work Flow of Orders in an Illustrative Firm

Neither the firm's sales volume nor its organization structure had changed significantly for several years. The delivery problem, however, had appeared only during the last year. Further study showed that somewhat prior to this time, the distribution of order *sizes* entering the plant had changed from few orders of a relatively large lot size to many orders of a relatively small lot size. The basic products had not changed, but the *average size* of orders had been reduced.

Although the organization had been able to produce effectively the large lot size mix, it was not able to handle as successfully the production of many orders of small size. The smaller lots required relatively more engineering time, tooling, scheduling, and set-ups per dollar of sales. Failure to coordinate these changed requirements among the firm's departments other than production constituted a basic reason for the late delivery problem that arose. While organization changes had been made in production to correct the *resulting* problems, no attention had been given to eliminate their *causes* in those departments *preceding* production in the work flow.

Once the real problems had been identified, several organizational redesign steps were undertaken in an attempt to correct them. Data on product mix were developed (and projected) by the sales department so that engineering, tooling, and production could anticipate the size and nature of their work forces. By also having these data, production was able to organize separate crews for off-shift maintenance and for set-ups, which permitted the reduction of overtime work. Organization adjustments of similar types in the engineering and tooling departments also helped make it possible to process orders into the shop on time.

As the above example illustrates, inadequacies in the structure of organizational tasks and information flows may manifest themselves in a host of resultant problems. Further, the inadequacies underlying such problems are often not immediately apparent, but may be uncovered only after considerable analysis. If management focuses attention solely on the resultant problems, without attempting to identify the variables underlying them, it may develop a "patchwork" organizational redesign which only scratches the surface, and effects little fundamental improvement in its operations.

Intervening Performance Indicators

In the example given in the preceding section, an organizational problem was ultimately manifested in a measurable output deficiency—an increasing number of deliveries were late. Managers are also sometimes able to uncover problems by examining what may be referred to as "intervening" measures of performance. These measures are so-named because they "intervene" between the firm's operations and such ultimate measures of operating performance as costs and profits. Among those intervening measures commonly examined by management are employee attitudes, labor turnover, absenteeism, number of grievances, and accident rates. Measures for many of the more commonly utilized intervening performance indicators exist, so that it is possible for managers to note both the development of trends and to compare the performance of particular departments with that of other departments or their firm's performance with that of other companies.

When intervening performance indicators are "out-of-line," the firm may or may not experience any basic problems in meeting its output objectives. For example, even though the number of employee grievances in a particular department has increased, its cost, production quality, and delivery schedule objectives all may still be met. When such indicators do give "negative readings," however, it may be a warning of impending difficulties.

If, for example, employee turnover or absenteeism in one department of a firm is significantly higher than in other of the company's organizational units, there is some indication that its employees do not wish to associate or identify with the department or other individuals in it. Although the reasons for such possible non-identification are not indicated by the intervening performance measures *per se,* the measures do give the manager a warning that certain problems may exist, or be in the making. These problems, of course, may not be due to inadequate organizational design alone; they might reflect poor supervisory practices or any one of a number of other conditions.

Periodic Surveys

In their day-to-day analysis of data concerning their operations, managers may often be able to pinpoint organizational problems, as we indicated previously. However, because of imperfect information, time pressures, and other limiting factors, many organizational problems or potential problems that might be uncovered in day-to-day operational analysis may go long undetected by the manager.

To help overcome this problem, managers sometimes obtain periodic reviews or surveys of certain facets of their operations by individuals or groups outside their department. Such reviews may be conducted by outside consulting firms or by staff groups within the organization. Such periodic surveys may focus attention on both direct measures of output, and upon intervening performance measures of the types discussed in the previous section. Illustrations of such reviews of organizations are provided by the periodic inspections held by the Armed Services, the periodic evaluation of university departments by outside experts, and employee attitude surveys which are conducted from time to time by many business firms.

Attitude surveys have often been used as a means of determining the sentiments and viewpoints of employees in a company. Replies from such surveys are often segregated and summarized for the subordinates reporting to each manager. This permits managers to compare the attitudes of their subordinates with those of subordinates in other departments and with the attitudes of all employees as a whole in the plant or company. In some companies, attitude surveys are conducted on a planned periodic basis—e.g., every two years. If the same questions are asked in each such survey so that the results from one survey to the next are comparable, not only may absolute "levels" of employee attitudes be determined, but also *changes* in attitudes may be discerned. In some attitude surveys, questions are asked about conditions in the employees' own departments and about overall plant or company conditions—e.g., attitudes may be obtained about employee benefit programs, the company newsletter, or the plant cafeteria.

Two final observations are in order concerning the value of attitude surveys in pinpointing problems which may call for organizational redesign. First, some of the problems revealed by such surveys may not be ones of organizational inadequacy. For instance, negative attitudes toward the plant's cafeteria may be due to nothing more than overly hot conditions in the summertime which could be corrected simply by the purchase and installation of an air conditioner. Secondly, as is also true of many of the intervening performance indicators discussed in the previous section, survey results frequently indicate only that an organizational problem may exist but do not give a complete picture of what the problem is or what its underlying causes are. For example, if most of the employees in a particular department express the opinion that they "are given little opportunity to express their ideas on the job," such sentiments might reflect the practicing of close supervision by their foreman. Or, on the other hand, the basic reason for these attitudes could be that work in the department has, through overspecialization, become so routine that little creative expression is possible.

RESTRUCTURING THE ORGANIZATION

As our discussion up to this point has indicated, there are many different kinds of problems which give rise to the need for organizational redesign, and many different ways of modifying the firm's organization structure to help resolve such problems. Our purpose in this section is to examine three types of important organizational redesign techniques to which we have not given explicit attention previously: (1) restructuring of information flows, (2) centralization and decentralization, and (3) shifts in line-staff responsibilities.

Information Flow Restructuring

In some cases, organizational problems have arisen because of inadequacies existing in the manner in which informational outputs from one organizational sub-system have flowed as inputs to another sub-system in the firm.

An example of this type of problem is provided by William F. Whyte's analysis of communications and work flow in certain restaurants.[8] Whyte has shown that inadequate informational structuring in some restaurants has been a source of organization conflict. Waitresses give customer orders to cooks. During busy periods, customers pressure waitresses resulting in the waitresses pressuring cooks for their orders. The work load of the cooks is most efficiently handled if it is bulked (i.e., if a dozen salads can be made at one time rather than individually). In contrast, the work load of the waitress is most efficiently handled if all orders for a table are batched together. Thus, the most efficient work flow in the waitress sub-system is different from that in the kitchen sub-system.

Another variable influencing the relationship between waitresses and cooks is status. The cook is a highly skilled, highly paid male. He enjoys a relatively high status in a restaurant's hierarchy of positions. On the other hand, waitresses are relatively low skilled, low paid, and females and hence of a lower status. In the work flow, the lower status waitresses give orders to the higher status cooks. This

---

[8] "Social Structure of the Whole Organization: The Restaurant," *American Journal of Sociology*, 54 (January, 1949), 302–08.

condition has been a source of many tensions and conflicts in restaurants.[9]

A third variable in the waitress-cook relation is the type of communication used between them. When oral communications are used, there is likely to be more disagreement and conflict when errors are made in orders than if the orders are written. Whether the waitress errs in obtaining the order from the customer or whether the cook errs in receiving the oral order from the waitress is often difficult, if not impossible to determine. Further, with oral communications, waitresses must often stand in line during peak periods waiting to call their orders in to the cook.

A restructuring of the work between cooks and waitresses has been accomplished in some restaurants through the use of a circular spindle upon which waitresses place their *written* orders and from which cooks establish their work sequence. This spindle turns so that the cook may scan all orders and batch together common items from all waitresses. This allows more efficient kitchen operation. Since the spindle intervenes between the cooks and the waitresses, the tensions and conflict occasioned by verbal orders being given from lower status to higher status employees are reduced. Direct face to face contact is eliminated as a necessary condition of communication. Further, the use of written orders tends to overcome errors arising from miscommunication by oral means; and when an error does occur, the person responsible for it can be determined by reference to the written communications. As Porter has pointed out,

> The waitress prepares the order slip and the cook works directly from it. If the waitress records the order incorrectly, it is obvious to her upon examining the order slip. Similarly, if the cook misreads the slip, an examination of the order slip makes it obvious to him. . . . [A function] . . . of the spindle, then, is to provide "feedback" to both waitress and cook regarding errors. The spindle markedly alters the emotional relationship and redirects the learning process.[10]

Additionally, the spindle serves as a queuing device in two ways:

> It holds the order in a proper waiting line until the cook can get to them. When dependent on his memory only, the cook can get orders mixed up. It

---

[9] For an explanation of the reasons for these tensions and conflicts in terms of both psychological, sociological and anthropological theory, see: Elias H. Porter, "The Parable of the Spindle," *Harvard Business Review,* 40 (May–June, 1962), 58–66.

[10] From *ibid.,* as reprinted in Max D. Richards and William A. Nielander, *Readings in Management,* (2nd ed.; Cincinnati, Ohio: South-Western Publishing Company, 1963), p. 135.

also does all the "standing in line" for the waitresses. They need never again stand in line to pass an order to the cook. This makes their jobs easier—especially during the rush hours.[11]

As the reader may note, the above analysis of the restaurant problem illustrates application of the systems concept which we discussed previously in Chapter 3. A central focus of attention was upon the flow of information from one organizational sub-system to another. This example also illustrates that organizational design decisions should take into consideration not only *what* information is transmitted to a particular sub-system but *how* it is transmitted. The introduction of the spindle did not significantly alter the *content* of messages transmitted from waitresses to the cooks. Rather, it helped overcome both psychological and work flow problems by modifying the form which the messages took (verbal to written), and the timing of the message transmission and receipt—i.e., the waitresses did not have to wait to transmit orders, while the cooks could *time their own receipt* of the informational inputs contained in the written orders, so as to plan their work more effectively.

Line-Staff Shifts

Sometimes problems which have arisen in an organization persist largely because no one has the time or competence to analyze and resolve them. In some such cases, firms will create a special staff group to study such problems and to recommend solutions to them. Then, quite often, after the problems have been reduced to tolerable levels, some of the work performed by the staff group may be reassigned to existing line departments; and/or the group may organizationally be absorbed by another broader-based staff department. The existence of such shifts in organizational responsibility as problems emerge and are subsequently reduced in magnitude is illustrated by the following example:

After World War II, many American firms discovered a shortage of qualified managers to meet the needs occasioned by executive turnover and of corporate growth. This shortage was often partially a result of the failure to hire men with potential during the depression and war years. To alleviate this problem, one company hired a consultant to study possible sources of new managers and the qualifications of its current management group. He confirmed that there was a need for a larger supply of candidates for higher-level managerial positions if the firm were to continue to operate effectively. Further, if the company were planning to acquire or build new facilities and to add to its product line, some accelerated methods for acquiring more managers and

---

[11] *Ibid.*, pp. 133–134.

for rapid development of those already in the firm's employ were recommended. Upon the consultant's recommendation, the company engaged a Director of Management Development. With the aid of the consultant, the president and the new director set up a management development department and developed programs to accomplish the desired results.

During the next ten years, the magnitude of the manpower problem was reduced considerably, and, in addition, each line manager was given greater responsibility for developing the potential of his own subordinate managers. In consequence, much less attention to management development was needed by the staff group; and with the scope of its activities thus reduced, it was eventually absorbed into the firm's personnel department.

We should also point out that line-staff shifts may also occur in business firms in a manner opposite of that described in the above example. As we mentioned previously, when organizations reach a size such that enough specialized work handled by line managers exists to justify the hiring of staff specialists, the work is often shifted from the line to a newly created staff group. In some cases, such staff groups are set up organizationally *within* existing line departments. Subsequently, however, the magnitude of work performed by the new staff group may become large enough to justify its being broken away from its "parent" department to form a separate organizational unit. For example, in some companies, executive manpower planning—i.e., projecting the firm's managerial needs in future years, the future movement of managers into higher level positions, etc.— was handled first by line management, subsequently assigned to the personnel staff, and finally made the responsibility of a separate organizational planning unit. This type of line-staff shift as contradistinguished from the type discussed earlier is illustrated in Figure 9–2.

FIGURE 9–2. Two Types of Line-Staff Shifts

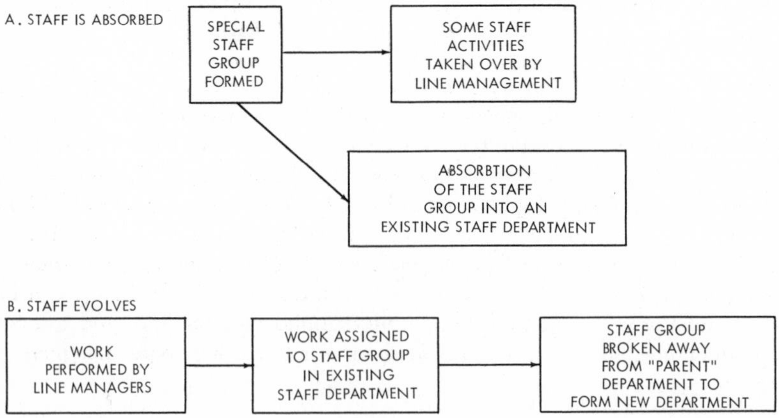

Centralization-Decentralization

Analysis of a firm's organizational problems may indicate that either greater centralization or decentralization of decision-making responsibilities is appropriate. That is, as we indicated in Chapter 8, decisions previously made at one organizational level may be shifted upward (centralization) or downward (decentralization) in the firm's managerial hierarchy.

There are many possible reasons for the desirability of shifting the level at which decisions are made. Enlarging the scope and importance of the decisions lower-level managers are responsible for may better prepare them to assume higher-level positions with greater responsibilities. Decentralization may be utilized as a means to allow quicker and more appropriate decisions. For example, in one large company, all grain purchases had to be approved by the president. On many occasions the firm's head purchasing agent had an opportunity, if he could act quickly, to make purchases at especially favorable prices; however, he could not contact the president for approval in time to take advantage of these opportunities. This problem was later overcome by giving full responsibility for purchases to the agent.

Two other observations are in order concerning modification of the organizational levels at which decisions are made. First, effective decentralization is possible only when lower level managers possess the skills and competence to handle those decisions formerly made at higher levels. If the purchasing manager mentioned above was prone to make poor decisions, continued approval of all grain purchases by the president might have been more appropriate, notwithstanding the problems of delay which the need for such approval sometimes created. Furthermore, shifting certain types of decision making downward may not be possible when the work performed by several functional departments is highly interdependent, and requires centralized coordination—e.g., manufacturing firms producing many small lots of different items, which flow from one department to another in their manufacture, have centralized production control departments in order to coordinate work scheduling among the various production departments.

Second, although many different types of technological change may give rise to a need for centralization or decentralization, one relatively recent technological development—computerization—appears to have far-reaching consequences for organizational design, especially at managerial levels. With electronic computers, it is possible to generate more and better data for decision making much more quickly than has heretofore been possible. In consequence, top managements of many firms are now often able to make more detailed decisions, which were formerly the responsibility of lower level managers. With the science of decision making and information processing developing at a rapid rate, the opportunities for top management to plan and control in detail the operations at lower levels are increasing. To the extent that these opportunities are taken advantage of, the decision latitude of middle level managers is greatly reduced, and the need for middle management is lessened. Leavitt and Whisler have predicted that middle management will assume much less importance within the next twenty years because top management, aided by computers and a staff of experts, will be able to make or to program in detail many of the decisions now made by middle-level managers.[12]

SUMMARY

Business organizations are dynamic systems in which structural changes frequently take place. Firms may find it necessary to modify their organizational structure as changes occur in the outputs which they produce and/or in the transformational methods which they utilize. Further, organizational growth *per se* may lead to the necessity for organizational modification. The need for organizational redesign may be pinpointed both in the manager's day-to-day analysis of his operations and from periodic surveys. In both cases, intervening performance indicators as well as such ultimate measures of performance as costs or profits may signal the existence of organizational problems. There are many different ways in which organizational restructuring may be effected. Among these are the restructuring of informational flows, the shifting of responsibilities from line to staff departments, or vice versa, and providing for either greater centralization or decentralization of decision-making responsibilities.

DISCUSSION AND STUDY QUESTIONS

1. If, as a firm expands, the number of its managerial and professional personnel increases at a faster rate than that of its nonadministrative personnel, why are not small firms more efficient than large ones?

---

[12] Harold J. Leavitt and Thomas L. Whisler, "Management in the 1980's," *Harvard Business Review*, 36 (Nov.–Dec., 1958), 41–48.

2. Evaluate: Decentralization of decision making to lower levels in the management hierarchy insures the development of more managers with competence to fill positions at higher levels in the organization.

3. Evaluate: When a firm reaches a size of 175 employees, it should establish a personnel department to obtain the benefits of a specially trained and competent professional personnel staff.

4. Indicate some of the organizational changes which might be required if General Motors decided to produce a new type of automobile that had no tires but rather moved upon an "air cushion."

5. What organizational changes might be necessitated in the following types of firms if the nation's defense budget were cut in half next year; (a) in a retail food chain? (b) in a stock broker's office? (c) in an aerospace firm?

6. What is likely to happen to a firm which establishes inflexible objectives and refuses to change its methods in light of scientific and technological innovation: (a) under the American capitalistic system? (b) under the Soviet system?

7. What advantages might accrue from having an outside consultant survey the operations of a particular firm or department? What disadvantages might there be to such an approach?

8. The decision making responsibilities of middle-level managers may be reduced in the future as a result of increased utilization of high-speed computers. Discuss.

9. What are some of the organizational changes that might be necessitated in a large supermarket chain with 14 geographical divisions by each of the following conditions?

   a) Top management has decided to establish delicatessens in each of the firm's stores in its Podunk Division.

   b) The firm has decided to computerize its accounting and payroll operations in all of its divisional offices.

   c) Due to competitive conditions, the firm has decided to give trading stamps in all of its stores.

   d) The firm has decided to hire only college graduates for its managerial positions, and to provide a 75-week managerial training program for newly-hired college graduates.

SELECTED REFERENCES

BLAKE, ROBERT R., and MOUTON, J. S.   *The Managerial Grid.* Houston, Texas: Gulf Publishing Co., 1964.

CARTWRIGHT, D., and ZANDER, A.   *Group Dynamics.* 2d ed. Evanston, Ill.: Row, Peterson & Co., 1960.

DUBIN, R.   *Human Relations in Administration.* 2d ed. Englewood Cliffs, N. J.: Prentice-Hall, Inc., 1961.

HAIRE, M.   *Modern Organization Theory.* New York: John Wiley & Sons, Inc., 1959.

LAWRENCE, PAUL R.   *The Changing of Organizational Behavior Patterns.* Boston: Division of Research, Graduate School of Business Administration, Harvard University, 1958.

LIKERT, R.   *New Patterns of Management.* New York: McGraw-Hill Book Co., Inc., 1961.

PORTER, DONALD E., and APPLEWHITE, PHILIP B.   *Studies in Organizational Behavior and Management,* Sections 8 and 9. Scranton, Pa.: International Textbook Co., 1964.

ROY, DONALD.   "Quota Restriction and Gold-Bricking in a Machine Shop," *American Journal of Sociology,* 57 (March, 1952), 430–37.

SAYLES, LEONARD.   "The Change Process in Organizations," *Human Organization* (Summer, 1962), 62–67.

TRIST, E. L., and BAMFORTH, K. W.   "Selections from Social and Psychological Consequences of the Longwell Method of Coal Getting," *Human Relations,* 4 (1951), 6–38.

WALKER, CHARLES R. (ed.).   *Modern Technology and Civilization.* New York: McGraw-Hill Book Co., Inc., 1962.

WHYTE, WILLIAM F.   *Human Relations in the Restaurant Industry.* New York: McGraw-Hill Book Co., Inc., 1948.

WOLF, WILLIAM B. (ed.).   *Management Readings Toward a General Theory.* Belmont, Calif.: Wadsworth Publishing Co., Inc., 1964.

VAN ZELST, RAYMOND H.   "Sociometrically Selected Work Teams Increase Production," *Personnel Psychology,* 5 (1952), 175–85.

CHAPTER 10

HUMAN FACTORS AND ORGANIZATIONAL CHANGE

O UR discussion in the previous chapter implicitly assured that organizational changes can be implemented, and will be accepted by members of the organization, once management has decided to effect them. In some cases, this assumption is a valid one, for the implementation of numerous forms of organizational redesign may meet little or no resistance on the part of individuals within the business firm.

In other cases, however, considerable resistance to organizational change may emanate from individuals, work groups, and/or unions. In the first part of this chapter, we will examine some of the reasons for resistance to change and some of the approaches which may be utilized by management to overcome such resistance. Then, in the second part of the chapter, we will focus attention on another salient characteristic of the organizational change process—that in many cases individuals (and groups) within the firm will, rather than resist change, initiate on their own modifications in organizational design in addition to those formally planned by management.

REASONS FOR RESISTANCE TO CHANGE

There are many reasons why members of the business firm may resist organizational changes. Sometimes an individual may not understand how a proposed modification will affect him, and be reluctant to accept the change essentially because he is "afraid of the unknown." Or, his perceptions of the implications of some organizational rearrangement may be inaccurate, and he may unrealistically and erroneously assume that the new arrangement will somehow threaten the satisfaction of certain of his needs. In still other cases, a particular form of organizational redesign may pose a *real* threat to the individual, of which he is aware and does perceive accurately; and he may attempt to take some actions to prevent such an occurrence. We will now examine some of the more specific factors which may give rise to resistance to organizational change. For purposes of exposition, we will classify these as (1) psychological and sociological, and (2) economic.

Psychological and Sociological Factors

Disruption of Interpersonal Relationships. As we pointed out in Chapter 6, friendship cliques are frequently formed in firms as a means of meeting individuals' belongingness needs, and the formation of such groups is conditioned by the formal task and command structure of the organization to the extent that physical proximity facilitates friendship associations.

Sometimes organizational redesign will mean that individuals who have been in association with each other will be assigned to other tasks and relocated to other departments, thereby effecting a disruption of bonds of friendship and common social activities which have developed over a period of time. Separated from those co-workers toward whom he has developed positive sentiments, the individual may find himself placed in association with new and unknown colleagues, whom he may or may not like, or who may like or not like him. Such uncertainties as to how one will be accepted by, and "fit in" with a new work group can, quite obviously, pose a threat to the belongingness needs of the individual.

Threats to Status. Organizational change may also effect, or, at least, be perceived to be, a threat to the individual's status position, and hence to the satisfaction of his esteem needs. That such may be the case may be illustrated by an organizational change which took place in one large accounting department of a firm. In this department, the rapid turnover of clerical personnel made it necessary for supervisors to spend considerable time training new clerks as replacements. Part of this turnover was planned in that some college graduates were assigned to clerical positions for training purposes and to ascertain their capabilities for advancement within the accounting management hierarchy. Many of the other clerks were women whose turnover often resulted from marriage or pregnancy. Further, the firm was located in an area where an acute labor shortage existed and where worker mobility was often generally high.

Top management in the accounting department believed that some of the clerks were not being trained adequately and that an excessive amount of learning time was often being required before new clerks achieved satisfactory performance levels. As a result of this belief, it was decided to establish a special staff group within the department to train new clerical and other accounting personnel. This organizational modification was strongly resented by a number of the supervisors in the department. Seeing that the scope of their positions was being reduced by transferring their training responsibilities to the staff group, the supervisors perceived this change as reducing their status, and anticipated that they might, in consequence, be less highly esteemed by their subordinates and other managers in the organization. Top management in the accounting department had not anticipated this reaction by the supervisors. When the reasons for the reactions to the change became clear, however, an attempt was made to overcome the resistance. Arrangements were made for the trainers to work under the direction of a supervisor whenever any of his new clerks required training.[1] This modification was perceived favorably by most of the supervisors, who felt that their "lost" status had now been regained.

Fear of Increased Responsibilities. Organizational changes may sometimes be resisted because individuals fear their own inability to handle the increased work responsibilities which such modifications may effect. It is for this reason that some non-managerial employees are reluctant to accept the job enlargement redesign approach which we discussed in Chapter 7. Such reluctance may be observed sometimes at the managerial level where an individual may balk at having the scope of his job expanded, or may even refuse to accept a promotion to a higher organizational level. In terms of the ideas which we presented in Chapter 5, individuals resisting such increases in responsibilities will tend to be those whose dependence needs are fairly strong.

Economic Factors

Members of the business organization may view organizational restructuring as a threat to their economic security, and hence to

---

[1] The trainers still also reported to the chief of the training group, thus violating a "classical" principle of management, unity of command, that a subordinate should report formally to only one boss.

their physiological, safety, and esteem needs. Such fears are not without foundation, for technological changes have on many occasions resulted in (1) jobs calling for relatively high skill levels being replaced by lower-skilled (and lower-paid) work on more highly mechanized equipment, and/or (2) the total elimination of some jobs, accompanied by layoffs.

As organizations have grown, with the volume of their operations becoming sufficiently large to justify mass-production methods, increased specialization with the replacement of highly-skilled jobs by those calling for fewer skills, has been common. Further, at the present time, considerable task restructuring is taking place in many firms due to automation. Although some newly created jobs in automated operations have called for *higher* skill levels than those required for many of the jobs existing theretofore, in many cases, however, the converse has been true.[2] In addition, at times considerable numbers of workers may be displaced by automation. In one electric power firm which expanded its operations by the addition of a new "automated" power plant it was reported that the man power required in the new plant was about half the number which would be needed in the older plants to generate the same level of output.[3] Although no workers were actually displaced in this operation since the power plant constituted an *addition* to the firm's capacity:

> The effects of these reduced personnel needs are reflected in a greater feeling of job insecurity for the workers in . . . [the firm's] . . . older plant. These men recognize that technological developments will soon force them to acquire new skills or to supplement their present skills. . . .[4]

Viewing the American economy as a whole in the longer run, the assumption that technological change and automation leads to greater unemployment or lower pay levels can be questioned. As Peter Drucker has pointed out, from 1961 through 1964:

---

[2] For a discussion of the extent to which automation lowers as opposed to raising skill levels, see James R. Bright, "Does Automation Raise Skill Requirements?" *Harvard Business Review,* 36 (July–August, 1958), 85–98. Bright holds that although it seems "logical that automatic machinery does result in higher work-force skills. . . . despite a number of exceptions here and there, the opposite is a truer picture of reality."

[3] F. C. Mann and R. L. Hoffman, "Case History in Two Power Plants," in *Man and Automation: Report of the Proceedings of a Conference Sponsored by the Society for Applied Anthropology at Yale University,* as reprinted in Charles R. Walker, *Modern Technology and Civilization* (New York: McGraw-Hill Book Company, Inc., 1962), p. 168.

[4] *Ibid.,* p. 169.

. . . the blue-collar manufacturing jobs that automation supposedly devours have been growing particularly fast—by 1,600,000 altogether since 1961; that is, at twice the rate of the other job classes. There has been no drop in the past 10 or 15 years either in the proportion of the American labor force employed on the factory floor (a third of total employment in the country) or in the number of man-hours per week needed to get the nation's work done. The average weekly take-home pay of the factory worker is at an all-time peak and likely to grow further in 1965 as a result of sharp pay raises in the new union contracts.[5]

However, in the short run, in certain specific companies and industries, numerous individuals have without doubt been adversely affected by technological change (albeit in some cases only temporarily so). Thus when mechanization and automation occur or are being considered, resistance to such changes is not unusual or irrational when viewed from the vantage point of the affected individual.

Not only does such resistance come from individuals, but also from work groups and from unions. Since union income is dependent upon the number of dues-paying members, union officers, both at the international [6] and local levels, may view changes which will mean lower levels of employment as a threat to their own (and the union's) economic security. Such threats are of special significance at the international level, of course, when technological changes portend the reduction of employment throughout an industry (e.g., the effects of dieselization of the railroads upon firemen). Further, union leaders may be under serious pressures to resist technological changes from their membership, for if they do not support member desires, they may lose their positions in the union at the next election of officers.

The reader should not infer from the above discussion that unions always resist organizational change; for, in fact, union leadership has sometimes given support to technological changes calling for worker displacement. For example, John L. Lewis, long the president of the United Mine Workers, considered technological change in the coal industry desirable since it would mean the removal of men working in undesirable coal mines and would permit an increase in productivity and pay of the mine workers. Although a considerable number of coal-mining jobs were eliminated, the average rate of

---

[5] Peter F. Drucker, "Automation Is Not the Villain," *New York Times Magazine,* January 10, 1965, p. 27. © 1965 by the New York Times Company. Reprinted by permission.

[6] National union organizations in this country are usually referred to as "internationals" since they may have members in Canada.

pay of the miners who continued to be employed rose considerably as mine technology advanced under encouragement by the union. Thus, the union viewed technological changes in the industry as desirable in an overall, long-run sense, rather than considering each such change as a threat to employment in a particular mine at a particular time.

INFLUENCING ACCEPTANCE OF ORGANIZATIONAL CHANGE

Individuals and groups will, quite obviously, exhibit different degrees of resistance to change depending upon the extent to which they perceive their needs being threatened, their predispositions of hostility towards management, etc. In some cases, the resistance may be major and widespread—e.g., a strike may be called by the union because of management's insistence on changing certain work procedures. In other cases, resistance to proposed organizational modifications may be relatively minor—e.g., a group of employees may simply gripe to their boss for a few days about a task reassignment but accept the restructuring without slowing down in their work or in any other way "fighting" management. Even such minor resistance, however, tends to be disruptive and to consume some time since it does represent a diversion from normal work activities.

Because of the disruptive effects of resistance to organizational change, considerable attention has been given by management thinkers to ways of dealing with and helping to overcome such resistance. We will now examine certain facets of the problem of dealing with resistance to change in organizations.

Psychologically, the process of attempting to influence employees to accept organizational restructuring is the same as that for inducing acceptance to *any* form of change. Influencing acceptance of organizational change is but one sub-type of influence in general—i.e., it represents one sub-set or sub-class of the universal set, "influence," which we discussed in our chapter on leadership. For this reason, we find it useful to discuss the problem of dealing with change in terms of some of the concepts presented previously in Chapter 5.

There are many different ways in which management can attempt to influence the acceptance of organizational restructuring. In choosing from among these alternatives, however, it is not very useful for the manager to seek answers in any "universal principles." Rather, a situationist approach, in which he takes into account such factors as the magnitude of resistance anticipated or expressed by various individuals and groups, the strength of his own bases of social power, etc., is preferable. In some cases, for example, a manager may be able, on the basis of his expert power, to allay certain unreal fears of his subordinates by discussing proposed organizational modifications with them. In such discussions, it is usually considered advisable to explain not only what the changes will be, but also *why* they are taking place. Or, even if organizational change poses a *real* threat to the individual (e.g., some loss of status due to task reassignment), he may still be influenced to accept the change if he identifies strongly with his supervisor (referent power) and/or if he believes that "because the boss says so, it's the right thing to do" (legitimate power). Additionally, the manager may draw on either his reward and/or coercive bases of power in gaining acceptance of organizational redesign. For example, he might promise to reward a subordinate by granting him certain special privileges in return for accepting an unwanted task reassignment; or he might threaten dismissal if an employee refuses to go along with proposed organizational modifications.

In addition to such influence efforts carried out in the form of face-to-face interpersonal relationships between the manager and his subordinates, more formally planned attempts to deal with resistance to change may be undertaken by organizations. In some cases when the resistance stems to a considerable extent from threats to economic security, firms will provide economic guarantees to their workers. For example, when, as a result of changes in job content, the pay rates for certain positions are downgraded, a company may guarantee the maintenance of the employee's past earnings as long as he remains on the same job. This practice is sometimes referred to as establishing "red circle" rates. Under this practice, if the employee is subsequently promoted or transferred, he will receive the pay rate for his new job. Further, when new employees take over any of the downgraded jobs, they will receive the new lower-level pay rates. Thus, such a policy results in different persons receiving different earnings for the same work. Over a period of time, however, labor turnover tends to eliminate the out-of-line rates, and the firm no longer has to pay some persons "more than their jobs are really worth."

Another practice undertaken by a few firms aimed at reducing threats to economic security is to guarantee that no employee will be released by the company as a result of technological change.

Such a policy, of course, means that the firm will have to transfer employees and retrain them in skills required for other types of work. Over a period of time employment levels in the firm may still be reduced by such an approach by the expedient of not hiring new employees to replace those who leave the company.

Two further observations are in order concerning economic guarantees of the type we have been discussing. First, they may be quite costly. Whether such costs are justified will, of course, depend on the variables involved in any particular situation. For example, in some cases, the granting of red-circle-rate demands by a union may prevent a major strike; while in other cases, a firm may "get by" without adopting such a practice and encounter no serious negative repercussions. Even so, management may still believe that these economic guarantees ought to be provided on the basis of its value system which holds that the firm has a moral obligation to its workers. Second, the downgrading of jobs, as we indicated previously, may not only provide a threat to the individual's economic security, but also threaten his status position. In consequence, to the extent that an individual's or a group's status needs are strong, resistance to change may not be overcome simply by providing economic guarantees.

Also useful in helping to induce employees to accept organizational redesign may be the group participation method which we discussed in Chapter 6. The efficacy of this approach under certain conditions has been demonstrated by several research studies. For example, in an experiment conducted by Coch and French at the Harwood Manufacturing Corporation, slight changes were made in the job content of four different groups of employees.[7] Three of these groups were permitted to participate in deciding how the jobs were to be redesigned; in the fourth (control) group, no such participation opportunities were provided. In the control group:

> Resistance developed almost immediately after the change occurred. Marked expressions of aggression against management occurred, such as conflict with the methods engineer, expression of hostility against the supervisor, deliberate restriction of production, and lack of cooperation with the supervisor. There were 17 per cent quits in the first forty days. Grievances were filed about the piece rate, but when the rate was checked, it was found to be a little "loose." [8]

In the experimental participative groups, on the other hand, no workers quit their jobs in the first forty days after the task changes

---

[7] Lester Coch and John R. P. French, Jr., "Overcoming Resistance to Change," *Human Relations*, 1 (1948), 512–32.

[8] *Ibid.* Quoted by permission of *Human Relations*.

had been introduced, and their average productivity *increased* over what it had been prior to the task restructuring.

As we mentioned in Chapter 6, the participation approach, notwithstanding its usefulness, may not be effective when the individuals concerned do not have the knowledge or skills to help make decisions or when they are apathetic or hostile towards management. Additionally, the efficacy of the participation approach can be seriously questioned in cases in which the necessary organizational changes pose a real, serious threat to the group—e.g., when, say, half of a group knows that they will lose their jobs, and the other half knows that their jobs will be downgraded due to a technological change. In the Harwood experiment, none of the workers was threatened by either loss of job or downgrading of skill levels— as mentioned previously, the changes in job content were only minor ones. Thus, conditions probably more conducive to the participative approach existed at Harwood than would be found in many cases where technological change necessitates job redesign.

WILLINGNESS TO CHANGE

Up to this point, we have focused our attention on negative reactions to change by organizational members. We will now give consideration to the converse of this phenomenon—the willingness of individuals in the business firm to initiate of their own accord modifications in organizational tasks, patterns of influence, communications flow and content, etc.

Underlying resistance to change, as we have pointed out, are perceptions (real or imagined) that the satisfaction of certain of the individual's needs will be threatened by organizational redesign. In many situations, however, it is *only by modifying* or elaborating upon formal organizational structures and processes that individuals *can* better meet certain of their needs and/or more fully attain certain organizational objectives which are congruent with these needs. In the following sections we will focus attention upon several facets of this "informal" initiation of organizational modification and elaboration by individuals.

Lag and Generality of the Formal System

There are many reasons why individuals may initiate modifications and elaborations of the formal organizational system. For example, a production worker may change the method of performing his job in order to reduce fatigue; or, a manager may develop a communications channel with a colleague in another department not specified by the formal organization in order to obtain quickly the information he needs to make a particular decision.

Among these many reasons for initiation of change are two fundamental ones to which we have not yet given explicit attention. First, is the *lag* of the formal system. In the previous chapter, we pointed out that environmental changes frequently give rise to formal organizational redesign. In some cases, however, environmental changes which call for redesign are *not* immediately recognized or effected by management; and individuals within the firm find it necessary to "step in" and initiate "informally" organizational modifications if their needs and work objectives are to be met. Or, to put it another way, individuals effect modifications in work procedures, information patterning, etc., because the formal organizational system has lagged behind changed environmental conditions. It should also be pointed out that in some cases, such informal modifications may ultimately become formalized within the organization. For example, one small firm established a new personnel department, without giving immediate, explicit consideration to many phases of information transmission and receipt between personnel and other departments in the company. Soon, numerous of the firm's production supervisors found it necessary to make frequent calls or visits to the personnel manager in order to obtain information about certain personnel problems—i.e., informal communications patterns were developed. Then, as patterns of informational needs became more clearly understood, formal information processing and communication procedures and processes were designed. Policy statements on certain matters were written by personnel and distributed to the foremen, periodic reports on labor turnover, grievances, etc., were developed, the foremen were notified that certain types of information could be obtained directly from one of the clerks in the personnel department, without going through the personnel manager himself, etc.

Elaboration of the formal organizational structure is also often necessitated due to the *generality* of the formal system—i.e., more specific *codes* and *rules* for behavior are needed by individuals and groups than those provided formally by management. Policies, job descriptions, and many operating procedures must usually be to some extent general in character because of management's inability to specify (or the cost of specifying) in detail all of the behavior the organization requires to accomplish its objectives. This is true even in those organizations which emphasize formalizing past precedents into procedures or decision-rules for future guidance, for *complete* specification of requisite behavior is usually not possible by such formal methods. Even on many routine, machine-paced production jobs, for example, workers have some latitude, albeit small, to go beyond formal job specifications in defining precisely the best way for them to perform their work. Further, high degrees of behavioral specification are sometimes undesirable for reasons which we have discussed in previous chapters—e.g., highly programmed work may lead to boredom and monotony and negate the possibility of creative expression on the part of the individual.

Forms of Initiated Change and Elaboration

In Chapter 7 we indicated that organizational design implies the structuring of (1) tasks, (2) information patterns, and (3) power and influence relationships among individuals holding various positions in the firm. In the following sections we will focus attention on some of the ways in which changes in each of these three facets of the design of the formal organization may be initiated by individuals "informally." Before doing so, however, two general observations are in order. First, we should emphasize that each of these facets of design is often interrelated with the others. For example, by informally developing new communications channels with another member of the organization, a manager may obtain information which permits him to become more knowledgeable and make better decisions, which, in turn, will enable him both to exert greater influence on others and to expand the scope of his job content. Second, the organizational changes initiated by individuals may not be congruent with organizational objectives; nor may they always represent "constructive" behavior, as defined in Chapter 4. For example, a manager may gradually enlarge the content of his job by taking on more and more tasks, many of which are quite useless in terms of meeting organizational objectives, largely because of a subconscious need to punish himself (by overwork); or, so that by spending many long evenings at work, he can avoid a nagging wife as much as possible.

The Job and the Individual: Task Restructuring. In previous sections, we have made reference to the fact that individuals in organizations will often informally redesign their jobs to some extent. We will now examine this facet of the individual's initiation of change in greater detail.

Formal organizational design attempts to develop a rational scheme of work division and coordination. Jobs and positions are specified so as to best meet the objectives of the firm. In the design of a particular job, consideration is usually given not only to the work which needs to be performed, but also to the qualifications that individuals ought to possess in order to be able to fill the position—e.g., education, previous related experience, etc. To aid in specifying these qualifications, firms often prepare job (or position) descriptions. These descriptions define the activities, duties, responsibilities, etc., that are required for particular positions.

In designing jobs, it is assumed that someone can be hired or trained to perform the duties so specified. But, from a purely theoretical view, jobs are designed formally without giving explicit consideration to the *particular* individuals who may be available to perform them. This is done so that the firm will not become dependent on a particular individual to the extent that when he is moved to another position or leaves the organization, a respecification of his duties and responsibilities will be necessary. From a practical point of view, however, the job duties and responsibilities as formally envisioned prior to the selection of any given individual to fill a position must frequently be modified to accommodate the person's particular abilities and limitations. This is especially true for managerial positions at higher levels in the organization, where the work performed is so complex and dynamic in nature that it cannot be highly preprogrammed—e.g., no specific procedures for the step-by-step performance of the job of president of a firm can be spelled out as they can for a machine-paced routine job on the assembly line.

In consequence of this need for accommodation of positions to the personalities of persons filling them, managers will often modify the task content of positions in their departments when new individuals are called on to fill particular jobs and/or when a subordinate's abilities, needs, or interests change to the extent that some restructuring of his task content seems desirable. For example, in one personnel department with which the authors are familiar, the department head restructured the jobs of two of his assistant managers by having them "trade" certain of their duties on a "permanent" basis because each expressed more interest in and seemed to possess more potential ability in performing those parts of the other's work.

Additionally, it is common for individuals (in positions in which the work is not highly specified in detail) to make subtle, gradual, and informal changes in their duties as their tenure in a particular position increases. When first moved into a new position, for instance, a manager may have to spend considerable time developing satisfactory interpersonal relationships with his new supervisor, subordinates, and peers. In addition, the demands of his job are probably more comprehensive and broader in scope than those of the positions which he has held previously. Initially, then, his performance tends to be limited by his lack of knowledge about and experience in dealing with the new work. If successful in dealing with these initial problems, the new manager then may begin to enlarge the scope and depth of his performance, and to seek out new ways of improving his operations. As a consequence of his own personal development, his scope of work may evolve from a minimal or sub-minimal one during his initial months on the job to one which ultimately exceeds that formally included in the specifications of his position. Sometimes, such changes as these in activities performed may be formally incorporated into the manager's position specification; the salary range for the position may be upgraded, and upon his leaving the job, a replacement may be sought who can perform the job as more broadly defined. In other cases, however, no such formal modifications are made, and the scope of activities performed by the manager's successor may be narrowed towards conforming with the original, and unchanged, formally defined specifications of the position.

The Restructuring of Power and Influence. Gradual expansion of a manager's activities, as described in the previous section, may often be accompanied by an increase in his status, prestige, and power to influence other members of the organization. Additionally, more overt and less gradual attempts to restructure power and influence patterns within the organization may also be found. An illustration of the initiation of power restructuring on an "informal" basis is provided by the following situation which occurred in one firm:

As one superintendent, a middle-level manager, neared the company's compulsory retirement age, he began to avoid any long-run binding commitments. He appeared to fear forthright action in risky situations. Soon, his subordinates concluded that he was "playing it safe" by avoiding decisions the consequences of which might jeopardize his position or might negatively influence his future retirement. Although no change in the formal organization structure was made and no personnel were reassigned, considerable modifications were undertaken in the actual departmental operations. His subordinates began to and were successful in by-passing him in obtaining authorizations for new programs from higher levels of management. Before long, the superintendent became a "figurehead" with little power and influence, recognition, status, or relevant information. Although they continued to socialize with him in deference to his past contributions, his subordinates and associates did not "bother" their boss with important information or decisions.

In this situation the informal operating changes were made to accommodate the lag in the formal structure by recognizing the still-existing necessities for accomplishing work. This delay in changing the formal structure was not entirely without benefit in spite of the problems which it posed. Maintaining the superintendent in his formal position was interpreted (or rationalized) as a willingness of the firm to "take care of" employees who had made substantial past contributions to company success. At the same time, the work was accomplished and the superintendent apparently was satisfied. As the reader may observe, this example also illustrates the interrelationships among the task content, informational flow and influence patterning aspects of organizational structuring which we emphasized previously. Not only was the superintendent's influence reduced, so also was the scope of his task content, and the number and significance of informational inputs which he received and messages which he transmitted to others.

Communications and Information Restructuring. Many different kinds of messages are transmitted through diverse communications channels within the business organization. In some cases, members of the firm are able to obtain the informational inputs which they need to meet their work (and personal) objectives. In other cases, however, information needed may not be obtainable through existing communications channels; messages may become distorted through transmission and receipt; and/or informational receipt may be delayed beyond the time at which it is needed to make decisions. In order to help overcome barriers such as these, individuals will frequently modify and elaborate upon the formal communications patterns established by the organization. In this section, we will discuss some of the more common communications problems which exist in organizations and some ways in which communications and informational restructuring is effected by individuals.

Vertical Communications Barriers. Communications experts frequently emphasize two points in discussing barriers to effective communications: (1) the level of difficulty of messages must be congruent with the capabilities of the receiver to understand them; and (2) the sender of messages must be empathetic towards (or understanding of) the needs of the receiver for information. These two communicational needs are often not met in organizations, perhaps especially in the vertical transmission and receipt of messages from superior to subordinate and vice versa.

One study, for example, showed that in one firm workers understood *"less* than 25 percent of what their managers thought they understood." [9] One reason for such problems is that when management communicates within its ranks and with workers, there is sometimes the tendency to use written media, since many consider it preferable to "have it in writing" in case anything goes wrong. Research findings reveal, however, many communicational inadequacies in typical written formal policies, procedures and manuals designed for the use of lower-level managers and workers. These weaknesses also exist in many house organs, supposedly designed to facilitate vertical communications between management and workers. One reason for the existence of such problems is that the semantic barrier is likely to be higher with the written word than when oral communications are employed. Not only do the usual differences in the *meaning* of words exist (e.g., "profit" as interpreted by a firm's board of directors as opposed to its interpretation by a union steward), but also management tends to write above the *level* of its readers. For example, it was reported that in an

analysis of 69 articles selected at random from 13 representative employee papers, 37—or over half—were on a readability level of difficult to very difficult, that is, above the educational level of 67 to 95 per cent of the adult population.[10]

Further, when writing, it is more difficult for the sender of a message to obtain *feedback* from the receiver as to the effectiveness of the communication. Face-to-face oral methods, on the other hand, tend to provide fuller mutual understanding since difficulties in comprehension and differences in meaning can be more readily identified and corrected on the spot.

Problems in vertical communications within organizations are also often created because of status differences among the senders and receivers of messages. As Schuyler Hoslett has pointed out:

The placing of persons in superior and subordinate relationships in the formal structure necessarily inhibits the free flow of information, ideas, suggestions,

---

[9] Ralph G. Nichols, "Listening Is Good Business," *Management of Personnel Quarterly*, 1 (Winter, 1962), 212–17; as reprinted in Max D. Richards and William A. Nielander, *Readings in Management* (2nd ed.; Cincinnati, Ohio: South-Western Publishing Company, 1963), p. 195.

[10] Schuyler D. Hoslett, "Barriers to Communication," *Personnel*, 28 (September, 1951), 108–14; as reprinted in Max D. Richards and William A. Nielander, *op. cit.*, p. 181.

questions . . . the subordinate tends to tell his superior what the latter is interested in . . . and to cover up problems and mistakes which may reflect on . . . [himself]. . . .[11]

Conversely, the superior may feel that:

he cannot fully admit to his subordinate those problems, conditions, or results which may reflect adversely on his ability and judgment. To do so would undermine his position as a superior being in the formal organization.[12]

There is some research to indicate that if a supervisor emphasizes his higher status, he is less likely to attain satisfactory face-to-face contacts with his subordinates as individuals or in groups. For example, Nichols reports a ninety percent reduction in grievances in a plant in which foremen were taught to de-emphasize status by "listening." This training emphasized utilization of the so-called "grunt rule" and "question rule." [13] When talking to their subordinates, the foremen were encouraged not to make declarative statements about the content of the conversation but to say "uh-huh" as the worker talked and to ask questions to encourage further conversation. This approach permitted worker "catharsis" in expressing opinions and grievances and generated more productive face-to-face communications because it indicated an attitude of understanding on the part of supervisors.

The "Grapevine" and Rumor.   Common to the business firm is the development of the so-called "grapevine"—the informal transmission of messages of interest to one's friends and associates in the organization. Basically, the grapevine emerges to satisfy informational needs of organizational members which are not met by the firm's formal communications—either because such communications do not "get through" properly to their intended receivers as indicated previously, or because certain information needed by individuals is never transmitted by management in the first place.

The grapevine carries information which is job-related and that which is designed to meet the "social and personal interests of people." [14] If subordinates are uncertain and in the dark as to where they stand or what they are to do, their security needs tend to be thwarted. In such cases, job-related information may be sought to allay fears. For example, the grapevine is often quick to carry job-related news (e.g., impending layoffs or new contracts, changes in

---

[11] *Ibid.*, p. 176.
[12] *Ibid.*
[13] Nichols, *op. cit.*, 198–99.
[14] Keith Davis, "Communication Within Management," *Personnel*, 31 (November, 1954), 212–18; as reprinted in Richards and Nielander, *op. cit.*, p. 189.

management assignments) which may affect such factors as the position, employment, or pay of workers. Since it constitutes a method of socializing, the grapevine also provides a means of ful- filling the *social* needs of employees. Bowling scores, births, sick- nesses, and impending social events are illustrative of grapevine subjects. Further, typical of the grapevine are the following char- acteristics:

1. People talk most when the news is recent.
2. People talk about things that affect their work.
3. People talk about people they know.
4. People working near each other are likely to be on the same grapevine.
5. People who contact each other in the chain of procedure, tend to be on the same grapevine.[15]

To what extent is the information content passed through the grapevine accurate? As we have indicated previously distortion of information is common when it passes from one person to another. Such distortion has frequently been illustrated by the classroom experiment in which a message is secretly whispered from one member to another around the class. A comparison of the original message with its interpretation by the person at the end of the com- munications chain is usually good for a laugh since the two are so different. Such classroom messages, however, are not directed to- ward fulfilling the security or social needs of group members as grapevine messages are. For this reason, it is not surprising that re- searchers have found that *actual* informal communications are much more *accurate* than messages transmitted in classroom experiments. In studying the informal transmission of messages among certain military personnel during wartime, for example, Theodore Caplow found that:

> The rumor process in the group observed was a fairly successful group de- vice for circulating desired information. Rumors tended to diffuse along defi- nite channels of person-to-person communication. The formation of channels decreased the number of rumors and increased their diffusion. The effect of transmission was to increase rather than decrease the validity of the state- ments.[16]

---

[15] *Ibid.*, p. 190.
[16] Theodore Caplow, "Rumors in War," *Social Forces*, 25 (October, 1946–May, 1947); as reprinted in Albert H. Rubenstein and Chadwick J. Haberstroh, *Some Theories of Organization* (Homewood, Illinois: The Dorsey Press, Inc. and Rich- ard D. Irwin, Inc., 1960), p. 287.

Caplow attributes the validity of observed rumors to strong group interests and the fact that the content of the rumors tends to satisfy group needs. When only social information (such as birth notices) is transmitted informally, however, there is likely to be more distortion in content.

Development of Horizontal and Diagonal Channels. Much attention in the design of organizational relationships has been focused on *vertical* communications within firms. Policies, procedures, operating reports, etc. are passed down from superior to subordinate; if a subordinate has problems he may communicate them to his boss, and so on.

A considerable amount of *work* in some organizations, on the other hand, *flows horizontally* cutting across departmental boundaries. For example, on the automobile assembly line, the "conveyor carries each automobile 'without a stop' through five departments, past the areas of 10 general foremen, through the sections of 50 or 60 foremen, and past the work stations of thousands of workers." [17] Because of the high degree of interdependence of work among departments under such conditions, it is often necessary for managers in dealing with problems to communicate horizontally with the managers of other departments and/or diagonally with workers who report to other managers. The foreman on the automobile assembly line, for instance, can theoretically:

. . . report any deficiency in services from supporting groups [such as maintenance men and inspectors] to his general foreman. . . . Time on the assembly line, however, is crucial; cars pass a given work station at the rate of one every 1.5 minutes. Unless an error is corrected immediately, the consequences can be far-reaching. The foreman cannot afford to spend time hunting down the general foreman; he has to attend to the matters immediately. To do so he has to deal with other foremen (on the horizontal plane) and also with materials handlers, maintenance men, inspectors, and other foremen's workers (on the diagonal plane). [18]

In some cases, those horizontal and diagonal communications channels necessary for the effective performance of work are formally defined by the organization. For instance, organizational procedures may be developed specifying that a foreman should directly contact another foreman's subordinate on certain matters as long as

---

[17] Frank J. Jasinski, "Adapting Organization to New Technology," *Harvard Business Review,* 37 (January–February, 1959), 79–86; as reprinted in Edwin A. Fleishman, *Studies in Personnel and Industrial Psychology* (Homewood, Illinois: The Dorsey Press, Inc., 1961), p. 443.

[18] *Ibid.,* p. 444.

the problems involved do not exceed a predefined magnitude. Often, however, it is necessary for managers to elaborate on such formal informational specifications and develop additional horizontal and/or diagonal communications channels if they are able to perform effectively. For example, in one firm manufacturing special-purpose machines, tool engineers often found that tool expenses could be reduced if changes in product design were made. Since the product engineers were responsible for the technical feasibility of machine design, it was necessary for the tool engineers to check out product changes with them in order to accommodate economical tooling and insure product performance. In some instances, this coordination went further than merely between tool and product engineering. The sales department and even customers were, at times, consulted about design changes. This type of coordination through horizontal communications was accomplished cooperatively without benefit of formal procedures. The persons involved believed informal methods were superior to and more flexible than highly defined written rules.

HUMAN BEHAVIOR AND THE ORGANIZATIONAL SYSTEM: SUMMARY AND OVERVIEW

In this, and in the previous six chapters, we have focused attention on human behavior and the variables influencing such behavior in the organizational system. Our purpose in this summary will be: (1) to provide an overview of these facets of behavior, and (2) to indicate some of the directions which we will take in the remaining chapters of this book.

The business firm is basically a dynamic organizational system comprised of numerous interrelated technological and human sub-systems. In Chapter 4, we examined the behavior of the most elemental organismic unit in the firm—the individual. Such behavior may be viewed as output from an open personality system, in mutual interaction with its environment. The individual receives information, makes decisions, performs physical work, and transmits information to other persons in the firm. Further, through his messages he often attempts to influence the behavior of others, as was a major focus of our attention in Chapter 5. As we pointed out in Chapter 6, through the association of individuals in the firm, various types of groups are formed. The behavioral and attitudinal outputs of these groups—which represent social sub-systems—are a function of their membership inputs and environmental factors. Our emphasis in this and the previous three chapters has been upon management's structuring of the organization to meet its objectives. Such structuring requires definition of: task content and the interrelationship among tasks, information channels and message content, and patterns of power and influence.

Our primary emphasis in this "behavioral" section of this book has been upon the relationships between technology, information, and influence flows, etc., and the behavior (and attitudes) of the organization's human sub-systems. In operating effectively, however, the manager must consider many variables other than human ones. Of special importance in a profit-oriented society are the economic implications of managerial decisions. In succeeding chapters, we will devote considerable attention to the economic aspects of decision making and will indicate a number of models useful in dealing with such problems. In doing so we will first examine in general the concepts of planning and control, and then explore such economic tools for analysis as the breakeven model, and such problems as the acquisition and maintenance of inventories.

Although for purposes of exposition, we have focused primary attention on human variables and will now begin shifting our attention more toward economic ones, it should be emphasized that both types of variables often stand in close interrelationship with each other. For example, a firm's scrap rate on a particular piece may be excessive partly because of a poor "economic" decision to purchase inferior materials, and partly because the employees working with the materials slow down their pace because the poor quality has caused them to lose some of their "pride of workmanship." Or, by making a series of "poor" economic decisions, a manager's basis of expert power may become diminished as a result of his subordinates' losing confidence in his abilities.

Recognizing that the manager must often give simultaneous consideration to numerous closely interrelated variables, both human and "non-human," we will next turn our attention to the planning process in the organizational system.

DISCUSSION AND STUDY QUESTIONS

1. "Formal policies from top management should always be communicated in writing so that they will not be misunderstood and so that lower level executives can be held responsible for their implementation." Discuss this statement in light of what you have read in Chapter 10.

2. What effects might the strength of the dependence needs of individuals in a department have upon the ability of their supervisor to introduce organizational changes?

3. Research indicates that it is just as effective to *explain* changes as it is to allow workers active participation in the change process. Do you agree with this statement? Explain.

4. In the history of technological change, it has often been the worker who has borne the brunt of implementing the changes. Comment on this statement. Explain your answer.

5. Resistance to change in an organization is inversely proportional to the rate of technological change which takes place in the organization. Do you agree? Explain.

6. Resistance to change in a firm is directly proportional to the average number of years that its employees have worked for the firm. Comment.

7. What reactions might be received by a management consultant explaining to the members of a firm's personnel department how the psychological tests which it gives to job applicants might be interpreted by a computer rather than by humans? Why?

8. What are some of the major reasons why some unions have tended to resist automation?

9. Both willingness to change and resistance to change can be motivated by a desire to satisfy any of the five classes of needs discussed in Chapter 4. Discuss. Give specific examples to support your discussion.

SELECTED REFERENCES

BENNIS, W. D.; BENNE, K. D.; and CHIN, R. (eds.). *The Planning of Change.* New York: Holt, Rinehart, & Winston, 1961.

BRIGHT, JAMES R. *Research, Development, and Technological Innovation.* Homewood, Ill.: Richard D. Irwin, Inc., 1964.

CARTWRIGHT, DORWIN. "Achieving Change in People: Some Applications of Group Dynamics Theory," *Human Relations*, 4 (1951), 381–392.

GUEST, ROBERT H. *Organizational Change: The Effect of Successful Leadership.* Homewood, Ill.: The Dorsey Press, Inc., 1962.

LAWRENCE, PAUL R. *The Changing of Organizational Behavior Patterns.* Boston: Division of Research, Graduate School of Business Administration, Harvard University, 1958.

LeBRETON, P. P., and HENNING, DALE A. *Planning Theory*, pp. 253–318. Englewood Cliffs, N. J.: Prentice-Hall, Inc., 1961.

LEVY, S., and DONAHUE, G. "Exploration of a Biological Model of Industrial Organization," *Journal of Business*, 33 (October, 1962), 335.

McMURRY, ROBERT N. "The Problem of Resistance to Change in Industry," *Journal of Applied Psychology*, 31 (December, 1947), 589–593.

PHILIPSON, MORRIS (ed.). *Automation Implications for the Future.* New York: Vintage Books, 1962.

PORTER, DONALD E., and APPLEWHITE, PHILIP B. (eds.). *Studies in Organizational Behavior and Management.* Scranton, Pa.: International Textbook Co., 1964.

ROSS, PAUL R. "How to Deal with Resistance to Change," *Harvard Business Review,* 32 (May–June, 1954), 49–57.

SHILS, EDWARD B. *Automation and Industrial Relations.* New York: Holt, Rinehart & Winston, 1963.

STARR, MARTIN K. *Production Management,* Chaps. xi, xii. Englewood Cliffs, N. J.: Prentice-Hall, Inc., 1964.

TAYLOR, GEORGE W. "Collective Bargaining," *Automation and Technological Change* (ed. Dunlop, John T.). Englewood Cliffs, N. J.: Prentice-Hall, Inc., 1962.

CHAPTER 11

THE PLANNING PROCESS

PLANNING for the future is an important aspect of almost all human behavior, both individual and organizational. The parent may begin developing financial plans when his children are young to help send them to college many years in the future; the student plans his college curriculum to prepare himself for a future vocation; individuals plan for vacation trips, parties, retirement, and so on. Similarly, within the business organization the manager develops many plans for future courses of action—the purchase of a new machine, the development of new products, forthcoming negotiations with the union, etc.

The purpose of this chapter is to examine the role of planning in the managerial decision-making process. We will first discuss the meaning of the term "planning." We will then turn our attention to the manager's need to predict future events in order to develop appropriate plans. Finally, we will examine three key factors in the planning process—time, programming, and repetitiveness.

PLANNING: A DEFINITION

There are many different ways in which one can view plans developed by business organizations. Our preference is to define an organizational plan as *any information output from a substantive decision transformation which either specifies or guides the taking of future actions by its members geared toward overcoming existing or anticipated problems.*

Several observations are in order concerning this definition of an organizational plan. First, by utilizing the term "information output" we are viewing plans as messages or communications. In many cases, we may observe such messages being transmitted by their developers to other members of the organization—as when a foreman's plans for assigning work are communicated either orally or in written form to his men. In some instances, however, planning may take place even though no observable outputs are generated and transmitted to others. For example, in developing his itinerary for any given week, a salesman might do nothing more than make a mental note of the calls which he plans to make. In such a case, the "information outputs" called for by our definition of a plan would simply be those mental messages generated by the salesman and fed back into his own memory system to serve as guides to his future actions during the week.

Second, the phrase "either specifies or guides" is utilized in our definition of a plan in recognition of the fact that not all organizational plans explicitly prescribe future courses of action to be taken. Rather, some simply indicate general directions to be followed by a firm. Such is the case with many basic company objectives—e.g., a profitability goal of $1,000,000 established by a company for a particular year would constitute a general plan, the realization of which would require the design and implementation of numerous more specific sub-plans. Thus, in terms of means-ends-means chains as discussed in Chapter 2, some plans assume the form of overall objectives, while others serve both as sub-objectives and means toward the accomplishment of overall firm goals.

Third, it should be recognized that the time interval which occurs between the statement of a plan and the actual taking of any actions so specified will vary considerably for different organizational plans. Some plans call for actions to be taken almost immediately, while others are geared toward guiding the undertaking of activities several years in the future.

Fourth, the rather obvious point should be mentioned that the course(s) of action specified in any plan may or may not ever actually take place. Unforeseen future events will sometimes occur which lead management to modify or retract completely its plans or otherwise prevent the organization from taking the actions which had been intended. As the poet Robert Burns once put it: "The best laid plans o' mice and men gang aft a-gley." [1]

Finally, we should emphasize that the planning process is a pervasive one in the business organization and that all managers are

---

[1] In his poem "To a Mouse."

called on to develop courses of action for the future.[2] Moreover, although we are treating planning (and control) separately from direction and organization in this book for the purposes of exposition, the reader should recognize that virtually all of the organizing and directing decision problems which we discussed in earlier chapters involve planning. The manager must develop plans for assigning work to his subordinates, considerable advance planning is required in the design of economic incentive plans, and so on.

PREDICTION AND PLANNING

The effectiveness of an organization's planning efforts will usually be a function not only of the actions undertaken by the firm itself, but also of the occurrence of other future events. As we suggested previously in Chapter 2, such events may be classed as states of nature and competitive strategies.

In organizational planning it is important to recognize that management may often have little, if any influence over the occurrence of those states of nature and competitive actions which may have an important bearing on the achievement of its objectives. For example, there may be nothing that a firm can do to prevent a strike against one of its raw materials suppliers, the occurrence of which would force curtailment of its production. Or, there may be no way to prevent a leading competitor from coming out with a new product, the introduction of which would seriously hurt the firm's own sales.

Even though the manager can have little or no control over the occurrence of many such future happenings, it is important for him to consider explicitly these variables in his planning activities. As Miller and Starr have pointed out:

> The fact that a large number of variables do not fall under the control of the executive does not mean that he should ignore them. On the contrary, it is the decision-maker's responsibility to examine all noncontrollable variables that affect his attaining the objectives. Although he can exercise no control over these variables, *he can make predictions about them.*[3]

---

[2] It might be noted that managers in higher level positions in the business firm usually spend more of their time in long-range planning than do managers at lower levels. For example, the president of a company may devote considerable time considering long-range plans for product diversification or expansion into foreign markets; while first line production supervisors are normally concerned with matters such as scheduling work for the following day or week.

[3] David W. Miller and Martin K. Starr, *Executive Decisions and Operations Research* (Englewood Cliffs, N. J.: Prentice-Hall, Inc., 1960), p. 25. Copyright © 1960 by Prentice-Hall, Inc. The italics are ours.

For example, by studying the position taken by the president and certain influential members of congress, a firm may be able to predict the passage or failure of a piece of Federal legislation which, if enacted, would have a significant impact on its operations.

It is, of course, also important that management attempt to forecast the outcome of its own decision alternatives should those states of nature and/or competitive strategies of concern to it take place, for objective attainment is a function of the firm's own actions *coupled with* the occurrence of such events. As may be recalled from our discussion in Chapter 2, the manager in utilizing payoff matrices to make decisions under risk ought to try to predict:

1.   What will happen in terms of attaining objectives should any of various possible states of nature (or competitor actions) occur along with his choice of different available decision alternatives, and

2.   The probability of occurrence of each such state of nature and/or competitive strategy.

One further observation concerning the role of prediction in the organizational planning process should be noted. Earlier we indicated that organizational plans represent outputs from substantive decision transformations. Managerial predictions, on the other hand, may be viewed as informational *inputs* upon which such decision transformations are based. For example, sales forecasts may serve as information inputs upon which a firm's monthly production schedules are predicated; psychological test scores, which are utilized as predictions of individuals' job performance, often represent important informational inputs in the making of personnel selection decisions, etc.

Bounded Rationality in Managerial Prediction

Some variables of concern to the manager are relatively easy to predict with a fairly high degree of accuracy. For example, by analyzing population data, elementary school textbook publishers are able to predict quite closely the number of children who will reach school age in any given year.

Other factors, however, may be extremely difficult to predict accurately, for the rationality of the manager is bounded in a number of ways. For one, it is rarely, if ever, possible to visualize the occurrence of *all* states of nature or competitive strategies which may have a bearing on the firm's objective attainment. Nor, even if the possibility of occurrence of a particular competitor's action or state of nature can be foreseen, may management be able to assign a probability to such a happening. For example, knowing that a competitor has started research on a new product idea, it may be next to impossible to forecast accurately when, if ever, the product will be ready to be marketed. Further, the manager may often find it necessary to settle for predictive data less accurate than he would like because of the excessive expense which would be incurred in obtaining highly precise information or because insufficient time is available to develop such data.

For example:

1.   In personnel selection, a management might find that the use of extensive psychological tests and depth interviews by trained psychologists improves slightly its ability to predict how successful job applicants will be in working for the firm; but this slight improvement in predictive ability does not justify the costs incurred by such sophisticated selection techniques.

2.   A soap manufacturer coming out with a new detergent may forego its usual practice of refining its new product demand projections by extensive test marketing because: (1) it knows that one of its major competitors is planning national distribution of a similar product shortly, and (2) the time required for its test marketing would prevent it from beating its competitor to the market.

In short, the predictive rationality of the manager is bounded by time, incomplete information, and imperfect foresight.

Prediction: Focus and Methodology

Most business firms attempt to predict the occurrence of many different kinds of events—economic trends, sales, costs, employee reactions to managerial policies, etc. Although the predictive efforts of firms engaged in different kinds of business will vary considerably, certain generalizations may be made about the variables focused upon and methodology utilized in managerial forecasting.

As far as the focus of prediction is concerned, fundamental to and providing a basis for much managerial decision making is the *sales forecast*. This is because the quantity and kinds of raw materials, parts, manpower, and capital equipment needed by a company will depend to a considerable extent on the quantity and types of goods and/or services which it believes it can sell. In attempting to predict sales for any given future period, companies will usually consider in relation to each other all classes of variables discussed earlier:

1.   *States of Nature,* such as population growth, changes in the age or income distribution of the population, government fiscal policies which may have an impact on consumer or industrial spending, etc. For example, firms producing military goods frequently develop market forecasts based upon "a long-term projection of GNP," a "projection of the military budget on the basis of the economic forecast" and a "statistical analysis of the composition of the military budget." [4]

2.   *Competitive strategies* such as the introduction of new products, price changes, or modifications in marketing and advertising programs (e.g., a competitor's anticipated introduction of trading stamps).

3.   The firm's *own possible strategies*—e.g., the impact of a proposed improvement in product quality on its sales volume.

As far as *approaches* to forecasting are concerned, many different methodologies are currently employed, depending upon the variables concerned, the degree of precision desired, the sophistication of management, the funds available for predictive analysis, and so on. In some cases, executives' intuition and judgment are relied on heavily in organizational prediction. Although managers are sometimes able to come up with quite accurate forecasts of what the future will bring by this means, the validity of the intuitive approach is open to serious question. This is because, as we indicated in Chapter 3, the manager's previous experience may not provide an adequate sample upon which to base predictions; his memory, observation, and interpretation of data may be fallible, etc.

In other cases, more sophisticated predictive tools are employed by managers. Frequently utilized in sales forecasting (and often in predicting other factors of concern to the organization) are methods such as trend, cyclical, or correlation analysis. For example:

1.   Statistical analysis of the composition of military research and development efforts indicated for 1955–60 a shift away from conventional weapons and aircraft to astronautics and missiles. These trends are illustrated in Figure 11–1.

2.   Sales in many industries often fluctuate according to some pattern that is at least roughly predictable—in relation to either the "business cycle," seasonal buying, or in some cases, daily variations

---

[4] Murray L. Weidenbaum, "The Role of Economics in Business Planning," *Business Topics,* 10 (Summer, 1962), p. 50.

FIGURE 11-1. The Changing Mix of Military R and D

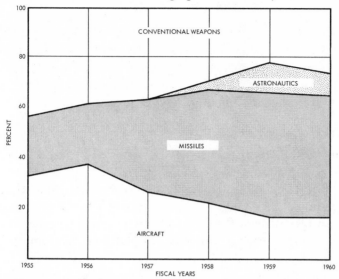

Source: Murray L. Weidenbaum, "The Role of Economics in Business Planning," *Business Topics*, 10 (Summer, 1962), p. 51.

in purchasing activity. In planning the size of their work forces, for instance, from the analysis of historical sales data, department stores may act on the premise that 40 percent of their total annual sales will be obtained during the Christmas season; or supermarket managers on the premise that 50 percent of their weekly sales will be made on Thursday and Friday evenings and on Saturdays.

Although reliance on predictive approaches such as these may sometimes be highly useful to the manager, caution must be exercised in their application. This is because many are essentially "static" models based on the not necessarily valid premise that the relationships between variables will be the same in the future as in the past. For example, in each of the past 10 years, 38–43 percent of a department store's sales may have been concentrated in the Christmas season; but this year a strike or major layoff at the largest manufacturing plant in town in September and October may have an important negative impact on Christmas sales.

Finally, as we indicated in Chapter 3, gaining increasing utilization as both predictive and prescriptive tools are the mathematical tools developed by operations researchers. We will devote attention in succeeding chapters to a number of such models.

THE TIME VARIABLE

As we indicated previously, under different conditions quite different *time intervals* may exist between the point at which planning statements are formulated and the point at which the actions so specified are actually carried out. In this section we will explore several aspects of the time variable with respect to planning.

The Need for Advanced Planning

A number of different values may be obtained by the organization from effective planning efforts. Underlying all of these, however, is one basic function which planning activities serve to perform—to help increase the probability of occurrence of those future activities which must take place if the firm's objectives are to be attained. Suppose, for example, that a firm has just finished developing a new product and wants to be able to sell 10,000 units of it eight months hence. If this objective is to be met, a multitude of appropriately sequenced activities will have to be completed prior to the sale of these units, some of which are illustrated in Figure 11–2. Moreover, these activities will obviously not "just happen," nor is it possible for many of them *to occur immediately* upon management's decision that it wants them to occur. Rather a considerable amount of advanced

FIGURE 11–2. Sequence of New Product Activities

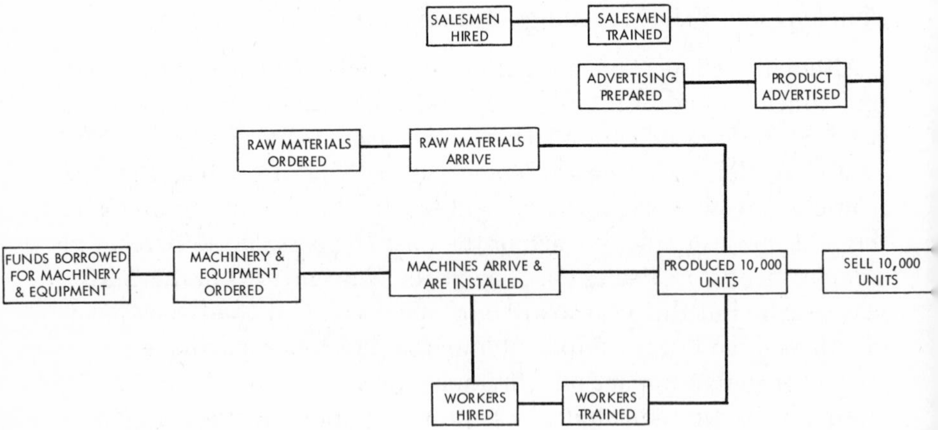

planning must be undertaken if the firm's sales objective is to be achieved. Such planning must recognize, that:

1. *Lead times* will be required for the acquisition of the resources necessary for the production and sale of the product. The new machinery needed for the manufacture of the product may not be ready for use until four or five months after it has been ordered; a lead time of two or three weeks may be required for the acquisition of raw materials, etc.

2. Certain activities cannot be initiated until others have been completed—e.g., the firm's new product cannot be manufactured until after its employees have been trained; the training cannot begin until after the employees have been hired, and so on.

In effect then, the attainment of the firm's objectives requires planning the design of *means-ends-means chains over time.* As is illustrated in Figure 11–2, attainment of the worker training sub-sub-objective, which must be planned prior to its occurrence in April for example, serves as a means toward accomplishing the manufacturing sub-objective which, in turn, serves as a means toward attaining the sales objective.

The Time Problem

In determining the time interval between the development of plans and the undertaking of the actions desired, the decision maker faces a fundamental problem—if this interval is either too short or too long, his objectives may not be (fully) met. We will now indicate some of the reasons why this is so.

Failure to Plan Far Enough in Advance. If the decision maker does not plan far enough in advance any one or more of problems such as the following may be encountered:

1. He may completely fail to meet his objectives, e.g., the failure of a retailing manager to plan sufficiently in advance in ordering goods he needs for a special sale compared to the acquisition lead time for them may result in his having to cancel the sale.

2. He may attain his objectives but only by incurring additional expenses in doing so. The retailing manager may still be able to obtain the goods in time for his sale but only by expediting their shipment by means of more expensive air rather than truck transportation.

302   Management Decision Making

3.   He may still be able to meet his objectives but only at the expense of his and/or his subordinates being subjected to additional psychological (or physiological) stress. Examples are legion about supervisors who fail to plan the work of their departments sufficiently in advance, and then, put all work on "crash" basis to get employees to speed up their work considerably as deadlines approach.

Planning Too Far in Advance.   Designing plans too far in advance may also be inappropriate for the decision maker. In general, as the time interval between plan and action increases, the conditions surrounding the specified actions and, hence, the outcome of such actions becomes more uncertain and unpredictable. For example, a retail department store manager can usually predict his sales for the following week much more precisely than those for the same week four years hence, by which time population may have shifted, competition may increase or decrease in the area, etc. Consequently, there is usually a greater probability that plans for the distant future will have to be modified or completely retracted than for those in the near future. Important to the organization in this respect is the fact that *planning costs* will tend to increase to the extent that planning statements need to be revised. By planning costs, we mean the time and expense involved in designing planning statements, putting them down on paper, communicating them to other members of the organization, etc. Moreover, when plans have been decided upon considerably in advance, there is the possibility that the organization will *commit* itself to certain of the actions so specified sooner than need be. For example, the supervisor who plans vacation schedules for his employees several months in advance, may find later that due to unanticipated heavy work loads he must either (1) back down on his commitment thus creating employee resentment, or (2) schedule overtime work to cover for certain vacationers.

The Time Problem: Opposing Costs.   From our above discussion, we may observe that in planning, the decision maker faces a set of *opposing costs* with respect to the magnitude of the time interval between the design of planning statements, and their implementation:

1.   As this interval becomes too small, the firm may fail to meet its objectives, incur additional costs in doing so, or added psychological stress may be incurred, while,

2.   As the time interval becomes too large, planning (and some-

times commitment) costs may increase.[5] These relationships are illustrated graphically in Figure 11–3.

FIGURE 11–3. Advanced Planning Opposing Costs

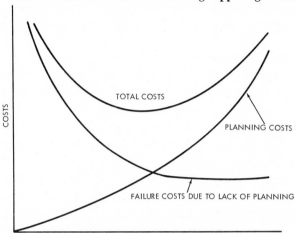

TIME INTERVAL BETWEEN DESIGN OF PLAN AND TAKING ACTIONS SO SPECIFIED

The model depicted in Figure 11–3, of course, is intended to portray only a generalized conceptualization of the planning problem with respect to time. Just what will represent an optimal time interval will vary considerably from situation to situation—as will also the nature of the planning and failure costs involved. For instance, longer acquisition lead times will force the decision maker to design his planning statements further in advance if his objectives are to be attained. Or, in decision problems in which a fairly high degree of certainty exists, plans can be developed farther in advance without facing the possibility of their major revision.

THE PROGRAMMING PROCESS

Business plans, as indicated previously, are comprised of sets of statements specifying or guiding future courses of action for the organization. In this section we will focus attention on the manner in which and degree to which the manager may want to program (i.e., spell out) such statements under varying conditions. We will first

---

[5] We should note that in some cases, planning costs may also increase if the time interval is too short. For example, if the manager waits too long before starting to plan a particular project, overtime work may be required on the planning *itself* if it is to be completed to meet necessary deadlines.

discuss two basic types of planning statements which may be utilized by the manager. We will then examine some of the conditions under which each has application. We will also turn our attention to management's consideration of the human variable in programming courses of organizational action for the future and to the utilization of standing plans to deal with repetitive problem situations.

Types of Planning Statements

The statements included in any business plan may assume either of two basic forms—(1) *do,* or (2) *if.* Although some plans designed by organizations may be comprised entirely of only one of these two types of statements, most all major and complex ones will include a number of statements of both types. We will now illustrate the characteristics of each.

Do Statements. Some plans call for certain courses of action to be taken regardless of the occurrence of any future events. For example, in negotiating with its union, a firm may devise a plan stipulating: "irrespective of union demands, pressures or threats, we will not agree to grant any wage increase this year." Or, the supervisor of an employee who has frequently come to work late over a prolonged period may decide: "I will discharge this man regardless of his plea for me not to do so."

That such categorical "do" statements have been developed, of course, does not necessarily mean that the actions so specified will actually be carried out, for as indicated previously, managerial plans may not be effected as originally intended. In our above illustration, for example, the firm might be forced to yield to union pressures for a wage increase as a result of a prolonged strike. Thus, the "do" of which we speak refers simply to a statement of intent, and in no way implies certainty that a specified course of action will be undertaken.

If Statements. In some situations, managers will develop what may be termed "contingent" plans—i.e., decide to follow one course of action if certain events occur, and to undertake other actions if other events take place. We will refer to such contingent planning imperatives as "if" statements because they take the form: "If *x* occurs, do *y.*" For example, in its union negotiations, management—rather than developing a categorical "do" statement as illustrated above—might design a plan incorporating the following "if" statements:

1. If the union agrees to *either* (1) our introduction of a new time-study-based incentive plan, or (2) the elimination of certain "featherbedding" practices in the maintenance department, agree to a five cent an hour wage increase.

2. If the union accepts both of these requests of ours, agree to a ten cent an hour increase.

3. If the union will not agree to either request, refuse to grant any wage increase.

As with "do" statements, the design of an "if" statement does not necessarily imply that the contingent actions specified will actually be taken—rather, the "if" simply represents an *intended* plan.

Utilization of Do and If Statements

There are many different variables which will influence the type of planning statements which the manager will find most appropriate in any given situation. In this section, we will illustrate some of the conditions under which do and if statements may be useful or necessary in organizational planning.

The Use of Do Statements. Do rather than if statements represent an obvious choice for the organizational planner under conditions of certainty—i.e., when he knows which states of nature and/or competitive strategies may have a bearing on his decision problem, when they will occur, and what will be the outcome of all possible strategies available to him in terms of objective attainment. Under such conditions, it is not necessary to develop any *contingent* plans since the values of all variables in his decision problem are known.

Rarely, if ever, of course, is the manager able to foresee the future so accurately. However, in many decision problems, he may be able to assign such a high probability to the occurrence of those states of nature and/or competitive strategies which may have a significant bearing on his decision problem that he may feel confident in proceeding to design plans comprised of do statements on the assumption that certainty does exist. For example, a retail store manager may go ahead and make definite plans to replace a clerk who has given notice of quitting his job based on the probability of the store's sales falling off sufficiently so as to obviate the need for the replacement is so small that it may be dismissed from consideration. Although many of the manager's day-to-day decisions are effectively made on the basis of such assumptions of near certainty, there is, of course, always the danger that his probability estimates may be grossly in error, and that, consequently, his plans may not work out as intended.

The design of do rather than if statements may also be more appropriate (or in certain situations, essential) under conditions in which considerable risk or uncertainty exists. Such is the case in those decision problems in which important future competitive strategies and/or states of nature are not known, but in which the manager must *commit* himself to taking certain actions *prior to* the occurrence of such events. For example, the farm manager cannot develop a set of contingent plans to specify which crops he will plant in any given spring on the basis of that year's summer weather conditions—i.e., if the weather in June and July is wet, plant crop *x;* if it is dry, plant crop *y.* Rather, he *must* plant his crops in the spring before the weather conditions which will have an important bearing on his success actually take place. In cases such as this, in which *prior commitment* is essential, the design of do statements based on payoff matrix analysis, as suggested in Chapter 2, may often be appropriate. Here, as the reader may recall, the manager first attempts to predict the outcome of each possible course of action available to him coupled with the probability of occurrence of each possible state of nature and/or competitive strategy (or under conditions of uncertainty employs one of the criteria suggested in Chapter 2). He then will develop categorical do statements specifying the actions which his analysis indicates should be taken. The nature of such prior commitment analysis and planning statement design is illustrated in Figure 11–4.

In addition to prior commitment situations, developing do, rather than if statements may be more appropriate under certain other risk and uncertainty conditions. One reason for this is that the design of a number of contingent plans obviously requires more time and expense than planning a single course of action. In consequence, the cost of developing and then revising do statements should unforeseen and/or adverse contingencies occur may often be less than that of developing an elaborate set of if statements in the first place. For example, a first line supervisor who plans the assignment of work for his 20 production line employees one day in advance, might have little time to do anything else if in his planning he considered the contingency of each employee being absent on the following day, coupled with that of each machine being down for repairs. Rather, his normal procedure would be to develop a single work assignment plan comprised solely of do state-

FIGURE 11–4. Payoff Matrix Analysis for Designing Do Statements
Specifying Prior Commitments

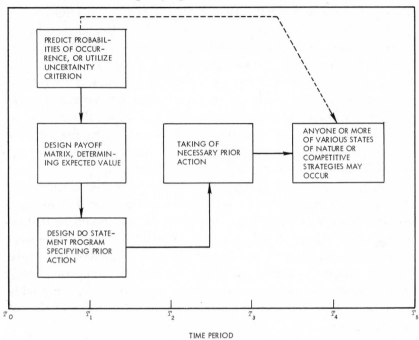

ments, and then reassign the work necessary to the extent that any
absences or machine breakdowns do occur.

The Use of If Statements. There are at least two basic kinds of
situations in which the utilization of if statements may be desirable
or essential in organizational planning. First, if statements may be
quite useful as a means of providing responses to certain kinds of
repetitive decision problems, as we will illustrate in a later section.
Second, the utilization of if statements is essential in organizational
planning situations which possess the following characteristics:

1. When the attainment of the firm's objectives is a function of
both certain future states of nature and/or competitive strategies
and organizational actions which must be taken *after* the occurrence of such events.

2. When the states of nature on competitive strategies are not
known for certain, and

3. When *insufficient time* will be available between the occurrence of the states of nature and/or competitive stategies and that
point at which the managerial actions must be taken to allow for
such actions to be planned for *after* the events have taken place.

For example, a supermarket operator might have reason to believe that his major competitor is considering the introduction of trading stamps and decide that if this happens, he ought to retaliate with stamps of his own as quickly thereafter as possible. If he is to do so, considerable planning and analysis must be undertaken—e.g., determining which stamps are available, their respective costs, the nearness of redemption centers, means of advertising and promoting the stamps, etc. If such planning were not initiated until *after* the competitor's introduction of stamps (should this occur) the quick retaliation would probably not be possible. Rather, only by means of the prior design of contingent planning programs would it be likely that this objective could be met.

Compound Planning Statements.   As we indicated earlier, most organizational plans are not comprised of single do or if statements. Rather, they are more complex, including sets of do and/or if statements linked in various ways. In this section, we will illustrate some of the forms which such *compound* planning statements may take.

Some compound planning statements may be comprised solely of do statements, assuming the form: "do *a, b, c, . . . n*"; while others include linked sets of if statements, such as those of the following forms:

1.   If *a and b* occur, do *v* and *w*, but if *c and d* occur, do *x* and *y*.
2.   If *a or b* occur, do *v* and *w*, but if *c or d* occur, do *x* and *y*.
3.   If *a or b* occur, do *x*, while if both *a and b* occur, do *y*, but if *neither a nor b* occur, do *z*.

An illustration of the utilization of such compound if statements is provided by our previous example of the company's contingent plan relative to meeting the union's wage demands (see p. 305 above). As the reader may note, this plan is of the compound if form (3) above.

Still other compound planning programs may be comprised of *both* do and if statements. For example, in many decision problems it is necessary not only to develop a set of if statements, but also to design do statements committing the organization to certain prior actions as a basis for effecting *each* such contingent plan. Such would be the case when, in planning their commencement exercises, colleges and universities design if statements as follows:

1.   If the weather is fair, we will hold our exercises outdoors in the stadium, and

2.   If the weather is bad, we will hold our exercises indoors in the gymnasium.

But, if it is to be possible for either of these strategies to be effected, the organization must commit itself to a number of prior actions which anticipate *both* possible weather conditions—e.g., set up the gymnasium in case it rains, instruct students, parents, faculty and staff on both alternative plans, etc. Such a planning program—which assumes the form: do *m, n, o* . . . , and then if *a* occurs, do *x*, but if *b* occurs, do *y*—is illustrated in Figure 11–5.

Programming: The Degree of Detail

Another problem which the decision maker faces is that of determining the degree to which his plans should be programmed —i.e., the degree of precision and detail in which his planning statements should be spelled out.

Under certain conditions it may be advisable for management to develop highly programmed courses of action. Such is almost invariably the case in *close tolerance* situations in which only a small margin of error from some precise specification is permissible if management's objectives are to be met. For example, highly programmed plans are required in the design and manufacture of many electronic components for this reason.

FIGURE 11–5. Compound Do, If Statements Program
(University Commencement Exercises)

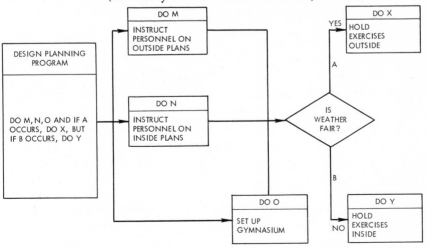

In other cases, however, more generalized planning statements may serve managerial objectives more appropriately. There are at least two reasons why this is so. First, the lesser planning time and costs required for their design may more than offset any advantages which might be gained from developing highly detailed plans. Or, to put it another way, the marginal value of highly detailed programs in terms of objective attainment may be less than the marginal costs of their development. For example, a salesman, in planning a sales presentation to a potential customer:

1.   May increase his probability of making the sale considerably if he spends some time in advance outlining his presentation in general terms (as opposed to going in to see the customer "cold"), but

2.   May be able to increase the probability only slightly (if at all) by spending many hours in developing a highly programmed word-for-word sales talk.

Since this time could be utilized to call on other customers, the salesman's objectives might be best met by developing generalized planning statements rather than either (1) highly programmed ones, or (2) none at all.

Secondly, the utilization of generalized, rather than highly programmed, planning statements may be advisable in order to permit *flexible* responses to problem situations when the plans assume the form of *instructions* from the manager to one or more of his subordinates. That is:

1.   Under conditions of risk or uncertainty, in which the manager cannot foresee all possible states of nature and/or competitive strategies which may influence the appropriateness of a subordinate's actions (and hence, cannot design adequate sets of if statements covering all contingencies),

2.   Spelling out in great detail the actions that the subordinate should take rather than allowing him some degree of judgment within the framework of a generally specified plan, may *bind him* to behavior which is inappropriate.

For example, the authors have observed some industrial trainers being bound by their superiors to highly detailed "canned" presentations in management training conferences, which "fell flat" because little or no consideration was given to the responses of the training groups involved. Much more effective in such programs is for generally specified training plans to be worked out in advance, permitting the instructor to use his own judgment in responding to any unforeseen reactions of the group.[6]

Programming: The Human Variable

Although highly detailed programs such as that in the above example may be ineffective because they place the subordinate in a "straight jacket" and do not permit him the flexibility that he needs in order to behave appropriately, there are also dangers involved in developing instructions for subordinates which are too generally programmed. This is because instructions which are too generally specified may not be understood by the subordinate, and/or because he may not have the ability or psychological inclination *to fill in the details* of the plan necessary for its implementation.

Just how highly programmed any instructions should be will, of course, vary from situation to situation. As we pointed out in Chapter 5 in discussing leadership directiveness, three classes of variables—the personality of the leader, that of the follower, and the nature of the situation—must be considered in relationship to each other in determining how highly detailed instructions aimed at evoking desired follower responses should be. The complexity of the decision problem, the costs of failure, the ability of the subordinate to "fill in" generally specified programs, his dependence and independence needs, the overall philosophy of the organization toward "general supervision" must be taken into account in the programming of planning statements which are to serve as sets of instructions to subordinates.

THE REPETITIVENESS VARIABLE

Planning theorists frequently distinguish between *single-use* plans which are designed to deal with unique problems and *standing* plans which are geared toward providing responses to *repetitive* situations. Most of the observations which we have made in the preceding sections have application to both of these two types of plans, although we have not explicitly treated the design of planning statements for recurring decision problems. It will be the purpose of this section to discuss some of the special characteristics of standing plans.

---

[6] Assuming that the instructor has the ability to respond appropriately in such situations.

Types of Standing Plans

Most business organizations rely on many different kinds of standing plans to aid them in their decision making. Some of these are made up of rather broad, generalized planning imperatives—as is the case with many basic company *policies,* such as the following:

1. We will not discriminate in employing personnel on the basis of race, religion, or color.

2. It is the policy of our (retailing) firm to sell only the highest quality products.

To implement policies such as these as well as to deal with other specific repetitive decision problems, business firms will also design a multitude of more highly programmed statements—in the form of *rules, procedures,* and *methods.* As a means of implementing the employment non-discrimination policy mentioned above, for instance, the following imperative might be formulated: "When interviewing a prospective employee do not ask him about his religious or ethnic background." A few of the many other kinds of rules, procedures, and methods commonly utilized by business firms are cited below:

1. Employees on production lines frequently are required to follow highly detailed work methods often developed by industrial engineering.

2. Practically all companies have developed a number of rules by which their employees must abide—reporting to work at specified times, no smoking in hazardous areas in the plant, etc.

3. Most firms rely on various standard operating procedures. For instance, union employees having grievances should first bring their problems to the attention of their shop stewards; customer refunds in a supermarket must be handled by the store manager; employee claims for medical benefits under the firm's insurance program must be processed by the personnel department, and so on.

Such standing plans, like single-use plans, may be comprised of either do, if, or compound planning statements. For example:

1. The above-mentioned statement requiring interviewers to refrain from asking prospective employees about their religious or ethnic backgrounds is of the form do (not).

2. Some firms have developed shop rules specifying that when an employee is absent from work without excuse, he shall be given an oral warning *if* it is his first such offense; a written warning *if* it is his second such offense; etc.

Thus, standing plans are similar to single-use plans in that they not only may be programmed to varying degrees of detail but also are comprised of the same basic types of planning statements.

Values of Standing Plans

There are several advantages which may be gained from the utilization of standing plans. We will now examine three of the more important of these.

First, the design of such plans provides the manager with *relief from decision making.* That is, the manager does not have to take time out each time a repetitive situation occurs to decide how to handle it—standing plans provide him with pre-programmed *decision rules* which he can apply whenever called for. For instance, the development of vacation policies by a firm—e.g., if an employee has been with the company one to ten years, grant him a two week vacation; but if he has more than ten years' service, give him a three week vacation—serves to relieve its managers of the task of deciding just how many days of vacation each of their subordinates should be granted each year. In short, the design of standing plans simplifies the whole decision-making process by transforming problems of the type: "when x occurs, *decide on* how x is to be handled" to ones of types such as: "When x occurs, do y"; "When x occurs, do y if condition a exists, but if condition b exists, do z"; etc.

Secondly, by *routinizing* many decision problems through the utilization of decision rules, standing plans provide an important vehicle for delegating responsibility to lower levels in the organization. For example:

In the absence of any decision rules for deciding upon the quantities of parts and materials needed by a manufacturing plant to be purchased, all ordering decisions may have to be made by the materials manager, or by one of his managerial assistants. With the availability of a quantitative model specifying how many units should be purchased at any given time, however, it may be possible for clerical help in the department to handle the ordering simply by plugging appropriate figures into the model, carrying out the calculations called for, and following the courses of action so generated.[7] Or, as is being increasingly done by business firms with such programmable decision problems, the standing plan may be programmed on a computer, thus obviating the need for human calculations.

Finally, standing plans provide a means of obtaining *uniformity* in the handling of like decision problems. The development of standardized work methods and procedures, for instance, helps in-

---

[7] We will illustrate the application of models of this type in Chapter 17.

sure that all units of production turned out on the assembly line will meet the same specifications. Or, the design of uniform accounting procedures makes it easier for management to compare operating results from one department to another. Moreover, uniform responses to recurring situations also may serve to provide equitable treatment to either the firm's customers or employees. For example:

1. The vacation policies mentioned above help insure that favoritism will not be shown to certain employees—e.g., *all* employees with more than ten years' service are granted three weeks vacation annually.

2. By developing standardized payment schedules, health insurance companies treat all of their customers alike. For instance, whenever the insured or a member of his family undergoes a tonsillectomy, he or his doctor may be paid $50; for all appendectomies, $75, and so on.

Problems Involved in Designing Standing Plans

Notwithstanding their values, there are a number of problems which may be encountered in the design and utilization of standing plans. First, as with single-use plans, such planning statements, if either too generally or too highly programmed may be either ineffective or actually lead to the creation of problems for the organization. Policies which are very generally stated, and not implemented with more specifically detailed rules and procedures may be, in effect, quite meaningless. This is sometimes true with respect to companies which proclaim themselves as "equal opportunity" employers in their basic policy statements, but which do nothing to see that discrimination is avoided in their employment practices.

At the other extreme, highly programmed standing plans may force organizational employees to be inflexible in their responses to certain decision problems. For example, many instances have been cited of the statutory and administrative requirements that call on civil servants to follow a number of highly detailed rules, regulations and procedures in handling governmental problems.

Additionally, requiring employees to follow highly programmed statements may lead to monotony and boredom on the job and a thwarting of the higher level needs. As we pointed out in Chapter 4, concern has been raised about the number of jobs in today's business organizations which are routine and call for the application of only a few simple skills—jobs which, in terms of our conceptual framework in this chapter, are structured around sets of highly programmed do or if statements, and which leave little room for employee judgment and ingenuity.

Finally, a problem which probably exists in all organizations to some extent is that standing plans may continue to be relied upon even though the conditions which led to their design no longer exist and the plans are no longer needed or appropriate. The authors have frequently observed, for instance, executives continuing to receive reports, accounting data, and other forms of written communications, which were perhaps once useful to them, but which have become unnecessary due to changing conditions within the organization. Such inertial tendencies to continue to follow prescribed methods, rules and regulations (often due largely to individuals' resistance to change) render it important for the firm to review its standing plans periodically.

SUMMARY

Central to management decision making is planning courses of action to be taken in the future. If the firm's objectives are to be met, it is also essential for the manager to predict as accurately as possible the outcome of his strategies in terms of the possible occurrence of those states of nature and competitive strategies which may influence the effectiveness of his actions.

In designing planning statements, attention must be given to the time variable, for plans developed either too far or too soon in advance of the actions which they specify may create problems for the decision maker. A second key planning variable is that of the manner and degree to which planning statements are programmed. Depending on the specific conditions involved, such statements may be couched in terms of either if and/or do, and may be spelled out to varying degrees of detail. Further, business plans may be either single-use, to deal with unique situations, or standing, to handle repetitive decision problems. In all cases, business plans may also serve another function which we have not yet discussed—to provide a basis for *control* decisions. It is to the facet of the managerial decision-making process—control—that we will turn our attention on the next chapter.

DISCUSSION AND STUDY QUESTIONS

1. In planning future actions, the manager need focus his attention only upon those variables over which he has control. Do you agree with this statement? Explain.

2. What factors must be considered when deciding how highly detailed plans should be?

3. a) Of what value may standing plans be to the businessman?
   b) How might standing plans interfere with the effective operation of the organization?

4. Develop plans for each of the following activities, indicating sequentially the major "if" and "do" statements incorporated in your plans in flow diagram form (as in Figure 11–5).
   a) The student council's publishing of a mimeographed brochure containing a biographical sketch of each professor in a college of business administration.
   b) Writing a term paper on the subject of "planning."
   c) Taking a vacation trip by yourself to Bermuda next summer.
   d) Expanding your fraternity house to accommodate ten additional members utilizing a surplus of funds existing in the fraternity's treasury.

5. Do you believe that it is possible to do too much planning? Explain.

6. "The staff plans; the line acts." Do you agree? Why?

7. In terms of the discussion of information-decision systems model in Chapter 3, what type of systems element would you consider a standing plan to be? Explain.

8. Evaluate: The use of standing plans in making decisions insures that all relevant variables are continuously considered. Explain your answer.

9. Evaluate: "All relevant variables should be considered in making planning decisions."

10. In what way may highly detailed plans for future activities be inconsistent with the leadership methods employed by managers in a firm?

11. Under what conditions might a firm which is not completely certain about future conditions utilize "do" rather than "if" statements in its plans?

12. Discuss: The need for periodic planning results from change. If the values of all variables affecting a system remain constant, future actions can merely be those undertaken in the past.

SELECTED REFERENCES

BRATT, ELMER C. *Business Forecasting*. New York: McGraw-Hill Book Co., Inc., 1958.

CHURCHMAN, C. WEST. *Prediction and Optimal Decision*. Englewood Cliffs, N. J.: Prentice-Hall, Inc., 1961.

GILMORE, F., and BRANDENBURG, R. G. "Anatomy of Corporate Planning," *Harvard Business Review*, 40 (November–December, 1962).

HARRISON, W. B. "Long-Range Planning in a Dynamic Industry," *American Management Association Management Report*, 3. New York: The Association, 1958, 47–53.

HOLT, C. C.; MODIGLIANI, F.; MUTH, J. F.; and SIMON, H. A. *Planning Production, Inventories and Work Force.* Englewood Cliffs, N. J.: Prentice-Hall, Inc., 1960.

LeBRETON, PRESTON P., and HENNING, DALE A. *Planning Theory.* Englewood Cliffs, N. J.: Prentice-Hall, Inc., 1961.

NOVIC, D. "Planning in the Department of Defense," *California Management Review,* 5 (Summer, 1963), 35–42.

REILLEY, E. P. W. "Planning the Strategy of the Business," *Advanced Management* (December, 1955), 8–12.

THOMPSON, STEWART. *How Companies Plan,* Research Study, 54. New York: American Management Association, 1962.

CHAPTER 12

THE CONTROL
PROCESS

IN the previous chapter we presented a conceptual framework for understanding the planning process in the organizational system. We will now turn our attention to another basic facet of organizational decision making—the control process. In doing so, we will first make some general observations about the nature of control. We will then examine two basic facets of control systems— (1) the development and use of performance measures and standards, and (2) the design of information systems to provide data for control decisions.

THE NATURE OF CONTROL

A number of different conceptions of control are reflected in the thinking of management scholars and in the practices of business managers. As a starting point for our discussion of control, let us examine Douglas S. Sherwin's definition: *"The essence of control is action which adjusts operations to predetermined standards, and its basis is information in the hands of managers."* [1] As may be noted, a central focus of this definition is upon *action* taken to correct performance, with action considered dependent upon information. In addition to acting, however, the manager must *decide* whether the information indicates that action should be taken, and, if so, just what actions are required. Consequently, intervening between information and action in the control process is the control *decision*.

---

[1] Douglas S. Sherwin, "The Meaning of Control," *Dun's Review and Modern Industry* (January, 1956), as reprinted in Max D. Richards and William A. Nielander, *Readings in Management* (Cincinnati, Ohio: South-Western Publishing Co., 1958), p. 423.

Also central to the control process are the performance standards indicated in Sherwin's definition. Essentially, such standards represent *desired* levels of performance with respect to any one or more variables in the organizational system. For instance, a sales volume of $500,000 or an average worker output of 110 units an hour on a particular operation might be established as performance standards. Thus, standards in effect represent *objectives* which the organization hopes to attain. Further, as in our examples of sales volume and average worker output, the utilization of standards involves the development of performance measures—e.g., *dollars* as a measure of sales volume, and *units per hour* as a measure of worker output. Once such measures and standards have been developed, management may then *compare* the *actual* performance of its operations with that level *desired,* and depending upon the extent to which the standard is not being met, decide whether corrective action is necessary to bring the system into conformity with the desired standard. These various phases of the control process are illustrated schematically in Figure 12–1.

FIGURE 12–1. The Control Process

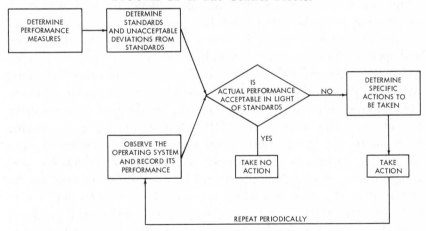

Certain other observations are in order at this point concerning the control process. First, with respect to the relationship between control and the planning process as discussed in the previous chapter, we suggest that control decisions may be thought of as a special class or *sub-set* of planning decisions. That is, like planning decisions, control decisions either specify or guide the taking of future action, but such decisions are *specifically geared* toward *correcting* deviations in systems performance from established standards.

As was indicated in our previous discussion, the control process involves both determining *when* (or, under what conditions) corrective actions are called for and specifically *what* actions should be undertaken if the performance of the system is inadequate. In some situations, both the when and what of control action may be specified in advance through the utilization of *if* statements. For example, in a quality control system, the following planning (and control) statement might be developed: "If rejects produced on a particular machine exceed 5 percent in any given period, replace the machine's cutting tool." Such preprogramming, of course, requires that management know in advance what should be done should the system get "out of control." In our example, for instance, the effective preprogramming of the retooling decision would be contingent upon management's knowledge that such a course of action would correct the reject problem.

In the previous chapter, we indicated that in the planning process if statements are useful: (1) for dealing with certain repetitive types of decision problems, and/or (2) when insufficient time is available between the occurrence of an event and the point at which managerial actions must be taken to permit such actions to be planned after the event has taken place. The same may be said for the utilization of those if statements which specify both when and specifically what corrective actions should be taken in the control process. An example of the use of such if statements in dealing with repetitive problems would be provided by our previous retooling example, assuming that, as in many production processes, the periodic wearing down of the cutting tool was creating a recurring problem of the production of an unacceptable number of poor pieces. Or, to provide an example of situations in which the preprogramming of if statements would be absolutely essential due to the need for quick action when a process begins to go out of control: when the temperature or pressure in certain chemical processes exceeds a predetermined critical level, the reaction must immediately be halted lest an explosion occur.

Our discussion in the preceding paragraphs has assumed that management knows in advance what actions will correct unacceptable deviations in systems performance. In many cases, however, such is not the case. A company may not know, for instance, just why its sales volume has fallen 20 percent below the desired level in a particular week, or why the absenteeism rate among its production workers has suddenly jumped considerably above acceptable levels. In cases such as these, if statements may sometimes still be preprogrammed to specify *when* corrective action should be considered (e.g., when absenteeism exceeds 5 percent); but it would not be possible to develop specific plans for correcting systems performance until after subsequent analysis had been undertaken to find out just why the performance was inadequate.

Three final observations are in order concerning the nature of the organizational control process. First, it should *not* be inferred from the previous discussion that control actions are taken *only after* systems performance has *already* become unacceptable. In many cases, management may note: (1) that while performance is still satisfactory, negative trends toward unacceptability are taking place, and (2) corrective action must be taken in an effort to *forestall* the continuance of these trends. For example, a firm may note that while its sales volume is still quite satisfactory, sales have been declining in recent months, and that steps should be taken in an effort to reverse this trend before the decline becomes a really serious one.

Second, some comments are in order concerning the nature of the control process in terms of our systems view of the organization. In systems terms, the data generated by management concerning the actual performance of the organization represents *feedback* to the control decision system. In the system are stored as *memory* the standards of performance which have been developed and the degrees of deviation from the standards which have been deemed acceptable. By comparing actual with standard performance and deciding whether control actions are necessary, and if so, what actions should be taken, the manager *transforms* the information at his disposal into a decision *output*.

Finally, we should point out that it may often be desirable for business organizations to provide for participation in the control process by their nonmanagerial members. If a manager's subordinates know what performance levels are expected of them, subordinate *self-control* may prove more effective in keeping performance within acceptable limits than if their supervisor specifies what corrective actions should be undertaken. Such self-control, of course, assumes not only a technical knowledge of the operation on the part of the subordinate, but also motivation to initiate corrective actions on his own. Further, if self-control is to be possible it is necessary that the control system be designed so that feedback data concerning the subordinate's performance is provided to him.

It may be useful to have the subordinates participate initially in establishing performance measures and standards. Such participation may not only help develop an awareness and insight into the control process but also stimulate motivation for exercising self-control.

⑴ MEASURES AND STANDARDS FOR CONTROL

As we indicated previously, the design and utilization of both performance measures and standards are essential facets of the control process. In this section we will explore these two aspects of control.

Performance Measures

Many different types of performance measures are utilized by business firms depending upon the systems variables in question. Performance may be measured in terms of dollars and cents, units produced, the number and/or frequency of certain types of human behavior taking place (e.g., number of employee grievances), etc. Further, as we will point out more fully in the next chapter, it is often most useful to frame performance measures in terms of relationships between two systems variables—e.g., number of grievances *per* 100 employees per month.

Since all organizational systems and sub-systems (of any magnitude) have multiple objectives, multiple measures of performance may be required for effective control. Further, constant or periodic monitoring of systems performance is often necessary so that any performance inadequacies or tendencies towards inadequacy may be noted and hopefully corrected before they become serious, as mentioned previously. For example, in examining the performance of one of his salesmen the sales quota for whose territory is $500,000 per year, a sales manager may want to keep track of sales made on a monthly, weekly, or even on a daily basis. Additionally, in order to pinpoint more precisely any performance inadequacies which may occur, additional information about the salesman's patterns of behavior may be useful—e.g., number of customers seen, frequency of calls on each customer, percentage of time spent travelling, etc. If the salesman is falling behind in meeting his quota, this information may help enable the salesman and the manager to determine why such is the case. Further, the sales manager may also want to develop and apply measures to other variables which are outside his or the salesman's immediate control, but which, nonetheless, may be influencing the latter's performance. For example, such factors as long delays in deliveries of the firm's product to certain key customers, adverse economic conditions, or increased competitive activity in the salesman's territory may be key contributing causes to negative trends in his performance.

Two other observations are in order concerning the utilization of multiple performance measures for control purposes. First, it is important for the manager to weigh the advantages of the control measures which he utilizes against their cost. In any organizational system or sub-system of any magnitude, the use of literally thousands of performance measures might be conceivable. To develop, maintain, and evaluate all such measures, however, would be prohibitively time consuming and expensive. In order to overcome the problem of excessive information costs while at the same time providing for adequate control, managers' commonly (and perhaps optimally) rely on *selective* control measures—i.e., attention is focused only on certain *key* systems variables. Just which variables are considered key ones, of course, will depend on what particular organizational system and set of decisions are under consideration. Further, additional measures may be developed and/or existing ones excluded from consideration as organizational conditions change. For example, our sales manager may record and examine only the total expense account figures of his salesmen, but should these expenses start getting "out of line" he may call for an itemized analysis of them (e.g., travel, entertainment, etc.) in an effort to find the causes of and ways to correct the problem.

Second, it should be pointed out that the extensive utilization of control measures by management with respect to the performance of particular individuals in the organization may be reacted to negatively by the latter. If a salesman, for example, is required to fill out reports indicating in detail his activities for each hour during every day, he may not only feel that he is not being trusted by his superior, but also resent having to spend considerable time filling out the reports—time which he may consider could more profitably be utilized otherwise. In terms of the conceptual framework which we presented in Chapter 5, the manager's close scrutiny of an extensive number of measures of his subordinates' performance represents one facet of close supervision; and the subordinates' reactions to such close control will be influenced by such aspects of his personality orientation as the relative strength of his dependence and independence needs.

Performance Standards

Once performance measures for a system variable have been selected, it is necessary to determine what standards of performance are to be considered acceptable for the variable. In this section, we will discuss three different facets of the development and utilization of performance standards. First, we will point up the need to consider systems variability in designing standards. Then, we will illustrate some of the approaches commonly utilized by managers in defining standards of acceptable performance for the organizational system. Finally, we will consider certain psychological aspects of importance to consider in establishing standards.

Systems Variability and Standards. In establishing standards, it is important to recognize that the performance of most systems will not remain constant over a period of time, but rather will be subject to some degree of variability. A machine operator, for example, may average 110 units per hour, but his performance might normally be expected to range anywhere from 100 to 120 units in any given hour, depending upon his motivational state, the degree to which he is fatigued, etc. Or, in manufacturing shafts of a desired diameter of 1.95 inches, the units turned out on any given day might be expected to range in diameter from 1.945 to 1.955 inches. Thus, in developing standards, the manager must define not only desired *levels* of performance, but also the *degree of variation* from these levels which is acceptable to him.

Certain other observations are in order concerning performance variability and control standards. First, for some systems variables, both *positive* and *negative* variations from standards would obviously be considered unacceptable if their magnitude were considerable. For example, for our shafts with a desired diameter of 1.95 inches, pieces turned out which are either too large or too small would be unusable.[2] For many other types of systems variables, however, the manager's primary concern would be in avoiding *negative* variations from standards, with positive variations being welcomed. For instance, if production standards for a particular job have been established at 100 units/hour, and a particular employee with high levels of skill and motivation is able to turn out an average of 170 units hour, his supervisor might be quite pleased with his performance.

Even where performance levels above standard are generally desirable, however, *extreme* positive variations may be indicative of

---

[2] It might be possible, of course, to rework those shafts which are too large.

organizational problems requiring corrective action. Some of the reasons why such may be the case are as follows:

1. If performance is consistently far above standard, it may be that something is wrong with the standards. For example, if all employees working on a particular operation are producing at 200 percent of the performance standard set for their job, it is highly probable that the standards were set unrealistically low.

2. High positive variations from standards on one systems variable may be indicative of the existence of a suboptimization problem within the organization—i.e., the high performance with respect to the one variable may have been attained only at the expense of some other organizational objective. For instance, a division in a large corporation may be showing an unusually good profit picture to a considerable extent because of cutbacks on research and development efforts—a move which may endanger its long-run profitability.

3. In some cases, individuals within organizations may make their performance look good by failing to report performance inadequacies. For example, cases have been reported of supervisors managing to avoid the reporting of minor accidents occurring in their departments in order to make their safety records look better.

One further observation is in order concerning variability in systems performance. For certain variables, performance may normally be expected to fluctuate according to some predictable pattern—e.g., consistently higher sales in a supermarket on Fridays and Saturdays than on Mondays and Tuesdays. When such is the case, definition of standards and acceptable variations for the variable under consideration would have to take into account the particular time period in which performance takes place—e.g., different levels of acceptability would have to be set for sales on different days of the week.

Establishing Performance Standards.   There are many different approaches utilized by managers to determine what levels of and variations in systems performance are acceptable. We will now examine several of these.

In many situations, managers find it useful to utilize data concerning organizational performance in previous time periods as a basis for setting standards of acceptability for the future. For example, if a firm's raw materials costs as a percentage of its total cost of goods sold have stabilized at about 32 percent over the past two or three years, this figure might be considered as an acceptable standard for future performance. Or, a firm might judge a reject rate of 5 percent for a certain part that it manufactures as good based on its prior experience in turning out the part.

The use of historically based standards is valid only under two general types of conditions. The first occurs when the factors influencing the performance of the systems variable under consideration are stable. For instance, if the price of raw materials for the firm mentioned in the preceding paragraph had just decreased by 10 percent, the historical standard of 32 percent would no longer be appropriate (assuming that all other variables influencing materials costs have remained the same). Second, historically based standards may also be valid under nonstable conditions if the key dynamic variables influencing systems performance are *predictable*. For example, a publisher of textbooks for the elementary schools might find that historically changes in the magnitude of its sales volume have closely paralleled increases or decreases in the number of elementary school pupils in the United States each year, and aim for a 5 percent increase in its sales for the forthcoming year based on a like projected percentage increase in elementary pupils.

When such historically based standards are utilized, managers, of course, may hope not simply to maintain previous performance levels (or increase them in proportion to market increases as with our publisher), but rather to improve upon their performance. For example, the book publisher might hope to increase its sales by 8 percent in the forthcoming year through the introduction of a number of new titles.

In addition to simply looking at the previous performance of a particular variable in their own organizational system, managers often find it useful in setting standards to compare their performance with that of other similar business firms. For example, in establishing levels of acceptable performance in the area of safety, management may find it useful to examine accident rate data for other like firms in the industry. Further, in setting standards for a particular sub-system in the organization some consideration may also be given to the performance of *other similar sub-systems* within the firm. For instance, in establishing a sales quota for a given salesman, management may give some weight to what other salesmen with similar sales territories have been able to do in the past. Or, cost standards for a newly opened store in a large supermarket chain may be based largely on performance levels achieved in the past by other of the firm's stores of a similar size and type.

When performance levels achieved by either other firms or other organizational sub-systems are being considered in setting standards, it is important, first of all, that such performance is considered adequate. That is, the manager would not want to use someone else's poor performance as a standard for his own operations. Additionally, it is important that the system or sub-system for which the standard is being set really is comparable to that from which the performance data is being derived. For example, the cost standards based on the performance of other supermarkets mentioned above may not be valid for the new supermarket in its initial weeks of operations, due to the fact that many "nonnormal" costs would be expected in getting the store started—e.g., unusually large training costs, an extensive advertising program to attract customers, etc.

Finally, it should be pointed out that in many cases managers will use more sophisticated, analytical, and statistical means for establishing standards and taking control actions than we have discussed thus far. For example, time study analysis is frequently undertaken by industrial engineers to provide (among other things) a basis for establishing incentive standards for workers.[3] Widely used, especially in quality control, are numerous statistical techniques for determining what degree of variation from standards is acceptable, and when control actions should be taken.[4] As with the historically based standards discussed above, those standards developed by analytical and statistical means are valid only for stable systems or when dynamic variables influencing systems performance are predictable. For example, if the work content of a production line job were to be modified, new incentive time standards would have to be developed to take into account this change.

Establishing Standards: Psychological Considerations. As we pointed out in Chapter 4, different individuals vary in numerous respects as far as personality orientation and need importance is concerned. In performing on the job, some individuals have higher *aspiration levels* than others—i.e., the levels of future performance toward which they strive is different. The individual's aspiration

---

[3] For a discussion of time study procedure see, for example, George Strauss and Leonard R. Sayles, *Personnel: The Human Problems of Management* (Englewood Cliffs, N. J.: Prentice-Hall, Inc., 1960), pp. 624 ff.

[4] For an introductory discussion of statistical quality control approaches see, for example: Franklin G. Moore, *Manufacturing Management*, 4th ed. (Homewood, Ill.: Richard D. Irwin, Inc., 1965), Chap. 33.

level is conditioned to a considerable extent by his past level of actual achievement. Further, his aspiration level over time "tends to adjust to the level of achievement." [5] For example, if a person's achievement is continually below that toward which he has strived in the past, he will tend to reduce his aspiration level downward in order to reduce feelings of failure.

In designing performance standards for individuals within the organization it is important to consider not only what is "fair" or physically possible with "normal" effort, but also what the aspiration levels of the individuals concerned are. If standards are set *below* the individual's own level of aspiration, they will quite obviously not serve to motivate him to improve his performance. Conversely, if standards are set too far above the individual's past achievement level and his related future aspiration level, he may perceive that his performance cannot meet the expectations set for him and become discouraged. In some extreme cases, discouragement may become so pronounced that his performance may actually deteriorate rather than improve.

The importance of considering aspiration levels in developing performance standards may be illustrated by the following example. In one firm, incentive standards were established for a job by the use of time study methods. The job that was studied and for which standards were set was that of accomplishing a major overhaul on a unit of operating equipment. The time standard developed indicated that an overhaul could be completed at a normal pace in 2,400 man-hours. A review of past records, however, showed that 6,000 man-hours had been needed on the average for each overhaul. The incentive plan based on the 2,400-hour standard was placed into operation despite the large discrepancy between it and past performance. The workers' aspiration level was so distant from the 2,400 "normal" level established that they considered the incentive plan ridiculous, and actual performance continued as before at about 6,000 hours per overhaul.

Subsequent management reflection on the problem led to an "adjustment" in the standard. A few minor methods changes were introduced, larger rest and fatigue allowances were added, and the revised standard was set at 3,000 hours per overhaul. At this level, the standard was effective in stimulating improved performance on the part of the maintenance workers. In fact, some subsequent over-

---

[5] James G. March and Herbert A. Simon, *Organizations* (New York: John Wiley & Sons, Inc., 1958), p. 182.

hauls were completed in as short a period as 1,900 man-hours, indicating that the original standard had not really been an unreasonable one.

This example illustrates that a "fair" standard may be ineffective in helping to improve organizational performance. If in the design of performance standards for a control system, a goal is to improve actual performance, the standards set must not be so far above the aspiration levels of the individuals concerned so as to engender rejection of the standards and/or discouragement.

We should also note that economic considerations are important in determining what levels of performance are deemed acceptable as standards. In most cases, higher levels of systems performance may be realized only through additional expenditures of effort and costs. For example, the percentage of pieces turned out on a machine which will be rejects may be a function of numerous variables such as operator skill, the quality of raw materials utilized, etc. By devoting more effort to operator training, and/or by purchasing higher quality raw materials, management may be able to reduce its average reject rate from, say, 8 to 4 percent. Whether such efforts would be advisable, however, would depend upon the marginal savings realized from reducing the reject percentage as compared with the marginal costs of attaining the improved performance.

Similar considerations, would, of course, also apply in determining what variations from standards should be considered acceptable. For instance, the percentage rejects turned out on our machine might also increase as the tooling utilized wears down over time. Although the magnitude of these variations in performance might be reduced by more frequent retooling, the costs of such an action would have to be weighed against the advantages of reducing performance variability.

THE INFORMATION SYSTEM FOR CONTROL

Once satisfactory measures and standards have been established, it is necessary to design a system for reporting feedback data concerning the actual performance of their operations to the managers. From the point of view of the manager, the information feedback system should be designed in such a way that it will increase his chances of identifying and correcting the most important problems which exist in his organization. On the other hand, it is also important to design the system so that the costs of recording and processing the data useful to the manager can be kept at a minimum and do not exceed their value in helping to make better control decisions. In this section we will consider three basic facets of the design and utilization of information feedback systems for control: (1) data relevance, (2) report format, and (3) the timing of feedback data.

Data Relevance

It is important to design information systems in a manner such that the feedback data reported to the manager is *relevant* to possible control actions which he may undertake. For example, information as to how each of a firm's salesmen is progressing in meeting his yearly sales quota would be of no value to a first line production supervisor in improving the performance of his operations.

In speaking of "relevance" it should be emphasized that we do *not* mean that the manager should be given feedback data *only* with respect to variables over which he has control. Often, information provided to the manager relative to states of nature and/or competitive strategies which are beyond his control may be useful to him in making better control decisions. For example, if a production supervisor is aware of the fact that the batch of raw materials which his workers are currently processing is of an inferior quality such that their work pace has to be slowed down, he may avoid taking the inappropriate control action of reprimanding them for poor performance.

Although the fact that control reporting should be relevant to possible control decisions is a fairly obvious one, it is sometimes ignored in the design of feedback systems. In one department store, for example, merchandise markdowns (to dispose of slow moving items) were reported periodically by stock number in numerical order. Each departmental manager in utilizing the markdown report would have to seek out and identify the items sold in his department. Much of the information in the report was irrelevant to his own decision making, since it concerned markdown activity in other departments. This particular report was a carryover from the time when the store was small and there were no separate departments. When departmental managers had been appointed to supervise the stores' various merchandise lines, the report was maintained in its old form which had served well prior to the departmentalization.

It should also be noted that the store manager could follow markdown activity on an overall store basis from the report and discern *when* control action was warranted. He could not, however, easily determine *where* action should be initiated. Without further analysis, he could not determine the extent to which, if any, the various departments in the store might be contributing to excessive markdowns.

Eventually, the store's markdown report was revised so as to feed back to each manager information on the items sold by his department. This not only helped to reduce each departmental manager's search activity, but also enabled the store manager (who received the various reports for all departments) to pinpoint those departments which appeared to need assistance in controlling their operations.

This idea of focusing control reports upon data pertinent to the operations for which each manager has responsibility is often referred to as *responsibility reporting*. This concept has in recent years been receiving considerable attention in accounting circles, where, in the past, cost data frequently had been reported solely on a product-by-product basis. For example, in one firm in which cost data had been reported by product but not for each department involved in making its products, management found that its accounting data were extremely useful in determining the profitability of each of its product lines. If the costs of manufacturing a particular product were found to be excessive, however, management was unable to pinpoint the departments responsible for the high costs. A revision of the accounting system to report the costs incurred by each department as well as by product was instituted, and this problem was overcome.

One further observation is in order concerning relevance of control data reported—in some cases irrelevant data may not only increase the manager's search activity, but it may also create other problems. For example, in one plant one item in the report given to each foreman for cost control purposes was the rent charged to his department on a square footage allocation basis. Although rent was a cost to the firm, and each department obviously used space for which rent was charged, the foreman had no control over the rental price or over the amount of space assigned to his department. Foremen soon learned to ignore the item. On their reports it continued as a sort of annoyance. Some people believed that reporting the rent figure actually constituted a disservice since a few foremen had refused to let other supervisors make use of unutilized space in their areas because they "had to pay" for it.

Control Report Format

In addition to determining which performance variables are relevant to the manager for control purposes, consideration must be given in designing control systems to the format of the feedback data being provided. The format of control reports can assume considerable importance since data relative to the same systems variable presented in one way will often provide greater insight and permit more rapid decision making than if it is presented in other ways.

In its simplest form, a control report may merely provide information as to the *actual performance* of the manager's operations. For example, a report to a first-line production supervisor relative to downtime on the assembly line in his department might be in the following format:

Actual Level

Line Down This Week: 43 minutes

With such information, the manager must compare in his own mind the actual performance to the standards which have been developed for the variable. This comparison forces him to *recall* what standard performance is supposed to be. In some cases, and especially when he is working in an operation with a complex control system generating many control measures, his personal recall may be incomplete, and, in consequence, a failure to take appropriate control action may result.

To remove the control system's dependence upon human recall of the standard, the downtime report could be expanded so as to include data relative to *both* actual and standard performance—e.g.,

Actual   *Standard*

Line Downtime This Week: 43 minutes   38 minutes

Reports such as this facilitate comparisons between actual and standard performance, but the manager must still evaluate the extent to which the two levels are in variance from one another, and determine whether it is necessary to redirect the system toward the standard. This evaluation process can be built into the control reporting procedure by providing the manager with *both* the standard level of performance *and* normal variations from it when the actual performance of the system is fed back to him. If, for example, the normal variation of downtime is ± 2 minutes from the standard of 38 minutes, the following form of reporting would allow the manager at a glance to determine that the system's performance is not within acceptable levels:

	Actual	Standard	Normal Variation
Line Downtime This Week:	43 minutes	38 minutes	36–40 minutes

To give the manager further insight into the performance of his operating system, it is also sometimes useful to provide him with feedback concerning not only the present status of the system, but also its status in the past. In our downtime report, for example, the following data might be provided:

	Average Last Month	Last Week	This Week	Normal Variation
Line Downtime:	57	52	43	36–40

In this example, the historical trend indicates that the performance of the system is improving as time passes. If we assume that this trend will continue (e.g., because forces have already been set in motion in the system to correct its performance), it might *not* be necessary to initiate additional corrective action even though the performance variable is still outside of the acceptable range.

One further method of highlighting areas of performance which are out of control is to restrict feedback data given to the manager only to those conditions which are abnormal. For example, if 25 different performance measures have been developed describing the status of a department's operations, a typical weekly control report might contain data only with respect to only two or three variables, the performance of which is abnormal and to which the manager needs to give immediate attention. This approach is often referred to as *reporting by exception.* It assumes that only exceptionally good or bad performance areas require managerial attention since the manager does not need to take control actions when his system is performing normally. Reporting by exception recognizes that the time and resources of the manager are limited, and that if he directs his efforts toward correcting inadequate performance rather than focusing his attention on all phases of his operation, the probability of improving his operations will be increased.

The Timing of Feedback Data

In addition to determining *what* performance data needs to be fed back to members of the organizational system, management must also give consideration to *when* the feedback information should be provided. We will now give consideration to several facets of the problem of feedback timing.

One will find considerable variation in different managerial control systems both as to (1) the duration of the time period encompassed in feedback reports, and (2) the immediacy with which the control data is fed back to the system after the performance has occurred. Illustrative of reports covering long durations and fed back slowly would be the annual financial reports of many firms which are sometimes not available to management until two or three months after the fiscal year encompassed has expired. At the other extreme, in certain automated or semiautomated production systems, performance may be measured every second or fraction of a second, and such data fed back to the system almost immediately. For example, at the Newark, Ohio plant of Owens-Corning Fiberglas Corp., a computerized control system was developed to run a glass furnace. The system

> . . . has run largely without attendants, monitoring the glass coming out of the furnace, making control decisions, and ordering adjustments to keep the process balanced . . .
>
> The system runs the furnace by detecting changes at a wide range of measuring points in and around the furnace. The computer scans the signals from the thermocouples and other devices at predetermined times. One crucial instrument is read 10 times every second; another instrument, far less critical to the process, is sampled only once every minute and a half.[6]

In defining the timing of feedback data in control systems, several factors may be of importance. One of the most basic of these for all control systems is, of course, costs. Quite obviously, all other factors remaining the same, the more frequently performance is measured and control data fed back to the manager, the more time and expense will be incurred. From a theoretical point of view, the basic question which should be raised relative to feedback frequency is: "Will the marginal returns of more frequent feedback (in terms of better control decisions) exceed the marginal costs of providing such feedback?"

As far as the *need* for frequent feedback is concerned, one key consideration is the *rapidity* with which it is likely that the system may go out of control. In an automated chemical process, for example, it may be necessary to measure performance and provide feedback data every few seconds because sudden temperature or pressure changes beyond critical limits are possible which would ruin the processing. On the other hand, in a quality control system in which an excessive number of defective parts turned out is normally due to the wearing down of cutting tools, which takes place

---

[6] "New Edge in Glass," *Business Week* (April 10, 1965), pp. 60, 62.

relatively slowly, sampling of pieces turned out once a day or every two or three days might be adequate in order to prevent the system from going out of control.

When considering the frequency of feedback to members of the organization (as opposed to that provided within nonhuman automated systems), certain psychological considerations may also be of importance. In learning situations, as we pointed out in Chapter 4, for example, immediate corrective feedback is usually desirable so that the trainee does not develop inappropriate habits, which may be quite difficult to unlearn at a later time. Also, as far as day-to-day supervisor-subordinate relationships are concerned, too frequent monitoring of subordinate performance may not only be disruptive but be resented as representing overly close supervision and control. For example, such was the case with one supervisor known to the authors who would sometimes check every ten or fifteen minutes on the progress of his secretary when she was in the process of typing certain lengthy reports. At the other extreme, of course, supervisory monitoring and feedback which is conducted too infrequently may result in the continuation of and failure to correct inappropriate subordinate performance. Just how frequently supervisory control should be exercised will depend upon the variables which we discussed in Chapter 5—the characteristics of the leader, of the follower and of the particular organizational situation under consideration.

One final observation is in order concerning the psychological aspects of feedback frequency. Some research has indicated that the individual's performance may be adversely affected if he is "*overloaded*" with too much *negative* feedback (or criticism) at any given time. In a study of the value of annual performance appraisals of subordinates at the General Electric Company, for example, the following conclusions were drawn:

> Employees seem to accept suggestions for improved performance if they are given in a less concentrated form than is the case in comprehensive annual appraisals . . . employees became clearly more prone to reject criticisms as the number of criticisms mount. This indicates that an "overload phenomenon" may be operating. In other words, each individual seems to have a tolerance level for the amount of criticism he can take. And, as this level is approached or passed, it becomes increasingly difficult for him to accept responsibility for the shortcomings pointed out.[7]

---

[7] H. H. Meyer, E. Kay, and J. R. P. French, Jr., "Split Roles in Performance Appraisal," *Harvard Business Review*, 43 (January–February, 1965), p. 127.

From these findings, it was concluded that corrective feedback from supervisors to their subordinates is more effective if it is carried on a day-to-day, rather than on a once-a-year basis.

SUMMARY

The control process centers around ensuring that actual systems performance is in accordance with that desired by the organization. In designing control systems it is first necessary for management to establish measures of performance. Then standards of performance and acceptable deviations from the standards must be defined. In order that members of the organization be made aware of the need to take corrective action, it is also necessary that information be fed back to them concerning the status of their operations. In designing information systems for control purposes, it is important to give consideration to the relevance of feedback data, the format in which the data is reported, and the frequency with which the feedback is provided. In all phases of the design and utilization of control systems, attention must be given both to: (1) the cost of generating and reporting information as compared with its value to improved decision making, and, (2) likely human reactions to the system—e.g., those of individuals to an "overload" of negative feedback. Thus, consideration of both economic and psychological variables is important in the control process.

DISCUSSION AND STUDY QUESTIONS

1. You are the manager of a large pizza house which specializes in home deliveries. Last week, demand for your pizzas was considerably higher than usual, and the number of customer complaints that the pizza was cold by the time it reached their homes doubled. Of what value would this feedback be to you as a basis for improving your firm's performance? How might you change your plans?

2. Continuously favorable variations from standard sometimes indicates corrective action is needed. Why? What types of corrective actions may be desirable?

3. Under what conditions is it valid to use historical-based standards?

4. "A manager should ignore those costs over which he has no control since devoting attention to such costs will only represent a waste of valuable time. "Do you agree with this statement? Support your opinion.

5. Design a control report showing final inspection results for a chair manufacturer. The report form should include, but not necessarily be limited

to, information on the nature and quantity of defects such as: scratches, screw heads showing, warp in the wood, and inadequacies in varnishing and gluing.

6. "When we set up a new assembly line, we always set work standards for our employees at a level somewhat higher than we expect them to achieve. This helps to motivate them to work harder." Evaluate this approach in terms of setting standards for control.

7. Evaluate the following statement in terms of planning and control theory: "My personal promotion in this firm is dependent upon how much profit my division makes. In the short run, I can maximize the profits of my division by minimizing expenditures for certain programs which do not pay off immediately, such as research and development, management training, and plant maintenance. If I can hold out two to four years, I will get promoted because I 'have performed.' When I leave the division, this approach will help make me look even better because my successor will be stuck with a run-down plant, untrained people, etc. Then his costs will go up. Isn't this a heck of a way to run a business?"

8. One foreman in a knitting mill expressed the following philosophy: "I want to know about everything that is going on in my department." Evaluate this statement.

9. "At our university, emphasis upon faculty research to the possible detriment of teaching is a result of the relative ease of evaluating research output—each year we can tell how many books or articles a faculty member has written, but it's very difficult to determine how good a teaching job he has done." Evaluate this statement in terms of control theory.

10. In our competitive free-enterprise economy, those firms whose managers and employees have lower levels of aspiration than their counterparts in other companies will eventually go out of business. Discuss.

11. What are some of the major advantages of a control system which is based on the "exception" principle?

SELECTED REFERENCES

Ashby, W. R.　*An Introduction to Cybernetics.* New York: John Wiley & Sons, Inc., 1956.

Bell, D. A.　*Intelligent Machines, An Introduction to Cybernetics.* New York: Blaisdell Publishing Co., 1962.

Bonini, C. P.　*Simulation of Information and Decision Systems in the Firm.* Englewood Cliffs, N. J.: Prentice-Hall, Inc., 1963.

Bonini, C. P.; Jaedicke, R. K.; and Wagner, H. M.　*Management Controls.* New York: McGraw-Hill Book Co., Inc., 1964.

De-Latil, P.　*Thinking by Machine: A Study of Cybernetics.* Boston: Houghton Mifflin Co., 1957.

Drucker, Peter F.　*The Practice of Management,* Chap. xi. New York: Harper & Bros., 1954.

GOLD, BELLA, and KRAUS, RALPH M. "Integrating Physical with Financial Measures for Managerial Controls," *Academy of Management Journal,* 7 (June, 1964), 109–127.

HYLAND, JOHN P. "The Demonstration of Statistical Control Problems by an Electronic Analog," *Management Technology,* (January, 1960), 81–85.

KAGDIS, JOHN, and LACKNER, MICHAEL R. "A Management Control Systems Simulation Model," *Management Technology,* 3 (December, 1963), 145–159.

PUTNAM, A. O.; BARLOW, E. R.; and STILIAN, G. N. *Unified Operations Management,* Section 3. New York: McGraw-Hill Book Co., Inc., 1963.

Quality Control in Action, Management Report No. 9. New York: American Management Association, Inc., 1958.

RICHARDS, MAX D., and NIELANDER, WILLIAM A. (eds.). *Readings in Management.* 2d ed. Section D. Cincinnati: South-Western Publishing Co., 1963.

STOLLER, DAVID S., and VAN HORN, RICHARD L. "Design of a Management Information System," *Management Technology,* (January, 1960), 86–91.

VAZSONYI, ANDREW. "Automated Information Systems in Planning, Control, and Command," *Management Science,* 11 (February, 1965), B–2–41.

WEINWURM, G. F. "Computer Management Controls Systems Through the Looking Glass," *Management Science,* 7 (July, 1961), 411–419.

CHAPTER 13

ANALYSIS OF
THE FIRM

I N Chapter 3, we pointed out how models, both quantitative and
qualitative, may be utilized by the decision maker to provide
understanding and insight, to predict the outcome of proposed strategies, and/or to prescribe future courses of action. Most of the models which we have discussed thus far have been essentially qualitative in nature, with a majority of them having focused attention on
the behavior of the firm's human sub-systems from a psychological
or sociological point of view. In this and succeeding chapters we will
place much greater emphasis upon quantitative models (and tools)
designed to aid the manager in analyzing and dealing with the problems of the firm from an economic point of view. A central focus
of these quantitative-economic models is upon the question: "What
profits and/or costs will be incurred by the firm or by one of its
sub-systems when different decision strategies are chosen under various conditions?"

The first section of this chapter will be devoted to a discussion of
several fundamental economic concepts, knowledge of which is
necessary for an analysis of the firm's cost and profit structure. Then,
we will turn our attention to a simple model for analyzing the profitability performance of the organizational system or one of its sub-
systems at various levels of output—the breakeven model. Finally,
we will point up some of the ways in which percentages and ratios
can be utilized by the manager for the comparative analysis of various systems variables, both economic and noneconomic.

FUNDAMENTAL ECONOMIC CONCEPTS

Many different kinds of costs will be incurred in the operation of
the business firm—labor costs, materials costs, the cost of borrowing

funds, etc. For the purpose of analysis, these costs may be classified into five basic types: (1) sunk, (2) opportunity, (3) fixed, (4) variable, and (5) marginal. In this section we will discuss each of these, as well as two other concepts basic to the economic analysis of the firm—marginal revenue and marginal profits.

Sunk Costs

(*Sunk costs* refer to those outlays which have been incurred by the firm in the past, and which are *unrecoverable.*) The important fact to recognize concerning such sunk costs is that they should be completely *ignored* as far as the making of *future* decisions is concerned. For example, suppose that:

1.   A company bought a machine last month for $40,000, only to find now that a newer one, which performs the same work much more efficiently, has become available, and that

2.   Only $5,000 could be realized by selling the old machine if the new one were to be purchased to replace it.

The fact that $35,000 of the $40,000 investment in the old machine would be "lost" if the new machine were purchased should not be considered in deciding whether or not to acquire it. Rather, the recent purchase of the old machine, which now appears to have been a mistake, should be ignored in making such a decision. The new machine should be evaluated only on the basis of its own potential value to the firm in the future (although the salvage value of the old machine should be considered). We will consider means for evaluating investment decisions such as this in terms of their future value to the firm in the next chapter.

Opportunity Costs

It is important to recognize that the term "cost" is *not* always used to apply only to expenditures which are *actually made* by the business organization. Such is the case with *opportunity* costs, which refer to those gains which must be *sacrificed* by choosing one course of action rather than another. A prime example of the existence of opportunity costs is seen in the management of the firm's inventories. By tying up funds in inventories, a company must give up the opportunity of investing, and hence realizing earnings on these funds elsewhere. As we will point up in greater detail in Chapter 17, it is important for management to consider these foregone opportunities as well as actual cash outlays in deciding on the levels of inventories that it wishes to maintain.

Fixed Costs

In producing and selling goods and/or services, certain of a company's costs may remain fixed regardless of the level of output generated. Such costs are termed *fixed* costs. For example, during any given month, expenses for rent in an insurance office may remain the same whether 4,000 or 5,000 claims are processed; or in a manufacturing plant, salaries paid to supervisors in a particular week may be fixed at $25,000 whether 40,000 or 50,000 units of production are turned out.

The reader should recognize, however, that such fixed costs do not remain "fixed" indefinitely—rather, they may be subject to variations from time to time. Supervisory salaries in the manufacturing plant, for example, although fixed at any given time, may be increased annually to reflect cost-of-living changes. Thus, when we use the term "fixed costs" we refer to the short run—in the long run, all costs are subject to change.

We should also point out that many of the firm's so-called "fixed" costs are really *semifixed*—i.e., although remaining fixed for *normal* variations in output, they will vary if output is either exceedingly high or low. For example, if production in a manufacturing plant which normally operates on a three-shift, five-day-a-week basis is cut back to the point where only one or two shifts are required, some production supervisors will probably be laid off. Or, if production is expanded so as to necessitate Saturday and Sunday work as well, additional supervisory personnel may be needed. For such an operation, the relationship between semifixed supervisory salaries and output may be described as a step-function, such as the hypothetical one illustrated in Figure 13–1.

Variable Costs

Other costs incurred by the firm will vary directly with output. These are referred to as *variable* costs. Each unit of production that a manufacturing plant turns out, for instance, might require (1) $4.00 in materials, and (2) under a piecework incentive system, $1.00 in wages paid to those employees directly involved in fabricating and assembling the product. As the reader may observe, the relationship between total variable costs (TVC) and output (X) may theoretically be expressed by a linear equation—as in our above illustration, where $TVC = \$5X$. (This relationship is shown graphically in Figure 13–2.) In actual practice, however, many of the firm's costs, although closely linked to output, are not directly and

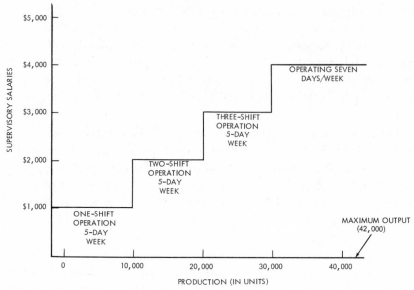

FIGURE 13–1. Semifixed Costs: Supervisory Salaries/Week
(Hypothetical Example)

Assumes: Maximum output of 2,000 units/shift per day.

linearly so related. To illustrate this point, let us return to our previous example and add some realistic qualifying conditions.

1.   There will probably be some newly hired fabricators and assemblers in the manufacturing plant who have not yet reached full proficiency in their work. As in many piecework systems, however, they may still be paid the "base rate" set for their jobs even though they do not produce up to standards. If so, labor costs for the pieces turned out by these individuals will be greater than $1.00 per unit.[1]

2.   If production were to be increased in the plant sufficiently to require overtime work, time-and-a-half pay would be called for, and the firm's variable labor cost function would look like that illustrated in Figure 13–3.

3.   If a number of overtime hours are worked, we might expect some of the plant's employees to become fatigued to the point where the quality of their work suffers. If their fatigue results in a greater

_____

[1] To illustrate more fully how this may be so, let us consider the following example. The hourly base rate for assemblers whose work standard is 20 pieces per hour, is $3.00, and an incentive wage of 15¢ per unit is paid for all units produced above the standard. Thus, direct labor costs for all work performed either at, or above the standard, is 15¢ per unit. A newly employed worker, who is able to produce only 15 pieces per hour, on the other hand, would often be paid the base rate of $3.00, so that direct labor costs for his work would be 20¢ per piece.

FIGURE 13–2. Relationship Between Variable Costs and Output

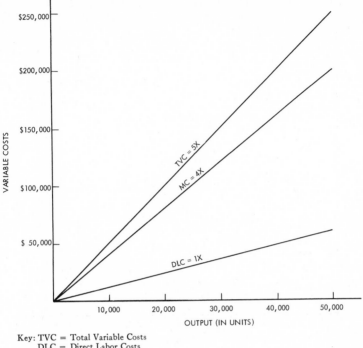

Key: TVC = Total Variable Costs
     DLC = Direct Labor Costs
      MC = Materials Cost
       X = Units of Output

percentage of pieces which have to be scrapped, increasing per unit materials costs such as those illustrated in Figure 13–14 might result.

In short, some of the firm's variable costs may not be directly and linearly related to output. In certain such cases, however, they may be considered directly variable for purposes of simplification, without appreciably distorting the analysis—i.e., relatively good approximations of the firm's cost structure may be obtained by treating the relationship between variable costs and output as a linear one.

Marginal Cost-Revenue Concepts

The concept of "marginal" is a basic one for the manager since it underlies all optimizing decision-making models. In the analysis of the firm's operations, the concept may be applied to costs, revenue, and profits (or, theoretically, to any goal). Marginal costs are defined as those *additional* or *extra* costs which are incurred because a particular course of action is undertaken. Frequently, the concept of marginal costs is used to refer to the additional costs which will

FIGURE 13–3. Variable Labor Costs and Output
(For Both Regular and Overtime Work)

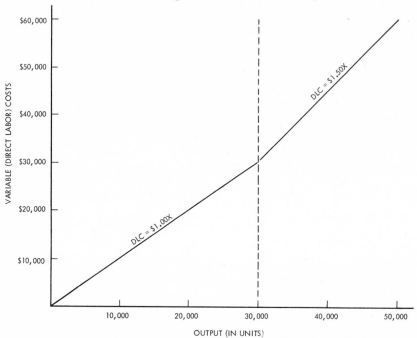

Assumes: Maximum output possible without recourse to overtime is 30,000 units.

Key: DLC = Direct Labor Costs
     X = Units of Output

be incurred when the organizational system produces *one more unit* of output. When such is the case, marginal costs will remain *constant* per unit of output at all levels of output *if all* the firm's cost relationships are *linear*. For example, in the illustration given previously in Figure 13–2, the firm's marginal costs are $5 at all output levels. When certain costs are related non-linearly to output, on the other hand (such as is the case with materials costs with an output of over 30,000 units as shown in Figure 13–4), the increased costs incurred by producing one more unit will *vary* at different levels of output.[2]

The marginal concept may also be applied in analyzing costs other than those associated with changes in levels of output. For example, in financial analysis, consideration may be given to the marginal cost of capital (the added costs of obtaining additional

---

[2] This is also true for the kinked function shown in Figure 13–3, in which marginal labor costs are $1.00/unit under a level of output of 30,000; and $1.50/unit at 30,000 units and above.

FIGURE 13-4. Materials Costs and Output
(Assuming Greater Scrap on Overtime Shifts)

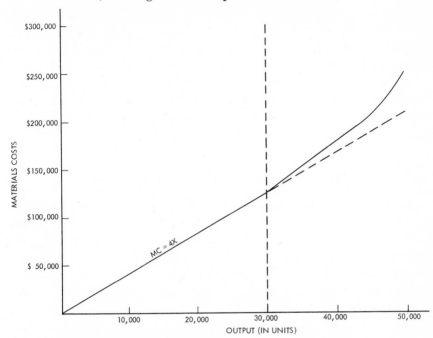

Assumes: (1) Maximum output possible without recourse to overtime is 30,000 units.
(2) Scrap rate does not appreciably increase until overtime hours are worked.

funds for financing).[3] Or, in dealing with other types of problems, attention may be focused on the additional costs which will be incurred by adopting the strategy of, say, hiring one more maintenance man in a production operation or the marginal savings incurred by eliminating one checkout operator in a supermarket.

Conceptually paralleling marginal costs is marginal revenue, which is defined as the extra or additional revenue generated by the firm as a result of undertaking a particular course of action. As with marginal costs, marginal revenue: (1) is often used to refer to the extra revenue gained by producing one additional unit of output; but (2) in a more general sense may be utilized to refer to the additional revenue generated from *any* course of action—e.g., the added revenue expected by a supermarket if one more checkout operator is employed.

The marginal *profit* accruing from any course of managerial ac-

---

[3] See, for example, Robert Johnson, *Financial Management* (2d ed.; Boston: Allyn & Bacon, Inc., 1962), pp. 207 ff.

tion is the difference between marginal revenue and marginal cost. Important to recognize with respect to marginal profit is that in making managerial decisions regarding levels of output, profits will be maximized according to economic theory when *marginal revenue equals marginal costs,* since it is at this output level that marginal profits are zero. At higher output levels, marginal costs increase more than do marginal revenues, so that marginal profits become negative, and total profitability is reduced. We will illustrate this point in greater detail in our later section on non-linear breakeven analysis.

BREAKEVEN AND PROFITABILITY ANALYSIS

A widely recognized deterministic model for analyzing the firm's cost and profitability position is the *breakeven* model. As its name implies, one function served by this model is that of answering the question: "What will be the *breakeven point* for either the company as a whole or for any of its individual products (or services)—i.e., the level of output needed for total revenues to meet total costs, and at which profits are zero?"

The usefulness of the breakeven model, however, is not limited solely to the determination of the firm's breakeven point. Rather, it may be utilized to answer such more general questions as: "What profits (or losses) will be realized at *any* given level of output?" Or, conversely, "What level of output must be generated and sold for the firm to realize any particular desired level of profitability?"

In the following discussion we will illustrate how the breakeven model can be utilized to answer such questions. In doing so, we will first deal with problems in which all relationships between both revenue and output and variable costs and output are linear. We will then demonstrate the applicability of breakeven when such relationships are non-linear. Finally, we will summarize some of the major values and limitations of the breakeven model.

Linear Analysis

As mentioned previously, a firm will just break even (have no profits) on its operations at that level of output for which total costs (TC) equal total revenue (TR). In the simple linear breakeven model, it is assumed that the firm incurs no semi-fixed costs, and that its total costs at any level of output will be equal to the sum of its fixed costs (FC) plus its total variable costs (TVC); or $TC = FC + TVC$. Total variable costs will, of course, depend upon the level of output produced by the firm. Assuming, as we will do in our linear model, that variable costs are directly and linearly related to output:

(1) $TVC = VC(X)$; where VC represents variable costs per unit; and X the number of units of output produced, and

(2) $TC = FC + VC(X)$

The total revenue generated by the firm, on the other hand, will equal the price per unit charged (P) times the number of units sold (X); or $TR = P(X)$. At the breakeven point, total costs will equal total revenue: $FC + VC(X) = P(X)$; and $X = \dfrac{FC}{P - VC}$. The solution of this equation for X will provide the level of output at which the firm will break even.[4]

The application of the breakeven equation can best be demonstrated by both (1) presenting a specific problem, and (2) depicting graphically the relationships between the variables involved on a *breakeven chart*. For our illustrative problem, let us assume that a company wants to determine how much sales volume will be required for it to break even on a new product to be priced at $2.00, and for which fixed costs are estimated to be $50,000, and variable costs $1.50 per unit. The breakeven point may be obtained by substituting these cost and price data in the breakeven equation given above, and by solving for X as follows:

(1) $X = \dfrac{\$50{,}000}{\$2.00 - \$1.50}$

(2) $X = 100{,}000$ units

That 100,000 units is the breakeven point for the new product may be verified by reference to Figure 13–5, a breakeven chart illus-

---

[4] Two observations are in order at this point. First, in speaking of "the level of output at which the firm will break even" here and in the ensuing discussion, we are assuming that the firm will be able to sell all units produced. Second, we should point out that for the firm as a whole which produces several products there will be no single breakeven point—i.e., with a different cost and revenue function for each product, many different combinations of output and sales for the various products would result in the company's just breaking even. Because of the enormous complexities of examining all such combinations when the number of products handled is large, formal breakeven analysis of the type we are discussing in this chapter may be prohibitive. However, many multi-product firms are able to utilize the basic cost concepts with which we are dealing to determine approximate break-even points. For example, supermarket chains, by estimating how total sales will be divided among meats, groceries, produce, soft goods, and so on, for any given store, and with a fairly good knowledge of fixed costs, labor costs, markups, etc., can approximate the store's weekly breakeven point in total sales dollars.

FIGURE 13–5. Breakeven Chart

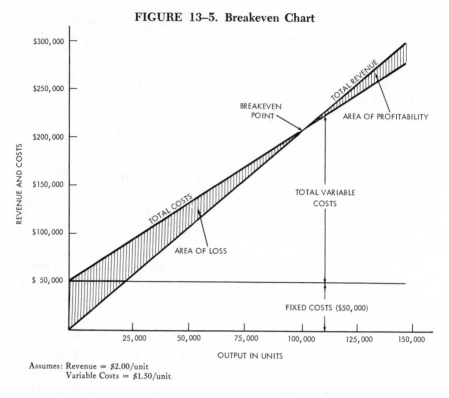

Assumes: Revenue = $2.00/unit
Variable Costs = $1.50/unit

trating the cost and revenue relationships involved in our problem. The reader will note here that the firm's losses decline at a constant rate of $.50 per unit as output is increased from zero up to the breakeven point of 100,000 units, above and beyond which point each additional unit produced and sold results in a marginal profit of $.50. This $.50 figure represents the *difference between price and variable costs per unit*. In effect then, up to the breakeven point the company "picks up" from the sale of each unit a $.50 contribution to the coverage of fixed costs; at the breakeven point, fixed costs are fully covered; and above this point, each $.50 per unit differential between price and variable costs represents a contribution to profits.

There are certain other important questions which our hypothetical firm manufacturing the new product can answer by utilizing breakeven analysis as presented above and/or with certain modifications. For example, it may determine that in order to earn an adequate return on investment [5] on the product, it must realize $75,000 in profit during the forthcoming year; and may want to know how

---

[5] We will discuss the meaning of return on investment later in this chapter.

much sales volume must be generated to meet this profit objective. This question may be answered by modifying the breakeven equation so as to include the desired profit *as well as* fixed costs as a sum which must be fully covered by the per unit difference between price and variable costs times the number of units of output. Thus, the level of output and sales at which any given profit will be achieved may be obtained by solving the following equation for X:

$FC + PR + VC(X) = P(X)$; where PR represents the profit desired.

Or, with a profit objective of $75,000, and the cost and revenue functions given previously:

1. $50,000 + $75,000 + $1.50X = $2.00X
2. $.50X = $125,000$, and
3. $X = 250,000$ units.

The reasoning behind the modification of the breakeven equation may also be visualized graphically by reference to Figure 13–6. The

FIGURE 13–6. Modified Breakeven Chart—Point of Desired Profitability

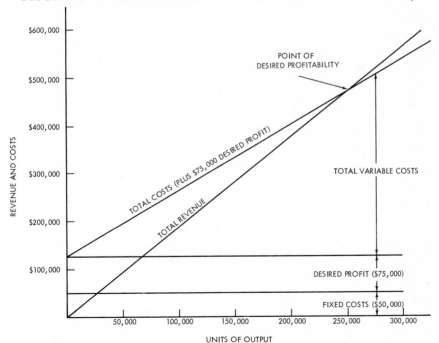

Assumes: Revenue = $2.00/unit
         Variable Costs = $1.50/unit

reader will note that the only difference between this "breakeven" chart and the one illustrated in Figure 13–5 is that the total costs line has now been "pushed up" by $75,000 (the desired profit), so that its intersection with the total revenue line represents the "break-even plus $75,000 point" rather than the point of zero profitability.[6]

Thus far, we have demonstrated how the breakeven approach may be applied to the analysis of a *single set* of cost data. It should be pointed out that this technique may also be utilized for (1) the comparative evaluation of alternative decision strategies and or (2) an analysis of the effect of changes in the firm's existing cost and revenue structure as far as the breakeven point and profitability are concerned. For example, a company might use this form of analysis to determine what impact its concession to a ten-cent-an-hour wage increase demanded by the union would have on its breakeven point, and/or how much its sales volume would have to be increased with the higher wages in order to maintain its existing level of profitability (assuming that it does not increase the price of its products). Or, a firm considering the purchase of either of two new machines each of which would alter its fixed and variable cost structure differently, might be interested in (1) the projected breakeven point for each, and/or (2) the level of sales volume at which the two strategies would be equally profitable.[7]

Non-Linear Analysis

Breakeven and profitability analysis are also applicable when either the firm's variable costs and/or revenue is not directly and linearly related to output. Such would be the case when:

1. The firm must lower the price of its product if it is to sell additional units of output.

2. Its per/unit variable costs increase or decrease as additional units of output are produced.

We will now illustrate the application of non-linear analysis by examining a situation in which the variable cost function is linear, but where total revenue increases at a diminishing rate as output is increased.

A firm's fixed costs for a particular product are $2,000, and its variable costs $.50 per unit. Previous experience has indicated that

---

[6] It should be noted that the 250,000 unit level of output needed to obtain the desired $75,000 profit could be read directly by extending the breakeven chart in Figure 13–5, without the need to draw up the chart shown in Figure 13–6.

[7] Which would be at the level of output at which total costs for each were equal.

consumer demand is sensitive to price, and that as the firm's price is lowered, an increasing number of units will be sold as follows:

Price	Units Sold	Total Revenue (price x units sold)
$10.00.............	100	$ 1,000
3.33.............	900	3,000
2.00.............	2,500	5,000
1.00.............	10,000	10,000
.50.............	40,000	20,000
.33.............	90,000	30,000

These cost and revenue data are illustrated graphically on the break-even chart in Figure 13–7.

The reader will note on Figure 13–7 that two breakeven points exist for the firm's product—one at 308 units, and the other at 31,492 units. These points may be obtained by equating total revenue with total costs, as we did previously with our linear analysis. Solution for the breakeven points now, however, becomes somewhat more

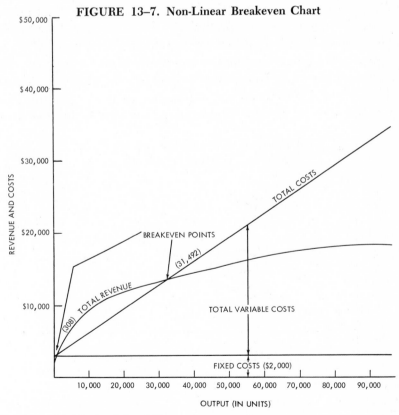

FIGURE 13–7. Non-Linear Breakeven Chart

Assumes: Variable Costs/unit = $.50

Total Revenue = $100 $\sqrt{X}$; where X represents units of output complex since the non-linear total revenue function in our example is expressed by the equation: $TR = \$100\sqrt{X}$, where X equals units of sales (and output). Equating $\$100\sqrt{X}$ with total costs ($\$2000 + \$.50X$) and solving for X as follows gives the two break-even points indicated previously (308 and 31,492):

1. $\$100\sqrt{X} = \$2,000 + \$.50X$
2. Squaring both sides of this equation:

    $\$10,000X = \$4,000,000 + \$2,000X + \$.25X^2$; and
    $\$.25X^2 - \$8,000X + \$4,000,000 = 0$

3. Next, employing the quadratic formula[8]

$$\frac{-b \pm \sqrt{b^2 - 4ac}}{2a}, \; X = \frac{+\$8,000 \pm \sqrt{\$60,000,000}}{\$.50}, \text{ or}$$
$$X = 308, \text{ and } 31,492.$$

Now that we have determined the two breakeven points for our firm's product, let us answer the question: At what level of output and sales will the greatest profitability be achieved? As we mentioned earlier, maximum profits are obtained at that point at which *marginal costs equal marginal revenue*—or, in our example, when the slope of the variable cost line is equal to the slope of the total revenue curve. Up to this point, as may be observed in Figure 13–8, the added revenue obtained from producing and selling one more

FIGURE 13–8. Non-Linear Breakeven Chart
(Point of Maximum Profitability) *

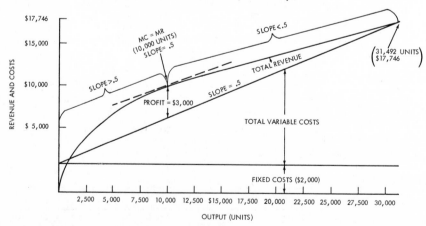

* From Figure 13–7

[8] As the reader may recall from his algebra, a in the quadratic formula represents the coefficient of the x^2 term (.25 in our example); b, that of the x term ($-8,000$); and c the constant (4,000,000).

unit of output is greater than the added cost incurred by doing so. Above this point, however, the costs necessary to produce each additional unit of output are greater than the revenue obtained from its sale.

The point of maximum profitability (which, as shown in Figure 13–8, is 10,000 units for our problem) may be determined either (1) by the trial and error method of calculating and comparing profitability for various levels of output or (2) analytically by setting the first derivative of the total revenue curve $\left(\dfrac{dTR}{dX} = \dfrac{50}{X^{\frac{1}{2}}}\right)$ equal to the slope of the variable costs line. This latter approach is detailed in the footnote below for those familiar with the differential calculus.[9] As may be noted in Figure 13–8, profitability at the optimum point is $3,000.

Breakeven and Profitability Analysis: Values and Limitations

The analytical approaches which we have described in this section represent simple deterministic *models* of the firm's operations. As such, they may serve any or all of the three basic functions of models which we pointed out in Chapter 3:

1. They may provide the manager with *insight and understanding*—e.g., What is the breakeven point for a particular product?
2. They may permit the manager to *predict* the outcome of proposed strategies—e.g., What effect would the acquisition of a new machine have on the breakeven point?
3. They may help *prescribe* courses of action for the manager—e.g., if projected sales for a proposed new product are below the level required to break even, perhaps the product should not be manufactured.

There are, on the other hand, a number of difficulties encountered in the application of breakeven and profitability analysis. The varia-

---

[9] (a) $\dfrac{dtr}{dx} = \dfrac{50}{x^{\frac{1}{2}}}$

(b) $\dfrac{dvc}{dx} = .5$

(c) Equating (a) with (b): $\dfrac{50}{x^{\frac{1}{2}}} = .5$, or $.5x^{\frac{1}{2}} = 50$

(d) Squaring both sides of the equation: $.25x = 2,500$, and $x = 10,000$

It should also be noted that this same method may be used to determine the point of maximum profitability: (1) when the firm's total revenue is linearly related to output, but variable costs are related to output curvilinearly, or (2) when both variable costs and revenue are related curvilinearly to output.

bles in the organizational system are much more complex than we have represented them in the models described above—which were made simple for purposes of exposition. In our simplified models, we have assumed precise knowledge of revenue and cost functions, which often is difficult, if not impossible, to obtain in a real business operation. For example, most firms do not know exactly how much sales volume will be generated at various prices, as we assumed in the non-linear revenue function problem presented earlier. Nor can many firms predict exactly what their materials costs will be during any given period—scrap rates, for instance, may change unexpectedly from time to time. Further, in attempting to utilize breakeven for a particular product, it is often far from a simple matter to assess just what percentage of certain overhead expenses (such as the salary of a company's president) should be assigned as fixed costs to that product. Finally, as we indicated earlier, precise formalized breakeven anaylsis is prohibitively complex when a firm produces many products with different costs and revenue functions. In short, the breakeven model, rather than being a highly precise tool, is simply one which, under conditions of imperfect knowledge, may provide the manager with answers representing relatively good approximations to some of his key questions.

COMPARATIVE ANALYSIS: RATIOS AND PERCENTAGES AS ANALYTICAL TOOLS

In analyzing the organizational system, a great many different variables can be examined—sales, profits, costs, employee productivity, number of lost-time accidents on the job, etc. In many cases, examination of any variable takes on significance *only when compared with* certain other variables in the system. For example, we cannot tell whether a monthly sales volume of $100,000 for a firm is good, bad or indifferent until we compare this figure with certain other information about the company. Quite obviously, such a figure would be disastrously low for General Motors; while for a small supermarket, it might be considered excellent.

Most business firms develop and make reference to a wide variety of *percentages* and *ratios* for the purposes of comparative analysis of their operating data. Profits may be examined as a percentage of sales, attention may be focused on the ratio between current assets and current liabilities, the number of lost-time accidents may be compared to total man hours worked, and so on.

Our purpose in this section is twofold. First, to add to the reader's insight into our previous discussion of profitability and to provide a basis for the understanding of some of the ideas which will be presented in the next chapter, we will examine a widely used comparative measure of the firm's profit position—return on investment. Second, we will present several examples to show how various operating ratios and percentages may be utilized in the analysis of non-economic as well as economic variables within the organizational system.

Return on Investment as a Tool of Analysis

As may be inferred from our previous discussion, the number of dollars *per se* that a company earns during any given period is a completely inadequate measure of its effectiveness as a profit-maker. Rather, in evaluating a firm's profit position, it is important to *compare* its earnings with the funds which have been invested in the company; for the more money that one invests in any enterprise, the greater would be the expected returns, other things being equal. Such a measure of profitability is referred to as the return on investment (ROI).

Several different methods have been devised for measuring the firm's return on investment. Our preference is to define ROI as follows:

$$ROI = \frac{\text{Net Income Before Taxes}}{\text{Total Tangible Assets}}$$

We choose to use income before, rather than after, taxes in order to provide a more uniform base for comparing a company's profitability with either (1) that which it realized in previous periods (when tax rates may not have been the same) and/or (2) that of other companies, which with varying levels of profit, may be subjected to different rates of taxation. By "total tangible assets" we mean the firm's total capital assets (both fixed and current) minus any intangible assets such as good will. Although sometimes calculated on a monthly or quarterly basis, ROI for the firm is most frequently thought of as an annual profitability measure—net income for the fiscal year is compared with total assets as of the end of this period. For example, if a company's income for a particular year were $500,-000 and its year ending total tangible assets, $2,500,000 its ROI would be: $\frac{\$500,000}{\$2,500,000}$ or 25 percent.

As a measure of profitability, ROI serves as an instrument of both planning and control. For example:

1.   A number of business firms define their profit objectives in terms of ROI—e.g., a 20 percent annual return before taxes—and gear their planning activities toward the attainment of such an objective.

2.   The ROI which a company actually attains during any given year is often compared with its returns in previous years to determine what trends, if any, are taking place. A steadily declining ROI from year to year, for example, might signal to management that an earnings problem exists which it somehow must attempt to resolve.

3.   Additional insight may sometimes be gained by comparing a company's ROI figure with that of other firms in the industry. Assume, for instance, that a company's ROI for the past four years has been 15, 16, 17 and 18 percent in that order; and that its objective is to attain a return of 15 percent. Although its profitability objective has consistently been met and the trend is favorable, knowledge that other comparable firms in the industry have been averaging a return of over 25 percent during the four-year period might indicate that the company's ROI objective is inappropriately low.

4.   Businesses often find it useful not only to examine their overall ROI but also to compare the rate of return earned on various segments of their operations.[10] A national supermarket chain, for example, comprised of 38 geographically decentralized operating divisions, may note that its ROI position is favorable everywhere but in its Denver and Atlanta operations, on which a return of only 2.5 percent is being attained. On the basis of such information, management might decide to give special attention to the operating problems of these two divisions in an effort to improve their earnings position.

5.   The concept of return on investment may also be utilized in making *specific investment decisions*—e.g., a new piece of labor-saving machinery may be evaluated by management in terms of the return on the investment which it will generate. We will discuss this application of rate of return in greater detail in the next chapter.

As the reader may note from the above discussion, one major application of ROI is that of helping management to pinpoint existing

---

[10] Such an analysis would require an allocation of a portion of the firm's total assets and certain corporate overhead costs (such as its president's salary) to each segment of its operation so examined.

problems. Knowledge that either its overall return, or that for any of its operating divisions, is inadequate, however, does not by itself indicate to management *why* such problems exist, or what should be done to resolve them. A company's ROI may be poor because it is being undersold by its competitors, the quality of its product is poor, its labor costs are out of line, or for any one of a multitude of other reasons. For this reason, managers will sometimes expand their analysis of ROI so as to make it a more precise analytical tool as follows:

$$\text{ROI} = \frac{\text{Operating Income}}{\text{Sales (\$)}} \times \frac{\text{Sales (\$)}}{\text{Total Assets}}$$

In this expanded form, which is sometimes referred to as the Du Pont formula:

1. The ratio $\dfrac{\text{Operating Income}}{\text{Sales}}$ is referred to as the firm's "margin," and

2. The ratio $\dfrac{\text{Sales}}{\text{Total Assets}}$ is referred to as "turnover," "asset turnover," or "capital turnover."

The utilization of this formula may enable management to determine whether it has problems with respect to margin, turnover, or both of these variables. If so, as Johnson has pointed out: [11]

1. Margin may be improved either by increasing sales revenue more than expenses, or by reducing expenses more than sales volume, while
2. Turnover may be increased by increasing sales revenue more than assets, or reducing assets more than sales.

With respect to improving margin, for example; "Meat markets find that the selling price of boneless meat may be increased by more than enough to offset the added labor cost required to remove the bones." [12] Or in many cases, firms have found it possible to improve turnover by reducing the level of inventories which they carry.

The Du Pont formula, as the reader may note, does not answer the question: "Why is the firm's margin and turnover high or low?" To help provide a better answer to this question, the formula may be extended to focus attention on other systems variables and relation-

---

[11] Johnson, *op. cit.*, pp. 37 ff.
[12] *Ibid.*, p. 38.

ships.[13] For example, a partial extension of the formula might include the following:

1. Operating Income = Sales — Cost of Sales
2. Cost of Sales = Factory Cost of Sales + Selling and Administrative Expenses
3. Selling Expenses = Salaries and Commissions to Salesmen + Travel Expenses + Expenses for Maintenance of Sales Offices
4. Total Assets = Fixed Assets + Current Assets
5. Current Assets = Cash + Accounts Receivable + Inventories

Working with series of equations such as these, management may be able to trace changes in its ROI back to changes in the more basic variables underlying ROI—e.g., costs, sales volume, inventory levels, etc. For example, this type of analysis may indicate that one reason why a firm's ROI has been declining is that it has been forced to liberalize its credit policy and hence increase its accounts receivable in order to compete effectively with the rest of its industry which has adopted a similar practice. Further, the utilization of series of equations such as those illustrated above may enable management to evaluate the impact of *proposed* policies. For example, a proposed investment in a new automated process might increase the firm's total assets, while at the same time lead to decreased operating costs and a higher margin. Whether the *net effect* of the investment would be to increase or decrease the firm's overall ROI may be determined by the type of analysis we have been suggesting. Also useful in pinpointing organizational problems and evaluating proposed policies are certain ratios other than ROI, to which we will now turn our attention.

Ratios and Percentages: Other Applications

Business organizations, as we mentioned earlier, rely on many hundreds of different types of ratios and percentages as analytical tools other than ROI. To cover these applications in any detail is beyond the scope of this book. However, the following examples will serve to illustrate some of the many possibilities of comparative analysis.

1. *Cost/Cost Relationships.* Business firms often find it useful to compare one type of costs with another. For example, in some manu-

---

[13] For a discussion of how profitability analysis has been extended by one firm to include consideration of numerous systems variables, see Kenneth R. Rickey, "How Accountants Can Help Management Manage," *NAA Bulletin,* 44 (July, 1963), 25–36.

facturing operations, certain employees (indirect labor) will assist
those workers actually operating the machines (direct labor) by
(1) setting up (adjusting) their machines whenever necessary due
to changeovers in production from one size or model of product
to another, and/or (2) providing the operators with materials
and supplies. In such cases, management may find it useful to
examine its indirect labor costs as a percentage of direct labor costs.
Experience may show that if this percentage is too high, those employees in the indirect labor category may not be performing up to
par; while, on the other hand, a percentage which is too low may
mean that not enough indirect labor is being employed to service the
direct laborers adequately.

2. *Cost/Revenue Relationships.* In analyzing a firm's income
statement, attention is frequently focused on various costs as a percentage of dollars of sales, and any significant trends noted. For example, we may observe on the income statements illustrated in Figure 13–9 for a hypothetical firm that profitability is declining as the

FIGURE 13–9

Income Statement for Hypothetical Firm

	196–	%	196–	%	196–	%
Net Sales	$100,000		$105,000		$110,000	
Cost of Goods Sold						
Materials	31,000	31	42,000	40	47,300	43
Labor	29,000	29	31,500	30	34,100	31
Other Manufacturing Expense	10,000	10	10,000	9.5	12,000	10.9
Total	70,000	70	83,500	79.5	93,400	84.9
Gross Profit	30,000	30	21,500	20.5	16,600	15
Operating Expenses						
Administrative Salaries	8,000	8	10,500	10	8,800	8
Offices and General	2,000	2	2,100	2	2,200	2
Selling and Advertising	4,000	4	4,200	4	4,200	3.8
Total	14,000	14	16,800	16	15,200	13.8
Net Profit	16,000	16	4,700	4.5	1,400	1.3

total cost of goods sold as a percentage of sales income is increasing;
and that much of this increase is due to proportionally greater materials costs. Such information may point up the need for management to scrutinize certain phases of its operations more closely—
e.g., perhaps materials costs are increasing due to a larger number
of rejected (scrap) pieces being turned out, or because of poor procurement decisions.

3. *Asset/Liability Relationships.* Financial ratios are frequently utilized as a measure of the firm's asset and capital structure position. For example, one commonly used measure of *liquidity*—i.e., a firm's ability to meet its financial obligations to its creditors—is the so-called *acid test ratio:* $\left(\dfrac{\text{cash and equivalent on hand}}{\text{current liabilities}}\right)$.[14] If this ratio is too low a company may experience difficulties in paying its bills on time. On the other hand, an acid test ratio which is too high is not desirable either, for some of the excess funds tied up in cash might be more profitably invested elsewhere.[15]

4. *Cost or Revenue/Asset Relationships.* In addition to the income/asset comparison provided by ROI, business firms frequently utilize certain other comparisons between revenue or cost items and assets for analytical purposes. For example, to determine how rapidly their accounts receivable are being converted into cash, managers often examine their receivables turnover, which may be defined as: $\dfrac{\text{Credit Sales During a Year}}{\text{Average Accounts Receivable}}$. A low receivables turnover may indicate that numerous of the firm's customers are lax in paying their bills and that its credit policies are not strict enough; while a very high turnover ratio may suggest that its credit policies are too strict, and that, in consequence, it is losing sales by refusing to grant credit to customers who would be fairly good credit risks. Or, also frequently examined by firms is their *inventory turnover,* which compares cost of goods sold to average inventories. We will discuss the application of this measure in Chapter 17.

5. *Noneconomic Variables.* All of the ratios and percentages which we have discussed thus far have dealt with dollars and cents comparisons. Comparative analysis, however, is frequently utilized with noneconomic data. In the field of safety, for example, companies are usually interested in their accident record—with respect to both the number and severity of employee accidents on the job. Quite obviously sheer numbers of accidents or man-days of work lost due to accidents is an inadequate measure of performance, since one must also consider how many workers are being employed. For this reason, many firms focus attention on both accident frequency and

---

[14] "Cash and equivalent" refers to cash, government securities, and other highly liquid assets.

[15] Although different firms will have different ideas as to what kind of an acid test ratio they would like to experience, some authorities have suggested a standard of 1:1 as a general rule of thumb. See, for example, J. Fred Weston, *Managerial Finance* (New York: Holt, Rinehart & Winston, Inc., 1962), p. 57.

severity *rates* as a measure of their safety performance. The frequency rate is commonly defined as the number of lost-time accidents *per* million man-hours worked; while the severity rate is defined as: number of working days lost due to accidents per million man-hours worked. As with many of the other ratios and percentages which we have discussed, firms often compare their accident rate experience over time, or with that of other similar companies as a basis for evaluating their performance.[16]

From the above examples it may be seen that ratios and percentages have wide applicability both for purposes of planning and control. Values defining desired relationships among systems variables are chosen by management as objectives to aim at—e.g., an ROI of 20 percent; or an acid test ratio of 1:1—with unacceptable variations from the standards indicating the existence of problems and the need for corrective actions.

SUMMARY

In the analysis of the business firm, reliance is placed on a number of fundamental economic concepts: sunk, opportunity, fixed, and variable costs; and marginal revenue, costs, and profit. An important managerial tool for carrying out various forms of profitability analysis is the breakeven model. This approach may be utilized to handle situations in which the cost and revenue functions involved are either linear or non-linear. Additionally, business firms utilize a number of different types of ratios and percentages for comparing the relationship among variables in the organizational system both as yardsticks in the setting of objectives, and as a means of pinpointing problem areas. For control purposes, these percentages and ratios may be utilized along the lines suggested in Chapter 12—historical comparisons of performance may be carried out, the firm's performance may be compared with other similar companies, and/or performance comparisons may be made among similar sub-systems in the organization. Utilized alone, no single analytical tool discussed in this chapter will provide a complete picture of the firm's operations or problems. However, multiple analyses which focus attention on numerous systems variables and relationships of the types we have been discussing can be useful in helping management to develop more satisfactory solutions to its problems.

---

[16] For figures on accident frequency and severity rates for a number of industries, see, for example: Edwin B. Flippo, *Principles of Personnel Management* (New York: McGraw-Hill Book Company, Inc., 1961), p. 558.

DISCUSSION AND STUDY QUESTIONS

1. A young economist working for the Jones Map Company reports to the firm's president that he is quite concerned since the company's marginal revenue is just equal to its marginal costs, and hence the firm is just breaking even. What action should the president take to remedy the company's problem?

2. Define and give an example of each of the five basic types of costs that are discussed in Chapter 13.

3. An office manager recently purchased a collation machine for $15,000. Two months after its installation, a salesman attempts to sell him on a new machine with more than twice the speed of the one just purchased. In determining the economic feasibility of purchasing the new machine, what economic data should be considered and what should be ignored?

4. When considering fixed costs, just what is meant by fixed? Under what conditions may fixed costs be considered variable? Explain.

5. What are some of the problems often involved in the application of breakeven analysis?

6. Assuming linear cost and revenue functions, it would appear that the more a firm produces, the more profitable it will be. Why, then, don't companies produce an unlimited quantity of goods or services to obtain an unlimited profit?

7. When a firm's revenue function is non-linear, two breakeven points may exist. Does this mean that if the firm produces above either breakeven point it will be profitable? Explain.

8. Is it possible for a firm which has accurately determined its fixed and variable costs, its revenue function, and its breakeven point, to lose money? Explain.

9. a) You notice in the Wall Street Journal an article stating that the Parke Kappa Company has announced a yearly profit of $750,000 before taxes. Is this good or bad? Why? What additional information would you like to have in order to evaluate the profitability of this company?

   b) Assuming that this information were available, how would you determine whether the company's profits were acceptable?

10. The Busad Company has a product, the revenue function for which is non-linear and has been determined to be $50\sqrt{X}$, where X represents the number of units sold. Its variable cost is $.10/unit, its fixed costs are $1,000 and its maximum production with existing facilities is 50,000 units. Determine the firm's breakeven point(s). At what production level would the company's profits be maximized? Is this level attainable? If not, at what attainable production level will the firm obtain the greatest profits?

11. The J.K.L. Washing Machine Company has set an ROI of 15 percent as its profitability goal. The firm's Income and Position Statements for the past three years are as follows:

	Three Years Ago	*Two Years* Ago	*Last Year*
INCOME			
Sales	$1,250,000	$1,400,000	$1,500,000
Cost of Sales	1,000,000	1,091,250	1,168,000
Gross Profit	250,000	308,750	332,000
Selling and Administrative			
Expenses	156,250	187,500·	191,750
Profit Before Taxes	93,750	121,250	140,250
ASSETS			
Cash	$100,000	$ 50,000	$125,000
Receivables	100,000	150,000	100,000
Inventory	125,000	175,000	150,000
Total Current	325,000	375,000	375,000
Plant and Equipment	300,000	300,000	400,000
Total Assets	625,000	675,000	775,000

a) What was the firm's breakeven point in each of these three years?

b) Utilizing ratio and percentage analysis, indicate any problems that you believe the company has faced in these years.

12. On its deluxe model, the Beardless Shaver Company has a variable cost/ unit of $15.00; a selling price/unit of $18.00; fixed costs of $630,000/ year; and total assets of $4,800,000.

a) What is the company's breakeven point?

b) What unit volume is needed to enable the company to attain a 20 percent ROI?

c) The firm's marketing department estimates that with an advertising campaign costing $250,000 per year it could maintain its present sales volume while increasing its selling price $.50 per unit. Would the advertising campaign be profitable if the firm were presently selling: (1) just enough units to break even; (2) the unit volume which generates a 20 percent ROI?

d) What would be the firm's marginal costs and marginal revenue in c (1) and (2) above?

13. Gillmor Enterprises produces a canned sauce for spaghetti that often has been referred to as "the hottest thing around." Yearly fixed production costs are $3,000,000. Its variable costs of production, canning, and shipping amount to $0.40/unit; while fixed selling, administrative, and general expenses total $1,200,000 per annum. One can· of sauce will serve approximately 8 people and sells for $1.00. Maximum production with the firm's present facilities is 3,500,000 cans per year. Determine the breakeven point and the profitability of the firm if it sells all the sauce it can produce. If it sells its maximum production, what would be the lowest price it could charge per can in order to attain an ROI of 10 percent on its total assets of $2,000,000?

14. The Andros Seaside Equipment Company produces a line of sea bathing and sun bathing supplies such as surf boards, water skis, underwater

goggles, duck feet, spear guns, plastic tubes, water balls, and other equipment.

Since the sale of most of these products is highly seasonal, the president of the firm, Aristotle Andros, is attempting to introduce various planning and control methods that will permit management to be more effective in allocating the company's capital. Each product department superintendent is being asked to develop a breakeven chart for planning and control purposes.

The superintendent of the water goggles department, Mr. Hercules, is somewhat disturbed at this request for the term breakeven analysis is "all Greek" to him. He knows that his fixed costs per year at present are $200,000 and that his variable costs (which are constant/unit) are $300,000 at a production level of 400,000 units. He also knows that goggles sell for $2.00/unit.

Mr. Hercules has come to you for assistance and wants to know how many units must be produced in the department annually for the department to break even on goggles.

In addition, the president has told Mr. Hercules that he will receive a bonus of $1000 next January if the goggles department realizes an ROI of 20 percent this year. (The goggles operation has required a capital investment of $200,000.) Mr. Hercules is very much interested in knowing whether or not he has a chance for the bonus. Again, however, unfortunately, return on investment is "all Greek" to him and he wants you to tell him how many goggles must be produced this year for him to realize his bonus.

(NOTE: Give all formulas you use to come up with your answers. Also portray and label your breakeven analysis graphically on a chart such as that illustrated in Figure 13–5.)

SELECTED REFERENCES

ANDERSON, C. W. "Disclosure of Assumptions, Key to Better Break Even Analysis," *National Association of Accountants Bulletin,* 39 (1957), 25–30.

BARISH, N. N. *Economic Analysis: For Engineering and Managerial Decision Making.* New York: McGraw-Hill Book Co., Inc., 1962.

BAUMOL, WILLIAM J. *Economic Theory and Operations Analysis.* 2d ed. Englewood Cliffs, N. J.: Prentice-Hall, Inc., 1965.

CROWNINGSHIELD, GERALD R., and BATTISTA, GEORGE L. "Cost-Volume-Profit Analysis in Planning and Control," *National Association of Accountants Bulletin,* 44 (July, 1963), 3–15.

DEAN, JOEL. *Managerial Economics.* Englewood Cliffs, N. J.: Prentice-Hall, Inc., 1951.

HARRISON, W. E. "The Contribution of Marginal Costing to Present-Day Problems," *The Cost Accountant,* 33 (1954), 128–131.

HAYNES, WILLIAM W. *Managerial Economics.* Homewood, Ill.: The Dorsey Press, Inc., 1963.

RAUTENSTRAUCH, W., and VILLERS, R.   *Economics of Industrial Management.* Revised. New York: Funk & Wagnalls, 1957.

SHILLINGLAW, GORDON.   "Guides to Internal Profit Measurement," *Harvard Business Review*, 35 (1957), 82–94.

SHUBIN, JOHN A.   *Managerial and Industrial Economics.* New York: The Ronald Press Co., 1961.

STETTLER, HOWARD F.   "Break Even Analysis: Its Uses and Disuses," *The Accounting Review*, 37 (July, 1962), 460–463.

THE 1955 COMMITTEE ON COST CONCEPTS AND STANDARDS, American Accounting Association. "Tentative Statement of Cost Concepts Underlying Reports for Management Purposes," *The Accounting Review*, 31 (1956), 182–193.

TUTTLE, FRED G.   "Dynamic Variable Cost Control," *The Controller*, 24 (1956), 62–65, 96.

CHAPTER 14

ACQUISITION OF RESOURCES

I N Chapter 2 we indicated that business organizations develop objectives geared toward providing both economic and non-economic values to society. The attainment of objectives depends to a considerable extent on the manner in which organizations direct the means at their disposal toward these objectives. If the resources of the firm—men, materials, money and time—were unlimited, the fulfillment of most business objectives would pose few major problems. However, since resources are always in scarce supply to one degree or another, a key managerial problem is that of determining their most effective acquisition and allocation to meet the firm's objectives.

The manager faces many different types of problems in planning and controlling the acquisition and allocation of resources. We will treat a number of these problems and decision-making approaches designed to deal with them in this and succeeding chapters. To provide a framework for understanding these facets of managerial decision making, we will now present a brief overview of resource acquisition and allocation in systems terms.

RESOURCE ACQUISITION AND ALLOCATION

The business firm may be viewed as a system comprised of a series of transformation cycles, in which both the acquisition and allocation of (1) financial resources, (2) men, materials and machines, or inputs, and (3) goods and services, or outputs, are closely interrelated. As is illustrated in Figure 14–1, each such cycle consists of three phases: the transformation of financial resources into inputs, of inputs into outputs, and of outputs into financial resources. To elaborate more fully:

FIGURE 14-1. Transformation Cycle

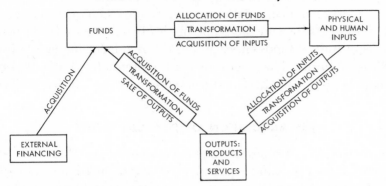

1.   Financial resources (or funds) are either (a) acquired externally by the business firm by borrowing or the issuance of stock, or (b) generated internally through the sale of goods and services.

2.   These funds are allocated to acquire the various factors of production—labor, materials and machines. Or, in systems terms, the funds are transformed into physical and human inputs.

3.   These inputs are then allocated for the production of outputs—i.e., human effort, materials and machine utilization are transformed into goods and services. Here again, both acquisition and allocation are involved—the transformation centers around input allocation to effect output acquisition.

4.   The sale of goods and services represents a transformation of outputs into funds. Some of these funds are paid out to the owners of the business firm; the remainder are available for transformation into inputs, thus permitting the above cycle to commence again.

As the preceding discussion indicates, resource acquisition and allocation are closely interrelated aspects of the decision-making process, and many decisions may be considered as being either type depending upon one's point of view. The decision to purchase a new piece of machinery, for example, involves the allocation of financial resources to effect the acquisition of a capital resource. For the purposes of exposition, however, we will treat separately various aspects of the business firm's transformation cycle, considering some of them under the heading "acquisition" in this chapter, and others as "allocation" problems in the following two chapters. This chapter will be devoted to two major aspects of the funds-input transformation—the acquisition of (1) physical resources, and (2) human resources (personnel selection). In succeeding chapters we will discuss certain facets of the input-output transformation, such as the allocation of men, machines and materials in operations planning and control and the application of mathematical programming techniques to resource allocation. It is beyond the scope of this book to consider in detail the acquisition of funds either by (1) external financing or (2) from the sale of output. These subjects most appropriately fall within the domain of texts in financial and marketing management respectively.

THE ACQUISITION OF PHYSICAL INPUTS

Several different types of physical resources are utilized by the business firm—plant and equipment, materials, machines and supplies. Further the acquisition of any of these inputs involves one or more of a number of different kinds of decision problems. Among the more impertant of these are the following:

1. What should be the *specifications* of the inputs utilized by a company to generate any desired output? For example, to manufacture television sets with certain desired characteristics (e.g., a 21″ picture tube, both treble and base audio volume controls), what kinds of machinery, materials and parts (capacitors, resistors, tubes, etc.) will be needed? Answers to such questions involve both (1) engineering considerations (the discussion of which is beyond the scope of this book) and (2) economic ones—e.g., can the company sell enough units of output at a high enough price to earn an adequate profit in light of the costs of the inputs utilized?

2. Having decided on its materials and parts specifications, how many units of these inputs should be produced or purchased at any given time? If a manufacturer of audio equipment plans to purchase 1,200,000 8-ohm resistors to meet its production requirements for the forthcoming year, is it more economical to buy all of them at once, or to order, say, one lot of 100,000 each month?

3. Should the firm manufacture itself, or purchase from other companies, the materials and parts which it needs? If the purchase alternative is chosen, from whom should the company buy, and to what extent should it rely on multiple suppliers? Cost is obviously an important consideration in resolving such questions; however, there are other factors which must be taken into account.

4. Are expenditures which the firm is considering for capital equipment economically justifiable? For example, should it purchase a new machine costing $80,000 which will effect labor savings of $12,000 a year for 10 years?

We have already discussed one approach for dealing with certain of these input acquisition problems—the breakeven model. In the following sections, we will focus attention on decision-problem types (3) and (4) above: make or buy decisions, and the assessment of proposed investments. We will reserve until Chapter 17 (Inventory Decision Making) discussion of the question of how many units of materials or parts should be purchased or produced at any given time.

Investment Decision Making (Capital Budgeting)

Business firms find it necessary to make many major decisions relative to the investment of funds—in new machinery, plant and equipment, and products. In this section we will first define what is meant by investment decision making (or capital budgeting, as it is often called). We will then point up a number of assumptions which must be incorporated into any capital budgeting model if it is to be "theoretically" correct. Finally, we will examine three approaches to making investment decisions: (1) payback; (2) present value; and (3) discounted rate of return.

Capital Budgeting: A Definition. Funds spent by the business firm for the acquisition of inputs are often considered as being either (1) *operating expenditures,* the primary returns from which are realized within a year (e.g., for labor and materials) or (2) *capital expenditures,* the major benefits from which are gained over longer periods of time (e.g., for plant and equipment). As the reader might suspect, this distinction is somewhat arbitrary. Moreover, it

. . . is not always applicable in practice. . . . most companies would consider the cost of advertising as a current tax-deductible expense, even though long-run benefits may result. To reduce the number of proposals for capital expenditures, management may decree that those involving less than, say $100, will be treated as operating expenses. Neither the tax treatment nor the accounting convenience is theoretically correct, but both are justifiable on the grounds of expediency.[1]

Recognizing that this distinction is somewhat blurred, but that capital budgeting generally refers to acquiring inputs with longer run returns, we will examine some of the basic assumptions made in making such decisions.

The Assumptions of Theoretically Correct Investment Models. Of the many investment models used by business firms today, some

---

[1] Robert W. Johnson, *Financial Management* (2d ed.; Boston: Allyn & Bacon, Inc., 1962), p. 174.

are considered by most observers as "theoretically" correct; while others, although their application may sometimes be justified on the basis of expediency, are regarded as being based on incorrect assumptions. The underlying rationale behind all "theoretically correct" assumptions is that attention be focused solely on the question: "Will the firm be better off financially if the asset is acquired than if it is not acquired?" Or, in economic terms, considering all oportunity costs, will the marginal revenues (or savings) realized from any investment exceed its marginal costs? Among the considerations which should be taken into account in the theoretically correct investment model are the following:

1. Only changes in future *cash flows* should be taken into account in capital budgeting. For example, suppose a manufacturing plant is considering the purchase of a new machine which will replace two present ones, and in doing so (1) effect annual labor savings of $5,000, and (2) reduce the floor space utilized by 300 square feet.[2] Suppose also that each department is "charged" $1.00 per square foot in rent each month for all floor space that it uses. Obviously, the labor savings represent a negative cash outflow (or return) of $5,000 and must be considered in evaluating the profitability of the new machine. However, the $300 less in rent which the department utilizing the machine would be charged would not represent any real cash savings to the firm, and should be ignored.[3]

2. As we pointed out in the previous chapter, sunk costs should be ignored in investment decision making since they do not influence future cash flows.

3. The *cost of capital* must be taken into account in evaluating investment proposals. Obviously, the rate of return realized on any proposed investment must exceed the rate of interest which the firm will have to pay to borrow any funds so utilized, lest the decision be an unprofitable one. Moreover, even if the firm is planning to use its *own* funds rather than borrowing, the cost of capital cannot be ignored. This is because, as we pointed out in Chapter 13, opportunity costs must be considered in managerial decision making—i.e., the firm must take into account the return that it could realize if it invested its funds elsewhere at going interest rates.

4. Money has a *time value*. That is, returns earned sometime in

---

[2] This example parallels one cited in *ibid.*, pp. 179–180.

[3] Unless, of course, releasing the 300 square feet of floor space would either reduce costs (e.g., lower rental payments made by the firm) or increase revenues (by its rental by the firm to someone else).

the future are not as valuable to the manager as those earnings which are realized today, and hence, must be discounted in evaluating investment proposals. This is again because of opportunity costs—e.g., $1,000 obtained today may generate additional earnings by being reinvested for the next 3 years; whereas such an opportunity would be foregone with $1,000 obtained 3 years from now.

5. Depreciation charges should be considered only to the extent that they influence taxes, which represent a future cash outflow. We will illustrate the effect of depreciation on taxes later with an example.

Keeping these assumptions in mind, let us now turn to the first of the investment models which we will discuss—the payback model.

The Payback Method. One commonly utilized approach to investment decision making is the *payback* method. Application of this approach tells the business firm *how many years* (or periods) will be required for its original investment to be returned from the savings realized on the investment. The savings so generated are usually computed on a *before depreciation but after taxes* basis. Although depreciation is not considered as savings, its *effect on taxes* must be taken into account, as we shall illustrate below. Mathematically, the payback model may be expressed as follows:

$$PB = \frac{I}{S},$$ where I represents the original investment, and S the net

yearly savings after taxes.[4]

We will illustrate the application of the payback model with an example.

A manufacturing plant is considering the replacement of one of its machines with a newer, more efficient one, which costs $20,000. The new machine would effect annual labor savings of $3,000 and a yearly reduction in the costs of materials of $1,000. The economic life of the new machine is estimated to be 20 years; and, if purchased, it would be depreciated by the firm for tax purposes on a straight-line basis—i.e., $1,000 would be charged for depreciation each year. The firm is taxed 50 percent on its earnings.

Gross annual savings on this investment would obviously be $4,000: $3,000 in labor and $1,000 in materials costs. All of these sav-

---

[4] For the purpose of simplification we assume here and in the following discussion that S remains the same each year. However, the payback approach can still be utilized even if expected savings vary from year to year. For example, if $I = \$10,000$, and savings were $3,000, $2,000, $4,000, $1,000, $3,000 and $5,000 in that order in future years, the payback period would be four years.

ings would not be taxable, however, because the yearly depreciation of $1,000 on the machine represents a tax-deductible expense. Thus, the firm's taxes would equal 50 percent of gross savings ($4,000) minus depreciation ($1,000): .50($4,000 — $1,000) or $1,500. Subtracting this figure from gross savings gives a yearly net after tax savings of $2,500. Or symbolically, $NS = GS — [(GS — D)(TR)]$; where NS represents net savings; GS, gross savings; D, depreciation; and TR, the tax rate (percentage). Utilizing these net savings in the payback equation: $PB = \dfrac{\$20,000}{2,500}$; the payback period for the new machine would be eight years.

At this point the reader may be wondering: Just what constitutes a "desirable" payback period? Is the eight years for the new machine in our example good, bad, or indifferent? These questions may be answered in two ways. First, if the payback period is longer than the service life of the machine or equipment, the firm will never fully recover its initial investment; and hence, any such investment decision would be a poor one. Second, assuming that this is not the case, many different payback period standards may be chosen, depending upon how rapidly the firm believes it must recover its initial investment, the type of investment being considered, the returns on other investment alternatives available to the company, etc. For example, in developing many new products, there may be *no returns* expected until several years in the future, whereas normally a new labor saving machine would begin paying off almost immediately. Illustrative of the variations which exist in payback standards are the following figures derived from a survey made by the Machinery and Allied Products Institute:

. . . 60 percent of the surveyed firms used the payback period. On equipment with a service life of 10 years or more, of those using the payback period, 28 percent used a 3-year payback, and 34 percent used a 5-year payback. Only 16 percent used a payoff period of more than 5 years.[5]

(The payback model, as the above survey indicates, is widely used) by American business firms. (However, it is not a theoretically sound one in light of the assumptions which we discussed previously.) (It does not take into account the time value of money by discounting future returns.) For example, consider two investment alternatives, each costing $10,000 and having an economic life of 4 years; but with different savings as follows:

[5] J. Fred Weston, *Managerial Finance* (New York: Holt, Rinehart & Winston, Inc., 1962), p. 125.

| | Year | | | |
	1	2	3	4
Savings from Investment A	$8,000	$1,000	$1,000	$1,000
Savings from Investment B	$ 0	$1,000	$9,000	$1,000

Alternative A would be a superior one in that a greater proportion of its savings are realized *sooner* than is the case with Alternative B; yet the payback period for both investments would be the same—three years. Nor does the payback model consider the cost of capital. Finally, the method does not take into account returns over the whole economic life of the investment. In some cases the savings realized from a machine, for example, may be considerable in those years toward the end of its service life *after* the payback period. To ignore these returns, as the payback model does, is to give an inadequate picture of future cash flows generated by the investment decision.

On the other hand, the payback method is simple to understand and relatively easy to utilize. Moreover, the use of the method may be defended when:

> a firm which is short of cash must necessarily give great emphasis to a quick return of its funds so that they may be put to use in other places, or to meet other needs. Where a situation like this obtains, the constraints are such that there is really no other alternative to the payback method. Here the . . . method is preferred, not because it leads to the best decision, but because the best decisions are not alternatives available to the firm because of the pressing need for return cash flows.[6]

In short, although used by many business firms, the payback model ignores several important considerations. Before discussing those investment models which are more theoretically sound, it will be necessary to examine more fully the concept of the time value of money upon which—unlike the payback model—they are based.

The Time Value of Money. As we indicated previously, it is important to consider the time value of money in investment decision making—a dollar earned on an investment sometime in the future does not have as great a present value as a dollar earned today. By utilizing a simple example we will now illustrate mathematically just how money does have a time value. This analysis will provide the basis for understanding the present value and discounted rate of return models which we will discuss later, both of which call for discounting the value of future returns.

---

[6] *Ibid.*, pp. 125–126.

'The idea that money has a time value may be grasped most readily
if, rather than beginning our discussion with the present value of
future earnings on an investment, we first consider the *converse—*
i.e., the *future value of presently held funds.* Let us assume, for example, that a manager has just invested $100 in some securities, and
that he will earn 10 percent on his money compounded annually. At
the end of one year, his $100 will have grown to $110: (a) the original investment (I), plus (b) the interest rate (i) times the $100.
Or mathematically, the future value of his investment after one year
(FV_1) may be represented as:

(1) $FV_1 = I + i(I)$, or
(2) $FV_1 = I(1 + i)$

Next, let us assume that our manager leaves all of his money (now
$110) invested in the securities for a *second* year. At the end of this
time, its value will be equal to: (a) the $110 which he had at the
beginning of the second year—$I(1 + i)$—plus (b) the interest earned
on this money *during* the second year, or $i(I[1 + i])$. Thus, the future value of the original investment at the end of *two* years may be
expressed as:

(1) $FV_2 = I(1 + i) + i(I[v + i])$, which simplifies to
(2) $FV_2 = I(1 + i)^2$;

and, for the manager, $FV_2 = 100(1 + .10)^2$, or $121.
The reader will note that the equation which gives the future
value of the investment at the end of year two (FV_2) is like that
which gives the future value at the end of year one (FV_1), *except
that* $(1 + i)$ *is now raised to the second power rather than to the
first.* Although we will not do so here, it can be shown mathematically that this type of relationship holds for *any number* of years or
periods—the future value of any present investment at the end of any
given number of periods (n) will equal the original investment
times $(1 + i)$ to the power n: $FV_n = I(1 + i)^n$.[7] That is, the future
value at the end of three periods equals $I(1 + i)^3$; at the end of four
periods, $I(1 + i)^4$; and so on. We are, of course, assuming that the
interest rate, i, remains the same during all periods.

---

[7] The period (n) can theoretically be of any duration, and does not necessarily
have to be a year. For example, if interest on money deposited in a savings bank is
compounded quarterly, the future value of any given sum saved after one quarter
would equal $(1 + i)^1$; after two quarters, $(1 + i)^2$; and so on, but in this case i
would be the quarterly rather than the yearly interest rate.

The Present Value Model. Above we saw that $100 invested to-day at an interest rate of 10 percent will have a future value of $121 at the end of two years. Conversely, it follows that $121 earned on an investment two years hence has a *present value* today of $100. Or, in mathematical terms:

(1) Since $FV_n = I(1 + i)^n$,

(2) $I = \dfrac{FV_n}{(1 + i)^n}$.

This latter equation lies at the heart of the present value investment model. However:

1. Since in investment decision making we are interested not in the future value of presently held funds, but rather in the present value of anticipated future earnings, the following notation is preferable: $PV = \dfrac{R_n}{(1 + i)^n}$; where R_n represents the returns expected in any given future period and PV, the present value of these returns.

2. Since a firm normally expects to obtain returns on its investments not only in a single future year, but rather *for several years*, we must expand our equation so as to account for any number of a *series* of future returns which management wishes to consider. As the reader might suspect, this may be done simply by *summing each appropriately discounted* future return—i.e.,

$$PV = \frac{R_1}{(1 + i)^1} + \frac{R_2}{(1 + i)^2} + \cdots + \frac{R_n}{(1 + i)^n},$$

where PV represents the present value of all future returns; R_1, returns in year one; R_2, those in year two, and R_n, those in the last year of the economic life of the investment.

This equation represents the basic present value model to investment decision making.[8] We will now illustrate its application by a simple example. Let us assume that a firm has the opportunity to purchase a new machine for $2,700 which will have a service life of 3 years, and that the gross savings (returns) realized by its use will be: $1,300 in the first year; $1,520 in the second, and $1,762

---

[8] This model assumes that all returns are realized at the *end* of each period, rather than continuously over the whole duration of the period, which would actually be the case with many investment decisions. For example, labor savings on a new machine would be generated continuously, and not all at the end of each year. The error introduced by making this assumption, however, is usually small. We should also note that there are methods involving the use of the calculus which do take into account the continuous inflow of future returns.

in the third. The going interest rate is 10 percent.[9] Taking into account taxes at an assumed rate of 50 percent, and depreciation *only* to the extent that it has a bearing on taxes, the present value of these future returns may be determined as follows. First, assuming straight-line depreciation as with our previous payback example, $\dfrac{\$2,700}{3}$ or $900 must be subtracted from each year's gross savings to give the taxable savings. Then, these savings must be multiplied by the tax rate (50 percent) to give the taxes which must be paid:

1. Year 1–$1,300 gross savings — $900 depreciation = $400 taxable income; $400 × 50% = $200 taxes.
2. Year 2–$1,520 gross savings — $900 depreciation = $620 taxable income; $620 × 50% = $310 taxes.
3. Year 3–$1,762 gross savings — $900 depreciation = $862 taxable income; $862 + 50% = $431 taxes.

Next, subtracting taxes from gross savings gives net after-tax savings for each year:

1. Year 1–$1,300 — $200 = $1,100 net savings
2. Year 2–$1,520 — $310 = $1,210 net savings
3. Year 3–$1,762 — $431 = $1,331 net savings.

Finally, utilizing these net savings figures in the present value equation, we have:

1. $PV = \dfrac{\$1,100}{(1+.10)^1} + \dfrac{\$1,210}{(1+.10)^2} + \dfrac{\$1,331}{(1+.10)^3}$
2. $PV = \dfrac{\$1,100}{1.10} + \dfrac{\$1,210}{1.21} + \dfrac{\$1,331}{1.331}$
3. $PV = \$1,000 + \$1,000 + \$1,000$; or $3,000.

Thus, the present value of all future returns (after taxes) on this investment of $2,700 is $3,000.[10]

---

[9] For purposes of simplification, we are assuming in this and later examples that the interest rate is known to the decision maker. In actual practice, however, determining of a going "cost of capital" presents many difficulties. For a discussion of the measurement of the cost of capital, see, for example, Johnson, *op. cit.*, Chapter 8.

[10] As the reader may have already observed, raising $(1+i)$ to powers as high as 10, 15 or more which is sometimes necessary in utilizing the present value model would be quite time consuming. Fortunately, tables have been prepared which give the present value of a dollar earned at the end of each future year (up to 50) at various commonly-employed interest rates. One such table is provided in Appendix B at the end of the text.

Now that we have demonstrated the mechanics of the present value model, let us turn to the critical question involved in this type of analysis: What represents a "good" present value on any given investment? (The answer is that an investment is generally — desirable if (1) the present value of all future returns is greater than the cost of the investment) (if $PV > I$)[11]; *provided that* (2) no more favorable investment alternatives are available. Thus, the new machine in our above example would represent a desirable investment since the present value of its future savings ($3,000) is greater than its cost ($I = \$2,700$) unless the firm could invest the $2,700 elsewhere and generate returns the present value of which would exceed $3,000.[12]

The Discounted Rate of Return Model. The final investment model which we will discuss, *discounted rate of return*, is theoretically quite similar to the present value model. As its name implies, it is also conceptually related to ROI, which we treated in the previous chapter. Rather than determining the present value of a series of appropriately discounted future cash inflows, as does the present value model, this approach answers the question: What return on the original investment will such inflows represent? The equation which will give the discounted rate of return resembles that utilized for present value, except that our unknown is now r rather than PV:

$$I = \frac{R_1}{(1+r)^1} + \frac{R_2}{(1+r)^2} + \cdots + \frac{R_n}{(1+r)^n}; \text{ where}$$

I represents the original cost of the investment; $R_1, R_2 \ldots R_n$, the future anticipated savings or returns; and r, the discounted rate of return to be determined.

We will now illustrate the application of this model by taking the same example as presented in the previous section. All variables such as savings, depreciation and taxes are treated *exactly the same*

---

[11] Because whenever $PV > I$ the future discounted returns to the firm obtained from the investment are greater than those returns which could be realized by investing the same sum elsewhere at the going rate of interest, i. We should also note that we have termed such an investment opportunity "generally" desirable, rather than always so, for there may be exceptions. For example, a firm whose financial position is strained and needs to generate returns quickly might deem it inadvisable to make an investment where most of the returns would be generated six or seven years hence, even though $PV > I$.

[12] Analysis of this problem would become more complex if another investment alternative costing other than $2,700 were available—i.e., if a present value of $2,500 could be realized on an investment of $2,200 as compared with the present value of $3,000 on our $2,700 machine. For an approach to ranking numerous alternative proposals when I is different in each case, see Johnson, *op. cit.*, p. 190.

with the discounted rate of return model as with the present value model. Thus, the net savings figures which are to be utilized in the discounted rate of return equation are:

$$I = \$2,700, R_1 = \$1,100, R_2 = \$1,210, \text{ and } R_3 = \$1,331; \text{ and}$$

$$\$2,700 = \frac{\$1,100}{(1+r)^1} + \frac{\$1,210}{(1+r)^2} + \frac{\$1,331}{(1+r)^3}.$$

The discounted rate of return may be obtained from this equation by means of trial and error experimentation with various values of r until one which provides a solution is obtained.[13] Such experimentation, as the reader may wish to verify, provides a value of just over 16 for r in the above example; and hence the discounted rate of return is approximately 16 percent.

Some additional observations are in order at this point to further clarify the meaning of the discounted rate of return model. First, the close relationship between this model and the present value one may again be noted by observing that, for any investment problem:

1. When $PV > I, r > i,$
2. When $PV = I, r = i,$ and
3. When $PV < I, r < i.$

For example, assuming an i of 10% again in our last problem, 16% > 10%; as was the present value of $3,000 > $2,700, utilizing the same data.

This observation leads us logically to a second one about the discounted rate of return model. Earlier we pointed out that an investment may generally be considered "desirable" when $PV > I$, provided that no other more favorable alternatives are available. Thus, since when $PV > I$, $r > i$, so also may an investment generally be considered desirable when $r > i$, with the same proviso.[14]

Finally, it should be pointed out that the present value and discounted rate of return models will not always yield the same results. A basic reason for this is that the present value approach assumes that all future returns will be reinvested by the firm at the interest rate i; whereas the discounted rate of return model assumes that these returns will be reinvested at the rate r. For example, consider an investment project which has a discounted rate

---

[13] This substitution may be simplified by the use of tables which give $(1+r)^n$ for commonly utilized ranges of r and n.

[14] Again, we use the words "generally desirable" for the same reason as indicated above in Footnote 11.

of return of 187 percent. The discounted rate of return model assumes that the returns obtained from this investment each period are immediately reinvested at 187 percent. While this assumption may be mathematically correct, it is unreasonable in its economic implications. It is beyond the scope of this book to delve deeply into this and other technical differences between the two methods.[15] However, it should be mentioned that:

1. When the firm is examining only a single investment proposal (e.g., replacing an old machine with a new one), generally the same conclusions may be obtained by utilization of either method.

2. When, on the other hand, various alternative proposals are being ranked, with the objective in mind of selecting the best of these, the present value model is theoretically sounder than discounted rate of return.

Present Value and Discounted Rate of Return: Values and Limitations. A major value of both the present value and discounted rate of return models in comparison with other capital budgeting approaches such as the payback method, is that each considers explicitly the time value of money. These two models are, however, not widely utilized in industry today. Rather, quite frequently:

Rougher techniques are used, sometimes because they are reasonably suitable to the needs of the firm, sometimes because more sophisticated techniques are not understood by management, and sometimes because management is still in process of training and educating its personnel in the use of rate of return or present value.[16]

Moreover, there are several difficult technical problems which have to be faced in the application of present value and discounted rate of return. For one, as indicated previously it is often difficult to determine just what value should be taken to represent the cost of capital. Furthermore, both the present value and discounted rate of return models which we have presented are based on the assumption that the manager possesses relatively accurate knowledge about the size of the future returns—i.e., both assume conditions of certainty. In actual practice, however, it may be very difficult to estimate how much in savings, for example, would be realized on a new machine 10 years hence. Recognizing this limitation, some

---

[15] For a more thorough discussion of these differences, see Michael P. Hottenstein, "An Analysis of Theoretical and Empirical Models of Capital Investment Decision Processes" (Chap. ii, Ph.D. dissertation, Indiana University, 1964).
[16] Johnson, *op. cit.*, pp. 192–193.

financial analysts have utilized Monte Carlo simulation techniques and other methods involving statistical analysis to evaluate investment proposals in which future savings are a function of numerous variables not known for certain.[17]

Physical Resource Acquisition: Make-or-Buy Decisions

An important question confronting many business firms is whether they should purchase their parts and materials from other companies or manufacture (or process) these inputs themselves. For example, should an automotive concern make or buy the tires and batteries used in manufacturing its cars? Or should a retail supermarket chain which sells its own line of private brand canned goods can and label the goods itself, or purchase them from another concern?

There are many factors which have to be taken into account in any make-or-buy decision. One prime question which must be asked in resolving make-or-buy problems is: Can the *quantity* of input desired at the specified *quality* level be obtained through *either* manufacture or purchase? In some cases a negative answer to this question may be obtained, thus dictating the decision alternative which must be chosen. For example:

1. A firm may not believe that it possesses the technical know-how to make a particular part; or it may be possible to make the part only by means of a special process, the patent to which is held by another company.

2. Conversely, there may be no other firms which have the plant capacity or technical knowledge to make the quantity of a particular input required.

In other cases, however, either the manufacture or purchase of the input may be technologically feasible. If so, cost will be a prime consideration—i.e., which of the two alternatives is cheaper? In answering this question, it is necessary not only to compare the purchase price of the input with the costs which would be incurred by its manufacture, but also to consider certain other factors. For instance:

1. The transportation charges which would be required to have the purchased input shipped to the firm's manufacturing facilities would have to be taken into account.

---

[17] See, for example, David B. Hertz, "Risk Analysis in Capital Investment," *Harvard Business Review*, 42 (January–February, 1964), 95–106.

2. If a company would have to purchase additional plant and equipment in order to make its own parts, the return on this investment must be examined. For example, assume that a firm could save $5,000 a year by making a part rather than purchasing it if it invested $30,000 in new machinery and equipment. Would the present value of these future returns justify the investment?

Nor are the above factors the only ones which management may want to consider in making make-or-buy decisions. In some cases firms will prefer to make a certain input themselves so as to be able to keep secret the processes required for its manufacture. Or, in other cases, the "make" alternative may be chosen by a company in order to provide it with a more closely controlled source of supply—e.g., to avoid being put in a position in which a strike against its supplier would force it to curtail or suspend its own production.

A second basic question which must be resolved with respect to procurement decision making is: should a firm rely on a single supplier or multiple suppliers for its inputs? Again, as with the make-or-buy decision itself, a number of variables must be examined in analyzing this problem. In some cases, multiple suppliers will be preferred:

1. In order to minimize the danger of the flow of inputs being cut off due to a strike against any given supplier, and/or
2. Because the quantity of input required is too large to be met by any single supplier, and/or
3. To minimize transportation costs. It may be cheaper for a firm with like plants in both Pennsylvania and California, for instance, to purchase parts utilized by the former from an East Coast concern, and those for the latter from a supplier on the West Coast. On the other hand, reliance on a single supplier may have advantages such as (1) making it possible to obtain quantity discounts by means of the placement of larger orders than would be possible with multiple suppliers, and (2) gaining preferential treatment in terms of delivery schedules by being a "big" customer.

As the reader may note, some of the above variables are fairly easily quantifiable, while others are not. What may be done in handling such decision problems in which both quantifiable and essentially qualitative factors are present is that suggested in Chapter 3—first, construct a model of the decision problem without the "soft variables," and then give the latter explicit consideration. For example, consider the following problem involving the choice between one or two suppliers:

A firm has two like plants—one in Oregon and the other in New York—each of which needs 5,000 parts of a particular type each year. Two suppliers are available, one on the West Coast and the other in the east. If the firm buys 5,000 parts from each supplier, its per unit cost from both will be $10.00; but if it buys all 10,000 parts from either supplier, its unit costs will be only $9.75 due to a quantity discount. Transportation costs will be as follows: from (1) the East Coast supplier to the New York plant, $1.00/unit; (2) the West Coast supplier to the Oregon plant, $1.25/unit; (3) the East Coast supplier to the Oregon plant, $2.00/unit; and (4) the West Coast supplier to the New York plant $2.10/unit. These costs are summarized in Figure 14–2.

FIGURE 14–2

Single- vs. Multiple-Supplier Costs

	Alternative A Buy 10,000 Units From East Coast Supplier	Alternative B Buy 10,000 Units From West Coast Supplier	Alternative C Buy 5,000 Units From Each Supplier
Unit Purchase Costs	$9.75	$9.75	$10.00
Total Cost of Part........	$ 97,500	$ 97,500	$100,000
Transportation Costs:			
To New York Plant.....	$ 5,000	$ 10,500	$ 5,000
To Oregon Plant........	$ 10,000	$ 6,250	$ 6,250
Total Costs.............	$112,500	$114,250	$111,250

As may be noted from Figure 14–2, on the basis of purchase and transportation costs alone, it would pay management to buy 5,000 units from each supplier. Suppose, however, that the firm believes that it would obtain a certain amount of "preferential treatment" (better delivery service, etc.) if it purchased all 10,000 units from either of the two suppliers. Assuming that the preferential treatment variable is not amenable to precise quantification, managerial judgment would then have to be utilized in deciding: Does the value of the preferential treatment which we would expect from either of the single suppliers more than offset the additional tangible costs incurred by such decision choices? A set of programming statements encompassing this decision problem is illustrated in Figure 14–3.

FIGURE 14–3

Preferential Treatment Program

If Value of Preferential Treatment, East Coast Supplier is:	And, If Value of Preferential Treatment, West Coast Supplier is:	Do
≤ $1,250.............	≤ $3,000	Buy 5,000 units from each supplier
≤ $1,250.............	> $3,000	Buy all 10,000 units from West Coast Supplier
> $1,250.............	≤ $3,000	Buy all 10,000 units from East Coast Supplier
> $1,250.............	> $3,000	Buy all 10,000 units from supplier, the value of whose preferential treatment is greater

Assumes tangible costs are those given in Figure 14–2.

THE ACQUISITION OF HUMAN RESOURCES: PERSONNEL SELECTION

We will now turn our attention to the firm's acquisition of human resources—the selection of personnel. As the reader will recognize from our previous discussion of human behavior, selecting people with certain desired characteristics to fill positions involves dealing with a number of complex and interrelated variables which defy precise definition. For this reason, business organizations have not found it possible to utilize formalized mathematical models in their acquisition of human inputs as they have with the acquisition of physical inputs.[18] Rather, personnel selection is a subjective process in which managerial judgment plays a central role.

Nevertheless, some of the basic concepts with which we have dealt previously in our discussion of quantitative models are often considered by management at least implicitly in making personnel selection decisions. For example, some contemporary observers place emphasis on the fact that the skills and knowledge of the members of the business organization

are a form of property or capital, which is part of the deliberate investment. In fact, this capital in western society has grown faster than the rate of accumulation of conventional, physical capital, and has a substantial effect upon the growth and productivity of the firm. This has become a distinctive feature of our economic system.[19]

[18] Statistical approaches are frequently utilized to measure the effectiveness of certain selection tools, such as psychological tests.

[19] George S. Odiorne, *Personnel Policy: Issues and Practices* (Columbus, Ohio: Charles G. Merrill Books, Inc., 1963), p. 156.

Moreover, it is often recognized that the acquisition and maintenance of human resources require both (1) an initial investment
(hiring and training costs) and (2) subsequent outlays of funds
for employee salaries and wages, fringe benefits, additional training and development efforts, etc. Managers also, of course, hope to
obtain an adequate *return* on their investment in human resources,
even though it may be exceedingly difficult, if not impossible, to
define precisely the benefits derived by the firm from the application of particular human skills. For example:

Many companies are cautious about hiring individuals who have
a history of frequent job changes. This caution is predicated on the
following assumptions. First, the probabilities are fairly good that
a person who has frequently changed jobs in the past will continue to do so in the future. Second, for many jobs, a period of initial
training is required during which the new employee will not perform at high levels of effectiveness (i.e., initially the returns to the
company on an investment in human resources will be low). Third,
the firm may, in consequence, never obtain a full "payback" on
its original investment if the individual's "economic life" with the
firm is relatively short.

Finally, as we will discuss more fully below, the concept of marginal analysis may often be useful in determining whether additional information should be obtained in making personnel selection
decisions.

Personnel Selection: An Overview

Our purpose in this and the following sections is not to present
a detailed description of personnel selection procedures which is
more rightly reserved for a text in personnel management. Rather,
our aim is to focus attention on certain fundamental aspects of the
problems involved in the acquisition of human resources in decision
making and systems terms.

There are several basic steps involved in the personnel selection
process. First, human input specifications must be determined—i.e.,
what kinds of people does the firm want to hire? Second, management must engage in one or more forms of *search activity*—it
must attempt to find people available for employment with the
skills and abilities desired. Third, attention must be given to obtaining specific and detailed information about all human input

alternatives available. For instance, if two recent college graduates are applying for the job of personnel assistant with a firm, management might want to know the age, marital and military status, grade point average, and business courses taken in college, etc., of each. Finally, these information inputs must be transformed into outputs—the decision must be made as to which individual(s) the firm will offer employment. We will now discuss these facets of personnel selection.

Input Specification and Search Activity

For our purposes, only a few observations need to be made about the input specification and search activity phases of the selection process. As far as the former is concerned, human input specification like that of the firm's physical inputs will largely be determined by the nature of both the output and the input-output transformations which are desired by management. If an aerospace firm has positions open which call for advanced design work on an intercontinental ballistic missile, it will need to hire engineers; in considering filling the position of head meat cutter in a supermarket, one important human input specification with which the firm may be concerned might be "previous meat cutting experience"; and so on. Further, economic considerations must be taken into account in human input specification—i.e., can the firm afford to pay the salaries or wages demanded by individuals possessing the characteristics desired? A company, for example, may want to hire only Ph.D.'s with five years of industrial experience in solid state physics for senior positions in its research laboratory, but have to settle for persons with lesser qualifications because of limitations on the salaries which it can pay.

With respect to search activity, human resources may be sought either (1) within the firm itself by considering individuals for promotion to higher level positions or (2) outside the company. It is beyond the scope of this book to delve into the relative advantages and disadvantages of promotion from within as opposed to external recruitment.[20] However, we should note that most companies utilize both of these two approaches to varying extents.

As far as search activity outside the firm is concerned, any one or more of a number of different approaches may be undertaken

---

[20] For a discussion of this problem see, for example, George Strauss and Leonard R. Sayles, *Personnel: The Human Problems of Management* (Englewood Cliffs, N. J.: Prentice-Hall, Inc., 1960), pp. 458–468.

by a company. Potential job applicants may be located through personal contact by the firm's managers, newspaper and journal advertising, utilization of employment agencies, recruiting trips to colleges and universities, and so on. Further, human inputs may sometimes be obtained without the firm's initiating any formalized search activity—i.e., from time to time it may receive unsolicited applications for employment.

Finally, we should reiterate a point which we made in Chapter 2 concerning the search for human resources: The manager's rationality to obtain the "best" possible candidates for employment is bounded by time and costs. That is, the marginal costs incurred by extending the search activity farther and farther may exceed the marginal returns in terms of obtaining possibly better candidates by doing so.

The Information Generating Process

After one or more potential candidates for a position have been located, it will be necessary to obtain detailed information about each to provide a basis for the final hiring decision(s). As means for obtaining such information, five basic selection "tools" or approaches are frequently utilized by American business firms today:

1. Application forms
2. The personal interview
3. Psychological tests, which attempt to measure the individual's skills, aptitudes, interests, personality characteristics, etc.
4. Reference checks
5. Physical examinations

Each one of these tools may be viewed as a "hurdle" which the applicant must "overcome" if he is to be given a job offer by the firm. That is, a negative showing by him at *any* of these stages in the selection process may result in his being dismissed from further consideration. For example, an individual may make a good impression when interviewed by management, and his test scores may be favorable, but he may be "washed out" when reference checks from one or more of his previous employers indicate poor performance in his past work. Thus, in terms of programming as discussed in Chapter 11, the information-gathering (and evaluation) process in personnel selection may be viewed as comprising a series of if statements: if the applicant looks desirable on the application form, give him the psychological tests, if not, dismiss him from further consideration; if his test scores are favorable, interview him, if not, dismiss from further consideration, etc.[21]

Two further observations are in order concerning the generation of information inputs in the selection process by means of the above approaches. First, the degree to which the information generating process is programmed will vary considerably from firm to firm. For example, in some companies managers who are called on to interview job applicants are allowed to structure their interviews in any way they may desire. On the other hand, some firms have developed a highly programmed interviewing procedure—the so-called "patterned interview"—in which each interviewer asks the same prescribed set of questions in the same order to each applicant. This approach has certain advantages, such as making it easier to compare responses given by the same applicant to each of several managers in the firm who may have interviewed him. On the other hand, the utilization of such highly programmed do statements has been criticized as preventing the interviewer from being flexible in adapting his questions to prior responses of the interviewee.

Second, the marginal costs of obtaining additional (or better) information must again be weighed against the anticipated marginal returns realized by doing so. For example, by spending $50,000 to design and validate a mental alertness test [22] of its own rather than purchasing one of the many such tests which have been developed by firms in the test design business, a company may have a slightly better predictive tool. However, in considering these two decision alternatives, management must ask itself: "Will the results which may be obtained by developing our own test be sufficiently better to justify the $50,000 expenditure?"

The Selection Decision

Transformation of the information inputs obtained about potential employees into the selection decision output involves many different considerations. We will now examine some of the more important of these.

---

[21] It should be noted that the sequencing of the various selection tools may vary from firm to firm. For instance, in some cases a job applicant may be given an interview before being tested; while in others he may be given numerous psychological tests prior to any formal interviews.

[22] Validation refers to evaluating the test to see that it measures what it is intended to measure. For example, to what extent are high scores on a mental alertness test correlated with successful managerial performance?

First, as we mentioned in an earlier chapter, it is essential in personnel selection to look at each individual's personality system *as a whole* rather than at just certain isolated aspects of his behavior and attitudes. This view, often referred to as the "whole man" concept, recognizes that almost all aspects of a person's life may have a bearing on his job performance. Financial difficulties at home, for example, may lead an individual to "moonlight" (take a second job) which may tend to impair his performance on his regular job. It is for reasons such as this that many companies feel justified in probing into many phases of the job applicant's personal life—especially for managerial candidates, who, if hired, may assume major responsibilities for the firm.

Second, we should reiterate another point emphasized in previous chapters—the individual's *basic* personality system is extremely difficult to modify once he has reached adulthood. For this reason, companies usually place considerable weight on patterns of an applicant's previous work behavior. The man who has enjoyed considerable success as a "creative thinker" in past jobs is likely to continue to contribute new ideas in the future; or, on the negative side, the "job drifter" is likely to continue moving about from job to job in the future.

Third, the personality system of the individual should also be viewed in relation to the organizational system in which he will function if hired. That is, in addition to determining whether or not an individual possesses the specific skills required for the job for which he is being considered, questions such as the following may want to be asked:

1. Are his expectations as to future promotional opportunities with the firm in congruence with the upward movement which it can offer?

2. To what extent are he and his family willing to accept the demands placed on him by the organization—e.g., extensive travel away from home, or the need for frequent transfers from one job location to another.

Fourth, due to the complexity of human behavior, it is usually not possible to predict with certainty the degree to which any particular individual will be successful on any given job; except perhaps to predict failure when a person is obviously highly unqualified—e.g., a low grade moron to do advanced design work on a ballistic missile. Thus, the selection process should be viewed as a probabilistic one, in which improving input generation and decision transformation is designed to *increase* management's *chances* of acquiring better human resources.

Finally, it is possible to develop certain types of programmed decision rules to aid management in evaluating applicants at the various stages of the selection process mentioned previously. For example, in assessing candidates for an engineering position, programmed planning statements such as the following might be appropriate:

1.   If the candidate does not have a college degree in engineering, or if he scores below 28 on our mental alertness test, dismiss him from further consideration, but

2.   If he meets both of these requirements, consider him further. As the reader may note, both of the above decision rules are of the "go, no-go" type. Further each prescribes a *specific* do (dismiss from further consideration) if the applicant *fails* to meet a given requirement; but only a *generalized* do (consider further) if he *does* meet the requirement. Such is generally the case with personnel selection decision rules, again because failure on the part of an applicant to meet a certain criterion may be a fairly good indicator of his being unqualified for a given job, whereas the converse is not necessarily true. For example, many individuals who both have engineering degrees and score above 28 on the firm's mental alertness test may not be qualified because of personality problems or for any one of a host of other reasons.

When two or more applicants for a job meet all of the firm's selection standards, of course, more than simple go, no-go decision rules are required in choosing from among them. What management must attempt to do in such cases is to weight its various criteria, measure each applicant against each criterion considered important, and then select the individual(s) appearing most suitable. For example, if two applicants for an engineering position both meet a company's selection standards, and one has less previous work experience but a higher degree of mental alertness as measured by the firm's tests than the other, management must decide which is more important, and how much so—the additional work experience or the higher mental alertness score. Decisions of this type, which may involve the simultaneous consideration of numerous variables, are generally not amenable to pre-programming, but rather call for the application of managerial judgment to each particular case. In short, personnel selection decision rules are primarily useful in helping the manager to *narrow down his range* of human input alternatives prior to the exercise of subjective judgment in making the final selection decision.

SUMMARY

A fundamental concern of the business organization is the acquisition of inputs, both physical and human. A number of formalized, quantitative, prescriptive models such as payback and present value have been developed to aid the decision maker in his choice of physical inputs. On the other hand, because of the complexity of the human variables involved, models of this type are not available for personnel selection. In consequence, managerial judgment assumes a greater role in human than in physical input problems. Nonetheless, programmed decision rules do have some application in dealing with personnel selection; especially in helping the manager to narrow down his range of decision alternatives. Further, the acquisition of both physical and human inputs is similar in that: (1) their specification is conditioned considerably by the types of outputs that the firm wishes to generate, and (2) the economic consideration of obtaining as favorable a return on the firm's investment in the inputs as possible is a paramount one.

DISCUSSION AND STUDY QUESTIONS

1. What are some of the major reasons why a firm might prefer to make its own parts and materials rather than purchase them?
2. Why might a company rely on a single supplier? Multiple suppliers?
3. Relate the "whole man" concept in personnel selection to what was said about individual behavior in Chapter 4.
4. What are the basic differences between the present value and discounted rate of return models?
5. Of what value may programmed decision rules be to management in the personnel selection process? May such rules be considered as standing plans as discussed in Chapter 11? Why?
6. "Depreciation represents neither a cash outflow or inflow. Therefore, it should be disregarded in making capital budgeting decisions." Evaluate this statement.
7. What are the major limitations of the payback method? Why is this method still utilized by many firms in spite of its limitations?
8. How may return on investment and marginal analysis be utilized in mak-

ing: (a) make-or-buy decisions? (b) personnel selection decisions? Give specific examples to illustrate.

9. Is the cost of capital as utilized in net present value model an opportunity cost? Explain your answer.

10. If a firm has cash balance which it considers excessive, are there any marginal costs of capital associated with investing a portion of the excess in a piece of new equipment? Explain.

11. A firm has the opportunity to purchase a new piece of labor-saving machinery for $27,000. The economic life of the machinery is 3 years, and expected gross savings on it are $10,000 during the first year, $12,100 in the second year, and $14,640 in the third year. The firm utilizes the straight-line method of depreciation. Its cost of capital is estimated to be 10 percent.
   a) What is the present value of the investment ignoring taxes?
   b) What is the present value of savings on the investment after taxes? Assume a 50 percent tax rate.
   c) Should the firm purchase the machinery? Why?

12. For an investment of $10,000, and given a cost of capital of 10 percent, which of the following statements could you be *sure* are *either* correct *or* incorrect even without undertaking either present value or discounted rate of return calculations? In each case, indicate why.
   a) If the present value of the investment is $12,000, its discounted rate of return is 8 percent.
   b) If the present value of the investment is $16,000, the discounted rate of return is 20 percent.
   c) If the present value is $10,000, the discounted rate of return is 10 percent.
   d) If the present value is $9,000, the discounted rate of return is 10 percent.
   e) If the present value is $8,000, the discounted rate of return is 7.5 percent.

13. In the past, all capital budgeting decisions made by the Un-Profitable Corporation have been based on the "intuitive" hunches of its president, Max A. Loss. Recently, the president, heeding the advice of his astrologer, hired a young financial analyst, Mr. I. Q. Sharp, who, since he has been with the firm, has spent considerable time extolling the virtues of present value analysis to Mr. Loss. In a recent conversation between the two on this subject, the president made the following comments: "Your present value model is theoretically unsound because it assumes that future returns realized from investments are known for certain; whereas, in real life they're not. For example, I have a chance to buy a new machine with an economic life of 3 years for $500 which will (a) effect labor savings of $220 in the first year, $363 in the second, and $266.20 in the third *if* business is good but will (b) effect savings of only $110 in the first year, $242 in the second, and $133.10 in the third if business is bad. Our cost of capital is approximately 10 percent. How can your model help me with the problem?" Mr. Sharp answered: "What probabilities do you

assign to business being "good" as opposed to being "bad"? "About 50–50," responded Mr. Loss. "Well, then," said the analyst, "solving your problem is not difficult at all."

a) What do you suppose Mr. Sharp's conclusion was? Why? Show all calculations.

b) What would the analyst's conclusion have been had the president assigned a probability of: (1) .3 to "good" business conditions and .7 to "bad" business conditions? (2) .4 to "good" conditions, and .6 to "bad" conditions?

14. Mr. Jones recently purchased a Lifetime muffler for his automobile. The initial cost of the muffler was $22.00, including installation. Had he purchased a Temp muffler, it would have cost him $12.00, including installation. The Lifetime muffler is guaranteed for the life of the automobile. The average life of Mr. Jones' automobile is six years. The Temp muffler will last for approximately three years. Mr. Jones has averaged six percent per year on his invested money in the past. Has Mr. Jones made a good decision?

15. Mr. Smith is considering the purchase of a cadmium-type battery for his fleet. The cadmium batteries are guaranteed for the life of the car, and cost installed, $40.00. Mr. Smith can purchase a cheaper battery for his cars for $24.00 installed, each with a 36-month expected life. Mr. Smith usually trades in his fleet every six years. Mr. Smith has averaged 10 percent per year on his invested money in the past. Which battery should he buy for his fleet on the basis of the above information?

SELECTED REFERENCES

AMMER, D. *Materials Management.* Homewood, Ill.: Richard D. Irwin, Inc., 1962.

ANYON, G. J. *Managing an Integrated Purchasing Process.* New York: Holt, Rinehart & Winston, Inc., 1963.

BIERMAN, H.; BONINI, C.; FOURAKER, L.; and JAEDICKE, R. *Quantitative Analysis for Business Decisions.* Rev. ed. Homewood, Ill.: Richard D. Irwin, Inc., 1965.

BIERMAN, H., and SMIDT, S. *The Capital Budgeting Decision.* New York: The Macmillan Co., 1960.

BURTT, HAROLD E. *Principles of Employment Psychology.* Rev. ed. New York: Harper & Bros., 1942.

CLAY, HUBERT. "Experiences in Testing Foremen," *Personnel,* 28 (1952), 466–70.

CODY, E. L. *Industrial Purchasing.* New York: John Wiley & Sons, Inc., 1945.

CROMBACH, L. J., and GLESER, G. C. *Psychological Tests in Personnel Decisions.* Urbana, Ill.: The University of Illinois Press, 1957.

DEAN, JOEL. *Capital Budgeting.* New York: Columbia University Press, 1951.

ENGLAND, W. B. *Procurement: Principles and Cases.* 4th ed. Homewood, Ill.: Richard D. Irwin, Inc., 1962.

HABBE, STEPHEN. "The Value of Five Screening Techniques," *Management Record*, 21 (July–August, 1959), 228–31.

HAYNES, W. W. *Managerial Economics*, Chap. xiii. Homewood, Ill.: The Dorsey Press, Inc., 1963.

HEINRITZ, STEWART F., and FARRELL, PAUL Z. *Purchasing*. 4th ed. Englewood Cliffs, N. J.: Prentice-Hall, Inc., 1965.

HIRSHLEIFER, J. "On the Theory of Optimal Investment Decisions," *Journal of Political Economy*, 66 (1958), 329–352.

MAIER, NORMAN. *Psychology in Industry*. 2d ed. New York: Houghton Mifflin Co., 1955.

MCKEAN, ROWLAND M. *Efficiency in Government Through Systems Analysis*. New York: John Wiley & Sons, 1958.

STONE, C., and KENDALL, E. *Effective Personnel Selection Procedures*. Englewood Cliffs, N. J.: Prentice-Hall, Inc., 1956.

TERBORGH, G. *Business Investment Policy*. Washington: Machinery and Allied Products Institute, 1958.

WESTING, J. H., *et al*. *Industrial Purchasing*. 2d ed. New York: John Wiley & Sons, Inc., 1961.

CHAPTER 15

ALLOCATION OF

RESOURCES

I N the previous chapter we pointed out that the operations of the business firm may be viewed as comprising series of resource transformation cycles involving both acquisition and allocation; and the acquisition of both physical and human resources was discussed. We will now turn our attention to two aspects of resource allocation of primary concern to management. We will first consider some of the problems involved in the periodic planning (and control) of the overall allocation of the firm's financial resources. In our discussion we will focus attention on the utilization of operating and cash budgets as instruments of planning and control. Second, we will turn to decisions involving planning and controlling the allocation of manpower, materials, and machine ultilization in generating the firm's outputs. We will indicate how the problems involved in planning and control vary depending upon the type of operations involved, and will discuss certain approaches useful in dealing with this phase of managerial decision making.

THE ALLOCATION OF FINANCIAL RESOURCES: BUDGETING

A key problem for the business firm is that of planning and controlling the overall allocation of its financial resources for future periods of operations. What sales volume is the company to anticipate for the forthcoming week, month, or year? How much revenue will these sales generate? How much money will have to be spent for the manpower, materials and other inputs necessary to produce the projected levels of output? How much profit will be generated by the planned level of operations? What can management do to help assure that its actual costs of operations can be kept in line with projected costs?

This problem can be an extremely complex one, especially for large corporations. Levels of future sales—which taken together with price will determine sales revenue—are dependent on many interrelated variables, and are often difficult to predict with a high degree of accuracy. Considerable difficulty may also be encountered in attempting to project many of the costs required to produce any planned level of output. In short, the overall allocation process is one in which many key decisions must be made under conditions of uncertainty. In light of these complexities, it is not surprising that, as yet, no decision approaches have been developed which will optimize the overall allocation of the firm's resources. The manager does, however, have at his disposal a useful satisficing instrument for planning and control—the operating budget. Further, as we will indicate in the following chapter, algorithms have been developed to achieve cost minimization for certain subphases of the firm's operations.

The Operating Budget

The operating budget is basically a formalized allocation of financial resources for a specified future time period, not uncommonly a year. Projections of several different systems variables may comprise the operating budget: sales, prices, sales revenue, costs, and profits. The inclusion of these projections in a simplified budget for a hypothetical firm is illustrated in Figure 15–1.

FIGURE 15–1

Operating Budget

Leslie Manufacturing Company

Operating Budget for 19—

Sales Revenue (100,000 units @ $10)		$1,000,000
Cost of Goods Sold		
Direct Labor ($4/unit)		400,000
Materials ($2/unit)		200,000
Factory Expenses		80,000
Total		$ 680,000
Selling and Administrative		
Expenses		100,000
Total Expenses		$ 780,000
Operating Profit		220,000

A basic step in developing the operating budget is that of projecting the firm's sales and sales revenue for the ensuing budgetary period. Sales will be a function of three basic classes of variables which we have discussed previously in mutual interaction: (1) certain states of nature, such as general economic conditions, (2) competitive strategies, such as competitors' prices, product quality, and advertising, and (3) the company's own quality, marketing, pricing, service, and other strategies. Projected sales revenue will, of course, be a function of both the firm's pricing decisions and its anticipated sales levels.

It is also necessary in developing an operating budget to define both in physical and financial terms the projected input-output relationships for the planning period under consideration—i.e., what levels of manpower, materials, and other inputs will be required to produce the planned level of sales output and how much money will these inputs cost? It should be noted that planned transformation levels may or may not be equivalent to planned levels of sales. For example, a firm with large inventories of finished goods on hand at the beginning of a budgetary period may decide to set its production at a level considerably below that of anticipated sales.

Further, in planning input utilization and costs, it is important to consider not only the expenditures required to produce the projected level of output, but also those financial resources necessary to produce the desired level of *sales*. Advertising, marketing, and sales promotional activities, for example, do not contribute to the production of goods and services per se, but they aid in transforming these goods into dollars.

In some cases, the costs which will be incurred in transforming the firm's inputs into outputs can be predicted with certainty. For instance, the firm may already be committed to certain fixed charges for the forthcoming year, such as interest or rental payments. Other costs, although not as certain to occur, may be projected with a fairly high degree of accuracy. If a company's production workers are being paid on a piecework incentive plan, under which each employee is paid a fixed sum for each unit of work he turns out, the direct labor costs per unit can be estimated quite accurately for any planned level of production. There are still other costs relative to planned levels of output and sales, however, which may be quite difficult to determine. For example, it may be far from a simple matter to determine how much money will need to be spent in advertising a particular product at a given price in order to sell the number of units desired.

Finally in the budgetary process the subtraction of projected costs from estimated revenues will provide estimates of the firm's profitability for the forthcoming budgetary period. Quite obviously, these profit projections will be only as valid as the other projections upon which they are based.

Several additional observations concerning the budgetary process are in order at this point. First, the firm does *not* first forecast sales, then set prices, then project sales revenue, and then its costs. Rather, all budgetary projections must be considered together in light of their mutual impact upon each other. A firm's sales, for example, cannot be predicted without knowing its pricing policies, the attractiveness of the quality characteristics of its product, etc.; while its costs cannot be accurately projected without good estimates as to what its sales will be. Further, because of the complex inter-relationships between the budgetary variables, numerous revisions may be necessary before a company is able to finalize its operating budget. The initial projections may indicate that planned costs are too high in relation to projected sales revenue to achieve the profit goals set by the company. If such were the case, certain programs might be delayed (e.g., research and development); the company's pricing policies might be modified either upward or downward depending upon management's estimates of the elasticity of demand; or additional expenditures might be planned for advertising if management believed that the added efforts would generate sufficiently greater sales revenue to improve profitability. On the other hand, certain programs deemed essential to the long-run success of the firm may be effected regardless of their short-run impact upon the attainment of profit goals. For instance, one firm hired a relatively large engineering force to update and improve its product line even though this course of action considerably increased its costs in the immediate future.

Second, it is important to recognize the close interrelationship between the operating budget, and the capital budgeting process which we discussed in the previous chapter. The decision to purchase additional machinery or to expand a company's existing manufacturing plant will be largely conditioned by its future sales projections. Further, once such a decision has been made, its effects upon costs should be incorporated into the operating budget. If a company plans to borrow $10,000 for a new piece of machinery in the near future, for example, the interest charges incurred, and any labor and/or materials savings realized can be accounted for in the cost projections for the forthcoming operating budgetary period.

Third, allocating funds among several programs, departments, and expense categories involves a series of decisions to determine the *relative values* of these alternative expenditures to the firm. Is a proposed $50,000 equipment overhaul program, for example, more important than a like expenditure for new product research? While from a theoretical point of view, an optimal allocation of resources would exist when the marginal expected present value is equal for all expenditures,[1] determining these values for many expenditures is not feasible. Bounded by the costs involved in accumulating the necessary data and by the time required to prepare such information, firms ordinarily can only hope to approach an optimal allocation.

As a consequence of the difficulty in obtaining data for optimal allocations, less sophisticated decision rules ordinarily are employed. Often, intuitive, subjective estimates of the relative worth of competing budget requests reinforced with incomplete objective data are employed. Or, in some firms, across the board increases or decreases from the previous year's budget may be utilized, irrespective of marginal values. Further, in some cases, the firm may be operating under certain non-profit constraints which would render it necessary to keep budgeted expenditures below most profitable levels—e.g., a lack of cash or manpower to carry out certain programs.

Fourth, emphasis should be given to the fact that the operating budget serves as an instrument of financial control as well as planning. As an instrument of control, the budget provides a *standard of performance* with which actual performance may be compared. As in the individual's personal life, significant variations from budgetary plans in organizations represent problems, and signal the need to take corrective action.[2] The operating budget of the type illustrated in Figure 15–1, however, only provides a standard of performance for the firm as a whole. It is not oriented toward providing a basis for controlling the performance of any of the company's operating units, such as divisions or departments, since it focuses attention on activities cutting across departmental lines, and for which no individual manager (except at the very top level in the organization) may be held singly responsible. In consequence, many companies break down their operating budget data

---

[1] Assume that $PV > I$.

[2] That is, to the extent that the budget is realistic. Exceeding one's budget may be impossible to avoid if it is unrealistically low, for example; in such case, the design of the budget, rather than the difference between planned and actual performance, would represent the problem.

by department so as to guide performance and permit a comparison between the planned and actual performance of each manager's entire operational area of responsibility. Such departmental (or divisional) budgets are frequently referred to as *responsibility* budgets. A responsibility budget for one department of a hypothetical firm is presented in Figure 15–2. The reader will note that

FIGURE 15–2

Responsibility Budget—Fabrication Department
April 19—

Controllable Expenses	
Direct Labor (400 units @ $2)........	$ 800
Indirect Labor.....................	200
Materials (400 units @ $1)..........	400
Tools............................	25
Supplies..........................	50
Travel and Transportation...........	35
Total.........................	$1,510
Expenses Controllable by Others	
Factory Overhead..................	200
Total Expenses...................	$1,710

this responsibility budget focuses attention only on those costs for which one department manager is to be held responsible. These budgeted costs provide both (1) performance goals to guide the manager in planning and (2) a basis for control. Note that this budget distinguishes between those expenditures which are within the control of the manager and those which are controllable by others. This distinction is made so that the manager will not be held responsible for those expenses charged to his department, such as factory overhead, which are beyond his immediate control.

Finally, brief mention should be made of two approaches often utilized by business firms in recognition of the fact that levels of sales, revenue, and costs may not turn out as forecasted. The first of these is simply to revise the budget at various intervals during the year (assuming a yearly budgetary period), such as each quarter or each month. The second approach is to initially develop a *variable* budget. The variable budget provides for the segregation of the firm's fixed and variable costs, and thus makes possible the projection of costs at various levels of sales and production. For example, if a department's fixed costs are budgeted at $10,000 per month, and its variable costs at $5 per unit of production, its total budgeted costs for a monthly production volume of 5,000 units would be $35,000; for a volume of 6,000 units, $40,000, and so on.

Although, as we indicated in Chapter 13, difficulties are often encountered in clearly defining some costs as either fixed or variable, the variable budgeting approach is helpful in providing budgetary control of departments when activity levels change.[3]

Cash Budgets

In addition to planning for profitability, it is important for business organizations to be concerned with their liquidity position. For this reason, many business firms also develop a *cash* budget along with the preparation of their operating budget. The cash budget, like the operating budget is a formalized financial plan for a specified future time period, and is a satisficing rather than an optimizing approach. Unlike the operating budget, however, the cash budget focuses attention on projecting the firm's cash needs for future periods, rather than on planned profitability.

A company's cash needs at any particular time will be conditioned considerably by its level of output. As sales and production increase, additional funds will be required for receivables, inventories, materials, wage payments, etc. Central to the cash budgeting process is an analysis of the flow of funds into and out of the firm in terms of the specific times at which various payments will be due and revenues received. Of special concern is the fact that large cash outlays are often necessary during the design, preproduction, and tooling phases of programs some time in advance of the sale of the product and the receipt of cash. Further, plans must be made to meet periodic cash payroll outlays, and dividend and tax payments. From the point of view of revenues, the firm's credit and collection policies and receivables turnover must be analyzed in order to project patterns of the inflow of funds.

An illustration of a cash budget for a hypothetical firm is presented in Figure 15–3. The reader will note that this budget includes projected figures for cash on hand at the beginning of the budget period, the inflow and outflow of funds during the period, and both planned and desired cash balances at the end of the period. That the desired ending cash balance of $100,000 is greater than the beginning cash balance of $75,000 for the period might be indicative of large cash needs for an expanded level of produc-

---

[3] For a more detailed discussion of variable budgeting, see, for example, S. Alden Pendleton, "Variable Budgeting for Planning and Control," *National Association of Cost Accountants Bulletin*, 36 (1954), 323–34. This article is reprinted in B. C. Lemke and James Don Edwards, *Administrative Control and Executive Action* (Columbus, Ohio: Charles E. Merrill Books, Inc., 1961), pp. 644–54.

FIGURE 15–3

Cash Budget

Wilson Company

Cash Budget for April 19—

Receipts
Accounts Receivable Collections........................ $500,000

Disbursements
Accounts Payable*......................... $150,000
Operating Expenses
Factory Wages........................... 270,000
Selling and Administrative................. 50,000
Insurance and Taxes...................... 8,000
Investment in Equipment................. 2,000 −480,000

Net Inflow–Outflow
Cash Generated from Operations:
(Accounts Receivable − Total Disbursements).......... $ 20,000
Beginning Cash Balance............................. 75,000
Projected Ending Cash Balance....................... $ 95,000
Desired Ending Cash Balance........................ 100,000
Projected Cash Needs................................ 5,000

* Includes payments for materials, supplies, etc., purchased prior to the current budgetary period.

tion during the following budgetary period. As the budget indicates, it will be necessary for the management of this firm to obtain an additional $5,000 in cash if it is to meet this need. Thus, cash budgetary projections play an important role in guiding managerial decisions to acquire funds from outside the firm.

As is the case with operating budgets, cash budgeting problems may often arise because actual levels of a firm's activity vary considerably from the budgetary projections. To help overcome this problem, some companies will develop more than one cash budget, each geared to a different possible level of sales. The following is a statement of one company's use of multiple cash budgets:

. . . we . . . establish a budget for a sales volume that is somewhat higher and another for a sales volume that is somewhat lower than the original sales forecast. We also prepare cash budgets based on all three of the operating budgets. The two extra budgets are primarily a safety factor. Our cash budgets may show a drop in profits and a decrease in cash to a dangerously low point and we may need to obtain loans in advance of normal requirements to be on the safe side. On the other hand, the cash budgets may show that an increase in profits will cause an excess amount of cash and we will then be prepared to invest this cash or to pay off any loans that are no longer needed.[4]

---

[4] Quotation from Grover E. Edwards, "Structure and Services of the Cash Budget," *National Association of Accountants Bulletin*, 39 (1957), 67–73, as reprinted in Lemke and Edwards, *Administrative Control and Executive Action*, p. 175.

In summary, like the operating budget, the cash budget is a tool for both financial planning and control. Courses of future action are charted, actual performance is compared to planned performance, and variances may signal the need for corrective action. Unlike the operating budget, the cash budget is oriented primarily toward the firm's liquidity objective rather than its profit objective. It should be recognized, however, that there is a close interrelationship between the operating and cash budgeting processes. The operating budget provides a basis for cash budgeting in that operating costs and revenues are (at least partially) reflected in cash flows. On the other hand, a projection of cash flows may indicate that a proposed operating budget is not feasible since it would require cash resources which are more than a company is able to acquire.

Budgeting: Human Considerations

We have indicated that the complexity of overall financial resource allocation for large organizations is considerable, and that no optimizing models have yet been developed to deal with this problem in its entirety. Thus, a considerable degree of value judgment is required by managers in making many budgetary decisions. Further, it is important to recognize that the interpersonal relationships among those individuals reponsible for the allocation of financial resources may be of considerable importance in budgetary decision making. In fact one may view the budgetary process not only as an economic process but as an influence process as well. Let us suppose, for example, that both the personnel manager and production control manager of a plant request larger budgets for the forthcoming year, but that the plant manager, who will rule on these requests does not believe that he can justify both increases to his superior. Each of the two managers making the requests has assembled and presented a considerable amount of data to support his position, but there are still a large number of intangibles involved and the reasonability of the requests is largely a matter of judgment. On what basis will the plant manager make his decision? Quite probably the decision will be influenced by such noneconomic considerations as his subjective opinion as to the relative importance of the two departments, his personal like or dislike of the two men, or his perceptions of the status, power, or influence of the two. In short, we are indicating that influence patterns, in terms of the bases of social power discussed in Chapter 5, may have an important bearing on allocation decisions such as those involved in the budgetary process. Such patterns of influence probably are of considerably less significance with regard to specific allocation problem decisions, in which the "authority of facts" may clearly indicate a particular decision strategy to be the optimum one from an economic point of view.

In the budgetary process, certain kinds of human relations problems may exist which deserve our attention. Research findings by Chris Argyris, for example, suggest that at least four such problems are fairly common:

1. Budget pressure tends to unite the employees against management, and tends to place the factory supervisor under tension. This tension may lead to inefficiency, aggression, and perhaps a complete breakdown on the part of the supervisor.
2. The finance staff can obtain feelings of success only by finding fault with factory people. These feelings of failure among factory supervisors lead to many human relations problems.
3. The use of budgets as "needlers" by top management tends to make each factory supervisor see only the problem of his own department.
4. Supervisors use budgets as a way of expressing their own patterns of leadership. When this results in people getting hurt, the budget, in itself a neutral thing, often gets blamed.[5]

To overcome such problems, Argyris has suggested permitting a greater degree of participation by supervision in the budgetary decision making, and training in human relations for the financial staff to enable them to perceive more accurately the human problems involved in the budgetary process.[6]

INPUT–OUTPUT TRANSFORMATION: OPERATIONS PLANNING AND CONTROL

In the previous section, we focused attention on the overall allocation of financial resources within the business firm. We will now center our emphasis on the problems involved in planning and controlling the transformation of the firm's inputs into outputs. Our concern here will be with the allocation of men, materials, machine utilization, and time in the production of goods and services; although as we will indicate later, input acquisition decisions must also be made by those responsible for the transformation processes.

Traditionally, many management texts have treated the problems

[5] Quoted from Chris Argyris, "Human Problems with Budgets," *Harvard Business Review*, 31 (January–February, 1953), 108.
[6] *Ibid.*, 108–110.

which we will discuss in this section as ones of "production planning and control." We prefer to describe this facet of managerial decision making, however, as that of "operations planning and control," so as to encompass both manufacturing and nonmanufacturing operations—for many of the basic types of decision problems involved both in the production of goods and services are conceptually quite similar.

Operations Planning and Control: Some Basic Considerations

Operations planning and control will vary considerably depending on the characteristics of the work processes involved. Planning and control efforts, however, will usually be comprised of a similar sequence of basic decisions. In manufacturing—working either from sales forecasts or from orders received—plans will first be formulated as to the number of units of each product to be manufactured over a given period of time. Similarly, in nonmanufacturing operations, estimates must be made as to the amount and kinds of work which will be required to service the firm's customers. In the claims department of an insurance company, for example, the manager may project the number of claims likely to need processing for the forthcoming year and the resulting work necessary to carry out this function. In short, regardless of the type of operation in question, the determination of output levels represents a primary step in operations planning.

Once general preliminary plans such as these have been developed, more intensive planning is necessary to ensure that adequate manpower, materials, tools, and machine capacity are available to meet operating needs. That is, certain input acquisition decisions are first made. Then, specific departmental work schedules can be formulated. The essential characteristic of scheduling, as opposed to other forms of planning, is that it centers around the *sequencing* of work in terms of chronological time. At what specific times will a particular piece of work be started and completed on a given machine? What piece of work will be scheduled next on the machine? What priorities will be established for various orders or batches of production?

After decisions such as the above have been made and the work planned is being performed, control becomes an important consideration. Actual performance must be compared with planned performance, and any important variances noted. Decisions can then be made as to what kinds of action are desirable to correct any excessive variances which may exist. If, in the key punch section of a computation center, for example, one operator is absent from the job, should the work originally scheduled for that operator be held up or transferred to another worker? If the latter alternative is chosen, to which operator should the work be rescheduled, and how will the work originally scheduled for this employee, but now displaced, be completed? These are among the kinds of questions which must be resolved in planning and controlling the allocation of resources for the production of goods and services.

As may be noted from the above discussion, many aspects of resource acquisition and allocation which we have discussed previously play an important role in the operations planning and control process. Projected input and output levels for a department may be developed in the operating budget process; the acquisition of additional machine capacity so as to be able to generate the levels of production planned for future periods may call for capital budgeting decisions; and the hiring of additional workers needed to turn out the planned output involves personnel acquisition.

These observations raise the question: To what extent do input acquisition decisions as opposed to those of allocation (input-output transformation) comprise or affect the operations planning and control process? In the very short run, the range of alternatives available to the manager is constrained to a considerable extent by resources which have already been acquired by the firm, and his primary problems center around the allocation of the inputs at his immediate disposal. That is, at any given point in time, he must work with the men, materials, and machines available to him; he is relatively restricted in his ability to acquire additional inputs in the short run. For example, in a department comprising four lathes, and twelve lathe operators, of whom four are working on each of three eight-hour shifts, the manager on any given day has at his disposal a maximum of ninety-six man-hours of input. In such a case, the manager's primary problems in planning and controlling production for the day would center around such questions as which jobs should be given priority and which men should be assigned to which jobs. If production were falling behind in the department with the available inputs, additional machine capacity or manpower could be obtained at some future time, but not immediately, because some lead time would be required for their acquisition. Of course, if we were considering a department operating on a single shift per day basis, the manpower input might be immediately augmented to a certain extent by scheduling overtime. In short, it is only in longer range planning that input *acquisition* becomes an important consideration in the operations planning process.

Generalizing from the above observations, we may state that in planning in the longer run, the manager's strategy space may be extended as he acquires additional resources as inputs. Even in future periods, however, his choice of alternatives will not be completely free, for his alternatives may be constrained both by lead time required for acquiring more resources and by budgetary limitations. For example, the manager in our previous illustration may wish to acquire two additional lathes for next month's production, but be unable to do so because either (1) funds are not available for their purchase, and/or (2) it will take three months for the lathes to be obtained from the company which manufactures them. These restraints and the role of input acquisition and allocation in the operations planning and control process are illustrated in Figure 15–4.

FIGURE 15–4. Input Acquisition and Allocation in the Operations Planning and Control Process

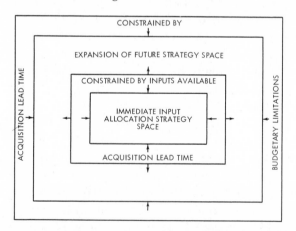

Finally, we should point out that the objectives sought in operations planning and control are usually both multiple and interdependent ones. In the allocation of resources for processing work through a system, management is usually interested in: (1) minimizing costs, (2) maximizing the amount of work (e.g., dollar volume) processed in a period of time, and (3) meeting the delivery promises that have been made to its customers.

These three goals are not independent of each other, and the attainment of any one may, and often does, affect the realization of the others. For example, to meet its requests for travel service at a particular time, an airline may schedule a second section of a flight, even though the capacity of the second craft will be only partially utilized. In doing so, costs may be incurred in operating the second plane which exceed the revenue obtained from its passengers. In such an instance, meeting the "delivery" objective would conflict with the firm's cost minimization goal.

As we indicated in Chapter 2, the handling of multiple goals can be simplified considerably if a single measure for all objectives can be developed. For instance, in our airline illustration, if management could estimate the revenue which would be lost due to dissatisfied customers switching to another airline in the future should the second section of the flight not be scheduled, it might be able to frame the scheduling problem in terms of a single profitability measure.

A further complicating factor in understanding the resource allocation process is that the variables which bear upon the three goals which we have mentioned vary considerably in different types of processing systems. In the following sections, we will illustrate some of the more basic of these differences by examining three different types of work processing systems: (1) job lot systems, (2) continuous-type processing operations, and (3) large, complex, limited-volume production.

Job Lot Processing Systems

In this section we will discuss the fundamental characteristics of job lot processing systems, some of the key variables which must be considered in planning and controlling such operations, and certain approaches utilized by management in job lot planning and control.

The Characteristics of Job Lot Systems. A fundamental characteristic of job lot operations is that many items or lots of items with different specifications are manufactured, each of which is characterized by a small yearly volume *relative to the processing capability* of the system. One optical firm, for example, estimates that it has the capacity to produce 20,000 units of one particular item per year should all its resources be concentrated on it. Yet, it has been able to sell only about 250 units of the item each year to its customers, who normally place orders of less than five units at a time; and the remainder of its capacity is utilized to produce many other items, each also with a comparatively small yearly demand.

Because the characteristics of the many different orders processed in a job lot system will vary from each other, processing equipment which is *flexible* enough to handle all types of items is employed. In machine shops, for example, most equipment commonly utilized is general purpose in use (e.g., engine lathes). It is not economical to use special purpose equipment designed specifically for the most efficient production of any one particular kind of item since the volume for any one item is relatively low. Further, since each piece of processing machinery in the system is employed in the production of many different items, the preparation or *setup* time necessary for producing each different lot is relatively high compared to manufacturing systems in which a large volume of a single product is turned out.

In some job lot systems, many different lots will be processed through the same sequence of operations, even though the specifications of each lot will vary somewhat. For example, in the manufacture of printing rollers, most lots of rollers are processed through essentially the same production stages, although variations exist from order to order in the length and diameter of the rollers, the type of rubber used in their manufacture, etc. In many cases, however, the processing sequences may vary from lot to lot. In a machine shop, for example, the production of an order of pistons, while being turned out on some of the same equipment as an order of axles, would require a different sequence of operations. When the processing sequence frequently varies from order to order, the machines utilized for production cannot be economically arranged to best accommodate the physical handling and flow of any one product, since the processing sequence of other lots will be different. As a consequence, the physical layout for job lot processing systems often does not, except in some very general way, attempt to match the processing sequences. Rather, similar types of processing equipment are often physically grouped together; and the operations may be departmentalized on the basis of process. In a job lot machine shop, for example, it would not be unusual for all of the lathes to be physically grouped together, with all lathe operators reporting to one supervisor, and for the same to be true for the milling machines, the planers, etc.

One final characteristic of job lot systems also deserves mention. Since the demand for any one item is small relative to processor capacity (although it may be steady), it is usually uneconomical to produce items on a continuous basis. In determining when the processing of particular lots should be scheduled:

1.   The firm may wait until a sales order is received before initiating the processing.

2.   It may wait until it has received several orders for an item, and batch these orders together so that they may be processed in the same lot in order to reduce the setup costs per item, or

3.   If the firm has experience to show that a particular item is likely to be reordered in the future, it may decide to carry an inventory of the item.

In the latter instance, the processing of lots would be initiated so as to replenish inventories which have been reduced by previous sales. When such is the case, lot sizes are usually determined independently of any particular sales order. Rather they are generally related to the total demand for the item in question over a period of time. We will examine methods for determining optimal lot sizes for the replenishment of inventories in Chapter 17.

Variables Involved in Job Lot Resource Allocation.   Now that we have discussed the fundamental characteristics of job lot processing the systems, we will examine some of the key variables which must be considered in planning and controlling in such operations so as to achieve the allocation goals of cost minimization, maximizing throughput, and the minimizing of delivery delays.

Lot Processing Sequences.   As we indicated previously, it is necessary to determine the sequence of operations which need to be performed on each lot in order to complete its production. The determination of the processing sequence for a lot—which is commonly referred to as *routing* since it involves defining the route along which the lot will travel as it is being produced—is conditioned considerably by the product specifications of the lot. In the manufacture of books, for example, the printing operation must precede the binding operation. Routing (and scheduling) decisions, however, may also be conditioned by economic as well as output specification factors. Some processing operations on certain products may be performed equally well (although not equally economically) on either of two alternative machines—e.g., a flat machined surface on a part on either a milling machine or a planer. In such cases, when a lot is being scheduled it may be assigned to that machine which can perform the operation most economically. If no capacity were available on the most efficient machine for the operation, however, the order scheduler might assign the alternative piece of equipment to the lot so as to avoid delivery delays.

Lot Processing Time per Operation. A second variable which must be considered in operations planning and control is the time it will take to process a lot through each operation in its sequence. For each operation, this time may be calculated by adding: (1) the setup time required for the lot to (2) the number of items in the lot multiplied by the processing time required for each piece. These times are often kept as data on a master route sheet compiled by the individual or individuals responsible for making the routing decisions.

Lot Delivery Date. In determining when a particular lot is to be scheduled on available facilities, the date when the lot needs to be completed is usually taken as a starting point. This date may represent that on which the items in the lot are to be shipped to the firm's customer; or, if we are scheduling the processing of parts which are later to be assembled into a final product, the delivery date for the lot may be set at the day prior to that on which their assembly has been scheduled to begin. If, on the other hand, the lot were processed in order to replenish inventories, the delivery date would be that when existing inventories are expected to be exhausted. In all such cases, provision may be made for scheduling the completion of a lot prior to its desired delivery date in order to help prevent any delay in its delivery should the processing time take longer than planned. We will discuss the provision for slack time in operations planning to cover such a contingency in a later section.

Processing Availability. Another important variable which must be considered in scheduling a lot to the different operations required for its processing is the amount and nature of other work already assigned to these facilities. If the delivery date for an order awaiting scheduling is 20 days, for example, and a piece of equipment necessary for processing the order has already been reserved for the next month because prior lots have been allocated to it, the scheduler obviously faces a dilemma.

When numerous orders must be scheduled on the same processing equipment, the problems of establishing priorities may become one of considerable importance. By giving processing priority to one lot, the delivery on another may be delayed, especially when the facilities are operating near capacity. In such cases, the scheduling of any given order must be determined in light of the processing requirements of all other lots utilizing the same equipment. To schedule one order requires knowledge not only of the equipment in the shop, but also of the times at which it will be free and available for additional work.

In-Process Inventories. The manner in which lots are scheduled will influence to a considerable extent inventory levels of the items being processed. For example, if it takes twenty days instead of ten to complete the processing of a particular lot, the raw materials utilized in turning out the lot must be "tied up" in production (or "carried" as in-process inventories) twice as long. Since there are costs associated with carrying inventories (which we will discuss more thoroughly in Chapter 17) attempts to minimize costs for a job lot operation involve keeping in-process inventory levels under control. It may, however, be more profitable to increase in-process inventories above minimal levels to help meet certain other objectives of the job lot system, as we will indicate in the next section.

Slack. The allocation of resources is a complex problem especially in large job lot operations; and many of the variables which affect production are not completely predictable. In consequence, allocation decisions frequently may not turn out as well as desired. A scheduler may not have been able to foresee that one large order should have been given priority over a smaller one. Because a worker is absent or a machine breaks down, delays in processing certain lots may occur. As a means of dealing with such contingencies, managers will frequently make provisions for allowing more time for the processing of lots then would be necessary if all work went perfectly according to plan—i.e., *slack* time is provided for. In some cases, extra slack time may be specified both prior to and after each processing step. Or, another method of allowing for slack time on an order is to schedule its processing in such a way that the last operation is to be completed a week (or some other duration) prior to its required delivery date.

It should be noted that providing for slack time increases the firm's inventory requirements and costs (since the lot remains in process longer) in order to increase the probability of meeting scheduled delivery dates. Slack scheduling may also permit supervision to sequence lots so as to reduce setup costs or to be able to utilize more highly skilled operators on complex operations. Thus, slack may help contribute to the reduction of operating costs as well as to the meeting of scheduled deliveries. That it leads to increase inventory costs in doing so, however, again points out that the different objectives sought in resource allocation may be in conflict with each other.

Job Lot Scheduling. As we mentioned previously, the allocation of resources in job lot systems of any magnitude tends to be quite complex. In fact, even in small shops, the amount of data which needs to be considered in routing and scheduling the processing of lots may be quite large. For example, consider a small job lot machine shop in which on the average 25 lots are allocated per week, with an average of 12 operations required for each lot. In such an operation, for each lot, the manager must consider the delivery date, 12 pieces of information about processing sequence, and 12 pieces of information about processing times required; or, *in toto*, 625 informational items must be considered. Further, for effective operations, the impact of scheduling any one lot upon the processing of all other lots being scheduled plus any lots already in process must be taken into account. Consideration of such interdependencies often poses difficult problems since the relationships between all variables in the system are not known precisely and are subject to change as the status of the system changes. For example, placing one lot on a "rush" basis may have little effect on meeting delivery dates for other lots in process when the system is operating at only 75 percent of capacity, but might delay the delivery of several other lots when the plant is operating at 98 percent of capacity.

Scheduling in job lot systems lends itself to the utilization of computers, the large memory systems and rapid computational abilities of which are ideally suited to handling masses of data quickly. Even with computerized scheduling, of course, the complex systems interrelationships must be defined and programmed; and in most cases it is not possible to attain such precise definition as to make possible any truly optimal scheduling-decision approach.[7]

Because of such complexities, many managers in job lot systems rely on one or more relatively simple scheduling rules to allocate processing resources. Furthermore, such rules are often applied sequentially, to one lot at a time, without giving consideration to all variables, lots, and processes in the system simultaneously.

One of the simplest scheduling rules utilized is to process each order on a first-come, first-served basis. If each order were assigned

---

[7] One method of developing satisfactory scheduling decisions is through computer simulation. This approach would involve developing a model of the operations and testing numerous decision rules which have been developed under typical processing conditions. With such an approach it may be possible to identify the conditions under which any given rule offers the greatest probability of achieving effective allocation. We will discuss simulation as an experimental problem-solving method more fully in Chapter 18.

an ascending lot number as it was received, foremen in the job shop could be instructed to process the lot with the lowest number first. Consequently, priority would be given to those orders which have been in the shop the longest period of time.

The first-come, first-served rule often may operate satisfactorily when the machines in the job lot system are operating at less than full capacity. A basic weakness of the rule, however, is that it does not give consideration to either the total processing time required for each lot or to delivery dates. For example, an order requiring 15 days of total processing time with a delivery date 16 days in the future, may remain in a department awaiting processing for 5 days while a prior order not due for delivery for three weeks, and requiring only 12 days of processing is being worked on. One way of alleviating this problem is by means of a somewhat different scheduling rule: "Give priority to orders which have the nearest delivery date." Although this rule gives explicit consideration to meeting delivery objectives, it does not give recognition to the processing time required for orders *in relation to* their delivery dates. A lot with a distant delivery date, for example, may await processing for so long that it may be too late to perform all of the operations required for its manufacture before the delivery date. As a consequence, some schedulers have resorted to still another allocation rule which states: "Give priority to lots with the smallest difference between the time remaining before their promised delivery date and the processing time still needed for their completion." Although this rule may be fairly effective in helping to minimize delivery delays, it is by no means an optimizing technique—for example, it does little to further the cost minimization objectives of the job lot system.

In addition to the utilization of scheduling rules, two other approaches are often employed to help facilitate the complex problems of scheduling in job lot systems. First, so as to give greater consideration to costs and to provide greater flexibility, numerous scheduling decision details may be delegated to supervisors of various departments in the plant, rather than attempting to plan centrally the exact start, stop, and handling times for all processing stages for all lots. Assuming sufficient lot slack is introduced, such decentralized scheduling may permit supervisors to employ scheduling rules which would be difficult to employ on a centralized basis due to lack of knowledge about the current status of all operations. Supervisors may gear their scheduling decisions so as to minimize setup costs, to match worker skills with available work, to assign any overtime work required to their employees on an equitable basis, etc. Thus, decentralized scheduling may allow more attention to be given to meeting the economic objectives of the system and to the human factors of importance.

Second, we should point out that various visual display and record maintenance aids are frequently utilized to aid schedulers in assigning lots to various machines and in keeping track of the progress of orders being processed in the system. Usually in job lot scheduling, the practice is followed of working backward from the lot delivery date, and scheduling the last operation first, the next to the last operation required, second, etc. In order to schedule the processing of lots in such a manner, it is necessary for the scheduler to have for planning purposes information showing the time periods at which each type of processing facility is available for assignment to unscheduled lots, and for control purposes, the progress made on lots already in process. One commonly utilized type of visual display device designed to provide such information is the Gantt Chart, to which we will now turn our attention.

The Gantt Chart is a form of schematic analysis designed to aid the manager in planning and controlling input allocation for the production of goods and services. Several different types of Gantt Charts have been developed—man and machine record charts, layout charts, load charts, and progress charts.[8] All are similar in form in that they enable the manager to visualize work to be scheduled and/or work actually performed in relation to the dimension of time. Although the Gantt approach has been used most widely for planning and control purposes in job lot manufacturing operations, some of the charts have been employed for other types of work—such as in the merchant marine to keep track of the movement of vessels, and in offices for the scheduling of clerical work. To illustrate the basic characteristics of Gantt analysis and its value to planning and control, we will examine one type of Gantt Chart, the project planning chart.

The project planning chart is a schematic model which enables the manager to visualize the times required for various stages of an operation and the interrelationship between the stages. It is designed with the time variable indicated horizontally, and the pro-

---

[8] The originator of the Gantt Chart was Henry Gantt, a pioneer in the scientific management movement. For a detailed discussion of each of the different types of Gantt Charts mentioned here, see Wallace Clark, *The Gantt Chart*, 3d ed.; New York: Pitman Publishing Corp., 1952).

duction capacity variable vertically. To illustrate the use of the project planning chart, let us consider the following example.

The foreman of a job shop is concerned with planning and scheduling the manufacture of a large piece of heavy equipment, the completion date for which has been set at February 16. The piece of equipment is comprised of two sub-assemblies; each of which, in turn, is made up of three parts which must be fabricated in the shop.[9] Final assembly cannot commence until each sub-assembly has been completed. Nor can the work on either sub-assembly begin until the fabrication of each of its three parts has been completed. The time required for each stage of the manufacture of the equipment is as follows:

Operation	Days Required
Fabrication Part #1	4
Fabrication Part #2	2
Fabrication Part #3	5
Sub-Assembly A (of Parts #1, 2, 3)	3
Fabrication Part #4	4
Fabrication Part #5	3
Fabrication Part #6	2
Sub-Assembly B (of Parts #4, 5, 6)	5
Final Assembly	3

Working backward from the completion date, the manager will first schedule the final assembly, then the two sub-assemblies, and finally the fabrication of the six parts. That the Gantt project planning chart is valuable in portraying these schedules schematically may be seen by the reference to Figure 15–5. Assuming no delays or slack time between operations, the chart indicates the fabrication of Part #4 must be initiated on February 1 if the order is to be completed on time, and that minimum time required for producing the piece of equipment is 12 days.

After the production has been scheduled and the work is in progress, the the Gantt Chart may be used for control and replanning by enabling the manager to visualize the progress of each stage of the operation. The chart illustrated in Figure 15–5 shows progress in the manufacture of the piece of equipment as of the end of Friday, February 6. The reader will note that work on Parts #2, 4, 5 and 6 and Sub-Assembly B has proceeded as planned, and that progress on Part #3 is one day ahead of schedule. The fabrication of Part #1, however, is one day behind schedule, and unless this delay is made up for before the scheduled initiation of work on Sub-

---

[9] We have included what would probably be an unrealistically small number of parts and sub-assemblies in this example for purposes of simplification.

416   Management Decision Making

FIGURE 15–5. Gantt Project Planning Chart

LEGEND:

⌐ JOB SCHEDULED TO START

⌐| JOB SCHEDULED FOR COMPLETION

| | TOTAL TIME SCHEDULED FOR JOB

▬ WORK DONE TO DATE

V TIME AT PRESENT

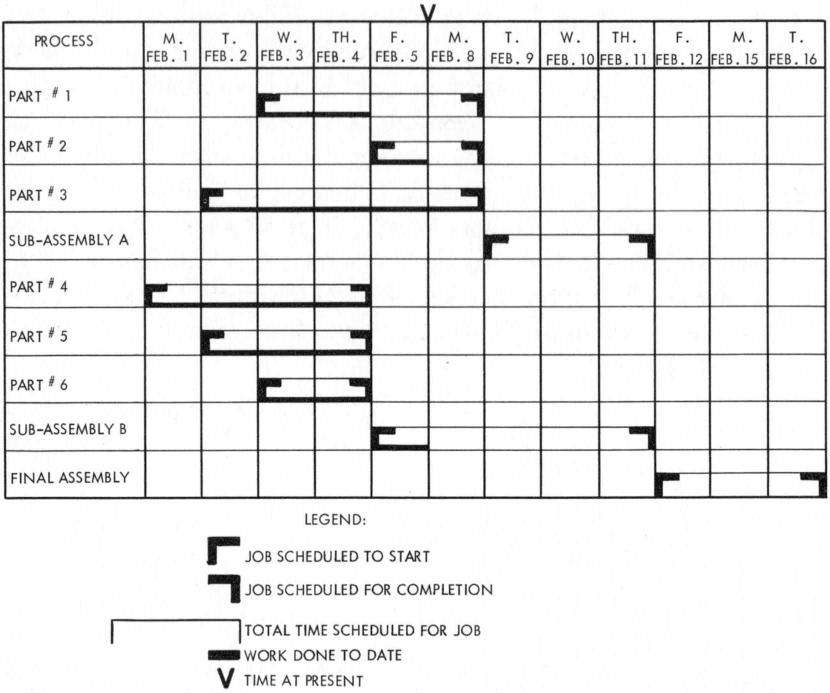

Assembly A on February 9, it will not be possible to complete the order on time. Faced with this variance between planned and actual performance, the foreman might decide to take corrective action by scheduling overtime work on Part #1.

As the above example illustrates, the project planning chart, by providing a graphic comparison of actual versus planned performance, represents a vehicle for facilitating control as well as a tool for planning and scheduling. Easy to design and read, Gantt Charts have been employed in many industries. On the other hand, keeping the charts up to date may require considerable time, particularly when the operation is a complex one. As a means of partially overcoming this limitation, various mechanical devices have been designed to facilitate Gantt-type analysis. Among these are peg boards which employ different colored pegs to represent the various Gantt symbols. Finally, we should reemphasize that notwithstanding its usefulness, Gantt analysis is not an optimizing approach and does not consider all key decision variables.

In our above illustration, for example, the Gantt analysis provided no answer as to whether slack time should have been scheduled with the operation to cover possible delays—but at the expense of an increase in in-process inventories. The various units of work may simply be blocked on to the charts on judgmental basis—no formalized search procedures or mathematically-based decision rules are prescribed. Although optimum schedules may be developed intuitively by means of Gantt analysis when the operations involved are relatively simple, the manager is not likely to achieve more than a satisfactory work program by this approach when the decision problem is a complex one.

The Focus of Control in Job Lot Systems. Control efforts in the job shop must center around keeping close track of the progress of *each* customer order. Each order must be turned out according to customer specifications by the delivery date promised, or else the manager faces the possibility of its cancellation. If a particular order is behind schedule, it is usually not possible to substitute in lieu thereof another order already completed—as would be the case in highly repetitive manufacturing in which large quantities of identical units are being produced—since different orders are different. Because attention in job shops is so strongly focused upon each customer order, planning and control procedures designed for this type of operation are often referred to as *order control systems.*

Data for control of operations in a job shop include the status of each lot as it progresses through the processing facilities. In some shops, these data are obtained at the completion of each operation and forwarded to scheduling for a comparison with the operation's scheduled completion date. In control terms, the schedule may be considered as a standard against which the actual performance is compared for purposes of deciding if a lot should be rescheduled or expedited. Corrective action may be indicated if it appears that a lot will not be completed in time to meet an important delivery date, or if subsequent processing on the lot will interfere with the processing of other lots. Overtime and Saturday work may be decided upon as a result of identifying performances which are behind schedule. At other times, it may be sufficient to designate a behind schedule lot as "rush" so that it may receive priority in the processing of lots at subsequent operating departments. As indicated above, a Gantt Chart, or its equivalent, is useful for visualizing the probable impact of each kind of corrective action.

Continuous Manufacturing

Characteristics of Continuous Manufacturing Systems. Quite different from job lot manufacturing are those operations which are highly repetitive in nature. Such operations are often referred to as continuous manufacturing. The key characteristic of continuous manufacturing—which is usually associated with mass production industries such as those making automobiles or cigarettes—is that long runs of highly standardized items are produced.

Also characteristic of continuous manufacturing is the production of items for inventories (or stock), as opposed to production to order—i.e., production is planned on the basis of sales forecasts rather than on the basis of specific orders received. Few, if any, manufacturing operations, however, are completely repetitive. In addition, some items are produced to order rather than for stock in many industries characterized as continuous manufacturing. In the automotive industry, for example, a number of different models with different options possible are produced each year, some of which are manufactured to customer or dealer specifications. To the extent that items produced are identical in design, each follows the same manufacturing or servicing operations. Consequently, there is no reiterative requirement to decide upon the *route* that items will take through the operations. Rather the product flow is standardized, going through basically the same operations for all items. Further, special equipment, perhaps designed especially for the manufacture of a single item may be economical. Such special purpose equipment is often relatively expensive in initial cost, but is designed to operate at higher speeds and with greater automatic control. The labor savings thus generated can, assuming sufficient product volume, justify the initial cost.

Since both the design of each item and its processing route through production are basically similar, the plant layout of machines can be based upon the processing sequences. In this manner, relatively little handling between operations is needed as work flows directly from one operation to the next. Since adjacent processors perform adjacent sequences, there is no requirement (in terms of minimizing handling costs) to await completion of a lot of parts prior to moving it to the next operation. Rather, each completed item can be moved individually for the relatively small distances involved. In addition, because of the fixed route that items follow through processing and the relatively large volume, automatic handling equipment (such as conveyors) can often be justified, in contrast to job lot operations in which different lots require different routes through production.

Planning Scheduling, and Control in Continuous Manufacturing. The allocation objectives in continuous processing are the same as those in lot processing, namely: minimizing processing costs, maximizing throughput, and minimizing delivery delays. Because of differences in the nature of continuous processing operations, however, the variables bearing upon the attainment of these goals operate in quite different ways. In continuous manufacturing, processing sequences and operating times are relatively unimportant since they are fixed during the layout of equipment. An electronics firm which plans to produce 1,200 table radios of a particular model each day can establish an assembly line for the model, determine the necessary sequencing of operations, and schedule the whole line as single unit. As long as the firm's production remains approximately at this rate, scheduling decisions are passive—i.e., no basic changes are required in scheduling work on the assembly line. When production requirements do increase or decrease, of course, a greater or smaller number of hours of work would have to be scheduled. Thus, the production scheduling decision in operations producing large numbers of identical outputs basically involves the number of hours that the whole unit will operate in order to meet its production requirements.

All outputs are not identical in most mass production processes, however. Automobiles, for example, may be purchased with a fairly wide, but limited and standardized, variety of options. Yet, the car with 20 extras goes through the same assembly line in the same length of time as does the stripped down model following it. Quite obviously, however, more man hours are needed to assemble cars with more options (e.g., installing a radio or air-conditioner).[10] Such variations in work load are accommodated in the original set-up of the assembly line by providing line space and manpower to produce the types of options expected.[11] This approach requires that sales forecasters not only estimate the number of cars sold, but also the number of each kind of option which will be required during the year prior to establishing the processing layout. Although some changes from the predicted mix of options may be accommodated on many assembly lines, the ability to deviate widely from pre-planned option mixes is usually not possible. Further, this basic adherence to pre-established plans is necessary not only over relatively long durations such as a month, but also during each day. For example, if all air-conditioned cars on an assembly line to be produced on a

---

[10] It should be noted that not all variations in options affect the workload of an assembly line. For example, it may take no longer to mount whitewall tires than blackwall ones.

[11] In addition, part of the extra work required with some options may be handled on sub-assembly lines. For example, much of the extra work required on a 4-barrel V–8 is done on the engine sub-assembly line rather than on the final assembly line.

given day were scheduled in the morning, the assembly crew for this operation might not be able to keep up with their work in the morning, and yet have nothing to do in the afternoon.

The focus of control is also different in continuous manufacturing from that in lot processing. Due to the high degree of standardization, it is the *total number* of units produced which is of primary concern rather than each specific order as in job lot operations. For example, a cigarette manufacturer does not have to keep close track of many different orders with various delivery dates to numerous customers; rather his control efforts are geared toward assuring that a specified number of packs be turned out each month. Although always of importance, maintaining close control over the quantity of items produced in continuous manufacturing is especially critical when there are a number of stages involved in the production process, and when production at any one stage is dependent upon a continuous flow of items from a previous stage. Suppose, for example, that the operations of a plant are geared for the final assembly of three sub-assemblies at a rate of 300 per hour. In such a case, the production rates for the final assembly and each of the sub-assemblies must be closely coordinated if there is to be a smooth flow of production. If production of one or more of the sub-assemblies is slowed down to 100 per hour, for example, the final assembly operatin cannot proceed as scheduled unless in-process inventories of the sub-assemblies exist. On the other hand, if the sub-assembling proceeds at a much faster rate than the final assembling, excessive in-process inventories will soon build up. In other words, the rate of output being turned out at each operations stage must be *balanced* if an optimum continuous flow of production is to be realized. For a graphic illustration of the production balancing problem, the reader is referred to Figure 15–6, which portrays both a balanced and an unbalanced production line. Because of the large degree of interdependence between each production stage, centralized planning and control is necessary if balancing is to be achieved. The scheduling of each operations process cannot be left to the discretion of each individual department head—coordination by the production control department is necessary. Systems designed to maintain a continuous rate of flow in highly repetitive manufacturing are often referred to as *flow control* systems.

Finally, some observations are in order concerning the difficulties involved in achieving the overall optimization of a continuous manufacturing operation. As we have indicated above, the high degree of repetitiveness and standardization in continuous processing renders its day-to-day planning and control less difficult than that in the job lot in certain respects—routing is not a major problem nor is it necessary to maintain close control over the progress of each customer order. Nonetheless, the decision variables and their inter-relationships in all but extremely small continuous operations entail such a high level of complexity that—as in the job shop—overall optimization is rarely attained. The manager must be concerned

FIGURE 15–6. Production Line Balancing

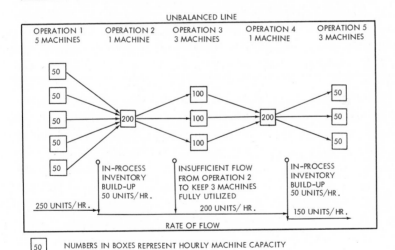

with such problems as the minimization of machine breakdowns, the rescheduling of production when breakdowns do occur, and the maintenance of optimum levels of raw materials, as well as in-process and finished goods inventories. Although it is possible to develop optimum solutions for many of these problems, such optimization usually leads to a less than optimum achievement for others, and suboptimization occurs.

Large Complex, Limited-Volume Production

Product Characteristics.   In contrast to lot processing or continuous production, the manufacture of some large complex products which are turned out in a limited volume does not lend itself to planning and control by the methods previously discussed. Examples of products of this type would be a jet bomber, a weather satellite, an apartment building, or a moon-landing vehicle. Such products are usually typified by the following characteristics:

1.   They are produced in relatively small volume, as indicated above.
2.   They are comprised of many small individual sub-assemblies and/or parts.
3.   The dollar value per item produced is *relatively* large.
4.   Whereas initiating some operations cannot be started until others are completed (e.g., the engine mounting on a plane must wait until the wings have been attached to the wing root), other operations can be processed in parallel. (E.g., wing sub-assembly may be done at same time as tail assembly.)
5.   A separate organization and facilities may be employed exclusively for the item. (E.g., a project manager and a project organization might be given overall responsibility and a separate plant to assemble a large missile.)

In scheduling large complex products, the allocation goals are sometimes not stated in the terms we have discussed previously: (1) minimizing cost, (2) maximizing throughput, and (3) minimizing delivery delays. In space projects, for example, on-time delivery may be preeminent and justify large costs and exclusive, although less than full, use of certain facilities. In addition, at the present time, there exists no operational method for optimal multi-project scheduling in those instances in which more than a few large complex projects are carried out using the same resources. Thus, we may characterize the operations planning and control methods for large complex projects as satisficing rather than optimizing in most respects.

Probably the most sophisticated project-type scheduling techniques which have been developed are the critical path methods originated by Morgan Walker and J. E. Kelly for scheduling large construction projects in Du Pont. The early versions of these methods concentrated upon meeting intermediate and final delivery dates. Some subsequent refinements of the methods, however, have also considered costs and cost-time tradeoffs. To illustrate such techniques, we will examine one popular version of critical path methods: PERT.

Program Evaluation and Review Technique (PERT). Developed by the U.S. Navy as a technique for planning the complex Polaris Fleet Ballistic Missile Program, PERT is a dynamic planning approach "for diagnosing and anticipating the integrated influence of time, resources, and technical performance on the outlook for achieving significant end objectives." [12] Since its inception, PERT has been found useful as a decision-making technique for handling numerous types of allocation problems in business such as those involving the planning of construction and research and development projects.

In this section, we will discuss the basic ideas underlying PERT and with a highly simplified example illustrate some of the ways that PERT may be useful as a decision-making approach. The reader should recognize, however, that although the PERT concept is relatively simple to comprehend, actual application of the technique to decision problems of considerable magnitude involves such a large amount of data that computer utilization is almost imperative.

The first step in the application of PERT is to determine (1) all of the significant activities involved in the project under consideration, and (2) the interrelationship between each activity. As mentioned previously, characteristic of most complex work programs is that many activities are often carried on simultaneously in parallel but that the initiation of some activities must wait until certain prior activities have been completed. In the construction and equipping of a new office building, for example, the installation of desks, chairs, office machines, and so on, cannot be initiated until after the flooring has been completed, but many of these activities can be carried on simultaneously as soon as their initiation is possible. In the language of PERT, the completion of any such project activity is referred to as an *event;* and in the application of PERT, the relationships between all activities and events are portrayed in a program *network.* An example of such a network is illustrated in Figure 15–7. Each lettered circle in the network represents an event, and each arrow connecting two circles represents an activity. With the time variable plotted horizontally on the program network, Figure 15–7 may be interpreted as follows:

[12] Willard Fazar, "The Origin of PERT," *The Controller,* 30 (December, 1962), 598.

FIGURE 15–7. PERT Program Network

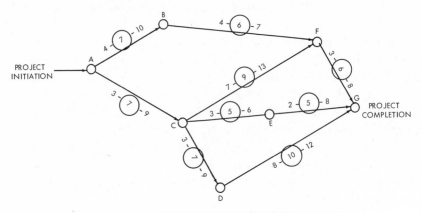

	PROJECTED TIMES (DAYS)		
PATH	OPTIMISTIC	MOST LIKELY	PESSIMISTIC
A – C – E – G	8	17	23
A – B – F – G	12	19	25
A – C – F – G	13	22	30
A – C – D – G*	14	24	30

*CRITICAL PATH

LEGEND:
⟶ = ACTIVITY
O = EVENT

Event A must occur before the activities represented by the A–B and A–C arrows can be initiated; event C (the completion of the activity represented by the A–C arrow) must precede the initiation of the activities represented by the C–D, C–E, and C–F arrows and so on until the event G, the completion of the entire project, has been accomplished.

Once the program network has been drawn up, it will be necessary for the decision maker to assess the time required for the completion of each activity. Because of the uncertainties involved in predicting how long it will take to complete future tasks, three time estimates can be made for each activity—optimistic, most likely, and pessimistic. Three such estimates for each activity in Figure 15–7 are indicated next to the activity arrows, with the circled numbers representing the most likely times. Assuming that these times represent points on a distribution curve, it is possible to develop statistical elapsed times for each activity and to determine the degree of uncertainty associated with each of the time estimates.

To undertake this type of analysis is beyond the scope of this book.[13] In our following illustrations of the values of PERT analysis we will deal only with the most likely times indicated in Figure 15–7. One final point should be noted with respect to the three time estimates—all are based on the same given set of inputs. If activity arrow A–B in Figure 15–7 represented a phase of an engineering project, for example, all three projected estimates (4, 7, and 10 days) might be based on three engineers working on a straight time basis.

The development of a program network in the manner described above may be of value to the decision maker in a number of different ways. First, it will provide a basis for pinpointing problems which are most likely to occur in the completion of a proposed project. A key feature of the PERT network is that it enables us to focus attention on the most *critical path* of activities in the project. The critical path is defined as the longest path (in terms of time) leading to any given event. The longest path leading to event F in Figure 15–7, for example, is A–C–F, which involves 16 days of work (using the most likely time) as compared with only 13 days for the other path leading to F:A–B–F. Similarly, the most critical path leading to the completion of the *entire* project (event G) is A–C–D–G, which takes 24 days. The key role of the critical path is indicated by the fact that any delays which occur on this path will *always* hold up completion of the project. This is not necessarily true for the other paths in the network. To illustrate, in Figure 15–7 a two-day delay anywhere along critical path A–C–D–G will set back the completion date of the project (event G) from 24 to 26 days. A similar delay along path A–B–F–G, on the other hand, will in no way retard the progress of the project. With such a delay, path A–B–F–G would entail 21 days of work, or three days less than that of the critical path. This delay will not effect a postponement of event G, since G cannot possibly occur sooner than 24 days after initiation of the project because of the constraint imposed by the critical path.

---

[13] For a discussion of the use of statistical elapsed times, see, for example, David G. Boulanger, "Program Evaluation and Review Technique," *Advanced Management,* 26 (July–August, 1961), 9–12. An expected time can be calculated as: $\frac{a + 4(m) + b}{6}$ where a, m, and b represent the optimistic, most likely, and pessimistic times, respectively. This formula represents a simplification of the beta distribution. As a consequence of the properties of this distribution, a and b should be estimates of those times that will occur once in 100 times. The resulting expected time presumably will give a better PERT analysis than use of a most likely time. See also, Charles E. Clark, "The PERT Model for the Distribution of an Activity Time," *Operations Research,* 10 (May–June, 1962), 405–406.

Analysis of the criticalness of the activity path in a PERT network will not only enable us to pinpoint those activities on which delays are most likely to hinder completion of a project—it may also provide a basis for a more efficient allocation of inputs to the project than that initially formulated. By more efficient input allocation, we mean the development of a program which will (1) hasten the completion of a project without requiring the application of additional inputs and/or (2) reduce the costs of input allocation without delaying the completion of a project. Depending upon the particular conditions involved in the problem, the critical path analysis may indicate the advisability of adding or taking away inputs from any given path, or of transferring inputs from one path to another. The following examples are suggestive of the types of program improvements which may be effected by such reallocation:

1. *Addition of inputs.* Managers sometimes encounter situations in which they desire to provide additional resources to a project so as to hasten its completion. Such a decision may be made during the preliminary planning stages in the development of a new project, for example because a firm's competition has just announced a new product development of its own. Or, delays encountered during the actual work on a project may necessitate the employment of additional resources (such as overtime work) if the project is to be completed by the planned deadline date. When such delays occur, managers are sometimes tempted to place the entire project on a crash basis, as for example putting employees working on all activities on an overtime schedule. Critical path analysis, however, may indicate that completion dates may be hastened by the application of additional inputs *only to the activities comprising one or a few of the paths in the program network.* Suppose, for example, that any of the activities indicated in the PERT network in Figure 15–7 could be speeded up by as much as 30 percent by scheduling overtime work, and that the manager has decided that he must reduce the overall project time from 24 to 22 days. This objective could be realized simply by scheduling enough overtime work on *any one* of the activities in critical path A–C–D–G to reduce the time needed to complete the activity by two days. No additional inputs need be applied to any of the other activity paths—the whole project does not need to be put on a crash basis. This is because the maximum number of days required by any of the other paths in the PERT network is 22 days (path A–C–F–G), which is just equal to the 22-day

completion time now desired. If the manager wished to further shorten the total project time, say to 21 days, however, he would find it necessary to shorten both paths A–C–F–G and the critical path to 21 days.

2. *Transfer of inputs.* In a somewhat similar manner, project completion may sometimes be hastened by the transfer of inputs from one network path to another. Suppose, for example, that the manager wishes to reduce the total project time as in our above example to 21 days and that the resources which determine the length of time required to complete both activities D–G and E–G are identical, and thus transferable from one to the other. Each activity, for instance, might be one involving the drafting of blue-prints, with all draftsmen equally capable of working on either. If such were the case, total project time could be reduced from 24 to 22 days by transferring two man-days of drafting work from activity E–G to D–G without applying any additional inputs to the project. Such a transfer would reduce the length of critical path A–C–D–G to 22 days, while increasing the length of path A–C–E–G to 19 days —which would still be three days less than the total project time available.

3. *Reduction of inputs.* In the above example we saw that it was possible to transfer resources away from a less than critical path without lengthening the time required to complete a project. In some allocation problems, it may be desirable for the manager to simply take away resources from one of the less critical paths in order to lower the costs of the project, rather than to effect a trans-fer to a more critical path to hasten project completion time. To illustrate this possibility, let us assume that the manager of our project had originally believed that overtime work would be neces-sary for activity E–G; and that the most likely time of 5 days planned for this activity was based on the employment of 5 draftsmen each working a 10-hour day. Assuming a straight-time rate for each draftsman of $2.50/hr., and an overtime rate of $3.75/hr., total labor costs for the overtime schedule would be as follows:

5 draftsmen @ 40 hrs. each straight time = 200 hrs. @ $2.50/hr. or $500.00
5 draftsmen @ 10 hrs. each overtime   = 50 hrs. @ $3.75/hr. or $187.50

                                                 Total labor costs $687.50

Critical path analysis indicates that the scheduling of the drafting work on a straight-line basis, which would require 6¼ days for com-pletion rather than 5, can be accomplished without delaying the completion of the project. Total labor costs for the straight-time work are:

5 draftsmen @ 50 hrs. each straight time = 250 hrs. @ $2.50/hr. or $625.

Thus, a saving of $62.50 may be effected by eliminating the use of overtime.

The examples illustrated above indicate that PERT is a highly useful approach for planning and controlling the allocation of resources. Analysis of the PERT network in the initial planning stages of a work project can both point up those activity paths which are most critical and provide a basis for the more efficient allocation of inputs. Further, analysis of the network as work on a project is in progress can focus attention on those areas in which actual performance is in variance with planned performance, and signal the need for corrective action.

SUMMARY

A fundamental management problem is the allocation of scarce resources in such a way as to achieve full realization of the firm's objectives. From a prescriptive point of view, the fundamental criterion for the allocation of resources should thus be the maximization of profit or its counterpart, cost minimization, to the extent that the objectives of the firm are economic in nature. In dealing with such broad allocation problems as budgetary decision making for the firm as a whole, and operations planning for complex work processes, the overall optimization of economic objectives (to say nothing of noneconomic ones) is an ideal, rarely, if ever, realized.

The rationality of the decision maker is bounded by the complexity of the key decision variables and their interrelationships in problems of such magnitude. Nor is his rationality in dealing with these problems simply bounded by the complexity of economic variables. Budgetary decisions, for example, often reflect political considerations as well as economic ones, and must be thought of at least in part in terms of the social power and influence of these members of the firm involved in the budgetary process.

Nevertheless, the application of such approaches as operating and cash budgets, as the Gantt Chart, and PERT may enable the manager to satisfice in dealing with his allocation problems. Further, optimization of certain sub-phases of complex allocation problems is sometimes possible by means of these approaches. Application of statistical techniques in the analysis of PERT program networks, for example, may permit the minimization of certain expected costs in the planning of work projects. Also of value in optimizing certain kinds of allocation problems is a class of new and powerful decision-making approaches—mathematical programming—to which we will turn our attention in the next chapter.

DISCUSSION AND STUDY QUESTIONS

1. Evaluate the following budgeting approach: "Our sales volume is expected to increase by 10 percent next year. Therefore, we will increase each planned expenditure in our operating budget for next year by 10 percent over what it actually was this year."

2. Not only must the development of a firm's cash budget be based on its operating budgetary projections; but the development of its operating budget must be based on its cash budget forecasts. Discuss.

3. Which budgetary approach—the variable budget, or budgetary revision at various intervals during the year—do you believe to be the more valid one? Why?

4. Indicate for each of the following types of operations whether PERT analysis, the utilization of Gantt Charts, or neither of these two approaches would be an appropriate resource allocation method. In each case, give reasons for your answer.
   a) The manufacture of cigarettes
   b) The construction of an apartment building
   c) A machine shop
   d) The manufacture of canned dog foods
   e) A printing establishment which prints handbills, posters, business calling cards, etc., to customer order.

5. What are some of the effects that the type of operations in which a firm is engaged—job lot, continuous manufacturing, or large complex limited-volume production—might have on the type(s) of departmentalization it chooses in designing its organization structure.

6. The introduction of slack into a processing system may effect both an increase in certain operating costs and a decrease in others. Discuss. Give specific examples to support your answer.

7. Evaluate the following statement made by a systems analyst: "In the utilization of simple critical path techniques, if you control time, you simultaneously control costs. By reducing the time required to complete a project via PERT methods, you will reduce the total costs of completing the project."

8. Why are operations planning and control methods for large complex projects characterized, in general, as satisficing?

9. Why do input allocation, rather than input acquisition decisions, assume greater importance for the manager in the short run?

10. The Bou Kee Company builds marine instruments to customer specification. An order is received on Friday, March 2 and company planners determine that work on the project can be initiated the following Monday. The particular instrument consists of two standard and one custom-built subassemblies. The standard subassemblies are purchased in completed form. The lead time for the first subassembly is known to be 21 days from the date on which the order is placed, while the lead time for the second, purchased from a local wholesaler, will only be four days. It takes two days to assemble the two standard subassemblies together after they have been received by Bou Kee.

Special machining is required on the third component taking 30 days including design, set-up time and fabrication, after which a three-day special finishing operation is performed. Final assembly of the custom and standard components can be accomplished in two days with an additional day required for installation. Before the instrument leaves the plant, it is given a special test. This test takes three days and is begun immediately after final assembly.

The customer is to be notified seven working days before the scheduled installation date in order that his boat may be properly readied for the installation. A company representative delivers and installs the instrument. The customer's boat is located two travel days from the Bou Kee assembly plant. Installation and testing of the instrument in the customer's boat requires one day. The Bou Kee Company operates on a 7-day week.

a) Draw a schematic diagram to aid in project planning and control.
b) What is the scheduled date for the completed installation?
c) Might the firm's scheduling decisions be different if the lead times and number of days to perform each operation were not known for certain by management? Why?

11. You are given the following network of activities and events. Based on this network, answer the questions which appear below. The activity times are stated in weeks, and represent optimistic, most likely, and pessimistic estimates. All individuals working on the project are paid $2.50 per hour.

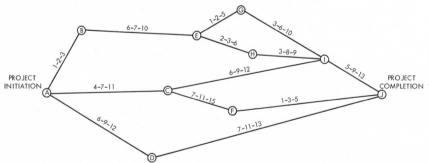

NOTE: The activity lines in the above schematic have not been drawn to scale.
a) Using the most likely estimates, determine the critical path for the network.
b) Which activity path has the most slack?

c) Assume that the resources utilized in each path are completely transferable to any other path. By how much time could the project be shortened by transferring resources from path A–C–I–J to the critical path?

d) Assume (1) that all time estimates are based upon the utilization of 5-man crews working a 40-hour week, (2) that *none* of the resources used in any path are transferable to another and (3) that the crew size is fixed.

(1) What actions would you take in order to complete the project in 24 weeks?

(2) What effect would your decisions have upon the total costs of the project as compared to your decisions had the project not required completion until 30 weeks after its initiation?

SELECTED REFERENCES

ARYGRIS, CHRIS. "Human Problems with Budgets," *Harvard Business Review*, 31 (January–December, 1953), 97–110.

BARTIZAL, J. R. *Budget Principles and Procedures.* Englewood Cliffs, N. J.: Prentice-Hall, Inc., 1942.

BIGELOW, C. G. "Bibliography on Project Planning and Control by Network Analysis: 1959–1961," *Operations Research,* 10 (1962), 728.

BOCK, ROBERT H., and HOLSTEIN, WILLIAM K. *Production Planning and Control.* Columbus, Ohio: Charles E. Merrill Books, Inc., 1963.

BOULANGER, DAVID. "Program Evaluation and Review Technique," *Advanced Management,* 26 (July–August, 1961), 8–12.

CLARK, WALLACE. *The Gantt Chart.* 3d ed. New York: Pitman Publishing Corp., 1952.

EVANS, MARSHALL K. "Profit Planning," *Harvard Business Review,* 37 (July–August, 1959), 45–54.

EVARTS, HARRY F. *Introduction to PERT.* Boston: Allyn & Bacon, Inc., 1964.

FORD, L. R., and FULKERSON, D. R. *Flows in Networks.* Princeton, N. J.: Princeton University Press, 1962.

FULKERSON, D. R. "A Network Flow Computation for Project Cost Curves," *Management Science,* 7 (January, 1961), 167–178.

HOLT, C. C.; MODIGLIANI, F.; MUTH, J. F.; and SIMON, H. A. *Planning Production, Inventories, and Work Force.* Englewood Cliffs, N. J.: Prentice-Hall, Inc., 1960.

JEWELL, WILLIAM S. "Risk-Taking in Critical Path Analysis," *Management Science,* 11 (January, 1965), 438–443.

McCRIMMIN, K. R., and RYAVEC, C. A. "Analytical Study of the Pert Assumptions," The RAND Corporation Memo, Rm–340A–PR (December, 1962).

McGEE, JOHN F. *Production Planning and Inventory Control.* New York: McGraw-Hill Book Co., Inc., 1958.

MILLER, ROBERT W.   "How to Plan and Control with Pert," *Harvard Business Review,* 40 (March–April, 1962), 93–104.

MITCHELL, WILLIAM E.   "Cash Forecasting: The Four Methods Compared," *The Controller,* 28 (April, 1960), 162–166, 194.

MOORE, FRANKLIN G.   *Production Control.* 2d ed. New York: McGraw-Hill Book Co., Inc., 1959.

MUTH, J. F., and THOMPSON, G. L.   *Industrial Scheduling.* Englewood Cliffs, N. J.: Prentice-Hall, Inc., 1963.

PENDLETON, S. A.   "Variable Budgeting for Planning and Control," *NAA Bulletin,* 36 (1954), 323–334.

STEDRY, A.   *Budget Control and Cost Behavior.* Englewood Cliffs, N. J.: Prentice-Hall, Inc., 1960.

WILSON, JAMES D.   "Dynamic Budgeting—Getting the Most From Your Program," *Dun's Review and Modern Industry,* 59 (1957), 62, 128–132.

CHAPTER 16

ALLOCATION OF RESOURCES: MATHEMATICAL PROGRAMMING

THE past two decades have witnessed the development and use of a number of mathematical techniques for arriving at optimum solutions for problems involving the allocation of resources. These approaches have made feasible the solution of many types of problems which heretofore could only be dealt with (if at all) by extremely lengthy, cumbersome, and trial-and-error methods. Utilization of the electronic computer has greatly facilitated the application of these techniques, and their use will probably become even more widespread in the future.

We will focus attention in this chapter on several of the better known mathematical programming methods: (1) the algebraic, simplex, and transportation methods of linear programming, (2) non-linear programming, and (3) dynamic programming. Specific step-by-step procedures will be presented for the solution to problems by the algebraic and transportation methods, both of which can easily be handled by those familiar with basic algebra. We will treat the simplex technique, non-linear and dynamic programming only in a general way because of the mathematical and/or computational complexities involved in their use.

Two conditions must exist for any of the mathematical programming techniques to be applicable. First, the decision maker must state explicitly the objective which he seeks in solution of the problems. This objective must be framed in quantitative terms, such as profit maximization or cost minimization. In programming problems, the objective chosen by the decision maker is referred to as the *objective function*. Second, there must exist one or more restrictions (or constraints) on the range of alternatives available to the manager. In other words, we are dealing with problems involving the allocation of *scarce* resources, in which *limited* supplies of men, materials, time, etc., are available. Thus, programming problems center around the optimization of the objective function within the constraints imposed upon the decision maker.

Unlike some quantitative approaches (such as breakeven analysis) none of the programming methods provides answers to decision problems through the solution of a *single* equation. Rather, each consists of a *formalized search procedure* by means of which the decision maker moves closer and closer to the optimum solution through a series of successive steps or iterations. It is this formalized, logically-determined sequencing of problem-solving steps which represents the major advantage of programming over previous trial-and-error approaches.

In addition to providing a powerful decision-making tool for the manager, mathematical programming represents an important area for study for at least two other reasons. First, like all quantitative approaches, programming enables the manager to visualize more clearly the key variables and relationships in decision problems. Second, a general understanding of these methods is often valuable even for those managers not directly involved in programming work if their organizations are to make most effective use of these tools. As Stockton has pointed out,

> Line managers—as differentiated from staff specialists or analysts—play an important role in the initial and final stages of problem-solving projects, that is, in the formulation of the problem and in the evaluation and application of the findings. They must, as a consequence, be capable of effective communication with any staff specialist, including the operations analyst.[1]

In fact, lack of understanding of the potential of mathematical programming by line managers is one important reason why its use is still somewhat limited today.

The reader should not infer from the above that mathematical programming, however powerful, represents a panacea which can be used indiscriminately for the solution of all allocation decision problems. An important consideration in the application of programming techniques, as with all decision approaches, is that of weighing the costs of using the tool against the returns derived from so

---

[1] R. Stansbury Stockton, *Introduction to Linear Programming* (Boston: Allyn & Bacon, Inc., 1960), p. 8.

doing. Employment of programming methods necessitates framing of the decision problem in quantitative terms, the gathering of relevant data and, in many cases, extensive calculations. If the total sum of money involved in making a particular decision is relatively small, the costs incurred by carrying out these programming steps may well exceed any possible savings or profits that might be realized by the use of programming in lieu of a purely intuitive approach to dealing with the problem.

Nor are the mathematical programming techniques applicable to all types of allocation problems. As will be indicated more fully in the following sections, only problems possessing certain fundamental characteristics may be handled by some of the programming methods. As their name implies, the linear programming techniques, for example, have applicability only to problems framed such that all relationships are linear ones. Further, many important allocation problems involve such a level of complexity that their solution is not possible by means of mathematical programming. For instance, although it is possible under certain conditions to optimize the assignment of men to machines in a job shop through the use of programming, optimization of the entire job shop operation cannot be achieved by the application of programming techniques. Thus, it is important for the decision maker to understand not only how mathematical programming may be applied to problems, but also the conditions under which such application is feasible.

LINEAR PROGRAMMING: ALGEBRAIC METHOD

The least complex of the mathematical programming methods designed to arrive at optimum solutions for resource allocation problems is the algebraic method of linear programming. The technique calls for the manipulation of a number of simple linear equations and inequalities. It is also sometimes referred to as the graphic-algebraic method, since the algebraic manipulation may be facilitated by the development of a graph to permit visualization of the constraints and the objective function. In fact, optimum solutions to the kinds of problems which may be dealt with by the algebraic method may often be approximated solely by graphic means. In the following sections we will supplement our treatment of the programming mathematics by their graphic presentation so that the reader may visualize the method both algebraically and geometrically.

Although the algebraic technique has applicability to a variety of problems, it is especially useful in handling *two-variable* product mix problems—i.e., problems in which the decision maker wants to determine the optimum number of each of two products to manufacture when the resources required for their production are limited. A major limitation of the method is its primary applicability to problems involving only two variables. Although three variables can be handled by the technique, their visualization in three-dimensional space is often difficult. (For *n* variable problems, the simplex technique is employed.) It should be noted, however, that the algebraic method can be employed to handle problems involving any number of *restrictions or constraints*. It is only the number of variables which must be so limited.

There are three basic steps involved in the application of the algebraic method: (1) determination of the restrictions or constraints, (2) the choice of an appropriate objective function, and (3) development of an optimum solution (or solutions). In addition, the problem under consideration must possess two fundamental characteristics if the technique is to be employed: (1) both the objective function and all of the restrictions must be expressed in linear terms, and (2) all of the profit and cost data relative to the problem must be known for certain. These two conditions are often referred to as *linearity* and *certainty*.

Application of the algebraic method may be illustrated best by the use of an example. As an illustration, we shall consider the following problem, and treat each of the steps in its solution:

The Atlas Chemical Company produces two chemical compounds, X and Y. The resources available for making the compounds are:

10 hours of labor
600 pounds of chemical element *A*
900 pounds of element *B*
1000 pounds of element *C*

Each unit of compound X requires: 1/50 hours of labor, 2 pounds of element *A* and 5 pounds of element *C*. Element *B* is not used in its production. Each unit of compound Y requires: 1/50 hours of labor, 1 pound of element *A* and 2 pounds of element *B*. Element *C* is not required. Profits obtained by the Atlas Chemical Company from each unit of compound X are $6.00; and from each unit of Y, $4.00.

Our objective is to determine the number of units of each compound which should be produced if total profits for the firm are to be maximized.

Expression of the Constraints

The first step in dealing with this problem is to develop mathematical expressions for each of the constraints and to illustrate these graphically. First, let us consider the labor restriction. Each unit of compound X requires $1/50$ hours of labor. Thus, if only X is produced, the 10 hours of labor available would permit the manufacture of 500 units. Similarly, enough labor is available for the production of 500 units of compound Y if no X is made, since the number of hours of labor required for the manufacture of each unit of compound Y is also $1/50$. Further, for every $1/50$ man hour taken away from the manufacture of Y and devoted to X, one additional unit of X, and one unit less of Y may be produced, and vice versa. For example, if all 10 hours of labor are allocated to Y, 500 units of Y and zero units of X can be produced; if 9 49/50 hours are allocated to Y, and $1/50$ to X, 499 units of Y and 1 unit of X can be manufactured, and so on. This constraint may be expressed in linear terms, since the number of units of either compound which must be given up to permit the production of the other is constant. In this case the *rate of substitution* is one for one.

The reader will recall from his study of algebra that the equation for a straight line may be obtained if two x values and two y values are known by substituting these values in the formula:

$$\frac{y - y_1}{x - x_1} = \frac{y_2 - y_1}{x_2 - x_1}.$$

Substituting in this formula the two sets of x and y values that are given in the chemical problem ($500x$, $0y$; and $0x$, $500y$), we obtain the following linear equation expressing the labor hours restriction: $x + y = 500.$[2] The reader should note, however, that, depending on

---

[2] These calculations proceed as follows:

1. $\dfrac{y - 0}{x - 500} = \dfrac{500 - 0}{0 - 500}$
2. $-500(y) = 500(x - 500)$
3. $500x + 500y = 250,000$
4. $x + y = 500$

We should note that this same equation can be determined more quickly by solving: $\dfrac{x}{a} + \dfrac{y}{b} = 1$; where a represents the point at which the line crosses the x–axis; and b, the point at which it crosses the y–axis. Or, for the labor requirements restriction:

(1) $\dfrac{x}{500} + \dfrac{y}{500} = 1$; and

(2) Multiplying both sides of the equation by 500; $x + y = 500$.

For further summary information regarding linear fractions which may be useful in dealing with graphic-algebraic problems, the reader is referred to Appendix A at the end of this book.

the other restrictions in the problem, the decision maker may choose to produce a number of units of X and Y, the sum of which is *less than* 500. The labor constraint equation only indicates the *maximum* number of units which may be produced with the labor resources available. Thus, this equation must be transformed to represent an inequality: $x + y \leq 500$. This inequality is illustrated in Figure 16–1. The shaded area to its lower left indicates the *strategy space* available to the decision maker with respect to the labor constraint. This area represents the ranges of possible combinations of units of x and y that can be produced with 10 hours of labor as a restriction. It should be noted that this area is bounded to the left and at the bottom by the x and y axes respectively, since negative units of production are an impossibility. We now turn attention to the available raw materials restraints.

Expressions of linear inequalities may be developed for each of the raw materials constraints in the chemical problem following the procedure outlined above. For element A, the expression is $2x + y \leq 600$; for element B: $y \leq 450$; and for element C: $x \leq 200$. These inequalities have the following meaning:

1.   A quantity of element A is available for the production of any combination of units of compounds X and Y as long as the number of units of Y plus two times the number of units of X does not ex-

FIGURE 16–1. Strategy Space Circumscribed by Labor Hours Constraint

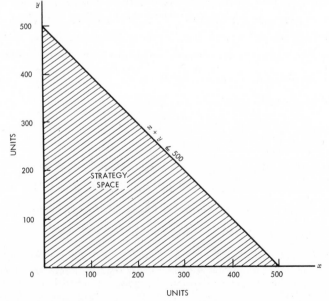

ceed 600. For example, if 400 units of Y are produced, the maximum number of X which can be manufactured is 100, since Y (400) plus two times X (200) equals the limiting value of 600.

2.   A quantity of element B is available for the production of 450 units of compound Y.

3.   A quantity of element C is available for the production of 200 units of compound X.

The reader should note that the reason the inequality representing the element B constraint contains no x term, and that for element C, no y term is that the production of compound X does not require the use of element B; nor does the manufacture of Y call for element C.

Graphing all the constraints in the problem will define the total strategy space available to the decision maker. This space which is represented by the shaded area in Figure 16–2 is often referred to as the *feasibility polygon*. The production of any combination of units of X and Y within this polygon is feasible with the resources available, although certain combinations will produce greater profits for the firm than others. It is the determination of that combination of production which will yield the greatest profit for the chemical company to which we will next turn our attention.

FIGURE 16–2. Feasibility Polygon

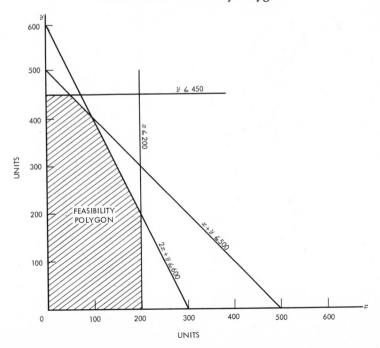

Expression of the Objective Function

As indicated previously, the chemical manufacturer will realize a profit of $6 from the manufacture (and sale) of each unit of compound X, and a profit of $4 from each unit of Y. To achieve any given level of total profits from the operation, any one of a number of different combinations of X and Y might be produced. For instance, a profit of $300 would be realized by the manufacture of: 50 units of X alone; 75 units of Y alone; 30 units of X and 30 units of Y; and so on. All possible combinations of X and Y which will produce any given amount of profit may be represented by a linear equation, which when superimposed upon the feasibility polygon is referred to as an *iso-profit line*. As will be pointed out below, it is *not* necessary to develop iso-profit equations or graph iso-profit lines to solve problems by the algebraic method. We illustrate four iso-profit lines for the chemical problem in Figure 16–3, however, to enable the reader to visualize the possible combinations of production of X and Y which will produce various levels of profit for the manager. As may be noted in Figure 16–3, the slopes of all of the iso-profit lines are identical ($-\frac{3}{2}$), which will be the case with all problems of the type we are considering. The existence of identical slopes is due to the fact that the per unit contribution to profits of

FIGURE 16–3. Iso-Profit Lines Superimposed on Feasibility Polygon

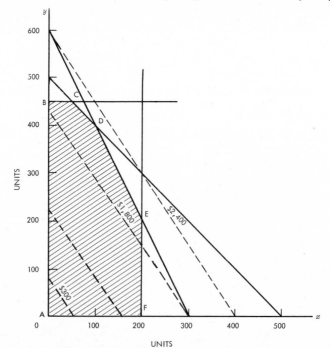

UNITS

both X and Y is constant regardless of the number of units produced In the chemical problem, each unit of Y always contributes $4 to total profits or ⅔ as much as the per unit contribution of X of $6.

Since profit maximization is the objective function, solution of the programming problem requires finding that iso-profit line representing the greatest profitability within the constraints of the feasibility polygon. A key characteristic of all linear programming problems is that *the optimizing iso-profit line will always intersect one or more of the corner points of the feasibility polygon.* For this reason, to solve the chemical problem we need only to: (1) examine total profitability at each of points $A, B, C, D, E,$ and F on the feasibility polygon illustrated in Figure 16–3 and (2) select that point which represents the most profitable product mix. Since point A represents zero production, it may be immediately dismissed as an optimum solution, and close examination of only the other five points is required.

Selecting the Optimum Alternative

The total profits which will be realized at corner point B on the y-axis, and at point F on the x-axis may be determined by inspection. At point B, 450 units of Y alone will be manufactured, and total profits at $4 per unit are $1800. The manufacture of 200 units of X and no units of Y at point F will yield a profit of $6(200) or $1200. The determination of production levels, and hence profits, at points $C, D,$ and E, on the other hand, will require some simple calculations. Each of these points represents the intersection of two of the constraint lines. Therefore, the values of X and Y at each of the points must simultaneously satisfy each of the two equations involved. The determination of these values by means of the solution of the simultaneous equations proceeds as follows:

1. Point C.
$$x + y = 500$$
$$y = 450$$
By subtraction and
$$x = 50$$
$$y = 450$$

2. Point D.
$$2x + y = 600$$
$$x + y = 500$$
By subtraction and
$$x = 100$$
$$y = 400$$

3. Point E. By substituting $x = 200$ in the equation $2x + y = 600, y = 200.$

The total profit realized from each of the product mix combinations at the corner points may be obtained by multiplying, for both X and Y, the number of units produced by the profit per unit. These calculations, which are illustrated in Figure 16–4, indicate that the

FIGURE 16–4

Evaluation of Allocation Strategies

Corner Point	Units of X	@	= Profit from X	Units of Y	@	= Profit from Y	Total Profit
A......	0	$6	$ 0	0	$4	$ 0	$ 0
B......	0	6	0	450	4	1800	1800
C......	50	6	300	450	4	1800	2100
D......	100	6	600	400	4	1600	2200
E......	200	6	1200	200	4	800	2000
F......	200	6	1200	0	4	0	1200

Source: Corner points, Figure 16–3.

optimum solution to the problem lies at point D, and that 100 units of compound X, and 400 units of compound Y should be manufactured at a total profit of $2200.

The Existence of Alternative Optimum Solutions

In some linear programming problems, unlike that just examined, a number of equally optimum solutions may exist. Multiple solutions will occur when, and only when, *the slope of the iso-profit lines is equal to the slope of any one of the lines representing the constraints.* In such a case, all feasible points on the constraint line with its slope identical to that of the iso-profit lines will represent optimum solutions (provided that the points represent whole numbers if the units being dealt with are indivisible).

The existence of multiple solutions may be demonstrated by modifying the chemical manufacturing problem so that the profit per unit for compound Y is $3 instead of $4. The slope of the iso-profit lines now becomes -2 since the per unit profit for compound Y ($3) is one-half of that for compound X. This slope is identical to that for the line representing the restriction for element A $(2x + y \leq 600)$, and the iso-profit line representing total profits of $1800 lies on top of the element A constraint line. As may be noted in Figure 16–5, all product mix combinations in whole units falling on these identical lines from point D (100,400) to point E (200,200) are both feasible, and will produce a profit of $1800. That these points represent optimum mixes may be noted visually, for:

FIGURE 16–5. Multiple Optimum Solutions

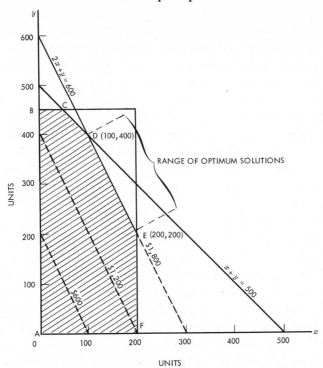

(1) moving the iso-profit line to the right brings it outside of the feasibility polygon, while (2) moving it to the left results in a smaller level of production, and hence lower profits, for both compound X and compound Y.

It should be pointed out that the existence of multiple optimum solutions in problems such as the above may be determined without developing and comparing the slopes of the iso-profit and constraint lines to see whether or not they are equal. Rather, the existence of alternative optima may be noted by inspection. All that is required is to determine whether any two corner points yield *identical maximum* profits. If so, all feasible points on the constraint line connecting these two corner points also yield optimum solutions. This is due to the fact that all such points fall on the same iso-profit line as do the two corner points.

LINEAR PROGRAMMING: SIMPLEX METHOD

The simplex method, which was developed by George B. Dantzig in 1947, is the most widely applicable of the linear programming techniques. Both the algebraic method and the transportation technique (which will be discussed in the next section) are but special cases óf the general simplex procedure. Among the many types of problems which may be dealt with by the simplex method are those involving: product mixes, job assignment, capacity allocation, production scheduling, transportation routing, and the evaluation of complex bids in purchasing.[3] The major advantage of the simplex technique over the algebraic method is that it is designed to handle any number of variables. On the other hand, the simplex method—although not necessarily involving complex mathematics—usually requires a lengthy and involved computational procedure even for problems with as few as four or five variables. Therefore, we will only outline in general some of the key characteristics of the approach.

Like the algebraic method, conditions of certainty and linearity are essential if the simplex method is to be applied. Simplex is further similar to the algebraic method in that the procedure first calls for framing the problem and explicitly stating in quantitative terms both the objective function and the constraints. Once this has been accomplished, an initial (trial) solution to the problem which satisfies the constraints is developed. Modifications of the trial solution are then formulated and examined, and the most favorable of these (in terms of the objective function) is incorporated into a second solution. This procedure is repeated until no further modifications improve the solution.[4] Thus, the simplex technique is a step-by-step search procedure in which the optimum solution is progressively approached. The procedure is designed so that the decision maker does not have to fully consider all possible alternative feasible solutions to the problem. This formalized shortcutting represents a major contribution of the method over trial-and-error approaches.

LINEAR PROGRAMMING: TRANSPORTATION METHOD

Another well known technique for developing optimum solutions for allocation problems is the transportation method of linear programming which is a special case of the simplex technique. Compared to simplex, the transportation method can be understood

---

[3] Edward H. Bowman and Robert B. Fetter, *Analysis for Production Management*, (rev. ed.; Homewood, Ill.: Richard D. Irwin, Inc., 1961), p. 101.

[4] For a discussion of this step-by-step procedure, see *ibid.*, pp. 82 ff., Stockton, *op. cit.*, pp. 43–72; or Harvey C. Bunke, *Linear Programming: A Primer* (Iowa City, Iowa: Bureau of Business and Economic Research, College of Business Administration, State University of Iowa, 1960), pp. 19–28.

much more easily with a limited background in mathematics. It does not call for the development and manipulation of linear equations, but rather involves only simple addition, subtraction and multiplication. On the other hand, application of the method is limited to a much narrower variety of problems than is the simplex. As its name implies, the transportation method is most applicable to problems in which the decision involves selection of optimum transportation routes. As we will indicate later, however, the method may be employed in the solution of other classes of problems as well.

Statement of the Problem

The transportation problem may be stated as follows: Given a number of sources of supply (origins) and destinations, and the costs of shipping a good from each source to each destination, the objective is to select that combination of routes which will minimize total costs. As with the use of both the graphic and simplex methods of linear programming, the transportation technique is applicable only to problems involving: (1) linear relationships between the decision variables and (2) conditions of certainty. That is, the per unit transportation costs from any source to any destination must remain constant regardless of the number of items shipped; [5] and these costs must be known for certain by the decision maker in advance. In addition, a third condition must exist if the method is to be applicable—homogeneity or one-for-one substitution. For example, if a manager gives up shipping 50 units from source A to destination X, the condition of homogeneity requires that he be able to substitute in lieu thereof the shipment of exactly 50 units from other sources to this destination. The reader will recall that this condition of homogeneity is not a requisite for the application of the algebraic method (nor is it for simplex). In our problem involving the chemical manufacturer, for example, the production of two units of compound Y had to be given up to release enough element A to produce one unit of compound X.

Developing an Initial Feasible Solution

Like the simplex technique, the transportation method is a formalized search procedure involving a number of successive itera-

---

[5] Some problems involving step-function costs may be dealt with by the transportation method by treating each step as a separate linear cost source. See, for example, Bunke, *op. cit.*, p. 15.

tions leading to one or more optimum solutions. The first step called for is that of developing an initial feasible solution. Then, unless this solution happens to be an optimum one, various alternative routes are considered and evaluated one by one until an optimum has been attained. To illustrate the application of the transportation method we will consider an extremely simple problem —one involving only three sources and three destinations. This problem can be solved more quickly by inspection than by use of the transportation technique. However, it will enable us to focus our attention on the basic aspects of the method without becoming involved with an unduly large number of calculations. Further, exactly the same procedure may be employed regardless of the number of sources and destinations comprising the problem.

For our illustrative example, let us assume that a manufacturer has three plants with the following monthly production capacities:

> Plant 1   200 units
> Plant 2   50 units
> Plant 3   200 units

and that the company has three warehouses which must be supplied from these factories, with the following monthly demand requirements:

> Warehouse A   100 units
> Warehouse B   150 units
> Warehouse C   200 units

Given the transportation costs from each factory to each warehouse indicated in Figure 16–6, our problem is to determine the number of units which should be shipped from each source to each destination to minimize these costs.

The first step in developing the initial feasible solution is to design a matrix indicating (1) all plant capacities and warehouse

FIGURE 16–6

Transportation Costs (in $)

Source	Destination		
	Warehouse A	*Warehouse B*	*Warehouse C*
Plant 1...................	4	1	2
Plant 2...................	6	5	6
Plant 3...................	3	7	4

requirements and (2) the transportation costs for each route in the upper diagonal halves of the matrix cells. Such a matrix is shown in Figure 16–7. The next step is to assign shipments of various

FIGURE 16–7

Initial Transportation Matrix

Source	Destination			Total Capacity
	Warehouse A	Warehouse B	Warehouse C	
Plant 1......	$4	$1	$2	200
Plant 2......	$6	$5	$6	50
Plant 3......	$3	$7	$4	200
Total Requirements	100	150	200	450

numbers of units in the lower diagonal halves of the cells in such a manner that the total number of units shipped from each plant will exactly equal its capacity, and the number of units shipped to each warehouse will exactly meet its requirements.

There are several different ways in which this initial trial assignment may be made.[6] The procedure we recommend is to first assign as many units as possible to the cell with the lowest transportation cost. Then this step should be repeated for the cell with the next lowest cost, and so on, until all capacity requirements are met. An initial solution to our problem developed by following this procedure is shown in Figure 16–8.

It should be noted that in following this procedure, sometimes cells with costs lower than others which are used have to be passed over, since their use would result in either the plant capacities or demand requirements being exceeded. For example, in the matrix in Figure 16–8, we first assigned as many units as possible to the three cells with the lowest costs—1B ($1), 1C ($2), and 3A ($3). The assign-

---

[6] One of the more widely known of these is the so-called "northwest corner rule" by which the decision maker assigns units first to the cell in the northwest corner of the matrix, and then proceeds "step by step, away from the northwest corner until, finally, a value is reached in the southeast corner." Churchman, Ackoff & Arnoff, *Introduction to Operations Research* (New York: John Wiley & Sons, Inc., 1957), p. 285. If the manager is analyzing the effectiveness of an existing distribution system, another approach for determining the initial assignment is to select the firm's existing routes, on the assumption that, although not optimum ones, they will probably be closer to an optimum solution than any arbitrary initial assignments.

FIGURE 16–8

Initial Feasible Solution

Source	Destination			Total Capacity
	Warehouse A	Warehouse B	Warehouse C	
Plant 1......	$4	$1 ⟋ 150	$2 ⟋ 50	200
Plant 2......	$6	$5	$6 ⟋ 50	50
Plant 3......	$3 ⟋ 100	$7	$4 ⟋ 100	200
Total Requirements	100	150	200	450

ment of 150 units to 1B and 50 units to 1C effected the full utilization of Plant 1's capacity of 200 units; and thus cell 1A ($4) had to be passed over. Assignment was next made of 100 units to cell 3C ($4). After this had been accomplished, the only remaining unused cell to which additional units could be assigned without exceeding the capacity or demand requirements was 2C ($6)—cell 2B with lower costs ($5) had to be passed over.

In making the initial assignment, it is also extremely important that the *number of cells used equals the rim requirements of the problem minus one.* "Rim requirements" is defined as the number of sources plus the number of destinations, which in our example is 6. This requirement is essential not only in the development of the initial solution, but for all succeeding solutions tried in working out the problem. If the number of used cells is either greater or less than the number of rim requirements minus one, a condition known as *degeneracy* will exist and the problem is not soluble. Methods for dealing with degeneracy, if it is encountered, will be dealt with in a later section after we have examined the fundamentals of the transportation procedure.

Development and Evaluation of Alternative Routes

By our following the procedure outlined above, the initial solution shown in Figure 16–8 happens to be an optimum one. This will often be the case with extremely simple transportation problems such as the one we have been considering; but will not usually be the case with more complex problems.

So that we may illustrate the full transportation procedure we will formulate another trial solution which is considerably less than

FIGURE 16–9

Initial Trial Transportation Solution

Source	Destination			Total Capacity
	Warehouse A	Warehouse B	Warehouse C	
Plant 1............	$4 50	$1 150	$2 0	200
Plant 2............	$6 0	$5 0	$6 50	50
Plant 3............	$3 50	$7 0	$4 150	200
Total Requirements........	100	150	200	450

optimum. This solution is illustrated in Figure 16–9. The reader will note that there are four unused cells in the non-optimum solution in Figure 16–9—no units have been scheduled for transportation in cells 1C, 2A, 2B, or 3B. The first step involved in developing an alternative, and possibly more optimum, assignment than that in the initial solution is to examine the effect on total costs of the *transfer of one unit* from any of the five used cells to each of the unused cells in turn.

First let us consider the transfer of one unit to unused cell 1C, which is illustrated in Figure 16–10.[7] Note that this transfer neces-

FIGURE 16–10

Transfer of One Unit to an Unused Cell

Source	Destination			Total Capacity
	Warehouse A	Warehouse B	Warehouse C	
Plant 1............	$4 ~~50~~ 49	$1 150	$2 ~~0~~ 1	200
Plant 2............	$6 0	$5 0	$6 50	50
Plant 3............	$3 ~~50~~ 51	$7 0	$4 ~~150~~ 149	200
Total Requirements.......	100	150	200	450

---

[7] A somewhat different approach for developing alternative routes is the modified transportation method, or *modi*. The difference between modi and the approach we are suggesting here is one of form rather than substance. For a description of the modi method, see Bunke, *op. cit.*, pp. 5–16.

sitates altering the assignment of units in three of the used cells, 1A, 1C, and 3C. These changes are mandatory in order to ensure that the capacities of each plant continue to be fully utilized and that the demand requirements for each warehouse continue to be fully met. For example, the demand requirements of Warehouse 3 (200 units) are now exactly met by the shipment of 1 unit from Plant 1, 50 units from Plant 2, and 149 units from Plant 3 rather than by 50 units from Plant 2 and 150 units from Plant 3.

Before evaluating the changes in total costs which will result from this transfer of one unit to unused cell 1C, two observations should be noted. First, the number of cells used at this stage of the transportation procedure does not necessarily have to equal the rim requirements minus one. This is because the transfer of one unit does not represent an alternative solution but rather a tentative exploration. In the above illustration, for example, the number of cells in use is 6 which is *equal* to the number of rim requirements. Second, in deciding which used cells to modify in effecting the transfer of one unit to an unused cell, it is desirable to choose the least cumbersome route—i.e., the one in which the fewest number of cells require modification. In many cases the simplest transfer procedure may be accomplished as follows: [8]

1. Select one used cell which is in the same row as the unused cell being evaluated, and another used cell which is in the same column as the unused cell; providing that a third used cell exists which is both (1) in the same row as one of the above-mentioned used cells, and (2) in the same column as the other. In Figure 16–10, for example, cell 3C is in the same column as the unused cell being evaluated, 1C; 1A is in the same row as 1C; and 3A is in the same row as 3C and in the same column as 1A.

2. Subtract one unit from each of the first two above-mentioned used cells (3C, 1A), and

3. Add one unit to both the unused cell being evaluated (1C) and the third of the above-mentioned used cells (3A).

Once the single unit has been transferred to one of the unused cells, evaluation of the effect of this modification upon total costs is a relatively simple matter. Reference again to Figure 16–10 indicates that the addition of one unit to cell 1C adds $2 to the trans-

---

[8] In other cases, such simple transfer routes as described here are not possible, and the reader will find it necessary to develop more lengthy routes. This will usually present no major problems as long as it is kept firmly in mind that all source and destination requirements must be exactly met.

portation costs, and that the costs of adding or subtracting one unit from each of the *used* cells which have been involved in the transfer are as follows: 1A, —$4; 3A, +$3; and 3C, —$4. Summing these four figures indicates that for each unit transferred to cell 1C, total transportation costs are reduced by $3: $2 — $4 + $3 — $4 = —$3. It would therefore be profitable for the decision maker to transfer *as many units as possible* to cell 1C. Before he decides to do so, however, each of the other unused cells should be similarly examined, for the transfer of a unit to any one of them may effect an even greater reduction in total costs than the transfer to 1C. Following the prescribed procedure we find that the cost changes effected by the transfer of one unit to each of the other three unused cells in Figure 16–9 are as shown in Figure 16–11.

FIGURE 16–11

Evaluation of Unused Cells

Unused Cell	Cost Change for Individual Cells Involved in Transfer (in $)	Net Change
2A	2A, +6; 2C, −6; 3A, −3; 3C, +4	+1
2B	1A, +4; 1B, −1; 2B, +5; 2C, −6; 3A, −3; 3C, +4	+3
3B	1A, +4; 1B, −1; 3A, −3; 3B, +7	+7

The reader will note that each of the above modifications results in *increased* transportation costs.[9] Therefore, only the transfer of as many units as possible to cell 1C should be given further consideration. Sometimes, however, *more than one* of the unused cells to which a unit is transferred may provide the basis for a more satisfactory solution than the initial solution. Or, the transfer of one unit to a particular unused cell may result in *no change* in the transportation costs from the initial solution. If so, the total costs which will be incurred if as many units as possible are transferred to this cell will be the same as they were for the initial assignment.

In deciding to which unused cell, if any, such a transfer should be effected, the following rules are recommended:

1. If the transfer results in a reduction in transportation costs for only one of the unused cells, that cell is to be chosen.

2. If the transfer brings about a reduction in costs for more than one unused cell, choose that cell for which the reduction is the greatest. Or, in other

---

[9] We should also note that the transfer route involving unused cell 2B is an example of the type mentioned above in footnote 8, in which a larger number of cells must be involved in the transfer.

words, select the cell for which the net change has the greatest negative value.[10] If this value is identical for two or more unused cells, evaluate the transfer of as many units as possible to each. Then, select from among these possible transfer routes the one which brings about the greatest reduction in *total costs.* For example, if the transfer of one unit to each of two unused cells results in a cost reduction of $2, and it is possible to transfer 100 units to one, but only 50 units to the other, in the reassignment, select the former. This will effect a reduction in total costs of $200 as compared with only $100 for the latter. If the greatest reduction in total costs is identical for two or more reassignment routes, either may be chosen.

3. If the transfer does not effect a cost reduction for any of the cells, *the initial solution is an optimum one.* If so, and the transfer results in *increased costs for all* of the unused cells, the initial solution is the *only* optimum solution. If so, but *no change in costs* is effected by transfer to one of more of the unused cells, the transfer of as many units as possible to these cells will provide *alternative optimum* solutions.[11]

The transfer of as many units as possible to the cell so selected may be accomplished quite simply. The transfer of 50 units to cell 1C in our example is illustrated in Figure 16–12. The reader should note that the number of units which it is possible to so transfer is always equal to the number of units in that used cell involved in the transfer containing the *smallest number of units of those used cells from which units are to be subtracted in the reassignment.*

FIGURE 16–12

Second Feasible Solution

Source	Destination			Total Capacity
	Warehouse A	Warehouse B	Warehouse C	
Plant 1............	$4 \qquad 0	$1 \qquad 150	$2 \qquad 50	200
Plant 2...........	$6 \qquad 0	$5 \qquad 0	$6 \qquad 50	50
Plant 3............	$3 \qquad 100	$7 \qquad 0	$4 \qquad 100	200
Total Requirements.......	100	150	200	450

[10] It is not essential that the cell with the greatest negative value be chosen; any negative cell may be selected. In some cases, in fact, choice of a negative cell which is not the most negative will result in the greatest improvement in the program over the previous solution. For an example of such a case, see Churchman, Ackoff & Arnoff, *op. cit.,* p. 289.

[11] If more than one optimum solution exists, the decision maker may make his choice among these on the basis of their contribution toward other non-economic objectives. He may prefer, for example, to give as much business as possible to a shipper handling one of the routes on the basis that this firm is a good customer of his company, all economic factors being equal.

In our problem, cell 1A—which contained 50 units—imposes this restriction. It is also important to reiterate that in the completed reassignment: (1) all of the rim requirements must be exactly satisfied, and (2) the number of cells being used must equal one less than the number of rim requirements. Further, none of the used cells may have a negative number of units assigned to it, since this would represent an impossible condition.

Further Steps in the Transportation Method

The above reassignment represents the second feasible solution to the transportation problem. Once this has been developed, exactly the same procedure as indicated above is *repeated* until the transfer of units to the unused cells effects *no further reduction* in transportation costs. When this stage has been reached, we will have one or more optimum solutions, depending upon the conditions indicated in paragraph (3) in the preceding section. As indicated earlier, any of the alternative solutions, including the initial feasible one (if the manager is fortunate), may represent an optimum.

These further steps may be illustrated by the evaluation of each of the unused cells in the second feasible solution in Figure 16–12. The transfer of one unit to each of the four unused cells effects the changes in the transportation costs (shown in Figure 16–13).

FIGURE 16–13

Evaluation of Unused Cells—Second Feasible Solution

Unused Cell	Cost Changes for Individual Cells Involved in Transfer (in $)	Net Change
1A	1A, +4; 1C, −2; 3A, −3; 3C, +4	+3
2A	2A, +6; 2C, −6; 3A, −3; 3C, +4	+1
2B	1B, −1; 1C, +2; 2B, +5; 2C, −6	0
3B	1B, −1; 1C, +2; 3B, +7; 3C, −4	+4

These calculations indicate that the second feasible solution is an optimum one, since in no instance does the transfer of one unit to any of the unused cells effect a reduction in transportation costs. It is only one of *two* optimum solutions, however, since the transfer of units to cell 2B results in no net change in the costs. By effecting the transfer of as many units as possible to this cell, as shown in Figure 16–14, we thus arrive at an alternative optimum solution. That total transportation costs are identical for each of these solutions is indicated in Figures 16–15a and 16–15b.

FIGURE 16–14

Alternative Optimum Solution

Source	Destination			Total Capacity
	Warehouse A	Warehouse B	Warehouse C	
Plant 1..............	$4 / 0	$1 / 100	$2 / 100	200
Plant 2..............	$6 / 0	$5 / 50	$6 / 0	50
Plant 3...............	$3 / 100	$7 / 0	$4 / 100	200
Total Requirements ..	100	150	200	450

FIGURE 16–15a

Transportation Costs—Second Feasible Solution

Cell	Units Shipped	Cost/unit	Transportation Costs
1B.........	150	$1	$ 150
1C.........	50	2	100
2C.........	50	6	300
3A.........	100	3	300
3C.........	100	4	400
Totals......	450		$1250

FIGURE 16–15b

Transportation Costs—Alternative Optimum Solution

Cell	Units Shipped	Cost/unit	Transportation Costs
1B.........	100	$1	$ 100
1C.........	100	2	200
2B.........	50	5	250
3A.........	100	3	300
3C.........	100	4	400
Totals......	450		$1250

Introduction of a Slack Variable

Throughout the previous discussion of the transportation method it was assumed that total plant capacity was equal to the total demand of the three warehouses. In many business problems, however, capacity will exceed demand, and it is important to know not only which transportation routes are optimum, but also which production facilities should not be utilized at full capacity. The answers to both of these questions may be determined by introducing a slight modification into the transportation method as we have presented it thus far. To illustrate this modification, the same data will be employed as in the previous example, except that we will now assume the capacity of Plant 3 to be 300 units instead of 200. This results in a total capacity of 550 units as compared to total demand requirements of 450 units.

To solve this problem, exactly the same procedure as outlined in the previous sections may be employed, except that a *slack variable* is introduced into the transportation matrix. This is slack Warehouse S, shown in Figure 16–16, which represents the hypothetical

FIGURE 16–16.

Transportation Matrix with Slack Variable

Source	Destination				Total Capacity
	Warehouse A	Warehouse B	Warehouse C	Warehouse S	
Plant 1........	$4	$1 150	$2 50	$0	200
Plant 2........	$6	$5	$6	$0 50	50
Plant 3........	$3 100	$7	$4 150	$0 50	300
Total Requirements.......	100	150	200	100	550

destination of those 100 units of excess capacity which will neither be produced nor transported. Since no units will actually be shipped to Warehouse S, transportation costs for each cell in its column are set at zero dollars. The cells in this column are treated in exactly the same way as the "real" cells in the matrix, and in each iteration the effect on total costs of the transfer of one unit to each unused slack cell must also be evaluated. Further, in the development of any feasible solution: (1) the demand requirements of the slack warehouse must be exactly fulfilled as must those of the real warehouses; and (2) if degeneracy is to be avoided, six used cells must be employed (since the rim requirements now number seven).

We will leave it to the reader to work through each iteration in the solution of this problem, since the procedure is no different than that outlined previously. A few words are in order, however, as to the interpretation of Figure 16–16, which represents the optimum solution. The capacity of Plant 1 will be fully utilized, with 150 units being shipped to Warehouse B, and 50 units to Warehouse C. No units will be produced in Plant 2 since all 50 units from this plant are assigned to the slack warehouse. Similarly, the 50 units from Plant 3 assigned to Warehouse S will not be produced—100 units of its production will be shipped to Warehouse A, and 150 units to Warehouse C.[12]

Degeneracy

Earlier we indicated that if the number of used cells in any of the transportation solutions is greater or less than the number of rim requirements minus one, degeneracy will occur and the problem is not soluble. In this section, both the causes of degeneracy and approaches for dealing with this condition will be discussed.

Degeneracy resulting from an excessive number of used cells can be caused only by an improper initial assignment in formulating the problem. In such cases, it is necessary to return to this assignment and modify it so as to satisfy the rim requirements minus one restriction. Degeneracy due to an inadequate number of used cells, on the other hand, may be brought about either by an improper initial assignment or by the normal mechanics of the transportation method itself. Degeneracy will occur during the normal processes of applying the method when: the number of units contained in two or more of the used cells from which units are to be *subtracted* in the transfer is equal to the number of units which will be subtracted from these cells to give the completed reassignment. When this condition exists, one or more of the used cells will be lost in the reassignment. In the reassignment illustrated in Figure 16–17, for example, all of the 100 units contained in both used cells 1B and 2A of the original assignment will be subtracted in obtaining the reassignment. In consequence, the number of used cells in the reassignment matrix equals rim requirements minus two, and the matrix is degenerate.

When degeneracy due to an inadequate number of cells is encountered, the reader should first check the initial assignment to ensure that it is not improper. If not, it will be necessary to add a

---

[12] We are assuming throughout this discussion that the manager is concerned only with present demand in the period under consideration. It may, of course, be desirable to fully utilize all plants in this example so as to be able to meet future demand. Determination of the desirability of such a course of action would require consideration of many other factors, such as inventory carrying costs.

FIGURE 16–17

Occurrence of Degeneracy

Original Assignment

		Destination		Total Capacity
		A	B	
S O U R C E	1	~~100~~ 101	~~100~~ 99	200
	2	~~100~~ 99	~~0~~ 1	100
Total Requirements		200	100	300

Reassignment

		Destination		Total Capacity
		A	B	
S O U R C E	1	200	0	200
	2	0	100	100
Total Requirements		200	100	300

"dummy" used cell to the transportation matrix. This may be accomplished either: (1) by treating one of the unused cells as a used cell with zero units assigned to it, or (2) by adding an artificial, infinitely small number of units (ϵ) to one of the unused cells so as to convert it to a used cell.[13] Both of these approaches accomplish the same objective—to increase the number of used cells so as to equal the rim requirements minus one. Further, treatment of either zero or ϵ cells is identical in the transportation procedure. Sometimes the zero or ϵ may drop out of the problem before the final solution is arrived at; in other problems, the zero or ϵ may remain in the optimum solution or solutions. If so, it is simply ignored. For example, if the final assignment to a particular cell is $100 - \epsilon$, the number of units to be shipped would be 100.

Transportation Method: Other Considerations

In this section we shall consider certain other significant aspects of the transportation method with which the decision maker should be familiar. First, it is possible for the manager to handle problems with the transportation method in which he wishes to rule out the use of one or more source-destination assignments on the basis of some other criterion than cost minimization. For example, the manager in our previous illustration may want to avoid shipping any units from Plant 1 to Warehouse C because lengthy delays are frequently encountered when this route is employed. In such cases,

---

[13] Treatment of one of the unused cells as a used cell with zero units assigned to it is suggested by Bunke, *op. cit.*, p. 12. The use of the artificial ϵ is suggested by Bowman and Fetter, *op. cit.*, pp. 125–27.

the undesirable cells may be eliminated from consideration simply by assigning extremely high costs to them, say \$50,000/unit.

It is also important to recognize that the transportation method is equally applicable to problems in which the objective function is profit maximation rather than cost minimization. When such is the case, dollars of profit, rather than costs, are assigned to the cells in the matrix. Nor is the method limited only to problems involving the selection of transportation routes. Many other kinds of problems may be dealt with by the technique providing that they can be similarly framed and possess the characteristics of linearity, homogeneity and certainty. For example, the method has been used in assigning manufacturing orders to work stations. Indeed, a key requisite for the successful application of the transportation technique is the ability to visualize ways in which business data may be modified so as to be amenable to treatment by the method. As Bunke has pointed out, a large number of problems "are subject to mathematical solution only when the data of the real world are so adapted that they can be fed into the programming model." [14]

NON–LINEAR AND DYNAMIC PROGRAMMING

Two further mathematical programming techniques which have been increasingly utilized in the solution of allocation problems in recent years are *non-linear* and *dynamic* programming. Application of the former requires a level of mathematical complexity beyond the scope of this book; while the latter—although often calling only for the use of simple arithmetic—usually involves a lengthy computational procedure. In consequence, we will treat these two approaches only in a general manner in this section.

Non-Linear Programming

Non-linear programming is designed to deal with problems in which the objective function and/or the constraints involve non-linear expressions. Or, in economic terms it "may be described as the analysis of constrainted maximization problems in which diminishing or increasing returns to scale are present." [15] As an illustration of a non-linear programming problem, let us consider the following simple example in which the objective function for one of two products under consideration is non-linear:

---

[14] Bunke, *op. cit.*, p. 13.
[15] William J. Baumol, *Economic Theory and Operations Analysis* (Englewood Cliffs, N. J.: Prentice-Hall, Inc., 1961), p. 98.

1. A company produces two products, X and Y, the manufacture of which is subject to the linear constraints shown in Figure 16–18.

2. The profit for each unit of product X sold is \$8; consequently total profit from X may be expressed by the following linear expression: $P_x = 8x$.

3. The per unit profit for Y (UP_y) declines as additional units are offered for sale due to consumer resistance in the following manner: $UP_y = 10 - .01y$. That is, if 100 units of Y are offered for sale, the per unit profit will be $10 - (.10)(100)$ or \$9; if 200 units are offered for sale, $10 - (.01)(200)$ or \$8; etc. The *total* profit obtained from any number of units of Y will equal Y times the unit profit function $(10 - .01y)$ or $y(10 - .01y)$, which simplifies to $10y - .01y^2$. This is a non-linear expression.

4. The total profit from both products equals the sum of the total profit from each or: $TP = 8x + 10y - .01y^2$.

Any number of non-linear iso-profit curves may be superimposed upon the restrictions indicated in Figure 16–19 in much the same way as were the linear iso-profit lines in our previous example of the chemical manufacturer faced with the linear allocation prob-

FIGURE 16–18. Linear Constraints for Problem with Non-Linear Objective Function

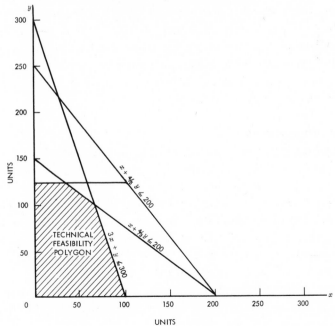

FIGURE 16-19. Non-Linear Iso-Profit Curves

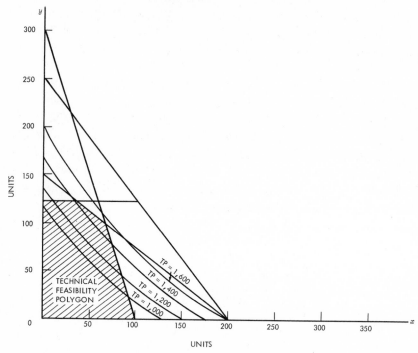

lem. Four such curves are illustrated in Figure 16-19. A major diffi-culty one encounters in solving non-linear programming problems arises from the fact that optimum solutions *will not necessarily be found at one of the corners of the technical feasibility polygon*, as is always the case with linear programming problems. In conse-quence, more sophisticated mathematical approaches are required to arrive at optimum solutions.[16]

Dynamic Programming

Each of the previous programming techniques which we have dis-cussed has been designed to develop an optimum solution for prob-lems calling for a single decision or set of decisions. Many business problems, however, involve *multi-stage* processes, in which se-quences of interdependent decisions are required. For example, sup-pose a company has $100,000 at the beginning of a year and wants to decide whether it should: (1) pay out the entire sum in the form of dividends, (2) reinvest the entire sum, or (3) allocate some por-tion of the $100,000 for reinvestment and pay out the remainder in dividends. If the company's objective is to maximize dividends for

---

[16] For a discussion of some of these approaches, see *ibid.*, pp. 109 ff.

the one year, it will obviously pay out the total sum in this form. Suppose, however, that the company is concerned instead with the proportional dividend payout from profits each year over a period of years, with its objective the maximization of dividends over the whole period of time. In such a case, the company will be faced with a series of interdependent decisions. Increasing the amount of money to be reinvested in any given year will result in added funds being available in future years either for dividend payments or further reinvestment, and vice versa.[17] It is for the handling of such multi-stage problems as this that dynamic programming is designed.

Like the other programming methods which we have discussed, dynamic programming is a formalized iterative search procedure. The fundamentals of this procedure have been summarized by Bowman and Fetter as follows:

> The basic feature of dynamic programming is that the optimum decision is reached stepwise, proceeding from one stage to the next. Stages in the problem need not be in terms of time. An optimum solution set is determined, given any conditions in the first stage. Then this optimum solution set (from the first stage) is integrated with the second stage to obtain a new optimum solution set, given any conditions. Then, in a sense ignoring the first and second stages as such, this new optimum solution set is integrated with the third stage to obtain still a further optimum solution set (or decision) under any conditions. This new solution is integrated with the fourth stage, and so forth. At each stage an optimum solution from all previous stages, under any conditions, is carried into the next stage. It is this optimum solution which is carried forward rather than all the previous stages.[18]

Unlike the other programming techniques which we have discussed, dynamic programming is designed to handle decision problems under conditions of both certainty and risk. It is also applicable to problems involving both linear and non-linear relationships. Among the many types of multi-stage problems which may be dealt with by dynamic programming are those involving production scheduling, equipment investment, and inventory decisions.

SUMMARY

In this chapter we have examined a number of mathematical programming methods designed to aid the decision maker in effecting the optimum allocation of resources. Each of these techniques is

---

[17] The dividend problem and its treatment by dynamic programming are described in David W. Miller and Martin K. Starr, *Executive Decisions and Operations Research* (Englewood Ciffs, N. J.: Prentice-Hall, Inc., 1960), pp. 328–34.

[18] Bowman and Fetter, *op. cit.,* p. 330.

applicable to constrained maximization or minimization problems in which the strategy space of the decision maker is circumscribed by some restrictions upon resources. Each represents an iterative process by means of which optimum solutions are progressively approached through a series of successive steps. Characteristic of all of the programming methods is the requirement that the objective function and all constraints be explicitly expressed in quantitative terms.

Notwithstanding these similarities, the programming methods vary both in mathematical and computational complexity and in the types of problems to which they may be applied. Figure 16–20 pro-

FIGURE 16–20

Comparison of Programming Methods

Programming Method	Ease of Application		Characteristics of Problems to which Applicable				
	Mathematical Complexity	Computational Work Required	Number of Variables	Number of Stages	Certainty Required?	Linearity Required?	Homogeneity Required?
Algebraic	simple	little	2–3	single	yes	yes	no
Simplex	moderate-complex	considerable	n	single	yes	yes	no
Transportation	simple	varies with size of matrix	n	single	yes	yes	yes
Non-Linear	complex	considerable	n	single	yes	no	no
Dynamic	moderate-complex	considerable	n	multiple	no	no	no

vides a comparison of some of the key characteristics of the programming methods.

Mathematical programming represents a significant contribution to management in that it provides an efficient formalized approach for handling resource allocation problems involving a considerable degree of complexity. By means of the use of electronic computers, even those programming problems requiring extensive computational work for their solution can be handled quite readily. With the rapid growth of computer availability in industry, we anticipate increased utilization of mathematical programming in the future. Programming, however, is not a technique which should be indiscriminately applied to all types of allocation problems. In some cases —as, for example, those in which the total costs involved in the decision problem are quite small—the marginal savings which may be realized by the application of programming may be exceeded by the marginal costs of doing so. Further, some allocation problems are so complex that their solution is not possible by the application of programming. Satisfactory solutions to some problems of this level of complexity, however, may be obtained by the use of simulation processes, the treatment of which we will reserve for Chapter 18.

DISCUSSION AND STUDY QUESTIONS

1. What characteristics must a problem possess in order for the algebraic method of linear programming to be applicable? The transportation method?

2. What advantages does the simplex technique have over the algebraic method?

3. What would be the rim requirements for a transportation problem involving 7 warehouses and 4 plants? How many cells in the matrix should be used in order to avoid degeneracy?

4. What do we mean when we say that mathematical programming techniques are iterative ones?

5. Your roommate, who has been observing you diligently working on the transportation method, makes the following comment: "Why bother with all that mathematical nonsense? Look, I can solve that problem of yours with the three plants and three warehouses in a couple of minutes without knowing anything about linear programming just by trying out a few different assignments." Evaluate his reaction.

6. Which of the following are requisite of all mathematical programming problems? In each case, give reasons for your answer.
    a) An objective function
    b) Degeneracy
    c) Scarce resources
    d) An explicitly defined strategy space
    e) Utilization of marginal analysis
    f) A slack variable

7. Personnel placement tests were given to 220 applicants to measure their aptitude for performing on each of four different jobs: A, B, C, and D. Each test was scored on a 10 point scale, with a score of 10 representing the greatest aptitude. Analysis of the test results showed the existence of four distinct applicant groups, as is illustrated in the table below. All 30 individuals in applicant Group 1, for example, had the same scores of 6, 9, 4, and 6 for Jobs A, B, C, and D respectively. Also indicated in the table below is the number of job openings for each of the four jobs in question. How should the applicants, if hired, be assigned to the existing job openings so as to maximize the total of all applicants' test scores (for the job to which each is assigned).

Scores Received

	Applicant Group				
Job Type	1	2	3	4	Job Openings
A.......	6	3	2	4	65
B.......	9	5	3	1	55
C.......	4	3	5	2	60
D.......	6	8	4	3	30
Number of Applicants...	30	65	45	80	

8. Mr. MacDonald, an elderly farmer, is considering the purchase this spring of new stock. Presently he has none. He has decided to buy only steers and pigs. He has steer pens which can accommodate up to 20 steers. His hog pens have a maximum capacity of 40 hogs. Young steers currently are selling for $400/head, whereas pigs are selling for $200/head. His available funds total $10,000. He expects that he will net $200 profit/steer and $50 profit/hog, after all expenses, when he sells the animals at the end of two years. In order to maximize profits, how many steers and pigs should he purchase?

9. A company fabricates and assembles two products, A and B. It takes 3 minutes to fabricate each unit of A; and 6 minutes to fabricate each unit of B. Assembly time per unit for Product A is 1 minute; and for Product B, 9 minutes. Six hundred minutes of fabrication time and 1800 minutes of assembly time are available. The company makes a profit of $2 on each unit of A it sells, and $1 on each unit of B. What quantities of A and B should be produced in order to maximize profits? What will be the profits earned at these production levels?

10. The per unit costs of shipping goods from each of a firm's three plants (A, B, C) to each of its three warehouses (1, 2, 3), the plants' monthly capacities, and the warehouses' monthly demand are shown in the matrix below. How many units should be shipped from each plant to each warehouse to minimize costs? What will these minimum costs be?

	Destination			
Source	W1	W2	W3	Capacity
P1	$5	$6	$5	25
P2	$8	$3	$4	15
P3	$9	$8	$5	25
Demand	15	20	30	65

SELECTED REFERENCES

BAUMOL, WILLIAM J. *Economic Theory and Operations Analysis.* 2d ed. Englewood Cliffs, N. J.: Prentice-Hall, Inc., 1965.

BOCK, ROBERT H., and HOLSTEIN, WILLIAM K. *Production Planning and Control.* Columbus, Ohio: Charles E. Merrill Books, Inc., 1963.

BOULDING, KENNETH E., and SPIVEY, W. A. *Linear Programming and the Theory of the Firm,* Chaps. iii–iv. New York: The Macmillan Co., 1960.

BROOM, H. N. *Production Management,* Chaps. xi–xii. Homewood, Ill.: Richard D. Irwin, Inc., 1962.

BUFFA, ELWOOD S. *Modern Production Management.* New York: John Wiley & Sons, Inc., 1961.

BUNKE, HARVEY C. *Linear Programming: A Primer.* Iowa City, Iowa: Bureau of Business and Economic Research, College of Business Administration, State University of Iowa, 1960.

CHARNES, A., and COOPER, W. W. *Management Models and Industrial Applications of Linear Programming,* Vol. II. New York: John Wiley & Sons, Inc., 1961.

CHURCHMAN, C. W.; ACKOFF, R. L.; and ARNOFF, E. L. *Introduction to Operations Research.* New York: John Wiley & Sons, Inc., 1957.

DORFMAN, R., *et al. Linear Programming and Economic Analysis.* New York: McGraw-Hill Book Co., Inc., 1958.

HEADY, EARL O., and CANDLER, WILFRED. *Linear Programming Methods.* Ames, Iowa: Iowa State College Press, 1958.

HENDERSON, A., and SCHLAIFER, R. "Mathematical Programming—Better Information for Decision Making," *Harvard Business Review,* 32 (May–June, 1954), 73–100.

MANNE, ALAN S. *Economic Analysis for Business Decisions,* Chaps. ii–vi. New York: McGraw-Hill Book Co., Inc., 1961.

MILLER, D. W., and STARR, M. K. *Executive Decisions and Operations Research.* Englewood Cliffs, N. J.: Prentice-Hall, Inc., 1960.

NAYLOR, THOMAS H., and BYRNE, EUGENE T. *Linear Programming, Methods and Cases.* Belmont, Calif.: Wadsworth Publishing Co., Inc., 1963.

SPIVEY, W. A. *Linear Programming: An Introduction.* New York: The Macmillan Co., 1963.

STOCKTON, ROBERT S. *Introduction to Linear Programming.* 2d ed. Boston: Allyn & Bacon, 1963.

VAJDA, S. *Readings in Linear Programming.* New York: John Wiley & Sons, Inc., 1958.

CHAPTER 17

INVENTORY DECISION MAKING

I N the previous two chapters we have examined a number of re-source allocation problems and decision-making approaches. We will now focus attention on a particular type of allocation problem—that of planning and controlling the inventories of a business firm. Although we are treating inventory decision making in this chapter as separate from other kinds of allocation problems for purposes of exposition, the reader should recognize that this distinction is an artificial one. That the maintenance of adequate raw materials inventories, for example, is just as important in the manufacture of goods as ensuring the availability of sufficient manpower or machine capacity, points up that inventory decision making is an integral part of the whole production planning and control process.

Only in recent years has the problem of controlling inventories come to be recognized as a critical one in managerial decision making. "In past centuries, inventories were considered an indication of wealth; even inventories greatly in excess of the amount needed to carry on the processes of production and distribution were considered beneficial." [1] With the development of modern industrialism and the growth of large-scale enterprises, however, inventories have come to represent very substantial investments for many business firms and their control has been recognized as mandatory. Beginning about 1915, attention was turned to the development of mathematical approaches designed to aid the decision maker in setting optimum inventory levels. Since that time increasingly sophisticated analytical tools have been brought to bear on the problems of inventory management.

---

[1] Thomson M. Whitin, *The Theory of Inventory Management* (2d ed.; Princeton, N. J.: Princeton University Press, 1957), p. 3.

The purpose of this chapter is to examine the functions that inventories perform for the business firm, the problems involved in their control, and the more commonly employed approaches to inventory decision making. In our discussion, attention will be given to certain of the simpler mathematical models designed to guide inventory decisions. Treatment of these models is intended to (1) focus attention on the key variables involved in inventory problems, and (2) serve as a point of departure for those interested in ultimately exploring more complex quantitative approaches to inventory decision making.

FUNCTIONS PERFORMED BY INVENTORIES

The basic function of inventories is to decouple, or make independent, successive stages in the manufacturing and distribution process so as to allow each to operate more economically. For example, inventories "make it possible to make a product at a distance from customers or from raw-material supplies" . . . [and] . . . "make it unnecessary to gear production directly to consumption or, alternatively, to force consumption to adapt to the necessities of production." [2]

The decoupling function may be performed in at least four different ways. First, *process and movement inventories* will be necessary if user demand is to be met when time is required to transport raw materials, goods in the process of being manufactured, or finished products from one location to another. An inventory representing an average week's demand would be needed in movement, for example, if one week were required to ship a finished good from a firm's warehouse to its retail outlet. Second, there is the *lot-size* inventory, where more units are purchased or manufactured than are needed for present use because certain economies may be realized from the larger lots. Quantity discounts or smaller per unit shipping costs due to avoiding less than carload (l.c.l.) shipments often may be gained by making larger purchases at less frequent intervals. Similarly, in manufacturing, the number of machine set-ups and resulting setup costs may be reduced by scheduling longer production runs of an item on a given machine. Third, when the demand for a particular item is known to be variable—perhaps seasonally—it may be more

---

[2] John F. Magee, *Production Planning and Inventory Control* (New York: McGraw-Hill Book Co., Inc., 1958), p. 17. For the material in this section, the authors have drawn heavily on Magee, pp. 17–20.

economical for a firm to absorb some of the variation by permitting its inventories to fluctuate, rather than its level of production. This is because such fluctuations in production would result in changing levels of employment—with attendant retraining, unemployment compensation, and other costs—and/or the need to schedule over-time work to meet the periods of peak demand. Inventories main-tained for such purposes are often referred to as *anticipation* inven-tories. Finally, because of *unknown* changes in demand for many items, *fluctuation* inventories may be necessary if an adequate sup-ply of items is to be available to the consumer when he wants them, and stockouts are to be minimized. For example, a supermarket may sell ten cases of a particular canned good per week on the average. Beginning weekly inventory, however—assuming stocks are replen-ished every Monday morning—would more than likely be kept some-what above ten cases so that normal fluctuations above the average demand could be met.

MINIMIZATION OF COSTS

A fundamental concern of the manager in developing inventory policies is to minimize the total operating costs of his firm. However, cost minimization may not be the only decision criterion, for other values and objectives may be considered important. For example, a company may maintain a stable level of production during periods of slack demand and thus permit its inventories to increase, in order to provide steady work for its employees because it considers this policy necessary to meet a social obligation. It should also be em-phasized that the costs directly incurred by carrying items in inven-tory are not the only ones which must be considered in inventory decision making. Rather, it is important to view the firm as a system and to recognize the mutual interdependence between inventory policies and many other types of decisions made by the company. The relationship between fluctuations in inventory levels and the stabilization of employment indicated above provides a good exam-ple of such interdependence.

The costs which a firm may incur as a result of the inventory lev-els which it establishes may be grouped into three categories. First, there are *inventory carrying* costs. These include the gains sacrificed by tying up funds in inventory which could have been invested else-where (opportunity costs). In addition, carrying items in inventory may require the rental of storage space and the payment of taxes and insurance and may result in losses due to the deterioration or obsolescence of the items being carried. Second, there are *procurement* costs which include both *setup* and *ordering* costs. Among the more important setup costs are the retooling and "shakedown" costs [3] which occur when a changeover is required from the manufacture of one item to another on a particular machine; while among ordering costs are those clerical expenses involved in placing an order. Third, losses may be realized by the firm if *stockouts* of items occur. Sales may be lost if inventories are not adequate to meet consumer demand or production may come to a halt if the inventories of critical raw materials or parts are insufficient to meet its needs.

Two fundamental and mutually interrelated inventory decisions which have a key bearing on the total costs which will be incurred by the firm are: (1) the size of each lot to be purchased or manufactured, and (2) the average inventory levels to be maintained. As the lot size and average inventory increase, certain of the costs indicated above will increase, while others will decrease. In the following sections, attention will be turned to one of the better known inventory models designed to minimize total operating costs—the economic lot-size model.

THE ECONOMIC LOT SIZE MODEL UNDER CONDITIONS OF CERTAINTY

The focal point of the economic lot-size model is the determination of that lot size for any given item—either purchased or manufactured—which will minimize total inventory costs for the item. If anticipated yearly demand for an item is 3,000 units, should all units for the year be purchased in one lot—or manufactured in a single run? Or, is it more economical to schedule two production runs, or the purchase of two lots during the year—each containing 1,500 units? In addition, application of the lot size model will also indicate both the optimum *number* of lots to be scheduled over a given period of time and the optimum size of the average inventory of the item under consideration.

Assumptions Underlying the Model

First, we will examine the economic lot-size problem by considering the purchase of a single item of inventory under conditions of certainty. We will assume that: (1) demand for the item is at a con-

---

[3] "Shakedown" costs refer to those costs often incurred because of diseconomies encountered initially in a production run—e.g., during the time required to bring quality under control, for workers to reach maximum efficiency levels, etc.

stant rate and known to the decision maker in advance, and (2) the lead time necessary for acquiring the item (elapsed time between the placement of the order and its receipt into inventory) is also known. Although these assumptions would rarely be completely valid for "real world" inventory problems, they permit us to develop a simplified model into which we may later introduce more realistic complicating factors.

The number of units in inventory at any given time under the above conditions may be portrayed graphically by what is frequently referred to as the "saw-tooth" model. This is illustrated in Figure 17–1. Here, letting Q represent the order size, we may note that the number of units in inventory is equal to Q at the time that each new order enters inventory; and that the inventory is gradually depleted until it reaches zero just at the point at which the next order is received. We may also observe that: (1) the average inventory of the item is equal to exactly *one half* the number of units in the lot size $\left(\dfrac{Q}{2}\right)$ and (2) because each new order is received into inventory at exactly the time at which the previous order is depleted, no stockouts will occur. This latter condition presupposes that the decision maker has taken full advantage of his knowledge of the constant acquisition lead time and placed each order appropriately in advance.

Opposing Cost Analysis

Since stockouts are assumed not to occur in our model, the only two sets of costs which must be considered in determining the lot size which will minimize total inventory costs for an item are the ordering and inventory carrying costs. A key feature of this model is that we are confronted with a set of *opposing costs*—as the lot size increases, the carrying charges will increase, but the ordering costs

FIGURE 17–1. The "Saw-Tooth" Model

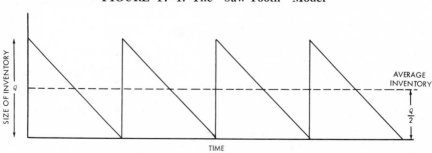

will decrease. A closer examination of these two costs will indicate why such a relationship exists:

1. (*Carrying Costs.* The annual cost of carrying one unit of inventory is frequently calculated by multiplying the value (cost) of the item under consideration)(C) by a percentage figure (I)—which represents management's estimate of opportunity costs, taxes and insurance on the items being carried, etc., per year as a percentage of the value of the inventory. Total carrying costs are equal to the cost of carrying one unit (CI) multiplied by the average inventory, which as indicated previously is equal to $\frac{Q}{2}$. Thus, total annual carrying costs are $\frac{Q}{2}CI$, and will increase as Q, the lot size, increases.

2. | *Ordering Costs.* The number of orders which will be placed during any given period of time is equal to the demand (R) for the period divided by the size of each order (the lot size, Q). Total ordering costs per period are equal to the cost of placing each order (S) times the number of orders per period $\frac{R}{Q}$; or, $\frac{R}{Q}S$. | As the lot size increases, fewer orders will be required to meet demand, and thus the ordering costs will decrease.

Figure 17–2 illustrates graphically the nature of the opposing costs involved in the lot size problem. It is important to note here that annual total costs—inventory carrying plus ordering costs

FIGURE 17–2. Opposing Cost Relationships

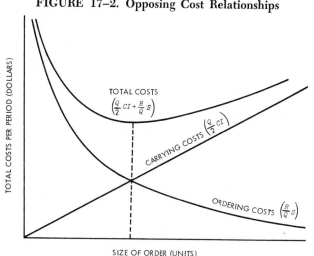

(or $\frac{Q}{2}CI + \frac{R}{Q}S$)—first decrease, and then increase, as the lot size increases;[4] and that our fundamental objective is to find a value for Q which will minimize the total costs. It should also be noted that, with any given demand, total *per unit* costs will be minimized by the same value of Q, since they are equal to $\frac{TC}{R}$.

Tabular Approach

One approach for solving the lot-size problem is by trial and error. This may be accomplished by:

1. Selecting a number of different possible lot sizes.
2. Determining total costs for each size chosen.
3. Selecting the lot size which minimizes total costs.

Development of a table of values, such as that illustrated in Figure 17–3, facilitates the employment of this approach.

FIGURE 17–3

Tabular Approach

Orders per Year	Lot Size Q	Ordering Costs $\frac{R}{Q}S$	+	Carrying Costs $\frac{Q}{2}CI =$	Total Cost TC
1........	8000	$ 30		$400	$430
2........	4000	60		200	260
4........	2000	120		100	220
8........	1000	240		50	290

In this example—letting $R = 8000$ units per year, $S = \$30$ per order, $C = \$1.00$ per unit, and $I = 10\%$ per year—the table developed indicates that an order size of 2000 units will result in the lowest total costs of the four decision alternatives evaluated. We cannot determine, however, whether any lot sizes *other* than those four chosen would represent an even more satisfactory solution. This points up a serious limitation of the tabular approach. By a judicious choice

---

[4] Assuming that ordering costs remain constant per order, and carrying costs constant per unit of inventory. These relationships also exist when the period under consideration is more or less than a year; although the value of I would have to be adjusted accordingly. For example, if management sets the annual carrying charges for an item at 12 percent of its value, and the period under consideration is three months, a value for I of approximately 3 percent would be used.

of decision alternatives for evaluation we might, with relatively little experimentation, approximate the optimum lot size. However, a relatively large number of alternatives often will have to be examined before the best possible solution is precisely determined.

The EOQ Formula

Fortunately, a formula has been developed which will enable us to determine the lot size which will minimize total costs without involving the considerable experimentation required by the tabular approach. This is the economic order quantity formula, which is often referred to as *EOQ*. This formula may be derived by utilizing the differential calculus, as is noted below.[5] Additionally, the logic underlying the *EOQ* formula may be demonstrated algebraically, due to the particular behavior of the variables involved in the model, as follows.

When a rectangular hyperbola such as that representing ordering costs in Figure 17–2 and a straight line such as that representing carrying costs in the inventory model exist, it happens that the minimum point on the total cost curve will be at the value for Q at which the *hyperbola and line intersect*.[6] Or, to put it another way, total costs for any period will be minimized with that lot size for which *carrying costs are equal to the ordering costs*. This relationship may be observed graphically by referring to Figure 17–2. Consequently, the economic order quantity may be obtained by equating the ordering costs and carrying costs, and solving for Q as follows:

---

[5] Total costs are minimized when the slope of the total cost curve is zero. Therefore, the *EOQ* formula may be obtained by setting the first derivative of total costs with respect to Q equal to zero, and solving for Q as follows:

(1) $\quad TC = \dfrac{Q}{2}\, CI + \dfrac{R}{Q}\, S$

(2) $\quad \dfrac{dTC}{dQ} = \dfrac{CI}{2} - \dfrac{RS}{Q^2}$

(3) $\quad$ Setting the first derivative equal to zero: $Q^2 CI = 2RS$; and $Q = \sqrt{\dfrac{2RS}{CI}}$

That this represents a minimum point rather than a maximum is indicated by the positive sign of the second derivative: $\dfrac{d^2 TC}{dQ^2} = \dfrac{2RS}{Q^3}$

[6] For the following reason: The magnitude of the slope of the hyperbola is negatively as great as the positive magnitude of the carrying costs line at the point of intersection. Thus, the sum of the two slopes is zero. Since the slope of total costs curve is equal to the sum of these two slopes for any value of Q, its value is zero for the value of Q at which the hyperbola and line intersect. The point on the total cost curve at which the slope is zero represents a minimum point.

Equating carrying and procurement costs:

(1) $\dfrac{Q}{2} CI = \dfrac{R}{Q} S$

Solving for Q:

(2) $QCI = \dfrac{2RS}{Q}$

(3) $Q^2 CI = 2RS$

(4) $Q^2 = \dfrac{2RS}{CI}$

(5) $Q = \sqrt{\dfrac{2RS}{CI}} = EOQ$

Equation 5 is the economic order quantity formula and will give us the lot size, Q, which will minimize total costs for the firm.

An application of the EOQ formula may be illustrated by taking the same set of data as used previously with the tabular example, where $R = 8000$, $S = \$30$, $C = \$1.00$, and $I = 10\%$:

$$Q = \sqrt{\dfrac{(2)(8000)(30)}{(1)(.10)}}$$
$$= \sqrt{4,800,000}$$
$$= 2191$$

Substituting this value for Q in the total cost equation, total costs for the year are $\dfrac{2191}{2}(1)(.10) + \dfrac{8000}{2191}(30)$; or \$219.09. Comparing these costs with the \$220 obtained by the tabular approach, we note that the latter gave us a close approximation of the lowest possible total costs. Once the most economic lot size has been so obtained, it is quite simple to determine both: (1) the number of orders placed per period: $\dfrac{R}{Q}$; and (2) average inventory for the item: $\dfrac{Q}{2}$. Since the acquisition lead time is assumed constant and known in advance, the date to place each order can also be determined. For example, if the economic order quantity for an item were 500 units, weekly demand 125, and the acquisition lead time one week, each reorder would simply be placed one week prior to the depletion of the existing inventories—or when the inventory level has fallen to 125 units. This number of units represents item usage during the delivery period. The reorder points called for in this example are illustrated diagrammatically in Figure 17–4.

FIGURE 17–4. Reorder Points

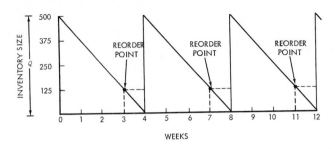

WEEKS

Further Development of the EOQ Formula

The *EOQ* model which we have been discussing is a highly simplified one and does not take into account many key variables which often must be considered by the manager. In this section, the effects of two additional variables—quantity discounts and a continuous inflow of items into inventory during production runs—will be considered. These are but two of many variables which analysts have introduced into the simplified lot-size model. They illustrate the ways in which elaboration of the simplified model is possible. In both cases, we will continue to assume that both the acquisition lead time and demand are constant and known in advance to the decision maker.

Continuous Inventory Inflow During Production Runs. In the *EOQ* model considered above, all items were treated as being received into the inventory at once. This is not uncommon when items are purchased from an outside supplier. When a firm itself is manufacturing the items, however, a situation may be encountered in which there is a continuous inflow into the inventory as the units are completed during each production run. Assuming a constant rate of inflow, the number of units in inventory at any given time may be represented graphically as in Figure 17–5. This illustration shows that the size of the inventory will increase during each production run to the extent that the inflow of items exceeds the number of items being withdrawn for use. Once a run has been completed, the inventory will decrease by the rate of usage until depleted at the time the inflow from the next run commences. For example, if the rate of inflow is 100 units per day during each run, and daily withdrawals to meet demand are 60 units, the inventory will: (1) increase at a rate of 40 units per day during each run; and (2) decrease at a rate of 60 units per day between runs.

FIGURE 17–5. Continuous Inflow into Inventories

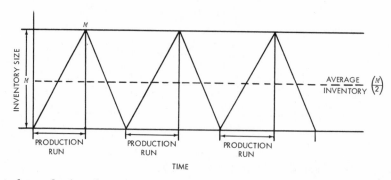

A formula for determining the optimum run size may be developed in much the same manner as the economic order quantity equation. Here, there will be procurement costs incurred by "ordering" the production of each run; these are the setup costs referred to previously. These costs are determined in the same way as the ordering costs in the purchase size model: $\frac{R}{Q}S$. As may be noted by comparing Figures 17–1 and 17–5, however, average inventory, and thus inventory carrying charges, are different when there is a continuous inflow of items into inventory than when the entire lot is received at once. In both cases, however, average inventory is equal to *one half* the maximum number of units in the inventory. In the purchase size model, the maximum number of units in inventory was Q, the lot size. In the continuous inflow model, on the other hand, inventory is at its maximum size at the time each production run is completed (point M on Figure 17–5). This maximum is equal to the number of days in the run (D)—times daily production (P) minus daily usage (U)—or $D(P-U)$. Thus, average inventory is equal to $\frac{D(P-U)}{2}$; which, as is noted below, may be simplified to read: $\frac{Q}{2}\left(1-\frac{U}{P}\right).$ [7] Following the same reasoning as in the purchase size model, annual inventory carrying charges are: $\frac{Q}{2}\left(1-\frac{U}{P}\right)CI$; and the total costs per year: $\frac{Q}{2}\left(1-\frac{U}{P}\right)CI+\frac{R}{Q}S$. This total cost equation may be manipulated in much the same way

---

[7] The number of days in a run (D) will equal the run size (Q) divided by the rate of daily production (P); or $D=\frac{Q}{P}.$ Substituting this term for D in the equation $\frac{D(P-U)}{2}$ gives us $\frac{\frac{Q}{P}(P-U)}{2}$, which simplifies to $\frac{Q}{2}\left(1-\frac{U}{P}\right).$

as the economic purchase size equation to give the following formula for determining the optimum size of a lot with a constant inflow production run: $Q = \sqrt{\dfrac{2RS}{CI\left(1 - \dfrac{U}{P}\right)}}$ [8]

It is interesting to note that—given the same procurement costs, carrying costs, and demand—a continuous inflow of items into inventories results in lower total costs for the firm than when the entire lot is received into inventory at once. This is true because the introduction of the continuous inflow brings about:

1. An increase in the optimum lot size, and thus, fewer orders (runs) and smaller procurement costs.
2. A decrease in the size of the average inventory, and consequently, smaller carrying costs.

A comparison between costs in the two models may be illustrated by taking the same demand and cost data as in our lot size example, but modifying for: (1) an inflow of 44 units per day while each lot is being produced and (2) a daily outflow (usage) rate of 22 units throughout the year (which for a 365-day year approximates a yearly demand of 8,000). Employing the continuous inflow formula:

$$Q = \sqrt{\frac{(2)(8000)(30)}{(1)(.10)(1 - \frac{22}{44})}}$$
$$EOQ = 3098$$

---

[8] The mathematical proof utilizing the calculus is as follows:

(1) $\quad TC = \dfrac{Q}{2}\left(1 - \dfrac{U}{P}\right)CI + \dfrac{RS}{Q}$

(2) $\quad \dfrac{dTC}{dQ} = \dfrac{CI}{2}\left(1 - \dfrac{U}{P}\right) - \dfrac{RS}{Q^2}$

(3) Setting the first derivative equal to zero:

$$Q^2\left[CI\left(1 - \frac{U}{P}\right)\right] = 2RS; \quad \text{and} \quad Q = \sqrt{\frac{2RS}{CI\left(1 - \frac{U}{P}\right)}}$$

Or, since total costs are minimized at the value for Q at which the ordering costs curve and carrying costs line intersect:

(1) $\dfrac{Q}{2}\left(1 - \dfrac{U}{P}\right)CI = \dfrac{R}{Q}S$

(2) $\left(1 - \dfrac{U}{P}\right)CI = \dfrac{2RS}{Q^2}$

(3) $Q^2 = \dfrac{2RS}{\left(1 - \dfrac{U}{P}\right)CI}$

(4) $Q = \sqrt{\dfrac{2RS}{\left(1 - \dfrac{U}{P}\right)CI}}$

Dividing the demand of 8000 units per year by this optimum run size, the (average) number of runs which should be scheduled during the year is 2.58; and total costs per year are minimized at approximately $154.92. This may be compared with the minimum total costs of $219.09 per year which were obtained with the simplified formula when each purchased lot entered the inventory all at once.

Quantity Discounts. Another common inventory problem is that of determining the economic lot size if one or more price discounts on all items in the lot may be obtained from the supplier when large quantities are purchased. For example, the per unit cost of an item might be reduced 5 percent if the purchase quantity is more than 1,000 units and 10 percent if the order size is 2000 units or more. Although it is possible to determine the economic lot size with any number of such successive discounts taking effect as the purchase quantity increases, we shall limit our analysis to the case in which only one discount price is offered.[9]

The basic costs relationships which exist in the quantity discount

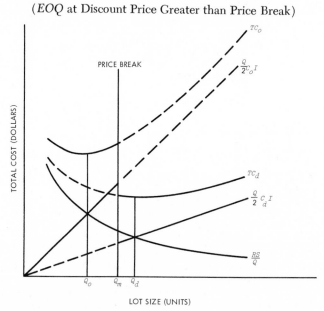

FIGURE 17–6. **Quantity Discount Model**

(*EOQ* at Discount Price Greater than Price Break)

[9] The approach presented here is one suggested by C. West Churchman, Russell L. Ackoff, and E. Leonard Arnoff, *Introduction to Operations Research* (New York: John Wiley & Sons, Inc., 1957), pp. 235 ff. For an approach to the quantity discount problem involving more than one discount price, see this same work, pp. 245 ff.

problem are illustrated graphically in Figure 17–6. The reader will note that procurement (ordering) costs are the same whether or not the lot size purchased is large enough to realize the discount; but that per unit inventory carrying costs are lower when the discount is obtained since the cost (and value) of each item in inventory is less. Minimization of total costs under such conditions may be determined by use of the *EOQ* formula developed previously, although in some cases certain additional calculations are needed. We will first indicate the steps required for the solution to this type of problem, and then will illustrate the application of this approach by treatment of a specific example.

1. Using the *EOQ* formula, and taking the cost of the item at the discount price (C_d), determine the economic lot size (Q_d). As Figure 17–6 shows, this economic lot size minimizes total costs. Lot size Q_d, however, will be feasible *only when it is equal to or greater than* the minimum number of units which must be purchased for the discount to take effect (Q_m). Such is the case illustrated in Figure 17–6.

2. If Q_d is less than Q_m and does not represent a feasible solution (as illustrated in Figure 17–7) the following additional steps are required:

    a) Using the original (nondiscounted) price (C_o), deter-

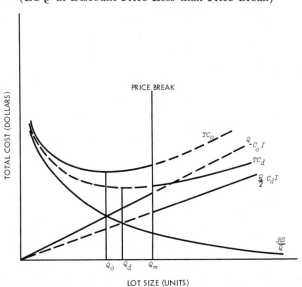

FIGURE 17–7. Quantity Discount Model

(*EOQ* at Discount Price Less than Price Break)

mine the economic order quantity (Q_o) and the total costs which will be incurred when this quantity is purchased (TC_o).

b) Determine total costs when the minimum number of items required to obtain the discount is purchased (TC_m). As Figure 17–7 illustrates, total costs *continuously increase* as the lot size increases beyond Q_m. Thus, it will never pay to choose a lot size greater than Q_m. Q_m may represent either a more or less economic lot size than Q_o, and the two must next be compared to see which provides better solution. In making the comparison, it is necessary not only to compare the total costs computed above $(TC_o$ and $TC_m)$ but also to consider the savings which will be realized from the discount price if Q_m is chosen.

c) Determine the savings which will be obtained if the discount is obtained. These will be equal to demand times the savings on each unit—which is the difference between the original price and the discount price. Or, mathematically, the savings may be represented by: $R(C_o - C_d)$.

d) If total costs at the minimum quantity needed to obtain the discount (TC_m) minus savings are less than total costs when the economic lot size using the original price is chosen (TC_o), it will pay to take advantage of the discount; and Q_m is the optimal solution. If not, Q_o is the optimal solution.

To illustrate the application of this method, let us consider the following example. Demand for an item is 8,000 per year, procurement costs are $25, the price of the item is $1.00 if less than 3,000 units are purchased, and $.99 if the lot size is equal to or greater than 3,000; and the percentage figure assigned to represent annual carrying charges is 10 percent. Proceeding step by step as indicated above:

1. The economic order quantity using the discount price is

$$\sqrt{\frac{(2)(8,000)(25)}{(.99)(.10)}} \text{ or } 2,009$$

This solution is not feasible since it is less than the 3000 units which must be purchased for the discount price to apply, and the following steps must be taken.

2. Using the non-discounted price, the economic lot size is

$$\sqrt{\frac{(2)(8,000)(25)}{(1.00)(.10)}} \text{ or } 2,000. \text{ Total costs} \left(\frac{Q_o}{2} C_o I + \frac{RS}{Q_o}\right) \text{ are}$$

$$\frac{2,000}{2}(1.00)(.10) + \frac{(8,000)(25)}{2,000}; \text{ or } \$200$$

3.   Total costs when the minimum number of units required to obtain the discount (3,000) are purchased

$$\left(\frac{Q_m}{2}\, C_d I + \frac{RS}{Q_m}\right) \text{ are } \frac{3,000}{2}\,(.99)(.10) + \frac{(8,000)(25)}{3,000}; \text{ or } \$217.25$$

4.   Savings of $.01 will be realized on each unit if the discount is obtained ($1.00 — $.99), and for 8,000 units, total savings are $80. Thus, although total costs at Q_m are $17.25 greater than at Q_o, the $80 in savings obtained by the discount more than offsets this figure and Q_m represents the optimal solution.

Values and Limitations of the EOQ Models Under Certainty

The most obvious limitation of the inventory models discussed above is that certainty does not exist in most business situations. For example, both acquisition lead time and the demand for items usually fluctuate in a manner not completely known to the decision maker in advance. In those cases in which these two factors are relatively constant and predictable in advance, however, these models will provide us with a close approximation of reality. Another problem which may often be encountered in the application of the models is that accurate cost information may be difficult to obtain. The clerical costs incurred by placing an order may defy precise measurement. Nor may it be a simple matter to assess accurately any losses due to obsolescence in determining the inventory carrying costs. However, relatively good approximations of minimal total costs may be arrived at even with quite crude cost data, for *"the total cost in the neighborhood of the optimum-order quantity is relatively insensitive to moderately small changes in the amount ordered."* [10]

This important characteristic of the *EOQ* model may be demonstrated by the use of an example. Let us assume that a firm's yearly demand for an item is 8,000 units, its procurement costs, $25, and its inventory carrying costs 10¢/unit (10 percent of the value of the item costing $1.00). Employing the *EOQ* formula, the economic lot size is $\sqrt{\dfrac{(2)(8000)(25)}{.10}}$; or 2000; and total costs for this lot size are $200. Next, let us suppose that management has erroneously estimated the procurement cost to be $12.50 instead of $25. If this erroneous figure were used instead of the correct one of $25 in applying the *EOQ* formula, the optimum lot size arrived at would be 1,414

---

[10] Magee, *op. cit.*, p. 66.

instead of 2,000. Using what we know to be the correct procurement cost ($25), total costs for a lot size of 1,414 would be $212. Thus, even with procurement costs in error by a factor of two, total costs in our example are only $12 or 6 percent more than they would have been had the correct cost figure been employed. This relative insensitiveness due to the flatness of the total cost curve on either side of the optimum lot size of 2,000 units in our example is illustrated in Figure 17–8.

FIGURE 17–8. Total Cost Curve Insensitiveness

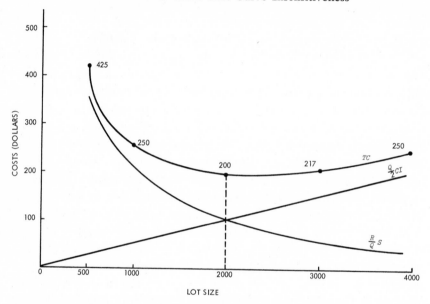

The inventory models, as is the case with most mathematical models, are also of considerable value to the manager in that they focus attention on and reveal the key relationships which exist between the variables in the decision-making problem. For example, the *EOQ* models indicate that under conditions of certainty, optimally both the order (or run) size and average inventory should vary in proportion to changes in the *square root* of the demand of the item. As demand doubles, for example, the new economic order quantity will equal the previous *EOQ* times $\sqrt{2}$; as demand triples, times $\sqrt{3}$; etc. Average inventory follows the same pattern since it is always equal to $\frac{Q}{2}$. These relationships are illustrated in Figure 17–9 which is based on the same cost data in the previous example ($S = \$25; C = \$1;$ and $I = 10\%$):

FIGURE 17–9

Demand	EOQ	Average Inventory
2,000...........................	1,000	500
4,000...........................	1,414	707
8,000...........................	2,000	1,000
16,000..........................	2,828	1,414

Another important relationship betwen the key variables in the inventory problem follows from the above analysis. Since the average inventory should optimally increase only in proportion to the square root of any increases in demand, a *smaller average inventory per unit of sales* is required as demand for an item becomes greater.

INVENTORY DECISION MAKING UNDER RISK AND UNCERTAINTY

As indicated previously, neither demand nor acquisition lead time for the items under control are constant or completely known to the decision maker in advance in most business situations. In some cases, the decision maker may have no idea whatsoever of what variations to expect in these two variables. In such cases we have the problem of decision making under uncertainty. More frequently, however, he will be in a position to estimate the probability of occurrence of various demand levels and acquisition lead times on the basis of past experience. This involves decision making under risk. With either risk or uncertainty the inventory decisions are considerably more complex than in the certainty models previously discussed. It is important to note, however, that it is *not* the lack of certainty about demand for the items under control alone which causes this added complexity. Rather it is the lack of certainty about demand *coupled with* the existence of an acquisition lead time. The maintenance of adequate inventory levels would pose few major problems, regardless of the degree of uncertainty and variation in demand, if *instantaneous replenishment were possible.* Such is usually not the case, however, and the manager—if he is to avoid stockouts—must protect himself against those occasions when inventories are being reduced more rapidly than anticipated, and a lead time renders replenishment impossible until after stocks are depleted.

In the lot size models considered previously—in which a constant known demand and acquisition lead time existed—both the size of orders (or manufacturing runs) and length of time between the placement of orders (or initiation of runs) were constant (see Figures 17–1 and 17–5). When variations in demand exist, however, both of these factors cannot remain constant if stockouts are to be avoided. The two most commonly employed approaches to inventory control under conditions of risk or uncertainty in which demand varies are: (1) to hold the lot size constant and vary the time between the placement of orders or scheduling of production runs, or (2) conversely, to hold the time between the placement of orders or initiation of production runs constant but to vary the lot size. A discussion of these two approaches will be found in the following sections.

Fixed Lot Sizes

First, let us consider the acquisition or scheduling of fixed lot sizes at variable intervals. This approach for purchased lots is illustrated graphically in Figure 17–10. The fixed lot size may be determined

FIGURE 17–10. Fixed Lot Size

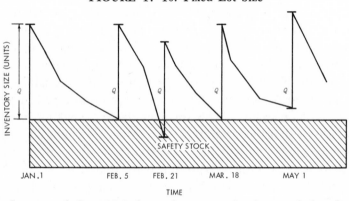

either by use of the *EOQ* formula, or on the basis of the decision maker's judgment. In either case, it is necessary to provide for a *safety stock*—as shown by the cross-hatched area in Figure 17–10—to protect against unpredictable fluctuations in demand and possibly also in the acquisition lead time. We will reserve discussion of the problems involved in setting safety stocks until a later section.

One form of the fixed lot approach—the two-bin system—has been used for certain types of items by many companies for a number of years. The items are placed in two bins. One contains the number of items needed to cover both: (1) average expected demand during the acquisition lead time, and (2) the safety stock. Initially, items needed for use are drawn from the second bin. The depletion of this bin signals that just enough items to cover expected demand during the lead time (plus the safety allowance) remain in the inventory (i.e., in the first bin)—and that it is time to place the replenishment order.[11] This system, which is "commonly used in parts warehouses, for manufacturing floor stocks and in similar circumstances where large numbers of low-value items are controlled," . . . [is] . . . "simple to operate and requires a minimum of record keeping."[12] The lot sizes chosen in utilizing this approach, however, should be reviewed periodically in order to make adjustments as changes take place in demand patterns, inventory carrying costs, etc.

Fixed Reorder Cycle

The second major approach employed in controlling inventories under risk and uncertainty is to vary the lot and size as demand changes, while keeping the interval between the placement of orders or production runs constant. This approach—frequently called the *order-cycling* method—is illustrated diagrammatically for purchased lots in Figure 17–11.

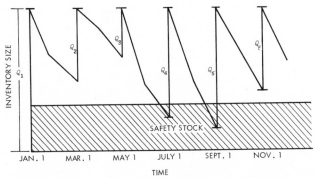

The fixed intervals when inventories are reviewed and orders placed or production runs scheduled may sometimes be quite lengthy —perhaps once every several months. Frequently, however, it is necessary to maintain close constant control over the inventories, and in such cases the review may take place as often as one or more times each day.

The mechanics of the order-cycling method may be illustrated by

---

[11] Sometimes, however, average expected demand during the acquisition period may exceed the purchase quantity, and inventories then would never be as high as the reorder point; in terms of bins, . . . [one] . . . is always empty and the . . . [other] . . . never contains the required quantity." (Whitin, *op. cit.*, p. 52.) For an approach to the treatment of the problem under such circumstances, see *ibid.*, pp. 52 ff.

[12] Magee, *op. cit.*, p. 70.

the use of an example. Let us examine a case in which: (1) the plant manager of a firm and his staff review inventories of a particular item on the last day of each month as a basis for scheduling the following month's production in light of anticipated demand, and (2) management has decided to set safety stocks for the end of each month equal to one-half of the forecasted demand for the following month.

Under these conditions, the number of items scheduled for production in any given month will be equal to expected demand for the month plus the desired ending inventory for the month minus the beginning inventory on hand. For example, let us assume that:

1. The firm's expected monthly demand for a six-month period is that indicated in Figure 17–12.
2. Actual demand will always equal expected demand.
3. No lead time is required for scheduling the production.
4. The beginning inventory for January is 2000 units.
5. The desired ending inventory for June is 2000 units.

In such a case, monthly production would be scheduled as follows using the order-cycling method:

FIGURE 17–12

Order Cycling Method

Month	Expected Demand	+	Desired Ending Inventory	=	Total Requirements	−	Beginning Inventory	=	Production
Jan.	4000		2100		6100		2000		4100
Feb.	4200		1800		6000		2100		3900
Mar.	3600		2400		6000		1800		4200
Apr.	4800		2300		6100		2400		3700
May	4600		2000		6600		2300		4300
June	4000		2000		6000		2000		4000

When actual demand does not equal forecasted demand—which is often likely—the variance may be adjusted by a review at the end of each month. For example, if actual demand during January in our example were 4200 units instead of the anticipated 4000, ending inventory would be 1900, or 200 short of the desired 2100. Since the desired ending inventory for February is 1800 and anticipated demand 4200 units, production for this month would be set at 4100 units rather than 3900 as in Figure 17–12.

Three other observations concerning the order-cycling method should be noted. First, the method is not basically an optimizing approach, although mathematical and statistical techniques may be employed to determine both the frequency of the acquisition intervals and the size of the safety allowances. Second, as in the fixed lot size approach, changing conditions may necessitate altering the frequency of review, and of the acquisition intervals.[13] Finally, essentially the same method used in Figure 17–12 for scheduling production may be applied to inventory problems when purchasing lots from an outside supplier. Acquisition lead time—assumed away in our production example—is normally an additional important consideration, however, and must enter into the calculations.

Determination of Safety Stocks

Under conditions of risk or uncertainty both the fixed lot size and order-cycling methods require the maintenance of safety stocks if stockouts are to be minimized. The fundamental question upon which the decision maker must focus attention in determining the size of safety stocks is that of whether the costs of carrying the items will be justified by the probable reduction in losses due to stockouts. Or, in other words, are the marginal costs of extra inventory exceeded by the marginal savings realized by avoiding lost sales as the size of the safety stock is increased? It is important here to emphasize *reduction* in losses due to stockouts, rather than complete avoidance of such losses. For many demand situations, the probability of extreme fluctuations above average demand will be quite small, and the costs incurred by carrying inventories large enough to cover *all possible* demand levels would greatly exceed the losses from stockouts which would be avoided by doing so. For example, let us assume that the annual carrying costs for each unit in the safety stock are $1.00; and that the probability that demand will exceed the number of items in inventory in any given week with various sizes of safety stocks is as indicated in Figure 17–13. If 1000 units are normally carried in the safety stock the probability of occurrence of an out-of-stock condition may be reduced by .30 (from .40 to .10) by adding 2000 items to the safety stock at an additional carrying cost of $2000 per year. However, if the size of the stock were increased by an additional 2000 items—and thus carrying costs increased by an additional $2000—the out-of-stock probability would be reduced only by another .06. These extra

---

[13] It should not be inferred from this discussion that an order must necessarily be placed each time inventories are reviewed, for sometimes the review may indicate that existing inventories are high enough to protect against stock-outs until the following review is to take place.

FIGURE 17–13. Probabilities of Out-of-Stock Condition Occurring

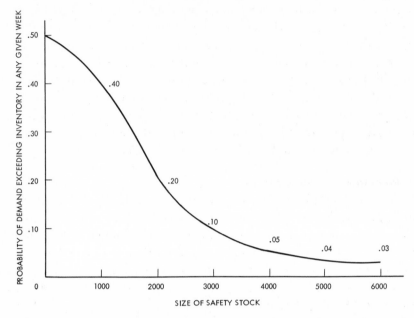

SIZE OF SAFETY STOCK

carrying charges should be balanced against the savings realized through the attendant reduction in stockout costs. Suppose, for example, that management has estimated stockout costs to be $200 per occurrence, and wants to know whether it should increase its safety stock from 1,000 to 2,000 units. Such an increase will result in additional carrying costs of $1,000 per year; while at the same time the probability of a stockout occurring is reduced by .20 for each week. As is shown in Figure 17–14, the marginal expected value of this reduction is $40 per week ($200 times .20), or $2,080 per year. Since this marginal value exceeds the marginal inventory carrying charges, the safety stock should be increased from 1000 to 2000 units. Optimally, the safety stock should be increased until the marginal savings are zero.

Certain other generalizations may be made concerning the establishment of safety-stock levels. All other factors being equal, the size of the stock should increase as: (1) stockout costs increase, (2) the inventory carrying charges decrease, (3) the fluctuations in demand increase, and (4) the acquisition lead time increases.[14] In addition, larger safety stocks will be required as the lot size decreases, since the possibility of depletion will occur more frequently.

---

[14] Whitin, *op. cit.*, pp. 55–56.

FIGURE 17-14

Marginal Savings for Selected Safety Stock

Safety-Stock Level (Units)	Marginal Inventory Carrying Costs	Probability Occurrence of a Stockout	Marginal Reduction in Probability of Occurrence	Expected Value of Marginal Reduction Per Week	Expected Yearly Value of Marginal Reduction	Marginal Savings (Marginal Expected Value — Marginal Carrying Costs)
0	—	.50	—	—	—	—
1,000	$1,000	.40	.10	$20	$1,040	$40
2,000	1,000	.20	.20	40	2,080	1,080
3,000	1,000	.10	.10	20	1,040	40
4,000	1,000	.05	.05	10	520	−480
5,000	1,000	.04	.01	2	104	−896
6,000	1,000	.03	.01	2	104	−896

Comparison of Fixed Lot and Fixed Cycle Methods

It will be useful to examine the types of conditions under which the fixed lot size and reorder-cycling methods are most applicable in the control of inventories. As a basis for this discussion, we will first need to treat the idea of selective inventory control.

Selective Control. It is frequently most economical for firms to employ different degrees of control for different classes of inventory items since the administrative cost of the control may exceed its value in some cases. It is not uncommon for a relatively small number of items in the firm's inventories to comprise a major portion of the inventory value. For example, 10 percent of the items may represent 90 percent of the total investment tied up in inventories. Consequently, a much greater portion of total inventory investment may be controlled by any given amount of effort for certain types of items—namely, the high-value items.[15] One approach for classifying inventory items in order to provide the basis for selective control is to establish three groupings: (1) close control for high-value items, (2) a moderate degree of control for medium-value items, and (3) relatively loose control for the low-value items.[16] It is important to note that when such selective control is employed, item value is not the only criterion upon which the

---

[15] By high-value items, we do not necessarily mean a high unit value; but rather those items whose total value contributes significantly to the firm's total inventory investment.

[16] See, for example, Howard L. Timms, *Inventory Management of Purchased Materials* (New York: National Association of Purchasing Agents, 1958), pp. 25–31. Timms considers degree of control as being "synonymous with frequency, accuracy, and completeness of review." (p. 27.)

degree of control to be established is determined. Both critical items and items which are subject to rapid deterioration or obsolescence are often placed in the high-value category, regardless of their contribution to total inventory value. Close control over a one-cent critical part, for example, would be justified if an out-of-stock condition might result in the complete breakdown of production. Similarly, a complete or near-complete loss in the value of certain items due to rapid spoilage or obsolescence would warrant close control of their inventories.

Comparison of Methods. It is possible to provide tighter, more frequent control over inventories with the order-cycling method than with the fixed lot size approach. Inventories may be reviewed daily, or even hourly, when necessary. Consequently, the order-cycling approach is frequently used for the control of high-value, critical, and rapidly depreciable items where close control is desired. The fixed cycle method is also applicable in those cases in which shipping costs can be reduced by ordering a number of items jointly from a particular supplier. Such joint orders would not be possible if fixed lot sizes for each item were ordered at variable time intervals.

The fixed lot size approach is employed most often for medium- and low-value items where a looser degree of control is permissible. The fixed order size may be determined either by using the *EOQ* formula or alternatively on a purely judgmental basis. The *EOQ* is more frequently used for medium-value than for low-value items. This is because the costs involved in applying the formula will frequently more than offset any savings which might be realized from its use when the total investment of the item being controlled is small. For example, if a company used fifty ⅛¢ (non-critical) bolts during the year, it would hardly pay to determine the carrying costs and setup or ordering costs necessary for application of the formula. This points up the fact that the decision maker needs to weigh the marginal costs of gathering and applying information against the marginal savings which may be realized by doing so.

OTHER INVENTORY CONSIDERATIONS

Total Dollar Limitations

Management may sometimes believe that some of the firm's funds tied up in inventories could more profitably be invested elsewhere

and that a total dollar limitation should be placed upon the value
of its inventories. Under conditions of risk or uncertainty in which
a safety stock is maintained, the average inventory value for an
item may be reduced to satisfy the limitation imposed in either or
both of two ways: (1) more frequent and smaller lot sizes may be
purchased (or shorter and more frequent production runs scheduled); or (2) the size of the safety stock may be reduced. For example, let us assume that yearly demand for an item is 8000 units;
that the item value is $1.00; that four orders of 2000 units are pres-
ently being placed each year; and that the safety stock is 500 units.
In this case, average inventory value is $\frac{Q}{2}C$ ($1,000) plus $500
for the safety stock; or $1500. If the manager decided to limit the
value of the average inventory to $1,000, he could: (1) reduce the
safety stock to zero, (2) maintain the safety stock at 500 units, but
place eight orders of 1000 units during the year, which would reduce the average inventory value of the "live" stock to $500; or
(3) reduce the safety stock partially and place somewhere between
four and eight orders per year.

When a total dollar limitation has been placed on an inventory
containing a large number of different kinds of items, the manager
must decide by how much the average inventory value of each
item should be reduced. A number of factors must be considered
in making such a decision. As Timms has pointed out,[17] the inventory reductions should normally be brought about primarily among
the medium-value items; for the high-value items are ordinarily
under close control anyway, and only a relatively small amount of
funds may be released by cutting back on the low-value items because of their small contribution to the total inventory investment.
Whether it is more desirable to order more frequently or reduce
the level of the safety stock for the medium-value items depends
on the relative importance that management gives to incurring
additional procurement costs as opposed to increasing the probability that stockouts will occur. Elimination of the 500 unit safety
stock in our previous illustration, for example, would increase the
probability of stock-outs without affecting the procurement costs.
Increasing the number of orders from four to eight per year, on the
other hand, would double the procurement costs, but would not
increase the probability of incurring stock-outs nearly as much as

---

[17] *Ibid.*, p. 62.

would elimination of the safety stock.[18] Finally, if the increased profitability attainable by releasing funds from the inventories is thought of in terms of a percentage return on investment, inventory reductions can be effected by manipulation of the *EOQ* formula in those cases in which it is employed. For example, if that portion of inventory carrying costs which has in the past been assigned to cover opportunity costs is 6 percent of the value of an item, and management decides that its funds can now earn 10 percent if invested elsewhere, a new economic order quantity reflecting this change can be determined by increasing I in the *EOQ* formula by 4 percent.

Inventory Turnover

An analytical tool which is often employed to determine inventory problems is the inventory turnover ratio. This ratio is computed by dividing the firm's annual cost of goods sold by its average inventory value. The average inventory value for the overall firm is usually determined by averaging the total value of the beginning and ending inventories for the financial year as given in the company's balance sheets. It is also possible to determine the turnover ratio for any single item in the inventory. Under conditions of certainty, in which no safety stock is maintained, the turnover is approximately equal to: $\dfrac{RC}{\frac{Q}{2}C}$, or $\dfrac{2R}{Q}$. [19]

With the addition of a safety stock (SS), the turnover becomes approximately: $\dfrac{RC}{\frac{Q}{2}C + (SS)C}$, or $\dfrac{2R}{Q + 2SS}$.

The reader may note that when only one item is being considered, its value (C) in both the numerator and the denominator cancels out, and the turnover ratio may be computed without reference to the item value. Computation of the turnover for the entire inventory of the firm, however, requires consideration of dollar values

---

[18] As indicated previously, the probability of incurring stock-outs will increase to an extent as smaller orders are placed more frequently, since the frequency of exposure to depletion is thereby increased.

[19] Where R represents the yearly demand, Q, the lot size, and C, the value of the item. The inventory turnover approximates $\dfrac{2R}{Q}$ to the extent that demand and the acquisition lead time are constant as assumed in our previous discussion of the lot size problem under conditions of certainty.

—since differently valued items invariably make up the inventory.

Turnover ratios vary considerably not only from industry to industry but also for different items carried by a firm. In the retail food industry, for example, produce items invariably turn over much more rapidly than any of the soft goods lines which a supermarket may carry. Consequently, there is no single turnover ratio which may be considered universally optimal. Comparisons of turnover figures with either (1) past ratios for the firm, or (2) current figures for other firms in the industry, however, may be useful in pointing up possible problem areas in the company's operations. A comparatively low turnover, for example, may indicate that too many slow-moving items are being carried. This may be due to the company making too many different sizes of models of a particular good. On the other hand, a comparatively high ratio may be an indication that insufficient inventories are being carried and that excessive stockouts are occurring. It should also be noted that turnover ratios—even for the same item—do not, and often should not, remain constant for long periods of time. As shown by the *EOQ* formula, for example, the average inventory for an item should optimally change only in proportion to the square root of changes in demand. Consequently, when the demand for a particular item increases, the turnover ratio should also increase.

SUMMARY

As the importance of adequate inventory control methods has gained increasing recognition, numerous analytical approaches have been developed to aid the decision maker in dealing with inventory problems. Although inventory decisions may serve to meet a number of objectives, the fundamental decision criterion on which all of these approaches center is the minimization of total inventory costs. Some of the techniques for handling inventory problems— such as the *EOQ* formula—are structured around mathematical models and are designed to develop optimum solutions. Because of the complexities encountered in dealing with inventories when demand and acquisition lead time are not certain, other approaches— such as the reorder-cycle method—are designed simply to satisfice rather than to optimize. In our presentation of all of these approaches, our primary focus has been upon decision making and analysis of the key decision variables and their interrelationships.

DISCUSSION AND STUDY QUESTIONS

1. What is the basic function performed by inventories? In what ways may this function be performed?

2. Explain how the two bin system functions. What cost, incurred when utilizing this system, is absent in the basic economic lot size model under conditions of certainty?

3. Which method of inventory control would you be more likely to use for each of the following items—the fixed lot size or order cycling?
   a) 14-karat gold wrist watches
   b) Ball point pens for use in clerical departments
   c) Lock washers (non-critical)
   d) Watermelons
   e) Text books carried by a university bookstore
   f) Paper clips

4. Under what conditions might you recommend that no inventory be maintained for a particular item?

5. In discussing his operations, the manager of a high-fashion dress shop stated that buying the right number of the right types of dresses at the right time to meet seasonal and style demands and to avoid excessive markdowns constituted his major decision problem. His friend, the manager of a firm manufacturing solid state electronic components, suggested that EOQ formulae be utilized by the dress shop as had been done in his electronics firm to deal with this problem. Do you agree? Explain.

6. A firm manufacturing phonographs, turntables, and loudspeakers recently installed a new inventory control system. The firm manufactures items both for stock and to meet specific customer orders. Its controller stated that a major advantage of the new system was that it provided accurate and timely information for controlling inventory levels. The system provides for daily reports on all items showing the number of parts, in-process and finished goods inventories on hand, the number of parts on purchase order, the number of items in process reserved for customer orders, etc. These reports are furnished to the inventory control manager, the controller, the purchasing agent, the production planning staff, the marketing vice-president, and the manufacturing vice-president.
   a) Comment on this system from the viewpoint of:
      (1) Information cost versus value.
      (2) Report format.
      (3) Exception reporting.
      (4) Differing data needs for different executives.
   b) Does this system as described assure optimal inventory decisions? Explain.

7. "An important feature of inventory management is that production and inventory decisions are rarely affected by minor variations in cost factors." Do you agree with this statement? Explain your answer.

8. "In some cases a firm may choose courses of action which do *not* minimize its inventory costs in order to effect minimization of its total operating

costs." Do you agree? If so, cite a specific example to support your answer.

9. The Richlaw Company, publishers of text books, buys engraved book contracts from an engraving company. It estimates that next year it will need 2,500 such contracts. The cost accountants estimate that the firm's ordering costs are $20.00 per order. Each engraved contract costs $1.00. The inventory carrying charge for such contracts is estimated to be approximately 10 percent per year of the value of the average inventory on hand.

    a) Evaluate by the tabular method each of the following order sizes. Which one would be the most economical order quantity?

    Order Size: 100   200   500   1,000   2,500

    b) One of these order sizes represents the *EOQ*. How could you determine which one this is without resorting to the *EOQ* formula?

    c) Utilizing the *EOQ* formula, determine the economic order quantity.

10. A manufacturing firm, with the following demand, output rate, and cost data is attempting to determine its optimum production run size.

Yearly demand.........................	36,000 units
Daily output	200 units
Carrying cost/unit	$1.50
Cost per set-up.......................	$15

    Assuming a 360-day year,

    a) What is the optimum size of each production run?

    b) What is the optimum length (in days) of each production run?

    c) If its daily output rate were 100 units rather than 200, what would the optimum run size and length be?

11. Yearly demand for an item is 15,000 units. Ordering costs amount to $30, and the item costs $.60 if purchased in quantities up to 6,000 units but only $.58 if the volume of a purchased lot is equal to or greater than 6,000 units. Annual carrying costs are equal to 10 percent of the purchase price. What is the most economical order quantity?

12. The Smith Company manufactures gear units for farm equipment. The nature of the demand for its product requires that the firm utilize intermittent manufacturing. The sales forecast for gear units the forthcoming year is as follows:

Quarter of Year	Estimated Number of Units
First.............	3,900
Second..........	4,100
Third............	4,600
Fourth..........	4,200

    The firm establishes production schedules on a quarterly basis. Its inventory policy specifies that the desired ending inventory of finished gear units for each quarter should be equal to one-half of its expected sales for the *subsequent quarter.* The firm's management estimates that the forthcoming year will commence with 1,000 units of completely assembled gear units in its finished goods inventories. Management has decided that it would like to end the forthcoming year with 2,000 units of finished goods in its inventories.

Using the order cycling method of scheduling, determine how many gear units should be produced in each quarter of the forthcoming year.

13. The Spoote-Nicht Television Company of Moscow, Idaho, has been developing color TV sets, and expects to have them on the market by May of next year. The Sales Manager has done a good job of market research and has prepared an estimate of monthly sales for the first full year of operations. It has been accepted as a valid basis for planning and is as follows:

May............	4,000 sets	November........	5,500 sets
June...........	3,500	December.........	7,500
July...........	2,500	January..........	6,000
August.........	2,000	February.........	4,500
September.......	3,500	March..........	5,000
October.........	4,500	April............	5,500

The firm is attempting to determine how large its production and warehousing facilities should be.

a) The personnel director would like to see a production schedule with a perfectly *level* productive output throughout the year, in order to provide stable employment, regardless of fluctuations in sales volume. Why is the personnel director interested in stable production? If maximum annual productive capacity is set at a level just large enough to meet expected annual sales, what will be the *warehouse size* necessary to hold the largest inventory which will exist at any time in the year?

b) The treasurer feels that the market will grow, and that any available capital should be invested in productive capacity instead of warehouse space. Therefore, he argues that productive capacity should be large enough to meet expected sales demand, without carrying any units in stock. What would be the minimum monthly *productive capacity* necessary in order to dispense with warehousing entirely? Is his position tenable? Explain.

c) The production manager believes that there should be a compromise, and that the installed productive capacity should be set at a maximum output of 5,000 units per month. The sales manager insists that in order to protect deliveries, the warehouse stock should never be allowed to fall below 500 units. If these suggestions are followed, what *size of warehouse* facilities in units would be necessary?

SELECTED REFERENCES

AMMER, DEAN. *Materials Management.* Homewood, Ill.: Richard D. Irwin, Inc., 1962.

CHURCHMAN, C. W.; ACKOFF, R., and ARNOFF, E. L. *Introduction to Operations Research.* New York: John Wiley & Sons, Inc., 1957.

FETTER, ROBERT B., and DALLECK, W. C. *Decision Models for Inventory Management.* Homewood, Ill.: Richard D. Irwin, Inc., 1961.

HADLEY, G., and WHITIN, T. M. *Analysis of Inventory Systems.* Englewood Cliffs, N. J.: Prentice-Hall, Inc., 1963.

HOLT, CHARLES C., et al. *Planning Production, Inventories, and Work Force.* Englewood Cliffs, N. J.: Prentice-Hall, Inc., 1960.

MAGEE, JOHN F. *Production Planning and Inventory Control.* New York: McGraw-Hill Book Co., Inc., 1958.

MILLER, D., and STARR, M. *Executive Decisions and Operations Research.* Englewood Cliffs, N. J.: Prentice-Hall, Inc., 1960.

MORRIS, WILLIAM. *Engineering Economy,* Chap. xiv. Homewood, Ill.: Richard D. Irwin, Inc., 1961.

STARR, M. K., and MILLER, D. W. *Inventory Control: Theory and Practice.* Englewood Cliffs, N. J.: Prentice-Hall, Inc. 1962.

TIMMS, HOWARD L. *Inventory Management of Purchased Materials.* New York: National Association of Purchasing Agents, 1958.

WHITIN, T. M. *The Theory of Inventory Management.* Princeton, N. J.: Princeton University Press, 1957.

CHAPTER 18

SIMULATION MODELS

I N the previous two chapters, we focused attention on the application of several different optimizing models to managerial problems. Certain of these, such as the simple *EOQ* and continuous inflow inventory models, provide optimal solutions to problems *directly* by the substitution of values in an equation. Others, such as the transportation model, do not provide for such direct solutions, but rather require the use of iterative methods. All of these models represent what we will refer to as *analytical* models. That is, they consist of known mathematical procedures or algorithms, which when manipulated, either directly or iteratively, provide an optimum solution.[1]

Many types of managerial problems are so complex that neither direct nor iterative analytical procedures exist for their solution, or, if such methods do exist, they present such great difficulties in application that their utilization is impractical. In such cases, the manager may turn to the use of a technique called *simulation*. In this chapter, we will explore several facets of simulation for managerial decision making.

THE NATURE OF SIMULATION

Simulation involves designing and utilizing a model which replicates some aspect of the firm's operations. Simulation models, like those which we have discussed in previous chapters, may be utilized to provide understanding about a system, to predict behavior, and/or to help prescribe courses of action. In general, simulation models may be distinguished from other operations research models

---

[1] It should be noted that some writers prefer to define "analytical" procedures in a narrower sense—e.g., as ones generally involving "the use of calculus to obtain the maximum point of a profit function or the minimum point of a cost function." Donald Clough, *Concepts in Management Science* (Englewood Cliffs, N. J.: Prentice-Hall, Inc., 1963), p. 372.

in that they are *nonanalytical* in nature, calling for an *experimental* approach, in which *numerous* trials or *iterations* are carried out by means of which workable, satisficing solutions rather than optimal ones are usually provided. We will now examine in greater detail these characteristics of simulation.

Nonanalytical Nature of Simulation

Simulation models, in their entirety, usually cannot be manipulated directly by mathematical means so as to arrive at an optimum solution.[2] As we mentioned previously, simulation models are utilized rather than those by means of which optimal solutions may be determined by one or more mathematical algorithms because the latter either do not exist or are not practically applicable. Illustrative of a problem of such complexity as to render simulation appropriate was that of one consumer goods manufacturer which attempted to determine whether or not it should initiate its own sales finance company. A simulation model of the proposed finance company was designed and run to estimate how profitable the operation might be under various possible conditions. Even though the model was "simplified" to the extent that no probabilistic functions were included in it, and certain elements which might have rendered it more useful were excluded:

> The model used . . . twenty-three input variables. . . . In total, forty-seven equations were developed to represent the operation of a finance company branch on a monthly basis . . . [and with an IBM 7090 utilizing FOR–TRAN] the entire simulation consists of approximately 8,000 program steps.[3]

Even in some cases in which a more straightforward mathematical statement of a problem can be made than in the finance model (with its 47 equations), there may be no known algorithm for determining an optimal solution, and simulation techniques may be called for. For example, in discussing one equation which describes the materials handling costs associated with the location of facilities in a plant, Armour and Buffa state:

> While this equation does furnish a mechanism for conceptualizing the problem, it unfortunately does not carry the analyst to a solution. The authors do

---

[2] Mathematical routines such as *EOQ* or linear programming may be incorporated into, and comprise one or more parts of, a total simulation model. See also Chapter 3, Figure 3–2, where both analytical and simulation techniques are applied to the same problem.

[3] Gordon B. Davis, Howard Ambill and Herbert Whitecraft, "Simulation of Finance Company Operations for Decision Making," *Management Technology*, 2 (December, 1961), 86, 87, 89.

not know of any algorithm which can *feasibly* be used to resolve this . . . problem.[4]

Illustrative of the usefulness of simulation techniques when analytical procedures do exist but pose such difficult computational problems that their application is not feasible, is with dealing with the so-called assembly "line-balancing" problem.[5] An optimum solution to this problem is computationally possible but the expense of analytical computational means is considered excessive. Through the use of heuristic line-balancing procedures which simulate the human thought processes of an industrial engineer when he balances a line, however, a "satisfactory" solution to this problem may be arrived at. Analytical balancing procedures probably could provide a better line balance, but the heuristic simulation techniques are almost as good and are considerably cheaper to operate.[6]

Simulation as an Experimental Process

A second basic characteristic of the simulation approach is that it is an experimental one. By experimenting with a number of variables incorporated into a simulation model, its user can compare the results from each experimental trial with those from other trials; and then select that set of decisions which the simulation results indicate would be most preferable. Although different simulation models vary considerably as far as the *specific* variables which are incorporated in them is concerned, they generally are structured around consideration of the *types* of variables which we discussed in Chapter 2—strategies which the firm may employ to meet its objectives; and states of nature in which the firm anticipates it may operate and/or competitive strategies which may be employed by other firms. Through such experimentation, several alternative strategies may first be tested under one set of possible competitor actions and states of nature. Then, the same alternatives may be tested under a second, third, and fourth set of external conditions, and so on. This process of systematically varying the firm's own alterna-

---

[4] G. C. Armour and E. S. Buffa, "A Heuristic Algorithm and Simulation Approach to Relative Location of Facilities," *Management Science*, 9 (January, 1963), 297.

[5] Balance "refers to the equality of output of each of the successive operations in the sequence of a line. If they are all equal, we say that we have perfect balance, and we expect smooth flow. If they are unequal, we know that the maximum possible output for the line as a whole will be dictated by the slowest operation in the sequence." Elwood S. Buffa, *Modern Production Management* (New York: John Wiley & Sons, Inc., 1961), p. 415.

[6] For a discussion of a heuristic approach to the line-balancing problem, see: Fred M. Tonge, *A Heuristic Program for Assembly Line Balancing* (Englewood Cliffs, N. J.: Prentice-Hall, Inc., 1961).

tives, states of nature, and competitive strategies can be continued for as long as considered necessary to determine which courses of action would be preferable.

An example of how various conditions of interest to management may be experimentally examined via simulation is provided by a simulation of the activities involved in operating a large airport developed by United Air Lines. In this simulation such factors have been included as weather conditions, need for maintenance, type and length of repair jobs, availability of spare aircraft, number of maintenance personnel, etc.[7] With this model:

> Management can change the number of spare aircraft, or the manpower schedule, and simulate operations under any new conditions which it would like to test. The computer is programmed to provide such data as expected idle manpower, expected idle equipment, utilization of maintenance docks, and delays in take-off. By comparing the expected performance in terms of these data with the cost of obtaining that performance, decisions can be arrived at that will produce the best over-all operation of the complex airport system.[8]

One final observation is in order concerning the experimental nature of simulation. While simulation is an experimental process, the experiments are performed on a model of the firm's operations rather than with the real operations themselves. In consequence, proposed courses of action can be tested *without disrupting* the actual operations of the firm. As the designers of the finance company simulation discussed previously have pointed out:

> Simulating a system allows those conducting the study to expand or compass real time . . . management . . . can simulate years of operations in a few minutes on a computer. Conversely they can slow it down to study special problem areas in detail. In short, they have a laboratory to analyze the proposed operation . . . simulation allows management to look before they leap and to test ideas in advance. The results can be evaluated and new ideas tried *without disrupting* current operations or incurring unnecessary costs for an uneconomical operation.[9]

Repeated Trials in Simulation

A third characteristic of simulations is that their utilization usually involves the carrying out of numerous trials or iterations. Repeated trials in simulation models may be necessitated for several reasons. First, as we indicated previously, management often desires to examine the impact of numerous possible strategies under a

---

[7] Franc M. Ricciardi, *et al.*, *Top Management Decision Simulation: The AMA Approach* (New York: American Management Association, Inc., 1957), p. 51.
[8] *Ibid.*
[9] Davis, Ambill and Whitecraft, *op. cit.*, p. 84. The emphasis is ours.

number of varied states of nature and/or competitive conditions. Additionally, it is necessary to simulate certain types of systems for numerous *time periods* if the impact of any given management decision, or of changes in external conditions are to be fully understood. Such would be the case in those dynamic systems: (1) the state of which in any time period is conditioned by their states in previous time periods and; (2) which take several time periods before reaching a new equilibrium state after having been "disturbed" from a previous equilibrium state. For example, in a simulation model of a production system described by Clough, the responses of certain system variables to a sudden 50 percent increase in customer order rates are long-term ones. With such an increase:

> The work-in-process level starts to oscillate and eventually settles at a level 50% higher than its original level. The warehouse inventory level begins to oscillate and then settles back to its original level. The interesting point is that the system does not reach equilibrium again until about 50 weeks after the step change in order rate.[10]

Systems such as that illustrated in the previous example requiring simulation over a number of periods of time because of their dynamic nature may be either stochastic or deterministic—i.e., they may or may not include any probabilistic relationships among variables. When a system being simulated includes probabilistic relationships, on the other hand, the necessity arises for repeated trials *regardless* of whether it is dynamic or not. This is because it is necessary to obtain an adequate *sample* of observations if statistical confidence is to be ascribed to the simulation results. Just how many experimental trials are necessary in utilizing simulations is a problem falling within the domain of statistical techniques, the discussion of which is beyond the scope of this book. It should be noted, however, that the number of iterations considered adequate may vary considerably from simulation to simulation depending upon their characteristics. In some relatively simple models, a sample size of less than 100 may be sufficient to produce useful estimates with a 95 percent level of confidence.[11] On the other hand, in one simulation with which the authors are familiar, about 50,000 iterations were considered necessary by its designer.[12]

---

[10] Clough, *op. cit.*, p. 378. Copyright © 1963 by Prentice-Hall, Inc.

[11] Murray A. Geisler, "The Size of Simulation Samples . . .", *Management Science,* 10 (January, 1964), 261–286.

[12] Richard L. Reich, "A Simulation Approach to the Solution of A Machine Interference Problem," Unpublished thesis (University Park, Pa.: The Pennsylvania State University, 1964), pp. 59–60.

TYPES OF SIMULATION

Now that we have discussed the fundamental characteristics of simulation models, we will indicate some of the different types of simulation utilized by management. There are several different ways in which managerial simulations may be classified. Our preference is to classify such models as (1) hand, (2) machine, and (3) man-machine.

With hand simulations, all calculations required in utilizing the model are performed by individuals either by hand or by the manual operation of calculating equipment, such as adding machines or comptometers. Machine simulations, on the other hand, are those in which calculations are carried out by an electronic computer. By man-machine simulation models, we mean those in which humans perform as *active participants* in the model, as we will illustrate more fully later.

Hand simulation may be used when relatively simple problems are being considered in which only a few variables or time periods are being examined. In such cases, it may not pay the decision maker to incur the expense of computer programming and operation. Further, hand computations are also frequently employed to test and "debug" a simulation model before it is programmed for a computer. For example, in the simulation of the finance company operations which we discussed earlier:

Since the simulation . . . involved the use of the computer to solve a relatively large number of rather simple equations, it was feasible to compute one solution by hand. This hand-calculated solution was compared against the same solution as calculated by the computer and any corrections or differences were rectified. Once the preliminary solution was completed, it was possible to proceed with additional problems using a wide range of input values.[13]

For large-scale simulated experimentation, utilization of computers is almost mandatory. Many such experiments are pure machine simulations—resort is simply made to computerization without introducing people into the model as active participants. Man-machine simulations, on the other hand, may be employed when: (1) it is necessary to simulate certain facets of human behavior if the simulation results are to be adequate; and (2) either the expense of or probable error resulting from developing a program to simulate such behavior on the computer is likely to be excessive. If the particular behavior which the simulation designer is interested in

---

[13] Davis, Ambill and Whitecraft, *op. cit.*, p. 89.

is overly complex, defining and programming it may exceed the cost of using people themselves in the simulation. Additionally, a pure machine simulation into which certain aspects of human behavior have been programmed may be in error due to an adequate knowledge of how this behavior is exhibited in the real system.

Man-machine simulations may also be employed for the specific purpose of determining how individuals will react in a *proposed* system. For example, management may want to know how much stress certain individuals will experience under a new organizational structure. Since the proposed organization does not yet exist, it might be very difficult to predict just which kinds of situations would occur in it. If, however, we are able to simulate the information flows, the interpersonal relationships and other factors which would exist in the proposed system, we may be able to determine how individuals would behave in it and whether its operation would be adversely affected because of the stress they experience. This type of man-machine simulation is sometimes referred to as *operational gaming*. The application of operational gaming may be illustrated by reference to a study of the supply systems for aircraft logistic support made by the RAND Corporation.[14] In this study, RAND developed new rules for making decisions about inventory levels, reorders to manufacturing plants, and other activities in a proposed defense supply system. Before recommending the new system to the Air Force, RAND designed a man-machine simulation of the proposed system to test its effectiveness. Air Force personnel were used as integral elements in the simulation, acting in the same capacities as they might in the real supply system if it were to become operational in the Air Force. Computer-generated reports necessary for logistics decisions were given to these people. Their decisions were fed into the computerized portion of the simulation and the impact of these decisions was determined. Usage rates under conditions of both war and peace were simulated to discover whether the supply system proposed and the individuals in it would be effective in both cases. Since Air Force personnel would eventually operate the system, their participation in the simulation was also helpful in determining how the selection and training of persons at different hierarchical and functional positions of the proposed supply system might best be effected.

---

[14] The RAND simulation experiments have been widely published. For a general evaluation of them, see Murray A. Geisler, "Appraisal of Laboratory Simulation Experiences," *Management Science*, 8 (April, 1962), 239–245.

Extending this RAND experience in designing new systems for the Air Force, Geisler and Steger have suggested that proposed business organizations can be tested by means of man-machine simulation.[15] When a firm reorganizes, modifications in existing power relationships, information patterns, and content of jobs often take place. If individuals can be placed in a system which simulates such changes, it may be possible to determine the adequacy of proposed information networks, work loads, influence patterns, etc. Appropriate improvements might then be made *before* the new organization is placed into operation. Such simulation may also serve the auxiliary function of providing *training* to potential incumbents slated for revised positions. Although such operational experiments have been proposed, their practical feasibility for business firms has not yet really been shown. Perhaps someday operational gaming will be widely used in business, but thus far its application has been almost exclusively limited to military systems.

THE STRUCTURE OF SIMULATION MODELS

The design of simulation models involves many of the same considerations as does the development of other types of mathematical models utilized in managerial decision making. Simulation models, however, are often structured somewhat differently from the models which we have discussed in previous chapters, due to their nonanalytical, iterative-experimental replication of often fairly complex systems. In this section, we will examine several aspects of the structuring of simulation models. The purpose of this examination is not to enable the reader to become proficient in simulation design. Rather, it is intended to provide him with greater insight into and understanding of the simulation approach.

Iteration Specification

As we indicated previously the simulation approach is characterized by iterative experimentation. The operations of a system may be simulated for numerous time periods and/or a repeated number of trials for any one or more periods may be carried out to ensure obtaining an adequate sample of data. When the simulation being utilized is a manual one, the experimenter can simply go ahead and

---

[15] Murray A. Geisler and Wilbur A. Steger, "How to Plan for Management of New Systems," *Harvard Business Review*, 40 (September–October, 1962), 103–110.

run the model for as many iterations as considered desirable, keeping track of each trial as it is carried out. When the simulation is to be computer-run, on the other hand, specification of the iterative procedures to be utilized must be programmed in advance. For example, suppose a firm is simulating certain phases of its production system in order to determine the effect of various proposed raw materials ordering rules on its inventory levels, and that it has been decided to simulate the operations on a weekly period basis for four years. If only one proposed ordering rule is to be tested at a time, the computer would have to be instructed to carry out 208 iterations (4 years times 52 weeks). Each such iteration is sometimes referred to as a model *cycle*. Further, it would be necessary in the programming to define the *end point* for each cycle—i.e., to specify that when the last necessary calculation for any given cycle has been completed, the computer should initiate computations for the next cycle (week). It would also be necessary to program the simulation so that the number of cycles already completed in the run are kept track of—this would be accomplished by building an *index* into the program which is incremented by one each time that a cycle of the model is iterated. After the index has reached the desired number of cycles (208 in our example) the computer would be instructed to terminate the run.

If our firm wanted to test numerous ordering rules as indicated previously, it might well not want to test them one at a time as we have been describing. Rather the computer program might be structured so as to permit several (or all) of the proposed rules to be tested in one run. This would obviate the necessity of setting up the experiment and reading the simulation program into the computer several different times. If such multiple-testing were undertaken, of course, additional end point and indexing specifications would be necessary—i.e., the computer would have to be instructed to initiate testing of the second ordering rule for the first week of operation after the last calculation for the 208th week with the first rule tested had been completed, etc.; and the computer would have to keep track of the number of 208-cycle tests already completed as well as the number of cycles completed in each test.

Input-Output Specification

In addition to specifying the iterative procedures to be utilized, it is necessary for the simulation designer to give attention both to the data which he plans to "feed in" to his model (input) and to the results which he wants the model to generate (output). In this section we will discuss some of the characteristics of simulation inputs and outputs.

Simulation Inputs. Some simulation inputs represent values which define the state of the system being simulated at a given point in time. In a simulation of a production operation, for example, an input value of 500 might be fed into the model to specify that 500 units of raw materials inventory are to exist for a particular item at the beginning of week one of the simulation. Other input values may be ones which help describe the relationships between certain variables in the simulation—e.g., in a production simulation the value $2.50 might be inputted to specify that labor costs are to be $2.50 for each nonovertime hour of work performed on certain operations in the system.[16]

In some simulations, all inputs are defined prior to the beginning of the first cycle of the run. In certain such cases, the outputs from the first cycle of the run may then serve as inputs to the second cycle, and so on. To use our production system as an example again, after week one of operations has been simulated, the raw materials inventories may have increased from an initial value of 500 to a level of 700 units, and this ending inventory level for week one (an output from cycle 1) would serve as an input into the second cycle. In certain types of simulations, on the other hand, it may be necessary to "plug in" new input values as the simulation progresses. For example, in a man-machine simulation of an air-defense direction center, numerous input data such as blips on a radarscope simulating the locating of aircraft were continually "fed in" to the system to be responded to by personnel participating in the experimentation.[17]

---

[16] It should be noted that values such as the one given in this example may or may not be structured as inputs to a computer program in a strict technical sense. In some cases, the $2.50 labor cost definition may be written into the computer program itself—e.g., as in the following equation $NLC = \$2.50\ NHW$; where NLC represents nonovertime labor costs, and NHW, nonovertime hours worked. It is often more convenient, however, to structure a program so that the $2.50 would represent an input —e.g., to write in the program the equation $NLC = C_n\ NHW$; where C_n represents the hourly nonovertime labor rate. In this way C_n the hourly nonovertime labor cost parameter can be *varied* any time the simulation user so desires, by simply punching a new input card (assuming the computer utilizes this type of input). If the $2.50 were specified in the program *itself*, on the other hand, it would be necessary to *recompile* the program every time this figure needed to be changed. (Compilation is a process in which programs written in such computer languages as FORTRAN are translated by the computer into machine language).

[17] See, for example, W. R. Goodwin, "The System Development Corporation and System Training," *The American Psychologist*, 12 (August, 1957), 524–528.

Simulation Outputs. The kinds of results generated from a simulation, or its outputs, will vary considerably depending upon the
objectives of the experimentation. In some cases, management may
be interested only in certain overall measures of system performance. For example, in a simple computerized simulation designed
by one of the authors, probability distributions for two variables
effecting cost savings with a new machine investment over a period
of years are fed into the model, and a frequency distribution of present values for the investment are outputted.[18] In this model, the
program was not written to print out cost savings data for each year,
since the objective of the simulation was simply to provide present
value data for the whole economic life of the investment. In other
cases, however, management may find it desirable to print out data
for each cycle of the simulation run. This would be the case when
a dynamic oscillating system was being simulated, and management was interested in the patterns of change in the system over
time. For instance, in testing new ordering rules in a production
system as we discussed previously, it might be important to know
how, and by how much inventory levels fluctuated each week.
Finally, with respect to outputs, we should point out that sometimes
it is essential to know something not only about overall system performance, but also about the performance of one or more of the
system's *subsystems*—either with respect to their state at each cycle
of the run or to their performance for the run *in toto*. It is to this
facet of simulation structuring that we will next turn our attention—
the design of subsystems.

Subsystems

Systems being simulated, especially more complex ones, may
often be comprised of fairly well defined subsystems, which are
linked together in one manner or another. For example, physical
production in a furniture factory moves sequentially through four
operational subsystems—rough mill to finish mill to assembly to final
finishing. It is useful in designing simulations of such systems to
segment the model into parts corresponding to these subsystems.
Such subsystem segmentation may permit greater flexibility both in
the design and operation of a simulation. For example, suppose the
management of a furniture factory wished to test among other things

---

[18] This model is patterned after the approach suggested in David B. Hertz, "Risk
Analysis in Capital Investment," *Harvard Business Review*, 42 (January–February,
1964), 95–106.

via simulation the advisability of purchasing kilns to dry green lumber as opposed to its present practice of buying already dried lumber. If the total simulation were segmented into subsystems paralleling those in the real operation, a subsystem representing the drying operation might easily be inserted into the model prior to the rough mill subsystem in place of the existing "purchasing of dried lumber" subsystem. Without this segmentation in the model, the simulation might require considerable redesign each time that management wanted to test the effect of such changes in the operations. In addition, subsystem segmentation may make it possible to test the effects of proposed policies on only one (or more) subsystems without the need to run the *total* simulation. The management of the furniture firm, for instance, may seek to test the impact of substituting improved machines for existing equipment in the finishing mill. This modification might have no impact outside of the finish mill subsystem. In such a case considerable savings could be realized by restricting the experimentation to just this one subsystem.

As we indicated in the previous section, it is often desirable to design simulations so that subsystem as well as overall system outputs are generated. The usefulness of such an approach may be illustrated by reference again to our furniture factory example. Suppose that management were simulating the impact upon its cost structure of increasing the variety of its furniture suites to be produced. Such a proposed course of action might increase labor costs considerably in the finish mill, moderately in rough milling and assembly, and only slightly in the finishing subsystem. Without the generation of subsystem cost outputs, the firm's only knowledge of its proposed policy would be with respect to total costs. Such overall data might, of course, be sufficient for evaluating the proposed course of action. Subsystems analysis, however, would permit a greater insight into the specific factors contributing to total costs. Management could determine, for example, the number and type of extra workers that it would need to acquire in each department. If no such information were generated from the simulation as to what would happen *within* the individual departments (subsystems), additional detailed studies would be required before the new policy could be effected.

Variables and Relationships

Of prime importance in designing simulations is specifying the variables which are to be incorporated into the model and defining the relationships which are to exist among the variables. We will now focus attention on these facets of simulation structuring.

Variables. As we have mentioned previously, variables may be classed as independent, dependent, or intervening. In simulations, independent variables—which represent experimentally controlled factors, the value of which affects the values of other variables— are invariably structured as model inputs. For example, if management were testing the impact of a number of ordering rules upon total costs in a production-inventory simulation, the quantity of parts or materials purchased as specified by the rules would represent an independent variable. Conversely, in such a simulation, total costs, which are determined by the quantities purchased (among other factors), would represent a dependent variable, and a simulation output. Intervening between total costs and quantities purchased would be a number of other variables—e.g., average inventory levels, which when multiplied by carrying costs/unit would give total carrying costs; and ordering costs, which when added to total carrying costs, would give total inventory costs.

Three other observations are in order concerning simulation variables. First, the dependent variables are invariably outputted from the model, since it is how they behave when any one or more independent variables are manipulated that the simulation designer is primarily interested in. Second, intervening variables, on the other hand, may or may not be so outputted, depending upon the objectives of the simulation. As we indicated earlier, for example, in simulating some dynamic production systems, management may be interested in examining the intervening variable "inventory levels" at the end of each simulation cycle. In other cases, however, it may be considered necessary only to output values for a dependent variable such as "total costs." Finally, we should mention that the distinction which we have been making between independent, intervening, and dependent variables is somewhat arbitrary. In some man-machine simulations, for example, certain human variables under study may be interdependent—e.g., positive sentiments among two or more group members may help contribute to "successful" performance, while successful performance may also serve to increase positive sentiments. Further, the *same* variable may be structured as one of a different type from one simulation to another. To illustrate with reference to a production-inventory system again, in one simulation an ordering policy may be the experimentally controlled independent variable as described earlier; while in another, management may frame the simulation problem as follows: "*given* an ordering rule that we have already decided to use, how would our total costs be influenced by different worker assignment decision rules?" In this latter case, the "given" set of ordering decisions would intervene (somewhere in the model) between the independent variable being experimentally tested (worker assignment) and the dependent variable, total costs.

Relationships Among Variables. In addition to specifying simulation variables, the model designer must define the relationships which are to exist among these variables. For purposes of convenience, simulation relationships may be classified as being either of the two types which we mentioned briefly earlier—deterministic, and probabilistic (or stochastic). In deterministic relationships, the value of the dependent variable is absolutely determined by the values of the other variables in the relation. Such relationships may be linear or curvilinear, or step- or kinked-functions may be utilized depending upon just what relations management is attempting to simulate.

A relation among two or more variables is classed as stochastic if at least one of the variables assumes multiple values, the frequency of occurrence of which may be described by a probability distribution. For example, management might find that the service life of one of the parts of a machine which it utilizes conforms to the probability distribution illustrated in Figure 18–1.

FIGURE 18–1. Probability Distribution
(Hypothetical Example)

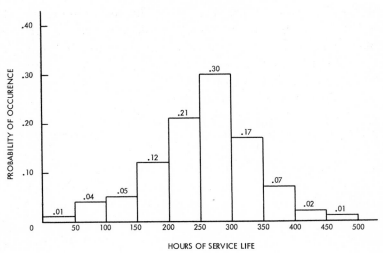

HOURS OF SERVICE LIFE

Probability distributions utilized in simulation models are sometimes standard mathematical ones, such as the normal or Poisson. In many cases, however, they are not. In fact, it is frequently for those situations in which actual distributions observed in the real system *cannot* be approximated by any standard distributions that simulation processes may be most useful.

One other observation is in order concerning the relationships among simulation variables. As we pointed out previously, simulation is utilized primarily when algorithms do not exist for the solution of managerial problems, or when the application of such analytical techniques is not feasible. Further, variables which are related stochastically involve more computational and manipulative problems than those related deterministically, *ceteris paribus*. For these reasons, it has been for systems (or problems) involving stochastic relationships that a great many simulation models have been designed. If the relationships among variables in a system can all be stated deterministically, the problem can often be dealt with analytically *unless* the system is a fairly complex one. Thus, simulation is primarily utilized with stochastic or *complex* deterministic systems; its use is rarely justified with simple deterministic problems.

Handling Stochastic Variables: The Monte Carlo Technique

In designing stochastic simulation models, it is necessary to have a means for dealing with those probabilistic variables, the values of which assume a frequency distribution. One commonly utilized method for working with stochastic variables in simulation models is the so-called Monte Carlo technique. This technique is one which both has application to an almost endless variety of simulation problems and at the same time, is relatively simple to comprehend and easy to utilize. In this section, we will illustrate the application of the Monte Carlo technique by utilizing an inventory problem under conditions of risk as an example.

Let us suppose that a retailing firm wants to develop an inventory ordering rule for a product for which both demand on any given day and the lead time required between its order and receipt are variable. Let us assume further that, on the basis of previous experience, the firm's management has derived probability distributions for both demand and lead time, as illustrated in Figure 18–2.

By simulating numerous days of experience given these probabilities, management could determine the impact of various pos-

FIGURE 18–2

Demand and Lead Time Probabilities

Daily Demand (Units)	Probability of Occurrence *		Lead Time (Days)	Probability of Occurrence
30	.10		1	.10
35	.20		2	.65
40	.40		3	.25
45	.25		Σ	1.00
50	.05			
Σ	1.00			

* These probabilities are assumed to be the same regardless of day of week for purpose of simplification.

sible ordering rules upon such variables as inventory levels, number of orders placed, and lost sales. Then, if costs could be assigned to these variables, a basis would be provided for evaluating the proposed ordering rules and choosing from among them a preferred course of action.

To illustrate the utilization of Monte Carlo with this problem, let us assume that management wants to test over a fifteen day period the following two ordering rules:

1. Whenever inventories at the beginning of a day have fallen to a level of 80 or below, reorder 80 units.

2. Whenever inventories at the beginning of a day have fallen to 200 or below, reorder 200 units.

In actual practice, of course, management would probably try out more possible rules than these two (the choice of which was somewhat arbitrary) and a simulated experience of more than 15 days would be required to obtain an adequate sample. However, this limited examination of two rules will serve to illustrate the application of the Monte Carlo technique.

A basic problem in running this simulation is to select values for lead times and demand such that they will represent or mirror the probabilities assumed to exist in the real system. This would mean that, as the model is iterated, lead times with a length of from 1 to 3 days, and demand levels of from 30 to 50 units/day be utilized *in proportion to* the frequency that each of these conditions is expected to occur in the real system. One method of achieving this objective would be as follows:

1. To simulate the demand distribution, place 100 balls in an urn: with 10 of them marked "30 units" (since this demand level occurs *10 percent of the time*); 20 marked "35 units" (which occurs 20 percent of the time); etc. Next, "select" a ball at random, and use the number of days indicated thereon as demand for the first day of the simulation. Replacing this ball, then draw another to provide a demand value for the second day of the simulation, and so on, for each of the 15 days to be simulated.

2. To simulate the lead times, place 100 balls in an urn, with 10 of them marked "1 day"; 65, "2 days"; and 25, "3 days." Then, each time that it is necessary to place an order (following the proposed ordering rule), draw a ball at random to obtain a value for the lead time required for that order.

As yet, computers have not been designed to accommodate either urns or balls, nor is it convenient for managers, professors, or students to carry such equipment around with them. Fortunately, however, an equivalent process for random sampling with replacement has been developed. This involves first taking 100 *numbers* (say 1–100) rather than balls, and assigning the occurrence of an event to a *proportion* of these numbers *equal to* the probability of the event's occurrence. Thus, in our problem, we would assign to the numbers 1–100, lead times and daily demand levels as is shown in Figure 18–3.

FIGURE 18–3

**Assignment of Lead Times
and Daily Demand Levels**

Lead Time (Days)	Probability of Occurrence	Occurrence Assigned to Numbers:	Daily Demand (Units)	Probability of Occurrence	Occurrence Assigned to Numbers:
1	.10	1–10	30	.10	1–10
2	.65	11–75	35	.20	11–30
3	.25	76–100	40	.40	31–70
			45	.25	71–95
			50	.05	96–100

Then, a number from 1 to 100 is generated randomly for each demand and lead time iteration (as one would draw a ball randomly if an urn were to be used); and the event assigned to the number generated is considered as having occurred in the simulation. This random selection of numbers may be accomplished:

1.   In manual simulations by using a *table of random numbers,* numerous of which have been published and are readily available.[19]

2.   In computerized simulations, by building a random number generator into the simulation program.[20]

These various stages of the Monte Carlo process are schematically diagrammed in Figure 18–4.

FIGURE 18–4. The Monte Carlo Process

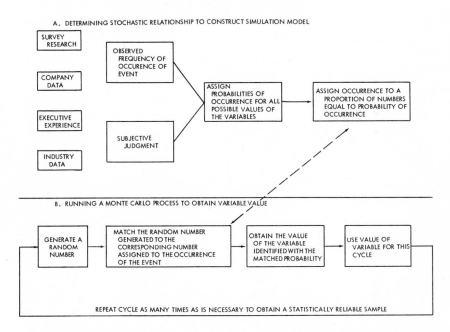

A. DETERMINING STOCHASTIC RELATIONSHIP TO CONSTRUCT SIMULATION MODEL

SURVEY RESEARCH

COMPANY DATA

EXECUTIVE EXPERIENCE

INDUSTRY DATA

OBSERVED FREQUENCY OF OCCURENCE OF EVENT

SUBJECTIVE JUDGMENT

ASSIGN PROBABILITIES OF OCCURRENCE FOR ALL POSSIBLE VALUES OF THE VARIABLES

ASSIGN OCCURRENCE TO A PROPORTION OF NUMBERS EQUAL TO PROBABILITY OF OCCURRENCE

B. RUNNING A MONTE CARLO PROCESS TO OBTAIN VARIABLE VALUE

GENERATE A RANDOM NUMBER

MATCH THE RANDOM NUMBER GENERATED TO THE CORRESPONDING NUMBER ASSIGNED TO THE OCCURRENCE OF THE EVENT

OBTAIN THE VALUE OF THE VARIABLE IDENTIFIED WITH THE MATCHED PROBABILITY

USE VALUE OF VARIABLE FOR THIS CYCLE

REPEAT CYCLE AS MANY TIMES AS IS NECESSARY TO OBTAIN A STATISTICALLY RELIABLE SAMPLE

Returning to our inventory problem, let us suppose that we have selected the random numbers shown in Figure 18–5, and assigned to them, following the procedures outlined above, the demand levels and lead times as are also illustrated in Figure 18–5.

Given these data we can simulate our inventory problem with both of the proposed ordering rules specified previously. Taking the "reorder 80 units when inventory falls to 80 or below" rule and assuming that the system starts with an inventory of just 80 units

---

[19] Frequently utilized is the RAND Corporation's *A Million Random Digits,* (Glencoe, Ill.: The Free Press, 1955). See, for example, Riccardi, *et al., op. cit.,* pp. 36–37; or Clough, *op. cit.,* p. 394. A table of random numbers is also provided for the reader's use in Appendix C at the end of this text.

[20] Or, with some computers it is possible to program the simulation so as to make use of a random number generating sub-routine incorporated in the computer system itself.

FIGURE 18–5

Monte Carlo Generation of Demand Levels and Lead Times

| | Demand Levels | | | Lead Times | |
Day	Random Number Chosen	Represents Demand* Level of:	Order	Random Number Chosen	Represents Lead* Time of:
1	77	45	1	80	3
2	18	35	2	62	2
3	47	40	3	75	2
4	91	45	4	83	3
5	22	35	5	02	1
6	09	30	6	41	2
7	02	30	7	39	2
8	37	40	8	07	1
9	19	35			
10	10	30			
11	88	45			
12	57	40			
13	62	40			
14	15	35			
15	51	40			

* From Figure 18–3.

(with the first order thus being placed at the beginning of the first day), our simulated system for the 15 days behaves as is illustrated in Figure 18–6. With the 200 unit reorder rule (and assuming an inventory of 200 units at the beginning of the first day), the system will behave as is shown in Figure 18–7.[21] As may be noted from these figures (and as would be expected from our discussion of inventories in the previous chapter), with the 200 unit reorder rule:

1.   Average inventories are considerably higher (209.5 as opposed to 42.2 units with the 80-unit rule),

2.   Fewer orders are placed (3 as opposed to 6), and

3.   No sales are lost, as compared with lost sales of 90 units with the 80-unit rule.

---

[21] With both of these ordering rules, we are assuming that no orders will be placed while any previous order is still outstanding—e.g., no order is placed in days 2 and 3 in Figure 18–6 since the order placed in day 1 has not yet been received.

FIGURE 18–6. Inventory Simulation with 80-Unit Reorder Rule

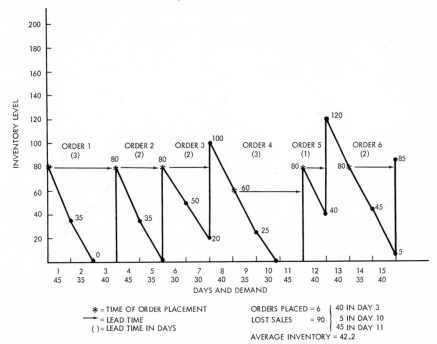

* = TIME OF ORDER PLACEMENT	ORDERS PLACED = 6	40 IN DAY 3
⟶ = LEAD TIME	LOST SALES = 90	5 IN DAY 10
( ) = LEAD TIME IN DAYS		45 IN DAY 11
	AVERAGE INVENTORY = 42.2	

To evaluate these two ordering rules, management would, of course, have to next define the costs which would be expected with each. For illustrative purposes, let us assume that it costs $5 to place each order; that the cost of each "lost sale" is estimated to be $1; and that, for a 15-day period, as simulated, inventory carrying costs are believed to be about $.10 for each unit of average inventory carried. In such a case, the total costs expected for each ordering rule would be computed as is illustrated in Figure 18–8.

One final observation is in order concerning this illustrative application of the Monte Carlo technique. As we indicated earlier, simulating the firm's experience for only 15 days would not provide a large enough sample to permit ascribing statistical confidence to the cost data given in Figure 18–8. If enough iterations are performed, however, the *simulated* frequency distributions of lead times and demand levels will tend to *approximate* the frequencies assumed to exist in the *real* system. When such is the case, Monte Carlo can provide a highly useful and flexible means of generating data upon the basis of which more effective managerial decisions may be made.

FIGURE 18–7. Inventory Simulation with 200-Unit Reorder Rule

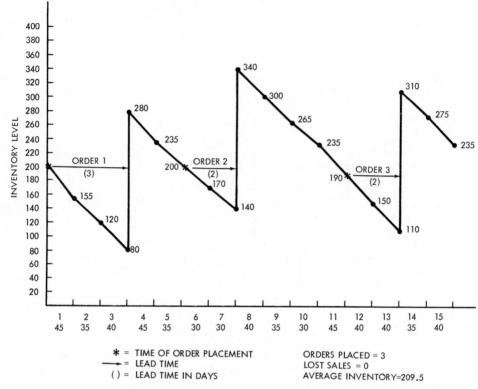

```
*       = TIME OF ORDER PLACEMENT        ORDERS PLACED = 3
——→ = LEAD TIME                         LOST SALES  = 0
(  )   = LEAD TIME IN DAYS               AVERAGE INVENTORY=209.5
```

FIGURE 18–8

Computation of Costs for Two Ordering Rules

	80-Unit Ordering Rule	*200-Unit Ordering Rule*
Lost Sales	90 × $1 = $90	0 × $1 = $0
Ordering Costs	6 × $5 = $30	3 × $5 = $15
Inventory Costs	42.2 × $.10 = $4.22	209.5 × $.10 = $20.95
	Total Costs = $124.22	Total Costs = $35.95

THE FUTURE OF SIMULATION

Bringing "Science" to Top Management

As we indicated previously, the design of simulations is quite flexible, and it is possible to enlarge their scope by incorporating additional subsystems into them. In consequence, it might be possible, over a period of time, to develop a simulation into a representation of the operations of the firm as a whole. In this way, simulation may evolve from a decision-making aid in relatively narrow areas of business to an instrument capable of providing insight and assistance to top-level managers holding policy-level positions. To date, most management science and operations research models such as mathematical programming have application only to relatively narrow problem areas and to lower-level operations. Literature addressed to top management is replete with new decision methods. Rather than providing top management with methods for improving its own decision making, however, many articles tend to implore top management to insure that their *subordinates* utilize one model for inventory decision making, another for optimizing production schedules and still another for determining the in-plant location of facilities. In contrast, it may be possible to design simulations for experimentally testing proposed decisions emanating from the executive suite.

The Decline of Simulation?

At the same time that additional opportunities for analysis of top-level problems via simulation may evolve, the utilization of the simulation technique for dealing with lower-level problems may decline. As more and more analytical solutions to problems are developed to states of technological and economic feasibility, the usefulness of simulation with such problems tends to lessen. Since simulation will not necessarily provide optimal decisions, analytical methods are preferred if they exist and their costs are not excessive.

The world of business management has seen the rapid development of analytical methods in the last decade. As this trend continues, solutions based upon simulation techniques may tend to become obsolete. However, many aspects of dynamic business operations may never yield to analytical processes (at least in the economic sense). It is precisely to these areas that simulation can, and probably will, be directed to an even greater extent in the future.

On Line Decision Systems

In Chapter 12, we discussed the possibility of providing instantaneous feedback of operating data for control decisions. If such an information system could be coupled with a simulation of the firm's operations, it would be possible to experiment with the simulation using current on line data from the operating system. If the feedback and simulation systems could be operating fast enough, it would be possible to test *day-to-day operating decisions* upon the simulated system *prior* to their implementation.

Often, however, considerable time is needed after the completion of an experimental test of proposed courses of action before the meaning of its results is known because lengthy analysis of the simulation outputs is required. The experiment may consume but a short period whereas the analysis of it may take weeks. To employ a simulation for on line operating decisions, therefore, would require construction of methods of data reduction and analysis such that rapid conclusions could be reached. Perhaps rapid mechanical and computer methods can never economically replace human beings completely at this stage. If creative and unique analyses are required, predetermined data reduction and analyses, obviously, will be insufficient for the task. Yet, similar methods of analysis tend to be used over and over in handling many types of management problems. As long as the operating characteristics of the real system undergo no fundamental changes, rapidity of analysis seemingly could be built into an integrated data processing and simulation decision system.

SUMMARY

Simulation provides an approach for dealing with managerial decision problems for which analytical methods either do not exist, or cannot be feasibly applied. Iterative and experimental in nature, simulation permits the testing of various proposed managerial strategies under different conditions without disrupting the real system. Further, simulation is a more flexible tool than are many currently used operations research techniques (e.g., linear programming)—the technique has been applied to many diverse types of managerial problems. In spite of this diversity, there are many general characteristics of model structuring common to most simulations—e.g., the specification of the iterative procedures to be utilized, and of the inputs, outputs, variables, and relationships among variables.

Simulations have been designed to replicate both deterministic and stochastic systems. When stochastic variables are being simulated, the Monte Carlo technique is often highly useful. Through random number generation, Monte Carlo provides a means of selecting values for the stochastic variables in the model so that they will approximate those probabilities assumed to exist in the real system.

Simulation is being increasingly utilized to deal with managerial decision problems. In the future, possibilities may be envisioned for building up simulations into representations of the operations of firms as a whole to deal with top-level policy decisions. Further, the possibility of the coupling of on-line informational feedback systems with simulation, offers prospects for testing day-to-day operating decisions in a simulated system prior to putting them into effect.

DISCUSSION AND STUDY QUESTIONS

1. What are the basic differences between simulation and other operations research models? What types of solutions are usually developed with simulation techniques?

2. Under what conditions would the utilization of simulation models *not* be appropriate for problem solving?

3. Why must simulations of stochastic systems, even though they are not dynamic, involve repeated trials in order to obtain valid results?

4. What is meant by the term "operational gaming"?

5. What advantages may be obtained from providing for subsystem analysis when designing simulation models?

6. The same variable, such as inventory carrying costs, might be defined as either a simulation input or output depending upon the specific objectives of the simulation. Discuss.

7. What are the differences between (a) hand, (b) machine, and (c) man-machine simulation models?

8. If all relationships in a model can be defined deterministically, why should there be any need to employ iterative simulation calculations?

9. Utilizing the same lead time and demand figures as given in Figure 18–5 for the Monte Carlo inventory simulation in the text:
   a) Simulate the effect of each of the following ordering rules over a 15-day period. Whenever inventories at the beginning of a day have fallen to:
      1) a level of 100 or below, reorder 100;
      2) a level of 125 or less, reorder 125 units; and
      3) a level of 150 or less, order 150
   b) For each of the above rules:
      1) draw a schematic diagram such as is illustrated in Figures 18–6 and 18–7; and
      2) determine what total costs would be incurred if the rule were followed, using the cost data given in the chapter.
   c) Compare the total cost results obtained with each of these three rules and with the two rules illustrated in the text. Do the results of your comparisons seem logical in terms of our discussion of inventory costs in Chapter 17? Why?

d) What additional ordering rules might be tested via simulation?

e) Assume that you are planning to develop a computer program to handle this inventory problem via the Monte Carlo method so that you can test a large number of ordering rules quickly. Develop a flow diagram for the program such as that illustrated in Figure 11–5 of Chapter 11. In your diagram, indicate sequentially all "if" and "do" statements required. Should the lead time and demand distribution figures given in this problem be written into the program itself? Or, should provision be made to read these numbers into the program as parameter inputs for each run? Why? (HINT: See footnote 16 in the chapter.)

10. A firm builds tables to customer specification. Following is a frequency distribution of the number of orders received each day for its product in the past:

Number of Tables Ordered Per Day	Frequency (%)
0	6
1	12
2	15
3	25
4	14
5	10
6	9
7	9
8 or more	0

Production is of the job lot type and the number of man-hours required to build each table varies between seven and ten. Following is a frequency distribution of times required to build tables in the past.

Number of Man-Hours Required to Build One Table	Frequency (%)
6 or less	0
7	10
8	25
9	40
10	25
11 or more	0

All workers are paid at a rate of $4.00 per hour. The firm operates on an 8-hour day, 5-day week basis with no overtime. The company has no way of accurately determining how much business it loses when it is forced to keep a customer waiting, but has subjectively approximated that for each hour of work backlog remaining at the end of any given day it incurs a "cost of lost sales" of $1.00.

The company wants to determine the optimum number of workmen which should be employed in the production of tables. If the company has too many workers, it must pay for idle time since there are no other jobs in the firm on which its workmen can be employed. Further, it is not possible to hire employees on a part-time basis because their skills are in great demand. On the other hand, if there are too few workers, order backlogs will build up and business will suffer because of customer dissatisfaction.

Assuming that the same probabilities will hold in the future as in the past for number of orders received per day and processing time per table, determine, by use of the Monte Carlo technique the number of workers which should be employed. There is no current order backlog.

Use twenty iterations. Begin your selection of random numbers at the top of column 1, line 1 in the Table of Random Numbers found in Appedix C at the end of this book. Proceed down column 1 until the column is exhausted; then go to the top of column 2 and repeat the same procedure. Utilize your first random number to generate the number of orders received in day 1; your second random number for the number of orders in day 2, etc. Then, utilize your next random numbers for determining the number of man-hours required to build each order received in day 1; your next numbers for man-hours required to build each order received in day 2, etc.

NOTE: Choice of the first random number should theoretically be made randomly rather than simply selecting the first number on the table as indicated here. We have suggested starting at the beginning of the table in order to enable all those working this problem to arrive at the same answer.

SELECTED REFERENCES

ALBERTS, W. E. "System Simulation," *Proceedings of the Seventh Annual National Conference of the AIEE* (May 17–18, 1956).

BAUER, R. A., and BUZZELL, R. D. "Mating Behavioral Science and Simulation," *Harvard Business Review*, 42 (September–October, 1964), 116–124.

BORKO, HAROLD (ed.). *Computer Applications in the Behavioral Sciences*, Chaps. xiv, xv, xxi, xxiii, xxiv. Englewood Cliffs, N. J.: Prentice-Hall, Inc., 1962.

BOWMAN, EDWARD H., and FETTER, ROBERT. *Analysis for Production Management*, Chap. xi. Homewood, Ill.: Richard D. Irwin, Inc., 1961.

CONWAY, R. W. "Simulation in Profit Planning," *Report of System Simulation Symposium.* (ed. D. G. Malcolm) Baltimore: Waverly Press, Inc., 1957.

CONWAY, R. W.; JOHNSON, B. M.; and MAXWELL, W. L. "Some Problems of Digital Systems Simulation," *Management Science*, 6 (October, 1959).

FLAGLE, CHARLES D. "Simulation Techniques," *Operations Research and Systems Engineering.* (ed. C. D. Flagle) Baltimore: Johns Hopkins Press, 1960.

FORRESTER, JAY W. "Industrial Dynamics—A Major Breakthrough for Decision Makers," *Harvard Business Review*, 36 (July–August, 1958).

GEISLER, M. A. "The Simulation of a Large-Scale Military Activity," *Management Science*, 5 (July, 1959).

GUETZKOW, HAROLD (ed.). *Simulation in Social Science.* Englewood Cliffs, N. J.: Prentice-Hall, Inc., 1962.

HOGGATT, A. C., and BALDERSTON, F. E. (eds.). *Symposium on Simulation Models: Methodology and Applications to the Behavioral Science.* Cincinnati: South-Western Publishing Co., 1963.

HOVLAND, C. I. "Computer Simulation of Learning," *American Psychologist,* 15 (1960).

JACKSON, J. R. "Simulation Research on Job Shop Production," *Naval Research Logistics Quarterly* (December, 1957).

MAYER, H. A. *Symposium on Monte Carlo Methods.* New York: John Wiley & Sons, Inc., 1954.

MALCOLM, D. G. (ed.). *Report of System Simulation Symposium.* Baltimore: Waverly Press, Inc., 1958.

SASIENI, M.; YASPAN, A.; and FRIEDMAN, L. *Operations Research.* New York: John Wiley & Sons, Inc., 1959.

SHUBIK, M. "Bibliography On Simulation, Gaming, Artificial Intelligence, and Allied Topics," *American Statistical Association Journal,* 55 (December, 1960), 736–38.

SHUBIK, M. "Bibliography On Simulation, Gaming, Artificial Intelligence, (September–October, 1958), 390–92.

Simulation and Gaming: A Symposium, Management Report No. 55. New York: American Management Association, Inc., 1961.

SPENCER, M. H. "Computer Models and Simulation in Business and Economics," *Business Topics,* 11 (Winter, 1963), 21–32.

TOCHER, K. D. *The Art of Simulation.* London: English University Press, Ltd., 1963.

CHAPTER 19

OVERVIEW

THE managerial process is a complex multi-faceted phenomenon. In the previous chapters we have explored several different dimensions of this process. At times, we have viewed management in "global," macrocosmic terms, examining such subjects as
stages in the decision-making process, the systems concept, and the
nature of planning and control decisions in general. At other times,
our focus of attention has been a more microcosmic one as we discussed numerous specific problem areas of concern to the manager
and techniques and approaches for dealing with these problems.
These specific problems have been of a wide variety and have encompassed many different types of systems variables, both economic
and psychological.

The purpose of this chapter is to present several concepts aimed
at providing the reader with deeper insight into how the many areas
which we have discussed thus far may be "tied together" into a more
integrated conception of management. In our overview, we will
focus attention upon four areas: (1) a dynamic, holistic view of the
organizational system; (2) the interrelationships among basic managerial decision types; (3) a classification of managerial problems,
and (4) some methods for dealing with complex decision problems.

SCIENCE, MANAGEMENT, AND DYNAMIC HOLISM

The Holistic View

In Chapter 1, we indicated that many similar ways of thinking
have emerged in numerous fields of modern science. One of the most
basic of these is that of viewing phenomena in *holistic* terms. This
view emphasizes that systems—whether they be physical, biological,
or social—are comprised of numerous interrelated elements; that the
behavior of these elements is influenced by and can be understood

525

only in light of the state of the system as a whole.[1] As von Bertalanffy has pointed out with respect to biological systems:

> . . . each individual part and each individual event depends not only on
> conditions within itself, but also to a greater or lesser extent on conditions
> within the whole, or within superordinate units of which it is a part. Hence the
> behaviour of an isolated part is, in general, different from its behaviour within
> the context of the whole.[2]

Such is also the case with organizational systems. In the previous
chapters, we have been compelled to break down our treatment of
management into several discrete "chunks" for purposes of exposition—motivation, organization, inventory models, etc. At the same
time, however, we have on numerous occasions emphasized that
many key interdependencies exist among the multitude of different
elements and variables in an organizational system. As we have
pointed out previously, for example, any particular aspect of the
individual's behavior can be understood only in light of his total
personality system; the behavior of individuals within the organizational system both influences and is influenced by the work group
subsystem(s) of which they are members; hiring, training, and firing
costs incurred by a firm's personnel department sub-subsystem will
be considerably influenced by production leveling decisions made
in the manufacturing subsystem of which it is a part, etc. Thus, a
true understanding of management requires an understanding not
only of the parts of the organizational system, but also of the relations between the parts. As with all fields of learning, the *integration* of knowledge about the phenomena with which we are dealing
represents a basic concern to management. The central problem of
such integration, as one scholar has pointed out:

> is always . . . [that] . . . of understanding how *many* parts, elements,
> items, things, events, generic classes, and so forth, are related to one another
> and to the whole such that they are *one*. The parts must in some significant
> sense constitute a meaningful whole, totality, system, or unity. The problem is
> always that of integration, organization, systemization, and unification. It seems
> to make little difference whether one is talking about tissue systems, nervous
> systems, personality systems, or social systems.[3]

---

[1] Also central to holistic thinking is the concept that the total system represents
more than and something different from simply the sum of its parts.

[2] Ludwig von Bertalanffy, *Problems of Life* (New York: Harper & Bros., Harper
Torchbook Edition, 1960), p. 12. As an example, von Bertalanffy points out, that:
"The reflexes of an isolated part of the spinal cord are not the same as the perform-
ances of these parts in the intact nervous system." (*Ibid.*)

[3] Ronald G. Jones, "The Unity of Knowledge and Liberal Education," a revision of
the paper "Holism, The Integration of Knowledge, and Liberal Education" read at

Our knowledge of how the many elements in the organizational system are related to each other and to the whole, is, of course, incomplete in many respects. Organizational processes, as we have said before, are extremely complex ones; and the serious study of management is relatively new. It has been our view, throughout this book, however, that by incorporating knowledge about the behavior of both human and economic variables from many disciplines into an information-decision framework, a considerable amount of integration is possible.

A Dynamic View

Also emerging in many fields of modern science is the viewing of phenomena not in rigid structural terms but as *dynamic* processes. A basic change in modern physics, for example, has been in

> . . . the resolution of rigid structures into dynamics. Classical physics considered the atoms as solid bodies like tiny billiard balls. According to modern physics, they are minute planetary systems, with a nucleus as the central sun, consisting of positively charged and uncharged particles . . . encircled by negative electrons. At the same time matter appears as a process, as dynamics. . . . An electron is not a tiny rigid body; it is a concentration of energy, a matter-wave or a wave-packet.[4]

Parallel changes in thinking have been taking place in the field of management. More and more, attention is being focused upon the business organization as constituting dynamic interrelated processes. In some earlier conceptualizations in organization theory, for example, relationships among members of the firm were portrayed almost entirely in static terms by means of organization charts, with relatively little or no attention being given to the dynamics of organization restructuring such as those which were discussed in Chapter 10. Or, as we illustrated in Chapter 18, considerable attention has been given in recent years to understanding the dynamic behavior of numerous interrelated systems variables over time via simulation processes. In short, we are coming more and more to viewing the business organization not only as a holistic system, but as a *dynamic* holistic one. From an operational point of view this approach allows the manager to conceptualize the relationships among the variables existing within the organizational system.

---

the Second Synopsis Congress of the International Society for the Comparative Study of Civilizations, Salzburg, Austria, September 1964, p. 2.

[4] von Bertalanffy, *op. cit.*, p. 179.

THE BASIC TYPES OF MANAGERIAL DECISIONS

As we mentioned in Chapter 1, management thinkers of the classical or functional school conceived of the manager's job as consisting of several distinct functions or processes, such as planning, organizing, and controlling. We have retained this classical conceptualization to an extent in this book, although we have conceived of the classical "functions" more as decision types. One of our primary foci in Chapters 4–6 was upon managerial decisions aimed at *directing* and *motivating* individuals to gear their efforts toward meeting organizational objectives; in Chapters 7–10 we gave consideration to types of *organizing* decisions which the manager must make; and in Chapters 11–18, we examined both the nature of *planning* and *control* decisions and numerous techniques, methods and models utilized for planning and control purposes. Our purpose at this time is to discuss the question: "What relationship is there between these different basic types of managerial decisions?"

In Chapter 12, we suggested that control decisions may be thought of as a specific class or sub-set of planning decisions—as those decisions specifying or guiding future actions which are specifically geared toward correcting unacceptable deviations in systems performance. Similarly, motivating, directing, and organizing decisions may also be conceived of as special sub-types of the general class, planning decisions. Both are designed to specify or guide future actions, with

1.   Direction-motivation decisions specifically geared toward inducing individuals (and groups) to work toward meeting organizational goals, and

2.   Organizing decisions specifically geared toward the *structuring* of tasks, informational content and flows, and influence and power relationships within the firm.

It is also important to recognize that directing, organizing, and control decisions do not represent mutually exclusive sub-sets of planning decisions. Rather there is a considerable amount of "overlap" among these three subsets. That is, although some specific managerial decisions involve only direction, but no control or organizing aspects, or only control but no direction or organizing aspects, etc., many decisions will fall into either two or all of the three sub-sets which we are considering. For example, a job enlargement decision, as discussed in Chapter 7, involves both directing and motivating employees and changing the organization of work content. Or, a manager's checking on the performance of a subordinate has both motivational-directional and control implications. The interrelationships among the types of managerial decisions we have been discussing are illustrated in Figure 19–1.

FIGURE 19–1. Interrelations Among Basic Decision Types

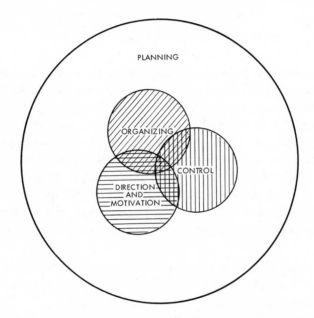

MANAGERIAL PROBLEM CLASSES

As we pointed out in Chapter 2, managerial decision making is directed toward the solution of organizational problems. In previous chapters we have focused attention on a wide variety of managerial problems and decision techniques for dealing with these problems. Our purpose in this section is to provide a framework into which these numerous problems and approaches may be incorporated.

In examining managerial problems and problem techniques, we find it useful to classify managerial problems as: (1) being comprised of either a *few* or *many variables*, and (2) being either *deterministic* or *stochastic* in nature. This framework is illustrated in Figure 19–2.

This classification is, of course, somewhat arbitrary in that complexity is dichotomized into few vs. many variables; whereas it might better be described as a continuum in which the number of

FIGURE 19–2

Classification of Problems

	Deterministic	Stochastic
Few Variables..........	Organized Simplicity	Disorganized Simplicity
Many Variables..........	Organized Complexity	Disorganized Complexity

Adapted from: *Tentative Recommendations for the Undergraduate Mathematics Program of Students in the Biological Management and Social Sciences* (Berkeley, Calif.: Committee on the Undergraduate Program in Mathematics, 1964), p. 12.

variables ranges from one to infinity. Somewhat similarly, one could differentiate various degrees of disorganization in stochastic decision problems—e.g., in one decision problem involving ten variables, only one might be stochastic; while in another with the same number of variables, all ten might be stochastic. Nonetheless, this framework provides a useful integrative conceptualization of the many different kinds of problems with which managers must deal.

Further, as all managerial *problems* may be grouped into the four classes illustrated in Figure 19–2, so also may the *decision techniques* available to management for dealing with these problems:

1. *Organized Simplicity.* For problems in which only a few deterministic variables exist, *analytical models,* such as the E.O.Q. model discussed in Chapter 17 are often available.

2. *Organized Complexity.* For problems comprised of many deterministic variables, *interative* models, such as mathematical programming, are frequently most useful—e.g., to determine optimal product mixes in oil refineries, where it is possible to process different types of crude oils in a variety of ways in order to produce different products yielding different profits.

3. *Disorganized Simplicity.* For decision problems consisting of only a few stochastic variables, payoff matrix analysis is available to the manager, as was illustrated in Chapter 2.

4. *Disorganized Complexity.* In dealing with multi-variate stochastic problems, managers frequently will rely on experience-based decision making (sometimes supplemented by research into the behavior of certain systems variables). In some cases, managerial judgments may also be formalized into "models" geared to aid in decision making—e.g., the Lockheed model for dealing with span of control which we discussed in Chapter 7. Additionally, with the

advent of the electronic computer, it is now possible to deal with disorganized complexity to a much greater extent than ever before through such approaches as PERT, heuristic programming, and simulation.

Two final observations are in order concerning managerial problems and problem-solving approaches. First, the problems which management faces in an organization tend to cluster in the category of disorganized complexity. This is due to a considerable extent to the large number of interrelated variables and their probabilistic nature in organizational subsystems. Further, most organizational problems of any magnitude involve one or more human variables, and human behavior can rarely, if ever, be predicted for certain. Secondly, fewer optimizing decision techniques are available for dealing with problems of disorganized complexity. Among those which do exist are certain stochastic programming techniques, which are advanced types of mathematical programming and which employ probability distributions rather than single values for variables.[5] Further, as we have indicated previously, it may be possible to approach optimum solutions to problems via simulation, which is one of the most basic techniques available for considering complex problems in a systems sense.

SIMPLIFICATION OF THE COMPLEX

One of our central themes in this chapter has been that the manager operates in a complex stochastic system comprised of many interdependent variables, equipped with decision-making approaches which are limited in their ability to cope with disorganized complexity. One basic approach probably utilized by all managers operating in such an environment is that of reframing complex disorganized problems into simpler, more organized ones with which they may more readily cope. Such a "simplification of the complex" occurs both in experience-based decision making and in the development and utilization of formalized quantitative models. Further, there are several different ways in which managers may reframe problems in more easily manipulable terms. We will now discuss some of the more important of these.

---

[5] For a discussion of stochastic programming methods, see, for example, *Mathematical Studies in Management Science*, ed., Arthur F. Veinott, Jr. (New York: The Macmillan Company, 1965), pp. 313 ff.

In some cases, managers find it adequate to assume certainty in dealing with a problem, even though it may be characterized by one or more stochastic variables. For example, we may obtain a relatively good approximation of minimal total costs in an inventory problem, by assuming that demand is known and constant, even though it is a stochastic variable; partially because total costs in the neighborhood of the most economic order quantity are relatively insensitive to small changes in the quantity of items ordered. Or, in making capital budgeting decisions, the variability in the firm's demand which would affect the present value of future returns from two proposed investment alternatives may be excluded from consideration if it is assumed that both alternatives will be operating under the same conditions. That is, the decision choice may not be based on the absolute profitability of each alternative, but only upon its profitability relative to the other assuming that both will experience the same type of variability.[6]

Another problem-simplification technique is to assume that the *relationships* among variables are simpler than they really are. In this respect, managerial decision models frequently assume *linear* relationships among variables, even though in reality such relationships are non-linear. For example, linear programming formulations may often be utilized to obtain quite good approximations of optimality, even though all relationships in the problem are not perfectly linear. As we mentioned in Chapter 16, non-linear methods of programming do exist. However, in some cases it may be more practical and convenient to assume the simpler conditions of linearity.

Still another method for dealing with disorganized complexity is to: (1) develop decision methods applicable to a particular segment of the business; (2) attempt to optimize the output from that segment, and, in doing so, (3) assume that the operations of the remainder of the organization will not be adversely affected. Basically, this approach assumes that one can isolate the operations of one segment of an organization from operations elsewhere. If we consider an organization as a system, however, we see that this approach may often be invalid. Yet, the operations of certain sub-systems may be relatively insensitive to certain decisions made in others. For example, the decision made in a supermarket chain to establish a delicatessen in one of its stores might have no effect on

---

[6] In this example, we are assuming that management anticipates $PV > I$ for both alternatives.

sales in its other stores (unless they were in close physical proximity).

Finally, we should reiterate a point made previously in Chapter 3 —that complex decision problems may be more easily coped with if they can be broken down into a series of simpler subproblems, for which there is a greater likelihood that problem solving techniques exist. This approach, as mentioned previously is relied upon in the design of heuristic programs for problem solving.

SUMMARY

Business organizations may be most appropriately viewed as complex, dynamic, holistic systems, comprised of numerous interrelated subsystems. The basic activity carried out by the manager in the organizational system is that of decision making. Of the basic types of decisions made by managers, those characterized as motivational-directional, organizing, and control may be conceived of as special types of planning decisions; for all organization decision making is geared toward specifying or guiding future actions. The problems toward which the manager's decisions are addressed may be classed as comprising either a few or many variables, which may be either deterministic or stochastic. Many managerial decisions and probably all major ones fall in the category of disorganized complexity. In order to cope with such complexity, managers often reframe their problems so as to render them more organized and less complex— by assuming conditions of certainty, by treating certain non-linear relationships as linear, by assuming away the interdependence among decisions, and by breaking up complex problems into simpler subproblems, for which solution methods are more likely to exist.

DISCUSSION AND STUDY QUESTIONS

1. What is meant by a dynamic holistic system?
2. How can models based upon the assumptions of certainty and linearity be of value to the decision maker even though their underlying assumptions are not met in a real world situation? Under what conditions will such models work best?
3. Indicate whether the following decision approaches are designed to deal with (1) problems framed in deterministic and/or stochastic terms, and (2) problems with few or many variables. Explain your answer in each instance.
   a) Dynamic programming
   b) Breakeven analysis

c) Discounted rate of return
d) Linear programming
e) Simulation
f) Expected value analysis
g) Laplace criterion
h) PERT
i) Gantt chart
j) Non-linear programming
k) Basic present value model
l) Criterion of regret
m) Variable budget
n) ROI
o) Basic E.O.Q. formula
p) The Lockheed span of control model

4. In Chapter 17, we observed that a basic function of inventories is to decouple, or make independent, various organizational subsystems. If inventories are used to decouple subsystems, couldn't we then optimize the total system by optimizing each of its decoupled subsystems? Explain.

5. If predictions of future events used for planning purposes are based on what has happened in the past, doesn't their utilization ignore the fact that business organizations are dynamic systems? Explain.

6. By assuming that the relationship among variables in the organizational system are simpler than they really are, the manager may actually be taking an optimal approach to decision making. Discuss.

7. The basic reason why we have to view business organizations as stochastic systems is that we do not know enough about the behavior of many of their variables. For example, we cannot predict precisely how a subordinate will react to being disciplined by his boss because we do not have complete knowledge about his personality system. With additional research, however, we will learn more and more about business systems, and as we approach having complete knowledge about them, we will approach the point of being able to consider all business decision problems as deterministic ones. Discuss.

8. A basic premise of the systems view is that of interdependency—the behavior of each variable in the organizational system both influences and is influenced by the behavior of all other variables in the system. Therefore, the manager must be aware of everything which is going on in his firm if he is to make effective decisions. Discuss.

SELECTED REFERENCES

Selected References for this chapter are included throughout the references in this book. See especially Chapters 1, 2, and 3.

APPENDIXES

APPENDIX A

A SUMMARY OF LINEAR FUNCTIONS*

The following will be an aid in review of linear equations.

1. A Standard Form of the Equation of a Straight Line is: $y = a + bx$

   Where: y = the dependent variable

   x = the independent variable

   a = a constant, called the "y intercept"; i.e., it is the value of y when x is equal to 0, or it is the value of y where the line in question crosses the vertical, or y axis.

   b = a constant, called the slope of the line; i.e., it is the amount of change in y with a given change in x, or $\Delta y/\Delta x$. This quotient is the slope or rate of change of y with respect to a given change in x.

Example A

Suppose that we have the following equation: $y = 1x$

   Here $a = 0$; i.e., when $x = 0$, $y = 0$

   $b = 1$

A plot of this line looks like the following:

POINT	WHEN x IS:	y IS:
o	0	0
p	1	1
q	2	2
r	3	3
s	4	4
t	5	5

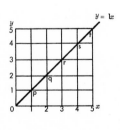

Notice that $a = 0$. Notice also that from any point on the line to any other point on the line, the change in y divided by the change in x is a constant, one; i.e., from point p to point q, the relationship is $1/1$; from q to s, it is $2/2 = 1$; from t to q it is $-3/-3 = 1$. This is of course the slope of the line (i.e., $b = 1$).

---

* A knowledge of the material in this appendix may be helpful in dealing with the subject matter in Chapters 13 and 16.

Example B

Let us look at another equation: $y = 2$. When plotted it looks as follows:

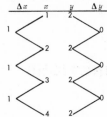 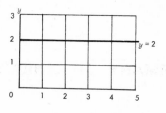

Notice that when x changes by 1, y changes by zero, hence $b = 0$.

Example C

Suppose that we now add these two equations together, calling the first, y_a, the second y_b, and the sum of $y_a + y_b$, y_c, so that $y_a + y_b = y_c$.

$$y_a = 0 + 1x$$
$$y_b = 2 + 0x$$
$$y_c = 2 + 1x$$

Plotting this we have:

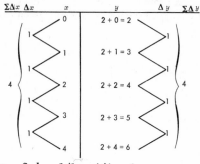 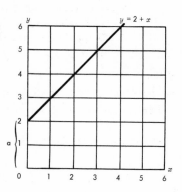

$a = 2; b = 1/1 = 4/4 = 1.$

Notice here that the line looks essentially the same as that in Example A above (i.e., it has the same slope) except that it has been moved up an amount equal to a.

Example D

The equation $y = \frac{1}{2}x$ looks like the following:

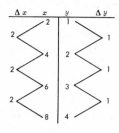 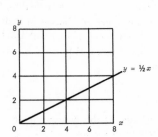

2. Non-Linear Functions

What distinguishes a straight line from a non-straight line? Let us take another example, $y = x^2$, and plot it.

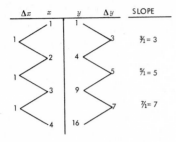 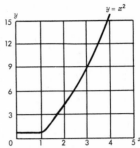

Notice that the change in y divided by the change in x ($\Delta y/\Delta x$) is *not* a constant between values of x and y. The main distinguishing feature of a straight line is thus illustrated; the change of one variable with respect to the other; i.e., the slope, is a constant.

Example

Let us look at another function. Given the following, do we have a linear or non-linear function?

We have a linear function. The slope $\Delta y/\Delta x$ is equal to 2 and is constant for each pair of values. The value of a by inspection is zero, thus the equation of the line is $y = 2x$.

3. Negatively Sloped Lines

The equations $y_a = -x$ and $y_b = 3$ look like the following:

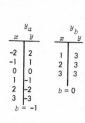 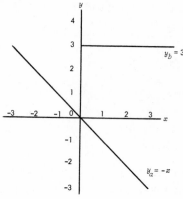

When the two equations are summed, letting $y_a + y_b = y_c$, we have the following equation:

$$y_c = 3 - 1x$$

Notice that this line slopes in a direction opposite to those previously considered, and that it therefore has a negative slope; i.e., $b = -1$.

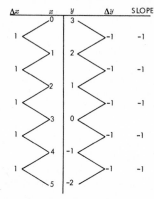 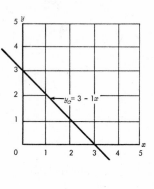

We can show that the slope of a line can have any real number for its value, that is, it can range from plus infinity through zero to minus infinity. The following diagram illustrates the point:

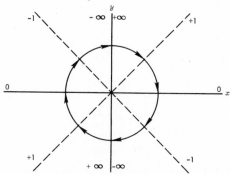

4. Point Determination

Another skill required is that of finding x and y when two lines cross or intersect. The key characteristic of the point of intersection which helps us locate these values is that at that point, $x_1 = x_2$, and $y_1 = y_2$. As an example, let us consider the following two lines:

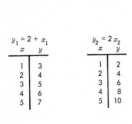

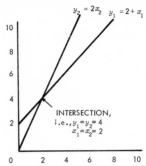

By knowing that $y_1 = y_2$, and $x_1 = x_2$ at the point of intersection, we can find the coordinates of the point by:

a. Setting the equations equal to each other, i.e., $y_1 = y_2$, which gives us $2 + x = 2x$, hence $x = 2$. Substituting in either y_1 or y_2 we have $y_1 = 2 + 2 = y_2 = 2 \times 2 = 4$. The values of x and y for the point of intersection are then $x = 2$, $y = 4$.

b. Subtracting one equation from the other:

$$
\begin{array}{l}
y = 2 + \quad x \\
- (y = \qquad 2x) \\
\hline
0 = 2 - \quad x \\
x = 2
\end{array}
\quad \text{OR} \quad
\begin{array}{l}
y = \qquad 2x \\
- (y = \quad 2 + \quad x) \\
\hline
0 = -2 + \quad x \\
x = 2
\end{array}
$$

5. Equation Determination Given Any Two Points

Suppose that we wish to write an equation, given the coordinates (i.e., value of x and value of y) for two points:

e.g., $y_1 = 4$; $x_1 = 6$
$\quad\;\; y_2 = 5$; $x_2 = 9$

A. One method of determining the equation would be by inspection.

$$
\begin{array}{c|cc|c}
\Delta x & x & y & \Delta y \\
\hline
 & 0 & 2 & \\
 & 1 & \cdot & \\
 & \cdot & \cdot & \\
 & \cdot & \cdot & \\
 & \cdot^{6} & \cdot & \\
3 & \cdot & {}^{4} & 1 \\
 & {}_{9} & 5 &
\end{array}
$$

We can quickly notice that the slope, or change in y divided by change in x, is a positive $\frac{1}{3}$.

$$
\text{Slope} = \frac{\Delta y}{\Delta x} = \frac{y_2 - y_1}{x_2 - x_1} = +\tfrac{1}{3}
$$

By back tracking we can find a; i.e., value of y when $x = 0$, which here is 2. Hence, we can write the equation which satisfies these points as $y = 2 + \frac{1}{3}x$. This is a laborious and inexact process. Other methods are preferred.

B. Another method is to learn and apply the following equation:

$$\frac{y - y_1}{x - x_1} = \frac{y_2 - y_1}{x_2 - x_1} \quad \text{Substituting:} \quad \frac{y - 4}{x - 6} = \frac{5 - 4}{9 - 6}$$

Hence our equation for the line is again $y = 2 + \frac{1}{3}x$.

C. The subtraction method is a third alternative.

$$\begin{array}{ll} y_1 = a + bx_1 & \text{substituting} \\ - (y_2 = a + bx_2) & \end{array} \qquad \begin{array}{l} 4 = a + b6 \\ - (5 = a + b9) \\ \hline -1 = -3b, \text{ or } b = +\frac{1}{3} \end{array}$$

Substituting in either of the original equations we have:

$$4 = a + \frac{1}{3} \cdot 6 \quad \text{OR} \quad 5 = a + \frac{1}{3} \cdot 9$$

Hence, $a = 2$, and our equation is $y = 2 + \frac{1}{3}x$.

6. Equation Determination Given Axis Intercepts

One final problem remains. Suppose that we know the values of x and y where one particular line crosses the axes, e.g.,

$$\begin{array}{ll} \text{Where } x = 0; y = 2 & \text{this is the } y \text{ intercept, or } a. \\ y = 0; x = 4 & \text{this is the } x \text{ intercept, or } c. \end{array}$$

There is a simple way to write the equation of the line which passes through these two points, the intercept form of an equation for a straight line:

$$\frac{y}{a} + \frac{x}{c} = 1 \qquad \text{Note: } b = \text{slope} = -a/c$$

We can quickly write:

$$\begin{array}{ll} \frac{y}{2} + \frac{x}{4} = 1 \quad \text{OR} & y = a + bx, \text{ where } b = -a/c, a = 2, \text{ and} \\ & \qquad\qquad c = 4, \text{ hence } b = -\frac{1}{2} \\ y = 2 - \frac{1}{2}x & y = 2 - \frac{1}{2}x \end{array}$$

This method is especially useful for dealing with algebraic linear programming problems as covered in Chapter 16.

SUMMARY

The above summarizes the requisite knowledge of linear functions. The student should develop and solve examples for each type of problem, so that recognition and manipulation of such problems become "second nature" with him. Some problems and answers follow.

LINEAR FUNCTION PROBLEMS AND ANSWERS

1. Plot the equation $y = 3 + 2x$.

   What is the value of the y intercept?
   (Answer: 3)

What is the slope of the line?
 (Answer: $+2$)
What is the value of the x intercept, i.e., when $y = 0$?
 (Answer: $-\frac{3}{2}$)

2. Determine the slope and y intercept of the following:

Equations	Put in standard form	Y intercept	Slope
$3y + 2x = 7$	$y = \frac{7}{3} - \frac{2}{3}x$	$\frac{7}{3}$	$-\frac{2}{3}$
$2y + 3x = 6$	$y = 3 - \frac{3}{2}x$	3	$-\frac{3}{2}$
$y - x = 2$	$y = 2 + x$	2	1
$4y - 3x = 12$	$y = 3 + \frac{3}{4}x$	3	$\frac{3}{4}$

3. Which of the following equations is (are) not linear?

	Linear	Non-linear
A. $y = \frac{1}{2}x + 6$	✓	
B. $y^2 = \frac{1}{2}x + 6$		✓
C. $y = x^{\frac{1}{2}} + 6$		✓
D. $y = \frac{1}{2}x + 6^2$	✓	
E. $3y + 2x = \sqrt{10}$	✓	

4. In words, what is the difference between a positive and a negative slope of a linear function?

Answer

For a line with a positive slope, as the value of the independent variable (x) increases, the value of the dependent variable (y) also increases.

For a line with a negative slope, as the value of the independent variable (x) increases, the value of the dependent variable (y) decreases.

5. Given the following sets of two linear equations, find the points of intersection first by setting the equations equal to each other and second by subtracting one equation from the other.

 A. $3y + 4x = 7$
  $4y + 3x = 12$

Method 1. Set the equations in standard form.

$$y = \frac{7}{3} - \frac{4}{3}x$$
$$y = 3 - \frac{3}{4}x$$

Set equations equal to each other.

$$\frac{7}{3} - \frac{4}{3}x = 3 - \frac{3}{4}x$$
$$\frac{7}{12}x = -\frac{2}{3} \qquad x = -\frac{2}{3} \times \frac{12}{7} = -\frac{8}{7}$$

Substituting in the value for x in either equation we have

$$3y + 4x = 7$$
$$3y + 4(-\frac{8}{7}) = 7$$
$$3y - \frac{32}{7} = 7$$
$$3y = 7 + \frac{32}{7} = \frac{49}{7} + \frac{32}{7} = \frac{81}{7}$$
$$y = 3\frac{6}{7}$$

Method 2. Multiply the first equation by 4 and the second equation by 3, yielding

$$12y + 16x = 28$$
$$-(12y + 9x = 36)$$
$$\overline{\quad\quad 7x = -8}$$
$$x = -\tfrac{8}{7}, \ y = \tfrac{27}{7}$$

OR

Multiply the first equation by 3 and the second equation by 4 yielding

$$9y + 12x = 21$$
$$-(16y + 12x = 48)$$
$$\overline{-7y \quad\quad = -27}$$
$$7y = 27$$
$$y = \tfrac{27}{7} = 3\tfrac{6}{7}; \ x = -\tfrac{8}{7}$$

B. $\quad y + \tfrac{1}{2}x = 6$
$\quad\quad 3y + x = 2$

Method 1. Set the equations in standard form.

$$y = 6 - \tfrac{1}{2}x$$
$$y = \tfrac{2}{3} - \tfrac{1}{3}x$$

Set the equations equal to each other.

$$6 - \tfrac{1}{2}x = \tfrac{2}{3} - \tfrac{1}{3}x$$
$$5\tfrac{1}{3} = \tfrac{1}{6}x$$

or

$$\tfrac{1}{6}x = 5\tfrac{1}{3} = \tfrac{16}{3}$$
$$x = (\tfrac{16}{3})(6)$$
$$x = 32$$

Substitute in either equation the value obtained for x.

$$3y + x = 2$$
$$3y + 32 = 2$$
$$3y = -30$$
$$y = -10$$

Method 2. Multiply the first equation by 3, holding the second constant.

$$3y + \tfrac{3}{2}x = 18$$
$$-(3y + x = 2)$$
$$\overline{\quad\quad \tfrac{1}{2}x = 16}$$
$$x = 32$$

by substitution $y = -10$

OR

Multiply the first equation by 2 holding the second constant.

$$2y + x = 12$$
$$-(3y + x = 2)$$
$$\overline{-y = 10}$$
$$y = -10$$

by substitution $x = 32$

C. $\quad 2y + x = 9$
$\quad\quad 3y + 2x = 7$

Method 1. Set the equations in standard form.

$$y = \tfrac{9}{2} - \tfrac{1}{2}x$$
$$y = \tfrac{7}{3} - \tfrac{2}{3}x$$

Set the equations equal to each other.

$$\tfrac{9}{2} - \tfrac{1}{2}x = \tfrac{7}{3} - \tfrac{2}{3}x$$
$$\tfrac{1}{6}x = -\tfrac{13}{6}$$
$$x = (-\tfrac{13}{6})(6) = -13$$

By substituting in the value obtained for x, the value for y will be obtained.

$$2y + x = 9$$
$$2y - 13 = 9$$
$$2y = 22$$
$$y = 11$$

Method 2. Multiply the first equation by 3 and the second equation by 2.

$$6y + 3x = 27$$
$$\underline{-(6y + 4x = 14)}$$
$$-x = 13$$
$$x = -13$$

by substitution $y = 11$

OR

Multiply the first equation by 2, holding the second equation constant.

$$4y + 2x = 18$$
$$\underline{-(3y + 2x = 7)}$$
$$y = 11$$

by substitution $x = -13$

6. Using the equation for determining a line given the coordinates of two points on the line, determine the equation of the lines designated by the following pairs of points.

A. $y_1 = 3$ $x_1 = 5$
 $y_2 = 4$ $x_2 = 6$

$$\frac{y - y_1}{x - x_1} = \frac{y_2 - y_1}{x_2 - x_1}$$
$$\frac{y - 3}{x - 5} = \frac{4 - 3}{6 - 5}$$
$$\frac{y - 3}{x - 5} = \frac{1}{1} = 1$$
$$y - 3 = 1(x - 5)$$
$$y - 3 = x - 5$$
$$y = x - 2$$

B. $y_1 = 2$ $x_1 = 3$
 $y_2 = 4$ $x_2 = 7$

$$\frac{y - y_1}{x - x_1} = \frac{y_2 - y_1}{x_2 - x_1}$$
$$\frac{y - 2}{x - 3} = \frac{4 - 2}{7 - 3}$$
$$\frac{y - 2}{x - 3} = \frac{2}{4} = \frac{1}{2}$$
$$y - 2 = \tfrac{1}{2}(x - 3)$$
$$y - 2 = \tfrac{1}{2}x - \tfrac{3}{2}$$
$$y = \tfrac{1}{2}x + \tfrac{1}{2}$$

C. $y_1 = 0$ $x_1 = -5$
 $y_2 = 5$ $x_2 = 4$

$$\frac{y - y_1}{x - x_1} = \frac{y_2 - y_1}{x_2 - x_1}$$
$$\frac{y - 0}{x - (-5)} = \frac{5 - 0}{4 - (-5)}$$

$$\frac{y}{x+5} = \frac{5}{9}$$
$$y = \tfrac{5}{9}(x+5)$$
$$y = \tfrac{5}{9}x + \tfrac{25}{9}$$

D. Using the same values for x and y, determine the equations of the lines using the subtraction method.

1) $y_1 = 3$ $\qquad x_1 = 5$ $\qquad$ Substituting in either equation
$\ y_2 = 4$ $\qquad x_2 = 6$ $\qquad$ we can get the value for a.

$\ y_1 = a + bx_1$ $\qquad 3 = a + b5$ $\qquad 3 = a + b5$
$\ \underline{-(y_2 = a + bx_2)} \quad \underline{-(4 = a + b6)} \quad 3 = a + (1)(5)$
$\qquad\qquad\quad -1 = -b \qquad\quad 3 = a + 5$
$\qquad\qquad b = 1 \qquad\qquad a = -2$

Hence, with $a = -2$ and $b = 1$, we have the equation
$$y = -2 + x$$

2) $y_1 = 2$ $\qquad x_1 = 3$ $\qquad$ Substituting in either equation
$\ y_2 = 4$ $\qquad x_2 = 7$ $\qquad$ we can get the value for a.

$\ y_1 = a + bx_1$ $\qquad 2 = a + b3$ $\qquad 4 = a + b7$
$\ \underline{-(y_2 = a + bx_2)} \quad \underline{-(4 = a + b7)} \quad 4 = a + (\tfrac{1}{2})7$
$\qquad\qquad\quad -2 = -4b \qquad\quad 4 = a + \tfrac{7}{2}$
$\qquad\qquad b = \tfrac{1}{2} \qquad\qquad a = \tfrac{1}{2}$

Hence, with $a = \tfrac{1}{2}$ and $b = \tfrac{1}{2}$, we have the equation
$$y = \tfrac{1}{2} + \tfrac{1}{2}x$$

3) $y_1 = 0$ $\qquad x_1 = -5$ $\qquad$ Substituting in either equation
$\ y_2 = 5$ $\qquad x_2 = 4$ $\qquad$ we can get the value for a.

$\ y_1 = a + bx_1$ $\qquad 0 = a + b(-5)$ $\qquad 0 = a + b(-5)$
$\ \underline{-(y_2 = a + bx_2)} \quad \underline{-(5 = a + b4)} \quad 0 = a + \tfrac{5}{9}(-5)$
$\qquad\qquad\quad -5 = -9b \qquad\quad 0 = a - \tfrac{25}{9}$
$\qquad\qquad b = \tfrac{5}{9} \qquad\qquad a = \tfrac{25}{9}$

Hence, with $a = \tfrac{25}{9}$ and $b = \tfrac{5}{9}$, the equation becomes
$$y = \tfrac{25}{9} + \tfrac{5}{9}x$$

7. Using the formula for line determination given the values of the variables at the points where the line crosses the axes, determine the lines for the following points.

A. $x = 0$; $y = 3$
$\ y = 0$; $x = 4$

$$\frac{y}{a} + \frac{x}{c} = 1$$
$$\frac{y}{3} + \frac{x}{4} = 1$$
$$\frac{y}{3} = 1 - \frac{x}{4}$$
$$y = 3 - \tfrac{3}{4}x$$

B. $x = 0$ $y = 5$
$\ y = 0$ $x = 2$

$$\frac{y}{a} + \frac{x}{c} = 1$$
$$\frac{y}{5} + \frac{x}{2} = 1$$
$$\frac{y}{5} = 1 - \frac{x}{2}$$
$$y = 5 - \tfrac{5}{2}x$$

OR

$$y = a + bx, \text{ where } b = -\frac{a}{c}$$

$$y = 3 + (-\tfrac{3}{4})x$$

$$y = 3 - \tfrac{3}{4}x$$

C. $x = 0 \quad y = -3$
    $y = 0 \quad x = 2$

$$\frac{y}{a} + \frac{x}{c} = 1$$

$$\frac{y}{-3} + \frac{x}{2} = 1$$

$$\frac{-y}{3} = 1 - \frac{x}{2}$$

$$-y = 3 - \tfrac{3}{2}x$$
$$y = -3 + \tfrac{3}{2}x$$

OR

$$y = a + bx$$

$$y = -3 + \frac{-(-3)}{2}\,x$$

$$y = -3 + \tfrac{3}{2}x$$

OR

$$y = a + bx$$
$$y = 5 + (-\tfrac{5}{2})x$$
$$y = 5 - \tfrac{5}{2}x$$

D. $x = 0 \quad y = -1$
    $y = 0 \quad x = 1$

$$\frac{y}{-1} + \frac{x}{1} = 1$$

$$\frac{y}{-1} = 1 - x$$

$$-y = 1 - x$$
$$y = -1 + x$$

OR

$$y = a + bx$$

$$y = -1 + \frac{-(-1)}{1}\,x$$

$$y = -1 + x$$

APPENDIX B

PRESENT VALUE OF $1

$$(1+r)^{-n}$$

n	1%	2%	3%	4%	5%	6%	7%	8%	9%	10%
1	0.9901	0.9804	0.9709	0.9615	0.9524	0.9434	0.9346	0.9259	0.9174	0.9091
2	0.9803	0.9612	0.9426	0.9246	0.9070	0.8900	0.8734	0.8573	0.8417	0.8264
3	0.9706	0.9423	0.9151	0.8890	0.8638	0.8396	0.8163	0.7938	0.7722	0.7513
4	0.9610	0.9238	0.8885	0.8548	0.8227	0.7921	0.7629	0.7350	0.7084	0.6830
5	0.9515	0.9057	0.8626	0.8219	0.7835	0.7473	0.7130	0.6806	0.6499	0.6209
6	0.9420	0.8880	0.8375	0.7903	0.7462	0.7050	0.6663	0.6302	0.5963	0.5645
7	0.9327	0.8706	0.8131	0.7599	0.7107	0.6651	0.6227	0.5835	0.5470	0.5132
8	0.9235	0.8535	0.7894	0.7307	0.6768	0.6274	0.5820	0.5403	0.5019	0.4665
9	0.9143	0.8368	0.7664	0.7026	0.6446	0.5919	0.5439	0.5002	0.4604	0.4241
10	0.9053	0.8203	0.7441	0.6756	0.6139	0.5584	0.5083	0.4632	0.4224	0.3855
11	0.8963	0.8043	0.7224	0.6496	0.5847	0.5268	0.4751	0.4289	0.3875	0.3505
12	0.8874	0.7885	0.7014	0.6246	0.5568	0.4970	0.4440	0.3971	0.3555	0.3186
13	0.8787	0.7730	0.6810	0.6006	0.5303	0.4688	0.4150	0.3677	0.3262	0.2897
14	0.8700	0.7579	0.6611	0.5775	0.5051	0.4423	0.3878	0.3405	0.2992	0.2633
15	0.8613	0.7430	0.6419	0.5553	0.4810	0.4173	0.3624	0.3152	0.2745	0.2394
16	0.8528	0.7284	0.6232	0.5339	0.4581	0.3936	0.3387	0.2919	0.2519	0.2176
17	0.8444	0.7142	0.6050	0.5134	0.4363	0.3714	0.3166	0.2703	0.2311	0.1978
18	0.8360	0.7002	0.5874	0.4936	0.4155	0.3503	0.2959	0.2502	0.2120	0.1799
19	0.8277	0.6864	0.5703	0.4746	0.3957	0.3305	0.2765	0.2317	0.1945	0.1635
20	0.8195	0.6730	0.5537	0.4564	0.3769	0.3118	0.2584	0.2145	0.1784	0.1486
21	0.8114	0.6598	0.5375	0.4388	0.3589	0.2942	0.2415	0.1987	0.1637	0.1351
22	0.8034	0.6468	0.5219	0.4220	0.3418	0.2775	0.2257	0.1839	0.1502	0.1228
23	0.7954	0.6342	0.5067	0.4057	0.3256	0.2618	0.2109	0.1703	0.1378	0.1117
24	0.7876	0.6217	0.4919	0.3901	0.3101	0.2470	0.1971	0.1577	0.1264	0.1015
25	0.7798	0.6095	0.4776	0.3751	0.2953	0.2330	0.1842	0.1460	0.1160	0.0923
26	0.7720	0.5976	0.4637	0.3607	0.2812	0.2198	0.1722	0.1352	0.1064	0.0839
27	0.7644	0.5859	0.4502	0.3468	0.2678	0.2074	0.1609	0.1252	0.0976	0.0763
28	0.7568	0.5744	0.4371	0.3335	0.2551	0.1956	0.1504	0.1159	0.0895	0.0693
29	0.7493	0.5631	0.4243	0.3207	0.2429	0.1846	0.1406	0.1073	0.0822	0.0630
30	0.7419	0.5521	0.4120	0.3083	0.2314	0.1741	0.1314	0.0994	0.0754	0.0573
35	0.7059	0.5000	0.3554	0.2534	0.1813	0.1301	0.0937	0.0676	0.0490	0.0356
40	0.6717	0.4529	0.3066	0.2083	0.1420	0.0972	0.0668	0.0460	0.0318	0.0221
45	0.6391	0.4102	0.2644	0.1712	0.1113	0.0727	0.0476	0.0313	0.0207	0.0137
50	0.6080	0.3715	0.2281	0.1407	0.0872	0.0543	0.0339	0.0213	0.0134	0.0085

Source: Bierman, H.; Bonini, C. P.; Fouraker, L. E.; and Jaedicke, R. K., *Quantitative Analysis for Business Decisions* (rev. ed.; Homewood, Ill.: Richard D. Irwin, Inc., 1965), p. 427. Reprinted by permission.

TABLE OF PSEUDO RANDOM NUMBERS

17	57	89	67	26	06	55	79	96	77
49	49	19	98	24	68	53	32	39	95
36	58	57	33	07	62	30	22	47	09
80	37	50	16	11	36	45	31	09	87
84	15	86	27	60	33	79	98	76	16
56	97	98	83	59	93	41	18	65	98
11	65	65	37	98	52	61	41	54	50
63	75	07	76	52	40	93	74	87	08
33	61	89	25	78	86	17	80	72	19
46	32	21	44	18	13	36	78	81	51
31	73	56	29	99	40	77	41	49	86
19	45	92	13	31	83	89	02	76	20
48	85	69	65	08	54	50	47	27	69
57	06	73	88	07	60	56	18	27	62
92	98	34	22	91	04	31	14	69	45
00	25	23	45	07	86	22	90	10	80
34	29	60	68	83	03	00	57	67	45
51	27	04	40	35	44	60	81	26	34
11	12	62	45	60	97	20	85	34	56
79	52	83	03	40	47	23	48	02	38
23	94	59	71	41	73	37	05	06	22
16	58	28	41	15	49	52	45	87	65
33	42	72	41	93	49	83	17	46	41
56	18	16	36	96	38	69	22	53	41
69	35	29	25	24	82	73	20	39	70
61	19	24	46	63	38	82	24	99	50
24	71	58	71	85	64	06	07	94	19
53	69	33	08	43	09	80	93	46	31
51	64	95	01	75	23	64	68	44	56
22	86	31	30	03	48	41	68	40	80
73	41	77	12	33	23	16	89	48	05
18	09	08	00	55	85	21	81	49	48
72	48	47	81	44	65	11	51	86	44
57	90	58	79	57	91	65	63	67	42
97	46	51	56	37	85	86	33	64	09
20	99	79	08	09	68	00	38	13	26
58	11	40	66	84	55	58	09	12	92
49	19	74	99	56	57	36	30	26	19
33	37	66	12	03	83	32	47	82	39
54	53	48	45	86	35	69	56	73	97
61	33	90	73	53	12	93	13	53	55
06	17	12	11	33	12	77	29	43	90
45	23	73	04	39	25	14	70	26	98
40	44	80	39	72	38	24	60	50	87
54	49	81	35	11	35	49	76	26	83
56	84	70	49	24	96	57	53	30	30
19	68	84	73	60	96	37	83	02	84
19	00	05	35	54	08	06	12	46	19
37	52	58	00	24	97	02	42	29	25

INDEXES

AUTHOR INDEX*

---

* This Index does not include the authors of the selected references given at the end of each chapter.

Reich, Richard L., 502
Ricciardi, Franc M., 501, 515
Rickey, Kenneth R., 358
Roethlisberger, F. J., 7, 126, 165, 180, 181
Rosenzweig, James E., 233

S

Sarbin, Theodore R., 179
Savage, L. J., 50
Sayles, Leonard R., 147, 173, 178, 182, 183, 185, 194, 195, 230, 327, 385
Schlaifer, Robert, 46, 52
Schmidt, Warren H., 158–59, 160
Scott, William G., 22, 179, 180
Seashore, Stanley, 183
Sherwin, Douglas S., 318, 319
Sherwood, Frank P., 236
Shewhart, Walter, 11
Simon, Herbert A., 27, 29, 30, 63, 92, 328
Smith, Adam, 2
Starr, Martin K., 48, 52, 65, 295, 461
Steger, Wilbur A., 505
Stieglitz, Harold, 212, 213
Stockton, R. Stansbury, 434, 444
Strauss, George, 147, 178, 182, 230, 327, 385

T

Tannenbaum, Robert, 135, 158–59, 160

Taylor, Frederick W., 4, 5, 234, 235
Terry, George, 6, 63
Timms, Howard L., 489
Thrall, R. M., 51
Tonge, Fred M., 91, 500
Towne, Henry, 5

V

Veinott, Arthur F., Jr., 531
von Bertalanffy, Ludwig, 21, 22, 526, 527

W

Wald, Abraham, 48
Walker, Charles R., 126, 200, 201, 274
Weidenbaum, Murray L., 298, 299
Weschler, Irving R., 135
Weston, J. Fred, 360, 372
Whisler, Thomas L., 268
White, Lancelot Law, 103
Whitecraft, Herbert, 499, 501, 503
Whitin, Thompson M., 466, 485
Whiting, C. S., 42
Whyte, William F., 117, 183, 184, 185, 200, 263
Wiener, Norbert, 22
Worthy, James, 209

Z

Zaleznik, A., 126, 180, 181

SUBJECT INDEX

A

Acquisition decisions; *see* Resource acquisition

Allocation decisions; *see* Resource allocation

Aspiration level, 114
impact upon standards, 327–28

Authority; *see* Power

Automatic systems, 87

Automation; *see* Organizational change

B

Behavior
cultural influences upon, 116–18
group; *see* Group behavior
learning, influence of, 122
organizational system, related to, 289–90
unmotivated, 111–12
functional autonomy, 111

Bounded rationality
in decision making, 29–30
in planning, 296–97
simplification of decisions, 531–32

Breakeven
analysis
linear, 346–50
non-linear, 350–53
values and limits, 353–54
chart, example, 348, 351–52
modified for profits, 349

C

Capital budgeting, defined, 369
discounted rate of return model, 377–79
payback method, 371–73
present value model, 375–77
time value of money, 373–74

Change, organizational; *see* Organizational change

Cohesion, 183

Communications
barriers, 286
data for coordination, 203–4
differences in understanding, 285
grapevine, 286–89
learning results, 123
restructuring, 284
restructuring formal flows, 263–65
rumor, 286–89
via staff, 237–39

Computer
control system example, 334
use in simulation, 503–5, 515

Control
data, 330–31
defined, 318
feedback timing, 333–36
information system for, 329
measures of, 322–23
the nature of, 318–22
reporting, 332–33
standards for, 322–29

Coordination, 203–4

Costs
fixed, defined, 341
marginal, 343–45
opportunity, defined, 340
semifixed, defined, 341
sunk, defined, 340
variable, defined, 341–43

Creativity, 41–42

Critical path analysis; *see* PERT

D

Decisions
acquisition; *see* Resource acquisition
allocation; *see* Resource allocation
under certainty, 43–44
control as subset of planning, 528–29

557

This book has been set in 11 and 9 point Caledonia, leaded 2 points. Chapter numbers are in 12 point Lining Gothic #545 and chapter titles are in 18 point Lining Gothic caps. The size of the type page is 27 × 46½ picas.